PLANNING
PARKS
FOR
PEOPLE

by

**Second
Edition**

John Hultsman
Richard L. Cottrell
Wendy Z. Hultsman

Venture Publishing, Inc.

PLANNING PARKS FOR PEOPLE

Second Edition

by

John Hultsman
Richard L. Cottrell
Wendy Z. Hultsman

Venture Publishing, Inc.

PLANNING PARKS FOR PEOPLE

Second Edition

by

John Hultsman
Richard L. Cottrell
Wendy Z. Hultsman

Venture Publishing, Inc.

Production Manager: Richard Yocum
Manuscript Editing: Richard Yocum, Diane K. Bierly, and Matthew S. Weaver
Cover Design and Illustration: Sikorski Design, 1998
Printing and Binding: Thomson-Shore, Inc.

Library of Congress Catalogue Card Number 98-84038
ISBN 0-910251-95-9

Dedication

The authors dedicate this second edition of *Planning Parks for People* to the memory of a most outstanding and unique recreation professional—Ralph C. Wilson.

Ralph was an active, hardworking, and involved member of numerous professional organizations (including a few beyond America's shores). He was, at various times, chair or president of most of them and the recipient of numerous prestigious awards.

At his passing in May of 1985 he had just retired as assistant director of the Ecological Science Division of the USDA-Soil Conservation Service. Since the mid 1960s he had essentially been Chief of Recreation for the SCS.

Unlike most professionals who work within one or two interest areas in the recreation realm, Ralph had broad concerns about and impacts on outdoor, municipal, therapeutic, military, sports, private, and international recreation. He was involved in the development of new technologies through research and continuing education, along with the arts and historical preservation. He also thoroughly enjoyed working with students and student consortia. Ralph advocated recreation progress and, in a broad sense, he disdained favoring advances for one user group at the expense of another (advocating both wilderness use and off-road vehicle riding, for example).

Perhaps his greatest service to the recreation profession was his ability to link people who had problems with people who had answers—always in a spirit of advancing the value of recreation, parks, and leisure services.

If during your career you have the opportunity to help, encourage, or perhaps be a mentor to one or two younger professionals, you will have been most fortunate. Ralph was a mentor and an example to dozens of professionals across America and around the world.

Years ago he and others suggested we write a book about the mistakes we had all made in outdoor recreation planning, design, and programming, focusing on the negative effects these mistakes have had on park users, administrators, and the resources themselves. Throughout our long association with Ralph, he made sure we didn't forget his professional request. Ten days before he died he asked one of us about our early writing progress on the first edition. He would be delighted with this expanded second edition!

Many of the comments on professionalism we've included in this book are a part of Ralph's legacy to us and you. He was a dynamic force in recreation, a professional's professional, and above all else a warm, close friend!

Biographical Sketches

John Hultsman is a professor of Recreation and Tourism Management at Arizona State University West in Phoenix, Arizona. He formerly taught in the Department of Physical Education, Health, and Recreation Studies at Purdue University and worked as a recreation planner for the Tennessee Valley Authority at Land Between the Lakes in Kentucky and in Norris, Tennessee.

Dick Cottrell spent 25 years in outdoor recreation with the USDA Forest Service and Tennessee Valley Authority at Land Between the Lakes. From 1981 to 1987 he was a part-time consultant in recreation and full-time partner in a wholesale nursery. He continues his consulting work, and is a lecturer, author, and co-host of two to three week-long workshops each year. He has worked with numerous federal, state county and city park organizations including the U.S. Army in the United States and NATO and the Japanese government. Dick also works as an "expert" witness and for the private campground sector. In his spare time he fishes and works on "honey do" jobs around the home. He and his family moved to Murray, Kentucky, in mid 1997.

Wendy Z. Hultsman is an associate professor of Recreation and Tourism Management at Arizona State University West. She taught in the Departments of Forestry and Physical Education, Health, and Recreation Studies at Purdue University, the Recreation and Parks Department at Bowling Green University, Clinton Community College, and Penn State University. In Wendy's spare time she is very involved in the team sport of dog agility with her furry son Sam, the golden retriever.

Table of Contents

Chapter One
Setting the Stage

"Whoever loves instruction loves knowledge, *but* he who hates criticism is stupid." This is a paraphrase of Chapter 12, Verse 1 of the Bible's Book of Proverbs which was written by King Solomon (who was described as an exceptionally wise man). Those of you who are college students should be eager (we hope) to learn all you can about planning parks for people, and you likely won't be offended by our criticism of poor park work. *However* (and this is a *big* however), we suspect the well-deserved criticism of all sorts of park folks—*including your professors*—will be far less than greatly appreciated.

Fact is, if you are using this text in one of your classes, your professor has lots of courage. *Note: We have, early on in the text, praised someone.* The authors enjoy giving praise where it is due—and you'll find praise for people throughout the book. However, of the many teaching tools used herein, the one we've leaned on most is the negative. Here's what park folks (including us) have done; here's what's obviously wrong with that work; and here's how to do it much better and oftentimes far less expensively. Teaching or writing in the negative—if carefully done—are rarely used, though marvelous, techniques. Since the authors have made numerous "mistakes" over the years and will share them with you while telling you about the mistakes of others, we have high hopes *you* will learn many good things.

Before you read further, you should understand the title of our book—*Planning Parks for People* (Second Edition)—is quite facetious. The authors (who collectively have over 70 years of experience in planning, administering, budgeting, designing, programming, researching, teaching, and enjoying parks in the United States and 10 other countries) *do not believe* many wildland parks anyplace have been well-planned *for people.* There are numerous reasons for this. Your challenge will be to find them somewhere in our 11 chapters, to understand why things have happened to harm outdoor recreation and parks, *and*—as a real professional—to make your numerous future contributions positive ones.

If you are a person who thrives on scholarly scientific writing full of profound, yet bewildering, wisdom, we suggest you stop reading now and ask the bookstore to refund your money. Our book won't be heralded as such a text. If, however, you appreciate "here's how to do something" stuff splashed frequently with axioms, guidelines, and illustrations including true and oftentimes tragic stories, read on.

The foundation of our recreation philosophy was given to us by some of the bright young people in the Kennedy administration when they wrote:

The outdoors lies deep in American tradition. It has had immeasurable impact on the Nation's character and on those who made its history. . . . When an American looks for the meaning of his past, he seeks it not in ancient ruins, but more likely in mountains and forests, by a river, or at the edge of the sea. . . . Today's challenge is to assure all Americans permanent access to their outdoor heritage.

The above quotation can be found on the back covers of all 27 volumes of the Outdoor Recreation Resources Review Commission (ORRRC) report, and, without a doubt, the most important guiding documents written in this half century were those 27 volumes. The ORRRC was established in 1958 by President Eisenhower, headed by Laurance Rockefeller, and completed and issued by the Kennedy administration in January of 1962. It set the stage for all sorts of great things in outdoor recreation. These include the Land and Water Conservation Fund Act; Wilderness Act; establishment of the Bureau of Outdoor Recreation (BOR); expanded funding in all federal park managing agencies; help for the private sector through the United States Department of Agriculture (USDA) Extension Service and National Resources Conservation Service (NRCS); greatly increased emphasis on outdoor recreation, national recreation and scenic trails; *Congressional* approval of many National Recreation Areas; Tennessee Valley Authority's Land Between the Lakes; accelerated public works; and more and more and more (Volume 27 is the summary chapter—the authors suggest you find a copy and study it). The last sentence in the quotation—"Today's challenge is to assure *all* Americans permanent access to *their* outdoor heritage" is, or should be, our guiding directive or principle. We've emphasized the two key words—*all* and *their.* For a number of years, things went quite well in the outdoor recreation realm for all Americans. More and more colleges and universities began to teach subjects in outdoor recreation. This helped meet the expanding needs for personnel in federal, state, county and local public agencies, and the fledgling private sector. Public parks were upgraded and expanded, and there was little or no special attention given to one sort of user over another. We realize we made too many mistakes in those days (which you'll learn about later) and spent too much money doing questionable things—such as building primitive campgrounds and unreinforced campsites *but,* all in all, many good things happened. Then along came the special interests and providing facilities and programs for all Americans slowed and finally stopped. Many of the tragic answers to the question *why* are in Chapters Two through Ten. We will also return to the *whys* in our last chapter.

What's different about this text as compared to the 10-year-old first edition? It's better written to help you avoid mistakes. Most of it is also written in conversational English, meaning that unless you are common sense challenged (as some highly educated folks appear to be), you will understand (perhaps not agree with, but understand) what you've read. Each chapter has been extensively upgraded, revised *and* greatly expanded. We've added a sizable new chapter on Family Campground Design. Hundreds of photos and drawings showing good items and mistakes are new. (In our view the first edition of our book and most other texts are long on words and short on showing you good and poor examples). Several new sections have been added including Native-American parks, group day use, Americans with disabilities pitfalls and pathways, visitor safety, maintenance, the rise and flop of outdoor recreation research, the wonders of carrying capacity (we wonder why it doesn't work), and customer service (or lack of it today).

We have been far more critical of agencies, groups and the private sector. If, for instance, a photo shows poor work done by the U.S. Forest Service (USFS), Tennessee Valley Authority (TVA), National Park Service (NPS), state parks, or others, we will likely tell you, *"Who done it* (Our thanks to TVA for all of its help!)."* In the last chapter, we've added a section on Heroes and Villains. Are you or your agency or group mentioned in either category?! The preservationists, environmentalists, and other similar rascals get lots of credit for what they've done but not much praise. Finally, throughout the book, we've added true stories illustrating good things and not-so-good things.

We'll pause now and answer some questions that should be of interest to you. Are the three authors (see biographical sketches at the front of the book) environmentalists? We are ardent protectors of our wildland environment, *but* hope no one ever "credits" us as being a part of the thoughtless anti-everything environmental movement. Early on, we all were drawn into the movement but dropped out when the movement's lack of knowledge, truthfulness *and* integrity became obvious.

Do we have any serious credentials in true conservation of natural resources, including recreation or parks and in doing things for both users and the environment? We think so, but *you* are the ultimate judge. Our collective academic backgrounds from seven universities include degrees in geography, planning, environmental education, recreation, and forestry. We've worked for both the public and private sectors; taught or teach at the university level; authored or coauthored textbooks and numerous publications; coordinated numerous workshops, symposia and institutes in continuing education; and have been asked to be "expert" (we don't like that word) witnesses at recreation-related trials. We enjoy recreational vehicle (RV) and tent camping, hiking, backpacking, fishing, gardening, wilderness, and active sports. Also included in our experience is hiking on the Appalachian Trail (with the

Appalachian Trail Conference chairman), the Pacific Crest Trail, and the Continental Divide Trail; establishment of national recreation trails, long-distance trails, and interpretive trails; doing the early planning for a later designated wilderness; attending a wilderness ride and planning session where the guidelines for all wilderness travel and use were imagineered; hiking in a proposed wilderness area with the then-*president* of the *wilderness society*(!); planning of the nation's first designated off-road vehicle area; co-originating the 30 university student consortium process; "designing" the impact-resistant universal campsite now used by the private sector *and* built by the hundreds in state, county, and federal park systems across the United States; pioneering the subtle movement of people (at least in campgrounds) through design psychology; interacting with all sorts of real user groups from wilderness to off-road vehicles, to athletic teams, to different types of persons with disabilities, to trail users, hundreds of students, campers, and more. We also have received numerous regional and national awards and commendations, including one from the Sierra Club.

Now have a close look at Figures 1.1, 1.2 and 1.3.

Welcome. Welcome indeed to some of the most beautiful and important lands and waters in the world: the parks, lakes, forests, streams, and other resources we use for outdoor recreation. Those of us who choose recreation as a career have a responsibility to develop and manage these resources in ways which will provide the best possible experience, including fun for people. The challenge for park and recreation professionals, however, doesn't end with this task. Working in recreation also requires a commitment to resource stewardship. By this we mean that provision of recreation areas and facilities must be coupled with careful management of the resources we develop. Thus, working in recreation implies a dual responsibility.

The first question we want to address is: "How well are parks and recreation professionals meeting this responsibility?" On the surface, it would seem our record is pretty good. Our resources are full of beautiful scenery, our trails are hiked, our campgrounds appear to be used, and our beaches are full. Unfortunately, a careful examination of our parks and other recreation areas would seem to indicate the real answer to this question is one many of us would rather not hear. All too often our resources, which originally looked like those pictured in Figure 1.1, end up looking like the areas

Figure 1.1

Figure 1.2

Figure 1.3

shown in Figures 1.2 and 1.3, with heavily compacted, poorly drained soil; erosion; dying old-growth trees; and no aesthetic appeal. Figure 1.2 is of an undefined campsite in an Indiana state reservoir property. Figure 1.3 is of a poorly designed and impacted pull-in campsite "designed" by the oldest author 30-plus years ago on the Cherokee National Forest in Tennessee. See Chapter Seven for the mistakes he made on this one. (It's no wonder he got promoted!) Too often we also tend to blame the users—the recreating public—for the environmental damage existing in our parks and recreation areas. Generally, the scenario runs something like this:

Time: Late September—after Labor Day
Place: A Texas campground (the song is the same in Virginia, Indiana, Colorado or Oregon)
Cast: The "ranger" and maintenance crew
Plot: The *annual* job of rehabilitating Possum Hollow Campground begins

"Boy, I'm glad the season's over! Seems like this poor ol' campground had 20 percent more of those city-born, city-raised critters called campers than ever before! Campers seemed even more determined than in past years to drive over and use any area they wanted. They even cut what few bar-

rier posts we had left to get their trailers onto our tent pads and nearer the picnic tables. Why would they want to do things like that? Some folks even want unnatural things like water and electricity at each campsite. They either ought to be happy with what we provide or stay home! Fact is, if a lot more would stay home, all this work wouldn't have to be done every year.

"The soil is hard as concrete—dusty in dry times, with mud aplenty when it rains. The grass we planted around the camp units last September has long since died—a victim of the pad, pad, padding of feet, feet, feet! It's a real shame, since the green grass sure looked good this spring *before* the campers arrived.

"You know, Possum Hollow sure doesn't look like it did when we first built the campground. Remember the big trees—oaks, hickories, dogwoods and pines? Low shrubs were sure thick and pretty. Now look around. Shrubs and small trees are mighty scarce, and the big, beautiful trees have all got some kind of disease and are dying. We've sprayed them with all kinds of chemicals and spent a fortune having dead tops and limbs cut out, but nothing seems to work. We've got a sad area from all this overuse!

"Well, folks, let's finish our lunch and get to work rototilling and spreading grass seed and fertilizer around these tables. Ya know, maybe we should get some research on what kind of grass grows best under those picnic tables!"

This sort of dialogue occurs in parks all over the world, including in parks managed by federal agencies like the National Park Service, Bureau of Land Management, the Forest Service, the Tennessee Valley Authority, and military installations. State parks, county parks, city parks, and private and commercial areas also face these maintenance and user challenges, and most of the good folks working in these parks make the same mistakes we described in our scenario. "Overuse" is a word we overuse! Parklands worldwide suffer from what is mistakenly called "overuse," meaning we blame visitors for our problems and maintenance woes. While users do create some difficulties for us, we frequently hold them responsible for far more damage than they cause. We usually react by eliminating park facilities such as camp loops because of problems we have ourselves created.

If it's not "overuse," then what's the problem? More often than not, *poor planning, inadequate design,* and *lax administration* combine to give this appearance. Conscientious planning can minimize user impact, and a thorough understanding of design techniques, attention to detail, and application of knowledge from related areas of expertise (including fun programming to help eliminate most park vandalism) can reduce maintenance costs drastically.

Over the years, resource managers have learned a good bit about stewardship. For example, they know how to handle water movement and to minimize erosion on agricultural land through the use of ditches and berms, how to analyze soils and use the results for prescribing treatment for mineral imbalances to maximize agricultural production, how to maintain domestic livestock and game species numbers to minimize environmental problems, and how to manage forest lands for timber production. But when it comes to applying these same areas of expertise to managing resources for people—which is one of the goals of recreation resource management—they have either failed to use the information available to us or simply haven't realized that other disciplines, such as forestry and soil science, have application for recreation. Consider the situation we described at poor old Possum Hollow Campground. The resources were in sad shape. What sort of "picture" did you get from the description? What were the *real* problems and what caused them? We see many things, including:

- Heavily impacted and compacted soils caused by foot and vehicular traffic over the entire area.
- Accelerated runoff and erosion—soil with only $^1/_{20}$ to $^1/_{120}$ the percolation or absorption rate of water it once had.
- Once beautiful old-growth trees now dead or dying because their root systems cannot absorb enough moisture and air through compacted soils.
- A continuing tendency to fight *effects* rather than *causes* by practices that include planting grass on known-impact areas such as campsites.
- A failure on the part of planners, designers, and administrators to blend together the *needs of the user and the environment* when developing and managing parks and other resource-based recreation areas.
- A failure to understand and use all of the applied research data available, universal sites, and design psychology.

It's easy to blame users for the types of problems we've just described. After all, Possum Hollow looked fine before it was opened to the public. Let's consider, however, others in the cast of characters—the planners, the designers and the administrators—and see how they may have contributed to these problems.

The planners caused the first real error when they picked the grove of big trees as the site for the campground. *You can't build* park facilities in such groves (particularly among some species) without killing your attraction—those big trees. Trying to save old-growth trees by cutting out dead tops and limbs and by using chemical sprays is another example of fighting effects of recreation impact rather than causes. Generally, planners have been treated well by the public and their agencies or organizations. Oftentimes, they've had their pick of lands for development and have had few constraints placed on them in terms of design guidelines. Given this freedom, have they investigated alternative sites for suitability? Once a site has been tentatively selected, have they tested soils for composition and percolation rate? Have they reduced the overstory shade factor to at least 50 percent? Have they eliminated the large trees and those unable to withstand user impact? And are they planning to reinforce all areas of known impact? Chances are, they aren't.

What about designers, including landscape architects? Can these good folks be at fault as well? Often, designers subscribe to a philosophy of "If I like it, it must be right."

This can lead to a failure to provide administrative and support personnel with alternative designs for park developments. With several alternatives to review, administrators and programmers responsible for managing an area can choose the best elements of each and synthesize them into a final, functional design. Most of the soil compaction described at Possum Hollow was a result of pedestrian and vehicular traffic—but not the fault of the user. The designers failed to *recognize* and *reinforce* areas they should have known would receive impact. Allowing users to drive over unreinforced areas changed the site environment. Also, areas *not* intended for impact need to be protected from it. This is partly the responsibility of the designer. Since we were told visitors even cut barrier posts to get to tent pads and tables, the design—by ignoring the needs of users—actually forced them to cause maintenance problems. Designing a barricade between a parking spur and the camping pad it serves is analogous to an architect building a locked fence between your garage and living room; yet in recreation areas, this kind of *hindrance* to visitors occurs quite frequently.

It will perhaps surprise you to know one of our most respected park agencies—the National Park Service—is guilty of the poor planning just described. (The authors plan to make sure you are surprised quite often throughout this text!)

If you routinely ask your designers for only one solution to a design problem, (e.g., a picnic area) more often than not they will accommodate you while "setting their feet in concrete"—insisting their design is the *only* feasible answer to your needs. Getting most of them to redesign or change their site plan, no matter how poor it is, will require quite a battle. Please take our advice and ask for three or four alternative solutions. With these in hand, *you* and *they* can find avenues of agreement while egos remain intact.

Another portion of the responsibility for protecting recreation resources lies with administrators. At times, these managers may make changes in plans and designs without adequate thought, justification, or awareness of possible consequences for the environment or for users. In fairness, political and budget problems may sometimes place constraints on managers and influence their decisions. However, park designs are periodically changed for the worse as a result of unnecessary managerial alterations. Also, a recreation area can be perfectly planned and designed, and still fall apart if managerial staff allow visitors to misuse the area. Inadequate regulations, or failing to enforce existing ones, can create problems no design could avoid. Parks are *planned* by, *managed* by, and *used* by people. At times, planners and designers of recreation areas have failed to recognize the need to balance planning, parks and people. As our title suggests, the authors will consider the *interrelatedness* of these topics. We'll discuss each of these briefly, to set the stage for later chapters.

Planning

Our recipe for successful planning consists of three ingredients. The first is the *technical knowledge*. To plan effectively, for example, it's necessary to understand contour lines and be able to interpret percent of slope. These types of skills, however, are relatively easy to acquire—slope is simply the change in elevation divided by the distance in which the change occurs. A four foot rise (or drop) in elevation along a line 100-feet long would equal a four percent slope. Other types of technical knowledge, such as interpreting soils, are not as simple to learn. In fact, planners *shouldn't try* to learn all the skills necessary for planning. They should, however, be aware of what skills are necessary and know how to get information about these from sources who *are* experts in various areas.

The second element required for successful planning is a healthy dose of common sense. If a planner routes a trail (hiking or interpretive) immediately adjacent to a smooth-barked tree such as an aspen or beech, he or she shouldn't be too surprised to find people will carve their initials on it. Every element in the plan for a recreation area should have a purpose the planner can justify. Further, the purpose should make sense. Planners should be able to explain, in nontechnical terms, how and why their designs function as they do. The architect Frank Lloyd Wright suggested that designs should adhere to the concept of "form follows function." In other words, while appearance (form) is a consideration, nothing is more important in design than *purpose* or *function*. At times, park planners seem to have amended Wright's concept to "form follows function—Phooey!" Consider the concrete drainage ditch in a TVA group camp in Tennessee shown in Figure 1.4. It has the *form* of a drainage ditch. It's also built above natural grade so water running down the slopes toward the ditch would have to rise above the sides of the ditch to drain into it, a fairly unlikely prospect. Elements of recreation plans must be functional.

While function must be the primary consideration for park designs, planners must also remember the recreational aspect of parks. To address this aspect, we need to include a third and final ingredient in our recipe for successful planning: a measure of *creativity*. Creativity in design is probably the most difficult element of planning to learn or to teach. Some people, and therefore some planners, are simply more creative than others. It is possible, however, to sharpen your creative design skills. The first trick is to *put yourself in the users' place:* How appealing is your design from their standpoint? The second method of improving your creativity is to make yourself *consider alternative designs.* Except for certain

Figure 1.4

functional standards—length of a regulation tennis court, for example—there are no "rules" governing creative design. There may be a dozen alternative locations for the tennis court, all of which can satisfy technical requirements.

By developing the habit of looking at alternatives, you can become more creative. Figure 1.5 shows two ways of designing a path from a parking lot to a scenic overlook. Both designs get the public to the attraction, but, from the standpoint of building anticipation, providing an aura of mystery, and *creating* a positive recreational experience, which is the better design?

We have tried, throughout this book, to take a practical, here's-how-to-do-it approach to planning. It's important to understand the steps necessary for developing master plans for parks and recreation areas. However, there are other sources of information addressing broad planning issues and needs assessments. *This text approaches planning from the standpoint of designing and building.* When we discuss campgrounds, for example, we assume the need for a campground has already been established as part of the master planning process. This book concentrates on the actual development of facilities: how to and how not to lay out and build parks and recreation areas.

Parks

Our use of the word "park" should be taken in the broadest sense possible. This book is concerned primarily with resource-based, outdoor recreation areas. However, the planning *principles* we discuss apply to a much wider range of areas and facilities. It may take longer, for example, to plan a 200-acre forest-based day-use area than it takes to plan an urban tot lot. But simply because the day-use area is larger

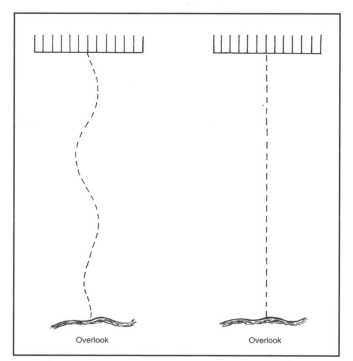

Overlook   Overlook

Figure 1.5

doesn't imply the tot lot deserves any less conscientious planning regarding its overall intended purpose. Conversely, the large day-use area should receive the same attention to detail and "fine tuning" as the tot lot. In fact, many of the planning concepts throughout this book may be applied to indoor settings as well. Designing a display area in a visitor center or environmental education building requires attention to factors such as intended audiences, zoning, circulation, entry/exit points, design psychology and safety. All of these and other considerations are discussed in the following chapters. The types of facilities and available resources may vary, but the *principles* remain the same, regardless of whether the facility being planned is a major park or a minor parking lot.

To illustrate this point, consider what is perhaps the single most important principle in recreation planning and design: the KISS principle (Keep It Simple, Stupid). Plans and designs for parks and recreation areas don't have to be, in fact *shouldn't* be, complex in order to be effective. Let's examine this principle for both a minor and a major design challenge. Figure 1.6 illustrates a potential problem at the exit point of a federal recreation area in Kentucky. Camping trailers and other recreational vehicles *exiting* the site tended to drive too close to the checkout building, striking the overhanging roof of the building. Figure 1.7 shows the design "solution" recommended by a staff planner. Extending the curb as shown would have interfered with traffic for several days, thus causing inconvenience to users. Additionally, construction, including materials and labor, would have cost several hundred dollars. The KISS solution, shown in Figure 1.8, was to place a four-foot length of orange-painted railroad tie perpendicu-

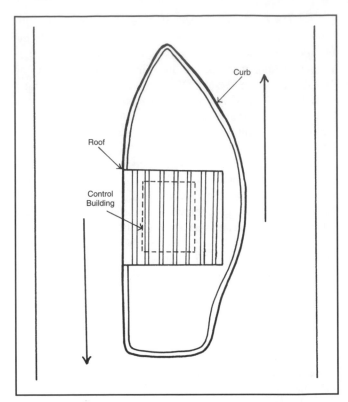

Figure 1.7

lar to the building. Drivers steered to avoid the tie and the problem was solved. This solution took 15 minutes to install at a minimum cost: Keep It Simple, Stupid!

On a larger scale, consider the design for the Indiana State Park campground shown as actually built in Figure 1.9. We'll discuss campground design in more detail in Chapter Seven; for now, let's concentrate on the problems created by the design. The road system has over 20 intersections, each of which is a potential source of confusion for users and an administrative problem for managers (safety, signing and traffic control). The design also spreads the potential for impact over the entire area. The KISS solution, shown in Figure 1.10, has reduced the number of intersections, simplified the circulation pattern, increased the potential for administrative control, minimized impact by moving users to and from toilet/shower buildings over the already hardened roadways, and reduced the cost of development by decreasing the amount of road (see Chapters Seven and Eight). As these examples illustrate, design challenges for parks, measured in square miles or square feet, may differ in scope but not in need for simplicity of function. We've also added the most important *zone* for bringing family use to this campground—the *play zone*. This, as you'll see in Chapter Nine, means play and fun for children *and* adults. It is missing in most public campgrounds in North America!

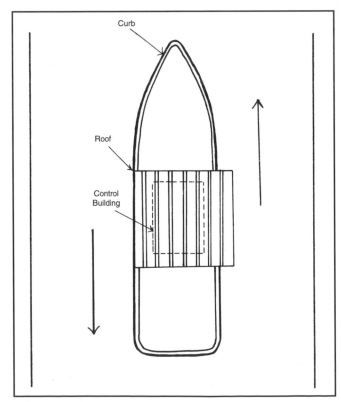

Figure 1.6

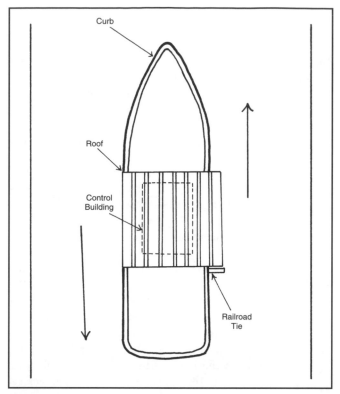

Figure 1.8

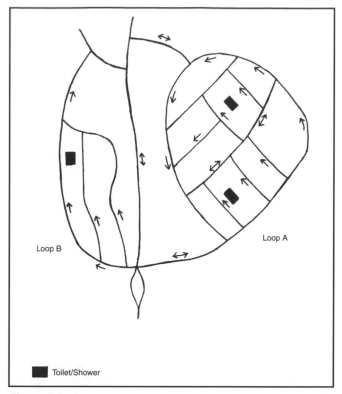

Toilet/Shower

Figure 1.9

People

Of the three elements in our title, people are the most important. Before we discuss the kinds of people who need to be considered in park plans and designs, let's start by talking about the types of people for whom this book is written. First, each chapter is designed to serve as a quick reference for people who are directly responsible for developing plans and designs for parks and recreation areas. For example, if someone assigns you the job of designing a campfire theater, you can turn to Chapter Nine and find answers to such questions as:

- How many people should I expect to attend programs?
- How many linear feet of seating per person should I allow?
- How can I locate the theater to *complement* rather than *conflict with* other use areas?

Second, *and more important,* this text is for people—both professionals and students—who aren't or don't expect to be recreation planners. This may sound like a different method of developing a book, which, after all, is about planning. There is, however, a reason

behind this approach. The majority of people who practice in and study about recreation and parks are not planners, yet everyone involved with parks depends upon the plans planners create. This book considers planning from the perspective of those who are, in effect, *consumers* of the planning process—managers, programmers and maintenance personnel.

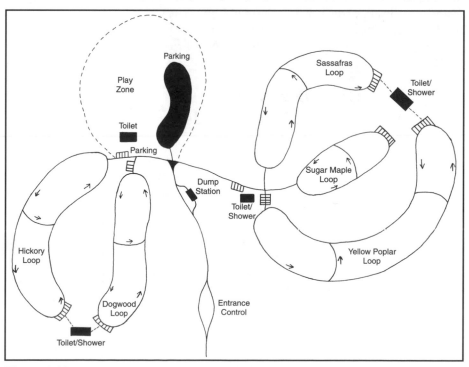

Figure 1.10

Far too often, these people are left out of the planning process. Ask yourself this question: Who is a park for? The obvious answer, the visitor, is only partly correct. Users are the most visible recipients of the efforts of planners, but others benefit or suffer from park designs as well. This brings us to the types of people who should be considered during the planning and design process: users and staff.

People go to parks and recreation areas to relax, refresh themselves, *and to have fun*. Plans for these areas should be developed to *enhance* the enjoyment of the user. Confusion should be minimized. Convenience, safety and usability should be maximized. The way you design a park can make the difference between an enjoyable or frustrating experience for visitors. It can also be discouraging to try to manage, maintain, or program a poorly designed recreation area. Park planners should remember their work is a *means* to an end rather than an end in itself. In other words, planning efforts should *support* the work of those who operate park facilities. When planners fail to consider the *consequences* of their designs, the results can cause a variety of problems.

Many of the headaches associated with park planning result from a lack of *balance* between attention to the needs of people and the technical requirements of design. Often, one of the two is emphasized at the expense of the other. We feel one reason for this problem is also one of the most critical issues in recreation planning today. The typical recreation planner is trained in either a technical discipline or a people-oriented discipline, *but not both*. For a recreation design to succeed, it must be functional *and* pleasing to people, and because technical and human needs are at times in conflict with one another, good design requires compromise. In order to compromise effectively, the planner needs a full appreciation of both aspects of design. Let's examine two case histories to illustrate how inattention to either human or technical considerations can cause problems in parks: problems for users, problems for staff, and problems for the environment.

Case History 1:
Inattention to Human Needs

Outdoor recreation came into its own in the 1950s and 1960s. A number of factors, including the strong postwar economy, urban growth and population growth, led to an unprecedented increase in demand for natural resource areas for recreation. The relatively sudden popularity of outdoor recreation caught many federal and state resource management agencies unprepared for such heavy use of their lands and waters. A case in point was the U.S. Forest Service. Prior to the passage by Congress of the Multiple Use Act in 1960, provision of opportunities for recreation was not mandated responsibility of this agency. Even before Congress acted, the Forest Service began taking steps to accommodate growing numbers of campers, hikers, picnickers and others who, almost overnight, began appearing on ranger districts nationwide. Since this high level of use was a new phenomenon, the first action neces-

sary was to provide facilities for the various types of users. Campgrounds, picnic areas and boat launches needed to be developed, and someone had to plan and design these areas. Since there were no recreation planners in the agency, the question was, who should get the jobs?

Perhaps, using the logic that building roads and other facilities for recreation should be no different than building roads and other facilities for timber management, the Forest Service first assigned the job of recreation planning to engineers. As you'll see in later chapters, engineering skills are critical to recreation design. Alone, however, they are not adequate to meet the needs of the people involved in recreation—users and recreation staff. Figure 1.11 shows a typical Forest Service campground designed by Forest Service engineers in Arkansas. From a technical standpoint, it works; the road intersection is functional and the turning radii in the curves are adequate. But from a human standpoint, consider the following problems. With only six camp units, most visitors can't find room to camp. Once these users enter the area, they have to turn around in order to exit; if they have a camping trailer, even a small one, there is no convenient way for them to reverse direction. Given the angles of the parking spurs and the dead-end road, exiting is also a problem for people who are able to find an empty site. From a management standpoint, the size of the area creates administrative problems as well. The campground is too small to cost-justify on-site management, security or programming. To meet the needs of an increasing number of users, more areas were needed, and thus numerous small campgrounds were devel-

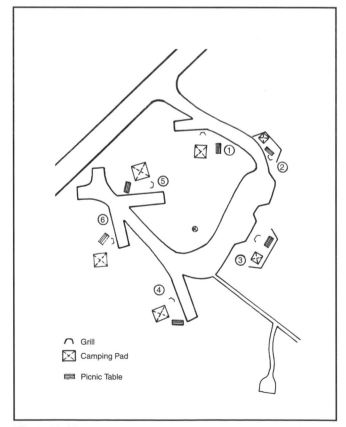

Grill

Camping Pad

Picnic Table

Figure 1.11

oped. But these areas are expensive to maintain and easy to vandalize. Because this type of design spreads use over a large area, a greater proportion of the environment is affected. From an engineering perspective, this type of design works. From a *recreation* perspective, it does not! It was obvious, even to the Forest Service, that the poor old engineers couldn't plan parks!

The Forest Service then gave the job of recreation planning to foresters. Overnight they, including one of the authors, became instant "experts" with little experience and even less technical education. Since their supervisors knew almost nothing about recreation, there was no one the untrained foresters could turn to for quality training. Figure 1.12, a camping area in a National Forest in Mississippi, illustrates a design typical of this group. The area exhibits many of the same problems discussed above: too few units to manage, maintenance and vandalism problems, and environmental damage. Additionally, this design wastes large amounts of potentially usable land in wide, or "fat" camping loop roads with few camp units. The roads themselves are a major mistake. There is no sensible system of circulation; the number of intersections and their relative locations are a source of confusion to users. (Remember, what you see in this bird's-eye view is not what confronts the user on the ground). From a management standpoint, the road system is difficult to sign and, more importantly, is extremely expensive on a per-site basis; that is, the amount of road per campsite is much too high. As in engineering, some of the technical knowledge foresters have is important to recreation planners. As is the case with the engineers, however, this area—planned by foresters—does not take into consideration the needs of people who use and manage the area for recreation. It was obvious (at least to some folks) that the poor old untrained foresters couldn't plan parks, either!

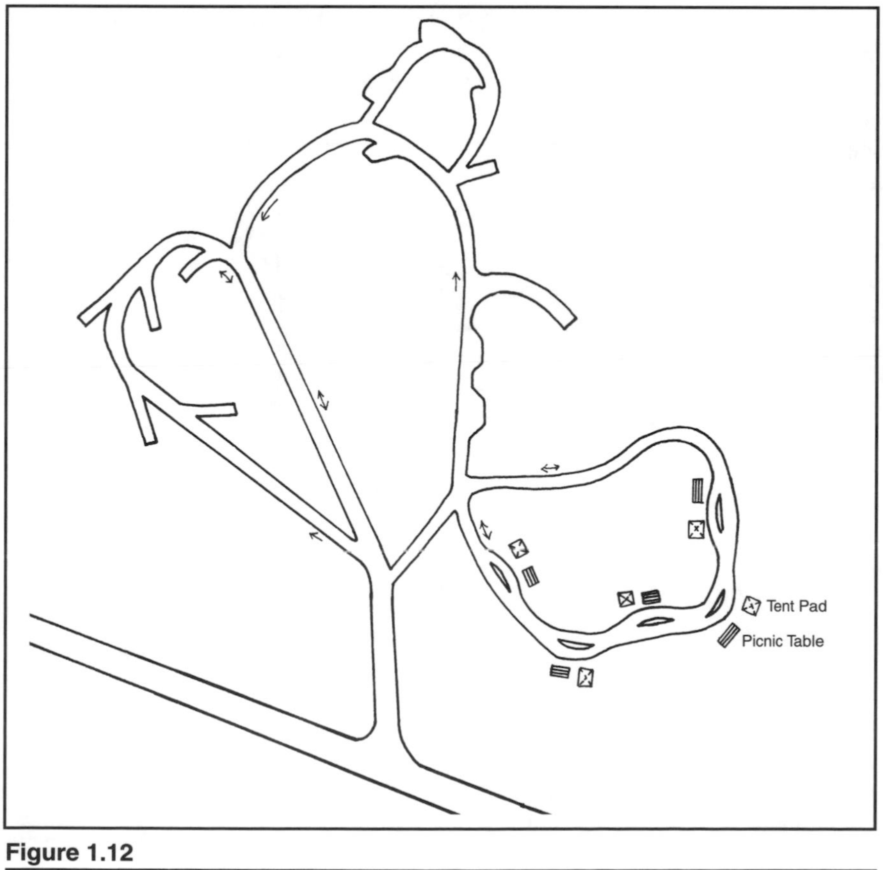

In the early 1960s, the Forest Service began hiring extensive numbers of landscape architects, and they were the next group to whom the agency assigned the job of recreation planning. Figure 1.13 depicts a sizable National Forest recreation area in Texas, designed by a landscape architect, which corrects some of the mistakes made in the previous two plans. More sites are included, so on-site management is feasible. The increased number of sites also reduces the expense of per-site construction and maintenance. Since all sites are centrally located instead of dispersed at several small areas, the potential for environmental damage is limited to one location. There are *big* problems with this design, however. The long, one-way loop precludes the opportunity to use a large portion of developable land between the upper and lower portion of the road. The one-way road is confusing enough but allowing day users to use the boating and swimming sites is even more of a problem. In this large area, both facilities could have been for campers only. From the user's standpoint, regardless of where you choose to camp, every person who launches a boat or who uses the swimming site is required, *by this design*, to drive by your campsite. Everyone drives by everyone else! Disregarding technical considerations for a moment, our goal should be to create a positive recreation experience for users. Routing *all traffic* by each campsite is not an effective means of accomplishing this goal (when you study Chapter Eight, you'll easily see most of the things wrong with this Texas area). *The major mistake made by the Forest Service was in thinking landscape architects had the expertise and academic park training to provide park design excellence—they did not!* An even bigger problem was that few of the previously mentioned engineers, foresters, and their untrained superiors realized that landscape architects didn't know how to plan parks either. Their mistakes were simply bigger and far more costly than those made by the persons they replaced!

In fairness to the Forest Service and their technical staffs who planned these areas, it must be stated other agencies have made similar and oftentimes greater mistakes. When the designs above were conceived, outdoor recreation itself was a new phenomenon, at least on a larger scale. There were no recreation professionals to whom agencies could turn for design assistance. Thus, much of the recreation planning during the 1950s and early 1960s became, by default, the responsibility of technical personnel. As the demand for outdoor recreation

Tent Pad
Picnic Table

Figure 1.12

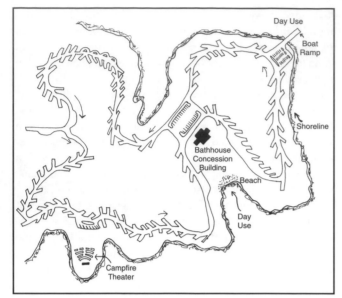

Figure 1.13

continued to grow, more universities began offering curricula in recreation, and graduates of these programs started entering the job market. Some of these new recreation professionals began producing designs for recreation areas, and this brings us to our second case history.

Case History 2: Inattention to Technical Requirements

Unlike their predecessors with backgrounds in technical disciplines, most of the new recreation graduates were trained in "people-oriented" skills. Courses in programming and leadership provided a better grounding in the needs of users; the new recreation professionals had a more complete understanding of management and program staff requirements in operating facilities for visitors. They did not, however, have the technical skills available to engineers, foresters and landscape architects. Concepts such as road alignment, drainage patterns, which trees will best withstand user impact, and spatial awareness were not, and *generally still aren't,* part of the recreation curricula. Thus, a new generation of individuals developing recreation plans emerged. These individuals were trained in areas where previous planners were weak, but unprepared in areas where their predecessors *were partially* competent.

In many instances, the new recreation graduates who produced designs had no training as planners. In this sense, they shared a common background with earlier planners, and made some of the same mistakes. Part of the problem has been a matter of economics. Most of the land available for outdoor recreation is managed by either the federal government or the states, and agencies at this level of government are more likely to have the funding capability to staff planning positions. Historically, however, these levels of government have not been heavily involved with intensive recreation development; most advancements have been made by county and munici-

pal governments and by private and commercial concerns. Yet many of these smaller recreation agencies and companies cannot justify the expense of a full-time planner.

Assume for a moment you've just graduated from college with a degree in recreation. Your first job is as the Assistant Director of Parks and Recreation in Median, Ohio (population 27,500). Your boss has a strong background in programming, so most of your responsibilities seem to fall in the area of park management and maintenance. The annual budget has funds earmarked for the development of a new park which will include a day camp, picnic area, playground and trails system. You are given the assignment of overseeing the design effort. If you can't afford to hire a consulting firm (and you probably can't), what do you do? In this case, you probably have two choices: Design it yourself or go to the city engineer for help. If you can afford a consultant, how do you know his or her plan has merit? Almost all consultants do an excellent job of *packaging* their products with professional drawings and presentations. But, the old saying about beauty being only skin deep is worth remembering. An attractive package, whether developed in-house or by a consultant, *does not guarantee a good design.* In fact, it often covers up a poor one.

The fact is, none of these solutions is ideal, yet all too often this is how park design evolves: The responsibility for planning falls to the person who is "least unqualified." To illustrate this point, let's examine the evolution of a campground in a *city park* in Kentucky. The campground was designed by an individual with a background in recreation programming, and this original development is shown in Figure 1.14. At this stage, the major problem with the design was the failure to take advantage of all of the usable land with five exceptions—no campsites were built on the outside loop. The

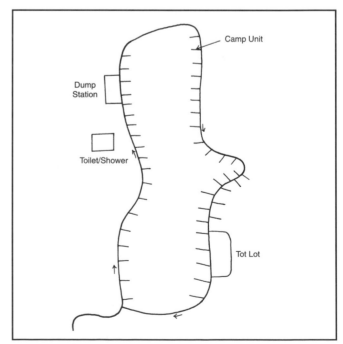

Figure 1.14

problems began to compound when a series of additions to the campground was built. The first addition, shown in Figure 1.15, was typical of developments of this type all over the world. The planner erroneously assumed *there was a need to extend from the roads already in place.* The difficulty with such an assumption is this: It takes for granted the original development was well-designed. If the original is bad, extending from it will usually make the situation worse, and whether you are adding to a campground, a trail, a playground, or any other recreation facility, this axiom of design applies.

The design in Figure 1.15 begins to create several problems we've already discussed. The number of intersections increases considerably, making the area confusing to users and difficult to administer. The new roads widen the use zone and increase the potential for environmental impact associated with increased use, thus creating additional maintenance problems. These problems are all compounded further with the completion of the next addition, shown in Figure 1.16. Once you start this type of addition sequence, it's difficult to break away from the pattern and salvage a functional design.

One final addition was also completed and the campground, as it exists today, is shown in Figure 1.17. For a simple example of the type of problem created by this design, consider the small loop in the upper left-hand corner of the design. The administration decided the campground should have an area reserved exclusively for tent-camping and designated this loop for that purpose. The question is, how does the on-site manager enforce this regulation? It is possible, through design, to limit an area to tent camping. (Although, as we'll discuss in Chapter Seven, this may be a poor management decision in developed campgrounds.) One way (though we don't think it's good) to accomplish this is to provide nearby parking and have users walk to their tent sites. If

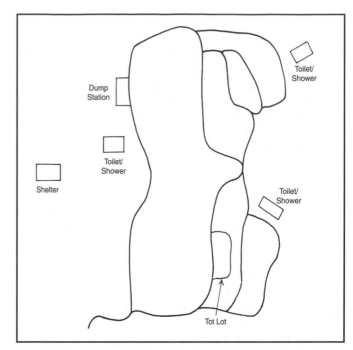

Figure 1.16

a road or other circulation system interconnects all areas, it is almost impossible to separate different types of users. This holds true for campsites, trails, play equipment, and most other recreation facilities. It may not be a management or design goal to separate areas, but if it is, they should be zoned without obvious circulation access between them. In Chapter

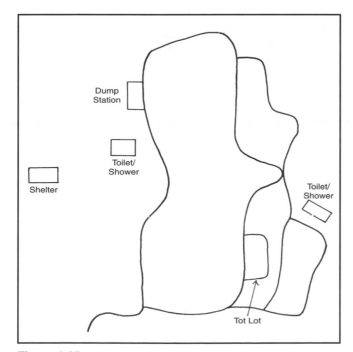

Figure 1.15

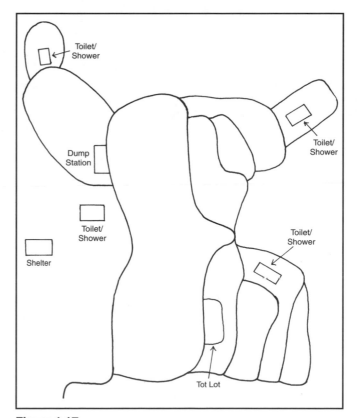

Figure 1.17

Eight, we'll give you the opportunity to redesign areas like this one. Major redesign of poorly designed parks is much more difficult than doing it right the first time. Although the person in charge of this park had a master's degree, he made the mistake of not starting with a rough, workable master plan. Thus, when users demanded expansion, he simply added to his problems without a clue as to where the design would end up. The authors see this sort of mistake worldwide.

From a design standpoint, we've been fairly critical of planners with either a technical or a recreation background. Most of the design problems in these two case histories caused these undesirable consequences. First, they encouraged environmental damage. Second, they created management and maintenance complications. Finally, the park areas weren't designed to beckon users. The primary problems for *users* we've discussed to this point have been confusion or inconvenience resulting from poor road patterns, but the examples in both case studies also omitted the most important aspect of recreation possible. This omission wasn't a facility—it was the philosophy that *recreation should be fun!* Surprisingly, most wildland parks and recreation areas seem to be designed without this idea in mind. None of the areas in either case study had play equipment, ball fields, hike 'n bike trails, or other areas to provide *recreation opportunities* for users. None of the campgrounds in either case study had campfire the-

aters, or other facilities to provide *program opportunities* for staff to share with users. The first two Forest Service areas we discussed were too small to justify these developments; the other, larger, campgrounds actually neglected to include most of these facilities.

If you seriously plan parks for people, you can't afford such negligence in recreation. As we suggested at the beginning of this chapter, recreation professionals have a dual responsibility: protecting the environment and creating an enjoyable experience for users. Provision of a facility such as a campground doesn't carry with it guarantees of enjoyment, and while recreation programmers shouldn't force their programs on park visitors, they should nevertheless offer opportunities for people to participate in planned activities. Programmers should also provide a pleasing environment—one which has aesthetic appeal and protection from environmental impact built into it. Programmers, managers and maintenance crews can all contribute to user enjoyment and environmental quality. In our opinion, however, none of these individuals has more potential for benefiting, or harming, these efforts than the recreation planner. To guarantee that the outcome of the planner's work is positive, he or she needs to be familiar with both technical and people-oriented skills. In the following chapter, we'll explore the specific kinds of knowledge planners should have.

Chapter Two

Tools of the Trade

Do you know:
- Water runs downhill?
- Shallow-rooted trees cause problems in parks?
- We rarely measure what we do in recreation?
- If possible, trails should begin on a slight downgrade?
- Years ago (in federal agencies) public safety received more emphasis and concern than it does today?
- Over 40 percent of developed site campground use comes as extended family or family and friends wanting to camp together?

Do you know:
- People should be hired and/or promoted based on qualifications—not on skin color, gender, age, political or religious preferences?
- *Within a campground* use of a campfire theater or other program area *is not* a function of distance to it?
- Parking lots are major sources of water pollution?
- Wilderness use in the 1990s is dropping (in some places drastically) all across the United States?
- All park planning should begin (but rarely does) with *people*—whom do you want?

Do you know:
- Which presidents (this half century) have done great things for outdoor recreation—*and* which of the rascals have done the most harm?
- Design of casino-related campgrounds is a major emphasis as we near the year 2000?
- Engineers, architects, landscapers, researchers, and planners are (or should be) service personnel with a "how can we serve you" attitude?
- Persons with disabilities visit parks to have fun (just as others do)—not just to use the toilet!?
- Universal campsites discourage fire ants?

We've provided a few *"do you know"* questions to give you a mini-idea of the answers you'll have to dig out as you plan parks for people. Somewhere in this book you'll find our answers to these questions and hundreds of others. You will also have questions for which we don't—as yet—have answers!

Our aim throughout this book will be to weave individual elements of recreation administration—planning, design, programming, maintenance, construction, and management—into a complete tapestry. The old saying about a chain being only as strong as the weakest link seems appropriate here. If you build facilities poorly, maintenance will be difficult. If management is lax, programs will suffer. If you do not provide site protection, families will not visit you in big numbers. The three authors agree, however, that the link causing most of the problems in parks and recreation areas today can be traced to poor planning and design.

This chapter has two purposes. First, we want to share with you some examples of problems created by inadequate planning. Second, we will examine the types of knowledge recreation planners need to consider in their work. Successful planning may depend on skills as diverse as engineering and political sensitivity. No individual can expect to master all the areas of expertise necessary for planning. Thus, part of the role of the planner should be to gather and synthesize information from various sources. Consider, for example, the recreation complex shown in Figure 2.1 (you should understand

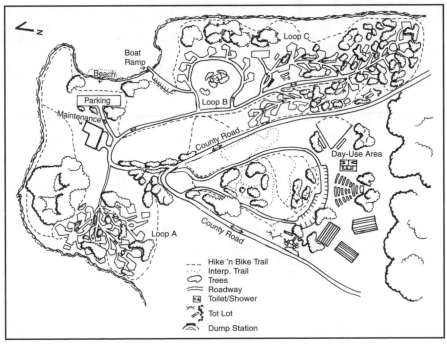

Figure 2.1

this is a poorly designed area). This area has at least 30 planning errors designed into it, ranging from landscaping and engineering to maintenance and programming. We have included a list of errors in Appendix A, and there are other errors we have not highlighted. How many can you find? To provide you with some help, let's explore some of the concerns facing planners.

Water

Water is one of the best friends outdoor recreation professionals have. Scenic waterfalls such as Bald River Falls in the Cherokee National Forest (Figure 2.2) are visitor drawing cards throughout America. Water provides the major attraction at many parks in the form of boating, fishing, swimming, skiing, and other activities. However, water can be one of our

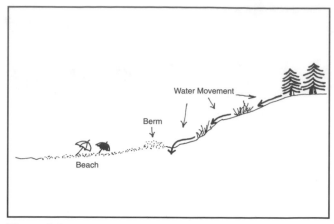

Figure 2.3

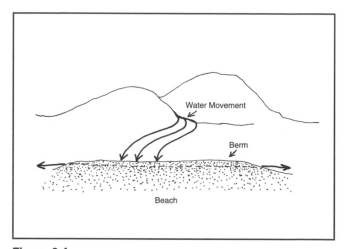

Figure 2.4

Figure 2.2

worst enemies if we fail to cope with it properly. For example, *water runs downhill,* often causing erosion problems. When you allow water to run downhill over extended distances, both volume and velocity increase. The results of this are evident around beaches and other waterfront attractions which, since they are at lower elevations than surrounding land, are particular victims of water-caused erosion. One method of coping with this "mysterious" property of water is to place a ditch and berm combination just above the beach, as shown in Figures 2.3 and 2.4. This moves runoff water to the side of the beach, preventing the buildup of a large enough volume of water to erode the sand. The velocity of the runoff water is also slowed by reducing the distance of the unchecked downhill flow. If you don't keep moving water away from fragile surfaces erosion can quickly occur. See Figure 2.5 where concentrated runoff has already cut a deep ditch on a then-new campsite at Stone Mountain, Georgia.

Polluting agents are another problem caused by runoff water around beaches and waterfront zones. Parking lots collect gases, oils and waxes spilled or leaked from vehicles. When these lots are uphill from beaches, rainwater collects the pollutants and carries them to the recreational water below. To avoid this problem, parking lots can be constructed with surfaces slightly tilted (at a two to three percent grade)

away from the beach zone, as shown in Figure 2.6. The tilt directs water away from the beach into a sump or rock-filled filter strip. If a parking lot is already installed (and the lower edge of the lot is facing the beach), the same sort of filter strip may be added to the edge of the lot, as shown in Figure 2.7. Such a strip should consist of a ditch two- to three-feet wide and four-feet deep that is filled with two inch minus rock and topped with crushed stone. As waterborne pollutants hit this strip, they percolate down through it instead of passing over to reach the shoreline below.

The roofs of buildings in parks—picnic shelters, rest rooms, entrance stations and other structures—act as mini-watersheds, too. Rainwater will drain to the edge of rooftops and then fall immediately below. Unless the ground surface beneath the eaves of a roof has been protected with crushed stone or other reinforcing materials, you'll have a muddy mess and erosion will occur here rapidly.

Another "mysterious" property of water is its tendency to *seek low places.* If a park has them, water will rarely fail to find them. Figure 2.8 shows a patio at a TVA group camp entrance zone filled with water after a moderate rain. Why? Design folks didn't include drainage outlets in their low rock walls. That's why!

Figure 2.5

Figure 2.8

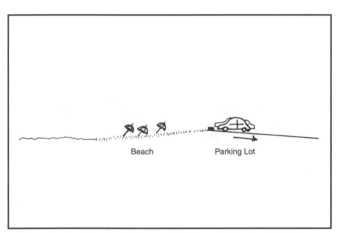

Beach   Parking Lot

Figure 2.6

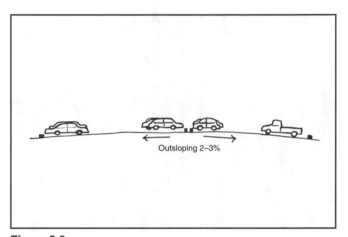

Outsloping 2–3%

Figure 2.9

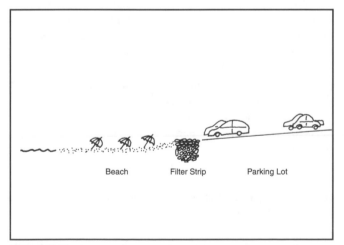

Beach   Filter Strip   Parking Lot

Figure 2.7

Parking lots, trails, roads, play fields, and play courts are among the other types of areas where water tends to pool. To avoid the problem in facilities such as these that are built on flat ground, crown them in the middle as shown in Figure 2.9. In other words, make the central portion of the surface slightly higher (two to three percent is enough) than the edges. This prevents water from standing, creating a nuisance for users,

becoming a potential breeding ground for insects, and causing inconvenience for maintenance crews.

A final "mystery" of water is this: *If recreational facilities are geared to waterfronts, they may get flooded,* as shown in Figures 2.10 and 2.11. Because so many recreation lands are located next to lakes, streams, and rivers, many parks are partially or entirely situated on flood plains. The possibility of periodic overflow should not necessarily prevent building recreation areas on flood plains. Athletic fields, golf courses, campsites, picnic areas, and similar facilities may not suffer a great deal of damage if they are subject to periodic flooding. Since they are relatively flat, flood plains are also well-suited for certain types of recreation facilities.

Caution should be exercised, however, if any of the following conditions are present. *Frequent flooding:* If an area is subject to flooding on a regular, cyclical basis, it may be best to avoid development entirely. *Rapid flooding:* In areas such as the narrow valleys and canyons of mountainous areas, flood waters may rise rapidly enough to create dangerous conditions. Sites where this danger exists should be posted as hazardous or avoided, and facilities such as campgrounds, where people could be caught unaware, should not be located here at all.

One of the most difficult tasks in planning is learning to identify potential water problems before developing a

Figure 2.10

Figure 2.12

Figure 2.11

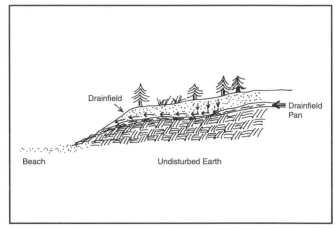

Figure 2.13

recreation area. Drainage patterns, minor changes in elevation, off-site conditions or problems, and potential sources of erosion and standing water are not easy to see. Additionally, construction may alter the water movement patterns on the site. If you have questions about preventing or solving water problems, we suggest you contact your local office of the National Resources Conservation Service (NRCS) for advice.

Soils

Probably more information is available about soils than any other element of recreation planning. Yet the characteristics of soil—its potentials and limitations—may also be neglected more frequently than other elements of the planning process. There are three basic types of soil: *clay,* which tends to absorb and hold moisture; *sand,* which does not; and *silt,* which covers all the gradations between clay and sand. The basic problem with soil, from a recreation planning perspective, is that certain types of facilities are not compatible with certain types of soil. If a recreation planner fails to incorporate soil information into his or her design, the results can cause a variety of problems. Make sure you seek aid from a soil scientist. If one isn't available in your organization, ask the NRCS for some additional help (a soil scientist explains his findings to a group of recreation designers in Figure 2.12).

A quite serious mistake caused by inattention to soil conditions is depicted in Figure 2.13. The plan for a recreation area in Texas called for a septic drain field to be located on a hill overlooking the beach. Effluent from the toilet's septic tank, as usual, moved downgrade through the drain field. With proper soil absorption, the effluent should have percolated through the field safely and harmlessly. Since soil information wasn't gathered prior to construction, planners and engineers weren't aware of a hard pan of nonabsorbent soil less than three inches below the *bottom* of the drain field. This pan sloped gently toward the beach zone and actually came to ground surface above the beach. The effluent hit, ran along the top of the pan, and seeped out on the slope above the beach (Figure 2.14—Effluent moves in a small stream towards the beach). As a result, the beach area became unsafe and unusable because engineers and planners didn't take time to gather adequate soil data!

It is not essential for recreation planners to be soil scientists. As with hydrology, your local NRCS office can help provide most of the information on soils you need. It is important, however, to understand the *implications* of this information for the design of recreation areas. Recreation planners should avoid placing facilities in areas where soils are inappropriate for them. For example, if you were a planner visiting the construction site in Figure 2.15 (with a heavy clay

Figure 2.14

Figure 2.15

Figure 2.16

base), would it surprise you to return a year later and see the finished road looking as it does in Figure 2.16?

A word of caution seems advisable here based on the authors' extensive experience. As planner, you must have enough expertise to know when and how to use soils, along with vegetative, hydrologic and other technical information. Soil scientists are likely to have little or no knowledge of recreation planning and design. Their advice may be helpful in curing the *effects* of problems (such as soil compaction), but may not address the true *causes* of your woes. The same sort of

caution should be exercised when dealing with foresters, hydrologists, engineers, researchers and others (including the public).

Vegetation

There are two basic problems with existing vegetation in recreation areas. One problem is having too much of it. The other problem is not having enough. First, let's consider some of the reasons why vegetation should be removed.

Plants and Hard Surfacing. Some recreational facilities, such as the paved parking lot in Figure 2.17, are not compatible with existing vegetation. Hard-surfaced lots and earth cut off the moisture and air needed for survival by the root systems of trees. Failing to cut most trees prior to building such facilities will lead to their death and the need to remove them within a relatively short period (one to two years) after construction is complete. This later removal is normally far more costly than a preconstruction cutting, as it leaves stumps which must either be removed or left as eyesores. As the tree dies, rotting limbs may also cause hazards during windy periods. Leaving big trees in new parking lots creates costly maintenance problems worldwide.

A word of caution here about the removal of trees (even those in Figure 2.17): it will make certain you are *attacked* by the save-everything environmental crowd. It is the reason the large oaks in Figure 2.17 were not cut when they should have been. Environmentalists don't have to pay the extra costs of the demands imposed by their rhetoric; you do. They do not have to have any knowledge to be an "aginner;" you do have to know what's right and wrong. Do so with courage!

Vista Cuttings. Parkways and roads within recreation areas often move through beautiful scenery, particularly in mountainous areas. In many instances, it is possible to enhance the experience of visitors by cutting trees that block vistas. Site-specific conditions dictate the appropriate type and amount of clearing. In addition to aesthetic views, the planner should also consider visitor safety when developing vistas. Safety may be increased by providing parking areas or turnouts with wide shoulders sufficient for vehicles to pull off the road. If you develop off-road parking facilities, plan and design them for travel trailers and other large recreational vehicles as well as for

Figure 2.17

cars. Where narrow right-of-ways or other factors prohibit off-road viewing areas, safe vista viewing is still a concern. Avoid vista cuts in areas near sharp turns, crests of hills, intersections, or other areas where driver attention should be focused entirely on the road.

Overshading. Particularly in warmer climates, recreation areas and shade go together like hot dogs and mustard. However, in some instances, thinning vegetation to reduce shade is appropriate. Campsites should be provided with morning sun for drying equipment (and warming campers). Beaches should have afternoon sun. Some areas, such as playgrounds and picnic areas should have a mixture of shade and open areas. Given this mixture, users can design their own experience, based on their preferences and the current weather conditions.

As a general rule, asking users what their shade preferences are *will not provide* you with a valid guide for deciding how much vegetation to cut. People tend to overestimate the amount of shade they actually prefer, so your own careful observation and common sense are useful tools when prescribing levels of shade.

In all park efforts you should do everything possible to beckon users and to help them enjoy your park environment, facilities, and program. Listening to the "save all the trees" crowd causes *unskilled* park personnel (and politicians) to make serious mistakes as shown in Figures 2.18 and 2.19. The first one "shows" (hard to see isn't it?) a state park campground in western Washington. The photo was taken about noon on a *bright, sunny* day. Yes, it's dark *and* frightening! The second dark area is the entrance to a private campground in northeastern Ohio. This photo was also taken on a bright sunny day. The dark entrance and 100 percent overstory shade in the campground *repulsed* visitors rather than beckoning them. The difference between the two areas was in the attitude of the managers—the private owner took our advice and intended to have a remedial timber sale immediately to correct the problems. And she did! The public area still "enjoys" the heavy shade! (Readers should ponder these challenges and discuss them with one or more of their professors.)

Figures 2.18 and 2.19 also are linked to our discussion (later in the chapter) about design psychology. About now you should have a glimmer of two parts of learning how to plan parks for people. These are: (a) you have lots to learn about a host of subjects, and (b) they are closely interrelated in that understanding one piece of the puzzle requires you to relate it to other pieces.

Susceptibility to Impact. Some species of trees are more prone to damage from recreation use than are others. Young, vigorous hardwoods, particularly the deep-rooted species such as hickory, are probably most compatible with recreation use. Species such as scarlet oak, American beech, Douglas fir, white pine, and aspen are quite shallow rooted and more subject to damage from impact. Knowing your trees has two implications for planning. For some recreation developments, it may be possible to devise planting plans prior to completion of facilities. In these instances, the planner should take steps to ensure the vegetation planted is capable of withstanding im-

Figure 2.18

Figure 2.19

pact. In other cases, recreation development may be planned in areas where vegetation is already established. Here trees likely to be damaged by use (such as large and shallow-rooted ones) should be removed prior to development. Remember, foot traffic creates impact as well as vehicular traffic.

Perhaps it is appropriate to raise an ecological point here. Recreation professionals are faced with a choice: protect the environment by *prohibiting* recreation use or protect the environment by *conscientiously planning* for recreation use. If we make the choice—both personal and professional—that using our natural resources for recreation is a good thing, then we *must accept* some alteration of and impact on these resources. However, as we suggested briefly in Chapter One (and as we'll discuss in later chapters) it is possible to minimize the impact of outdoor facilities. Cutting trees subject to impact is an example of this. If, in the name of protecting the environment, a planner chooses not to cut an impact-susceptible tree in the middle of a new playground, he or she has condemned the tree to slow death by moisture and oxygen starvation, created a maintenance problem, and encouraged a potential safety hazard. If you do this, you're not a good steward of resource use. Trees should not be removed indiscriminately; however, when the situation warrants it, they should be cut down!

Tunnel Effect. Another instance when it is desirable, from an aesthetic perspective, to manipulate levels of vegetation is to control a tunnel effect. Vegetation along the sides of roadways and trails may grow up and over these corridors, creating a tunnel-like enclosure. A tunnel effect in itself is not bad; however, the old proverb about too much of a good thing should be invoked here. One key to aesthetically pleasing design is *visual variety*. Long, unbroken sections of road or trail which are enclosed become oppressive. Conversely, long open stretches can be monotonous. Other prescriptions for visual variety are suggested under the Design Psychology section discussed later in this chapter.

"Invisible" Effects. Some problems that result from failing to cut vegetation may not be readily evident. An excellent example of this is the attraction some species of trees, such as willows, have for water and sewer lines. In an effort to find moisture, the roots of these trees will, in effect, "attack" utility lines. Another often unseen problem with vegetation is dead limbs on otherwise healthy trees. Thus, a good motto for planners (as well as maintenance crews and other field personnel) is to "learn to look up!"

During the extensive revisiting of *Planning Parks for People,* we've learned numerous things or at least have had a few revelations. One of these revelations is most of a park's problems with vegetation are invisible to most park planners and managers. Building park facilities and private houses in groves of big trees or in species which can't stand construction or pedestrian impact are good (bad) examples. The planned community of Reston, Virginia, near Washington, D.C., is one of those examples (Figure 2.20). Developers and home builders damaged shallow-rooted trees and big trees, and the home owners who also added foot-traffic impact watched the trees slowly die. Along the way families spent thousands of dollars trying to save trees they had little chance of saving. (Note, the "save-the-trees rascals" zapped us or ya'll again!) This sort of foolishness has been repeated all across America.

Although the problem does not arise in as many instances, it is possible to remove too much vegetation. While it is not directly related to recreation, an excellent example of overclearing may also be found in many housing developments. Often, developers purchase a large tract of land, clear it of vegetation, grade the area, and build homes. Home buyers must then purchase topsoil, seed grass, and plant trees and shrubs in order to have yards. While this is likely preferable and less expensive to home owners than the Reston example, *why* can't we learn to use the tools (or knowledge) available to save some vegetation and minimize impact? An appropriate principle to remember when you plan parks is: "Cut what must be cut but *only* what must be cut." Vegetation should be left in place or planted to accomplish the following goals:

Screening. Trees with dense, low limbs as well as thick understory vegetation are useful for providing physical and psychological screens between areas you wish to separate. For example, if a design goal is to maximize the number of camp units per acre, vegetative screening around units can provide a sense of privacy for campers while allowing the

planner to develop a high-density camping area. A campground with sites carved out of a dense stand of young spruce can average 10 to 12 camp units or more per acre without producing a feeling of being crowded. Screening can also be used effectively to "channel" people from one area to another. For example, if you wish to have people use a reinforced trail between a lodge and a camp-

Figure 2.20

fire theater, cut only the vegetation necessary to construct the trail. This makes it convenient for the public to use the trail and inconvenient for them to stray from it, meeting users' needs and protecting the environment at the same time. Walking on a trail or camping on a site surrounded by vegetation also tends to create a "natural" atmosphere.

Some words of caution follow. We've provided considerable guidance in later chapters concerning vegetation, screening, and design psychology particularly to camp units, visitor protection, and trails.

Noise Reduction. Leaving vegetation between facilities can also help minimize obstructive sounds. If, for example, an area is limited in size, it may be possible to develop a wide variety of facilities and programs that might otherwise conflict with one another by leaving or planting vegetation strategically.

If a "grass mower" decides to cut this sound barrier later (as they often have done), you will have problems aplenty.

Advance Planting. If an area has been designed for future development in a long-range plan, it is a good idea to consider future levels of vegetation. For instance, if the plan calls for construction of a picnic area in five years, will there be adequate shade? Long-term advance planning of recreation sites is not always available, but if it is, additional plantings should be implemented as needed. This is another great opportunity to involve user groups in the planting of small trees and shrubs.

Cover Planting. Development and maintenance of vegetation in parks and recreation areas can benefit users in a variety of ways. Grasses, trees, and understory vegetation help prevent the erosion caused by both water and wind. Many species of shrubs also provide browse and shelter for deer and other wildlife. And shrubs bearing fruit and berries can be planted along the edge of an open field pathway to create a songbird walk.

Mowing. A tragic axiom in far too many parks involves grass—yes, acres and acres of grass. This axiom states that parks are run by grass mowers, a bit facetious sounding, but containing a ring of expensive truth. (TVA and the U.S. Corps of Engineers spend big bucks mowing [in our view] far too many acres inside of their [our] park areas.)

When given a choice, most maintenance personnel love to mow, mow, mow. Compared to most other maintenance tasks, mowing is not a difficult job, and as a result, they tend to mow more than is necessary. However, if you want to establish screening around individual camp units, you should instruct maintenance crews to cut *nothing* or *only* one mower width around the perimeter of each unit. This gives a well-kept, groomed look to the site without eliminating desired vegetation before it has a chance to develop into a screen. Mowing patterns should be prescribed specifically by administrative personnel with advice from the planner, rather than left to the discretion of maintenance crews.

A Final Word About Vegetation. During the late 1960s, outdoor recreation was enjoying an unprecedented popularity. With increasing numbers of users, many recreation areas began to take on a trampled, overused look. In response to this, government agencies began investing research funds into ways of coping with recreation impact. The research arm of the U.S. Forest Service spent considerable time and effort attempting to determine which kinds of grasses grow well around picnic tables receiving high impact. The answer, which in retrospect should have been obvious, was that none will. Grasses will withstand impact more readily in sunlight than in shade; however, if the potential for use is fairly consistent, the planner should recognize this and reinforce areas where impact will occur.

There are several sources available to help provide expertise on questions concerning vegetation. Each state has an agricultural extension service. Central extension offices are generally located on the campuses of land grant colleges or universities. Additionally, the extension service maintains branch offices throughout the United States. Often, help may be available through the various district or regional offices of the U.S. Forest Service and the National Resources Conservation Service. State governments support departments of forestry, and many colleges and universities have schools or departments of forestry or natural resources.

Topography

Developing recreation plans and designs on a flat piece of paper is quite different than designing facilities in the field. One skill essential for creating plans and assessing the merit of alternative designs is reading and interpreting topographic maps. These maps contain imaginary *contour lines* indicating elevations above sea level. For example, on a topographic map all points on an area elevated 1,250 feet above sea level would be connected by the same line. Normally, contour lines are drawn in intervals of two, five, or ten feet, depending upon the scale of the map. Along with the contour interval, this scale, which typically shows that one inch equals 50, 100, or 200 feet, allows you to determine the percent of slope of the land. Assume the contour interval is five feet and the scale is one inch equals 100 feet. If there are approximately three contour lines per inch on the map, the slope is (5 x 3) ÷ 100 or 15 percent—too steep for most recreational facilities. Figure 2.21 illustrates contour intervals, scale, and other features commonly found on topographic maps.

While topographic maps are important, they should not be relied upon exclusively to provide information for developing plans. Unlike maps drawn on paper, real topography is not entirely static. Streams may change course and lakes may vary in "pool" (the elevation of the lake surface). Features such as road or adjacent housing developments may also have been developed after the survey that produced the map was carried out. Actual contours or other features in the field may not be located exactly as shown on the map, either. The au-

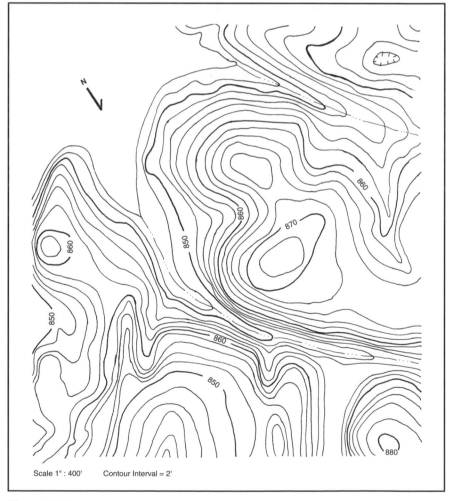

Scale 1" : 400'   Contour Interval = 2'

Figure 2.21

thors (who, of course, never make mistakes) once located a camping loop road adjacent to a tree line shown on a topographic map. Our intent was to provide shade for the campsites. While studying the map in the field, we realized the actual tree line was over 100 feet away from where it was indicated on the map.

Remember, on a scale of one inch equals 200 feet, a hiking trail six feet from side to side is indicated by a line the width of a pencil mark. As a result, mistakes are not difficult to make, and information drawn from topographic maps should be supplemented by other, more reliable sources. One such source, particularly if the area to be planned is larger than a few acres, is aerial photography. In some cases, your local NRCS office may be able to provide you with aerial photographs of your area. If not, commercial agencies are available to conduct photogrammetric surveys, usually at a reasonable cost. There is no substitute, however, for a hands-on approach. A recreation facility—whether a vest-pocket park or a 1,000-acre complex—should *never* be planned without on-site visits. There are too many intangibles which, without field planning, might be left unconsidered. Fact is, we believe most park facilities should be carefully field designed.

One design error we have seen a number of times relates to the inattention planners sometimes give to the interaction of people with topography. A common mistake is to choose a site for a recreation complex based on its proximity to a lake or reservoir, then develop the site on a hill or bluff overlooking the water. From an aesthetic perspective, this may be appealing. However, there are two program-related problems associated with this approach. First, the lake is the primary attraction associated with the facility. If the recreation complex is several hundred yards away from the lake—as well as 50 feet higher in elevation—then access to the water becomes a problem.

Second, a design goal may be to provide active play areas such as ball fields and play courts. Generally, when lakes are present, most of the developable (i.e., flat) land will be immediately adjacent to the shoreline; therefore, access from the main complex, if it is located on an overlooking hill, may again present a problem. The severity of this problem depends on the type of population for which the facility is intended. College students and young adults might find a half-mile walk down a 150-foot high hill with an 11 percent grade an inconvenience at most; for most other users such a path might present a real barrier.

We know of two recreation complexes in Indiana built on bluffs overlooking lakes. One is a university alumni camp catering to senior citizens and families with young children. The other is a resident camp specifically for children and adults with severe physical disabilities. All travel from the living zones to the lakes is difficult. In our view both camp locations were poorly planned.

There are several sources of information and assistance if you have concerns about topography. In addition to the NRCS and photogrammetric services mentioned, the United States Geological Service, with regional offices across the country, may provide help for you. Also, many colleges and universities have departments of geography and/or regional planning capable of providing topographic assistance.

Programming

Chapter Nine provides a more detailed look at the implications recreation programming has for planning. However, we mention programming here briefly for two reasons. First, let's reemphasize programs and the benefits they provide to people should be, but rarely are, the ultimate goals of recreation. Planning, administration, construction, and maintenance should *all* be oriented toward facilitating *program* delivery. In other words, the programs you plan to have should dictate overall design of your campground or park. Before you do any of this, however, you should decide and describe who you want in *your* parks. If it is the good ol' boys, families whose teens stay at home, and maybe old folks, programming isn't important. If you want extended families, teens visiting your park with their families, single-parent families, minorities, persons with disabilities, and more, then programming is a must! Second, we mention programming because it illustrates, through two simple examples, the need to seek a balance in planning. While there are exceptions, a good starting point from planners is to balance "too much" with "too little;" "too expensive" with "too cheap;" and, as illustrated in Figure 2.22, "too near" with "too far."

Figure 2.22 shows the design for an activity area in a developed site, a family campground operated by the Tennessee Valley Authority (TVA) in Kentucky. The play court, which consists of volleyball and basketball courts, is lighted to permit play after dark. The courts are popular, and normally attract a mix of 20 to 50 children, teenagers and adults each evening. Another popular campground attraction is the campfire theater. Passive programs, including movies, puppet shows, and sing-alongs, were once held in the theater four to five evenings each week. Often, several hundred people attended these programs. The theater and play courts were built within 50 feet of each other with no physical or vegetative screening between the two facilities. As a result of this design, the noise from the games on the play court made it impossible to conduct quiet programs in the campfire theater, and turning the lights off on the enjoyable play court in order to host a campfire theater program did not make for happy younger campers.

The point is both types of recreation—the passive campfire program and the active court sports—provide enjoyment for campers and are valuable assets to the campground. However, the design provided by the planners creates a situation where it is impossible to take advantage of both facilities *at the same time*. We'll talk more about concurrent programs in Chapter Nine; however, keep in mind one goal of design should be to maximize the use of *all* facilities. If one program will conflict with another, the design should allow for this by separating the areas designated for each one. Placing the campfire theater too close to the play court is an excellent example of not planning parks for people.

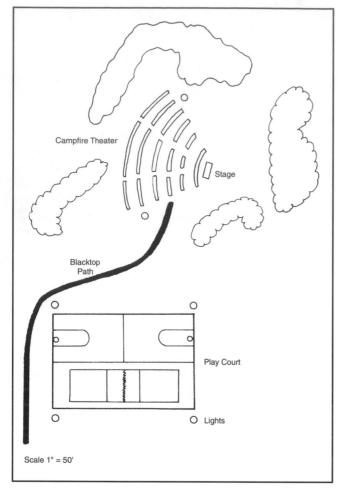

Figure 2.22

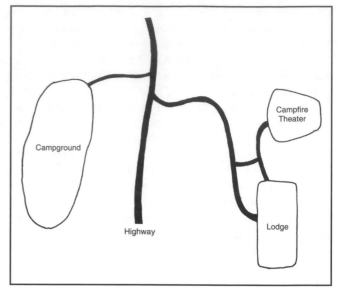

Figure 2.23

Separating use areas by too much can also create problems. Part of Paris Landing State Park in western Tennessee is depicted in Figure 2.23. In this case, the park campground is on one side of a busy highway. The park lodge and campfire theater are on the opposite side. Along their parkways, the National Park Service, as well as many state systems, make this same mistake. The distance between the campsites and a campfire theater is between one-third and one-half mile. On our visits to the theater, we found the evening programs to be quite entertaining; however, we rarely met people from the campground who attended the programs. Two comments are worth making here. First, program facilities should be relatively close to the areas supporting them. This close proximity should be physical, although, if this is not possible, it may be psychological. Large theme parks such as Disney World, for example, use shuttles in their parking lots; the attraction thus seems close because it is easily accessible. Second, program areas function more effectively when they are perceived to be a part of the recreation complex people are using. The TVA campfire theater discussed above is in a large campground. Some campsites there are farther from the theater than is the case in the complex at Paris Landing, but attendance from these distant TVA campsites was *once* as good (before they deemphasized programming) as that from campsites near the theater. There was no perception of *leaving the*

campground, and the program area was well-attended. Experience and applied research tell us participation at various program facilities *within* a campground is not a function of distance from campsites. This allows you considerable latitude in deciding where you locate such facilities.

A few sources may be able to provide you with advice if you have questions about planning outdoor recreation areas to enhance programming. Most "direct programming"—where agency staff actually interact with users on a face-to-face basis—occurs at the local level in municipal parks and recreation departments. As a result, city personnel are more familiar with programming than the majority of state and federal recreation staff, and may be able to advise you. Likewise, college and university *recreation departments where courses in programming are taught* can provide assistance.

A final means of gathering information about programming need—and one too frequently neglected—is to develop a working relationship with user groups. Local chapters of the National Campers and Hikers Association, the American Motorcyclist Association, horseback organizations, hunting and fishing clubs, and similar groups can provide you with a wealth of advice about their needs and preferences. In addition to gathering information, the public relations benefits make working with user groups worth your time. As we mentioned earlier, programs should be supported by planning. However, other concerns, including those of maintenance crews and administrative personnel, need to be addressed as well.

Administration

Parks can be planned to work for or against effective management. Conscientious planning can make recreation areas easy to administer. Failure to consider the needs of management personnel can create administrative problems throughout an area or in specific locations. Experience tells us most designers, planners and consultants are not knowledgeable

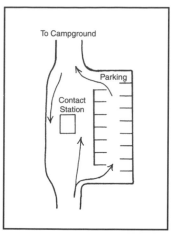

Figure 2.24

about many of your administrative needs and challenges. Our advice is set the rascals down and tell them! Consider, for example, the design in Figure 2.24. This shows the entrance to a campground within a state recreation area on Lake Monroe in central Indiana. Immediately across the road from the campground fee station (where campers register), the planner installed a large parking lot. The problem? The parking lot has two entrances/exits, one just before you get to the fee station and the other just beyond it. This design makes it possible to drive around, as well as past, the entry point. A parking lot may have been a necessary feature at this location, but the designer has given us an additional administration problem.

Interestingly enough, the entrance road to the campground at McCormick's Creek State Park, also in central Indiana, had exactly the opposite design problem and created another type of administrative headache. As shown in Figure 2.25, the approach to the fee station had only one lane for incoming traffic. The zone had a parking lot for visitors to the campground (which may or may not be a good idea, depending on your hosting and beckoning skills or the lack of them), with a single entry/exit point outside the fee station. The problem? Because of the one-lane entrance, campers who had already registered and who displayed a registration ticket on their vehicle must wait in line for newly arriving campers to check in. Assume, on the average, it takes two to three minutes to register; on Friday evenings there may be times when previously registered campers are required to wait in line behind 10 to 15 vehicles just to go back to their campsite after a day of sightseeing. This may not, on the surface, seem like an administrative problem, but would you like to greet a family of preregistered campers at your fee station after a 45-minute delay in central Indiana in July?

In our view this was a designer-insensitive mistake and we were among the hot and tired and angry users who complained. Wonder of wonders, the State Park folks listened *and* did something about the visitor unfriendly design turning it into one of the best camper

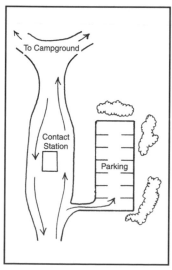

Figure 2.25

beckoning entrance zones we've ever seen! (See Chapter Eight for more details.)

Figure 2.26 shows an alternative design which solves this type of problem. The parking lot is accessible only from outside the entry point, and a dual entrance lane past the fee station lets newly arriving campers check in, using the inner lane, while those who have already registered may enter via the right-hand lane. (Note the turnaround we've added to the parking lot; dead-end parking lots in parks should be a no-no).

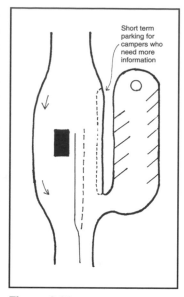

Figure 2.26

Campgrounds and other use areas with entry stations where only newly arriving vehicles are required to stop should have a minimum 200-foot, double-lane road on the right-hand side of the entry station. In addition to this minimum, planners should allow one foot of double-lane road for every potential user group beyond the first 100 feet. In other words, if an area has a maximum capacity of 300 vehicles, the double-lane portion of the entry road should be 200 feet for the first 100 vehicles plus 200 feet for the next 200, or a total of 400 feet. One final thought about camper or visitor check-in zones: They should always be far enough away from the highway intersection to allow for backup traffic. The larger the park or campground the more space for backup traffic is needed.

Poor planning can affect your ability to manage entire recreation complexes as well as specific areas such as entrance zones. This is illustrated by the multiple-use area shown in Figure 2.27, which depicts a park built on a broad peninsula of land. Prior to planning and developing the park, the only existing human-made feature on the peninsula was the county road. Over the years the area was built in phases (Figure 2.28 was the first phase). Each addition then added to visitor and administrator confusion. Consider the following administrative problems resulting from the "design" of the area. It is quite obvious ease of administration wasn't considered in the initial design and in the numerous expansion phases.

Traffic Control. A good axiom of design is to have only one entry/exit point in a recreation area. This minimizes user confusion (Where am I? How did I get here?), as well as reducing the number of points which must be controlled by management. If, for example, a design goal was to prohibit entrance to this park after 10:00 P.M., five intersections on the county road would have to be staffed or barricaded.

User Safety. Once the area between the county road and the shoreline was developed, the only place to install the new use area was on the other side of the road (area A in Figure 2.27). In addition to creating a safety hazard for users who want access to the lakefront, this area creates other problems.

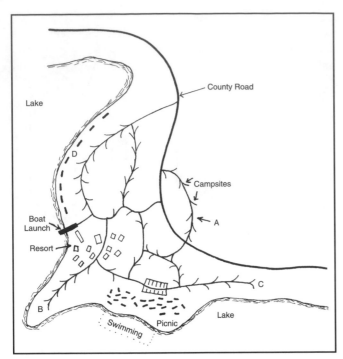

Figure 2.27

Since it is outside the rest of the complex, it may be more difficult to control vandalism and rowdiness in area A. It also requires either the costly installation of additional toilet/shower buildings and utilities, or forces users to cross the county road for these facilities.

User Convenience. Designs such as the one in Figure 2.27—which are surprisingly common in parks—are extremely disorienting to users. Each road juncture presents a new challenge. (Do I turn here, or go straight?) You could argue that directional and informational signs at each intersection would eliminate confusion; our response to this argument is: phooey! Extensive numbers of signs are a symptom

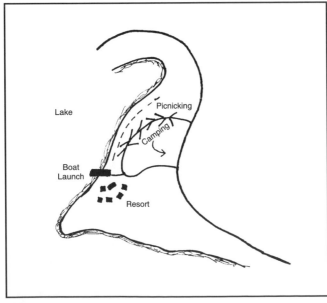

Figure 2.28

of poor planning and design; they help cure *effects,* but not *causes!*

Consider also the dead-end camping roads (areas B and C in Figure 2.27). Once a camper, towing a 22-foot trailer, reaches the end of these roads, how does the camper turn around? Pretend you are the park manager who must tell them what to do. (We certainly don't care to.) This suggests two other points to remember: Determine whom you want to visit the area and build to anticipate your clientele. If you plan on attracting users with large recreational vehicles or boats on trailers or extended families or teens or sizable diverse day-use groups or kids in wheelchairs, be sure you design for them. (Much more on this later.)

Zone Management. When you plan recreation areas, it is important to remember a concept called *simple zoning of use areas.* Design and locate facilities *near* other, similar areas and *away from* dissimilar ones, as with the play courts and campfire theater we examined earlier. The design of the park in Figure 2.27 did not follow this principle. For example, to reach or exit the boat launch zone, it is necessary to drive through and disturb part of the campground, inconveniencing users. From the manager's point of view, assume you want to close the campground after Labor Day, but keep the boat and launch ramp open. How would you route traffic? Don't ask us—we're just authors and planners. Similarly, both the swimming and picnic areas—day-use activities—are zoned near overnight camping areas, but campers and day users may have different recreational goals. We suggest these types of areas be zoned separately. User conflicts are thus avoided and management difficulties reduced.

Some areas within recreation complexes should be planned as "neutral zones." For example, the picnic sites (area D in Figure 2.27) violate this principle. Because of poor planning, a few individuals or groups are able to monopolize an entire section of shoreline which should be open to all park users. Camping or picnicking immediately next to the edge of a lake or river is an enjoyable experience; however, placing use facilities too close to a shoreline may also encourage erosion. Further, it tends to limit maximum use and enjoyment of the resource to the few groups who happen to arrive first. We suggest "primary attraction" such as shorelines, scenic vistas, and overlooks be designed so all visitors have an equal opportunity to enjoy them. To accomplish this, individual-use areas—picnic sites, camp units, and the like—should be kept a minimum of 75 feet away from such attractions.

One of the most difficult but necessary tasks of developing and assessing plans for recreation areas is to step back and view the "big picture." Most of the design errors in Figure 2.27 were committed because of three basic mistakes committed early on. Can you identify them? Here are some hints: They created safety hazards; forced dissimilar areas to be zoned together; and placed a severe limit on the opportunity to take advantage of usable land. Remember, look at the entire area.

This park design was doomed before it was ever constructed because planners allowed the existing county road to *dictate design to them.* Using roads and other support facilities already in place is cost-effective if, *and only if,* existing facilities serve the needs of the design. In this case, the county road ran through the center of the peninsula, splitting the available land into two marginally usable pieces. The other big mistake was in adding new features to phase one without having a well-designed master plan. (Where are we going and why?)

Figure 2.29 shows the same peninsula with the offending county road relocated and a host of other planning and design goodies you'll learn more about in the following chapters. The first planning job (one which is almost never done) is to decide whom you want to use the area. In our example we want extended families, nuclear families, single-parent families (all with teens), older Americans, persons with disabilities, international visitors (particularly if we are in a far western state), camping clubs, sizable day-use groups (such as company picnics or bus tour groups and church groups—several at a time), family picnickers, swimmers and boaters. We aren't keen on just attracting the good ol' boys, families whose teens stay at home, and the vandals and rowdies.

A primary concern was to build administration capability through zoning of uses. These zones include:

- Management zone with beckoning safe entrance, park office, maintenance/seasonal housing, dumping station (with a generous turnaround for those with trailers who decide they—after all—don't want to enter and pay) and entrance station.
- Boating use zone located immediately after the entrance control area. Note the main road just beyond this can be gated in winter allowing the boating zone to be opened (if you wish) while other areas are closed. The gate attendant can—*through design*—see who goes there.
- Group theme pod day-use zone. The three-group cluster is gated so other users won't penetrate the zone and each theme pod is gated. See Chapter Four for some user pleasing and money-making ideas on group day-use pods. Note again gate personnel can see who goes there.
- Family picnic/beach zone. Again the gate attendant can easily direct these users to their zone or area *and* see them drive toward the beach parking lot. Chapter Four covers beaches.
- Camping zone. Ease of administration is built in here with five gated loops the manager can open and close, including a special loop designed to beckon groups. Total units would exceed 200 which should provide a profitable area. Camp loops point to the water attraction and the toilets or toilets/showers (see Chapters Seven and Eight). The two sizable toilets/showers include family assist rooms which

are outstanding features for persons with disabilities. The same toilet/shower can be used by those enjoying the active and passive campground play zones.

- Campground amenity zones. We've broken these into two areas or zones though you wouldn't have to do so (see Chapter Nine). "Windows" created by mowing vegetative vistas along the county road give the potential visiting public the tantalizing opportunity (design psychology here) to see fun opportunities in this recreation complex. Since the two play zones are located apart from the bedroom and area camp loops, the manager *could* superimpose a sizable industrial picnic here without causing penetration of the camp loops. This would work well with the day-use theme pod zone. Again, the gate attendant can easily direct all overnight users to the first road to the left and see where they go. Facilities in the active play zone might include sizable shelter/equipment checkout, snack building, lighted multipurpose play court, tot lot, figure eight-paved radio controlled race track, eating and feeding area, and lighted softball field. The passive play zone could include shelter, skills area, tot lot, shuffleboard courts, boccie ball area and horseshoe pits (see Chapter Nine).
- The final zone is one located between the day-use zone and overnight use zone yet easily accessible to both. This is the interpretive zone with three to four theme trails or areas, and a campfire theater. The campfire theater thus could be used for all sorts of things including the final award ceremonies often planned by large day-use groups.

Making all these zones work for management and users means *careful* planning, coordination, and management are all imperative. Figure 2.29 could be designed better, but as designed, it would give staff persons an excellent, profitable

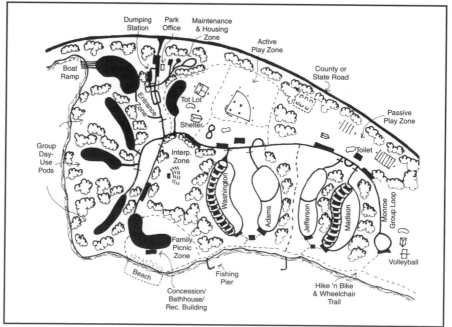

Figure 2.29

area to manage. And that, too, is what outdoor recreation is all about.

Elements showing you good and less-than-good designs for administrative purposes are a part of each chapter in this book. You are the key person in seeing that designs and rehabilitation plans include ways to improve park administration. Don't expect your designer to do it for you. Designers *do not have* the training and park management experience to do so.

Maintenance

There are several types of maintenance involved in parks and recreation areas. Typically, we think of *ongoing,* or *periodic,* work such as mowing, minor repairs and the like, and *long-term tasks* such as planning for new roofs for structures or resurfacing roads. *Preventative maintenance* is another type which, over time, is more important in terms of money and effort saved or spent. Since the planner can have a positive or negative effect on all types of maintenance, let's examine how this happens.

Ongoing Maintenance. As with administration, maintenance can be affected by planning on both a large and small scale. To illustrate, think about a basic maintenance task: collecting garbage. Figure 2.30 shows three ways a planner might design garbage disposal locations on a portion of a camp-loop road. Design A shows 12 campsites and 12 garbage collection points. (Remember, maintenance crews are generally paid by the hour.) Design B shows the same campsites, but with the garbage cans clustered to permit fewer stops for collection. In terms of benefits to users, there is a trade-

off here. On the negative side, campers might have to walk a little farther to deposit garbage. However, with this design, cans are available and odors removed from the "living area" of the campsites. Design C consists of the same 12 sites serviced by a single bulk-waste container, or "dumpster." With this design the number of collection stops is reduced even more, although the average distance from campsite to dumpster has increased. There is no "correct" answer to which of these designs will best suit the needs of a particular area, but both B and C are better than A. With clusters of cans, it is normally correct to group between a minimum of three and a maximum of five together to balance ease of collection with user convenience. Bulk-waste containers will service, depending on frequency of collection, size of containers, and campsite density, from 25 to 50 camping units. We prefer this system and recommend you have two dumpster locations on a 50-unit camp loop.

As we rapidly approach the year 2000, there is a fourth approach now used by many public agencies—providing no garbage collection facilities at all. It seems to work in some places and be less than successful in others. Our view is this is *not* a user-beckoning/user-friendly idea.

The same type of logic can be applied to ongoing maintenance on a larger scale. Continuing with our example of garbage collection and with the hourly paid workers, look at the design shown in Figure 2.31. This design depicts one way of planning camping areas in a large resource area, perhaps on a Forest Service ranger district. (A typical ranger district in the eastern United States might contain 100,000 acres of land.) Figure 2.31 illustrates the way most resource-based recreation areas have been planned historically. The design contains a combination of 10 small picnic and camping areas with a total of 70 camp units available for use. As you might imagine, the cost-effectiveness of collecting garbage from 70 units at 10 sites spread over 100,000 acres is not particularly high. In addition to being difficult to maintain, this type of planning violates sound principles of resource stewardship and, indeed, people management and protection. By providing small facilities throughout the resource base, the planner has scattered use, including that by vehicles, over

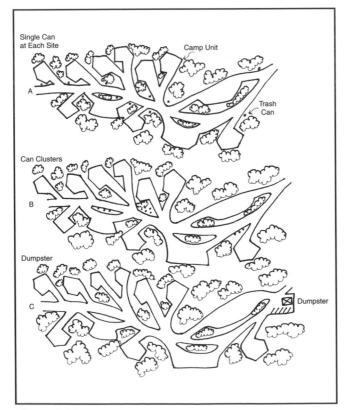

Figure 2.30

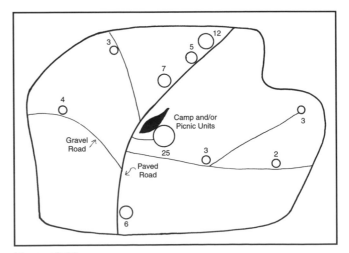

Figure 2.31

the entire area. This error will increase the proportion of the resource subject to impact and consequently environmental damage as well. This type of design thus suggests the need for another planning principle: areas subject to use and potential impact should be localized. Most federal agencies, including the Forest Service, the Corps of Engineers, and the Tennessee Valley Authority, have not approached recreation planning from this perspective. As a result, their recreation areas tend to be expensive to maintain, difficult to program, and hard to manage. For instance, one Corps of Engineers friend of ours has a 300-mile drive just to visit the campsites for which he is responsible.

The plan in Figure 2.32 shows how areas can be localized. Here the number of campsites had been increased from 70 to 815 while the number of areas have been reduced from 10 to four. There is a small remote area with 15 dispersed sites for users who desire a backcountry experience. *Note:* In the authors' view as the year 2000 approaches, there are far more folks who say they want a wilderness/backcountry camping experience than there are folks who will come out and enjoy it! This site can be managed, because of its placement, as an addition to the adjacent area with little increase in effort. The three large areas are sizable enough to cost-justify on-site management and maintenance crews, so potential for support facilities and programs enhancing the experience of users is increased. The planning principle involved here is: "Think big, plan big, and build big." Large areas benefit the manager, the maintenance crew, the program staff, the user, and the environment. From an ecological standpoint, this type of design allows us to identify where high levels of use will occur and enables management to take steps to prevent environmental damage.

Long-Term Maintenance. One excellent example of how planners can increase or decrease problems of long-term maintenance is in replacing roofs on park cabins. Planners in the environmentally charged 1960s placed countless rental cabins in densely vegetated areas where tree limbs covered and even touched roof tops. This led to rapid rotting of roofs and far too frequent replacement. These cabins needed more sunlight and much less shade.

Preventative Maintenance. Perhaps one reason it isn't difficult to find maintenance problems "designed into" recreation areas is the nature of the planner's job. Once an area is planned, designed, and constructed, the planner is finished with it. The planner doesn't have to worry about how well or how poorly the area functions. Trails deteriorate, erosion occurs, campsites are compacted, vegetation dies, signs get knocked down—these couldn't be the result of planning! Or could they? Twenty years' experience at hosting workshops on park design and rehabilitation tells us three unfortunate facts:

- Planners and designers rarely attend continuing education courses on planning and design.
- In far too many public agencies, planners and designers rarely work closely with or seek input from managers.
- Most planners aren't users of the facilities they plan, and they rarely interface with real park visitors.

Let's explore a few results of these planner characteristics. Some trails, because of the volume of use they receive, need to be reinforced with a hard surface. In parts of the country where frost heave is not a factor, hot-mix asphalt is one of the more popular hard surfaces used on trails. Asphalt holds up fairly well with one exception: it tends to crumble along the edges, especially in hot weather, when people step on it. The maintenance "solution" (again this addresses effects rather than causes) would be to patch the edges with new asphalt on a periodic basis. Yet the *preventative* maintenance solution, which is the responsibility of the planner, occurs during construction. As the trail is built, a border of crushed rock can be placed along the edge of the asphalt surface and tapered to ground level, as shown in Figure 2.33. This keeps weight along the sides of the trail, which in turn, prevents crumbling. As an added benefit, the gravel border prevents users from stepping off the edge of the trail, which is above ground level, and falling or spraining an ankle. As this example shows, planning techniques aimed at solving one problem will frequently prevent other types of difficulties as well.

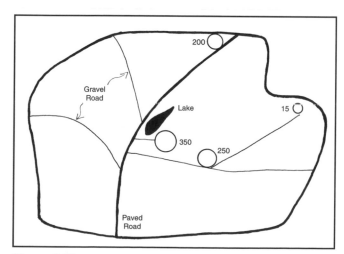

Figure 2.32

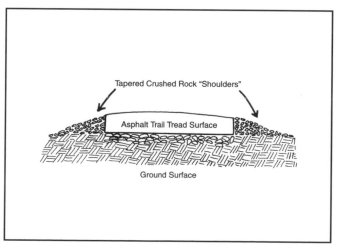

Figure 2.33

Figure 2.34

Staying with trails for a moment longer, let's continue with preventative maintenance. Figure 2.34 shows a trailhead leaving a Forest Service parking lot on the Cherokee National Forest in Tennessee. A few months before this picture was taken, the trail was covered with a three-inch layer of sawdust, which remained there until the first big rain. Due to some interesting design, the only outlet on the paved and curbed parking lot was located where the trail began. Water in Tennessee, as in other places, runs downhill. In this case, it ran away with the trails' sawdust surface. As you can see, planning for preventative maintenance requires anticipating what will happen as well as knowing what current conditions are. One of the authors, by the way, designed the trail and the parking lot, and was quickly promoted again, but the other two of us never make mistakes!?

In our discussion of administration, we talked about the need to localize potential areas of impact. The question here, from a maintenance standpoint, is rather like catching a cranky bull by the tail: Now that we have it, what do we do with it? Once areas subject to impact have been localized and identified, the answer is to take steps to reinforce them. To illustrate this point, let's look at three different ways of designing campsites. Because campsites receive impact from recreation vehicles as well as foot traffic, the potential for damaging the environment and creating maintenance problems is among the highest of all park-related facilities. Figure 2.35 shows a campsite with its facilities—the picnic table, grill, and garbage can—on the right-hand side of the parking spur as you face the site. We'll discuss campsite design more completely in Chapter Seven; for now, let's concentrate on the area of impact, shown in Figure 2.36, *caused* by designing the site this way.

One of the more unfortunate aspects of this type of design is the tendency for park administrators, as well as some members of environmental "awareness" groups to blame

users for the damage to the site. While campers and other recreationists do cause some problems in the natural environment, there are few that professionals can't control through conscientious planning and administration (i.e., designing preventative maintenance measures into park plans and enforcing regulations). Also keep in mind if we didn't have a recreating public using our resources, we wouldn't have jobs either!

Figures 2.37 and 2.38 show why it's easy to blame users for environmental damage, but Figure 2.37 also shows a poor campsite layout at Hungry Mother State Park in Virginia. *Note:* These photos at Hungry Mother State Park were taken years ago. There are two things you should know about the park: (1) In spite of the lack of camp-unit definition and dead and dying trees, the campground was full because users had all sorts of fun things to do (see Chapter Nine); and (2) unlike its sister state West Virginia, Virginia State Park folks haven't adopted user-friendly, environmental-saving universal campsites.

Vehicles were allowed to drive throughout the camping area, over nonreinforced surfaces, so the ground has been stripped of grass and compacted. The picture in Figure 2.38 was taken from the same vantage point as shown in Figure 2.37 to illustrate what this compaction does to trees. Users "caused" the problems here, but are they at fault or should we blame the planner?

Figure 2.39 illustrates a *somewhat* better (though still far less than good) campsite design. The shaded area of impact had been reduced by moving facilities to the opposite side of the spur from where they were in Figure 2.35. To understand why this reduces impact, it's necessary to know a little about users and their equipment. Almost all recreational vehicles and camping trailers have doors on the *passenger side* of their body (except pickup truck shells which open in the rear, and

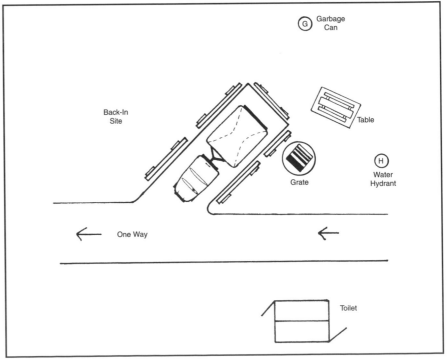

Figure 2.35

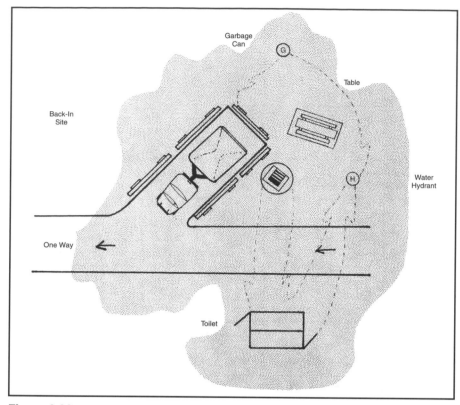

Garbage Can

Table

Back-In Site

Water Hydrant

One Way

Toilet

Figure 2.36

as we said, it is a better campsite than the one shown earlier in Figure 2.35.

Figure 2.40 shows a campsite designed to reduce impact, cut maintenance costs, and meet users' needs even more efficiently. It is one form of what is now called a universal campsite. In addition to aligning the facilities on the passenger side of the site, the entire camping area is *defined* and *reinforced*. Unlike those in Figures 2.36 and 2.39, the parking area (or spur) is not barricaded from the "living area" of the site and the table is movable. This allows users the opportunity to decide where to park on the site and thus how to design their own space. Site definition and reinforcement identifies and localizes impact on the area, helping to protect the surrounding environment. Figure 2.41 shows the result of designing sites this way. When the photograph was taken the site had been in use nearly 10 years. The field-designed campsite is tucked in behind the trees. It is generous, safe, level, and usable by tenter, wheeled-vehicle user, *and* persons with disabilities. The one fixed piece of campsite furniture is the on-the-ground grill. Table and lantern hanger are portable, meaning users can locate their camping equipment and vehicles anywhere they wish. You do not see a sea of barricades around the site and the parking zone. Nor do you see "overuse!"

some new trailers and fifth wheelers with doors on both the driver's and passenger's sides). The campsite in Figure 2.39 takes this into account and aligns campsite furniture to accommodate the movement of visitors between the site and their recreation vehicle. Maintenance and environmental concerns aside, isn't this *more convenient for the users* as well? In this illustration we've also moved the water outlet adjacent to the toilet building to remove another potential path of impact.

A critique of what isn't so good about the site includes a fixed table isn't user-friendly, the tent pad is an unnecessary relic of past years, the parking spur (unless it is 50-plus feet long is too short), and the barricades between the spur and furniture zone aren't necessary or user beckoning. Otherwise,

Grass still grows, surrounding trees are still healthy, ongoing maintenance costs are minimal, since most maintenance problems have been built "out" of the site, and what's most important tent campers and wheeled vehicle users alike are happy with the site. The principle to remember here is *operation and maintenance costs of recreation areas, as well as environmental damage, can be reduced significantly by building preventative measures into plans and designs for these areas.*

Before we leave the subject of maintenance, let's look at a few general considerations with implications for both planning and management. First, maintenance areas need to be *a part of* but *apart from* the park or recreation complex they serve. Figures 2.42 and 2.43 show two alternative locations

Figure 2.37

Figure 2.38

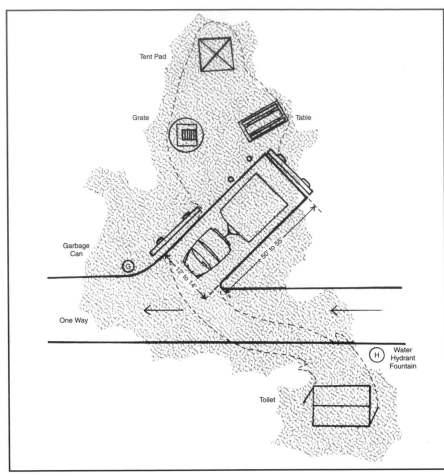

Figure 2.39

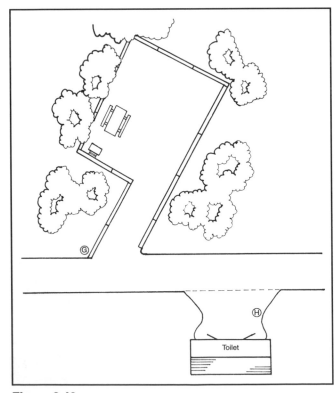

Figure 2.40

for a maintenance complex in a park. The maintenance yard in Figure 2.42 is slightly closer to the areas which need to be maintained. However, with this placement, the maintenance zone is the first thing visitors see upon entering the complex. This *is not* a good design. Generally, maintenance areas are not among the most aesthetic visual features parks have to offer. Also, they tend to be noisy, particularly early in the morning when many campers enjoy sleeping late, and in some instances hazardous. The design in Figure 2.43 removes the maintenance complex from the viewing area open to visitors as they enter the park. Planting a screen, or better yet, using existing vegetation to shield the complex makes it even less obtrusive. Note how the angle between the park-entry road and the maintenance-access road at point (A) prevents users from having to decide which is the right road to take as they enter the park. There is much more information about maintenance yards in Chapter Eight.

Other maintenance challenges may result from a lack of familiarity by recreation staff, particularly program-oriented personnel, with maintenance problems. Thus an occasional short seminar on the kinds of problems likely to need attention may save maintenance costs and other problems. You will likely have to teach most staff folks to "see things." A program leader or an interpretive specialist may walk past a plugged drainage culvert several times without noticing it (until it rains and the program area floods due to the lack of drainage). Encouraging communication among different types of staff can help make everyone's job easier.

One interesting aspect of working with maintenance personnel is their tendency to resist change. If a grass-mowing pattern has been in effect for 10 years, it likely will be difficult to convince maintenance personnel to change the pattern in order to establish screening around the new campfire theater or to minimize mowing around campsites, or to make whatever change is in order. Most staff persons at the Land Between the Lakes were big on grass mowing. When one of the authors was chief of recreation there and curtailed mowing around campsites, one of those maintenance folks wrote to his Congressional representative. Maintenance staff are generally excellent at what they do and their input into planning is, and should be, valued. *However,* like other groups— managers, programmers, construction crews and users—they tend to see things from a single perspective, one which is often unfavorable toward new ways of doing things. The fact is, our chief maintenance person at Land Between the Lakes at that time wanted a new maintenance structure to be located in the middle of a sizable campground so his grass mowers would always be close to their work (an extremely bad idea!).

Figure 2.41

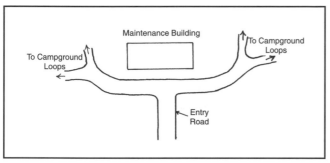

Figure 2.42

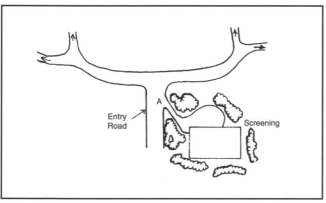

Figure 2.43

The planner has the responsibility to consider the perspective of maintenance folks along with the ideas of other consumers of the planning process, but the final plan should be his or her responsibility.

In addition to maintenance personnel, there are sources available to provide advice for building maintenance into park designs and facilities. The journal *Grist,* published quarterly by the National Park Service in cooperation with the National Recreation and Park Association, is a valuable maintenance tool. The U.S. Forest Service's Equipment Development Center located in San Dimas, California, also conducts research on maintenance equipment used in parks. Representatives from maintenance equipment manufacturers may additionally

serve as sources of information as long as you remember that they have products to sell, too.

Building or designing maintenance problems out of your parks should be a goal of every responsible park professional. Maintenance considerations, like administration, are woven into nearly all subjects and chapters of this book. Historically, though, park personnel haven't been taught to minimize maintenance problems and thus millions of dollars of *your* money got spent curing effects rather than causes. For additional information specifically about maintenance see Chapter Ten.

User Protection

Not so many years ago the Tennessee chapter of the National Campers and Hikers Association voted to "blacklist" a campground in the Cherokee National Forest in eastern Tennessee. In other words, it recommended their members discontinue using the campground. For some time, the Forest Service, along with many other federal and state agencies, followed a formula that provided parks and recreation services based on *access* and *attraction;* that is, if a natural resource had some appealing feature—a lake, a river or beautiful scenery—it was an attraction. Add to this an adequate system of roads and small, unobtrusive areas for camping (access), and the needs of recreationists would be served. In fact, this approach did and does serve the needs of a few outdoor recreationists—those who prefer an undeveloped, backcountry—a quasi-wilderness experience. This does not include most camping families and the small areas are not family campgrounds. Moreover, and this is one of the most important statements we'll make in this book, backcountry recreation enthusiasts make lots of noise and are well-publicized, *but they are a small minority of the population who use outdoor resources for recreation.*

In order to serve the entire spectrum of users—from the backpacker to the camper in an air-conditioned trailer—access and attraction are not enough. The formula must be expanded to include administration, which includes visitor protection. Administration has a number of implications, many of which can be enhanced or made difficult by the work of the planner. Ironically, the blacklisted campground had only recently been built, and, for the Forest Service, it was a large one—100 camp units. There were three gated loops which could be opened or closed, a residential area for seasonal or protection personnel, and a single-gated entrance/exit. In its first two years of use it also had a history of excellent visitor protection. Moreover, only campers who had paid the required fees were allowed inside the campground.

However, because of forest supervisory and ranger district staff changes, day users (noncampers) were allowed in and encouraged to use the beach inside the campground, and enthusiastic evening and late-night patrols by rangers and forest supervisory staff became a thing of the past. Instead of shouldering responsibility for visitor protection, the Forest Service, at that time, on a national basis shifted it to the local county sheriff. This policy change and the infusion of day use in an area previously designed for campers only "opened wide the door" for local rowdies. No longer were the campers welcomed and protected by the agency. Thus a once heavily used campground built on the shores of a beautiful 100-acre mountain-framed lake became blacklisted by what was then the nation's largest camping organization. This is of particular interest and concern to us, as one of the authors designed the 100-unit campground, *and* early on made sure it was adequately administered. Since then the Forest Service has built up a sizable law enforcement organization. Its lack of emphasis on visitor hosting is discussed in Chapter Ten.

In the past 20 years the Forest Service and some other agencies have backed away from strong visitor contact in developed sites. Unpaid hosts, hiring the local sheriff, concessionaires, and a shift of operations money to wilderness activities have all been negative elements. The one-on-one contact between uniformed Forest Service personnel (not storm troopers or "hosts," but real, live, interested and sincere Forest Service folks) on their extensively developed sites was one place where they could build a solid power base. This, in our view, can't be done in wilderness. With the demise of on-site personnel that greatly needed political power base is gone just at a time when it's needed most. Today's visiting public is above all else, interested in security. We will have more to say about this in Chapters Seven, Eight, Ten, and Eleven.

Planners can have an influence on park security with such things as sizable, manageable areas, a single entrance/exit to the park, quality location of entrance control station and personnel, careful zoning of uses, providing the ability to easily open and close camp loops, and not placing facilities and amenities inside of these loops. *But* they rarely can stop the political winds or aginner schemes that harm developed site use.

Recreation Programming

Earlier we said there were four real keys to heavy family use of parks, particularly campgrounds—access, attraction, administration (which implies protection), and fun programming. If the planning staff have the training and interest (most planners and designers have neither), they can enhance user enjoyment, minimize many maintenance problems, and ensure your area is a revenue-producer by properly zoning program amenities into your parks. The opportunities are endless.

By being aware of these opportunities, planners can thus consider *fun* as well as access, attraction, and administration to parks. In our view, this has rarely been done in our (your) nation's resource-based public parks. We believe design efforts aimed at providing program opportunities should address both a *broad spectrum of users and a broad spectrum of programs.*

Given the diversity of the recreation interests of people who use parks and resource areas, planners should work to facilitate opportunities for all user groups—from the hunter to the preservationist. Program facilities also need to complement one another; the nature trail should not be developed instead of, but in harmony with, the play court. The issue

here is a *principle of professionalism: It is not the planner's role to decide what the needs of the recreating public are.* Too often in the past, planners have developed facilities based on the attitude that, "if I like it, it must by right; if I don't, it must be wrong." This is not an appropriate approach to the development and delivery of recreation services. The planning function should support rather than dominate programming and administration.

During the early phases rewriting this book the authors ran into a "planner" (we question the title) who didn't like users—particularly persons who camped in anything but small tents! These undesirable people were environment-destroying pigs to this person. This "planner" is in the same anti-everything, environmentalist mode as the person in Chapter Eight who thinks old folks pulling trailers are road maggots! For a more in-depth look at outdoor recreation programming, see Chapter Nine.

Engineering

It would be difficult to imagine developing recreation areas without the expertise of engineers. The fact is, the authors wouldn't want to do so. We have considerable experience working with excellent engineers and a little experience trying to work with two or three who were far less than excellent. One of the big problems is engineers are not trained in the "people" aspect of recreation. As a result, the recreation planner should be responsible for integrating user needs with the technical aspects that design engineers provide.

Like other professionals whose expertise is necessary for the planning process, engineers can increase or reduce the cost of developing parks. To demonstrate this point, consider the alternatives for sewage disposal shown in Figures 2.44 and 2.45. The first alternative shows a sewage line running from a toilet building to a septic drain field located *at a lower elevation* than the toilet. The effluent flows by gravity unaided to the drain field. Conversely, in Figure 2.45, the drain field is located at a higher elevation than the toilet. In this case, the sewage must be pumped uphill, via a lift station, to the disposal site. In all instances, site-specific conditions will influence this type of challenge. Perhaps the only suitable soils for the drain field are above the toilet building so that the expense of lift stations is justified. However, *all other*

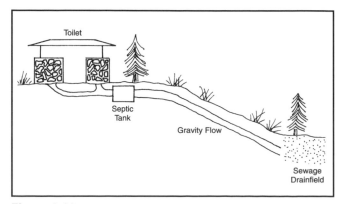

Figure 2.44

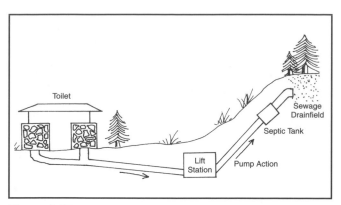

Figure 2.45

things being equal, the planner should work to keep the cost of engineered facilities to a minimum.

Another example of how engineered features can increase both development and maintenance costs in recreation areas can be found in several state parks in central Illinois. Designed by the Corps of Engineers, these parks included drainage ditches along roadsides. In flat areas such as central Illinois it is usually not necessary to provide any type of ditching system if roadways, including final surfacing, are built at ground level. If the land gently tilts downhill, so should the road surface. Yet, in addition to the cost of digging the ditches, each road intersection or branch or campsite spur required a culvert be installed so water would pass under the adjoining road, a particularly expensive operation if you add a culvert at each parking pad. Not only did these installations create unnecessary construction costs, the ditches had to be mowed by hand because of their slope, and the culverts tended to clog with leaf litter and other debris. Thus maintenance costs were increased by unneeded engineered facilities.

Our 20 years of experience hosting countless workshops and seminars (particularly on campground design) have provided some interesting trainees with all their strangeness. Some years ago we had a less-than-bright desk-type engineer (as a trainee) who became indignant with us. According to him no roads, anyplace, should ever be built without ditches and culverts. Like the abovementioned planner, no amount of "gentle" training or thoughts of the other trainees changed his mind.

The planner should take responsibility for limiting engineering to a role supporting recreation services and programs. Engineered features such as waste areas should not be allowed to dominate the park landscape. While these types of facilities are necessary to support the operation of a park, the planner should work to balance them with the aesthetic appeal of natural resources. Occasionally engineers, architects and other service folk are placed in a position of authority where they have the final "say" as to where facilities are to be located. In some cases this may be (due to personnel strengths, training or experience) the proper way to do things. Oftentimes it isn't—particularly when they say it's cheaper to do it this way than your better alternative. An extremely insensitive example of this is the location of the sewage treatment plant in Figure 2.46: next to a group camp swimming pool. Yes, it

was cheaper but . . . again that's TVA. As shown in Figure 2.47 at a nearby campground they also "saved" by building a campsite up against a sewage facility. The unit shown in Figure 2.47 does not appear to be a popular campsite! Engineered support facilities like maintenance yards should be designed as *a part of* but *apart from* recreation areas.

Another problem planners oftentimes run into with engineers is trying to get a few curves in roads, parking lots and other facilities rather than a "well-engineered" straight line or tangent such as the one shown in Figure 2.48. Tangents, particularly in park roads, should be short ones.

Another example of how engineering expertise can be misdirected is shown in Figures 2.49 and 2.50. The pictures are of campsites at the Edgar Evans State Park in Tennessee. Someone decided to locate a campground on the side of an extremely steep area overlooking a lake. The slope on the ridge was too severe to develop conventional campsites, so the "solution" was to build wooden platforms supported by concrete and steel pilings, cantilevering approximately 100 campsites over the side of the ridge. Because the platforms are wooden, the users' evening companion, the campfire, is prohibited. From the standpoint of engineering principles, the sites are sound. But when you consider the need to plan for *people,* they fail to get a passing grade. If you park a

Figure 2.46

Figure 2.47

Figure 2.48

Figure 2.50

Figure 2.49

trailer on the deck (and it's certainly sturdy enough to do so) all of the site furniture is located in the wrong places.

This was a "cooperative" effort between the U.S. Corps of Engineers and Tennessee State Parks. Each group will gladly tell you the other is responsible for the unique campsite's design. (In Chapter Seven we seriously question the cost of some campsites which, interestingly enough, is about 10 percent of the amount spent on these monsters!)

As we suggested earlier, use engineers and others with technical expertise, but keep their help in line with the recreation experience. There is an old saying called "the rule of the tool"—"Give a small child a hammer and suddenly everything in sight will need pounding." Perhaps this applies to some who depend too heavily on engineers in recreation resource areas as well. Engineers—we need them, love them, and have a record of working well with them. However, as a planner, *you* need to carefully guide them.

Design Psychology

When you enter the serving line in an upscale cafeteria, what comes first: the cooked carrots and spinach, or the pies, cakes and other desserts? Dessert is the obvious answer. Restaurant owners know if they locate the desserts near the end of the food line rather than at the beginning you will be far less

likely to add them to your nearly full tray. Walk through a sizable grocery store or supermarket and you'll be constantly subjected to all sorts of enticing displays beckoning you to buy many more goodies than you had intended. In both examples you have "enjoyed" the aura of design psychology. The fact is, throughout daily living you will experience examples of smart psychology getting you to buy this or that, view this rather than that, or move this way or that. If park professionals have any smarts at all they will use design psychology to beckon users, make them happier, and move them where they wish them to go.

Design psychology is one of the *big tools* of the trade you should add to your storehouse of skills. Experience tells us most park professionals *aren't* aware of the opportunities they have to use this skill to improve visitor experiences. We will share our thoughts about this subject throughout the book.

On a subconscious level, visitors are turned away from the entrance to the county park in Washington State shown in Figure 2.51. In contrast, the entrance to Indiana's McCormick's Creek State Park, shown in Figure 2.52, welcomes park users to a comfortable environment. The feelings generated by these two entrance zones are examples of what the planner can accomplish or lose through attention to aspects of *design psychology*. The park entrance in Washington, built at a right angle to the main road, consists of a nar-

Figure 2.51

row, 16-foot roadway, completely enclosed within a full canopy of overhanging trees. Because of the almost total shade cover, the narrow, constricted entrance is dark, frightening and uninviting. Compare this to the entrance to McCormick's Creek. Here, the juncture of the park entrance road and the highway is curved to produce a more natural approach to the park. The entryway is also built in the shape of an inverted "U," with the narrow end facing the interior of the park. Psychologically, this design says, "Hey folks, come on in" and "pulls" the users' vision and interest into the park. The effect is reinforced by pruned vegetation alongside the entryway, a manipulation designed to repeat the "U" shape of the entrance road. (In all fairness, though, the excellent beckoning psychology technique now stops at the gatehouse and you experience a less than enjoyable tunnel effect throughout most of this sizable park.)

Design psychology can have a significant impact on park visitors. If used effectively, the results are highly positive, as along the Natchez Trace through northern Mississippi, northwest Alabama and southern Tennessee. This parkway, developed by the National Park Service, passes through a part of the country having far less than outstanding scenic qualities. A few hundred feet to either side of the Trace, the land is characterized by open fields and low hills, typical of this part of the South. However, driving along the parkway itself is one of the most re-creative visual experiences you can find anywhere.

The key to the visual appeal of the Natchez Trace is in the way the planner employed *visual variety*. The tree canopy over the parkway alternately opens and closes to produce a sensation of changing environments. Plantings of pines have been employed to create contrasts in color. Variations in topography and sweeping curves are used to prevent long line-of-sight visuals along the right-of-way and to avoid monotonous views. Grass-mowing crews, instead of cutting on straight lines along the edge of the road, create naturally shaped patterns on the shoulders of the Trace. In sum, the parkway was planned with design psychology in mind. The attention

given to the interplay of *color, texture, form* and *line* has resulted in an overall backdrop capable of creating a meaningful recreation experience. Perhaps the most successful aspect of the Natchez Trace is this: The effects created by the design, while refreshing, are *so subtle* that the typical visitor passing along the parkway will rarely perceive the techniques used to enhance the environment. This, in fact, is the key to design psychology: The effects created by park design are felt by the *subconscious mind.*

A few paragraphs earlier we noted the excellence of the McCormick's Creek State Park entrance followed by the lack of attention given to providing visual variety in roadside vegetation throughout the park. We were quite surprised to find a big-time error amid the excellence on the Natchez Trace Parkway. Figure 2.53 shows a dark cave-like entrance down to a heavily shaded picnic area on a south Tennessee section of the Trace. In all of our trips by that roadside stop and picnic area we never saw or heard anyone down in that dark hole. It is similar in example to the dark threatening entrance to the county park in Washington State.

Unfortunately, inattention to principles of design psychology can produce negative effects on park users as well. For a number of years, TVA's Land Between the Lakes has operated a nature center as a focal point of its 5,000 acre environmental-education complex. The center contained a small, perhaps 30 by 60 feet, interpretive room with both historical and nature exhibits on display. The design mistake was to try and develop far more interpretive themes than the physical space was capable of supporting. The area's cultural history, iron mining, wildlife management, local environment and alternative energy sources were all interpreted here, and the staff planned on adding at least 20 percent more to the existing displays. Negative psychology forced visitors to move quickly through narrow aisles from one exhibit to another, tending to minimize both their quest for new knowledge and their enjoyment. Most of the exhibits were well-done; however, the quality of the exhibits themselves is not the point—the spatial arrangement of the room created an uncomfortable environment for visitors.

The purpose of design psychology is to make users feel comfortable in the park environment without calling attention to the techniques used. We'll discuss specific applications of design psychology as we talk about different types of recreation facilities in later

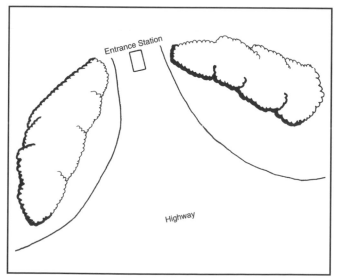

Figure 2.52

Figure 2.53

chapters. There are, however, a few general concepts you can apply in most park plans and designs—techniques aimed at enhancing *visitor receptivity* to the recreational environment.

Park planners, designers, managers and programmers often cause many other negative psychological elements which either completely repulse visitors or make them quite uncomfortable. Unfortunately, many of those same park professionals will not see or understand what is happening. Three examples of what we mean are shown in Figures 2.54, 2.55 and 2.56. Figure 2.54 shows several camping units in an Indiana state park built away from or without shade. Building campsites with little or no shade in most of the United States is a real negative (see Chapters Seven and Eight).

Figure 2.55 shows a campground bulletin board littered and trashed (you'll see lots of these on college campuses). Instead of beckoning users, this cluttered bulletin board will likely cause you and others to move quickly by rather than causing you to pause, read and learn.

Figure 2.56 is a bit more subtle than the others but nonetheless gives us all sorts of negatives. It is a primary entrance trail, to a Designated Wilderness in Colorado. (Note the edge of the parking lot). If we begin all planning and design with the question, "Whom do we want?" and our answer includes families, older folks (perhaps some with health problems), young children, and even persons with disabilities *as well as* the rugged good ol' boys *and* backpackers, this trail entrance with its obvious steepness (adverse grade) is not at all beckoning! The oldest author with gimpy knees wanted to explore *a little* of the wilderness. The steep trail for him wasn't hard to climb up but it was hard on the knees when he returned. Among the hundreds of potential visitors to a wilderness (or Appalachian Trail), you will have numerous folks who want a short hike so they can "experience" the wilderness *and* be able to tell others about it! Anyhow, beginning a recreation trail on an upgrade discourages many users. If possible, begin it on a slight downgrade and open the vegetation around the entrance. Both elements are excellent examples of using design psychology. *Note:* We realize gaining access to the wilderness from this parking lot zone didn't

Figure 2.54

Figure 2.55

Figure 2.56

provide the Forest Service with that downhill option. *However,* there were two better places to begin the trail nearby, both with far more favorable grades for a trailhead.

Other Design Psychology Considerations

Curvilinear Design. Few straight lines occur in nature. As a complement, our park design should avoid straight lines also. Curvilinear walkways, trails and roads not only repeat natural shapes, they create an aura of mystery and anticipation for the user: What new scene waits just outside of view around the next curve?

Blending Human-Made With Natural Colors. In most instances, our designs should intrude into the natural environment as little as possible. Signing schemes and paint on buildings can take advantage of earth tone colors. Exceptions to this do exist; some signs such as those indicating dangerous conditions should be brightly colored to draw attention to them readily. A color scheme might be developed for a park in which all trailheads are indicated by signs painted with brown backgrounds, signs for campgrounds with green backgrounds, and so on.

Designing to Avoid Confusion. Circulation patterns inside parks should be kept as simple as possible (KISS). Haven't heard of KISS? It's *Keep It Simple, Stupid!* It is likely one of the most important planning principles known to the authors (see Chapter One).

Designing Facilities Compatible With Adjacent Uses. This includes the principle we discussed earlier of zoning use areas simply and expands the concept. Adjacent facilities should avoid conflicting with each other's intended uses and should complement one another in terms of anticipated use. A picnic shelter placed next to a nature center may encourage picnicking. A tennis court next to the same nature center will probably not attract many players.

Designing to Human Scale. The scale, or size, of area and facilities can have an effect on park users. Some facilities and areas (e.g., the height of bulletin boards and the length of tennis courts) are dictated by intended use and/or standards. Keep in mind, however, scale can be psychological as well as physical. Particularly in an area where people stay for long periods of time, scale the design to make them comfortable. For example, a picnic table on top of a small hill with no shade in the middle of a Kansas prairie would not have a high comfort factor.

Lighting Aesthetics. Different types of artificial lighting produce different types of effects. Thus your choice of lighting depends upon the intended use of the area to be lighted. For sports and other areas where visual accuracy is needed, high-intensity discharge lamps such as metal halide, mercury vapor, or high-pressure sodium are appropriate. On the other hand, color *rendition*—the accurate reproduction of shades of color—is probably more important for producing human comfort in outdoor recreation areas where the natural environment is dominant. On pathways and other unstructured sites, incandescent lighting produces the best color rendition.

The number of sources to enlist for help and advice on design psychology is somewhat limited. College and university departments of landscape architecture often include a staff member with an interest in park planning and design. The Forest Service, particularly in the western regions of the country, has also developed guidelines for the visual management of resources. Their emphasis, however, is limited to designing extensive areas rather than fine-tuning site-specific resources that beckon visitors into and through small parks and facilities. The fact is, in our view, they have spent far too much time, too much of your money and unneeded staff effort on extensive area visual management while further deemphasizing building, renovating, enlarging, programming and managing developed sites for "all Americans." Their attention to scenic resource management and managing what they now call *view sheds* (used in the same sense as watersheds) was called into question recently by the public and a local Congressman (Pacific Northwest) when they had to restudy a $30,000-plus proposal for painting rocks in an avalanche area on a scenic highway. Painting rocks while curtailing family use is a good example of two things: appeasement of environmentalists, and running amuck.

We believe the best guidelines for developing parks according to the principles of design psychology are common sense and practice. Questions such as Whom is it for? Does it fit the environment? Is it a functional design? and Does it invite rather than repulse? should be answered affirmatively before construction begins.

Landscaping

Closely related to design psychology and nearly everything else in this book, landscaping fundamentals are key tools of the trade for the recreation planner. More importantly, however, the planner must understand the *implications* of landscaping *for recreation* rather than know the fine points of the discipline. To make the point clear, consider the example of a National Park Service recreation area some miles below Boulder Dam in Arizona. Here the designer used a plant called oleander to provide a screen between campsites. As you will learn in Chapters Seven and Eight, it is desirable to provide some intersite screening in campgrounds. Armed with a knowledge of landscaping and plant growth patterns, the designer knew oleander is capable of developing this screening and knew oleander is an especially attractive flowering plant. However, the designer did not know, or didn't consider, the implications for recreation; campers like to roast hot dogs on sticks they can find around the campsite. Oleander is dense (for screening), it is attractive (for aesthetics), provides lots of just-right roasting sticks (for hot dogs), and is *poisonous* (for campers).

Landscaping can be an effective tool for the park planner. It can enhance the natural attractiveness of an area, beckon users to "come on in," channel people along reinforced pathways, and help disguise maintenance areas and other human-made structures. But the planner also needs to remember the relationship between landscaping and recreation planning. Unless the design goal is to create a formal, landscaped area, landscaping should *support* rather than *dictate* planning efforts. We know of a small city in western Tennessee where exotic plants, species not naturally occurring in the area, were used to landscape a riverside community park. The results make the park look completely out of place with the surroundings. To remain consistent with the natural environment, use indigenous plants for landscaping.

There are other human needs besides aesthetics which should be considered when you landscape. Design decisions should not focus exclusively on the form of the area; the function is your primary concern. You should address the effect landscaping has on user safety and convenience. For instance, tall, dense shrubs along quiet walkways may create dangerous conditions (the same thing can happen with too many plants around buildings and play spaces), particularly in some urban areas; poisonous plants or those with thorns are inappropriate in most use areas; some plants, such as the female ginkgo, bear fruit which emits an offensive smell. One of the low-growing junipers commonly used around walkways has a strong smell like dog urine. Placed where people pass by, it is offensive. Placed at a distance, it isn't. Factors such as these do not always preclude the use of certain plant materials. The planner, however, should either know or take the responsibility for determining the potential effects plants may have on areas.

As with other topics discussed in this chapter, landscaping decisions should incorporate not only recreationists but other "users" of the park: the managers, programmers and maintenance staff. We know of a park which has a shower building completely surrounded with attractive shade trees and low understory vegetation. It has 100 percent overstory shade. At the end of each summer, a maintenance crew must spend several days scraping mold from the interior walls and repainting the inside of the building. The reason? Shade from the attractive trees prevents the walls from drying, allowing mold to grow throughout the summer. Managers may also need to keep some areas free of vegetation in order to reduce the amount of time it takes to patrol for vandals or muggers. And programmers may require a mixture of sunny and shaded areas for various activities.

Generally, the planner will have to compromise to address the needs of all concerned. The important point to remember is how landscaping will affect all these groups both immediately and some time after newly introduced plants reach maturity. The planner's role is to ensure that landscaping in parks and recreation areas remains a *means* to an end rather than an end in itself. University departments of landscape architecture may prove helpful to you in this decision-making process.

Earlier in this chapter we discussed the importance of engineers as a "tool of the trade" for planners. *Trained* landscape architects are another of those key tools. Many years ago they were far more skilled as plantsmen than as designers. During the last 45 to 50 years, though, earning a landscape degree involved courses in design useful to planning parks. We have worked with numerous landscape architects—most of them quite ready to *work with you and learn with you*. (Beware of LAs who already know it all, however!) The know-it-alls will not gain the basic knowledge in an academic classroom to guide you in such things as camp loop design, varied unit densities, careful location of play amenities so as not to conflict with each other or cause visitor unhappiness at night, design to ease administration and other park planning concerns. With additional continuing education training specific to outdoor recreation and careful study of this book landscape architects can be marvelous additions to your storehouse of tools of the trade.

User Involvement

A planner can develop an excellent design for a recreation area and watch it fail miserably if the public, for whatever reason, doesn't like or use the area. Fortunately, there is a way to help ensure people will take an interest in and accept areas for recreation use. The key is to *involve users in the planning process*. This action has several benefits: It provides a needed source of information since nobody can tell you more about a group's needs than group members themselves; it is an excellent public relations tool, particularly for public agencies which are frequently seen as insensitive bureaucracies; and, most importantly, it gives users a sense of having a *vested interest* in the area being planned.

We have had federal park planning experiences where we got considerable user input (mainly because we knew very little about specific user wants and needs) and experiences (many years ago in the U.S. Forest Service) where getting park and planning input from users was unheard of. Since it is impossible for any sort of planner to know everything about every possible design challenge the planner must get input from users. (Some of our challenges have included planning wilderness areas, facilities for persons with disabilities, wrangler's camps, the first federal off-road vehicle area in the United States, and a trail depicting General Grant's troop movements in the early spring of 1862.)

This need not be a nine-step process taking 16 months and ending with fist fights between conflicting users as is experienced by some federal agencies. And it should not be couched in terms of How do you want us to design this area for you? but rather in How do you function while using such an area? You are the planner/designer. It is your job to provide the plans and designs to meet those functions.

When the Hillman Heritage Trail was developed in a campground in TVA's Land Between the Lakes, the local chapter of the National Campers and Hikers Association was invited to help, both in planning and construction. The local press was notified, and it became something of an "event" for the club. The trail was later designated as a National Recreation Trail, and more publicity (and positive public relations for the agency) ensued. The approach taken encouraged benefits beyond physical development. Since a local group had a high degree of interest in the project, programming opportunities emerged. Group-hike weekends could be organized, with the hikers using campgrounds and thus adding to revenue and program potential. Maintenance costs were even minimized because one program during the weekend was centered around periodic trail maintenance—with assistance from the hikers. The single act of inviting users to become truly involved, rather than simply holding a required public meeting, can benefit management and program staff, maintenance crews, and, most importantly, visitors.

When involving users, planners should also try to draw operations and maintenance crews into the planning process. These people are responsible for managing recreation areas on a day-to-day basis, so they can have a strong influence on successful facilities. In the real world, there are two ways operations and maintenance crews do their jobs. They can accomplish tasks assigned to them at a minimal level of performance, or they can do the same tasks more efficiently and effectively. A number of factors, from salary to length of coffee breaks, influence their level of performance. Many of these factors are beyond the control of the planner; however, if operation and maintenance crews are made to feel a sense of responsibility for parks and recreation areas, they may be more concerned about their upkeep. One way to instill this sense of *responsibility* is to involve these individuals in the planning process. Their opinions are important and you should let them know it.

One problem we have encountered on numerous occasions concerns the renovation of old established areas. If a campground, picnic site or other area has been in service for some time, it likely needs extensive rehabilitation. We can guarantee some users, particularly those who have frequented the old area on a regular basis, will be opposed to this renovation. Frequently, they will protest strongly. Sometimes a patient explanation of the need to protect the environment will help and sometimes not, but it should at least be offered. Ultimately the planner has the responsibility of protecting the environment, and one means of accomplishing this is to rehabilitate deteriorating sites. In our experience, most users don't stay away permanently. A few do, but if you hope to please everyone all of the time, we suggest you look for work outside of recreation.

Applied Research

The final tool of the trade we suggest is *applied research.* You will read about research answers, needs, suggestions and problems throughout this book, particularly in Chapter Ten. There is a tremendous treasure house of already available research to meet some of your needs. Problem is, most planners don't have a clue where to find it or how to use it. The academic community requires research data be gathered in most master's degree programs and in all doctorate degree efforts but much of this isn't too helpful nor is it often related to planning, construction, maintenance, management, design, or programming concerns. It also will be reported in a sort of language unrelated to the linguistic skills of most managers.

One ironic and interesting type of research does occur in about a 10-year cycle. A relatively young (inexperienced) professor will encourage a master's degree student to carefully study "overuse" in campsites on public lands. If it's well-done the student will be encouraged to write a journal article and/or submit a learned paper at a research conference. We liken this to the wheel shown in Figure 2.57. It's been invented! It's been invented! When you thoroughly read this book you'll see why we question research such as this.

Figure 2.57

Conclusions

Traditionally, the role of the recreation planner has been to develop plans and designs. In recent years there has been a move to expand the role of the planner to one in which the synthesis of information is of importance as well. This is a step in the right direction. As we've tried to illustrate in this chapter, there are simply too many substantive areas of knowledge involved in planning for one person to master. We feel it is time for the role of the planner to evolve one step further: Planners should be recognized (and recognize themselves) as fulfilling a *service function.* Far too often, we have seen instances in which a planner produces a single design for an area, oversees the construction, and then turns over the finished and highly flawed product to managers, programmers, and maintenance staff. In effect, this says "here's the design for this area, now bend your programs and policies to fit it!" In fact, there is no single "right" design for a recreation facility. There are always *alternatives.* Functioning in a service role, the planner should (with input from those who will work and recreate in the area) develop several alternative plans for a given facility. Given these alternatives, staff responsible for managing, maintaining, and programming the facility can choose the best possible combination of components to meet their needs.

Speaking of alternatives, we hope you were able to find some poor ones in the recreation complex shown in Figure 2.1. We've reproduced the complex in Appendix A, with a listing of mistakes keyed to the numbers appended. We purposely designed in 31 errors; if you find additional ones, no one said we were perfect!

Chapter Three

Trails: Pathways for People

In the preface to *Planning Parks for People* we suggested your numerous skills would be tested throughout the book. Have a close look at the photographs in Figures 3.1 to 3.8. What does each picture represent? Is it a design or maintenance problem, a solution, a programming opportunity, an example of design psychology, or something else? We'll answer these questions as we move through Chapter Three. For now, happy hunting!

Figure 3.5

Figure 3.6

Figure 3.1

Figure 3.2

Figure 3.3

Figure 3.7

Figure 3.4

Figure 3.8

A Trail Truism:
Most Folks Are Not Trail Designers

This is the first of several chapters discussing specific types of recreation facilities, and we'd like to start by asking you a question: What do you think makes a good trail? Before giving you our answer, we'll provide you with a hint. The correct response to this question would be the same for the subjects of the remaining chapters as well: What makes a good day-use area, play area, or camping area? If this is beginning to sound like a trick question, that's because it is. It's also an important one since it emphasizes the point implied by the title of this chapter—trails are, or should be, pathways for people.

The answer to our question—what makes a good trail?— is actually two more questions. To determine if a trail is well-planned, you must first ask: What kind of a trail is it? What's "good" design for an interpretive nature trail is often poor, poor planning for a hiking trail. As we'll see shortly, some principles of planning and design remain the same, regardless of the type of trail involved.

For example, measures to prevent erosion should always be considered when developing trails. However, different types of trails may require different techniques to accomplish the same goal. Trails for dirt bikes and trails for wheelchairs would not always fight erosion with the same methods. Further, the nature, or intended use, of a particular kind of trail may require some design strategies unnecessary or undesirable on other types of trails.

To illustrate this, consider a short interpretive trail paralleling a Confederate Army line of defense at Shiloh National Battlefield and maintained by the National Park Service. The purpose, or design goal, of this sort of trail should be to take users back in time for a firsthand perspective of an era in our history when families were divided on two sides of an issue that tore the nation apart. This is clearly not the design goal a planner would have in mind when developing a jogging path in a city park. Both are examples of trails, but each needs a different planning approach to function effectively. Gertrude Stein said, "A rose is a rose is a rose." We say, "A trail is not a trail is not a trail." In part, the type of trail determines how it must be planned and designed.

Trail type, however, is not the only criterion for determining whether a trail is well-planned or not. The second part of the answer to our question, "What makes a good trail?" is this: "Who's going to use the trail?" Designing trails would be easier if trails with similar uses had similar users. This is not, however, always the case. For example, hiking trails may be found both inside and outside of developed recreation facilities. Those inside of areas such as group camps and family campgrounds need one set of design goals, strategies, and characteristics. Hiking trails outside of developed areas, such as the Appalachian and Pacific Crest Trails, require a different planning approach. Even two trails with the same design goal in the same area may differ, depending on the intended users. A group camp visited by a variety of user groups might have two interpretive trails: one accessible by groups with members in wheelchairs and the other for groups whose members are all ambulatory.

As you might expect, the types of people we need to consider when designing trails are not limited to the recreating public. As with other kinds of facilities, the planner can make trails easy or difficult to administer. Preventative maintenance measures built into the trail or neglected during construction can have a positive or negative impact on the expense and difficulty of ongoing maintenance. The potential for recreation programming can be designed into or out of trails by the attention the planner gives to his or her work. Many of the skills we discussed in Chapter Two—user protection and safety, design psychology, programming and others—have specific applications in making trails "pathways for people." As we suggested in Chapter One, however, recreation planners who design facilities have a dual responsibility. The trails we develop must consider resource protection as well as provision of positive experiences for people who use them.

More often than any other type of recreation facility, trails seem to be designed by persons with few skills in planning or resource stewardship. On the surface, designing a trail appears simple. From the standpoint of meeting program requirements, it isn't difficult to provide a minimally effective one. Disregarding standards for special populations for a moment, all you really need to do to construct a trail is clear a path wide enough for people to travel on. Unfortunately, there is a considerable difference between clearing a trail—which anyone can do—and designing a trail that minimizes environmental damage. Even more unfortunate, it seems this distinction has not been made frequently enough, particularly among recreation programmers and interpretive specialists. Too often, these individuals take it upon themselves to develop trails because they think they understand what needs to be done from a programming perspective. When this happens, environment and visitors both suffer.

As we've stressed before, it takes more than one type of expertise to plan facilities which are both usable and environmentally sound. This holds true for trails, too. Shortly we'll discuss the types of general concerns you need to consider when developing trails. We'll also explore how and how not to design several specific types. Before getting into these topics, however, we'd like to share a mistake with you. Starting with trails, each of the next seven chapters deals with a specific type of recreation development. In each of these chapters we'll include a description of one or more actual areas or facilities which have been poorly planned and/or designed.

There are two reasons for taking this approach. First, we feel the recreation profession has a tendency to perpetuate design errors. Planning mistakes made in the 1950s are still being made commonly today. This may be a result, in part, of the service orientation of our profession. The mission of recreation is to improve the quality of life. Thus everything we do must be well-intended. Unfortunately, there is often a wide gap between good intentions and good results. Recreation professionals need to be idealistic and enthusiastic. However, these qualities must be combined with pragmatism. Our resources are too limited to continue making errors we should have stopped committing 20 years ago. The second reason for providing what we intend as constructive criticism is to demonstrate the need to ask why. Most of the mistakes we'll share with you in this and later chapters didn't have to happen. They occurred because no one held the planner accountable for his or her designs. Much of our criticism in these "mistakes" sections will be directed at planners for what we feel are flawed designs. However, much of the blame for these designs actually being implemented lies with the programmers and administrators who deferred to the "expertise" of the planners.

The Blue-Gray Complex

The Setting: Near the southern end of TVA's Land Between the Lakes (LBL), recreation staff developed a complex of hiking trails called the Fort Henry Trails System. The trails were named for a Confederate defense installation constructed on the banks of the Tennessee River. When Kentucky Lake was built nearly 80 years after the Civil War, Fort Henry was completely flooded, except for portions of three sets of trenches or earthworks. The trailhead for the hiking complex was located at a midpoint among these sets. (Figure 3.9 shows how the trailhead and support facilities were designed.)

There are several positive aspects of trail design shown in Figure 3.9, including those keyed to the following legend:

A. A single entry/exit parking lot for ease of administration.
B. A turning circle on the upper end of the parking lot to facilitate use by large recreational vehicles and buses.
C. Toilets located inside a "pocket" of screening where they are both unobtrusive and easy to locate.
D. A wide trailhead narrowing toward the interior of the trail to attract users' vision.
E. Vegetative screening cut to reinforce the shape of the trailhead.
F. An enclave containing a bulletin board with a map of the trail system and other information for hikers. (Note how the enclave is set back from the trail entrance and screened from the parking lot. Both of these tactics are aimed at minimizing visual contact from the parking lot and, as a result, reducing vandalism.)
G. The trailhead, the enclave and the first few hundred feet of each trail (where use will be heaviest) reinforced with crushed stone to reduce impact.
H. Signs bearing the names of the two paths leading from the trailhead located at the point where hikers need to choose which route to take. (Each sign

is numbered and color-coded to the map on the bulletin board to reduce confusion and placed slightly to the sides of the intersection to screen them from the parking lot.)
I. Screening between the trails and the remaining Fort Henry trenches maintained to minimize impact on the trenches. (The vegetation provides a psychological barrier between hiking trails and possible interpretive zones.)

Recreation staff planned the historical hiking system with the help of National Park Service personnel, making certain the three sets of earthworks (interpretive zones) *wouldn't be penetrated* by hiking trails. This approach was taken to allow later development of the interpretive zones to fit a functional, overall planning scheme. Several years after the hiking complex was built, interpretive services staff at Land Between the Lakes decided to develop one of the three potential interpretive zones—the one with earthworks leading down a narrow ridge and terminating at the lake edge. To develop this, they built an interpretive trail, named the Blue-Gray Trail, as shown in Figure 3.10. The on-the-ground results of their planning have given the authors a host of major and minor mistake illustrations to share with you. Since Land Between the Lakes is designated as a demonstration area in outdoor recreation, including interpretation, part of its original mission was to share mistakes with other professionals and students when they occurred. Unfortunately, neither interpretive staff nor

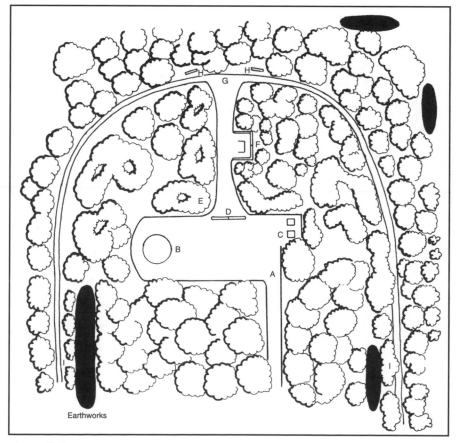

Earthworks

Figure 3.9

their supervisors had the planning background to recognize or understand the errors committed during development of the Blue-Gray Trail. In fact, they were quite pleased with what were, from a planning perspective, negative results. (In later chapters, you'll read more about the lack of outdoor recreation expertise in many public agencies, particularly at the federal level.)

The Blue-Gray Trail was initially intended to be an adventure in historical interpretation. Unfortunately, the results of poor planning gave management, and you, the taxpayers, an extremely costly collection of errors in design, design psychology, interpretive messages and maps, and architectural features. The new trail also eliminated previously completed work aimed at helping to prevent vandalism. However, these errors were minor compared to four major planning mistakes. These included the following:

1. Borrowing some excellent National Park Service trail construction ideas, but using them in the wrong place.
2. Building an expensive facility with electronic gadgetry in an isolated, unprotected area.
3. Creating an outstanding short-distance hiking trail rather than meeting the objective of developing a quality, history-flavored interpretive experience.
4. Failing to coordinate the interpretive development with previous planning efforts.

Let's explore these mistakes in detail.

Misplaced Ideas. During the planning phase of the Blue-Gray Trail, LBL's interpretive staff borrowed an idea from South Florida's Everglades National Park. This idea involved the outstanding Anhinga Trail located just behind a staffed, and thus protected, visitor center. The Anhinga Trail moves gently through a low, freshwater marsh. Since the area is naturally wet, visitors oftentimes travel on elevated wooden walkways. You can be quite close to the freshwater marsh environment with its bounty of unusual plant and animal life, including snakes, water birds and alligators, as you enjoy a relatively safe and dry experience on the walkways. The more important natural features along the trail are even interpreted by small signs located on upper safety rails.

Unfortunately, LBL's interpretive staff decided this idea was just the thing for the Blue-Gray Trail. So instead of developing the loop on an inexpensive, solid-ground location, TVA built over 100 feet of costly, elevated walkway across a wooded low area of a Kentucky lake embayment even though there was no water under the walkway for much of the year. The original location for the trail before the discovery of the walkway

idea and the "as built" location are shown in Figures 3.11a and 3.11b. While the walkway added considerable spice to the hiking experience, it provided no relevant interpretive features and no views of open water. It did offer some opportunities for environmental interpretation; however, these couldn't be used since the focus of the trail was the historical interpretation of the Battle of Fort Henry.

Management—including budget personnel—shared some of the "credit" for this expensive mistake that no one thought to ask why—why the elevated boardwalk was needed, how it would enhance the trail's historical interpretation objective, and, most obvious, how it re-created the aura of the history being interpreted? Was such a walkway used by the soldiers in 1862? The moral (and a good planning axiom): Borrowing planning ideas from others oftentimes enhances your facility or program. Make sure, though, that what you borrow accomplishes this. Does the idea enhance your facility or program, or does it—in your setting, with your objectives—detract from it?

Unprotected Facilities. Most of the interpretive messages for the Blue-Gray Trail were on cassette recordings activated by pressure sensitive rubber pads hidden a few inches under the trail surface. The recordings were sequential, mean-

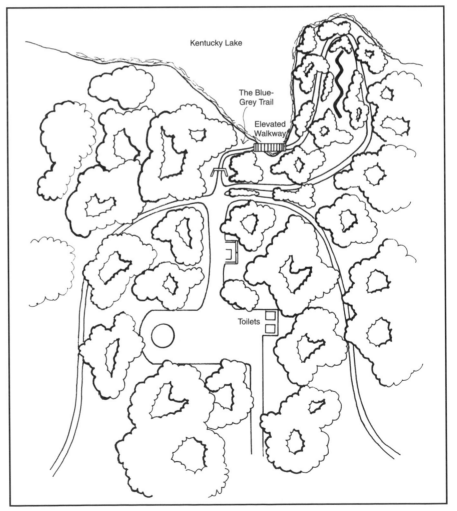

Figure 3.10

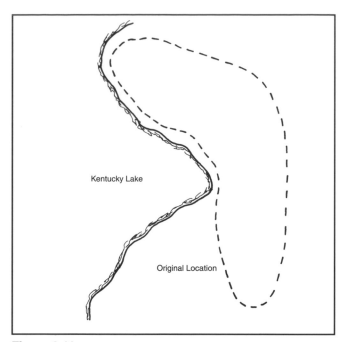

Figure 3.11a

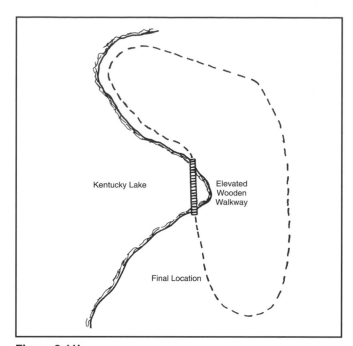

Figure 3.11b

ing the information at each station built on the message from the previous station. We believe this sort of interpretation can be an excellent technique in highly protected, carefully monitored areas. However, the Blue-Gray Trail was in an isolated area over 20 miles from interpretive personnel. The cassette installations were subject to vandalism and tended to malfunction due to moisture accumulation in their belowground boxes. Since the interpretive messages were sequential, malfunctioning stations caused visitors to miss important parts of the story. The moral (and another good planning axiom): Don't locate expensive facilities, particularly those requiring constant care, in remote areas.

Mixing Incompatible Uses. The authors believe the most common of all trail-related errors made by recreation planners, interpretive specialists, and others is the mixing of interpretation trails with other types of trails such as those for hiking, those built to link facilities, or those leading around or to scenic vistas. This mixing, whether intentional or not, causes the same drastic results all across America. Adding the unneeded elevated wooden walkway which provided lakeside access for viewing and fishing at the western end of the loop helped make the Blue-Gray "Interpretive" Trail the best short-distance *hiking experience* in Land Between the Lakes.

The basic difficulty in mixing hiking and interpretation lies in the inherent conflict between the two types of use. The primary functions of a simple hiking or walking trail are to cover distance on the ground, to move from one point to another, or to move by foot to points of interest such as scenic vistas or observation towers. The motivation may differ from person to person and include exercise, being out-of-doors, and viewing wildlife or scenery, but the common denominator is the hike itself. Conversely, with interpretive trails the opportunity to gain new knowledge is the primary reason to participate. As a result, visitor interests, their pace or speed, and their moods are different on hiking and interpretive trails. Mix-

ing hiking and interpretation also increases vandalism by those who simply aren't interested in the trail's educational aspects. Most naturalists, as well as planners who should know better, get an evangelical gleam in their eyes when they see visitors walking pathways to scenic points, strolling along lake or stream sides, or moving from campgrounds and picnic areas to other features such as beaches. Far too often, these professional folks decide to make sure that all visitors get to enjoy and learn from interpretive messages whether or not some give a hoot. We never learn; this type of poor planning always leads to recurrent replacement of interpretive installations due to excessive vandalism caused by trail users disinterested in such force-fed education.

Back to TVA's Blue-Gray Trail: Had one of the other two woodland-based earthworks been selected for a simple historical interpretation experience, the trail would have been void of water views, beckoning fishing sites and fun-to-walk-on elevated wooden walkways. Thus, the primary reason for walking through the earthworks would have been to learn a bit from the interpretive messages. Use of simple inexpensive signs, or numbered posts and a self-guiding brochure, rather than electronic devices in a remote area would have meant minimal vandalism.

The moral (and yet another good planning axiom): Please, please, resist the temptation to mix interpretation with other types of trails!

Coordinating Efforts. The fourth major mistake involved the issue of coordination with other staff who had a stake in the planning and management of the Fort Henry trails complex. At no time during the development of the Blue-Gray Trail did the interpretive staff request to review or discuss the potential impact of the interpretive trail on the existing facilities. The TVA recreation staff who managed the hiking complex were faced with new maintenance challenges. As a result of this communication failure, management and maintenance problems were amplified and, perhaps even worse, from the visitor's standpoint, opportunities to maximize the benefits of both interpretive and recreation programs were missed. Unfortunately, this failure to communicate happens all too frequently in most agencies. It seems to us this represents one of the many missing elements in the training of recreation personnel and, indeed, those in natural resource and related disciplines. We feel what's missing is an academic emphasis on the need for inter- and intra-agency coordination. The moral (and for now, a final axiom of good planning): Keep others abreast of your current and planned actions; be mindful of the possible impacts, both positive and negative, that these actions may have on staff in related disciplines and agencies; and expect and ask for the same courtesy in return.

As we suggested earlier, there were other errors associated with the planning and programming of the Blue-Gray Trail. Refer to the numbered locations on Figure 3.12 and consider the following problems. During construction, the vegetation at point 1 was removed. This provided a direct line of sight from the parking lot to the bulletin board and the entrance zone of the trails, so the rate of vandalism in these areas increased shortly after the new trail was opened. Expensive, easy-to-vandalize facilities such as bulletin boards and sign installations near trailheads should be easy to find *once people leave their vehicles.* However, they should also be screened from the sight of vehicles passing through the parking lot whenever possible. People who stop their cars, get out and walk into a trail zone tend to be interested in enjoying the experience on the trail. People who are inclined to vandalize may not go to the trouble of stopping if they don't see something worth breaking or shooting at while still in their car.

The entrance zone of the Blue-Gray Trail had several design problems. All of them were created because one human factor was neglected in the design. People, when given a choice of directions, tend to move to the right instead of to the left. This phenomenon occurs in movie theaters, on sidewalks, in hallways, and on interpretive trails and should be reinforced by the planner. If at all possible, loop trails with a single entry/exit should be designed with a counterclockwise traffic flow. The Blue-Gray Trail was not designed this way. Instead, interpretive messages were sequenced to have users walk the trail clockwise (2), so they had to enter the trail to their left instead of to their right, against their natural tendency.

In some instances—because of topography or other constraints—it may be necessary to encourage people to move to the left. When this is the case, there are design techniques

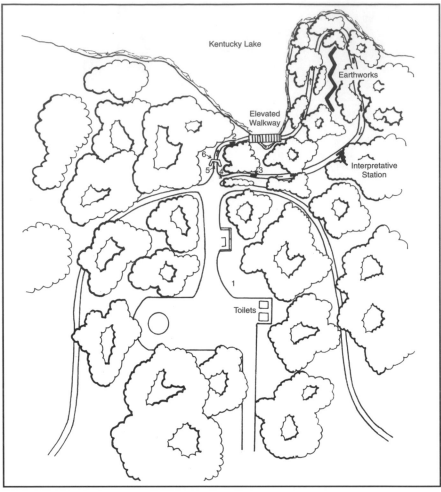

Figure 3.12

available to reinforce the movement. However, on the Blue-Gray Trail there were no such physical constraints, and some additional factors compounded the confusion for trail users at the entrance zone. The last audio pad in the sequence (3) was relatively close to the entry/exit point. When it was activated, people just entering the trail could hear the recording, although it was far enough away that the words could not be understood. The message, which was fairly long-playing, tended to "beckon" users to the right out of curiosity to find the source of the sound, reinforcing their tendency to enter the trail where the planner intended for them to exit. Unfortunately, the last audio station tended to malfunction and come on even though no one was there to activate it, so the beckoning problem was even further compounded.

Turning right was further encouraged by the wide throat and open angle (4) at which the exit was built. Neither discouraged users from moving in this direction. To compound the problem, the intended entrance to the trail (5) was designed to move users through a narrow constriction, a poor planning technique. The trail, which at this point was not widened, passed through the metal frame (6) shaped like an inverted "U" shown in Figure 3.13. Similar in design to an airport metal detector, the frame contained background information about Fort Henry's role in the Civil War. This and

Figure 3.13

other interpretive installations had several problems associated with them. From the manager's perspective, the metal frame was an attractive target for vandalism. It could be seen from the parking lot and was defaced soon after the trail was completed. It could also be seen from the rustic bulletin board describing the Fort Henry Hiking Trail complex, causing a serious and clearly visible conflict in architectural styles.

From the user's standpoint, the metal frame added to the confusion over which direction to take upon entering the interpretive trailhead. Only as wide as the trail itself, the frame added to the feeling of constriction brought on by the narrow entrance to the trail.

A final error does not relate to design, but mentioning it helps raise an important point. Some of the interpretive information on the trail was incorrect. A map showed the city of Nashville located on the Tennessee River (which it isn't). One of the interpretive messages referred to the Union forces who attacked Fort Henry as being under the command of "Admiral Foote," a rank which, at the time of the battle of Fort Henry, was nonexistent in the Union Navy.

The point is this: The planner neglected to pay attention to detail when designing the trail. None of the errors made created safety hazards for users. In fact, most people who walked the trail were probably not aware, beyond a vague feeling of confusion, of its problems. The question, then, is, "So what? A few minor mistakes were made, but no one was hurt by them." The answer to this question is a matter of professionalism. One of the major challenges facing those of us who work in recreation today is to be accepted as professionals by the public. To provide anything less than the best possible programs and facilities we know how to develop detracts from our professional image. If only one person in 100 notices a mistake we made, our stock as professionals goes

down in the public eye. If we make an avoidable error and no one notices, it still diminishes our standing as professionals—perhaps even more so.

There are ways the Fort Henry complex could have been changed to function as an effective interpretive zone. As we discussed earlier, the Blue-Gray Trail, as built, was a better hiking trail than an interpretive one, but Figure 3.14 shows an alternative concept which makes this type of trail viable. With this design, there is nothing to compete with the interpretive function. Further, the flat topography and nearness of the earthworks to the parking lot would allow the planner to design a barrier-free pathway.

This solution was fairly simple, but let's assume for a moment that the design in Figure 3.14 wouldn't work; perhaps the new area isn't flat enough for an interpretive trail. If we should want to use the same entrance zone for both hiking and interpretation, can we improve the design in Figure 3.10? Let's assume the program staff needs traffic on the interpretive trail to flow clockwise (to the left). This may not be a good idea from a design standpoint, but perhaps the story being told or the history being interpreted "fits" a left-hand entrance. In this case, as always, the program needs should take precedence over the general rule of design.

Figure 3.15 shows some design techniques aimed at simplifying the original entrance for users and reducing vandalism problems for management. Here, we've left the vegetation (1) to help screen both the bulletin board and the trailhead from the parking lot. A small directional sign (2)

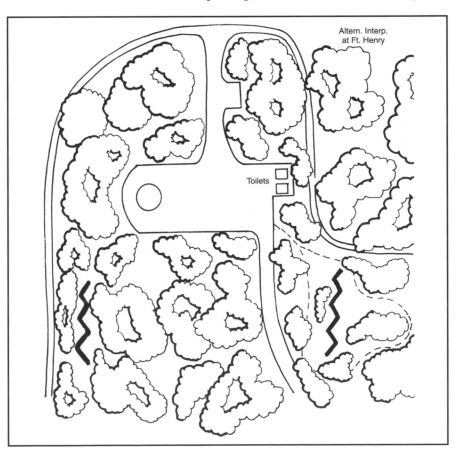

Figure 3.14

perpendicular to the parking lot, and thus less obtrusive, points to the interpretive trail. The metal frame (3) has been moved around the corner from its original position, also out of sight of the parking lot. The point (4) where the exit rejoins the trail has been designed as a reverse curve. This technique involves a very sharp right turn adjacent to a gentle curve moving to the left, making it psychologically easier for people to take the path to the left. It may necessitate a sign (5) pointing to the exit to avoid confusing users who have completed the loop. The last audio pad (6) has been moved further toward the interior of the trail to reduce the chance of hearing the recording from point 4. (An unsophisticated, but effective design technique when faced with situations such as this: Before the trail is built, have one person stand at point 4. Have another person walk toward point 6, stopping every few yards and speaking loudly. Where the person's voice can no longer be heard from point 4 is safe to place the audio pad.) Finally, the section of the interpretive trail at point 7 has been moved away from the parallel section of the hiking trail to prevent potential contact between users.

Interestingly, none of the solutions to the original problems required more effort, more expense or more technical knowledge. The needs of the programmers were still met, management problems were reduced, and user convenience was enhanced. The only element added to the original design was attention to detail—a necessity for conscientious planning. We have improved the overall design shown in Figure 3.10, but this trail—with its view of the lake—is still an outstanding hiking experience as well as a great pathway for bank fishermen. These conflicting uses can lead to considerable vandalism from users not interested in interpretation. Consequently, the lakeshore set of earthworks is still an extremely poor choice of locations for interpretation.

The greatest tragedy in the Blue-Gray Trail adventure, however, was this: Neither the interpretive staff nor the TVA managers recognized any of the "major" or "minor" mistakes. Further, when the problems were described and explained, *there was no attempt to correct them.* The photograph in Figure 3.16 is the one we showed you in Figure 3.3. Within five years of its opening, the Blue-Gray Trail was closed, leaving the public with a $40,000 mistake.

Basics and Standards

It's difficult to talk about basic concepts and design standards for trails because of the diversity of trail types and users. There are, however, some general guidelines we can apply to trail

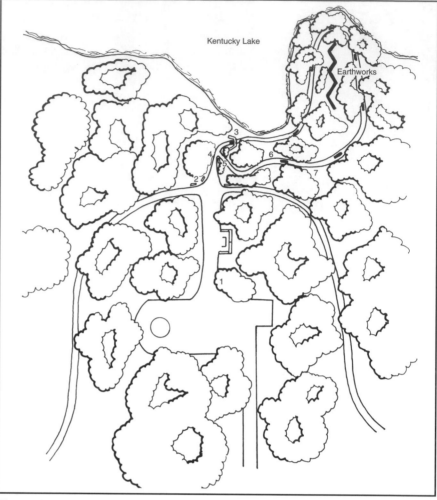

Figure 3.15

planning and development. The methods used to implement these guidelines may vary depending on the intended use of the trail. For example, a general guideline might be to "reduce impact on the trail surface." The method or type of surfacing material might depend on trail type, intended clientele and expected level of use. In our discussion of different types of trails a little later in the chapter, we'll focus on specific kinds of concerns for each. For now, let's consider some general guidelines for a variety of trail settings. You should keep

Figure 3.16

four topics in mind, and, although there will be some overlap, their general order is: zoning, design psychology, field design and construction, and administration.

Zoning. A trail can be superbly designed, built and managed, and still fail to function effectively if it is not properly zoned. Three areas of concern must be addressed during the zoning phase of trail development. The first is to determine the function or functions to be served by the trail. Will the trail be devoted to a primary function, such as hiking, interpretation or horseback riding? If so, which use or combination of uses will the trail serve? Who will use it? If the trail is not intended for primary use, it can serve a secondary function such as access to an area, connection between two areas, or circulation within an area. For example, we might design an access trail from a roadside parking lot to a scenic overlook, connect a play area to a picnic shelter, or develop a circulation system within a campground. Knowing how a trail is supposed to function allows us to make informed judgments on how to implement later phases of trail development. As with other types of facilities, the decision regarding intended trail function should not be the responsibility of the planner; administrators and program staff should take the lead in this phase of trail design. Figure 3.17 shows a tree diagram you may find helpful in determining trail function. Remember that planning decisions are too site-specific for any diagram to be all-inclusive; this is only a guideline.

Don't let the diagram in Figure 3.17 lead you to think that determining trail function is a complex process. Remember, KISS! If you're a programmer and you know you need a hike 'n bike trail in your campground, for example, a diagram

isn't necessary. The point is this: Consider all the options (is a hike 'n bike trail better in this setting than just a hiking trail?) and make a decision regarding function based on your needs and those of your users. Don't leave the decision regarding function to a planner or you may end up with a trail he or she wants to see developed.

Once the trail's function has been determined, the second zoning consideration is how does this trail relate to other trails in the area? As we suggested earlier, some types of trails (hiking/interpretive, horseback/off-highway vehicle) conflict with each other. Other trail functions (hiking/biking, dirt bike/four-wheel) may, in some instances, complement each other enough to permit combined usage. Even if there are no other trails in the area, the issue of conflicting or complementary use must be addressed if future developments are anticipated.

Consider, for instance, the trail development complex in a national forest in Colorado shown in Figure 3.18. Initially, the trail had four uses: access to the trout stream, hikes to the scenic vista and lake, short walks from the parking lot toward the lake for photographing, and hiking and horseback riding into a designated wilderness area. Even though there was considerable use on the trail, the functions were thought to be compatible. The major cause of extensive vandalism came when the interpretive specialist decided to add interpretive stations from the trailhead parking lot to the beaver dam. This is another misguided example of trying to make sure that everyone gets to "enjoy" some environmental education. When the interpretive specialist was asked by one of the authors if she wanted to know why her signs received so much

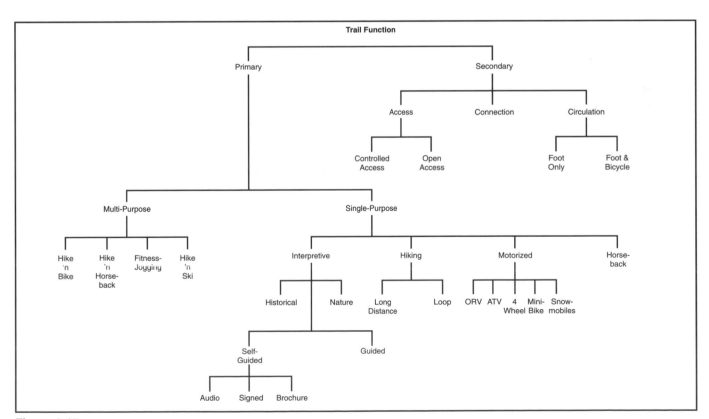

Figure 3.17

vandalism, her curt reply was, "No!" The old "I did it, it was the right thing to do, and I'm glad" syndrome.

Figure 3.19 shows an alternative to the original design with more attention given to zoning of trail uses. There are three trails leading from the trailhead parking lot. The lakeside trail provides lake access for fishing, photography, and alpine scenic enjoyment. The interpretive trail leading to the beaver dam is for those users who really have an interest in learning about the little flat-tailed critters. Finally, the main trail is for wilderness access and long-distance hiking.

There is another lesson to be learned from the design shown in Figure 3.18, however. This lesson has less to do with trails than with overall park planning and deals with a basic design error common in public and private parks worldwide. The campground in Figure 3.18 would be poorly designed even if it didn't have the multipurpose trailhead zone at its upper end. What is basically wrong? The designer has given the users and managers of this recreation area numerous administrative, safety, and harmony problems because dissimilar uses and users are mixed in with one another.

Figure 3.20 shows how the various features should be zoned. Visitors to the alpine lake, wilderness area, and even the interpretive beaver trail can access these zones via the main road into the large terminal parking lot. They do not penetrate the three-loop family campground.

The facilities associated with the wilderness trail (hitching posts, horse trailer unloading ramp, horse tack and gear loading dock, wilderness regulations, and other signing) can be carefully located at the wilderness trailhead. A good idea here, too, would be to physically restrict the horses to the main trail with fencing, vegetation, berms and cattle guards. This would keep the other trails and campground free from horses and their droppings. If a small number of camp units are needed for the wilderness horseback users, they could be zoned near the upper left edge of the parking lot.

The final zoning consideration to address is how does a trail relate to other facilities? As with many types of trails, some use facilities are compatible with pathways and others are not. "Quiet" facilities such as campsites and campfire theaters should be far enough away from motorized trails to avoid conflict. Even hiking and other trails which don't normally generate high noise levels can disturb certain areas such as popular fishing and bird-watching locations. On the other hand, some types of facilities and trails complement each other. Campers who use recreational vehicles often carry bicycles with them to provide transportation within the campground. By providing a hike 'n bike trail system, you may be able to offer (1) safer routes for bicycle circulation, (2) less congestion on roads (we've seen campgrounds with as many as 500 bicycles on busy weekends), (3) a host of program opportunities,

Figure 3.18

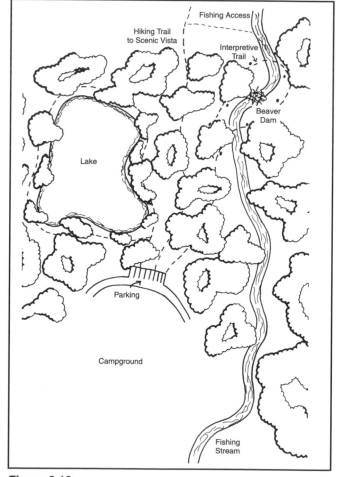

Figure 3.19

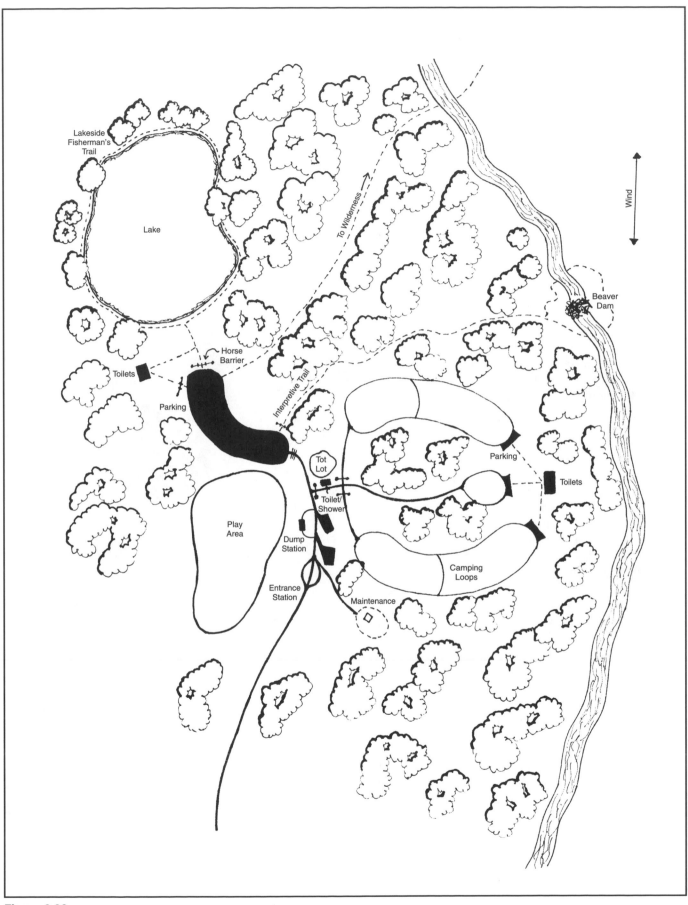

Figure 3.20

and (4) an increase in the number of campers who bring bicycles with them. All of these options provide more program participants for you and more fun and exercise for campers. Programmable facilities, such as trails, tend to create "snowball" effects if they are designed and managed properly. More facilities means more uses; more uses means more users; more users means more facilities. All of this adds up to more revenue!

Another example of a trail-compatible facility is a campfire theater. Since the theater requires a passive, quiet zone, it can be surrounded by an interpretive trail system as in Figure 3.21. These trails provide a buffer zone for reducing noise that would otherwise reach the theater. In addition, the theater can serve as a focal point for interpretive programs; for example, a naturalist might meet a group at the theater to talk about "night sounds in the forest" and then lead a walk on the trail to listen for them. Remember these two critical elements when thinking about zoning: First, look at the big picture and don't limit your planning to the trail itself (think about how the trail fits into the entire surrounding area) and second, learn to think program, program, program (how can the trail be used to provide fun experiences for users). Trails aren't merely cleared strips of

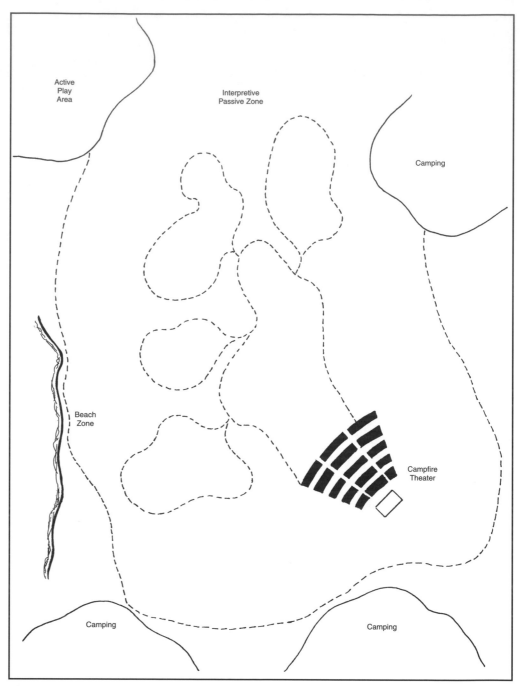

Figure 3.21

land, but vehicles for your creative programming ideas. Hike days and bike days are excellent examples of using trails for programming. Figure 3.22 (the photograph you saw originally in Figure 3.4) shows the "rewards" of hiking a trail loop for six Girl Scouts and their leader. The certificate given is for enthusiastic participation at a special hike day. This is a special remembrance for the participants *and* it can serve as good public relations for you by prominently displaying your logo.

Design Psychology. Once the function of a trail is set, it's time to think about how to enhance the experience of the users. While this depends upon the type of trail, certain elements of design psychology apply to most situations. The ultimate goal of design psychology is to make the user feel comfortable in the natural environment. When used correctly, design techniques should be subtle enough so trail users aren't aware that the environment is being manipulated for their benefit. For example, with the exception of secondary use trails and long-distance hiking trails such as the Appalachian Trail, a loop design is almost always preferable to a linear one. Even long-distance trails can be improved by the addition of loops, as you can see in the section on hiking trails below. A loop eliminates the need for backtracking and seeing the same scenery twice, reduces the number of other people the user is likely to see on the trail, and, from a management perspective, decreases trail wear since people walk around the circuit once

Figure 3.22

Figure 3.24

instead of out and back as they would on a linear trail. Unless the planner makes the loop design obvious by "forcing" corners and turns when they aren't necessary, users may be pleasantly surprised to find the trail ends where it began.

Loop design also lends itself to supporting another good rule of trail planning: Whenever possible, use a single entry/exit point. Single entry/exits, as we discussed earlier, are easier to administer and control—whether the facility is a trail or a state park. From a design psychology perspective, they benefit the users as well. Many people, especially those who only use trails on an occasional basis, may become disoriented in natural environments. If you design a loop with a single entry/exit, as in Figure 3.23, visitors finish the trail where they started it. At times, difficult terrain or other factors may keep you from developing a single entry/exit point. As an alternative, try to place the exit within sight of the parking lot, picnic shelter, or other facility from which the trail started. If this is not possible, and there is any chance trail users may become disoriented upon leaving the trail, signing may be necessary.

Before moving away from the entry/exit zone, let's discuss several other techniques of design psychology that you may find useful. Does your trail entrance zone beckon users to enter the trail and enjoy the experience, or does it repulse the potential user like the entry shown in Figure 3.24 (originally shown as Figure 3.8)? This lake trail entrance zone is located at an environmental education area in Pennsylvania. Most people who use outdoor recreation facilities—wherever they are lo-

cated—come from cities rather than farms or ranches. Figure 3.24, with its darkened interior and vegetation-shrouded entrance, "says" to users "if you enter this dark zone, something is gonna get you." This uncomfortable feeling may or may not discourage use, but as professionals, shouldn't we make sure that recreation visitors (in this case, trail users) are beckoned rather than repulsed?

Figure 3.25 shows a good example of how to beckon users. The trailhead is generous and wide while the trail clearing narrows after users get acquainted with the trail. A key element in the psychology of people movement on trails and roads is the creation of visual variety. So, it is a good idea to widen and narrow trail side vegetation slightly as the pathway moves through the forest.

Another design technique aimed at making the user more comfortable with your trail entrance is to try to avoid starting a trail on an adverse grade. This is a technical way of saying "don't start trails by going uphill." In some situations, uphill entrance zones are impossible to avoid. The problem with uphill starts is again psychological; if users see a climb waiting for them at the entrance, they may decide the trail isn't going to be worth the effort and avoid it entirely.

The photograph in Figure 3.26 (remember Figure 3.2?) shows a rather steep entrance and continued steep grade on a U.S. Corps of Engineers interpretive trail in California. The large rocks are vehicle barriers located along the trailhead parking lot. If you want users to enjoy and learn from your interpretive efforts, it seems to us you should plan, design and build your facilities (in this case, a trail) using the resource base to your best

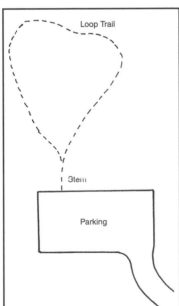

Figure 3.23

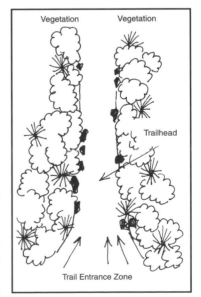

Figure 3.25

Figure 3.26

advantage. In this instance, a small draw (valley) with a gentle three percent natural grade intersected the road just to the right of the entrance shown in the photograph. Thus, the planner had the opportunity to direct the trail up that gentle valley for 200 or 300 feet and then locate a switchback to gain the elevation necessary to gain the ridge top. Instead, the potential user sees the steep grade from the trailhead and may be discouraged from walking the trail at all. (This is even more critical because the trail is an interpretive facility. Hikers interested in walking for exercise might be less put off by this entrance, but level entries to trails, or those that slope gently up or down, are always a better bet than are steep grades.)

A final point on entrance zone psychology. Earlier, we mentioned the tendency people have to move to the right when a choice is available. When developing a loop trail with a single entry/exit, you can reinforce this tendency through design. By moving people in the direction they prefer to go naturally, you can eliminate any vague feelings of anxiety they may have and reduce the chances of them entering what you

designed as the trail exit. As shown in Figure 3.27, three aspects of design are used in conjunction with one another to move users to the right on the trail. First, a gentle curve extends from the "stem" of the trail through the right-hand entrance. This encourages a natural continuation of the direction users were going while on the trail stem. Second, a reverse curve connects the left-hand trail exit to the stem. To enter the loop via this reverse curve, users would need to turn nearly 180°, a very unnatural movement, particularly with the gentle curve as an alternative. Finally, the trail is designed with a barrier, a pile of rocks, a large tree, or a bush, between the trail stem and the left-hand exit. The barrier and reverse curve are not intended to prevent users physically from turning left at this point; they do, however, serve as effective psychological blockades to move people onto your trail in the direction you want them to go.

The photograph in Figure 3.28 (originally shown as Figure 3.7) uses many of the techniques depicted in Figure 3.27. The picture shows some minor maintenance being performed on the reverse curve exit zone on the Paw Paw Path at TVA's Land Between the Lakes. The trail, which served several populations, was an interpretive loop trail describing various species and elements in a beautiful small hardwood zone in a group camp. There was a short (200 yards), essentially flat paved loop designed for use by the numerous elderly and disabled groups who used the camp. This loop was inside a somewhat longer (one-quarter mile) interpretive loop with some moderate climbs and descents.

The paved entrance section coming from the bottom of the photograph is generous, level and beckoning. This entrance zone contained several design challenges: It was necessary to gain elevation for the longer loop, keep the entry to the shorter loop level, move as quickly as possible away from the stream shown just behind the sign post in the picture, and separate the interior paved loop in as short a distance as possible from the longer unpaved loop. Further, the grade moving to the right was the maximum allowable for wheelchairs. Thus, while moving to the right is a positive design technique (and going uphill isn't) it was necessary to make sure that users weren't pulled to the left by the more level grade. This was accomplished by locating the pile of rocks as shown (this

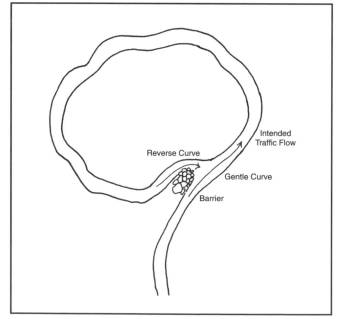

Intended
Traffic Flow

Reverse Curve

Gentle Curve

Barrier

Figure 3.27

Figure 3.28

54

is referred to as a *moment of force*) where the exit trail rejoined the entrance zone. Also, the reverse curve shown in Figure 3.27 was used to reduce the tendency to move to the left even more. Note how the trail could have been shortened by coming downgrade and straight from just to the left of the largest tree in the picture and tying back to the entrance just behind the back of the kneeling man (see the dashed line). This would have been less expensive, but would have reduced the recreational (and aesthetic) value of the trail by creating a lengthy tangent.

Once users enter the trail, it is generally a good idea to reduce the number of encounters they have with other people. On most trails not designed for motorized use—hiking, interpretive, bicycling, skiing—the planner should try to create a mood of being in a secluded natural environment. One way of reducing the potential for contact with others on trails is to use a curvilinear design, which decreases the linear distance people can see. A trail that avoids long tangents, or straightaways, and "snakes" through the woods will also increase user anticipation of what lies ahead. In flat areas, trail loops can be designed with a "fat" or broad layout to increase the distance between parallel points on the trail. If a trail is developed in an area with ridges and valleys, a narrow loop can be created by placing the trail below and on both sides of a ridge top as in Figure 3.29. In this case, the elevation of the ridge top provides a screen between parallel sections of the trail. In some environments, existing vegetation can be used as screening between sections of trail where people might otherwise see each other. Keep in mind, however, that deciduous trees and plants lose their leaves and will not provide a screen throughout the entire year. For this reason, and for ease of design, it is often a good idea to work on the trail layout in these environments during the months when trees and shrubs have lost their foliage.

To sum up, design psychology should be used to invite users onto trails by providing appealing entrance zones, to reduce confusion on the trail and at the exit by removing the choice between directional options, and to eliminate contacts with as many other users as possible by manipulating loop design, topography, and vegetation. A final aim of design psychology should be to create as much visual variety as possible, particularly on trails where foot travel is used. Remember, people move at a fairly slow pace on foot trails. As a result, scenery can become monotonous rather quickly. Moving in and out of forests and meadows, using frequent and gradual curves, and taking advantage of interesting scenery can all enhance the user's experience. And that's what design psychology is all about.

Field Design and Construction. In practice, the actual laying out and construction of a trail can't be separated from design psychology. In the last section, we talked about what techniques to consider for enhancing the user's experience. The construction phase of trail development is where these techniques are actually implemented. For example, if a loop trail is being designed in hilly country, the planner should try to construct the first half of the loop on an upgrade (excluding the entrance zone) and the last half on a favorable, or downhill, grade. With this layout, users who exert themselves will have an easier trip on the second half of the loop. While this is really a technique of design psychology, it is actually implemented during the construction phase.

In-the-field design of trails is also the time at which to apply techniques of resource stewardship. We could ask another trick question at this point: When, during the life of a trail, is consideration of maintenance most critical? The answer is during the design and construction phase. The level of attention we give to building preventative maintenance into our trail will determine the ease or difficulty we have maintaining it after it is completed.

Let's consider some of the preventative measures the planner can take during design and construction. Problems caused by water depend on whether trails are built on flat ground or

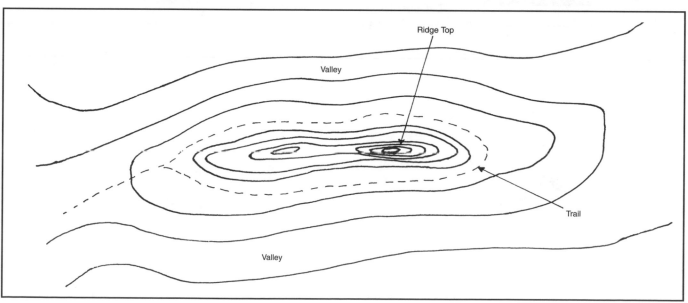

Figure 3.29

on slopes, and the measures you can take to prevent water-related damage are fairly simple but important. In flat areas, the sides of the trail should be designed with drainage escape channels. These are simply "gutters," or mini-ditches, which provide a path for runoff water to take. In order to move water to these escape channels, trails built in flat areas should be center crowned—two to three percent higher in the middle than along the edges. If possible, although this will increase costs of construction, trails should be built slightly above natural grade. These techniques prevent water from pooling on trails in flat areas and in the centers of ridges.

When trails are built along the sides of ridges, the challenge is to minimize damage from water movement. In moving downhill, water seeks the path of least resistance. Clearing and grading a trail down the side of a ridge is an invitation for water to use your path as its own, as shown in Figure 3.30. The solution is to move water off the trail surface as soon as possible to prevent the buildup of *volume* and *velocity*. One less than good trail construction technique used frequently that actually encourages erosion is the installation of stabilizer bars (Figure 3.31) along the lower side of the trail tread. As water moves down the ridge side and across the width of the trail, it strikes the stabilizer bar, usually long sections of log or railroad tie. Instead of continuing down the ridge side, the water is forced by the bar to remain on the trail surface, where it encourages erosion. The use of these stabilizer bars is shown in Figure 3.32 (origi-

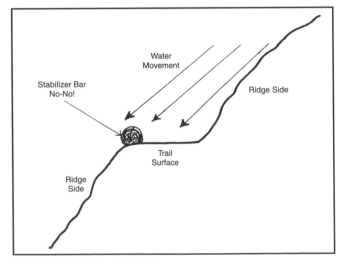

Figure 3.30

nally shown as Figure 3.1). Here, for a short distance, they are located on both sides of a steep trail section. This keeps the water trapped on the trail and leads to extensive erosion. There is an irony in both Figures 3.30 and 3.32 in that these construction mistakes are both located on steep grades in "environmental education" areas—one in TVA's Land Between the Lakes and one in a state-managed area in central Kansas.

While stabilizer bars should be avoided, you can use several other methods for moving water from the trail surface. One of the most effective ways of removing water from ridge side trails is shown in Figure 3.33. By constructing your trail so the downhill side is slightly (two to three percent) lower than the uphill side, the natural tendency for water to move across the trail is increased. This is called *outsloping*. Conversely, if the trail were constructed on the level or, even worse, insloped, water would tend to pool on its surface.

Another means of preventing water buildup on trail surfaces is shown in Figure 3.34. Water bars can be made with a log six to eight inches in diameter laid on the trail at a 30° angle and fastened with heavy stakes, posts or steel pins. The trail surface downhill from the water bar should be level with the top of the log, and the outslope should be slightly increased immediately above the water bar to permit water release. If your trail must make a slow, steady climb, it may be advisable to install *grade dips* (Figure 3.35). These are sections of trail where a short segment (not over five

Figure 3.32

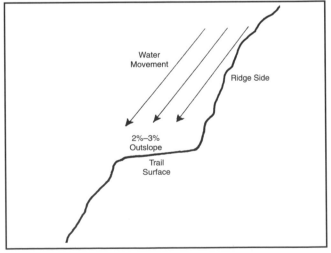

Figure 3.31

Figure 3.33

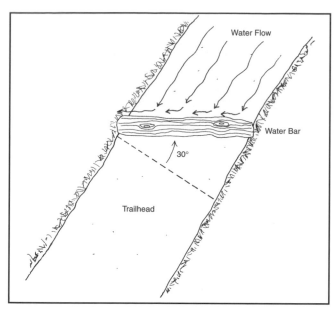

Figure 3.34

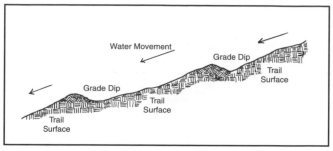

Figure 3.35

to six feet) has been built with a grade slightly adverse to the prevailing one. As with other techniques used when changes of topography are present, grade dips are employed to slow the downhill flow of water and remove the water from the trail surface at suitable intervals before it builds up an erosive force. A combination of all these methods usually provides the best erosion control.

Occasionally, you may find it necessary to construct your trail across the path of a major natural drainage. Often dry except for brief periods after rainstorms, these drainage courses and pathways can cause major damage to trail surfaces during short periods of wet weather. The best solution is to armor plate such drainage areas with asphalt, stone, or tile, as shown in Figure 3.36. Except for the need to place a hard surface across major drainage paths, the material used for surfacing trails depends on the type of trail and the anticipated amount of use. Preferred surfacing materials, along with other design specifications, are shown for various types of trails in Figure 3.37.

Although vandalism would seem to be more the problem of the administrator, there are steps the planner can take to reduce vandalism on trails. In our experience, we've found vandalism seems to occur most frequently within 500 feet of the trail entrance. (Perhaps people who enter a trail intending to vandalize it don't feel it's "worth the trouble" to walk the entire trail.) As a result, you may be able to reduce damage to more expensive facilities, such as benches, by placing them more than 500 feet into the trail. One of the most common forms of vandalism is initial carving in smooth-barked trees— usually aspen in the West and American beech in the East. By developing trails immediately adjacent to such trees, the planner invites such scarring. Trails should be kept at least seven to 10 feet from smooth-barked trees, and understory vegetation between these trees and the trail should be encouraged. If people are really intent on defacing trees, they will leave the trail and do so; the design goal here is to create a *psychological barrier* of distance and screening.

At times, people may cause damage to trail side signs without meaning to vandalize them. Part of human nature is curiosity, and curiosity is satisfied by touching objects. While on trails, people may reach out and touch, hold, or hit posts simply because they are there. Thus planners should consider such quirks of human nature and place sign installations close enough to be read but far enough off the trail so they can't be easily reached from the trail surface. This won't stop vandals from damaging signs, but it will prevent casual users from loosening sign posts over time. While it is easy to blame damage to recreation facilities caused by people on the individuals responsible—whether the damage results from vandalism or unintentional misuse—the real culprits are generally poor planning, design and administration.

One feature sometimes encountered on trails is the *switchback* (Figure 3.38). The purpose of a switchback is to reduce the percent slope, or grade, of the trail by increasing the linear distance traveled relative to the change in elevation. (Remember, slope is a function of rise over run, or elevation over distance.) In general, switchbacks should be avoided whenever possible because if the slope is steep enough to require one, it may be too steep to develop a trail. Severe grades discourage people and encourage erosion, but if switchbacks must be used, they should have a minimum turning radius of four feet on walking trails and a minimum turning radius of eight feet on multipurpose use trails. The area

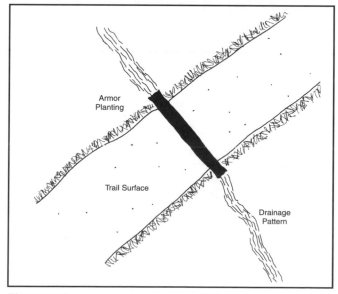

Figure 3.36

Trail Type	Clearing Width	Clearing Height	Tread Width	Surfacing[2] Material	Maximum Grade
Hiking—Backcountry—Distance	6 Feet	8 Feet	New tread 24" Existing tread (old road) variable	Natural with rock added in wet areas.	Variable—Can have steps and steep grades for short distances.
Hiking—Internally within a campground or other facility	Single lane 6–10' Double lane 10' (Traffic both ways)	8 Feet	Single lane 3' Double lane 6'10"	Natural if possible, gravel woodchips, or a combination of all three.	12% with 6% being general grade.
Horse[1]—Including pack animals	8 Feet	10 Feet	New tread 24" unless a wider tread is required for administrative vehicles.	Natural if possible, gravel in wet areas.	10% broken at short intervals by "rest" grades.
Bicycle[1]	8 Feet	8 Feet	Single lane 3' Double lane 6'10"	Paved if possible, Limestone Fines acceptable.	10% for short distances.
Interpretive	Single lane 6' Double lane 8'	8 Feet	Variable Single lane 2'6"	Dependent on use—Blacktop, woodchips, sawdust. (Gravel not acceptable.)	8% with 5% or less preferred.
For Persons With Disabilities	Variable but generous	8 Feet	Loop—3' (single lane) Double lane 5' minimum.	Blacktop almost a Necessity.	5%—Trail should be as flat as possible.
Off-Road Motorcycles	Single lane 6'	7 Feet	12"–18"	Natural	Variable

[1]If trail is other than a single-purpose trail (multi-purpose) the design requirements should be geared to the most demanding specifications within the planned uses.
[2]If asphalt paving is used, be sure to provide a gravel border along each side to keep the edge from crumbling.

Figure 3.37

where turning radii are placed should be graded nearly level, with enough slope to prevent water from being retained. This also provides a rest area. One of the problems with switchbacks is the tendency of foot travelers to take shortcuts across the tips of each curve or landing. This erosion-causing practice can be discouraged by a technique of environmental design: placing a cluster of four-inch high or larger stones in the neck of each switchback, as shown in Figure 3.38. These are quite uncomfortable to walk on and most folks don't!

When stream crossings are necessary, the planner has several options. Whenever possible, a ford is the method preferred because of minimal construction and maintenance costs. At times, some improvement in the stream channel may be necessary to improve footing at a ford, like placing large rocks in a straight line on the downstream edge of the crossing. Large rocks should be removed from the actual trail crossing. If a stream is too deep for fording, footlogs are the next best alternative for walking trails.

When a footlog is used, its top surface should be planed flat and a safety handrail or cable provided. Each end of the log can be secured by cable to the stream banks. For bridges on walking trails, two or three footlogs making a 24-inch width are usually adequate. Larger bridges and those for multipurpose or motorized use require individual design.

When users approach the end of a trail, they may be tired or ready to leave. As a result, the planner should avoid designing the trail so they can see the end of it from the interior. If users can spot the parking lot or whatever facility is at the exit point from the interior, they may be inclined to cut across country to reach it. Remember, we want to localize impact through design. Giving users visual encouragement to leave the trail before reaching the exit spreads impact rather than containing it.

Although we've reached "the end of the trail," the planner's job isn't over. There are several aspects of administration yet to consider, and the planner is at least partly responsible for these.

Administration. Generally, trails require less active, on-site management than many other recreation facilities. Less active, however, doesn't mean trails should be given less conscientious attention than other types of areas. Policies for use must be set and enforced, periodic maintenance schedules devised, and program opportunities developed. One of the first administrative tasks should be naming the trail, and the planner can advise management regarding appropriate names since he or she should be familiar with the pathway. The name should meet two objectives. First, it should provide a description of the character of the trail. Second, it should be something users will remember. Both these objectives can be met by using a little creativity. One excellent technique is *alliteration*—using words which all begin with the same letter or sound, such as: Shoreline Stroll, Tulip Tree Trail, or Paw-Paw Path.

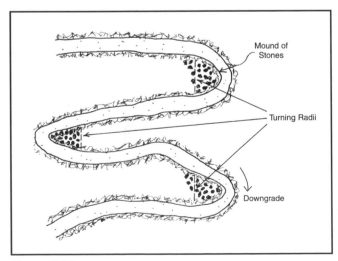

Mound of Stones

Turning Radii

Downgrade

Figure 3.38

Part of administration is keeping the user informed and oriented while on the trail through the use of signing. Because of their familiarity with the trail, planners should serve in advisory roles when these decisions are made. As a general rule, signing should be kept to a minimum, though it must be adequate to warn, restrict, or inform trail users. The following suggestions may prove helpful when considering how to sign trail systems. Schematic signs, which incorporate maps of the area the trail traverses, should be placed at major termini and intersections. These signs may be metal photo, painted, routed, Scotchlite, or laminated paper. A sign with the trail name and a matching symbol should be located at all trail termini, and trail and road intersections; the symbol alone can be used at other points along the route. The symbol should be easy to associate with the trail name; for example, Telegraph Trail might use *T* as a symbol (see the discussion on blazing which follows.)

Information on distances to shelters, water, campsites and other important features should be provided on termini and intersection signs, trail brochures, or both. When necessary, termini and road crossing points on foot, bike and horse trails should be marked with a sign prohibiting all motorized use (except administrative). Other prohibitions, as required by the type of trail or local conditions (e.g., no open fires), should be posted at these points as well. Gates, steps, stiles, posts or fences may also be required in some places to limit misuse, and markers with slogans like "Pack it in, Pack it out," along with adequate garbage disposal facilities, should be located at the termini and major road crossings. These types of signs may be located 100 feet or more from intersections to minimize sign pollution and vandalism. All springs located on or near the trail should, if possible, be boxed in and signed "safe only after suitable treatment." If they cannot be boxed in, they should be signed "unsafe without treatment." Too much signing can produce a negative experience for trail users, so when signs are necessary, mount them on posts as low as possible to avoid a high profile.

Often signing, or at least verbiage, can be avoided by blazing or painting symbol stencils on trees. When you use this type of marking, be sure the blazes are intervisible; from each tree marked, you should be able to see one blaze in either direction. In some instances, it may be necessary to place a blaze on opposite sides of a tree so it can be seen from either direction. The planner should walk the trail in both directions to determine appropriate locations for blazes. The interval between blazes will vary with terrain, type and density of vegetation, and trail alignment. The bottom of each blaze should be located about five feet above ground level. The frequency of blazes should increase as the trail approaches intersections, particularly those with other trails or logging roads. Blazes should also be used more frequently near trail termini and road crossings. If trees are not available at critical trail junctions or in sections of trail crossing extensive open areas, blazes may be marked on four-by-four-inch posts. These should be visible above tall grass or weeds.

Trees must be prepared for blaze stencils carefully. Smooth-barked species such as beech, aspen and yellow pop-

lar require little or no preparation, but the bark of other species should be scraped or smoothed *lightly* to provide a flat, clean surface for the marking template. The cambium, a thin layer just beneath the tree bark, must not be exposed, and the template should be made of flexible material to conform to the rounded shape of the tree. Marking paint should be applied with a one-and-a-half- or two-inch brush, and the paint should be color-coded so each trail is designated by a different color. A five- to 10-year forestry boundary paint should be used to ensure long life. The best colors for trail use are white, blue and yellow.

Zoning, design psychology, construction, and administration are all critical elements of trail development, regardless of the type of trail being discussed. We now need to shift our focus and briefly consider some aspects of design pertaining to specific kinds of trails commonly developed in parks and recreation areas. In the following sections, we'll look at trail design strategies for hiking, hike 'n bike, interpretation, minibikes and persons with disabilities.

Hiking Trails

There are two basic types of hiking trails. One is the *linear corridor,* the best examples of which include the Appalachian and Pacific Crest Trails. The purpose of this type of trail is to make a long-distance backcountry hiking experience fairly accessible to a large number of people. Being avid recreationists, we think this purpose is commendable. As planning critics, however, we feel the design of these trails could be improved and use extended to a wider variety of clients than those who currently hike them. Remember that access to an area doesn't ensure widespread use of the attraction.

Figure 3.39 shows a typical section of a linear corridor trail. The distance between the two access points on the roads might be 20 or 25 miles, thus the design of the trail has, in essence, limited use to serious, long-distance hikers. These people may leave one access point, hike all day to the shelter, stay the night, and hike to the next access point the following day. But the design in Figure 3.39 creates logistical problems for even this type of user. Hikers have the option of bringing

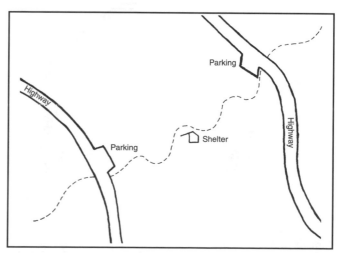

Figure 3.39

two vehicles to shuttle between their beginning and end points, or hiking back the way they came. As we discussed earlier, doubling back has its disadvantages: an increased potential for contact with more people, twice the impact on the trail, and/or seeing some of the same scenery over again. Shuttling is not an ideal solution either because of difficult logistics and doubling fuel expenses. Also, parking two vehicles in two safe spots is, more often than not, a problem. You may find nothing but tire tracks or a hub cap when you arrive after a two-day hike to that unprotected parking area.

The key to improving the type of design shown in Figure 3.39 is the key to successful planning of any type of recreation facility, which is understanding and accommodating the needs of users, including potential users. There are really two types of people who use linear corridor trails: the serious, long-distance hikers described above who are both willing and physically able to use these trails as the designers intended, and the "typical tourist," perhaps on a family vacation, who stops at an access point, walks in one-quarter of a mile or so and then returns. Planners generally don't understand this second phenomenon; the Appalachian and similar trails, because of their nature, have an aura of adventure about them. The same aura is true with entrances to wilderness areas. The average person may want to experience this briefly just to be able to say, "I was on it."

How can we, as planners, take the needs of these two groups and develop a better approach to linear-corridor trail planning? One solution is shown in Figure 3.40. In this design, the linear experience is left intact for those people who want to use two vehicles and hike in one direction only. The design also meets the needs of the casual user by providing a series of short connector loops (dashed lines). Now, instead of walking in one-quarter mile and returning back the same way, this group can walk a loop trail tailored to fit their preferences for short distances. The planner might develop one very short loop (one-quarter to one-third mile) on one side of the road where the main trail crosses. On the other side, a longer loop—perhaps one to two miles—could be constructed.

This approach would be aimed at expanding as much as possible the potential types of users.

The longer loops, shown by dotted lines, create an opportunity for a third type of hiking experience. These loops may be used by the long-distance hiker who can't or prefers not to use a shuttle system. With long connector loops, it's possible to leave your car at a parking lot, hike in, stay the night, and hike back without retracing your steps. In the southern United States, where linear trails pass through national forests, the existence of old logging roads gives the planner some real help.

The type of development shown in Figure 3.40 is important for two reasons. First, it creates the potential for additional types of hikes on a linear corridor trail. Second, it begins to present the opportunity for users to design the type of experience they want. This is an important point. Instead of the planner saying, "Here's a linear trail—take a long walk or don't use it," he or she says, "Here are some choices; pick the one meeting your needs and preferences." (Planning parks for people again.)

Most of the trails on federal public lands (Forest Service, National Park Service, Bureau of Land Management) were built in the early part of this century. User convenience, design psychology, recreational hiking and riding, and even concern for the environment were generally not included in trail planning, location, or construction. Trails then were foot and horse transportation arteries linking fire towers, line camps, guard stations, and ranger stations. The "users" included fire guards, fire tower personnel, telephone line and trail maintenance crews, and packers with pack horses taking supplies to towers, stations, and camps. The trails were nearly always as straight and narrow as possible. Location to enhance user enjoyment of topography, vegetation, and scenic views wasn't considered. Trail grade or steepness was determined by a loaded pack horse walking without undue strain. The thought that persons with disabilities or the elderly might want to hike a short loop or section or that the challenge of climbing steep grades is a common desire of many hikers were never part of that early trail planning process. This means that the large land managing agencies have thousands of miles of trails requiring upgrading similar to that suggested in Figure 3.40.

The Trail System

A system or complex of hiking trails such as the one shown in Figure 3.41 has certain advantages over a linear-corridor system, particularly for recreational users. From the standpoint of trail management, these include the following:

1. *Right of way:* Linear-corridor trails may be hard to develop because they require long, narrow tracts of land. Corridors adequate for trails may alternate between public and private ownership, making it difficult for public agencies to acquire title or easements and even harder for private concerns to attempt linear-trail development. Conversely, a hiking loop system incorporating consid-

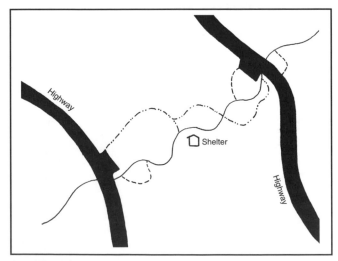

Figure 3.40

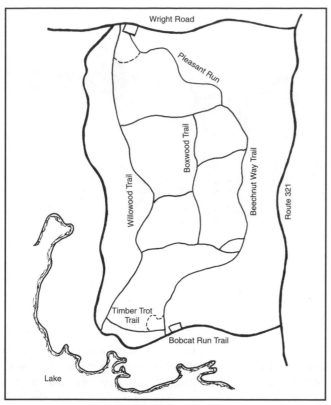

Figure 3.41

erable distance can be developed on a relatively small plot of land.

2. *Control:* Because hiking systems can be contained on single-ownership properties such as state parks, it is easier to manage access and use of the trails. Systems may be designed with fewer entry access points and road intersections than linear trails, and, in most instances, on-site management need not be as far removed from the system.

3. *Maintenance:* Linear corridors, because of their length, have to rely on several different maintenance operations. Hiking loop systems can be maintained from a single point, permitting more uniform maintenance and less need for coordination among crews and supervisors.

Users and management may both benefit from the opportunity to program trail systems. Since the trail system is geographically contained in one area, it is likely to receive more repeat use by local hikers as well as the transient use from out-of-area visitors. A local base of support gives any facility, including trails, an advantage in terms of program development. With area hiking clubs and branches of conservation-oriented societies drawn into cooperative relationships with the agency or organization managing the trail system, hike days, litter collection walks, and overnights with Scout troops can be planned. The chief advantage of trail systems is the opportunity for users to design their own experiences. As shown in Figure 3.41, the trail system, with its honeycomb of short, intermediate and long loops, can accommodate walks lasting from several minutes to two to three days.

Accessible from connectors to a nearby campground, linear trail, and park entry station, as well as the trailhead, the system "invites" users from a variety of sources. In northern climates, the complex can double as a cross-country ski system.

The management key to making trail systems convenient for users is adequate signing. One challenge with signing a hiking complex is to reduce cost, and the method we suggest is shown in Figure 3.42. As we discussed earlier, location signs need to be provided at each trail intersection. Instead of producing a separate map for each of the numerous intersections on a hiking complex, the signing system shown in Figure 3.42 uses a master map with numbered locations. Corresponding numbers are then placed on the sign posts, eliminating the need for 30 or 40 original maps, each with a "you are here" indicator on it.

Hike 'n Bike Trails

Inside of developed recreation areas such as state parks, and adjacent to campgrounds, there is an excellent opportunity to design a system of walking and bicycling trails. These systems, if designed carefully, can serve a *dual function;* providing circulation among the various facilities within the area—campsites, play courts and fields, beaches, campfire theater, and the like—and increasing program opportunities as well. The actual design and use of hike 'n bike systems are site-specific. Such factors as type of other facilities and physical characteristics of the site will help determine what you can and can't do with the system. There are, however, some general guidelines to consider.

Trails with more than one purpose need to be planned for the use with the most demanding requirements. For example, hiking trails need only a four-foot turning radius on curves and, unless use is heavy, can function with a natural ground surface. When bicycling is added, however, the turning radius should be eight feet and a surfacing material should be added. Ideally, an asphalt surface is best but also quite expensive—several dollars for each linear foot of trail. Depending on the situation, there may be an alternative. In most parks and campgrounds, users bring bicycles with them for internal transportation and recreation. For instance, recreational vehicle (RV) campers often bring one-

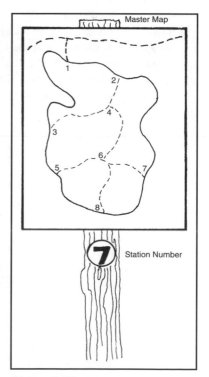

Figure 3.42

or three-speed bikes as opposed to 10-speed models with narrow gauge tires. If this type of user predominates in the camping area, we have found that finely crushed limestone works well, at a considerably lower cost than asphalt.

Hike 'n bike trails should be designed to connect major use zones with each other. Since circulation is one aspect of this, it may be possible to take advantage of part of the road system within the park or campground. There are two ways of developing hike 'n bike trails, both of which should be used in most instances. Portions of the system can follow roads connecting areas by developing signing schemes and painting bike lanes, though additional paths for circulation may be necessary to supplement those using the road system. In designing the circulation function into a hike 'n bike system, it's important to remember that motorized vehicles will be using the roads and crossing the paths. Keep in mind that speed is a design requirement that must be considered from the standpoint of safety. A cyclist needs more advance warning of an impending intersection than a hiker requires. Departing slightly from our need for curvilinear design, an occasional straightaway safe for passing should be included for faster bikers.

There are several aspects of trail design useful in enhancing program opportunities on hike 'n bike systems. *Variety* should be included in the system as much as possible. Design the trail so it moves in and out of stands of timber, through open meadows, along lakeshores—whatever resources are available in your area. Varied length loops are important to hike 'n bike systems. A loop taking two hours to walk leisurely may take an industrious 10-year-old less than half an hour to bicycle. Organized bike hikes can be planned by program staff if the trail design takes this need into account. Developing the trail near scenic views, abandoned cabins, or interesting geologic features will create opportunities for program staff. Programs can also take advantage of the connector function of hike 'n bike trails. The program areas connected by the trails can serve as bases for starting and completing hikes and bicycle tours. The photograph in Figure 3.43 shows a paved hike 'n bike trail in and near a campground.

Minibike Trails

During the mid 1970s, minibikes became popular additions to the recreational equipment users brought to parks and campgrounds. Adults used them for transportation, and children and teens used them (when they were permitted) for recreation. We mention them here to add another program element to outdoor recreation areas. This fits well with our philosophy of planning and designing areas with all users in mind.

Minibike areas and other recreational facilities that may be a nuisance to some users require the same zoning given to maintenance yards. They should be a part of, but apart from, the rest of the recreation complex. They should be far enough away from other types of areas so the noise created will not be noticeable. Sound level tests should be conducted to determine how great this distance needs to be, given local to-

Figure 3.43

pography and levels of vegetation. (You may be surprised at how close they can be located to other uses.) If a minibike isn't available for testing how far noise will carry, you, as a planner, can borrow a chain saw from the maintenance crew. The chain saw noise will approximate the sound of a minibike.

To reduce development costs, the ideal setting for a minibike area is in a once open field that is now covered with high grass, shrubs and scattered small trees. Once the appropriate zoning and distance factors have been determined, all that remains is to develop the trail complex. We suggest a design similar to the one shown in Figure 3.44. This complex, which can literally be built in one day, requires only minimal development. A parking area large enough for five or six vehicles serves as an entrance zone. Vegetative screening should be left here to help minimize the visual effect of the area. Using a bush hog, clear a long trail stem from the parking area to the minibike zone. This stem should be made as fairly straight and level as possible. The goal here is to provide access into the area rather than to create a zone where people will ride recreationally. Past the entrance, the design shown provides three areas for use. A staging area where riders can view the field and make minor repairs leads to a circular trail with gentle curves, which can be used by novices, and as a warm-up area. A trail of intermediate difficulty and an advanced trail are also included here, and a sign at the juncture of the three trails informs riders about the difficulty level of each trail.

The trails themselves require little more preparation than cutting a swath with a bush hog, assuming a suitable open field is available for development. The trail should be walked and inspected before use, for any woody plants, such as sumac, cut by the bush hog will leave sharp protruding stumps that should be dug out at ground level. All vegetation between the trails should be left to discourage users from cutting across between trails, and periodic mowing is normally the only maintenance the area will require.

Minibike areas are easy to design, develop and maintain. If an area has a suitable zone and the potential for use, it can add another dimension to program opportunities.

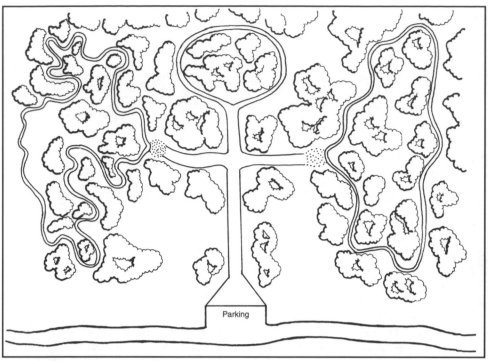

Figure 3.44

Interpretive Trails

This single type of facility, like several others in this text, has been addressed extensively in numerous other books and publications. However, with rare exception, these sources have focused on the development of the interpretive elements of the trail and not on the needs of the users or on the protection of the environment itself. As with other types of recreational areas and facilities, interpretive trails require attention to people and the resource base as well as the program element in question—in this case, interpretation.

Developing a successful interpretive trail depends on several factors. The most obvious criterion for judging a trail is the quality of its historical, cultural, or natural elements. However, this judgment must be made in light of the question: Who is the intended audience? An interpretive trail in a campground should not be expected to function the same way as one outside a nature center.

People go to visitor centers at national parks, museums at Civil War battlefields, and nature centers at state parks for the same reason: They are interested in them. People go to campgrounds to relax and enjoy themselves. Campers, then, generally don't have the same level of motivation to take advantage of interpretive services. This does not suggest that people who camp aren't interested in interpretation; only that interpretation is the primary reason people go to visitor and nature centers. Camping and having fun are the primary reasons people go to campgrounds, thus the key to developing successful interpretive facilities, including trails, is introspection. Think about who your users are (or better yet, who you want them to be) and develop displays and trails with them in mind. Interpretive messages wouldn't be designed the same way for children as they would be for adults. Likewise, they

should allow for different adult motivations in different settings.

Once you target an audience, design of interpretive trails is not difficult. For best results, we suggest that an interpretive specialist and a planner develop the trail together to ensure that both program and planning requirements are considered. The first step in the field planning process is to locate the two types of control points. The first is the set of features to be interpreted—specimen trees, geologic features, gunnery sites from a battle, and the like. The second relates to physical layout; the trail needs to start gaining elevation here, cross the stream just ahead, rejoin the loop over there, etc. Once you identify these points, the layout becomes rather like a game of connect the dots. How can we best design a pathway from the first to the last point?

Interpretation should be the primary focus of an interpretive trail. Walking it can be a good source of exercise, but you should avoid building excessive physical challenge into interpretive trails. Grades should not be overly steep and routes should not be too long. Depending on the audience and the features to be interpreted, one-quarter mile is probably a good length for most interpretive trails. The experience should be educational, but also enjoyable, and too much walking can spoil the mood you want to create for interpretation. Another way of detracting from this mood is to surface interpretive trails with gravel. When people walk on gravel, it crunches underfoot and the noise can detract from the experience you want users to have.

Poor maintenance can also cause interpretive trail users to be distracted. The photograph in Figure 3.6 (repeated here as Figure 3.45) shows a well-designed, paved, curvilinear trail in a National Park Service historical park in Massachusetts. The tree branches in the middle of the photograph are so low that adults have to move to the right-hand trail edge; then, the unpruned shrubs in the foreground force them to move back to the left of the walkway. The growth rate on both problem plants is quite slow, meaning once again maintenance and administrative personnel don't see too well!

Interpretive trails, to enhance the quality of the experience, should be as *convenient* as possible. Widened areas for people reading messages, such as those shown in Figure 3.46, should be provided at stations. If signs are used, place posts just out of reach to reduce casual damage. This will require using a larger typeface or print. Messages printed on signs or brochures should also be kept relatively short and nontechnical. People may remember that the wood of the Osage orange is used to make bows if you tell them the tree is also known as

Figure 3.45

a bowdock. They probably won't remember *Maclura pomifera*.

One effective technique when using interpretive signs is to spray a paint spot on the sign and a corresponding spot on the object being interpreted. This is helpful if there is any chance that the user might not be able to distinguish between the object being interpreted and other nearby features. For example, a person not familiar with nature might read an excellent message about poison ivy and then look knowingly at a nearby grapevine. If a paint spot is used, we recommend white; some bright colors look out of place in a natural environment, and others—reds and greens—are difficult for color-blind individuals to discern.

Trails for Persons With Disabilities

Whenever possible, avoid building trails "for disabled people." Designing specifically for those who happen to be blind or in wheelchairs reinforces the perception that these individuals are somehow "different." We feel a better approach is to plan trails for interpretation, hiking, circulation or some other purpose, and then design them so they can be used by as many people as possible, including those with disabilities. The only difference between an accessible trail and one with barriers is careful attention to standards. Trails designed to accommodate wheelchairs should not exceed a five percent grade[1] and should be hard-surfaced. Bridges on these trails should have railings. (We suspect that a trail built to these specifications wouldn't be recognized by most people as being for the "disabled.") Accessible trails should be marked with the international barrier-free symbol, but planning trails specifically for the disabled is demeaning.

Attempting to design trails for persons with disabilities can also limit the potential for trail use. Braille trails may be well-intended, but only a small proportion of visually impaired persons use Braille. Designing a trail with Braille symbols and regular-sized typeface for sighted people may actually hamper use by most of the visually impaired, but large type-

[1]Students with expertise in therapeutic recreation are quick to point out trail-grade standards for wheelchair users; however, in testing the same students the authors found that most of them had no idea of what a five percent grade looked like or how to attain it.

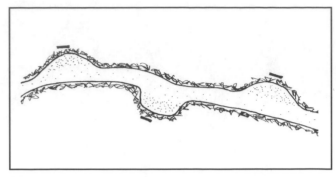

Figure 3.46

face and audiocassettes can be enjoyed by all users, regardless of their visual capabilities.

At times, it seems that planning trails or anything in the park realm for people with disabilities stops with good intentions. There are numerous instances of trails built "for the disabled" where the planner apparently thought of but didn't plan for the expected clientele. We've seen Braille trails with a four-inch drop off along the edges of the paved trail; trails surfaced for wheelchairs without a curb cut in the adjacent parking lot; trails three miles long for people with ambulatory problems. When possible, trails designed to accommodate persons with disabilities should be developed to allow them to choose the extent of their own experience. Building hard-surfaced loop trails with connectors, like the one shown in Figure 3.47, is a way of accomplishing this for individuals in wheelchairs. Our experience indicates the shortest trail can be about one-eighth-mile long. Longer loops provide a variety of options.

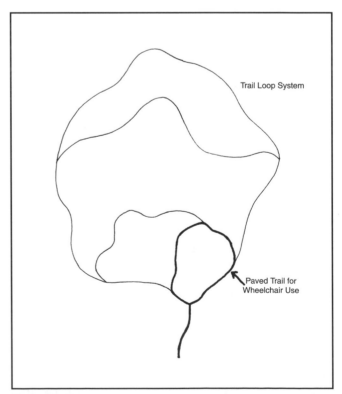

Figure 3.47

Synthesis

Regardless of the type of trail you need to develop, the critical aspects of planning are to fit the design to the needs of users, protect the environment, minimize management and maintenance problems, and enhance program opportunities. At times, some of these goals may conflict with each other. When this happens, the best solution is to compromise on the basis of common sense. Ask yourself, or your planner, why the trail is designed as it is, and make sure the answer is satisfactory. Be sure a trail is needed before you build it. Consider, for example, the trend in building jogging paths with fitness stations at intervals along the trail. We don't suggest these shouldn't be built, yet they are relatively expensive. We see people jogging on them fairly frequently in college towns and large cities, but in some locations, like campgrounds, the number of people using the exercise stations seems to be low. Do enough people use these trails for exercise to justify the expense, or would the jogging function alone on a hike 'n bike trail meet the needs of most users? Do fitness trails need to stand alone or could exercise stations be combined with trails designed for multiple purposes? We don't know how to respond to these questions, other than to say the answers probably depend to some extent on the location and other available opportunities. The point is twofold: First, we shouldn't assume that demand for a new type of trail or any other facility exists just because other parks or communities are beginning to install them, and second, to determine demand it is first necessary to assess need. When we suggest ways to help design trails, we assume you have already justified development.

More on Programming

The "flip side" of making sure that a particular type of trail is needed is taking advantage of existing trails for additional uses. The most outstanding example of adding exciting programming to an otherwise less than sensational trail we've seen is in Indiana's Lieber State Recreation Area. On the Friday and Saturday nights immediately preceding Halloween, a lightly used interpretive trail becomes a place where horned monsters, ghosts, trolls, mad doctors with their mutilated patients, and other assorted beasties roam the Trail of Terror!

It takes the staff about five working days to build the 17 scenes and train the 100-plus volunteers who help conduct the program (among the volunteers are judges, executives, state police officers, employees from Lieber *and* other state parks). Along with the volunteers staffing the 17 scenes, there are 22 roving costumed monsters, aliens, and critters who see to it that the groups of 30 persons (with leaders in front and back) are suitably stimulated between scenes. These rovers also make sure that all props and equipment keep working and that the supply of "blood" is flowing to the mad doctors and numerous gore-oozing unfortunates. Another of their jobs is to make sure that the 100 luminaries (large grocery bags weighted down with sand and lighted with a large candle) stay upright and lit—an idea borrowed from the southwestern part of the United States.

At the beginning point, the trail guide welcomes each group, explains the simple rules (for example, no flashlights allowed), and assures them he or she can guide *most* of them safely through the trail, reassuring them by saying that they seldom lose more than five people per group. Some, the guide explains, become choice monster morsels, others pass on to another world, and some, well, it's just too terrible to talk about what happens to them. Unfortunately, we know a number of state and federal recreation personnel in parks and resource areas who would be completely shocked at the prospect of turning a less than heavily used interpretive trail into a program zone, even for one weekend out of the year, *but* over 4,000 people of all ages have a delightful experience and Lieber Recreation Area gains more positive public relations than most sites get all year. This should tell us something about the value of programming, shouldn't it? (For your review and enjoyment, we've included eight photographs, Figures 3.48 to 3.55, of monsters and users on the Trail of Terror. For more information about this program, you can contact the Property Manager, Lieber State Recreation Area, Route 1, Box 712, Cloverdale, Indiana, 46120, telephone 317-795-4576.)

Figure 3.48

Figure 3.49

Trail Design Exercise

At the end of each of the next few chapters, you'll find an opportunity to design an area or facility similar to the one discussed in the preceding pages. Here's your challenge for trails.

The setting: Haunted Hill Campground (Figure 3.56) is located in a large state park in the Midwest. The area is built on the shoreline of a Corps of Engineers project, Veronica Lake. There are 300 campsites, 200 of which have electrical hookups. Users are mostly families with children ranging in age from a few months old to high-school age, although retir-

Figure 3.50

Figure 3.53

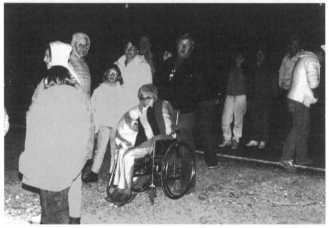

Figure 3.51

Figure 3.54

Figure 3.52

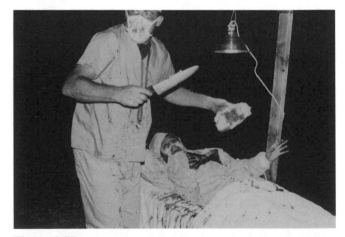

Figure 3.55

ees use the area regularly. The nearest community has active Scout troops and a chapter of the National Audubon Society. As an experienced consultant or team of consultants with a background in planning, management and programming, your job is to develop a conceptual plan for a comprehensive system of campground trails.

Givens:

1. Topography slightly rolling and sloping toward lakeshore. Land suitable for facility location anywhere.
2. Soils excellent. No problems with heavy clay content and frost heave is not a concern.
3. Vegetation: Overstory already thinned to a 50 percent shade factor with a mixture of high-quality, young vigorous hardwoods. Understory 10- to 15-foot dogwood, redbud, and other young hardwoods; three- to 15-foot material in shrubs and small trees adequate for good screening.
4. Public land ownership.
5. Features: No outstanding cultural, environmental, or historical features located on the land base. South side of southernmost bay of lake has interesting limestone bluffs, but no developable land between bluffs and shoreline. Bluffs are visible from northern shore.
6. Other park features outside campground: Linear corridor hiking trail one-and-a-half miles beyond campground entrance and fee station.

Your conceptual plan should include:

1. Connections between camping areas and program areas, including the beach zone.
2. Recreational trails for all types of users, including hikers, bicyclists, three-wheelers, and nature enthusiasts (indicate proposed surfacing materials.)
3. Locations where directional and information signs should be installed.

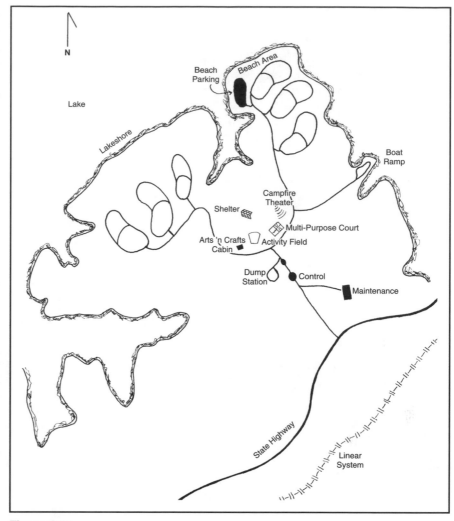

Figure 3.56

4. Any necessary support facilities. (There's at least one we haven't discussed yet, so here's your chance to apply some common sense.)
5. Something innovative—a special program using the trail system, an additional use for a conventional trail, a type of trail use we haven't discussed. Be creative!
6. Names and any necessary regulations for your trails.
7. A map legend distinguishing among the various types of trails you develop.

Obviously, there is no "right" answer to this exercise. We have included one solution in Appendix B, but since we've told you everything we know about trails, you should do better than we did. Good luck!

Chapter Four

Day-Use Areas: Hosting Through Design

There are some good items and some far less than good ones shown in these photographs. What do you see? Are you looking at problems or solutions? Are the facilities shown user-friendly or do they present barriers to full use and enjoyment? Take some time and have a close look before you read on. As you study Figures 4.1 through 4.7, try to think like a user.

Figure 4.4

Figure 4.1

Figure 4.5

Figure 4.2

Figure 4.6

Figure 4.3

Figure 4.7

Introduction

On the first page of this chapter, you have the challenge to view and study photographs of several park areas from around the United States. Some are good, and some are poorly planned, designed, administered or all three of the above! As we move through this chapter we'll discuss each one of these and other issues, but our main emphasis will be on the second part of the chapter title—"Hosting Through Design." If there is an underlying theme for this book it likely is that park systems need to be better hosts to their users.

As we reviewed the first edition and our materials for preparation of the chapters in this book, two issues evolved. First, we realized we had, in the earlier edition, been remiss by failing to emphasize hosting. Second, we neglected to focus on the extent to which elements in any of the facility-oriented chapters—for example, trails—are closely tied to other chapters with a focus on facilities—campgrounds, day-use areas, and the like. Principles of design or programming or administration or hosting—most of which is simply good old-fashioned common sense—should be similar in all sorts of park endeavors. For instance, how you plan (or how you should plan) to provide beckoning, fun programming in camping areas should guide area and facility planning and design. We touched on this in the first edition, though not nearly enough, but what we failed to point out is that this axiom holds true for trails, day-use areas, special-use areas and play areas as well. The fact that programming hasn't been a dominant criterion (or in most cases a nonexistent consideration) in the design of most state and county parks and most certainly those in the federal realm means the public has been shortchanged big time. Getting you to be concerned—or better, excited—about hosting, programming, and different sorts of users is one of our goals. Each of the authors has extensive teaching experience in continuing education for professionals currently working in the field; however, only in very recent years have we found a limited number of park folks willing to listen to this hosting message. Perhaps the most effective aid in getting the attention of professionals who have been reluctant to do much for users besides provide facilities, and which are, in general, poorly planned and designed, has been the Americans with Disabilities Act (ADA). Agencies are now required by law to provide accessible hardware (facilities) and programs for persons with disabilities. So, we ask in our typical naiveté, why not extend this logic to its natural conclusion and build, manage, and program recreation areas to meet the demands and desires of *all* users?

In this chapter we briefly discuss planning several special recreation areas. Chapters—and even entire texts—have been or could be written about these special areas (e.g., visitor centers). However, our challenge in a text like this is to give you as much guidance as possible within a reasonable number of pages and chapters. Your challenge is to learn the basics of planning parks for people and then use them to help solve most of your park design problems. This means determining as many facts as possible about potential users and their program needs and, indeed, any special park areas; then based on analysis of these facts you must plan facilities to meet the needs of users, managers and programs. In the real world, it rarely has been done this way; thus we again emphasize that historically most of our parks have been poorly designed.

Day-use areas, the focus of this chapter, include boat ramps, beaches, picnic areas, and visitor centers. In previous chapters, we've tried to stress the importance of program, program, program. This is still an excellent philosophy; never miss a chance to design or manage for the enjoyment of your users. Keep in mind, however, that the opportunity for programming won't always be present—at least not to the same extent for all types of facilities. How, for example, would you program a boat ramp? Actually, there are several ways. The main problem is a lack of creativity on the part of the planner. Ask yourself what a boat ramp is. If you conjure up a mental image of a broad slab of concrete sloping down into a lake, river or bay, you're at least as creative as most planners.

Instead of imagining what a boat ramp or other facility is technically, train yourself to think creatively, about what potential it has. A boat ramp is a slab of concrete, but it is also a use zone for people. And whenever you have people, there's an opportunity to program. Given a few extra dollars, perhaps you have room for a fishing pier next to the ramp; a little care taken in design and the pier is barrier-free. Anchor a number of old tires near one side of the fishing pier and your program staff can teach casting techniques. Suddenly your lonely slab of concrete is hosting, through design, 75 children and their parents, for an all-day fishing rodeo. Add some simple props such as gunny sacks and spoons for relays and egg races, and you have a full-fledged recreation program! If this boat ramp is in a campground and has available lighting, it may also be an excellent location for a large square dance or teen dance—perhaps while other potential dance surfaces (e.g., the multipurpose play court or shelter building) are being used for other programs.

There are two points to make here: First, the scenario we've just described doesn't happen on its own. It requires a commitment to programming on the part of management, a creative planner, an enthusiastic program person, marketing and organizational strategies, and a willingness to work with local media and user groups. We'll never tell you successful programming is easy. Second, programming—as important as it is—isn't always appropriate. If the boat ramp or other type of facility isn't convenient to reach, or if physical site conditions dictate "a slab of concrete and nothing else," you shouldn't try to force a program on the facility. Remember, our recipe for successful planning includes common sense as well as creativity. This brings us back to the point in the chapter title: Hosting Through Design.

Whether programs are feasible or not, the primary purpose of day-use areas is to provide enjoyment for those who use them. One way to increase people's enjoyment is to decrease the potential for hassles within the area. This is a function of design. If an area, whether boat ramp or day camp, is well-designed, it will be convenient, safe, and easy to use.

On the other hand, if you often see visitors who appear frustrated or who violate regulations (such as driving the wrong way on a one-way road), or if facilities are heavily vandalized, much of the blame can be traced to the person who planned the area. Before discussing specific types of day-use areas, it may be helpful to consider these types of issues from the perspective of *zoning*.

Earlier, we discussed the topic of simple zoning of use areas—how they relate to each other. There are really two types of considerations to keep in mind when you focus on zoning, and the first of these is *inter-area* zoning. In other words, how well (or how poorly) does the area in question "fit" with other use areas within the same complex? For example, a large lakeside park might have a picnic area, a beach, a boat-launching ramp, ball fields, play courts and playgrounds. The concern of inter-area zoning is the relationship between two or more of these areas: Do the locations of the picnic area and the playground complement one another? Are the beach and boating site zoned so they don't conflict with each other?

The second type of zoning to consider is *intra-area*. For intra-area zoning, we want to ensure that major and support facilities within a given use zone relate to one another in a reasonable manner. Within the area designated for play equipment, are the swings and the drinking fountain on the same side of the road? At the picnic shelter, are the garbage containers a part of, but apart from the eating area?

Note how one concept was repeated in both inter- and intra-area contexts: relationships. Relationships between use areas and among facilities within a single area are a crucial element in conceptual planning. A helpful tool for determining the sensibility of alternative ways of fitting use areas together is the relationship diagram. Examples of these diagrams are shown in Figures 4.8 and 4.9. The purpose of the relationship diagram is to help you conceptualize how "pieces" of an area can best be joined to each other. When placed on a base map of the site to be planned, these simple drawings are easier to interpret than formal plans. Indeed, relationship diagrams can often help form the basis for more sophisticated designs. For example, if the "fit" of facilities in Figure 4.8 seems to be the most logical of several alternatives from the standpoint of relationships, you might next consider the feasibility of various park entry points. If you have a firm idea of where the parking lot will be, you can "work backwards" to plan alternative road alignments and, ultimately, the best possible entrance zone. "Best" implies a compromise of several elements, including user safety, aesthetics, cost of development, and resource protection.

A final point to remember concerning relationship diagrams is this: "Relationship" doesn't always imply proximity between areas. A passive sitting area and a tot lot may be

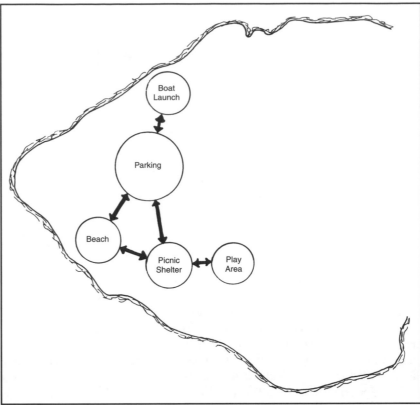

Figure 4.8

placed adjacent to each other if the purpose of the sitting area is to provide a vantage point to supervise children playing. If the purpose of the sitting area, however, is to provide a quiet enclave for contemplation, it should be removed from the tot lot.

Boat Ramps

In keeping with the theme of sharing mistakes, consider the facility shown in Figure 4.10. This drawing depicts a boat ramp built by the Corps of Engineers near Louisville, Kentucky. The ramp provided access to the Ohio River, which

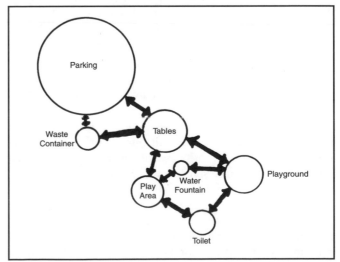

Figure 4.9

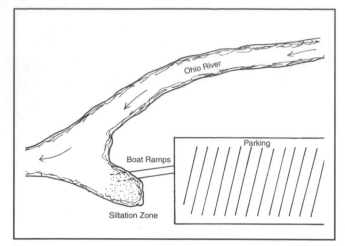

Figure 4.10

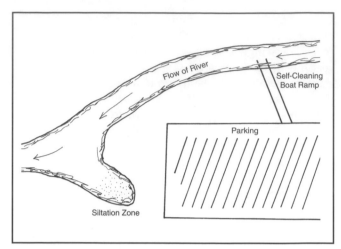

Figure 4.11

flows in the direction indicated by the arrows. The mistake resulted from the planning decision to place the ramp in a small inlet which was not in the path of the current. The lack of current in the inlet meant water moved slowly there, creating a siltation zone at the boat ramp. In other words, the natural flow of water moved silt into, but not out of, the inlet. As the silt settled, the inlet quickly filled in, and before long boats could no longer be launched. The initial solution to this problem, incidentally, illustrates a point we discussed earlier. After recognizing the problem, staff attempted to solve it many times by dredging the silt out of the inlet. As you know by now, however, such action would cure the effects of the problem for a short time rather than cure the cause of it. The final—and correct—solution, shown in Figure 4.11, was to close the original ramp and replace it with one where water movement provided a "self-cleaning" action. Figure 4.12—which you originally saw as Figure 4.1—shows another Corps of Engineers ramp with excellent self-cleaning potential. The Corps has done a good public safety job, too, with their Danger and Caution sign. In our view, the Corps of Engineers is now by far the best of all federal park managing agencies in operationalizing their concern for user safety.

There are some instances in which the solution in Figure 4.11 could create hazards to users. If the current is particularly swift, or if the boat ramp is for human-powered boats (canoes), a put-in point exposed to direct swift current might be unsafe. You can still avoid siltation zones in these situations by providing a breakwater immediately upstream from the launch point, as shown in Figure 4.13. The point to remember is this: A critical aspect of boat ramps is their slope. To maintain the degree of slope needed, you must keep the base area free of silt deposits. Allowing natural water movement to wash these deposits away is the most effective (and efficient) maintenance solution we know.

Although the previous example discussed a situation on a river, lakes are also subject to siltation. If you build a ramp at the base of a sheltered cove with a predominantly incoming wind, as in Figure 4.14, siltation may occur fairly rapidly. Ignoring soil studies and normal wind direction, along with a lack of attention to erosion control measures above the lake

shore, can also contribute to siltation. Soil washed down to a sheltered inlet may remain near where it enters the lake if wind and wave action aren't sufficient to remove it. Thus boat ramps on lakes should be built along the main shoreline (safety permitting) where the self-cleaning movement of water can be permitted to keep siltation in check.

Features of Boat Ramps. Finding a location naturally suited for a boat-launching ramp can often be quite challenging. The desirable slope, or grade, for a ramp is 12 to 14 percent. This slope is needed both above and below water level. The length of the ramp is also a concern if the surface elevation of the water is subject to change. Reservoirs may drop and/or rise several yards during the course of a season. The length of the ramp is not especially critical during a launch as long as there is room to back the boat or craft to the water. With a 14 percent grade, users should be able to launch most boats when the rear wheels of the tow vehicle reach the water's edge. The ramp should be long enough, however, to extend several feet below the lowest expected lake elevation, permitting launching when water levels are low. A few Corps of Engineers (USCOE), TVA, and Bureau of Reclamation lakes have elevation changes of 100 feet or more. Obviously planners can't realistically provide access at all ramp sites throughout the year.

Figure 4.12

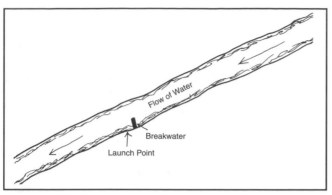

Figure 4.13

During most hours of the day, you can drive through the parking lot serving a boat ramp and not experience heavy launching traffic, even if the lot is nearly full. People launch their boats at different times of the day depending on their type of recreation use. Fishing parties tend to launch their boats early in the morning and/or late in the afternoon. Pleasure craft and power boats usually launch later in the morning and earlier in the afternoon. However, many people, both pleasure boaters and fishing parties, want to stay on the water as long as possible, leaving just before dark. As a result, many boat ramps suffer through a late afternoon/early evening "rush hour." If you expect this phenomenon to occur, you should plan a ramp wide enough for two boats or more, depending on the expected amount of use, to be taken out at one time. Figure 4.15 shows an example of a single lane ramp at low water. If the ramp is lightly used, this may be adequate; however, in a high-use boating zone, it is an example of poor hosting because a line may form here at dusk. Minimizing the

time users have to wait in line to get their boats put ashore will reduce their aggravation. Reducing hassles should be a goal of planning parks for people!

The problems users encounter on and around boat ramps can be decreased considerably through careful attention to detail. Since wet ramps can be slippery, the surface of paved ramps should be grooved perpendicular to the direction of the ramp to provide better traction. When building a ramp, you may want to include a series of iron rings three to four inches in diameter anchored along either side. This provides a convenient spot for boaters to moor temporarily while they drive their vehicle from the ramp to the parking lot upon launching and back again when they land.

The parking lot should be as close to the launch area as possible for convenience, but also should be located with environmental protection in mind. If the parking lot is built too close to the shoreline, construction may alter the site environment and make the shoreline more susceptible to erosion. When you design or build a new parking lot, remember to tilt it, if possible, two to three percent away from the launch. If rainwater is carrying pollutants from an existing lot to the launch area, you may also need to add a rock filter strip, as discussed in Chapter Two. (For a view of the pollutants deposited by vehicles on a paved parking lot, see Figure 4.6.) Regardless of the placement of the parking lot, the increase in wave action and vehicle and foot traffic around the launch area can create shoreline impact. Areas subject to considerable foot traffic should be reinforced. If the shoreline has a steep pitch or lacks vegetative cover, *riprap* may be needed. Riprap is large rock (six inches or larger in diameter) laid along the slope of the bank. The riprap receives the energy or force of wave action and thus helps prevent soil erosion.

When designing the parking lot to serve the boating site, remember the flow of traffic to and from the ramp as well as into and out of the area. Local conditions will have a bearing on what you can and can't do, but in all circumstances try to make the parking and launching maneuvers as simple as possible. Individual parking slips must be long enough to park vehicles towing boat trailers. Given the conditions existing on a particular site, try to design the parking lot and launch area to eliminate as much backing up as possible. Figure 4.16

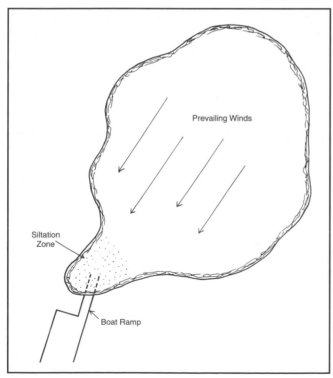

Figure 4.14

Figure 4.15

shows one excellent method for reducing backing between the parking lot and the ramp. (We'd love to claim credit for this, but we saw it at a Corps of Engineers campground on Barren River Lake, Kentucky). With this type of a turnout system, vehicles can drive two-thirds of the distance between the parking lot and the launch point in a forward gear. They need only back a short distance and, if you've ever backed a trailer, you can appreciate the convenience of this design.

Two excellent examples of hosting are shown in Figure 4.17. The ramp is a double, and here the Corps of Engineers has added a floating courtesy dock. (Note, too, they have minimized erosion with riprap.) The courtesy dock allows boaters to load and unload equipment, as well as themselves, from their craft without having to wade alongside it, another example of hosting through design, particularly for senior citizens and users with disabilities. The dock should be close enough to the ramp to reach by paddling, but far enough away to avoid interfering with the actual launch. If a dock is provided and the water elevation is subject to fluctuation, the dock should be hinged where it joins the shore. If the lake frequently rises above normal elevation, a dock can be designed to glide up and down on steel poles. These designs will permit the dock to change elevation with the water level.

As with all recreation areas, user safety and security should be incorporated into the design of launch-ramp areas. Swimming near the ramp should be prohibited, and signs indicating unusual safety problems (e.g., snags) should be posted. Regulations such as no wake speeds near the ramp should be clearly signed and enforced. Since boaters are often away from their vehicles for several hours at a time, parking lots should also be as secure as possible. Area lights may be needed if the lot will be used after dark. Underbrush and other areas for vandals and thieves to hide in should be eliminated. Area or security lighting at boat ramps is also a good program feature and is often critical as a safe destination beacon for late night fishing parties and other boaters (good hosting again!). If commercial electric power isn't available, the boating site is an excellent location for a solar-powered photovoltaic light.

Developing a recreation area or facility such as a launch ramp is a minimum level of service provision. As a professional, you should make every effort to maximize the use of resources allocated to recreation. There are at least two reasons for this. From a practical standpoint, recreation budgets are usually tied to quantitative measures: more users mean more dollars. From a somewhat more idealistic perspective, spreading the qualitative benefits of recreation to as many

Figure 4.17

people as possible is a worthwhile goal. The point is, don't stop with building a boat ramp. Imagine ways of increasing the use of the facility. For example, if fishing is one use of your water resource, work with a state or federal fisheries agency to provide fish attractors. A pile of brush or several old tires held together with bailing wire make an excellent environment for the small fish that attract larger fish. By sinking a number of these and making their locations available to fishing parties, you will enhance the recreation experience, and word of mouth will enhance your use figures. People who fish also appreciate the availability of depth charts, or underwater contour maps, as aids in locating game fish. If you can provide these, do so. An on-ramp bulletin board is a good location for the contour maps and other fishing information. Anything you can do to improve the recreation experience means a better hosting job. One result of quality hosting can be a wealth of public good will for your organization. If this isn't one of your management goals, it should be!

One of the more subtle elements of hosting is providing convenient places for users to deposit trash *and* to do a bit of recycling. We're certain you will have trash receptacles at your boat ramp but will you provide a beckoning, easy to see and use place to deposit aluminum cans? The homemade basket shown in Figure 4.18 is located at a Forest Service boat ramp in Colorado. More often than not, boaters will have several empty cans in the bottom of their boat by the time they return from their outing. Four things can happen to these cans: They get thrown out on and around your ramp; they are

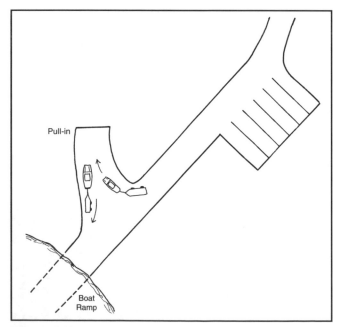

Figure 4.16

tossed into your on-site dumpster with other trash (and thus wasted); they blow out of the boat on our highways as users travel home; *or* they can become part of your hosting and agency goodwill program. The convenient wire cage shown in Figure 4.18 is a great place to drop those off *and* if you're smart and allow specific youth (or other) groups to glean the cans, you have an outstanding hosting facility. Making friends with the group that collects (and gets rewarded for) the cans adds to your oft-neglected political power base.

Beaches

Each spring, the maintenance crew of a parish park we know in Louisiana has a dredging job. During the year, rain water runs downhill, picks up the sand on the beach, and deposits it in the swimming area. So before the beach opens, the crew has to dredge the sand out of the lake and "put the beach back on the beach," another case of fighting effects rather than curing causes. Instead of an annual corrective action, a better solution would be to employ a one-time preventative measure. How simple it would be to provide a ditch and berm combination above the beach and route the runoff surface water away from the area where it causes damage!

The problem facing the parish park maintenance crew wasn't highly technical, they simply didn't look beyond the *surface* (effects) to see the real *problem* (causes). In addition to the phenomenon of water running downhill, beaches are

Figure 4.18

subject to damage because of the erosive potential of sand. Sand will not stay by itself on a slope greater than two to three percent. If you need to develop a sand-surfaced beach, or already have one on a steeper slope, a little preventative maintenance is in order. Figure 4.19 shows an existing grade leading to the water line. (We've exaggerated the slope somewhat for the sake of the figure; as drawn, the slope is too severe for a beach, although we've seen several even steeper.) Figure 4.20 shows a solution to this problem; a cut has been employed. Using a bulldozer or other earth-moving equipment, the original slope (dashed line) has been cut down to a grade of two to three percent, acceptable for a beach. Just above the beach zone, the angle of the cut has been increased and a low vertical wall installed.

Earlier in discussing boat ramps we suggested that the parking lot be tilted away from the boat ramp to eliminate the flow of pollutants from the lot to the ramp zone. This is particularly important with parking lots at beaches. The Forest Service, Tennessee Valley Authority, and a host of other park providers, including the private sector, have designed countless parking lots which act as collection areas for gases, oils and waxes from automobiles and have allowed these pollutants to flow directly into their beach areas. In most instances their designers didn't realize this was a potential problem.

The TVA Recreation Branch was a latecomer in the federal recreation realm. About 10 years after Land Between the Lakes became a reality, staff in the main recreation branch decided to build recreation areas on Tennessee Valley lakes in the upper South. One of their big problems was a failure to learn from the mistakes of others, including the Forest Service and Corps of Engineers, who had told TVA small areas were *big* trouble. So, during the 1970s, they built a series (over 140) of small and difficult to manage areas across the region. Most of these had poorly designed campgrounds, picnic areas, beaches, and boat ramps. Zoning of uses often worked against management and the users. (We'll share some of their costly mistakes with you throughout this text.) These areas are excellent examples of how *not* to plan parks for people. Figure 4.21—which you saw earlier as Figure 4.5—shows the pollution potential of a typical TVA beach with a sizable parking lot tilted toward the beach. The TVA Recreation Branch also did its best to help the private sector with pollution; they once recommended a design for a private campground in Tennessee with a beach located at the base of a watershed that drained a large (and operating) hog lot!

Often, recreation planners tend to equate a beach with an expanse of sand, bordered on one side by water and the other side by a road or parking lot. This is unfortunate, because designing an area like this limits the potential for user enjoyment. In the first place, you should ask yourself: Why do

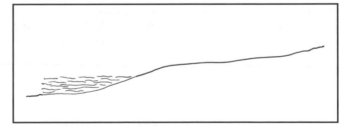

Figure 4.19

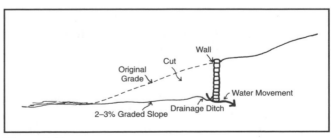

Figure 4.20

Figure 4.21

people go to beaches? Many go to swim, but others go to sunbathe, socialize, watch others, read, play, and pursue a variety of other recreation activities that aren't necessarily water related. Designs for beaches should encourage multiple uses of the waterfront zone. Ideally a beach should consist of a strip of sand between the water and an expanse of grass since people who don't care to swim may find it more convenient to sit on grass than sand. To protect the sand from erosion, placing a low wall or ditch-and-berm combination between the sand and grass is good practice. A portion of the seating area should be shaded so users have the option of sunbathing or not. The design should also include benches and tables for seating as well as open areas where people can sit on the ground on towels or blankets.

This topic—designing a beach for "landlubbers" as well as for swimmers—brings up an important point: The use of a given recreation facility is not necessarily limited to people who actually use it. This sounds like a contradiction, but it's really just an extension of what we suggested earlier. There are at least three types of people who go to a beach: those who go primarily to play in the water; those who go primarily to play on the beach; and those who go primarily because the person or group with them wants to go to the beach. Young children, who really want to enjoy the water and sand, may have parents who find little pleasure in sitting in hot sand under a hotter sun. Providing a few benches, tables, and a little shade may enhance the experience for these "unwilling users." When recreation planners develop formal or structured use areas, they generally attend to the needs of nonparticipants. Providing bleachers at a ball field is an example of this. The same consideration, however, is rarely extended to informal, nonstructured areas and facilities such as beaches. As you develop plans and designs for recreation areas, stretch your thought process to incorporate the needs of all people who may frequent the area, whether they are typical "users" or not. Ah, yes, we are again asking you to plan parks for people!

Design of a beach zone shouldn't stop at the water's edge. The planner needs to consider swimmer safety. Questions to ask should include: How deep is the water? How steep is the slope? (Around six percent is ideal.) Are there any ledges or

holes in the area? Are there large submerged rocks a swimmer might strike? Is the bottom free of broken glass and other debris? Are there dangerous currents, undertows, or unusual temperature changes due to underwater springs? Physical conditions in the water should be made as safe as possible. Other issues, such as how to define the beach (e.g., buoy lines, lifeguards, and necessary signing), should be made in accordance with state regulations or standards. We also recommend that you seek the advice of your legal counsel.

On a happier note, design in the water should also provide opportunities for play. Two old tires, each filled with concrete and a metal post, make an inexpensive, hard-to-vandalize set of water volleyball standards. Make sure you set these standards at a depth of no more than 30 inches so all family members can play. You can purchase floating basketball standards as well, although these should be limited to areas with on-site supervision to prevent theft. We've seen the addition of a few simple water play amenities increase both the amount of use at beaches and the fun people have there. Play equipment, however, doesn't need to be limited to the water. Beaches generally mean children, and children enjoy play equipment. Zoning a play area adjacent to a beach can multiply the opportunities for creative use of both zones.

Along with a water volleyball area, a volleyball "court" on your sand beach, such as the one shown in Figure 4.22, is also an excellent hosting facility. These two types of volleyball installations will provide countless hours of pleasure for children, teens, and families. They are also great places for the ever popular three-on-three contests.

Figure 4.23, which is also Figure 4.2, shows a sand beach during a family sand sculpture contest. Having these types of beach amenities and programs will enhance both your use and revenue.

There are several factors to consider when determining where to locate a new beach. The first of these is the availability of land and water suitable for the beach zone. It is, as Figure 4.20 shows, possible to "create" one next to good water by making a cut with construction equipment. This approach, however, is comparatively expensive if another, more suitable piece of land is available. A second criterion for locating a beach is the set of nearby site conditions. Ideally, a beach should have a western exposure for afternoon sun and should not be located directly in the path of incoming wind. As a general rule, beaches developed on lakes will be less subject to erosion and collection of stagnant water if they are placed along the side of a bay or inlet. Beaches exposed to the main channel of a lake are more subject to wave action and incoming wind, both of which contribute to erosion. Conversely, the mouth, or upper end of a bay or inlet, may not get enough wind and water motion to provide cleansing action. Trash and pollutants may thus tend to collect here, creating unpleasant conditions for swimming.

The potential for placement of other use areas also plays a part in determining where beaches should be located. As with other facilities, a beach should be zoned to complement nearby areas. Beaches fit together well with other active-use zones such as play areas and picnic grounds. Swimming and

Figure 4.22

Figure 4.23

other beach activities may conflict, however, with passive recreation pursuits such as a nature center or interpretive trail, and these areas should be zoned apart from one another. Thus the potential various sites have for a nature area may have a significant impact on where to locate a beach.

Recreation planning doesn't have to be difficult, but it is often quite complex. The perfect "spot" for a beach may be less than ideal once you consider the other pieces of the design puzzle needed to make up a functional area.

Over the years, planners and designers (who tend not to be users of what they plan and design) have given us thousands of park facilities, including beaches and boat ramps, that are downright user unfriendly. These folks are often not skilled in asking managers, programmers, maintenance crews, or users to define design criteria for them. Fact is, there is often an elitist attitude in the planning and design realm, meaning they really don't want input from you or anyone else. The authors believe that architects, landscape architects, engineers, wildlife specialists, planners, and some others are to be of service to managers, administrators, maintenance staff, and programmers. Far too often, though, design staff tend to dictate single solutions without thought to how these designs will (or will not) function for those who have to manage, program, maintain, and use the resultant area or facility. This approach

has traditionally been the underlying cause of most poor park planning and design. We further feel the basis for this approach to planning and design is mostly the fault of recreation curricula for not providing students with an adequate enough background in planning and design to at least question the solutions foisted on them by technically-trained landscape architects and others of this ilk.

Working together as a team is the only way to develop the quality designs deserved by users and tax payers. If your planning and design staff, including any consultants, doesn't ask for or want your input, make sure they get it anyhow. A better alternative, particularly with consultants, may be to get rid of the rascals.

Visitor Centers

Visitor centers should be designed with their name kept carefully in mind. By developing one conscientiously, you can create a positive experience for visitors and a wealth of good feelings for your agency or company. Visitor centers are often the initial contact point for people coming into your area. Whether it's their first stop or not, users often base much of their opinion of an area on their reaction to the center. A clean rest room, an easy-to-interpret wall map, a friendly greeting— paying attention to details like these—can result in more good will than an expensive display or audiovisual presentation. (See Chapter Ten for a less than friendly TVA visitor center experience.)

Failure to attend to "minor details" can leave a lasting impression as well. Not long ago, we visited a National Park Service visitor center in northern Indiana. The building had been altered to make it accessible to persons in wheelchairs, and barrier-free signs were prevalent. Inside, one prominent display employed magnifying glasses to show the contrast between two local soil types. The display had one pair of magnifying glasses set at a height suitable for an average adult, and another set at a height appropriate for small children. Most adults in wheelchairs would not have been able to use either display.

Ask yourself three questions: If you visited this center in a wheelchair, would you find it barrier-free? Would you leave with positive feelings toward the center? Would you accuse the center personnel of being good hosts? *Attention to detail* is a critical aspect of the total recreation job.

Before you reach the stage of designing displays, however, you should consider some more basic concepts. The first to address is developing a visitor center with one central theme in mind; you and your staff should determine what this will be well before you design the center. Also, the need for form to follow function is especially important. Amount of space needed, location of permanent interior walls, and circulation patterns all depend on the function of the center. Generally, most will be designed around one of three purposes: geographical and activity orientation in the area the center serves; environmental education conducted inside and near the center; or historical interpretation of the area surrounding the center.

Visitor centers often play more than a single role. One might, for example, contain an excellent display on local history. But users could enjoy this considerably and still leave with a sense of frustration if information on nearby campgrounds were not available or out-of-date. Focusing on one central purpose or theme doesn't mean ignoring all others. Certainly every visitor center should serve a "hosting" function: Personnel, displays and facilities should all be oriented toward making the user feel welcome and comfortable. Further, visitor centers will normally provide a number of secondary services as well—comfort stations, a place to meet friends traveling in another vehicle, a spot to refill a thermos of water. The point is, you should determine which major theme best suits your particular situation and make this your central focus. A common planning mistake is to attempt to develop an "all things to all people" visitor center. Generally, focusing on a number of major attractions will result in failing to achieve any purpose with successful results except for confusion and lack of consistency in displays.

Determining which of several alternatives should be your central focus depends upon two factors. On one hand, the needs of your clientele will influence what function you develop. If most anticipated use will originate from a long distance, orientation to the area and to local recreation opportunities may need to be the primary focus. Also, the potential of the site affects your decision. Theoretically, any site can be interpreted from historical or environmental perspectives. However, planners and programmers shouldn't try to force, for example, a major set of historical interpretive displays on a center where nothing of particular historical interest has occurred. This is an excellent reason for determining function or your basic theme before designing the site for the center. If you and your staff agree, prior to development, an environmental orientation is what your center needs, you have some basis for proceeding with design: You know you need to look for an area where interpretive trails can be incorporated into the plan; you can anticipate, and design for, the type of display space and circulation patterns best suited to environmental education.

Another common error in designing visitor centers is the "too much of a good thing" syndrome. This affliction seems especially likely to attack educational and interpretive staff, and the symptoms sound something like this: "If it's a good thing to teach people something, it must be better to teach them a whole lot more." Unfortunately this logic breaks down beyond a certain point for two reasons. First, people can only absorb so much information before calling a halt to the process. Second, attempts to provide as many displays as possible can create a cluttered, "busy" look. From a design psychology standpoint, such a look should be avoided when you provide a recreational experience. For instance, we know of a visitor center in central Pennsylvania with an environmental orientation. The main room of the center measures approximately 20 by 30 feet for an area of 600 square feet. Figure 4.24 shows a scale drawing of this room, with the circulation aisles indicated by dashed lines. The problem isn't the room or the circulation pattern; it's the displays. On the day

we visited, the room contained 78, all environmentally oriented. Figure 4.25 illustrates the visual effect that 78 displays have on a 600-square-foot room. Too much of anything, including a good thing, is simply too much.

Keep in mind the primary function of any recreation-related facility, including a visitor center, should be to provide enjoyment for users (being a good host). A crowded, claustrophobic appearance resulting from attempts to fit too many displays into a limited amount of space is not a good means of accomplishing this.

One of the standard operating procedures we strongly advise you to embrace as a professional is to constantly find out how you are doing—get a measurement of exactly what is happening. This type of self-evaluation is not conducted often or well throughout the recreation realm, particularly in the fringe areas involving interpretation and the environment. Interpretive staff often put 47 exhibits in a room or design and build all sorts of poorly conceived interpretive trails, pat themselves on the back for their good work, and then get quite upset when their peers don't fall all over themselves complimenting the interpretive masterpiece. Users tend to be even less impressed, if that's possible. It sometimes appears we care very little about what our visitors think or want or, in fact, if they are beckoned to or repulsed by our work. Part of being a professional means having the integrity to use applied research to find out if our work is well-done and well-received. If we find it isn't, we should take steps to correct the problem. If we find we are doing a good job, we should look for ways to do even better!

Regardless of the subject of your displays—orientation, history or the environment—you can use a few "tricks" to maximize the benefits of your efforts for visitors. One important concept is to limit your displays. Take a critical look at both the amount of space you have available and at potential circulation patterns within the center. Circulation patterns for interior spaces should use the same principle as for outdoor areas. Relationship diagrams, traffic flow and alternative layouts should all be employed to make an informed decision on locating displays. Avoid the temptation to add too many. Let common sense tell you when enough is enough.

If you are building a new center, it's probably a good idea to exclude any permanent walls from the display space except those around the outside of the room. This allows you considerably more flexibility both initially and after you de-

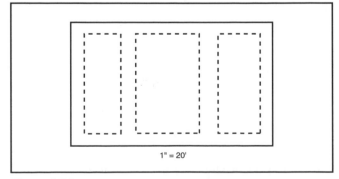

1" = 20'

Figure 4.24

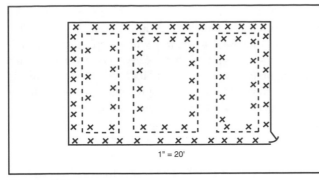

Figure 4.25

cide to make alterations later. If you're renovating an existing space, you may want to consider removing an interior wall or cutting in doorways if there is a barrier to your circulation needs. Before altering an interior wall, make sure it isn't load bearing (supporting the weight of the building). And remember the suggestion from Chapter Two regarding existing features in an area or building: Incorporate existing features or structures into your design when it makes sense to do so, but don't allow these to dictate design.

Movable displays, including floor-to-ceiling panels, tables and cases, are useful for directing circulation patterns within a display area. Tall panels tend to create a feeling of enclosure, but you can counteract this by using wide aisles and by alternating panels with lower displays. Some of the techniques applicable to moving people on trails will work in display areas as well. Figure 4.26 illustrates how they can be used to create a functional traffic flow within a room. In this instance, a display (A) to the right of the entry/exit has been angled toward the path people will take coming into the room. This display, coupled with the tendency people have to move to the right, will "pull" visitors in the direction of the arrow. Such movement is reinforced by orienting a panel display (B) so that people entering the room see the back of the panel rather than a display which might move them to the left. By encouraging a single-direction traffic flow like this one, you can reduce the perception of crowding.

Another way to create a feeling of spaciousness is by designing some display areas as alcoves off the main aisles, as in Figure 4.27. With alcoves, people viewing a display can move out of the aisle; however, this technique will require more space since the areas at points A and B are not functional. Whether you use alcoves or not, aisles should be wide enough for viewing and for circulation. If you plan to use both sides of an aisle for displays, it may help to "stagger" the panels, cases or tables so two exhibits aren't directly across the aisle from one another. This may help prevent "traffic jams" as people move from one to the next.

Traffic problems can also be reduced by developing displays with simplicity and clarity of meaning. Pictures with brief captions, artifacts like a soldier's pack, naturally occurring items like a hornet's nest, and three-dimensional displays like a papermâché relief map are all effective. Long, wordy explanations emphasizing scientific names and "73 uses for the wood of the American beech" are less than effective. The

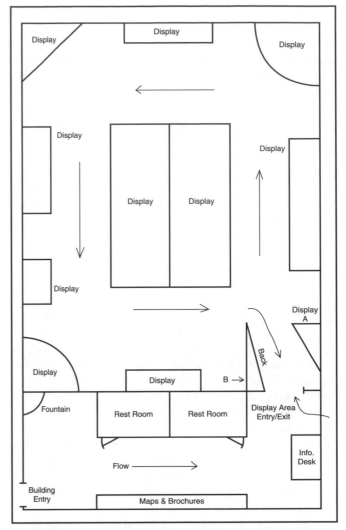

Figure 4.26

best way we know to teach people something is to entertain them: Make them smile at the close-up color picture of the "cute little beaver," and then tell them briefly why beavers build dams. This approach will help visitors retain more information and enjoy your displays, as well as keep traffic from getting congested. The subject matter and the number of exhibits your available space can support will help determine content. As a rule of thumb, visitors should be able to absorb the information in a single display in 20 seconds or less without hurrying.

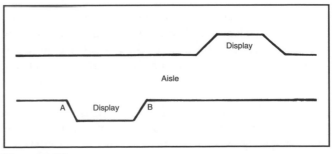

Figure 4.27

Visitor centers, because they are often an initial stop for people entering your area, are excellent locations for policies regulating use. However, remember visitors are your guests and as such they should be made to feel welcome in as many ways as possible. You should avoid emphasizing things people shouldn't do, or at least avoid telling them in a negative way. Given a little thought, it's usually easy to provide information in a manner users will find helpful instead of restraining. For example, you may want people to keep pets away from the entrance to the center. Instead of posting a "No Pets Allowed Here" sign, post one reading "Pet Area Is Located at End of Parking Lot." If you must prohibit a particular act, such as building fires during dry seasons, it often helps to explain the problem and request users' cooperation in abiding by your policies. Users should be informed, but you should avoid overwhelming them with negative wording.

Visitor centers, in addition to focusing on a major function like historical interpretation, are usually more successful if they are designed around a central theme. While the purpose lets visitors know why the center exists, the central theme explains what its purpose is. If, for example, you are developing a Corps of Engineers visitor center on a reservoir, the central theme might be the water resource. A center in a state forest, on the other hand, may concentrate on forest resources.

A central theme can be oriented to any of several major functions, including education, interpretation, or information. To support the Corps example from above, with its central theme of water, you might provide information on recreation facilities and activities surrounding the reservoir; education relating to the objectives met by the reservoir (power, fisheries management, recreation); or interpretation relating to the history or environment surrounding the reservoir.

The point is a central theme provides an *umbrella* for the center functions. An excellent example of this concept is the visitor center at Blanchard Caverns in the Ozark National Forest in Arkansas. Here managers and planners started with a theme—the caverns—and then built a center to complement it. Unfortunately this process is often reversed: Someone builds a visitor center and then administrators must try to figure out what to do with it. Most of the visitor centers we are acquainted with, such as the one at Georgia's Chattahoochee National Forest (Figure 4.28, also shown as Figure 4.4) were developed without having a basic theme. Agency architects get a perverse gleam in their eyes and off they go, without rhyme or reason, and we end up with a one of a kind structure and nary a clue as to how it is supposed to function. The Corps of Engineers, U.S. Forest Service, Tennessee Valley Authority, and many state parks have been guilty of this approach. As it happened, all three of the authors were working at Land Between the Lakes when the visitor center there was built. Suggestions to get some advice from the folks at Blanchard Caverns and to build around a central theme were not welcomed. We believe the public deserves better.

The structure you build should be designed to accommodate the exhibits and the needs of the clientele you anticipate. By anticipating uses and users in advance, you can make a center responsive to your aims and those of your users. Too

often, for example, in areas where camping is popular, we've seen visitor centers built with dead-end parking lots. What does this design "say" to visitors with camping or boat trailers about consideration of their needs? Have you ever tried to back a trailer out of a dead-end lot? Will visitors show up with boats and trailers, bicycles, or recreation vehicles at your visitor center? (The same problems and questions apply at administrative sites and other park areas where visitors are likely to go. These are all great places for us to flunk Hosting 101.)

This raises a final point about the purpose of visitor centers. In addition to whatever you want your center to accomplish for users, ask yourself, "What do we want the center to accomplish for us, the management?" A visitor center, by design and administration, serves a quasi-political purpose. It reflects what you think of users and helps determine what users will think of you. Whether you intend it to be or not, a visitor center is a public relations medium. Presumably, you want people to leave your area with positive feelings about what a good job is being done there. You should encourage them to feel that their money, whether tax dollars or admission fees, is being well-spent. Unfortunately this does not happen frequently enough, particularly in the public sector, for three reasons. First, visitor centers are often poorly designed in terms of user needs. Second, some centers tend to leave visitors confused because there is no central theme and/or major function. Finally, management frequently ignores the public relations potential of a visitor center.

Figure 4.28

In general, people who visit parks and recreation areas are, for some reason, quite naive about the management of these areas. Try asking people in a state or national forest, at a Corps of Engineers area, or at a state game preserve where they are. You may be surprised by how many people tell you they are in a national park. Perhaps this is because they associate the Park Service with the provision of outdoor recreation opportunities.

Earlier we suggested evaluating facilities was a necessary standard operating procedure. Interestingly, this happened several years ago at Brasstown Bald Visitor Center (the facility shown in Figure 4.28). The Southeastern Forest Experiment Station found only 50 percent of the persons exiting the center knew it was managed by the Forest Service (and those leaving the visitor center had just been zapped with a "heavy" Forest Service slide program). This brings up a further point in that instead of giving visitors a positive image about the agency, the Forest Service (in their slide program) gave a hard-sell push to the virtues of multiple use of forest resources. Instead of creating a warm glow about the agency, they made sure at least 50 percent of the shell-shocked visitors didn't know who managed the visitor center. (Although given the quality of the program, in retrospect this may not have been such a bad move on the part of the Forest Service!)

We aren't suggesting the Park Service shouldn't get credit for doing a good job in its own areas. We do suggest you're missing the public relations boat if it gets credit for your good work and you happen to be employed by someone else. Visitor centers should be a focal point for generating good public relations. The opportunity for public contact with your personnel is high, as is the chance for you to impress the public with the quality of your facilities and displays. Creativity, conscientious design, attention to detail and a sensitivity to the needs of people can have a lasting, positive effect. Visitor centers, by their nature, attract people; it's up to you to attract their favorable impressions.

Picnic Areas:
For Families, Large and Small Groups

Most North Americans enjoy picnics and most of these folks (which sadly includes many planners and designers) aren't too knowledgeable when it comes to how picnic areas should be designed, managed or programmed. When picnic areas are developed, the scenario usually goes something like this: Let's put some tables here (plunk!) and some more out here, 400 feet from the parking lot (plunk!), plop the toilet over there, locate our shelter—with group reservations available—in the nice, heavily shaded stand of old-growth trees, sprinkle some tot lot equipment around wherever we feel like it, drop in one large, centrally located parking lot like the one in Figure 4.29—this approach is always good for budget savings (damn the users, full speed ahead!)—*and* plan the entire area to make sure all the picnickers have to drive through at least one campground loop to get to the picnic area. We've seen—and enjoyed—this type of anti-hosting day-use disaster area all over North America!

Is this area zoned so families and various sizes and kinds of user groups can use it without conflict? Is the area a good revenue enhancer (can you charge for various types of day use and make money)? Into the foreseeable future, we predict agencies will increasingly need to recover their operations costs at a minimum; given the designs of existing areas planners like you will inherit, this may well be one of your greatest challenges. For many day-use areas, the only way to recoup operations costs will be to redesign them. We'll provide you with some suggested techniques for doing this shortly, although we will also caution you it is much more difficult to fix a poorly designed area than it is to do it right the first time.

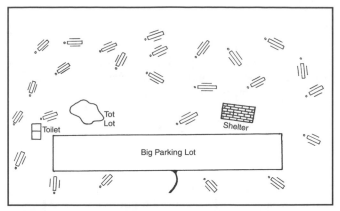

Figure 4.29

If you are an employee in an agency planning and building new parks, we feel your tasks will be much easier than those of your predecessors who have had to try to unscrew the disasters of the last several decades. This assumes, of course, you know some of the basics of zoning, administration, and programming contemporary planners either neglected to learn or felt were unnecessary to apply.

As we write this chapter, the Clinton administration is telling (as in mandating, not suggesting) federal agencies they are now to charge for day use as well as camping. In many instances, these day-use areas are poorly zoned. Most of these—without extensive redesign work and added amenities—will produce far fewer revenues than the costs associated with fee collection. Many will require relocation of entrance zone facilities to permit control and fee collection. These challenges are further complicated in numerous parks (particularly Corps of Engineers areas) with marinas and other privatized facilities inside of zones traditionally free of charge. We are not, incidentally, particularly critical of this administrative decree to charge for recreational day use; the basic problem—and the target of our criticism—is the planners and designers who simply failed to consider the potential impact of their designs on management personnel if, or when, fees were imposed.

For an example of this dilemma, have a look at the small Corps of Engineers day-use area (Figure 4.30) located in western Kentucky next to a beautiful stream *and* tucked up against a rural Kentucky town. The egg-shaped lagoon connected to the stream is a borrow area used by the highway department to excavate soil for use as fill material for the adjacent highway. The toilet building is not centrally located because it needed to be placed on the highest elevation, out of the 100-year flood plain. The shelter (which can be reserved for groups) is near the playground and a parking lot. Space isn't available near the shelter for open play or even a sand volleyball court. The park (other than the shelter) has been managed as a nonfee area. It would be difficult to manage with agency personnel, because the local Corps headquarters is over an hour's drive away. The local police and sheriff's office cruise the area as time permits. Cleanup of the area is contracted. All in all, it is a delightful area to visit and enjoy.

PLANNING

Who does this visiting and enjoying? Some of the users include fishing parties; boaters; nature enthusiasts; local individuals and families; tourists passing by on the adjacent highway; organized groups from local churches, businesses and civic organizations; elementary, middle-, and high-school classes; and probably a dozen other types of folks we've neglected to mention. This last type of user—the medium size or large group—presents one of the biggest challenges created by the type of design used here. The shelter—a key element for group use—is located amid the family picnic units and doesn't have the play amenities or open space needed and wanted by almost all day-use groups. (Incidentally, if the Corps is required to charge all persons entering this area, without considerable redesign, there would likely be a sizable drop in use and lots of poorly hosted and unhappy local residents.)

Figure 4.31 shows an improved design for this area. This design assumes the entire area remains a nonfee use zone. We'll consider the design challenges inherent in adding fees a bit later. In this first redesign, administration will be minimal and only a few group amenities will be available other than the reservable shelter. Incidentally, the original design of this area mistakenly had the boat ramp located in the lagoon, which led to siltation problems; the agency—at taxpayers expense—had to relocate the ramp to its present location in the stream to provide a self-cleaning action. (This was a planner's mistake corrected by a manager.)

In our minor redesign we've moved the shelter and the potential group zone to the far edge of the area where it doesn't conflict with the family units. The new location also provides considerable open space for group play. We've added a sand volleyball court, two sets of horseshoe pits and a sizable barbecue grill near the shelter. Because on-site administration is minimal, groups will be expected to bring their own play equipment. The sizable playground can stay where it is currently located which, in this design, is adjacent to both the family and group-use areas. We also suggest several benches be located in shade areas in the group-use zone, particularly adjacent to the play amenities.

In the family-use zone some picnic tables should be located singly, while others should be clustered in groups of two or three with various types of upright picnic grills at each table location. A good base design for the clusters of tables is a curvilinear segment such as the Corps design shown in Figure 4.32. The curved segments with the grill in the center on the outside edge make for far better intimate hosting zones than the straight line areas.

How many of what to locate in any family picnic area depends on the site, your current and expected construction dollars, your capability to manage, agency policies and the

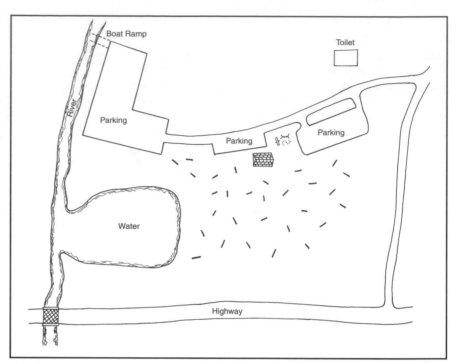

Figure 4.30

type of user you want to attract. We suggest you add a children's playground located in a defined sand base area. A large ($2\frac{1}{2}$- to 3-feet tall) sand pile located adjacent to the play zone is excellent, too. Play opportunities for children of all ages will cut down on the boredom leading to vandalism and other forms of depreciative behavior.

In Figure 4.31 we saw how the group shelter and area could be relocated to minimize conflict with family users. Suppose, though, you were faced with these two basic and realistic challenges (or opportunities): You are expected to break even or even make some money on your park *and* several groups want to use your group facilities at nearly the same time. This takes us back to the notion of form following function—our concept of designing with an eye to people's needs first, followed by programs for these people, and finally hardware (or facilities) to support these people and programs.

Even though we have, over the last several decades, devoted countless hours to planning, designing and rehabilitating park areas, it is only in recent years we have done a bit of imagineering on group picnicking. We've learned, as you should, to think about how people, including various types of groups, function as they picnic. Add a little common sense to this knowledge, and you'll do a better job of planning group picnic areas than 99 percent of the designers working today.

Groups come in all sizes and kinds, but there are two common threads that tie almost all of them together (with the possible exception of elderly and infirm groups from resident care centers). These two threads are the desire for active play of some sort (and the available space to play in) and the opportunity to engage in the passive enjoyment of watching friends and family members have fun during the active play. Unfortunately, most of the so-called group picnic areas we've seen in outdoor settings across North America are far less than

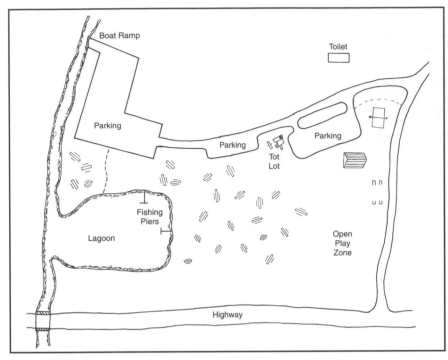

Figure 4.31

The photograph in Figure 4.34 (originally shown as Figure 4.7) shows a similar "group" picnic area in a state park in the mid-South. The picture was taken on a bright, sunny day in late winter. The park planners here were again up to their old tricks as they placed the sizable picnic shelter in a dense stand of pine and hardwood. If you were highly skilled, you could stand adjacent to this shelter and throw a Frisbee perhaps 30 feet without hitting more than four trees. There is no formal open space, a design parameter nicely complemented by a total lack of play equipment. Unless arrangements can be made to have the gate unlocked—which causes administrative and user problems— group members, including the elderly and persons with disabilities, have a long way to walk, and carry their chairs and other heavy picnic goodies. Are we good hosts here? No! Does this particular shelter generate considerable revenue for the park? Surprisingly, it does. The heavy use this facility gets, in spite of the poor hosting caused

great places for groups to come enjoy themselves. Figure 4.33 shows us a portion of a shelter located in a Midwestern county park. The shelter is sunlit in winter *but* surrounded by brush and heavy shade during most of the warmer, normal use season. There was no open space, other than the small parking lot, no lighting for night use, no electrical outlets for cooking or programming (e.g., for use with amplified musical instruments for a teen or square dance), and no playground equipment within one-half mile of the group picnic shelter. Pause a moment here to think about the implications of this design for hosting.

Apparently, the designers and managers of this county park group picnic area—and we use the term loosely—feel their job is well-done because group members can park in the parking lot, eat their picnic meal, perhaps identify a few leaves and sit in the heavy shade until they get terminally bored and leave.

by an equally poor design, tells us group facilities are greatly needed. Such demand, however, is no excuse for poor planning. This begs one last question: Can we achieve group picnic area designs capable of providing positive recreational experiences for users, environmental integrity, increased revenue, and positive public relations benefits (through user satisfaction) for the managing agency? We honestly don't know. From the standpoint of capability, the answer is a resounding yes; these design goals are actually fairly simple to achieve. The problem—traditionally and bluntly—has been a lack of professionalism on the part of public agencies. Whether increased accountability or, more likely, the mandate to generate revenues, will motivate park planners to improve their products remains to be seen. To the extent that current designs are any bellwether, we aren't terribly optimistic about the prospects for the future.

Figure 4.32

Figure 4.33

Figure 4.34

Getting down from our soapbox and back to basics, consider shade for a moment. Shade is an important element for most of the year in picnic areas and campgrounds all across North America. As Figure 4.35 (originally shown as Figure 4.3) indicates, there are sections of the continent where natural vegetative shade simply isn't available. Here in an Arizona state park, management has added human-made shade over the individual picnic sites via the use of ramadas. As we've seen, parks can, for a number of reasons, have too much shade. We'll discuss shade factors, which trees can withstand use pressures, and park timber thinning in a later chapter. Getting park personnel, including foresters, to cut trees (even the dangerous ones) is, strangely, a most difficult challenge.

Let's give some further consideration to the questions we raised earlier about the Corps of Engineers area in western Kentucky regarding the challenges to see if we can replan it to be more profitable and to host several groups at one time. To set the stage for these questions, let's fantasize briefly.

Pretend for a moment you're the recreation director in Gerrymander, Oklahoma, and this is your picnic area. The president of the local chapter of the Young Republicans Club calls you on Monday to reserve the area for a get together on Saturday afternoon. With the area designed as it is, you really can't control access (people need to get to the boat ramp), so you can only suggest that the club get to the park early.

Figure 4.35

Meanwhile, the Democrats are planning an open-air fund raiser to begin at noon—at the picnic area, of course (but they forgot to notify you). Have you created a confrontation? No, you're saved because Inez Independent and her 87 relatives descend on the site at 10:00 A.M. for their annual family reunion (and they normally like to stay until 8:00 P.M.). Of course there isn't any room left (or right) for individual families to picnic now, either.

The area simply doesn't meet the needs of several groups, does it? Fact is, few of our day-use parks in the public sector do meet the needs of two or more sizable groups who want to use the area at the same time. As a viable solution to this problem, we believe one form or another of something called the *pod system* will meet the needs of multiple user groups. One such system, applied to our western Kentucky Corps of Engineers area, is shown in Figure 4.36. Here, our entrance road has been moved to the north edge of the property; thus, we now have the potential to have a fee area with a staffed entrance facility. Inside the entrance are two basic zones, including a combination boating access/family picnic area and the gated area with four manageable group pods.

Each of these pods would have a gated parking area, shelter (preferably of different sizes in each pod to accommodate different sizes of groups), a playground, open space, sand volleyball area, and two sets of horseshoe pits. All groups would use the sizable toilet facility (remember, its location is out of the 100-year flood plain). Zones between the pods could be defined with low shrubbery and decorative post and rail fences. Perhaps one or two of the pods—depending on management objectives—could have security or other lighting for evening use. Groups too large for a single pod could rent two or more to fit their needs.

When your available space is more generous than the small Kentucky area described above, a more innovative approach to the concept of theme pods is a design similar to the one shown in Figure 4.37. These pods could be located near each other like those shown in Figure 4.36 or as much as one-eighth of a mile or more apart (along ridge tops, for example). Each of these areas should have the basic pod facilities, including a lockable entrance gate, a parking lot designed to accommodate bus and recreation vehicle parking, a playground, a shelter with a large food-serving zone and barbecue grill, a water hydrant/fountain, a dumpster, horseshoe pits, open play space, volleyball court, a fire circle with rustic seating, and easy access to a toilet (preferably flush). This last item is important; experience tells us an accessible toilet is needed in each theme pod unless the pods are designed in close proximity to each other and around a centrally located service area with a toilet located in it. Parents want and need to be able to see where their young children are and what they are doing. Each pod, if designed with the amenities described above, would be quite functional in terms of meeting the basic needs of any group. This assumes, of course, all the pods are designed with an eye to accessibility for all types of users.

In addition to the basic pod amenities described above, each pod could have three or four added features to make it especially appealing to particular types of groups. Now we are focusing seriously on hosting, because our point is to suggest you design theme pods to target specific user groups who are likely to use the area. We can't tell you who these groups are; it's up to recreation staff at the local level to know their clientele groups. We can tell you it's less than professional to assume every park in every location has exactly the same types of users with the same needs. Involving user groups in the planning process is, point blank, necessary. Aside from the input gained, which is reason enough to make the effort, the positive public relations accrued will do more for you than you can imagine—until you need it. We can also tell you to expect certain basic traits in potential user groups. For example, a group pod design in Texas had better accommodate fishing clubs and *big* barbecue grills.

Other theme pods truly do depend on your expected clientele. Some potential themes, though, may be appropriate regardless of regional forms of recreation. A sports theme pod, for example, could include—in addition to the basic pod amenities—a lighted softball field, a paved multipurpose play court, more horseshoe pits (lighted), a jogging path, a fitness trail, or whatever other facilities you wish. A passive theme pod might include the basic amenities and lighted shuffleboard courts, boccie ball area, lighted and fenced horseshoe pits, and a small interpretive zone with a tree finder or two. An interpretive theme pod could add several interpretive trails, an area planted with bird- or animal-attracting vegetation, a small shelter-type nature center, tree finders, and areas for nature crafts added to the basic pod facilities. Regardless of the theme, provision of the basic amenities at every pod means each one is usable by any group. For example, if a group wants to rent the passive sports pod but it has already been reserved by another group, the interpretive pod would have

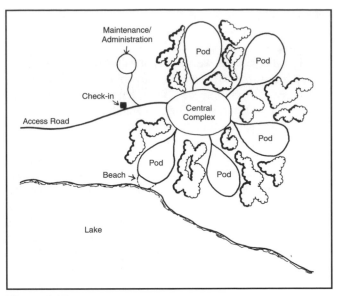

Figure 4.37

enough recreational potential to serve as an alternative. This, again, is good hosting.

The possible theme ideas are limited only by your users' needs and your imagination. If you are skilled at working with the public to build positive public relations—and if you aren't, you're going to have problems—you can enlist all sorts of monetary and in-kind help with the development and care of each pod. Service clubs, various industries, governmental offices, the military, professional groups, civic organizations, and churches are some examples of groups that could help finance the cost of a particular pod, help name it, and adopt it as a clean up or maintenance project. Groups thus invested in a pod will also be quite likely to be one of its most enthusiastic renters. Figure 4.38 shows what a passive theme pod might include.

It isn't difficult to appreciate the benefits of having four or five group theme pods in a day-use area. The pods serve as revenue builders and several groups can be accommodated—hosted—at one time. You can, perhaps for additional fees, provide a program coordinator and staff (student interns or senior citizen volunteers) to help groups plan and conduct their outing, arrange catering services, and do whatever else is necessary to ensure a successful outing. When this concept of theme pods is properly designed, programmed and managed, park use, revenues and public good feelings about the park will increase; we guarantee it! If it sounds, incidentally, like we are talking as much about programming as planning, we are; since both are critical elements of hosting. Experience tells us, however, a poorly planned and designed area with excellent program support will be much better

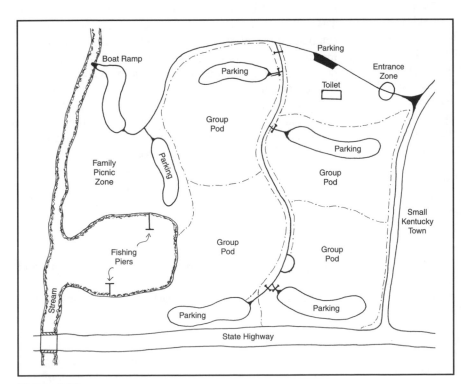

Figure 4.36

received by the public, and produce considerably more revenue for you than will a perfectly designed area with no thought given to programming.

The theme pods we've described here should be different types and sizes to accommodate perhaps 100 to 200 people in a relatively small space. What happens, though, if 487 Shriners or 500 employees of a local industry and their families need a place for an all-day picnic? Simple. You design and build an area to meet this need (making certain first there will, in fact, be demand for it). An Indiana state park property manager friend of ours and his program coordinator have developed the area, the program planning skills, and the staff to provide for these larger groups, so we asked them what such an area needed. Their advice included a gate-controlled area with numerous small parking lots throughout instead of one large, central lot; a large shelter (up to 150 feet in length) with plug-in electrical outlets, portable tables (groups like to design their own table arrangements), and concrete floor for dancing and games (if, by the way, you want to add shuffleboard courts, make sure you take into consideration the necessary location of the expansion joints in large concrete surfaces—your engineers can help you here); a large cooking and serving area with vehicular access for bringing in food and drinks (*hint:* before building this area, get together with your construction person or metalsmith and a professional barbecue cook to design a cooker); an area where large program tents can be erected; open play space; two or three smaller shelters for nature crafts and passive games; a large bulletin board for schedules and messages; an elevated stage with seating area or an outdoor theater; a flagpole; three or four sand volleyball courts in two or more locations (two with lighting); a lighted softball field; an interpretive area with one or two tree finders; a centralized flush toilet building, possibly with showers[2]; a boccie ball court (with a fine gravel surface to minimize ball scarring); four sets of lighted and fenced horseshoe pits; lots of benches sprinkled throughout; and a sand area with water sprinkler heads on seven-foot posts for children to play in. Our friends also suggested miniature golf, Frisbee golf, and hike 'n bike and fitness trails located near (but not in) the group zone. This park manager is now building four theme pods so he can accommodate that large group and four smaller groups all at the same time. (Current "higher" state park managers think this idea is a poor one!)

For both large group areas and smaller theme pods, play equipment such as horseshoes, croquet sets, volleyballs and nets, and softballs and bats should be available for checkout to all groups. Most of these items can be dispensed in canvas bags, although the amount of equipment needed for large groups may make it necessary to provide a small covered and

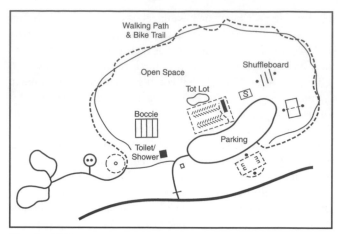

Figure 4.38

locked storage unit or trailer. One or more of the parking lots in your group-use zone might have electrical outlets at one end so scout groups and others interested in overnight experiences can be accommodated. Entrance signs at the theme pods and group area should have changeable lettering capability so you can personalize a welcome to each group entering. Another nice technique for hosting is to take photographs of groups enjoying themselves and then feature these pictures in a display the next time the group uses the area. Theme pod group day-use areas are now being built or planned in several areas around the United States. Try some; you'll be pleased with the results.

Day Camping

Earlier in this chapter we discussed the facilities and zoning, or "hardware," of use areas to beckon user groups effectively. The pod system, theme pods and large group areas we conceptualized and described to you would already serve as drawing cards for all sorts of groups. While the following section does touch a bit more on hardware, our main concern will be with users and programs.

Those of us who work in outdoor recreation fight a seemingly continuous battle between quality and quantity. On one hand, our mission is (or should be) to provide a meaningful and enjoyable experience for as broad a range of potential clients as possible. Yet when it comes time to account for this year's expenditures and justify next year's budget requests, the bottom line is numbers. How many picnickers? What percentage of the campsites were occupied? Did visitation rates increase or decrease? Sometimes philosophical debates over the quality versus quantity issue miss the point. Both are legitimate concerns and both can be addressed by the same strategies.

Let's consider another scenario. You're the manager of Possum Paw State Park in northeastern Iowa. The park is typical in terms of resources and facilities: a mix of forest and open land, flat fields and a low ridge system, a small lake, a campground, picnic area, boating site, nature center, play fields and courts, trails, and open space. Your location is excellent, 50 miles from the Quad Cities area, near an interstate

---

[2]Part of hosting, by the way, is making sure toilet facilities are adequate to meet user needs. Men and women tend to spend different amounts of time in toilet buildings, so the old agency standard of "two stalls, two urinals for men and four stalls for women" shouldn't be considered sacred just because "we've always done it that way." Make sure you build facilities based on user needs and behavior rather than dogma. We suggest you build 50 percent more facilities on the women's side.

highway, and close to five or six small towns ranging in size from 2,000 to 15,000 residents. There are several issues hidden in this brief description which, if addressed in combination with one another, can change the complexion of your park completely.

First, if Possum Paw is a "typical" state park, the chances are good that visitation figures are less than earth-shaking. Holidays and pleasant-weather weekends may fill the park, but during the week it often seems as if staff outnumber visitors. Consider also the surrounding population. Many small towns simply don't have the financial or other resources needed to maintain a diversified parks and recreation program. The Quad Cities, like many urban areas, maintains city parks and has a broad spectrum of recreation opportunities but lacks the natural environment of a large, rural park.

One final aspect of this scenario needs to be considered. Most large parks and resource-based recreation areas have a tendency to orient their facilities and programs toward individual visitors and families. These users should be a concern, but not at the expense of organized groups. The development of a well-conceived day-camping program for organized groups at Possum Paw could increase use and revenue, particularly during traditionally low visitation periods such as summer weekdays, and meet a need left unfulfilled by local communities. (Wouldn't the previously mentioned day-use theme pods be great places to host all sorts of day campers?) If the five towns near Possum Paw average only 7,500 residents each, a potential clientele of over 37,000 people exists, not counting the urban center less than an hour away. A brief listing of the types of organized groups you might find in these small communities could include scouts, 4-H clubs, youth and adult groups from perhaps a dozen religious organizations, school parties, senior citizens clubs, fraternal organizations such as Elks and Moose, civic clubs such as Lions and Rotary, employee organizations, persons or groups with disabilities, the YWCA and YMCA, and special-interest groups such as garden clubs and local chapters of national societies. A successful day-camping program may also be developed in conjunction with an assembly area or large group area for special events such as arts and crafts fairs, large family reunions, Easter egg hunts, Civil War reenactments, industrial picnics, and the like.

There are several ways of providing successful day camping, but they all have one requirement in common—the need for a thorough knowledge of programming and marketing skills. Organized groups likely will not seek you out, so it's possible to develop excellent facilities for a day-camping program and have them sit idle because of a lack of initiative on your part. You should be prepared and able to approach local group leaders and "sell" your facilities and programs, so both design and management of day-camping areas require you to understand and provide for the different needs of Boy Scouts or the League of Women Voters; the Kiwanis Club or Ms. Pinbug's tenth-grade biology class; the local chapters of the Audubon society or a trade union. If you work in a resource-based agency like a state division of forestry or the Department of Natural Resources, you may not be blessed with large numbers of staff possessing recreation programming skills. When this is the case, one solution is to develop cooperative ventures with municipal agencies. Local park and recreation systems are typically program-oriented. Quasi-public agencies such as the YMCA/YWCA also fit this description as well. Local-level professionals often have a good sense of community, they may know where and how to market a day-camping program to local groups most effectively.

If you lack an available resource base or are limited by funding constraints, an alternative to developing a site specifically for day camping is to superimpose day use on an existing facility such as a campground or picnic area. A word of caution is in order here: In many cases, trying to alter an existing area may result in creating more problems than it solves since existing use may be heavy enough to interfere with attempts to program for day-camping groups.

The professional friend we mentioned earlier has a sizable campground with adjacent open space, shelter, multipurpose play court, horseshoe pits and playground. It is used by family picnickers and campers alike. Since our friend has had numerous requests from groups wanting to day camp or have a large picnic—and given his park had no other suitable place—he decided to superimpose some group use on the previously described play amenities. He not only reserves the area but provides the staff to conduct programs for adults, teens and children throughout the day and evening. No one in the group, other than the coordinator, need worry if program and game materials, prizes for contests, or, in some cases, food, is available. Groups provide prizes and funding for tent rental, food and drinks; each person in the group pays the normal area entrance fee. Depending on your management philosophy, you could, in this situation, choose to charge a special fee for group use. Our friend doesn't do this, but the area does accept donations to be used for park program materials and in some cases new facilities. One such donation, from an anonymous group pleased with the opportunities our friend provides for recreation (with an emphasis on fun programs rather than hardware), was for $300,000. Do you know of any comparable gifts made to folks who manage small, unprotected, unprogrammed areas? We don't, and nobody has to hit us over the head with a two-by-four for us to see the connection here.

Many times areas such as campgrounds are *accidentally* designed so managers could use them for special group events. The program zone is located near the entrance; thus, day campers need not penetrate the camping loops and conflict with campers in order to reach facilities. The central program site contains a variety of active and passive program facilities, including a campfire theater, play courts and field, a shelter building, a crafts cabin, and a network of trails radiating out from this central complex. The primary advantage of this type of design is its ability to function in a dual role. The facility can be devoted entirely to the overnight camping clientele if demand justifies it. When camping use is low, groups of day users can be brought in on an advance schedule basis—another revenue enhancer. As director of a sizable park system you should understand not all of your staff will appreciate new ideas, particularly your superimposing a sizable day use group on them.

Another alternative for developing a day camp is to design the necessary facilities adjacent to an existing site such as a picnic area or campground. Some, indeed far too many, existing areas have been built without adequate programming facilities. For these, it may help to justify development of the facility needed for day camping by arguing in favor of benefits added to the existing site. If you can add program amenities adjacent to campgrounds and/or family picnic areas, you will likely be making prudent use of hard to find construction dollars, providing an excellent spot for group use or day camping, and continuing to build a reputation as a good host. As with a superimposed day-camping experience, the addition of a day camp adjacent to an existing facility must be carefully planned. A poorly designed addition can compound problems already in existence.

Your Chapter Four Problem

Now you should have some ideas for creating day-use opportunities. Figure 4.39 shows the resource base available to you. Your design challenge is to develop the area for a combination of overnight use, organized day camping and informal day use. You can assume all land is suitable for development. The shoreline is also usable all along the property and vegetation is good, with shade increasing as you move from south to north. There are only two constraints you need to consider. First, most program facilities you install must serve both overnight and day users. Second, the only access to the property is from the county road, as shown. Since we haven't discussed overnight camping facilities yet, you may want to limit your efforts to a simple zoning of this portion of the area. You should, however, consider circulation, separation

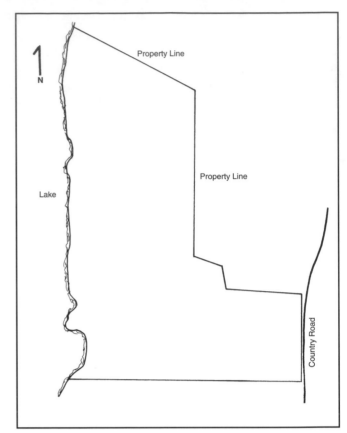

Figure 4.39

of use areas, administration and program potential in your design. We suggest you enlarge the base map to $8\frac{1}{2}$-by-11 inches before starting. One solution to this problem is shown in Appendix C.

Chapter Five
Special Uses for Special Users

There are some things either right or wrong with the subjects of Figures 5.1 through 5.6, but we're not too sure what they are. They do describe several of the special areas discussed in this chapter. Maybe after reading the following pages, you can tell us what's good—or less so—about these subjects.

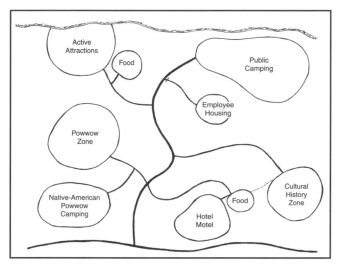

Figure 5.1

Figure 5.2

Figure 5.3

Figure 5.4

Figure 5.5

Figure 5.6

In this chapter, we'll consider six types of use areas: living-history complexes, off-highway vehicle areas, wrangler's camps, group camps, military recreation complexes, and Native-American parks. The earlier edition of this book didn't include planning and design thoughts concerning Native-American parks. Most of the challenges faced in these parks are similar to those in other government-managed areas. We are going to devote some attention in this chapter to Native-American parks for two reasons. First, dozens of tribes all across the United States either now have tribal parks or are in the process of developing them. Second, the authors have only recently begun to learn of the extent of Native-American park work and the ways we as professionals might help them from repeating the planning errors made by so many others in this field.

The term *special-use area* may be a bit inappropriate in one sense since these types of facilities aren't any more "special" than others. They're only different because they provide opportunities for people who share something of a common interest or background. For example, folks who use military recreation complexes are similar in most respects to visitors to "public" parks—except for an affiliation with the Armed Services. Additionally, after reading this chapter and the discussion of campsite design in Chapter Seven, you'll find there aren't many differences between "mainstream" campers and those who visit wrangler's camps, except that the latter group enjoys combining camping with horseback riding (including keeping their horses on or near their campsite). Because of the children, bicycles, and heavier traffic in large family campgrounds, it may be unwise to allow horseback riding in family campgrounds, and the same is true for off-highway vehicles. However, both horseback and off-highway riding are legitimate uses of outdoor recreation resources. Recreation professionals, because they are professionals, have a duty to provide opportunities for all types of uses.

The solution to meeting the needs of users whose recreation preferences are specific or may conflict with one another rests in the development of special-use areas. The principle behind this solution isn't complex; in fact, it's one you've heard before. Just as incompatible program areas such as a lighted play court and a campfire theater should be separated, conflicting uses should be zoned apart as well. As Chapter Four suggested, day-use and overnight camping will both function more effectively (for users and management) if they are zoned separately. The same logic applies to horseback and off-highway enthusiasts, organized group and individual family campers, and certain other combinations of outdoor recreationists. When you first begin to consider special-use areas, the idea of providing separate resources for different groups may seem prohibitive. However, most individuals who visit special-use facilities such as wrangler's camps or off-highway riding areas are more concerned about pursuing their particular interest than expensive program amenities contained in a developed, family campground or day-use area. Organized group camps may be developed in a number of ways, from rustic to highly modernized, depending on the needs of potential clients and your budgetary considerations. The point

is, special-use areas for off-highway riders, horseback enthusiasts, and many organized groups can be developed with a relatively small expenditure of capital dollars. The only high-cost requirement is an adequate land base, though other expenses like developing campsites, support facilities and trails, will also be incurred. Often some of these costs can be offset by enlisting the help of user groups during the early stages of planning and development. Further, unless you happen to ride off-highway bikes for leisure, you won't know as much about the needs of bikers as someone who does ride them. Local riding clubs and interested individuals can provide a wealth of information about design needs, as long as you remember theirs is only one of several perspectives to consider. These groups may, in some instances, also be willing and able to help with construction and ongoing maintenance of areas. It's been our experience special-interest groups are quite responsive when asked to cooperate in these ways. More often than not they are willing to help because they aren't used to being asked or to having recreation folks, especially those in the public sector, pay attention to their needs. As a planner your job is similar to that of a consultant, only in this instance your clientele is a user group rather than owners or managers. So, you need to ask all sorts of questions about the group and how they function throughout the day and evening. Don't go to the special groups and ask them how they want their special use area planned and designed. This is your function. They aren't planners and designers, although if you ask them to function as such they will likely try. The two potential outcomes of such an approach are a poor design if you take their advice or an angry user group if you don't.

Living-History Complexes

Living-history complexes haven't been included in our discussion to this point, because they are somewhat different from other special-use areas ("special" special areas, so to speak). Living-history resources differ in one respect because they don't include overnight use, as do the others considered in this chapter. This characteristic in particular has implications for the planner and designer. Entrance zones, parking, circulation, visitor contact points, and other facilities need special attention. As with other special-use areas, living-history areas should serve a *hosting* function; they should make visitors feel welcome both explicitly and implicitly. Explicit forms include the attitude of the staff, including the historical characters. Implicit forms include carefully managing and maintaining the area and designing the complex to balance the needs of the user with the need for historical accuracy. This point is important enough to elaborate on through an example of another of our mistakes.

The Homeplace 1850. Located in TVA's Land Between the Lakes, the Homeplace 1850 is a living-history area developed to portray farm life in the early nineteenth century. Figure 5.7 shows a schematic of the developed complex. The interpretive function, as is usually the case in living-history areas, was developed conscientiously here. Buildings are authentic, having either been moved from nearby locations or

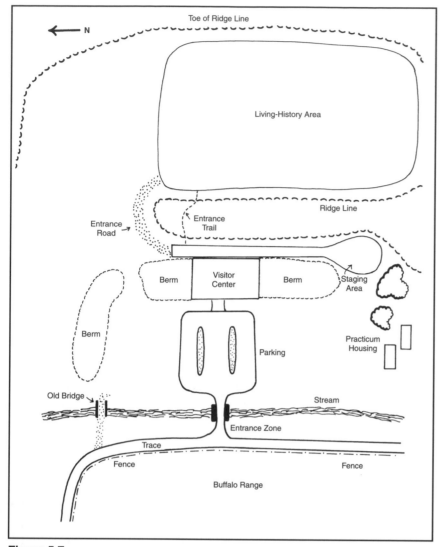

Figure 5.7

bridge in Figure 5.7). This entrance was located in a sharp bend in the Trace (the main north-south road running the length of Land Between the Lakes) and the potential hazard of developing an entrance in the curve was complicated by two factors. First, southbound traffic on the Trace entered the curve at the base of a long hill and tended to be moving rapidly. Additionally, a large field along the west side of the Trace contained a herd of about 50 buffalo, which would have attracted the attention of drivers away from the proposed intersection leading to the Homeplace. Fortunately this extremely unsafe entrance zone was rejected and an alternative site located in the middle of a long straightaway was selected. Obviously, no one on the interpretive staff would have advocated developing a hazardous intersection, but neglecting to consider the potential effects of the design would have produced a dangerous situation all the same.

Unfortunately, other design problems did find their way into the final construction plan. While these problems didn't create hazards, they reduced the potential for maximizing the experience of visitors. Take another look at Figure 5.7 and try to develop a mental image of what visitors would experience as they move into and through the area. As you move through the entrance zone, several features may capture your attention. One is a large, earthen berm, constructed to serve as a buffer between the initial contact area (the parking lot for the visitor center) and the interpretive zone (the living-history area). On the right are two house trailers for practicum student housing, and a modern visitor center stands in the center. These are the features meeting your eyes, but from the standpoint of design psychology, what do you see?

We see several things. First, the earthen berm is an excellent design tool. Once visitors enter the Homeplace itself—the living-history area—you want them to experience a step back to the past as quickly as they can with as few intrusions from modern times as possible. The berm helps to limit these intrusions and, since it is made of natural material (earth and sod), it is not intrusive itself. The rest of the initial contact zone, however, contains several errors—some of omission and others of commission. Consider the practicum student housing. Two white house trailers, in the original layout, were in plain view of the entry point. These are necessary components of the complex, but there is no reason to place them where visitors entering the area have clear views of them. Since every design decision should have a justifiable reason behind it, this argument goes beyond our current example. Two questions should have been asked and answered here: Why were the trailers located where they were? and Why couldn't they be placed some place less obtrusive?

reconstructed from portions of original structures. The history of the area was also researched thoroughly and in detail. For example, individuals who settled here originally, according to all available records, did not build outhouses, which were characteristic in other areas from the same period. Thus the Homeplace 1850 omitted outhouses as well. The interpretive staff, both those in period costume and others, are competent and personable. So what's the problem?

The problem with the Homeplace 1850 is a matter of design psychology. Several factors combine to reduce its potential to make a highly positive impression on users. People are favorably impressed by the experience they have here; the fact is, most may not even be aware that it could be improved. But—and this is important—whether the public will notice the difference or not, we should make every effort to do the job "as right as we are able." As we've suggested before, interpretive staff are generally good at interpretation, but this quality does not speak to designing for people. For instance, early in the planning of the Homeplace, the interpretive staff suggested using the existing entrance to the valley where the complex was to be located (the site of the old

In Chapter Three we discussed some of the more serious planning and design errors made on Land Between the Lakes' Blue-Gray Trail. The Homeplace 1850 (planned by the same group) has its share of planning, design psychology, and interpretive errors as well. Fact is, most interpretive areas we've visited around the country show similar signs of a lack of basic planning. The point of mentioning this is to make sure you understand expertise or competence in one area, interpreting history and culture, for example, does not automatically mean you will do a good job of planning and designing an interpretive area. The logic is somewhat like saying, "because I can speak Spanish, I can write like Cervantes." If you take courses in interpretation, you should challenge your professor to deal with planning, design, and management issues pertinent to interpretive areas as well as the interpretive issues. Putting it bluntly, some of the most serious environmental impact we've seen in recreation areas around the country has been in interpretive and "environmental education" areas.

From the first moment visitors enter a living-history complex, they should begin a transition taking them from the present back to the period being interpreted. A split-rail fence or perhaps a rustic welcome sign mounted on a period-piece wagon or other artifact can begin to set an appropriate mood just inside the entrance. In addition to having visitors begin to "enter" the

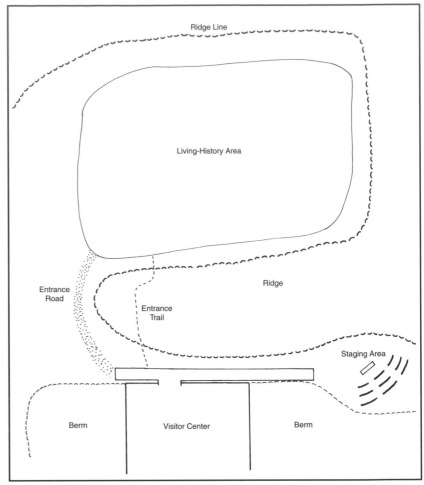

Figure 5.8

past, you should gradually draw them out of the present through design psychology. One way of accomplishing this is to physically separate the parking area from the visitor center. This technique gets users out of their automobiles and continues their transition back in time. The distance from the parking area to the visitor center shouldn't be too great, and it may be a good idea to provide an alternative to walking—perhaps a mule- or oxen-driven wagon to aid the transition even further. At the Homeplace 1850, the parking lot is immediately adjacent to the visitor center, which, as suggested earlier, is a modern structure. This point is worth emphasizing: The initial contact point of a living-history complex, often a visitor center or interpretive building, should complete the transition back to the period in time being interpreted. The visitor center at the Homeplace 1850, both inside and outside, is completely out of character with the aura of the early nineteenth century. Thus instead of "easing into" another culture, visitors are thrust there. (At the time the visitor center was being designed, a "new" TVA-LBL "idea" was to demonstrate all types of energy conservation. The frantic efforts to do so and to show the manager's expertise and "sincerity" overshadowed interpretive needs!)

Figure 5.8 focuses on the portion of the facility between the visitor center and the living-history area. After users have completed touring the visitor center, which contains displays

and a brief orientation program, they exit to the rear of the building into a staging zone. This paved area is used primarily for organizing the formal groups, particularly school groups, who often tour. From this point, a road and a trail lead into the interpretive zone, but both entrances have design errors. As shown in Figure 5.8, the staging area is between the visitor center and a low ridge. The ridge tapers into level ground to the left of the staging area, where the entrance road curves into the interpretive zone. As with the earthen berm discussed above, the ridge helps to buffer the living-history area from the present; however, consider the trail confronting the users. As we discussed in Chapter Three, you should avoid starting trails on an adverse (uphill) grade. The narrow trail leaving the staging area climbs steeply and presents, at the least, a psychological challenge. To many individuals, the trail is inaccessible. This is poor design!

Visitors who do not take the trail by choice enter the living-history facility via the road as shown. To understand the design error here, you need to consider the layout of the interpretive zone itself, shown in Figure 5.9. According to the history of the area, as told in the interpretation, the Homeplace evolved as follows. About 1830, a family settles the valley and builds a home at site 1. A generation later the children of the original family, now grown, build the house at site 2. By 1850, the period being interpreted, the family spans three generations; the original settlers at site 1 and their children and grandchildren at site 2. Other structures like the stable and tobacco barn are typical of the period.

Can you identify the design problem hidden in this narrative? The story doesn't evolve in the same sequence as the design does. Instead of following a physical trail of the family history, the visitor follows a reversed version of it. The visitor first learns about the way of life in 1850 from the point of view of the children of the original settlers. Then, by moving toward the interior of the interpretive zone, the story from

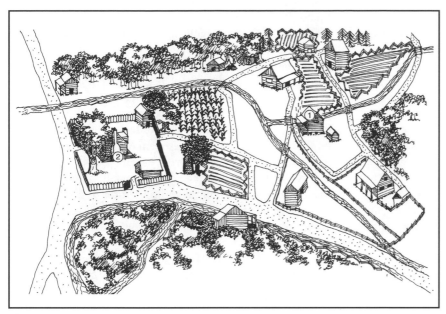

Figure 5.9

20 years earlier unfolds. Wouldn't it be a more effective experience if the design matched the chronology? It could quite easily have done so.

There are several design considerations left to discuss about living-history areas, but this mistake serves to focus on the most important one and points out a good axiom of planning, regardless of the facility type. Prior to developing any facilities, managers, planners and program staff should come to agreement on a master plan for the area that incorporates several elements. The first should be a conception of what you and other staff responsible for the living-history area want to accomplish. From a programming perspective, how do you want the area to function for users? Ask yourself and other staff what themes will be involved in the area—agriculture, family life, energy, community, recreation, education, and others. While the focus shouldn't be too narrow, it's usually a good idea to select a central issue and arrange complementary ideas around it. In the case of the Homeplace 1850, the program goal, or theme, was to show the evolution of a mid nineteenth century farm from generation to generation. Yet the physical design of the area conflicted with this program. Design elements should be developed to complement program considerations.

Once you have determined a tentative program goal, take the physical capabilities and limitations of the site into ac-

count. If you refer to Figure 5.7, you'll see the interpretive zone of the Homeplace 1850 is in a broad valley surrounded by ridges. The only logical entrance to the historical area was used; however, the physical limitation of being surrounded by ridges with only one usable entry point should have suggested placing the original homestead at the mouth of the valley (near the entrance) instead of in the center of the developed complex.

Figure 5.10 shows a graphic depiction of these last two points. Concurrent determinations of program goals and on-site conditions should lead you to a beginning idea of the development to follow, a process that should be followed regardless of the type of area being designed. Once you have addressed these preliminary aspects, design can become more specific. Also, a concern for anticipated types of users must permeate the entire design process. The needs of organized groups of school children will differ from those of smaller, family-oriented parties. Are there plenty of shaded benches for groups and individuals to stop, rest, and reflect about the area? In working toward a final design, visitor movement to and from the living-history complex and circulation within the interpretive zone are important. Consider concurrently the paths people should take, from the standpoint of design psychology, and the locations of specific features—houses, barns and the like. In other words, you shouldn't attempt to develop a circulation pattern and then add facilities.

While the internal elements of a living-history complex and their interrelationships are critical, it's important to remember support facilities as well. The master plan should account for the relationship of the historical zone to administration, parking, the initial visitor-contact point, where the transition to your historical period begins, and other support facilities. Depending on projected use, the addition of one or

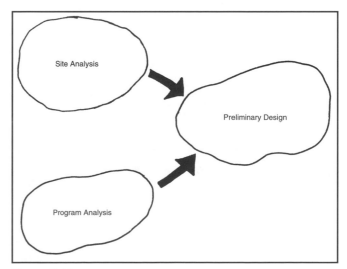

Figure 5.10

more group picnic areas (see Chapter Four) may also be a good idea. Regardless of what support facilities are involved, all need to relate in some way to the historical complex and to each other. They should also be convenient to, but not intrusive in, the interpretive zone.

As we stated earlier in the book, there are numerous challenges and benefits to park providers and users due to the adoption of the ADA (Americans with Disabilities Act). Most of the living-history complexes we've visited across the country require considerable (and costly) retrofitting to accommodate persons with disabilities. Figure 5.11 (earlier shown as Figure 5.3) shows a sizable, well-built log cabin in a complex of historical buildings in an Indiana state park. The wife of one of the authors has firsthand knowledge of some of the challenges we mentioned. She had charge of a seventh grader in a wheelchair as her school group visited the park—during a rainstorm. The girl wanted to move quickly (as other students were doing) from one inaccessible building to the next one. As you'd expect, the experience was less than user-friendly for the young girl, the author's wife, and others with similar challenges.

Living-history areas normally represent a major investment. They can also be enormously popular attractions. Both of these considerations are strong arguments for a conscientious and combined design effort on the part of planners, programmers and managers.

Off-Highway Vehicle (OHV) Areas

In two respects, OHV areas represent the opposite end of the design spectrum from living-history complexes. In the first place, developing an off-highway complex requires a relatively small investment of capital dollars. The facilities necessary for off-highway riding can be minimal, and the required ones are not particularly expensive to build or to maintain. A reasonably large resource base of several hundred acres is desirable, but not absolutely necessary, especially if variable terrain such as a ridge and valley system is available. The major challenge in generating an OHV area lies in the political realm, and this is the second difference between OHV and living-history areas. Unlike the latter, OHV developments

Figure 5.11

can be enormously unpopular—at least with individuals and organized groups who are opposed to off-highway riding in principle. Off-highway riding can and has caused environmental damage in some areas; however, the activity itself is a valid form of outdoor recreation. As professionals, you should thus be sensitive to the needs of OHV enthusiasts to the same degree as you are to the needs of other groups.

The three authors are not OHV users or enthusiasts, but all three have been involved in planning, managing, monitoring and conducting applied research on the nation's first federally designated off-road vehicle area—Land Between the Lakes' 2,350-acre Turkey Bay. During the 1960s and early 1970s, off-highway vehicles, particularly motorcycles, were becoming an explosive challenge on many of the nation's public and private resource-based lands. At the same time, the environmental movement began gathering momentum. While the environmental movement has brought about some positive changes in our parks and forests, it is our view that, on balance, environmentalists have had a negative net effect on outdoor recreation for mainstream Americans. As the chapter unfolds, we'll explain what we mean.

As for Turkey Bay, the environmentalists made dire predictions concerning complete destruction of all plants and animals wherever OHVs went near lands they said should be kept free of all uses and users (except, interestingly, themselves).

When planning for Turkey Bay began, the nonregulated OHV use at LBL was concentrated in a few areas. However, there was a growing amount of use coupled with an agency concern for the impact beginning to show from this use. Riders were starting to crop up on hiking and nature trails, in or near developed campgrounds and picnic areas, the environmental education area and special wildlife habitat areas. Since off-highway motorcycle users liked to see—and enjoyed being seen by—other users, they tended to ride in the busy areas of LBL. How to deal with this challenge was a management dilemma.

The best answer among several alternatives was to select and provide a sizable tract of land where all off-highway use could be localized, managed, monitored, buffered from other users and restricted. The site had to be located where management felt impact to soils, vegetation and wildlife would be minimal. Finally, it had to be desirable, acceptable and challenging to this "new" type of user. Turkey Bay met these criteria.

As early as the winter of 1970, a TVA planner became an *ad hoc* member of the Secretary of the Interior's OHV planning committee. This committee's function was to provide the background data and guidance for what later was to become a presidential Executive Order on OHV use on America's public lands. Since LBL had been established by President Kennedy as the nation's only federal outdoor recreation demonstration area (and little had been done to that time in the LBL demonstration realm), TVA offered Turkey Bay to the committee as a place to establish baseline information about impact measurement and user profiles. The committee accepted this idea, which led to LBL being identified as having a federally designated OHV area in President Nixon's 1972 Executive Order on OHV use.

Fortunately from a developmental standpoint, this happened just prior to the call for environmental impact statements (EIS) being required for nearly all developments on federal lands. This was fortunate because at the time, there was no research data anywhere in the country concerning the impact of OHV use on the environment. Had an EIS been required, *there would not* have been a scientific basis on which to establish the probable impact of developing an OHV area. Chances are, the project would have been blocked on the basis—which would not have been grounded in data—that it would have caused too much impact. Since the area did get developed with a built-in monitoring plan, it was possible to establish scientifically what impact did occur as a result of OHV use. This data base, gathered primarily by university researchers, became the foundation for EISs conducted by several other agencies.

The key to the successful provision of off-highway opportunities is one you've heard before. Most of the damage (and therefore the controversy) caused by off-road riding is the result of poor planning, design and management. (Remember the discussion of "overuse.") Shortly we'll discuss some design techniques aimed at minimizing the potentially harmful effects of OHV use and enhancing the experience of riders. First, however, let's examine some of the concerns raised by environmentalists and others, perhaps including you, who are critical of off-highway riding opportunities. These concerns cover damage to the environment, impact on wildlife, and—probably the greatest misconception—the difference between the perceived and actual profile of off-highway enthusiasts.

The Off-Highway Rider. People who enjoy all-terrain vehicles, four-wheel-drive trucks and jeeps, snowmobiles, and dirt bikes have an image problem. Mention the term "biker" to people unfamiliar with off-highway riding, and chances are the image they conjure up will be a leather-jacketed hoodlum. Some bikers fit this impression; fortunately most don't. Too often the image is applied to all people who like to ride off the road, mostly by opponents of OHV areas. In our experience, and we've spent a fair amount of time working with rider groups, these folks are just about like everyone else, barring their fondness for the challenge of their chosen activity. A profile of riding groups at Turkey Bay showed most riders participate as members of family or multifamily groups. Fact is, researchers found these users were interested in viewing scenery, sunsets, and wildlife, and enjoying quiet times in camp doing nature crafts, socializing, and eating. The old saying about "one bad apple spoiling the barrel" is especially appropriate when applied to OHV enthusiasts. If you visit an off-highway area, you may see black leather jackets, but you might not understand why riders wear them unless you've had the pleasure of turning a bike on its side and sliding downhill on a stretch of gravel.

Environmental Impact. Distinctions you should keep in mind are the differences between environmental impact, environmental damage, and environmental emotionalism.

Camping in a designated wilderness area for example, regardless of how careful you are, affects the environment. Many sections of the Appalachian Trail have been heavily impacted by hikers, many of whom will be among the first to criticize motorized use of natural resources for the impact this use creates. We see a certain irony here. The trick is for recreation participants and professionals to cooperate in ways designed to nullify, or at least minimize, the incidence of damage created by OHV use. As we'll discuss here, there are ways the professional, through design and management, can address this challenge. Many OHV enthusiasts are conscious of their image problem. As a result they will generally make efforts to pursue their activity in an ecologically sound manner. One of the riding club members who helped with sound level measurements prior to opening Turkey Bay did ask what this Sierra Club was and why were they upset with him and his group of OHV enthusiasts? He further wondered if Sierra Club folks knew anything about OHV use. We had no research data then to answer his questions. For the moment, let's consider one example of how much damage stems from OHV use.

Harm to the environment was a major concern of management after TVA opened Turkey Bay in the early 1970s. Consequently, when TVA personnel developed the area, they implemented the monitoring plan we mentioned earlier to assess future impact. Staff conducted a baseline survey of the 2,300-acre area and then repeated the survey to monitor impact, as shown in Figure 5.12. After four years of use, approximately 1.2 percent of the area (about 28 acres) showed evidence of riding. The wheel-to-ground impact monitoring indicated 2.5 percent (or 59 acres) in 1984, and the latest monitoring by Dr. Ken Chilman of the Southern Illinois University School of Forestry found the impact in 1990 (18 years after Turkey Bay was opened for use) was 3.5 percent (82 acres). By 1995, the impact was still less than five percent! Use levels, which obviously play a role in the extent of impact, have stayed constant there since the mid 1980s at about 30,000 visits per year.

Impact, however, is not the same as damage. Trails were evident, but erosion was not prevalent and surrounding vegetation did not exhibit particular stress. Once the trails became too rough or too muddy for use, the riders simply moved over a bit, made a new trail,

Figure 5.12

and continued to enjoy their activities. The users were allowed—within the boundaries of the Turkey Bay area—to build trails wherever they wished. We'd be shading the story unfairly if you weren't told the reason for this: The impact was minimal because the soil type at Turkey Bay is predominantly chert. Cherty soil has a high rock content and isn't particularly subject to high wheel-to-ground damage. This may sound as if we're drawing an unfair conclusion, but one reason Turkey Bay was selected in the first place was the low potential for damage because of the soil type! Here a conscious planning decision led to a situation in which user needs were met with minimal problems for the environment. Our dual responsibility, remember, is to enhance the experience of users while providing resource stewardship.

Soon after Turkey Bay became established, one of the authors took an older, personal friend who was a local officer of the Sierra Club into the area. Before the author could explain why he believed Turkey Bay was the way to go, his friend got extremely angry. "Why would you," he exclaimed, "a person so interested in trails and the environment, be a party to such destruction?" This was his first comment. His second was, "This area will be a biological desert in 12 months!" After some calming time and a careful description of why LBL personnel had taken this approach, the Sierra Club friend said, "Hey, what you've done makes good sense."

Many of the numerous environmentalists and environmental "educators" we hosted at LBL later were of the 1960s to 1970s vintage who did not have the wisdom or maturity to see, listen, learn, and change their minds. Unfortunately for outdoor recreation, these individuals are the parents and teachers of the 1990s. It isn't difficult to understand why school children are not knowledgeable about the facts—not myths—of resource management. The fact that after 18 years of use only 82 acres—3.5 percent—of the 2,350-acre area was impacted instead of the predicted total destruction of Turkey Bay in one year should make you—indeed, all of us—question much of the environmental rhetoric we hear so frequently.

One final environmental note may interest you. According to Dr. Chilman, Sierra Club officials have visited Turkey Bay in recent years and were quite upset that wheel-to-ground measurements of impact were so low. They were not pleased with his findings and, in fact, asked him to change them.

Impact on Wildlife. As with soil and vegetative concerns, the issue of off-highway riding and wildlife needs to be viewed in the context of impact versus damage. OHVs are relatively noisy and as such probably disturb wildlife. Damage, however, is another matter. We aren't aware of any studies which have shown that off-highway riding has injured wildlife. Soon after the Turkey Bay area was opened, TVA conducted a test using a volunteer rider and a technique called biotelemetry. This procedure involved capturing a mature male wild turkey and fitting it with a small radio transmitter, then mounting the receiving unit on the handlebars of an off-highway bike. The rider followed the signal (and the bird) for a two-hour period. To avoid the noise, the bird led the rider on quite a chase, but ended the test period only a few hundred yards from where it began. It's possible the turkey

suffered some trauma from its experience, such as a disruption of its reproductive cycle. However, the wildlife biologist involved found no outward signs of damage (at least on the bird; the rider was beaten up from the ride through the underbrush).

The Turkey Bay area, which is managed as a wildlife unit by TVA, is also opened seasonally for deer hunting, and the deer harvest there has been comparable to surrounding units where OHV use is prohibited. An interesting habitat management benefit came to Turkey Bay after it became an OHV area. One of the goals of wildlife management at LBL was to provide a small pond or water hole located within a mile of all animals within the Turkey Bay project. So, management built numerous water holes in what was to become the OHV area. One of these, located in a dry valley, wouldn't hold water until OHVs began to ride over, in, around and through it. The riding stirred up the clay, silt and rotting vegetation enough to form and maintain a "plugged" bottom, which kept the water in the water hole. These arguments aren't intended to suggest OHV use isn't in some way harmful to wildlife. They simply fail to prove that damage is associated with riding. If someone tells you that off-highway riding is harming wildlife, ask him or her to show you the proof, preferably in the form of an article in a scientific journal. We'd like to see it too.

Impact on People. There are two types of people who are affected by OHV use: those who don't ride and those who do. Controlling the impact on individuals who don't ride is simple—simply zone use areas. As with other activities and facilities, OHV areas need to be separated from areas with which conflict may occur. If you're working with a relatively large area like a state forest, this should not be a problem. The major "people impact" of OHV use is noise, which doesn't always carry over long distances, especially in a wooded environment. Terrain, atmospheric conditions, ground cover, and number of vehicles all affect noise levels. One way of reducing the potential for a problem here is to provide a buffer zone as shown in Figure 5.13. By containing OHV use within a bordered area and buffering this area from other uses, noise and user conflicts are both reduced. If your resource space is limited, you may have to choose between OHVs and one or more other forms of recreation. This decision, however, should be based upon (1) the needs of the people in your area, and (2) the opportunities available through other agencies and private/commercial concerns nearby. The decision should not be based on your personal preferences, biases, or opinions of what people want. You will be called upon periodically to make professional judgments, but these should be just what the term implies: professional.

Off-highway riding can also have quite an impact, literally speaking, on the participant. Therefore one legitimate concern of management should be the potential danger of this and other forms of recreation, and the possible legal liability involved. Not being lawyers, we won't pretend to give you a definitive answer to this one. We do, however, have our opinions and a couple of comments. First, be careful and conscientious in your approaches to planning and management.

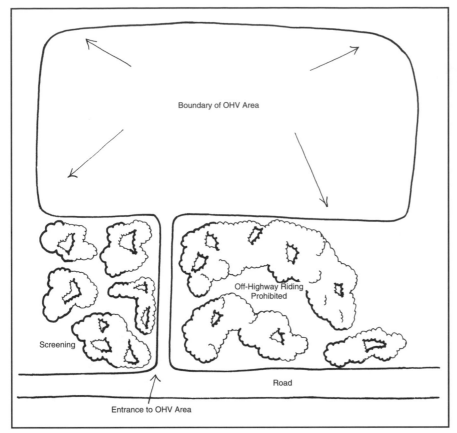

Figure 5.13

For example, one of the authors was involved in designing the area shown in Figure 5.14. This plan called for the development of a warm-up area—a broad, flat area for riders to check out their equipment before taking to the trails—associated with several campsites for other groups. Users had indicated they needed both these facilities, so the design challenge seemed straightforward. It turned out to be another of our mistakes. Given an audience (the people at the campsites) riders began using the warm-up area as an arena for showing off. After a few near-accidents, it was necessary to relocate the campsites in order to create safe riding and camping environments. The problem wasn't design; the warm-up area and campsites were developed correctly from a technical standpoint. The error was one in planning. A lack of understanding of the psychology involved created a problem for users and management.

As it turns out, you need to know a little about the organization of off-highway riding groups in order to develop camping facilities for them. You may find local clubs in your area, but this doesn't always provide an indication of how riders utilize an area. In our experience, OHV user groups tend to consist of fewer than 10 individuals who don't belong to any sort of riding organization, and a typical group might include two families. This suggests a need to develop camping facilities with some opportunity for separation of user groups built into the design. A "pod system" similar to that suggested for group picnic areas also functions well in OHV areas, and Figure 5.15 shows such a design. Note how, in this design, the camping area has been developed with a series of pods or enclaves. Each unit is separated from the others by vegetative screening for privacy, and the camping zone is removed from the warm-up area. With this design, a club can request use of the entire camping area if your management plan includes a reservation system. Conversely, individual user groups—whether they belong to a riding organization or not—can use an enclave and retain a sense of privacy.

Individual camping units should be designed with attention given to both environment and type of user group you anticipate. You'll find a more complete discussion of camp unit design in Chapter Seven covering issues such as coping with topography. For now let's consider some basics. Since natural ground cover won't hold up under vehicular impact, each campsite should be reinforced with gravel and defined along the borders with railroad ties or similar material. The defined borders seem to function as "property lines" for users and help to provide an indication of where management expects vehicles to be parked. The sites themselves should be relatively spacious, perhaps 30-feet wide by 50-feet long, since user parties tend to be large. It's been our experience most

OHV enthusiasts seem to appreciate the opportunity for challenge, but this doesn't suggest that you create or maintain hazardous conditions. Second, we've found off-highway riders to be fairly stoic about injuries. If a biker "hits the dirt," he or she tends to get up, brush off, and keep on going. Again, this should not encourage lax management on your part. Safety and challenge are not mutually exclusive.

Getting Help. It's probably a good idea to get legal advice during the process of developing an OHV area. Another source of help you should not fail to seek is the rider. There are two levels of aid available here, and you should use them both. First, solicit help from riding clubs, if they exist, and from individuals. As with other activities, participants tend to know their own needs, and many of the design techniques discussed here grew out of meetings and conversations we've had with riders. On a broader level, you can and should contact the American Motorcyclist Association. Located in Westerville, Ohio, this national organization encourages conscientious use of resources and can provide technical advice, literature, contacts within your area, research data, and other valuable assistance. Let's turn our attention now to what to do once you've made the decision to develop an OHV area.

Designing off the Road. It's not difficult to provide the types of facilities OHV enthusiasts need to pursue their riding. It would only be a slight oversimplification to suggest that the only amenities they need are places to camp, warm up, and ride. Like most other recreation areas, however, designing OHV facilities is a bit more complex than just listing them.

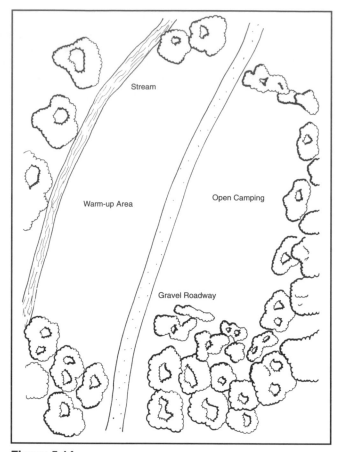

Figure 5.14

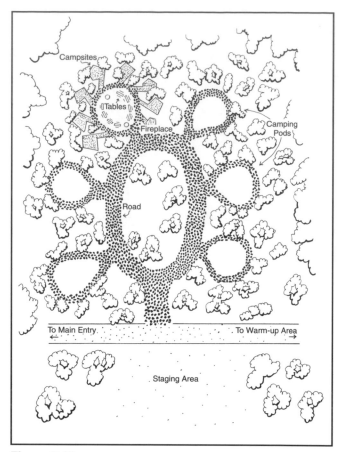

Figure 5.15

OHV groups camp in vans, pickup campers, small recreation vehicles or tents. Large camping trailers and motor homes are rare. Small, two-wheel trailers for off-highway bikes, however, will be used frequently and should be anticipated. For example, the "mouth" of camping pods should be broad enough to permit easy access when backing a trailer.

On-site facilities can be minimal—a picnic table, fire pit/grill, and lantern hanging device (see Chapter Seven), should suffice. Your expected volume of use and the amount of space you have available will help determine the number of campsites you need. A cluster of six to 10 pods should be enough in all but heavy-use areas, since many riders may come for the day without plans to camp. You should also provide toilet facilities and potable water. The physical characteristics of the site and probable use patterns (the number of day users versus campers) will help determine whether toilets should be in the camping zone, warm-up area, or both.

The warm-up or staging area for OHVs is quite simple to develop. The critical aspect of this portion of the complex is zoning. In addition to being separated from the camping zone, the staging area should be developed in conjunction with the entrance to the system of riding trails. Other than the trailhead, the only facilities needed in the warm-up area include a loading/unloading ramp, a garbage collection point, toilets, and an information-posting station or bulletin board.

Figure 5.16 shows a possible layout for a staging area. While design requirements are minimal, they deserve careful attention. Consider the following details which are given attention in this figure. The entrance to the staging area is quite broad, making the zone easy to locate and enhancing safety. Off-highway vehicles, trail bikes, and motorcycles also accelerate quickly, so your plan should avoid narrow constrictions and blind corners where a bike might meet a four-wheel-drive vehicle or a truck transporting other bikes into the warm-up zone. The road leading to the staging area is an exception to the curvilinear design need; a fairly long, straight section of road approaching the warm-up zone may help prevent accidents. The trash collection point is near the entrance to the area. This is convenient for users and reduces the distance traveled by trash collection crews. Also note the placement of the dumpster on the side of the staging area opposite the direction of incoming traffic. This should further reduce the chance of accidents.

Next to safety for users, the most important management consideration for OHV areas is controlling use. Off-highway riding has received a good deal of "bad press" and the activity does have the potential to damage the environment. Both managers and planners, however, can take steps to minimize physical impact and prevent negative feelings toward off-highway riding. Posting and enforcing clear and reasonable regulations is one preventative measure. Figure 5.17 shows a possible set of rules for OHV use. Note the wording; the rules prohibit several kinds of behavior, but negative language ("do not . . ") is minimal. These regulations emphasize the provi-

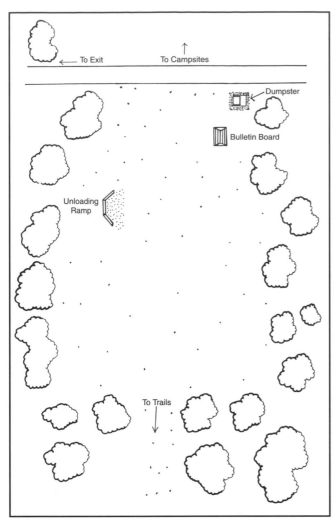

Figure 5.16

sion of an exclusive area for OHV use and safety practices recommended by the American Motorcyclist Association. Remember to check wording and specific regulations with legal counsel.

The role of the planner in controlling use lies in the ability to develop facilities that can be managed effectively. In Figure 5.16, the bulletin board where rules, area maps, and other information are posted is in clear sight of the entrance to the staging area. The unloading ramp is near enough to the entrance to be convenient, but is located off to one side of the staging area. To build this ramp, use a three-sided border of railroad ties, stacked two high and filled with gravel. Taper the gravel to ground level behind the ramp. Figure 5.18 shows two views of this construction, a profile (A) and a top view (B). Users soon discover the ramp works nicely as a jump as well as for loading and unloading; thus it must be located out of the main flow of traffic. The planner should also place clearly marked boundary signs around the perimeter of the OHV area that face into the riding area so riders can see them. Locations for signs must be intervisible as well. (You should be able to see one sign from both directions.)

The development of a trails system for an OHV area depends on site-specific conditions, and the help of a soil scientist is critical in choosing one. Avoid ecologically sensitive areas and sites subject to erosion; soils with a high gravel content are generally good choices. From the rider's perspective,

---

Sample Rules and Regulations Governing Motorized Vehicle Use

- All properly licensed motor vehicles may be operated on paved gravelled, and graded roads unless otherwise posted.

- Driving in woods, fields, utility right of ways, or trails is prohibited except in areas specifically designated for off-road use.

- All vehicles must be equipped with properly functioning mufflers.

- All motor bikes must have a properly functioning spark arrester.

- Drivers must hold a valid drivers license to drive on improved roads, although neither vehicle nor operator's license is required for off-road riding in designated areas.

- Motorbike riders are required to wear safety helmets and protective eyewear.

- In areas provided specifically for off-road riding:

  Riders must operate within posted boundaries;

  Use is allowed only during daylight hours;

  One-way trails must be traveled in the direction indicated;

  All garbage and debris must be placed in the containers provided;

  Users must refrain from harassing people or wildlife;

  Riders should observe the safety practices recommended by the American Motorcyclist Association.

Figure 5.17

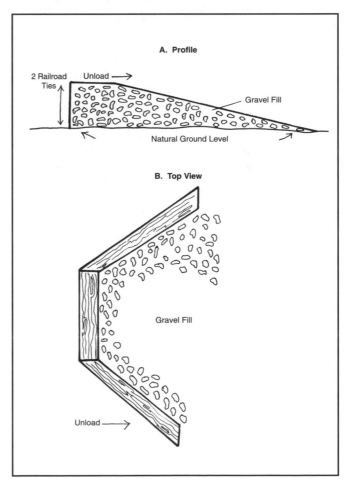

Figure 5.18

there are several other factors to consider in design. Build OHV trails with attention to variety in degree of difficulty. While the staging area provides a flat area for warm-up and for novices, the trails should offer differing challenges for more advanced riders. The key here is to avoid designing diverse obstacles into adjacent sections of trail. In other words, don't follow a broad, gentle curve with a tight, hairpin turn, but do plan hill climbs, dips, and other changes in elevation. If at all possible, avoid having the trail cross stream beds and narrow ravines. These abrupt changes in elevation can be dangerous, and such zones are particularly subject to erosion. Solicit help from off-highway riding clubs and individuals who pursue the activity whenever you can. In some instances you may find them willing to help with layout and construction. In all instances you should find that asking user groups for help and providing facilities for them to use will buy you a major dose of positive public relations.

The photographs in Figures 5.19 to 5.24 help to provide you with a sense of what the OHV experience—at least at Turkey Bay—is like. Figure 5.19 (originally shown as Figure 5.2) shows a couple with their children viewing the Turkey Bay bulletin board, showing other LBL attractions and current program information. Figure 5.20 shows one of the riding trails leading from the unloading area to the rugged,

challenging hills beyond. Note the natural chert (rock) base. Figure 5.21 depicts a small, vegetation-screened camping pod providing privacy for campers at Turkey Bay. Figure 5.22 demonstrates one of the joys of off-highway motorcycle riding: challenge. Figure 5.23 shows a flexible plastic OHV area boundary sign. Signs like these, facing into the area, encircled the 2,350-acre area. Most were stapled onto trees; in treeless areas, the signs were mounted on four-by-four posts. Where possible, they were intervisible. Boundary markers should

Figure 5.21

Figure 5.19

Figure 5.22

Figure 5.20

Figure 5.23

be checked and replaced as necessary at least once every year. Figure 5.24 (originally shown as Figure 5.5) is of the lakeshore bordering one side of Turkey Bay. This zone turned out to be a favorite spot for riders, particularly in winter and during periods of low lake pool. As the lake receded toward low pool, it exposed several acres of shallow mud flats. These flats provided a marvelous mud ride area for riders. The flats also were used for impromptu races and as a skills sharpening area.

Figure 5.24

Wrangler's Camps

The authors have been involved with the planning and management of wrangler's camps on national forests and at LBL. We feel many wildland park managers should give careful consideration to this type of recreation and its revenue-generating potential. As with other types of outdoor recreation opportunities (trails, campgrounds, day-use areas, and all sorts of programs for all sorts of users), we've made numerous mistakes working with wrangler's camps, learned from our errors, and made sure much of our learning came from applied research.

Planning facilities for recreational horseback riding, as with other types of activities, requires you to become familiar with your clientele. As it turns out, the main thing you need to know about horseback riding is where it occurs; the primary distinction in riding is a geographical, or, more specifically, a sectional one. In general, riding in the western portion of the country, from west of the Rocky Mountains, is a wilderness-oriented, long-distance, linear activity and the basic trail design can be similar to that for linear hiking discussed in Chapter Three. It's a good idea to provide connector trails, as shown in Figure 3.41, so users have the option of shorter rides that begin and end at the same point. Other features discussed in the section on long-distance hiking—parking, signing, trail marking, and the like—apply to this type of riding experience as well.

The topic of this section is the wrangler's camp, an experience more aligned with the recreational preferences of horseback riders in the East and South. A wrangler's camp is a destination facility. By this we mean it's a location where users plan to stay for a period of time, unlike "way stations" or overnight camping spots on a linear trail. A destination

facility, like OHV areas and developed campgrounds, is characterized by a central complex. In the case of the wrangler's camp, this must include facilities for camping, having fun, keeping horses, and riding. For example, Brown County State Park, Indiana's largest and most popular state park, is among the 25 most visited public parks in the United States (including the large national parks!). One of the reasons for this is the sizable—and quite profitable—horse camp, which we would call a wrangler's camp. It is not zoned as part of a family campground.

Camping. The number of campsites you need to provide in a wrangler's camp depends on a wonderful acronym, popular in recreation literature, that we've been waiting to use: PAOT. In English, this means persons at one time. The more popular riding is in your locale, the more PAOT you should expect, but we'll leave it to you to determine PAOT and limit our discussion to the types of camping facilities you may need to consider. People seem to arrive at wrangler's camps in one of two types of groups: small, as in a family or a group of friends; and large, as in an organized group of several families. Since you may find some of each wanting to use your facilities at the same time, it's a good idea to design your camping area accordingly. To avoid reinventing the wheel, we'll refer you to the section on campsite design in Chapter Seven for site specific information (construction materials, topographic challenges, and similar considerations). For now, let's consider campsite design from the standpoint of layout for wrangler's camps.

There are three ways to develop campsites for wrangler's camps. Since groups consisting of one family or a few friends may visit your area, some of the campsites you build should be individual units. These are smaller sites, perhaps 30 by 30 feet of reinforced living space plus attached parking large enough for a vehicle and a horse trailer, along with a single movable picnic table, on the ground grill, and lantern-hanging device (see Chapter Seven). You should build these sites together to localize impact, but apart to provide a sense of privacy for users at each site. Figure 5.25 shows a section of a camping area devoted to individual use, and three aspects of this design contribute to a psychological sense of privacy: the screening between sites, the "staggered" spur-to-highway junctures, and the "property lines" created by edging the sites with a defined border.

A second type of campsite design, shown in Figure 5.26, functions for larger groups. This type of site is distinguished by its larger living and parking space and by a collection of several tables and grills. (A single, large fire pit is also an alternative here.) Users can arrange their tables and the remaining space to suit their own particular needs.

Figure 5.27 shows a compromise between the types of sites shown in the previous two figures. Here they are built adjacent to one another to allow groups of several families to congregate if the families make up a larger party. Since they are individual, these sites will function for separate parties of users as well. Though you may not know what type of user groups to expect in advance, they are a good hedge against uncertainty.

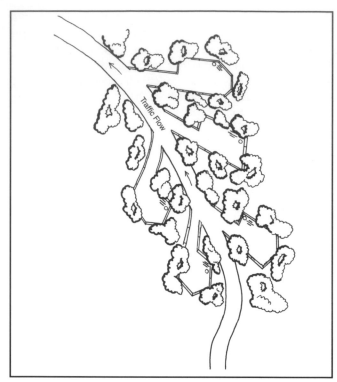

Figure 5.25

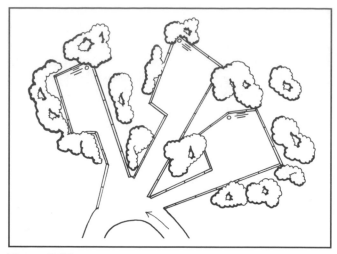

Figure 5.27

program zone for example, need not interfere. (Intensive programming may not be a design goal at all special-use areas. However, we advocate a philosophy of never passing up an opportunity.) A program zone at a wrangler's camp would include a small shelter with a concrete floor and five or six portable tables, a multipurpose play court, two sets of horseshoe pits (most appropriate), a campfire circle with seating, and a playground. Some of these features would be separated from one another and all should be fenced and have security lighting. The multipurpose play court shown in Figure 5.29 (originally shown as Figure 5.6) has simple security lighting, adequate electric plug-ins for dances, and a basketball court all surrounded by a horse-proof fence. If the one light shown had been placed near the center edge of the paved area and had portable volleyball standards and net been added, this would have been an excellent wrangler's camp facility. Campers do bring their own play equipment with them as evidenced by the photograph of the badminton game in Figure 5.30. Campers who visit a wrangler's camp have after-dinner program needs the same as campers in a family campground. Country music, line-dancing, square-dancing, guitars and fiddles at the campfire circle, as well as evening and late-night court games would be welcome additions to most wrangler's camps.

Designing Space for Horses. We promise not to stoop to any comments about horse sense, but there are a few things you need to consider in planning space for these animals. First, common sense tells us to avoid common space, the corral, which functions quite well in the western dude-ranch environment. At a wrangler's camp, most of the animals won't know each other. Unlike people, for whom recreation is a social experience, horses need their private space. Providing a corral may create a situation in which one or more horses could be injured, so this leaves you with a couple of alternatives. First, if you have the budget for it, stables with individual stalls are a possibility. A less costly alternative is to provide facilities for riders to tether their horses near their campsites.

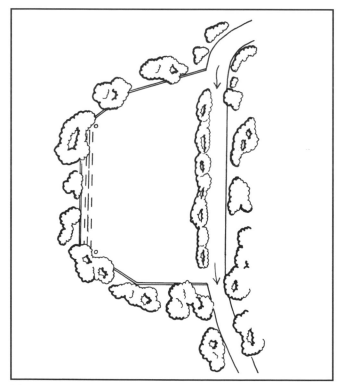

Figure 5.26

Figure 5.28 shows a possible layout for one loop of a wrangler's camp. Here the three types of campsites have been combined, and the impact from camping (vehicles, campfires, and the like) has been localized. Also, the sites are zoned into a single area so that potentially conflicting activities, in the

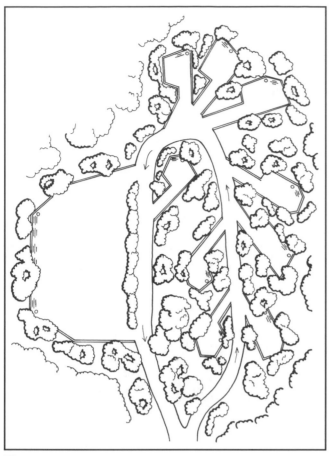

Figure 5.28

Figure 5.30

Our old friend "attention to detail" comes into play here. Particularly in the warmer months of the year, horses will need shade when tethered outside. The KISS principle by itself would tell us to use the straightforward solution and let users tie their horses to trees. However, there's a problem with this; horses will quite happily eat the bark off the trees to which they're tied, so unless you want your trees destroyed, you'll need an alternative. The best one we know is to use a series of four-by-six-inch posts anchored in the ground 15-feet apart with rope attached between them. You can place these tethering posts near trees to provide shade but far enough away to keep your bark intact. The 15-foot spacing of posts also al-

lows enough room for horses to be kept separate from one another.

Figure 5.31 is located at the LBL wrangler's camp. It shows a water trough and hydrant/fountain with a fixed table camping unit and horse tie rack in the background. The sign reads, "Do not tether horses near trees. $1,000 maximum fine strictly enforced." Figure 5.32 was photographed the same day within 500 feet of the sign. The horse is tethered to a rope tied to three trees. Soil impact around the trees and bark bites indicate administration there is less than good. (We were not surprised!)

Riding. The wrangler's camp experience seems to consist of two main components. Riding is obviously one reason people are attracted to these types of facilities. The other—and this is important to know from a design standpoint—is the social component. Riders seem to enjoy meeting and being with other riders, and this tendency has implications for the development of camping areas, as we discussed above. It should also influence how you design trails for wrangler's camps. Since most of the socializing occurs at the camp, rather than on the trail, users will want to begin and end their rides at camp. In fact, this "out and back" preference is what makes the wrangler's camp a distinctive recreational experience.

Length of ride depends on several factors, including the weather, time of year, who is riding (e.g., older riders, adults, young children), expected meal times and other available

Figure 5.29

Figure 5.31

Figure 5.32

activities. Interestingly, applied research tells us LBL wrangler's camp riders ride a total of six hours per day, which is the same riding time as users of Turkey Bay OHV area. This total tended to consist of two or three short outings rather than one ride three hours out and three back. This type of information demonstrates how the results of applied research should be used in planning and design, for it tells us to design a series of varied length loop trails to accommodate the riding habits and preferences of users.

The best way to design trails to meet this need is with a series of loop trails radiating out from the central complex, as shown in Figure 5.33. The important point to consider about the trails shown here is their varied length. As loop trails,

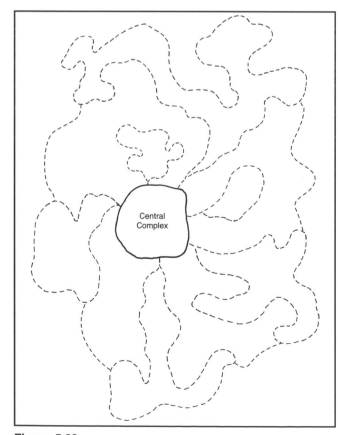

Figure 5.33

they allow users to begin and end at the central camp. With varied lengths, as well as information about riding times and distances posted, riders can also design the length of their experience to meet their needs. Trail-riding times might vary from two or three hours to all day, and some riders might even appreciate a loop trail long enough to offer the opportunity for an overnight excursion.

Figure 5.34 is of a schematic map in the center of the LBL wrangler's camp showing trail options, springs, and water holes. Some trails can be tied together to provide longer riding opportunities. The loop systems allow riders to travel one way (generally counterclockwise) around the trail with little likelihood of meeting other riders. The schematic also shows the location of and how to access the five major loops.

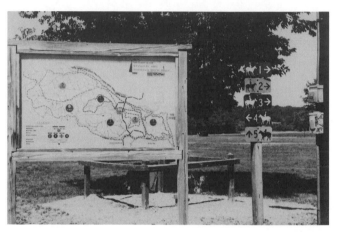

Figure 5.34

Trail 1 for example, which moved gently toward and around the shore of nearby Lake Barkley, was signed with the number 1 painted on trees around the entire loop. User groups helped with the initial marking and later remarking of these trails.

As with designing other types of recreation areas, you should make it a point to get to know local horseback riding groups and work with them to design facilities to meet their needs. More importantly, through provision of facilities and program opportunities, you can demonstrate to user groups your responsiveness to their needs. Figure 5.35 shows a Forest Service response to those needs in Colorado. Here staff have provided a place to unload saddles and other gear up out of the dust, mud and manure.

Group Camps

In the preceding sections on wrangler's camps and OHV areas, you've already been introduced to group camps. We now need to generalize a bit and discuss some basic concepts—ones you should consider regardless of the type of group you're planning for. These concepts aren't new. They involve nothing more than plain old common sense, but they often get ignored in the planning process.

When you begin to plan for a group-oriented facility, you need to ask yourself three questions: Who is the camp for?

Figure 5.35

How do you and users want it to function? and What are your program goals? Group camps can be developed along a continuum from the primitive to the highly modernized, but we'll limit our discussion of design techniques to a few general considerations since we don't have the space to consider all types of group camping. First, however, let's consider two examples to illustrate the importance of our three questions.

For 20 years, a Girl Scout council in northern Georgia had saved its money to develop a camp and finally they had raised enough to buy a piece of property. The council commissioned a plan for the area and formed a committee to review the plan. The property featured a fairly large flat field and several surrounding steep wooded slopes. The plan called for a stream running through the field to be dammed to create a lake, with facilities for the camp itself to be built on the ridges and slopes. Total development cost would have been approximately $2 million—half for the property, dam, and lake, and half for the facilities to be built.

As good fortune would have it, the review committee vetoed the plan and our story has a happy ending. The council ultimately sold the property to a timber company at quite a profit and bought another property with excellent county road access, and a preexisting camp and lake, then modified it to meet their needs. The important point is this: The decision to veto the new development was not made on the basis of how well the plan was packaged, but rather on our three questions. The camp was to be for Girl Scouts; it was to function as a resident camp, and program goals included developing space for a variety of activities. The lake planned for the original property would have flooded the only developable land available for both activity areas and "bedroom" space. Also, while this body of water was desirable from a programming perspective, creating it would not have been worth the trade-off in opportunities lost for building other types of areas. The decision to move the camp was the correct one since the committee made it on the basis of users, function, and programs. (The committee included a trained recreation person as a volunteer, which is quite rare for a group like this!)

The second example we'll share with you is a Boy Scout High Adventure Base in Kentucky. The function of this camp differed from the previous example in that the High Adven-

ture site was a base camp. The program called for scout groups to arrive at the site on Monday for orientation and then camp overnight at the base. The next morning, the group would begin a several day trek, either sailing or hiking. At the end of the week, the group would return, spend one night at the camp, during which preparations to leave were made, and depart the following day. As with our other illustration, the program provided the information necessary to design and administer the High Adventure Base Camp. Since groups did not use the facility in residence, there was no need for a major programming zone. Thus it was possible to develop the site on a relatively small, and fairly marginal, piece of land.

Major considerations from a planning perspective included administration space, office, departure points, equipment storage, a staging area for arriving groups, and a "departure camp" for groups spending their last night at the base. This arrangement—and the considerations for planning that accompany it—exemplify the potential diversity of group camp experiences. In one small area, three types of camping needs were met: the first night orientation, the extended trek and the checking-out camp. The approach used to meet these needs at the High Adventure Base was excellent in its simplicity. Upon arrival, groups checked out an appropriate number of small, two-person tents. They then set up camp for the night in the staging area and made final preparations for the upcoming outing. The next morning, the group would break camp, keeping the tents to use during the trek. Upon their return to the base several days later, they would bivouac at the departure camp, which consisted of larger tents set on raised wooden platforms. With this arrangement, there was no need for the group to spend time setting up camp their final night or breaking camp the morning of their departure. Instead, this time could be devoted to making any necessary equipment repairs, cleaning gear and recreating, including enjoying a final evening of skits and fun. Figure 5.36 shows a schematic of the base arrangement. Again a knowledge of user needs, camp function, and program dictated appropriate development.

In creating a group camp the most basic consideration, and the test of how successful the camp will be, is the program. In order to function effectively, a group camp must feature appropriate activities and zoning. Figure 5.37 illustrates the layout of a group camp designed to function for user groups and for management. Separation of use areas plays a primary role here. The central complex housing administrative functions such as group check-in and the dining area is immediately adjacent to the arrival point. Bedroom areas are zoned next to the central complex to simplify maintenance and cleanup, as well as camper setup and departure. This example shows a dormitory system, although camping pods for a more rustic experience could be developed with the same spatial arrangement.

The central complex and bedroom zone serve another function as well—they provide a buffer between active and passive program zones. With this arrangement, it is possible to program, for example, an interpretive hike and a basketball game at the same time. The design, in other words, encourages

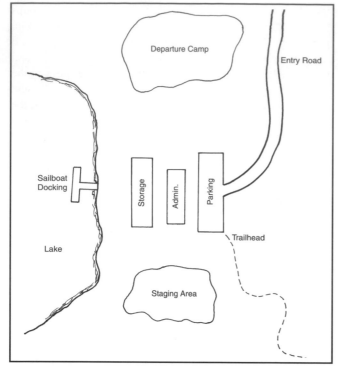

Figure 5.36

program flexibility. If the size and capacity of the camp are large enough, it is also possible to open the camp to two or more groups at the same time. If this possibility exists, you will need to consider one management issue: some groups may be incompatible with others. We recall one instance (although we'd prefer to forget it) in which this concern wasn't given enough attention. While working in the federal sector, we reserved space in a group camp for two sets of teenagers from different religious denominations. Although the camp was well-zoned, there were opportunities, such as in the dining hall, for the groups to interact. Before their stay was finished, they were literally throwing rocks at each other.

This story reminds us of one final point about group camps since many such camps are owned and operated by religious organizations. All too often, group camps are poorly maintained, unprotected, subject to vandalism, and unoccupied for much of the year. In the case of camps operated by service and religious organizations, there are probably two reasons for this. First is an inadequate operations and maintenance budget. Capital investment fund drives to buy or build camps are often quite successful, but can neglect the need to operate and maintain a camp once it is built. Figure 5.38 shows a shelter-assembly zone at a Midwestern group camp. The camp is used intensively for a few weeks each summer. The shelter needs extensive repairs, the benches around the fire circle are rotting and quite hazardous, the entire zone is compacted and

eroded, and the equipment in the foreground has a makeshift/make-do character to it. This is a scene duplicated in low-budget group camps all across North America.

A second problem with service and religious camps involves comprehensive program planning. Building a camp so a youth group can have an annual two-week retreat is a commendable purpose, but what about the other 50 weeks of the year?

It really doesn't matter whether the camp is owned privately or operated by a public, quasi-public, or commercial concern. What does matter is maximum use through as much of the year as possible. Ideally, maximum use means more opportunities for recreation; pragmatically, we're talking return on investment. We wish there were a simple, straightforward solution to this problem for you, but if there is, we aren't aware of it. One possible answer might be cooperative ventures in which several groups combine forces and resources to develop a single facility to be shared by all. This approach can create a few extra hassles—sharing property titles, scheduling, accounting, and the like. However, these problems are preferable to an underused, poorly funded, heavily vandalized facility.

Between writing the first and second edition of this book, one of the authors was asked to critique three church camps owned by one denomination. The owners wanted answers to questions such as: Should we keep all three or sell one and keep two? What sort of impressions did the author have about the camps? How should money be spent on short- and long-term improvements?

As visitors entered the most accessible of the camps, they were asked (by signs) to drive to the left on a narrow, gravel, one-way road. This took them on a one-and-one-half-mile ride along the property boundary (which was not particularly scenic), to and through the back of the property where the camp's quiet retreat outcamps were located, across the top of a dam on a narrow road where views on both sides were a bit frightening (the dry "lake" had been a mistake itself, for the

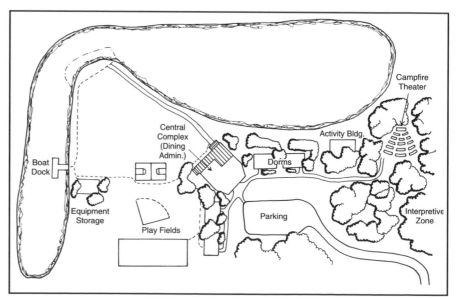

Figure 5.37

Figure 5.38

Figure 5.39

limestone bottom was full of fissures), and finally into the program/cabin zone—which was quite near the main entrance. When the layperson governing committee was asked why traffic flow didn't move to the right and immediately into the fun program zone (which would have eliminated extensive travel where casual visitors weren't wanted in the first place), the reply was, "We've always done it the way it is now."

Let's experience the entry from the viewpoint of, say, an elderly couple driving their 10-year-old granddaughter to camp for the first time. They enter the camp expecting a safe, uncomplicated, beckoning experience. Instead, they drive around and through the entire camp. Moving to the left on a narrow, one-way gravel road lowered their comfort factor. Instead of friendly waves and offers to help the couple find the program zone where new campers are supposed to go, folks in the retreat/quiet areas were distracted with the noise and dust of the unwanted intrusion into their area. Then comes the drive over the long, narrow "mountain lake" dam with its steep and frightening drop-offs right at the road's shoulder. Finally they arrive at the activity area, by now wondering why they brought their precious granddaughter here in the first place! Throughout this book, we've discussed design psychology, and how to beckon and repulse park users. What negatives do you find in this verbal drive-through? One you may miss is the uneasiness these grandparents will experience anticipating their repeat drive into the camp two weeks later to pick up their granddaughter after her camp ends. To the credit of the camp's governing board, they understood the problem and corrected it by making the short stretch from the entrance to the program zone a two-way road.

The second camp had all sorts of negatives too, including an extremely steep road from the activity area to the lodge and cabins. This would have been a negative experience for our grandparents mentioned above, many of their peers, and lots of other folks as well. The entrance zone to this camp was less than beckoning at this camp. The entrance road was narrow, graveled, and rutted; the first structure users encountered was the bright metal maintenance building (which wasn't signed, so new users didn't know what it was; see Figure 5.39); around the next turn was the entrance structure—an old, two-colored metal trailer with both colors different than that of

the maintenance building. The shelter, campfire circle, and eroded area, as shown in Figure 5.38, was also part of this recreation area. From a design psychology standpoint, were you beckoned into and excited about visiting this area? One hint here is to keep maintenance structures and yards from being focal points in parks—whatever kind of park it is. These areas should be judiciously located to balance the need for maintenance zones to be reasonably close to the areas they service with the need for them to be zoned and screened from general public view: a part of but apart from the rest of the park.

The third camp—shown in Figure 5.40—had a beckoning, landscaped entrance. Moreover, once you entered the camp, the first thing you saw was the fun and amenity zone with swimming pool, basketball court, playground, volleyball court, shelter, and other fun areas. Which of the three camps would you prefer? (Incidentally, the governing committee sold the third camp—not our recommendation, but another good lesson for you and one that goes beyond planning parks: You win some, you lose some.)

One of the greatest challenges most existing group camps now face is compliance with ADA standards (which are now being written, interpreted, and applied, more often than not, quite poorly—see Chapter Ten). Many of these camps and camping programs have difficulty paying their bills now. Strict enforcement of the ADA may require some camps to close

Figure 5.40

which, in many instances, will be unfortunate. Camp personnel and their lay volunteer committees will have to retrofit countless structures and rehabilitate others as funds permit (see Figure 5.41).

Figure 5.41

Why are there such extensive problems with so many group camps around the country? One obvious answer is the shortfall of operation and maintenance dollars. Another reason is governing committee members generally have good intentions but poor skills in camp planning and operations. Often, too, the good ol' boy they hire as caretaker/maintenance person begins to make decisions that shouldn't be his to make. Park professionals who work for committees have big challenges of all sorts and they are often inexperienced and alone. The American Camping Association has training sessions and numerous texts about group camps (not family campgrounds); we suggest you seek its help. Otherwise, the best pathway through the maze of group camp challenges is to learn all you can about basic park planning and design; watch and learn how users function, and use a bunch of common sense.

Military Recreation Complexes

As we suggested in Chapter One, outdoor recreation entered a period of unprecedented growth and popularity during the 1950s through about 1965. Public agencies at all levels of government—and later in the commercial sector—witnessed increases in staff, funding, areas, and programs in response to new demands. Generally speaking, this trend has reversed itself in the public sector during recent years. Particularly at the federal level, recreation agencies have experienced hiring freezes, cutbacks in funding, and, fortunately—as we'll discuss toward the end of the book—in cases such as the Heritage, Conservation and Recreation Service (the former Bureau of Outdoor Recreation), dissolution of programs altogether.

Until about 1990, one exception to this reductionist trend was the provision of outdoor recreation opportunities by the U.S. armed forces. Recreation services for military personnel are not, in themselves, new phenomena. In fact, histories

tracing the growth of recreation in general often point to the emphasis on physical fitness in the armed forces as one of the major causes that increased recreation services during the first quarter of the twentieth century. Outdoor recreation, however, is something of a "new kid on the block" as far as the military is concerned, and the 1970s were its "early days." Somewhat surprisingly, outdoor recreation in the military has not followed the same pattern of program provision—or lack of it—that we discussed in reference to other federal agencies. From the beginning, the military has made excellent strides in providing outdoor recreation programs and facilities.

In the early 1990s, the American military—including their recreation facilities and programs—came full tilt under the budget-cutting ax. The fall of the Berlin Wall, the abrupt end of the Cold War, the breakup of the former Soviet Union, coupled with a long-term buildup of domestic funding needs and a new administration less friendly to things military, all combined to cut military spending drastically. Throughout NATO and U.S. overseas bases, military recreation complexes were closed or turned over to other governments. Similar closings occurred at military bases all over the United States. Some of the remaining bases saw increased troop strength and the need for more recreation personnel but where bases were closed or their recreation mission deemphasized, recreation personnel were laid off. Figure 5.42 shows the entrance to the Chiemsee area in southern Germany, which, before closing, had been one of the most popular park and recreation areas in Europe.

The authors believe (and we're pretty stingy with our compliments) that the U.S. Armed Forces are unique among federal agencies in their approach to recreation services: They do great things for people! It seems to us there are three reasons for this. First, armed services recreation personnel are people-oriented. Below a top echelon of military personnel, a large proportion of the people involved are *trained in the profession* (isn't that unique?!). The armed forces hire graduates of recreation curricula, and, as we've suggested before, these folks tend to have good backgrounds in people-related skills: administration and programming. Thus recreation staff in the military tend to be sensitive to the needs of users. In fact, they are required to do so!

Figure 5.42

A second factor contributing to the success of armed forces recreation programs and facilities is their mission. Their very reason for existence is to meet the recreational needs of the clientele they serve, and although each branch of the military has its own recreation arm, the professional staff involved use this mission as a guiding force. It's been our experience that various branches of the military are relatively efficient in holding their recreation staffs accountable. Recreation service is their function, and they are expected to perform effectively.

In our view, the public's tax money used for recreation and parks would be better spent if public servants responsible for recreation were held accountable (like those in the military) for the satisfaction of a broad spectrum of users. In the outdoor recreation realm we see continued—in fact, increased—emphasis on the good ol' boy user, the glamorous winter sports enthusiasts, and wilderness types. This emphasis *excludes* most Americans. Personally, we enjoy fishing, backpacking, wilderness, and winter sports; what we enjoy personally, however doesn't—or at least shouldn't—have one whit to do with what we provide professionally. Nothing we know of is less professional than the attitude of: "If I like it, it must be right for everyone." In many federal agencies, however, promotions and personnel evaluations have little to do with a person's quality or quantity of work; until, or if, public servants are held accountable for their work, the public will continue to be shortchanged.

A final and related factor leading to effective recreation services for the military is the spectrum of users for whom professional staff provide areas and facilities. Consider for a moment the population at or near a typical military base. This may consist of retired service personnel and their spouses, career servicemen and servicewomen who have served several tours of duty and their families (including teenagers), young married personnel with smaller children, single officers, and enlisted men and women ranging in age from teens to sixties. In other words, the recreation clientele at a U.S. military base, whether in the United States or overseas, resembles a microcosm of society. With such a diverse population, military recreation staff have a need (remember their mission) to provide a broad spectrum of programs and facilities in order to meet the demands of all users (see, for example, the buddy campsite for multiple family groups at Fort Campbell, Kentucky, shown in Figure 5.43).

As we've noted, military recreation personnel are quite successful when it comes to providing programs and facilities because of two factors. The first is something we feel is essential in a professional: If you're doing a good job, accept the fact you are doing a good job, and the praise accompanying it. Second, never be complacent about your work. It's one thing to perform a task well; it's quite another to assume you can't do any better. We believe part of being a professional involves never being entirely satisfied, and while this does not imply you should downgrade yourself, it does suggest that you should always ask yourself and others, including users, how you can do even better next time.

In the case of military recreation services, one of the strong points contributing to their success is also a hindrance to improved performance: the background of many of their personnel. The programming and administrative expertise of armed services recreation staff does not often translate into effective planning and design skills. As a result, many recreation facilities at military installations are laid out ineffectively.

Another way of looking at this problem is to suggest that all the pieces of the puzzle are present, but that the "assembly" doesn't fit together as well as it should. To illustrate this point let's consider the evolution of a military recreation complex in Europe we've seen. This particular complex was operated by the Army, but branch affiliation is incidental.

First, we need a brief "history lesson." As early as the mid 1970s, Army recreation services became involved with providing facilities called "travel camps," particularly in Europe. These were high-density campgrounds, some of which now contain up to 35 campsites (like the ones shown in Figure 5.43) per acre. In comparison, a Forest Service campground might have three to four units per acre, a National Park Service area 10 to 15. As outdoor recreation services in the military became more sophisticated, these travel camps underwent an evolution of sorts. Today an Army recreation complex has become known as a "community park," which offers a wider variety of program opportunities and facilities, one of which may be a campground. Other facilities are also oriented toward day use and might include play fields and courts, picnic areas and pavilions, playgrounds, game areas, a recreation building, and similar developments you might expect to find in a typical municipal park.

Figure 5.44 shows the area allocated to recreation development at the Army base we mentioned above. Before recreation development began, portion 1 of the site had been fenced in and used to park tanks. Since a road and parking spurs were already in place here, the planner decided to add a recreation vehicle campground in the first stage of development. Proposed facilities included (2) an indoor lounge area, (3) a picnic area and pavilion, (4) a miniature golf course, (5) a multipurpose building, (6) a tent-camping zone, (7) a playground, and (8) two softball fields. The design also called for a toilet/shower building at the entrance to the RV camping area.

Figure 5.43

There are several problems with this design. First, the various facilities don't fit together in a cohesive fashion; the tent camping area seems more a part of the day-use zone than of the overnight use development; the playground doesn't relate to day-use facilities and, indeed, is in a rather dangerous location. A second problem occurs in circulation and use of space. Aside from the one parking lot and the campground, all movement within the area would require walking, and the areas above and below the softball complex are wasted. A third problem concerns administration and support facilities. Since the campground is reached via a separate entrance, control problems exist. The location of the toilet/shower keeps you from taking full advantage of this facility and, as placed, it won't serve any area except the RV campground.

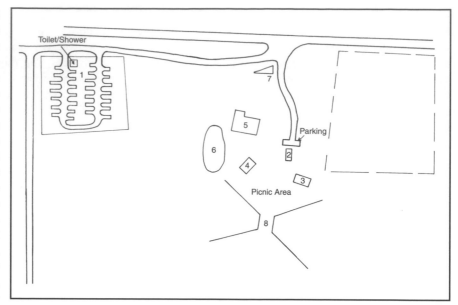

Figure 5.44

Let's try to redesign this area so it functions more effectively for users and management. Since it's quite easy to design just about anything on a piece of paper, let's also put some real-life constraints on our design: (a) area 1 must be used for camping, since the parking spurs are already in place; (b) the road leading to and beyond this zone must be kept open to traffic; and (c) the (2) lounge, (4) miniature golf area, (5) multipurpose building, and (8) softball fields must be built as shown in Figure 5.44. Our design goals should be to improve circulation, to provide better zoning of use areas, to build in ease of administration, to allow for an expansion of the campground, and to use space more effectively. It turns out these constraints don't force us into a more complex design solution; as is so often the case, the KISS principle can serve as a guide to improving the design.

Figure 5.45 shows one alternative solution to our problem, though other approaches could accomplish the same goals as well. This design meets the constraints we imposed. Area 1 is used for camping and the road past it has been kept open while the two former entrances to the campground have been sealed off, allowing us to use a single entry/exit to the entire area and control use with the addition of a (2) small entrance station. We've also provided both vehicle circulation and parking at the lounge, multipurpose building, miniature golf course and softball complex. The screen planting shown separates day-use facilities from the camping zone, which has been expanded. Note how the new location of the toilet/shower serves both the "old" camping area and the new loops added to the design. Within the camping and day-use zones, more of the previously "dead" space is now devoted to functional use areas.

Probably the most important feature of the design shown in Figure 5.45 is the addition of theme pods for day use. We've talked about pod design before, and the principle works as well in military recreation complexes as it does in civilian parks. Fact is, watching a military unit party near the area in Germany shown in Figure 5.45 gave us the idea for theme pods in the first place. Notice how the new design has eliminated the poorly placed playground and the original picnic area and pavilion. In their place, we've added a series of day-use pods (A through E; you would, of course, give each one a special name, based perhaps on some central theme reflecting something unique about the area). These pods function as group-use areas. Depending on the needs at a particular military base, each of these can be devoted to a specific theme. One might be designed for group picnics, including unit par-

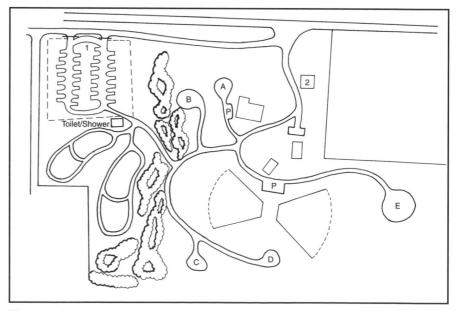

Figure 5.45

ties; another might be planned around a large playground for younger children; still another could be built for adult play space, tennis, volleyball, and the like; and so on. The contents or themes of the pods might vary from one military base to another, but the logic is the same: The design follows the principle of zoning of use areas (see Chapter Four).

Overnight use is separated from day use as well. Note how the original tent camping area—point 6 in Figure 5.44—has been removed. (In general, separating tent and trailer camping isn't a good idea and it creates a management problem; however, if this separation is a management objective, one of the camping loops in Figure 5.45 could also be designated for tents only.) Further, within the day-use zones, potentially conflicting uses are kept separated by the development of pods.

In military recreation complexes, as in civilian parks, form should follow function. Providing a broad spectrum of recreation opportunities is the ultimate program goal, and careful application of design techniques is, as always, a means to an end. By attending to the basic principle of zoning of use areas, military recreation personnel can improve what is already a good example of planning parks for people.

For the last 20 years and more, we have been involved in dozens of park planning and design workshops, some of which we've hosted and others for which we've been resource speakers for various groups. Wherever and whenever we've had the opportunity, we've espoused the need for programming and its companion, truly planning parks for people. Having program-oriented military recreation professionals in our "student" groups has been a real joy. These folks know why they need to develop park facilities (remember their people-favored mission!). While most military recreation professionals are inexperienced in the basics of planning and design, they are eager participants in the learning process, probably as a result of recognizing programs as a goal and planning as a support function. Those who aren't trained in the program realm—foresters, landscape architects, wildlife biologists, and other rascals—are oftentimes quite reluctant to embrace or even believe in the need to consider people and programs in the planning process. Unfortunately, their designs litter our parkscapes worldwide!

The sizable Fort Campbell community park shown in part in Figure 5.46 (and seen originally as Figure 5.4) was planned, designed and built (and quite effectively) by two individuals who, although they didn't have degrees in recreation planning, had availed themselves of continuing education opportunities—you're never too old to learn. The building in the center has a combination toilet/shower/laundry/arcade zone for the campground and day-use area, houses the outdoor recreation staff office, and serves as check-in/out location for campground guests and play equipment. Camping is zoned directly behind the structure where day users can be kept from driving through the campground. The campground contains double sites like the one shown in Figure 5.43: back-ins and pull-throughs. All sites are defined and generous, and all are universal sites, by which we mean they are usable by campers with any type of camping equipment, including trailers or

Figure 5.46

other wheeled-vehicle rigs, tents, and by campers with disabilities.

To the right of the campground is a large picnic shelter with sanitary facilities, equipment storage room, and a raised stage. A cooking/barbecue structure and both fixed and portable picnic tables are located adjacent to the shelter. Nearby play amenities include a softball field, football and soccer field, basketball and volleyball courts, a large playground, trails, and, to our knowledge, the U.S. Army's only nature/environmental education building.

There are numerous other group picnic areas located around this large fort, but the user-beckoning design of this community park means most of the army units want to reserve this one rather than the other areas. If land were available here, the addition of four or five sizable theme pods would solve most of the site's scheduling problems. If you're interested in military recreation, you might wish to visit Fort Campbell if you find yourself in the upper South. For those of you in the far West, Fort Lewis is also worth a visit.

Here's a digression from planning military facilities you may want to think about a bit. In the summer of 1993, we had the opportunity to visit Fort Hood in central Texas, the nation's largest military base. There, we had the chance to review and critique extensive outdoor recreation areas and facilities developed in recent years. It seems the three-star general responsible for the fort during those years was a big backer of recreation facilities and programs for his troops—a situation, unfortunately, not always true. At any rate, this general was also quite adept at finding extra dollars in Washington. He would "find" the money and then buy shelters and other facilities and then tell his recreation staff they had two weeks to figure out how to integrate the new goodies into the existing area. Now this approach obviously bypasses a sound planning process and some possible environmental concerns. It's also true that if the staff were better trained in planning and design, they would likely make fewer mistakes. However, actually doing something for people is, in our view, far more desirable than writing thick "how-to" manuals and spending seven years planning and designing something on paper and then doing absolutely nothing. If you're wondering what in the world we're talking about, there seems to be a disturbing—

and growing—trend in many public agencies (the Forest Service's response to the ADA is a good example) to expend major amounts of energy planning and talking about planning for change and then putting minuscule, or no, efforts into implementing the fruits of all this planning. Planning parks for people is professional when it precedes developing parks for people; planning parks for people as a stand-alone exercise is an easy way to look busy without having to make any tough decisions or do any real work!

Native-American Recreation

There are 500 Native-American tribes or confederations of tribes all across North America. Two-thirds of these are located in Alaska and California. Some have extensive land holdings of 500,000 acres and more, while other tribes have little or no land. Some tribes live on reservations while others do not. Their land ownership patterns are similar, in many respects to those of public recreation agencies in that there is no consistent pattern followed.

The Bureau of Indian Affairs (BIA) has technical responsibilities on most tribal lands but some tribes are self-governed with resource staffs of their own. Some of the tribes without self-governance also have staffs of their own. From what we've learned in recent times, about 200 tribes are involved in outdoor recreation planning, design, administration and programming as we write this chapter; others are gearing up to begin involvement. Our guess is another large contingent of tribes will start to think about and get involved in recreation in the next several years. There are few academically trained recreation professionals either at the BIA level or on tribal lands. Several federal agencies—the U.S. Corps of Engineers, the Forest Service, the National Resources Conservation Service, the USDA Extension Service, the National Park Service, the Bureau of Land Management, and others—have offered limited recreation help to tribal managers who request it. (In our view, the help these agencies are capable of providing, at least with respect to planning, design and management for recreation, is often just as well done without anyway.) Generally, the tribal recreation managers and staff we've met are enthusiastic about their work and, unlike some bureaucrats we know, want to provide parks for people.

In our view, recreation professionals, faculty and students need to be more aware of the challenges and opportunities associated with Native-American recreation. Academically speaking, curricula, particularly those with tourism components, would do well to consider adding course content geared to the particular, and at times unique, needs of tribal recreation. Some Native-American parks are quite profitable (often because of casinos) and extensive. In some (unfortunate) respects, many are similar to county, state, and federal parks: Some were built too small for prudent management and visitor protection; because of poor planning and design, many appear worn out or overused; on-site administration is lacking in some; most do not have proper zoning of use areas; others don't speak to the need for fun programming; and some attract only the good ol' boys, vandals, and rowdies.

In other respects, Native-American parks have unique characteristics. A few tribes, for example, have parks reserved for exclusive tribal or other Native-American use. Other tribes may have this exclusive type of use in some areas and open other sites to the general public. What are the special or unique design needs of each of these types of areas? We suspect, with the exception of certain administrative challenges centered on controlling access, the professional needs of Native American–administered areas are much the same as those for other parks, at least from planning and design perspectives.

Native-American recreation begins to depart from the norm of other outdoor recreation developments when we consider some of the types of special facilities you may find on tribal lands coupled together with the kinds of amenities found in typical public agencies. On tribal lands, you may expect to find casinos, large powwow areas, active attractions such as water slides and wave pools, and extensive cultural facilities. Some of these may be found as single attractions, while other areas may have two developments in combination, and other sites may support three or more of the types of recreation opportunities noted above. The planning and design concerns raised in this and other chapters relative to trails, day use, group facilities, family camps, wrangler's camps, programming, and simple zoning of use areas apply to Native-American areas as well as to the contexts in which the points were originally made; here, we want to focus on some aspects of planning, design, and administration unique to the challenges found in Native-American parks.

Let's start by considering some of the characteristics of a "typical" Native-American park (although, as with parks managed by other agencies, site-specific conditions play a large role in determining what you can and can't do developmentally). Our typical area is remote. It is 10 miles from a small town and 75 miles from a major western city. The state highway through Native-American lands is adequate and safe for current and future needs. The nearest connection to an interstate highway is 45 miles away. The main recreation attraction is a large federal reservoir that provides excellent boating and fishing. The area, while near mountains, is in a low valley warm enough for use 10 or 11 months each year.

The tribal council wants a casino perhaps combined with a hotel/motel and adequate food service to cover both needs. The council also wants a public campground located near the lake, as well as a housing zone for seasonal employees who will work in the total complex. Figure 5.47 shows a starting point relationship diagram among the various facilities. There are, of course, a host of possible variations of this general theme, based in part on considerations such as available funds, site conditions, and tribal council agendas. For example, the hotel/motel complex could be part of the casino structure. This portion of the development could be tied physically and thematically to the lake or located inland. One given is the location of the campground; to be most successful, it should be located near the lake. The employee housing zone should be *apart from* the other features (and visually screened from them) to provide privacy for the off-duty employees. Dorms, small

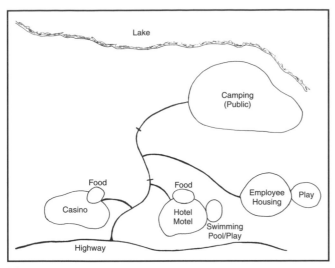

Figure 5.47

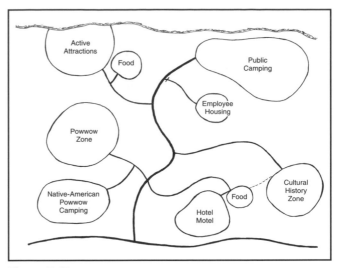

Figure 5.49

cabins, trailers, or other forms of efficient and inexpensive housing can be used here.

One of the greatest challenges for the tribal council and their planners will be to plan for the ultimate maximum expected use of the area. Will the area shown in Figure 5.47 be expanded to include an active attraction zone (e.g., water park, carnival-type rides), powwow area (if so, what size and how should it be administered?), and a cultural history zone? Figures 5.48 and 5.49 show two potential solutions to these questions. Figure 5.49 (originally shown as Figure 5.1), which has a sizable powwow zone and other attractions but does not have a casino, shows another possible alternative. You could literally fill pages with possible options to this planning challenge, contingent upon tribal needs, site conditions, target markets, and other factors.

The master planning problem the tribal council faces is—in our view—the greatest park planning problem worldwide. Far too often, we plan and build a small campground or picnic area and then, over the years, enlarge or expand it, expand it again, and then expand it some more until almost nothing functions as it should; to draw an analogy from Harriet Beecher

Stowe's *Uncle Tom's Cabin,* most of our areas, like Topsy, "jest growed." Our advice on planning is to think initially about long-term development. Start by assuming you will expand (and this holds true for all sorts of areas) and plan for your ultimate development when you begin to build. You may never build out to your original expectations; you may also alter your original plans. But don't get caught repeating the mistake most of us have made in the past of planning and building an area and waiting until later to start to think about how to expand it. Without being psychic, you should know where you are heading and anticipate your final destination with a route map (a master plan), even if it is a bit crude at this stage.

Getting back to concerns specific to Native-American parks, consider the relationship diagram in Figure 5.50. The powwow area, whether located as an isolated feature or with other aspects of the area such as a cultural history site or campground, calls for zoning within the overall powwow portion of the site. Public parking, entrance control, official and entertainer parking, an assembly area, play zone with playground equipment, volleyball courts and other adult play amenities, a group picnic area, sales and food zone, nearby camping (with toilet and shower facilities) for food and sales people, and sanitary facilities for day users all complement and surround the bleachers and stage areas. We've added a high impact zone for a nonpublic camping area open only to Native Americans. The tribal council would decide whether such an area should be part of the master plan.

Several decisions would also have to be made about the public camping zone (see Chapters Seven and Eight). As Figure 5.51 suggests, a Native-American public campground would involve family camping, group camping (particularly if the tribal council wanted to beckon camping clubs to the casino or Native Americans to powwows), a special amenity area exclusively for campers, and possibly a campground with seasonal sites. Figure 5.52 shows an expanded version of the possible camping areas.

The amenity zone might include a beach, bathhouse, concession/snack structure, recreation building, several sand

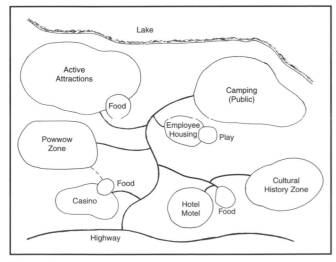

Figure 5.48

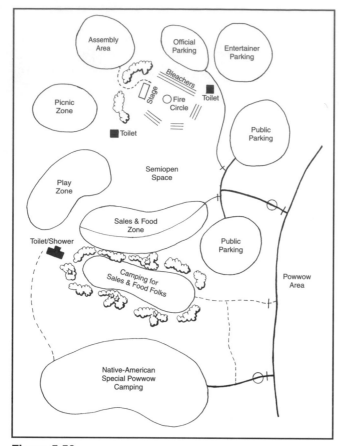

Figure 5.50

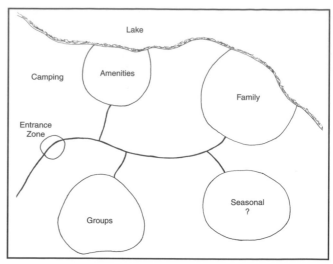

Figure 5.52

volleyball courts, multipurpose play court, shelter with equipment checkout capability, toilet structure, skills area, playground, fenced horseshoe pits, boccie ball and shuffleboard areas, hike 'n bike trails, campfire theater, and parking adequate for the expected use. Figure 5.53 shows one solution to this design challenge. Note how the amenity area is zoned so you could bring in portable tables and superimpose (on a limited basis) group day use on the site. Notice, too, how this could be accomplished without users having to move through any of the camping zones to reach the amenity area.

The family campground loops would all be water oriented and designed so users would move to both the lakeshore

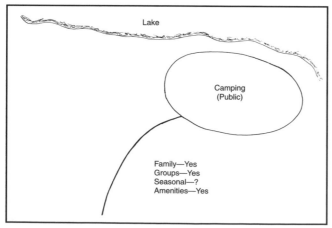

Figure 5.51

and toilet/shower structures on reinforced surfaces (roads and trails). This demonstrates the basic principle of design psychology of channeling people along routes you need them to follow in order to maintain the integrity of the environment and avoid the appearance of overuse. The loops could also be constructed in phases as the demand for use increased over a period of years. The first phase of development should include a boat ramp for exclusive use by individuals staying on the campground.

The group-use area, highlighted in Figure 5.54, has three to six group pods capable of supporting groups of various sizes. Each of these pods is oriented to one or both of the two toilet or toilet/shower structures indicated on the figure. Each pod should contain some basic amenities, such as a small playground, two horseshoe pits, a shelter with portable tables, a campfire circle, and sand volleyball court. These pods are designed so they could be used as overflow areas for the family campground if needed (assuming they weren't rented for group use).

Figure 5.55 shows the seasonal camp loops. Because we do not advise mixing seasonal and family camping in the same zone, the seasonal area could be zoned either where we've shown it or near the entrance where the group area is located in this figure. Seasonal sites can occupy the least desirable portion of your land base (away from the water attraction). The road into the seasonal area could be a half-mile or more in length to separate the seasonal area from other parts of the campground. User access could be provided through the use of a card-activated electronic gate, which would reduce the need for on-site administrative personnel. The seasonal area should have a collection of amenities similar to those described for the group-use zone. This set of support areas and facilities should be zoned at the end of the camping loops rather than between two loops to minimize the impact associated with pedestrian travel to and from the zone.

Since we still have lots to learn about special facilities for Native-American parks, we expect some of the suggestions we've made here will turn out to be additions to our extensive collection of design errors. It seems to us, how-

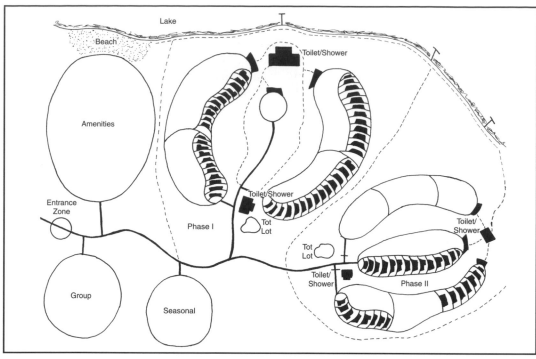

Figure 5.53

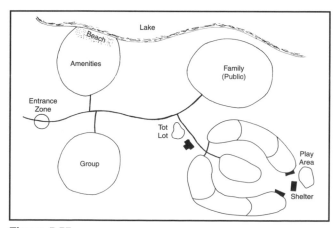

Figure 5.54

Figure 5.55

ever, many of the basic principles of design that work for other types of recreation areas hold true on tribal projects as well. Certainly one basic axiom of design applies: Find out how the folks who you want to use the area function and how the site managers will administer the area. With this knowledge and a master plan to guide phased development, you won't stray too far from a good overall design; certainly you'll be two steps ahead of the rascals responsible for most of the recreation areas we currently have spread across the country like a bad case of chicken pox.

Special-Use Areas: An Exercise

The problems at the end of the previous chapters have been design oriented. You've been given a set of guidelines and asked to plan a recreation area to meet a specified use. For a change of pace, this exercise takes a somewhat different approach. This chapter has considered the development of recreation areas for special uses. Since the spectrum of "special uses" entails a broader range of groups than those discussed here, we'll leave it to you to determine the type of group and thus the type of area for whom you're planning. Your plan should consist of several steps. First, identify a special-use group in your area in need of a recreation facility. To do this, you need to consider what types of recreation opportunities already exist within reasonable proximity to your location. (*Hint:* What is "reasonable?") Avoid duplicating services; your challenge is to meet a currently unfulfilled need.

Once you've determined that the need for a particular type of use area exists, your second task is to specify how you would go about getting the information necessary to make planning decisions, i.e., what do the users want in the area? The questions for you to address are: How would you collect the information? Would you meet with individuals, use a questionnaire, meet with the special-interest group, or hold a public meeting? You should be able to justify your approach.

A parallel task you need to tackle in addition to assessing user needs is considering potential resources for the development of the area. You'll need physical resources in the form of a land base suitable for the area, and fiscal resources in the form of development funds. Finally, after taking needs and resources into consideration, you should develop two or preferably three alternative concept plans for the area.

Here's a final note to consider before you approach this as just another sterile textbook exercise: Do it. We strongly believe in applying information, in receiving firsthand, real-world experience, and in getting recreation facilities built. Make this assignment a class exercise. Find a real user group with a need, and a local agency or corporation willing to co-operate with you and make something happen. You don't need a lot of funding or a large piece of land; a passive sitting area at a retirement home can be a real design challenge if you're conscientious about meeting user needs. You may be surprised how much you can learn by doing. You may also be surprised at how challenging it can be to translate a plan into a reality. We never claimed design was easy, just enjoyable and rewarding. Try it and see for yourself.

Chapter Six

Getting Serious About Play Areas

Here we go again! Figures 6.1 through 6.6 introduce Chapter Six: Getting Serious About Play Areas. What do you see in the six photos? Are there safety problems, design problems, problems of omission, indications of "we don't care" attitudes on the part of park providers, good ideas or designs . . . ?

Some theorists have suggested play is the "business" of children. It would seem that a bigger problem for the recreation professional is the tendency for these roles to be reversed in too many adults who make business their play. We'll leave this concern for the leisure educator, however, and confine the discussion in this chapter to another serious aspect of play: design of areas and facilities devoted to the pursuit of fun. We'll consider a variety of types of play areas in the next few pages, some of which you may be surprised to find. We'll also discuss play areas for adults as well as for children.

Figure 6.1

Figure 6.2

Figure 6.3

Figure 6.4

Figure 6.5

Figure 6.6

There are excellent resources, including video- and audiotapes, and textbooks available to serve as guides for outdoor recreation professionals interested in developing playscapes. Our intent in this brief chapter on play areas is to introduce the when, where, how, and why of playground design, as well as speak to safety concerns and basic concepts associated with play for students and professionals who may not have encountered these ideas previously. As with other types of park facilities discussed throughout this text, the planning, design, and development of playgrounds are (or should be) tied closely to the development and programming of other use zones within the overall recreation complex.

Let's start with the why of playgrounds, at least in the context of outdoor recreation areas. Experience tells us natural resource organizations across North America appear to be quite reluctant to focus serious effort on the development of play areas in their so-called family picnic areas and campgrounds. This doesn't mean you won't find play equipment sprinkled throughout some, though not all, of these areas; you will. As is the case with trails, however, installing pieces of play equipment is one thing; developing well-thought-out play areas integrated into the total design picture, coupled with a commitment to providing fun activities for children, youth, teens, adults and senior citizens is quite another—a missing component of most resource areas.

This lack of attention to play areas and program opportunities usually translates into several results: a high proportion of use of these areas by rowdies and good ol' boys rather than families; young children who do join their parents become bored quickly (and therefore prone to depreciative behavior); a general absence of teens (at least accompanying their parents); and extensive vandalism. Once during a workshop, a recreation director for the Spokane tribe told us, "The play equipment is awfully expensive, but we had extensive vandalism in our picnic areas until we added play areas and equipment, and then it stopped." In our view, this lack of attention to the fun aspects of outdoor recreation has been one of the primary factors leading to the decline of camping in the eastern United States and eastern Canada over the past decade or so. Sadly, most natural resource practitioners don't realize (or, in some instances, don't seem to care) that neglecting fun opportunities discourages families from using their areas. We'll develop this theme throughout the text.

Since most people (grown-ups, anyway) tend to think of play in terms of youngsters, let's start our discussion about design by thinking about the traditional playground. At several points in this book, we've tried to stress the dual responsibility recreation professionals have: the need to develop and maintain spaces which function for people and the need to protect the environment. Nowhere is this need more evident, and perhaps more frequently forgotten, than in play areas. Consider for a moment the area shown in Figure 6.7. The designer, a friend of ours, was working with a series of knowns.

He knew, for example, children were going to use the play equipment he provided. He knew he wanted to maintain a stand of grass in the area surrounding the play space. He

Figure 6.7

knew the average annual rainfall in Boulder, Colorado, the location of this playground, was only 14 inches per year—not enough to grow grass on land subject to the impact associated with play. He knew, therefore, that he had to recognize and reinforce the area of impact, which he did. As a result of this careful planning, the children and the grass both thrived.

The twist in our story is this: The designer of the Boulder playground wasn't a recreation professional at all. He worked in a factory, the children were his, and the play space was his family's backyard.

The play space shown in Figure 6.8, however, is in a public park, it does suffer from a lack of attention to people and environmental needs, and was designed by a "professional." The planner responsible for the area shown in Figure 6.8 had access to the same set of knowns available to our friend in Boulder, yet failed to attend to the potential problems associated with the intensive use inherent in a play area and likely blamed its later appearance on users!

It may seem as if our constant nagging about impact is akin to beating a dead horse, but you should consider ways to reduce impact associated with play areas as well as how to make play spaces functional from the standpoint of people. In fact, an excellent starting point for designing play areas and facilities is the topic of function.

Figure 6.8

The Question of Purpose

As with other types of recreational developments, play areas should be considered from the basic perspective of *why*. Why is the area designed as it is and what is the function to be served? Play areas can be, although they don't have to be, planned for a primary use. In other words, provision of a play space may be the main reason for the development of a given resource base. If this is the case, one set of design questions and considerations needs to be addressed. In some instances, however, play areas may serve a secondary use. Perhaps the best example of this is the development of play space as a support area. Consider the construction of play equipment at fast-food restaurants. Here play is used to draw people into the eating establishment. This same logic is often ignored in parks where play areas could be developed to support other types of recreation facilities.

Family-oriented recreation areas like picnic sites and campgrounds can be enhanced for all family members if planners give careful consideration to play areas in a supportive role. Drive-in theater operators recognize this secondary function when they provide space and apparatus for children to use during parent-oriented movies. However, we frequently see parks where this isn't considered, where adult play spaces are often designed without attention to the needs of children. What is there, for example, for a six-year-old to do at a soft-ball complex during adult league play? We don't advocate putting a swing set in the third base coach's box, but we do suggest that you consider zoning use areas with the relationship between areas for adults and children in mind. If a play space is to serve a secondary function, design questions and considerations may not be exactly the same as those for play spaces intended as primary-use areas.

Another concern you'll need to address is the question of *who*. Play areas and equipment for younger children need to be designed differently than those for older children. Teenagers have a different degree of motor control than six-year-olds. Levels of imagination also change as children mature, and, more obviously, children grow as they age. Therefore the age range for which you develop a play area means considering safety, creativity and scale in design. Too often, we limit our concept of play to children. All of us play, but in varying degrees and in different ways. Recreation professionals often react to the recognized need for children's play by providing children's play equipment. We should take the next step, however, and create opportunities for players of all ages by being proactive: A bench in a city park provides a place for adults to sit. A bench in a city park with an adjacent checkerboard table provides a place for adults to play.

In our numerous workshops and lectures on wildland park design, programming and administration, we touch on providing safe tot lots within a broader context of providing amenities for all sorts of family-beckoning programs and facilities. (We'll cover this broader context in considerable detail later in the programming chapter.) During these training sessions, we tend to be quite outspoken about the importance of programming in beckoning family groups to campgrounds and picnic areas. Most of the people who attend these sessions tend to be natural resource management types (as a group, folks who are, at best, indifferent toward recreation programs and program facilities as we suggested above). Their perspective means most of our preaching about programming falls on deaf ears. On occasion, however, a small percentage of our audience will take our comments to heart, return to their parks or management areas, and try to add some amenities to beckon family groups by enhancing program and play opportunities. This is particularly true if we have private campground owners in our group.

This brings up a cautionary note: What often happens is these converts to fun in the out-of-doors think they can implement our recommendations by simply sprinkling a few pieces of play equipment designed for young children around their area, sitting back, and waiting for the laudatory comments from the newly attracted hoards of families who have simply been waiting for a teeter-totter to be installed before swearing their undying fealty to the area and its forward-thinking manager. Not!

Figure 6.9 (also shown as Figure 6.4) illustrates the negative result of this approach. With no recreation programs or other play opportunities (such as play courts, ball fields, or beach volleyball) for the teenagers who do visit these areas, they tend to gather at whatever playscape is provided—in our example, the play equipment meant for much younger children. This can cause all sorts of social and safety problems (we've seen teens taunting younger children to try dangerous stunts on slides and simply taking over the equipment from smaller kids). The moral here is to understand the consequences of your design decisions; if you can't—or philosophically won't—support play opportunities for youth and adults of all ages, we think you're better off not adding any amenities at all. You'll do more harm than good.

A Mistake

The play area we'll discuss as an example of flawed design is truly a comedy of errors. In fact, the mistake serves to illustrate two problems, for once the initial difficulty was recognized, the "solution" compounded the original problem. Figure 6.10 shows the design of a playground complex built in

Figure 6.9

central Pennsylvania. As indicated in the drawing, the original plan primarily provided a number of pieces of traditional or conventional play equipment spread over a roughly rectangular area. If you're beginning to get a "feel" for design and for the need to think in terms of total concept planning, you should recognize one problem immediately. The play area in Figure 6.10 is rather sterile. There is little or no continuity in the relationship of one piece of apparatus to another. Thus the opportunity for creative play tends to be discouraged. Given the imaginative abilities of children, however, let's assume they can outsmart the planner and create enjoyable play scenarios here.

From the standpoint of the user, the playground is the proverbial accident waiting to happen. Note where the two sets of swings are located. In theory, it is a good idea to tuck equipment with motion involved into corners of play space because of the potential for collisions with passersby. However, one entrance to the playground is located so the circulation pattern into the area forces users to cross dangerously close to the larger set of swings. If we wanted to be sarcastic, we'd suggest that children in the swings "bail out" in the direction opposite the playground entrance if they anticipate a collision with a pedestrian. However, this probably wouldn't work too well since both sets of swings are quite near the fence surrounding the playground. Did we mention the fence just happens to be topped with barbed wire? Believe it or not, it is.

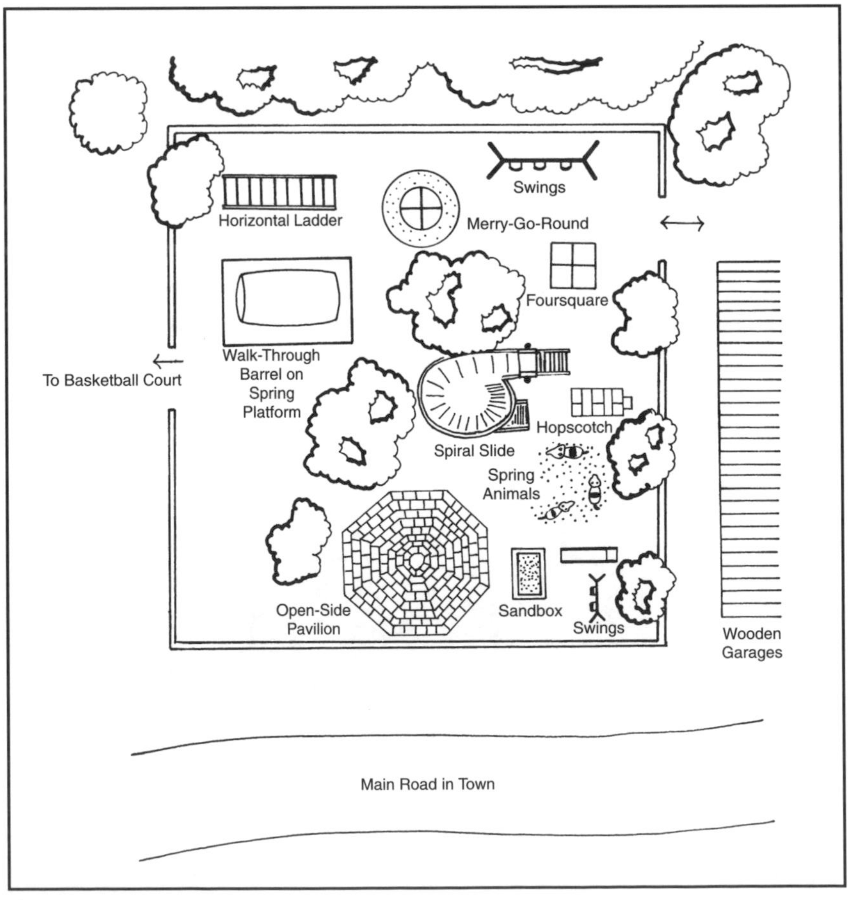

As if user safety weren't enough of a problem, the agency responsible for this playground has to contend with a resource concern as well. As we suggested in Chapter Two, planners often fail to borrow expertise from disciplines related to recreation. In this case, the forgotten element was soils information. The playground was built on soil with a heavy clay content. Using the area (in fact, just building the site) compacts the soil, and the point was soon reached where moisture was not being absorbed into the ground. Since, during the planning and construction phases, no one provided for drainage, like center crowning the area, water began to pool after every rain. The plot—and the mud—now thickens, for someone eventually realized that water standing in a playground was a problem in need of a solution.

The solution? Pave the playground. No more standing water? Right. No more hassles with compacted soil? Right. No more concerns? Wrong. Let's look at the problems created by this solution: First, by paving over the entire area planners sealed the fate of the trees, though chances are, unless the trees were young, vigorous, deep-rooted species, the impact from play would have killed them eventually anyway since they weren't protected from impact in the initial design. However, paving over the entire root system cut off their supply of water and air, condemned them to an early death, and removed the only source of shade in the playground.

Second, perhaps in an attempt to seek revenge, the trees struck back, creating costly short- and long-term maintenance headaches. Soon after the playground was surfaced, root systems began to break through the asphalt, creating mounds and humps in the pavement. As trees began to die, dead limbs also became a hazard, and ultimately there was the costly process of removing entire trees. This tended to leave rather obvious holes in the pavement. It really doesn't pay to mess around with Mother Nature.

Third, in addition to destroying the resource base, paving created a new hazard for children using the area. Underneath existing play equipment, it increased the potential for serious injuries severalfold. The spiral slide in the center of the playground, for example, was over 15-feet high. If a child fell from this height onto natural ground, or onto a padded surface, the chances of sustaining a serious injury would be high. Falling from this height to a paved surface would make the odds even higher.

Fourth, putting an asphalt covering on the playground created another potential hazard where none had existed before. Hard surfaces permit you to paint permanent lines for courts and games, and a foursquare court was added after the playground was surfaced (Figure 6.10). We applaud the attempt to create new program opportunities, but balls roll under the swing set if the player fails to catch them because of the placement of the court. Since foursquare is

Figure 6.10

aimed at very young children (remember the motor development issue mentioned earlier), the chance of missing a catch is considerable. Younger children are also the least likely to be conscious of potential hazards, so the problem is compounded further.

As with the mistakes discussed in previous chapters, the real tragedy associated with the playground problem described above is simple error. It doesn't require a technical degree to question the wisdom of placing a swing set next to a barbed wire fence. You don't need 20 years of experience to understand why water won't drain from a concave surface. All you need in order to plan safe and environmentally sound areas is common sense, an open mind, a willingness to pay attention to detail, and some knowledge of a few facts pertinent to the type of area being considered. If you've never thought much about the basic considerations necessary for developing play spaces, the following section should provide you with a few starting points.

Some Basic Considerations

Types of Play Equipment and Their Interrelationships. In an earlier chapter, we introduced the concept of relationship diagrams because area interrelationships must be considered relative to user circulation. While circulation is an important aspect of how play areas fit together, two other concerns need to be raised as well. First, play spaces should provide users, especially children, the opportunity to *create creativity*. Fantasy is an important element of play, and play areas can either encourage or discourage it, so pieces of play apparatus should relate to each other in a fluid rather than in a static sense. In other words, the positioning of play equipment should encourage flow throughout the play space. As with other types of areas, play-space planning can benefit by input from potential users. Successful playgrounds have been developed by giving children scale models of play equipment and asking them to position the pieces as they would like to see them installed. Remember, however, if you ask children for design help they won't think of safety requirements.

A second consideration of equipment relationships should be balanced against the need for creativity. In play areas for children, *safety* is a primary concern, and to balance this need with convenience and creativity you need to consider the various types of play equipment. Generally speaking, there are three types available for children: *stationary, manipulated* and *motion*.

Stationary play equipment includes apparatus and environmental features like climbers, horizontal ladders, balance beams, tunnels, hills, and pathways. With this type of play opportunity, the child interacts with the structure or equipment. The play experience doesn't require or rely on any motion of the apparatus. Playground design should encourage movement among stationary features. For example, a tunnel might connect a horizontal ladder with a hill, as in Figure 6.11. Since stationary equipment by itself is static, play movements depend on the child and on the way the pieces relate to one another. The primary safety consideration for

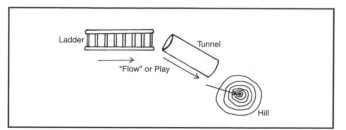

Figure 6.11

stationary play apparatus is how the child will move on and through the environment.

Manipulated equipment, not surprisingly, means wagons, tricycles, bicycles, scooters, balls, toys and the like. Because of the potential for vandalism and theft, most play areas will normally not provide manipulated equipment as such. This should not, however, imply that children don't need it since this type of play aids in developing fine motor skills. Sharing toys and similar manipulated equipment with other children may also help to generate a sense of cooperation and other social skills.

Planners developing a play area should compromise between offering opportunities for manipulative play and avoiding equipment damage or loss. This can be accomplished by designating spaces exclusively for manipulated equipment. The old playground standby, the sandbox, serves as an excellent example of this type of environment. Interestingly, many of the newer "creative play" developments seem to be built without sandboxes, raising a question about playground planning and design: Have children passed an evolutionary turning point beyond which they no longer need the simple pleasures of traditional playgrounds? Perhaps, just perhaps, the proliferation of expensive, modern playgrounds could be partly a function of the need some park professionals have to keep up with the Joneses. In other words, if our neighboring city builds a creative playground, will we be viewed as non-progressive if we don't follow suit? It is important to develop new and exciting play opportunities for children. However, remember that playgrounds are there for youngsters to enjoy; they aren't vehicles to enhance our professional reputations.

As is so often the case, the appropriate planning response to this question would seem to be a compromise. We don't know of any rules preventing you from mixing traditional and creative play apparatus in the same playground. You should provide opportunities for all types of play experiences, but for some types of manipulated equipment like tricycles, the best design is no design at all.

Motion equipment includes play apparatus which a child moves or rides on. Swings, merry-go-rounds, slides, and spring-mounted balancing boards and animals are examples of this. In terms of safety considerations, these types of apparatus require the most conscientious planning for two reasons. First, the child and the equipment both may be in motion (with the exception of slides), so the potential for injury increases. Second, the possibility exists for motion equipment to injure a child who does not interact with it. A neutral zone can solve these problems by defining the area devoted to motion equipment. Traffic patterns into the play area and among various pieces of motion equipment should be developed outside of these defined zones.

Manufacturers of play equipment should provide you with safety standards that tell you how much neutral space is required around each piece of equipment. Standards for neutral space, however, will not tell you how children move in and among apparatus. Traffic flow depends on how your design connects each piece of play apparatus to others and where your entry/exit points are, so this aspect must be considered in the planning stage of playground development. If, for example, you installed a swing set with a recommended amount of neutral space directly in front of the entrance to a playground, you'd be asking for an accident.

Before moving on to specific types of safety measures you can take when building playgrounds, consider one more general point about design. Integrating safety features into play facilities shouldn't be equated with building sterile environments. Learn to think of play areas as miniature adventure worlds. Rather than merely installing several pieces of play equipment, try to create a complete experience in which, as the saying goes, the whole is greater than the sum of its parts. Also build on a scale appropriate for the age group for whom you're planning. Use changes in elevation. Mix openings and enclosures. Suggest alternative routes (up and down as well as forward or sideways). Be creative. Let the child in you be the parent to your design.

Creating Play Environments. It's unfortunate to start a new section of this chapter on a pessimistic note, but the issue of playground surfacing materials refuses to go away. When trying to decide on an appropriate one, you need to consider *safety, wearability,* and *cost*. Natural turf is somewhat resilient, at least compared to asphalt, and is certainly inexpensive, but it doesn't hold up well under impact. In fact, it can become quite hard as extended use compacts it, so you need to consider alternatives.

When balancing safety, wearability, and cost factors, you should always put safety first, and there are some general guides to follow when you assess surfacing needs. As a rule of thumb, some type of safety surfacing should be used under apparatus where children are elevated to a height greater than their own, and areas receiving constant impact need durable surfaces. For example, the perimeter of merry-go-rounds, the bases of slides (front and rear), and the areas beneath swings need firm but cushioned surfaces. These kinds of areas should also provide good footing surfaces. Rubberized mats meet our criteria for safety and durability, but are extremely costly. Shredded tires are cheaper, but individual pieces tend to spread out, leaving piles in some places and exposed ground in others. Reinforced surfaces are durable and fairly cost-effective, but are too dangerous under elevated apparatus. If you're wondering what the point is, it's this: There is no good surfacing material, to our knowledge, capable of meeting all of the criteria outlined above. Sand surfacing or a 50-50 mixture of sand and sawdust are two good alternatives; pea gravel is another. We stress again the need to put safety first. If you can't afford to buy a cushioned surface to put beneath a piece

of equipment you know needs one, you should consider an alternative type of apparatus.

Putting aside the issue of surfacing material, there are other aspects of design and construction you should consider in the interest of creating safe play environments. Consider Figure 6.12 (originally shown as Figure 6.2). Placement of play equipment (in this case teeter-totters, which we recommend be eliminated from your playscapes due to their history of causing injury) needs to consider existing features capable of creating hazardous conditions. The diagonal line in the foreground of the picture is a metal guy wire. Any questions?

Figure 6.12

Although it seems almost unnecessary to say, you should avoid sharp edges on and around play equipment. Most manufacturers of play apparatus will "design out" potentially sharp corners and surfaces before the equipment reaches the playground; however, you should always check before you buy. Some potential locations for sharp edges do not involve equipment, either, and these are the sites you should check during construction. If, for example, you build a railroad tie border or use ties to create a series of steps, you should be sure the edges are beveled as in Figure 6.13. This is especially critical at the ends of ties where front, top, and side surfaces come together to form a point as in Figure 6.14. However, all exposed edges where two surfaces join should be beveled for maximum safety.

Other safety features can be designed into play areas as well. You can avoid bolt protrusions by countersinking as shown in Figure 6.15. Be sure to fill over the countersunk bolt with caulk to prevent water damage. Remember, also, to think ahead in your design as well—nails hammered flush with a wooden surface will eventually work loose and become exposed, and should be countersunk also (see Figure

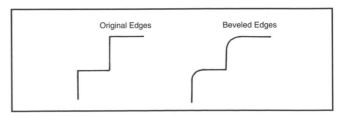

Figure 6.13

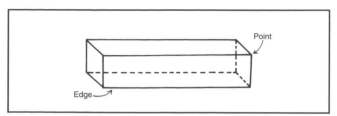

Figure 6.14

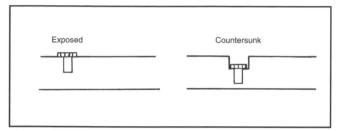

Figure 6.15

6.16, originally shown as Figure 6.6). If you use chains on swings or climbing equipment, make sure the links are fused to adjacent links rather than wrapped together. It may even be advisable to encase chains in metal tubes to avoid the possibility of pinching. Flat metal surfaces can grow extremely hot when exposed to sunlight, and fiberglass or other soft surfaces can circumvent this problem. If you inherit metal equipment, it is possible to retrofit for safety as demonstrated by the wooden ramada built for shade over a slide in a Corps of Engineers campground in California (Figure 6.17; ask yourself, though, is the height of this slide a safety hazard?). Most importantly, remember that equipment wears out. Periodic checks for wear and tear, particularly at stress points, are a necessity. Another necessity, particularly given how quickly things change in the workplace, is to be sure playground safety is an integral part of your in-service training, continuing education or professional development efforts (Figure 6.18, originally shown as Figure 6.1; here a group of professionals study features of play equipment at a workshop in Illinois while one of the authors [in dark glasses] ponders either where all the moose went or how far is up).

As we mentioned at the beginning of this chapter, there are sources of information readily available to help you make informed decisions about safety issues concerning play equipment. The Consumer Product Safety Commission, for example, can suggest strategies such as the following for playgrounds and play equipment (they can be reached at 800-638-2772):

- Providing continuous handrails over the full length of the access on both sides of stairwells, regardless of their height.
- At the entrance to a slide, there should be a means to channel a user into a sitting position, such as a guardrail, hood, or other device that does not encourage climbing.
- Stairs on a ladder should be close enough together for children to negotiate, but be spaced far enough apart to keep them from becoming trapped.
- Rung ladders and climbing components, such as nets, arch climbers, and tire climbers, should not be used as a sole means of access.
- Climbing equipment should be outside the play structure so a child does not fall onto anything but the softer playground surface.

Figure 6.17

Figure 6.16

Figure 6.18

- Allow at least six feet of clearance in all directions around equipment.
- Swing structures should be located away from other structures and fenced in, to prevent children from running into the path of a moving swing.
- Guardrails or protective barriers should be used to prevent falls off elevated platforms.

The issue of building versus buying playground equipment is a difficult one. In many instances, it may be less costly to construct certain types of equipment than it is to purchase it. The problem with building apparatus in-house is mainly one of legal liability. Given the prevalence of lawsuits over playground injuries, we recommend you buy equipment from a reputable manufacturer. Company representatives, like the one shown in Figure 6.19, will help you select and install play equipment within your budget and can also help with your in-service education.

Generally, play equipment manufacturers do a good job with construction and design safety. This does not guarantee, however, that purchased equipment will always meet the play needs of children. Sometimes, it seems the apparatus chosen for a playground depends more on the selling ability of the manufacturer's representative than on the needs of the park or the children, so make sure you have a good idea of your design and management goals before you begin the process of bidding and selecting a manufacturer.

Figure 6.20 (originally shown as Figure 6.3) shows a likely outcome of failing to provide playscapes and opportunities in resource-based areas. Don't fall into the trap of thinking people visiting wildland parks won't want to engage in recreation; they will. And, if you don't design areas to accommodate their desires, they will find ways to play in spite of you. The trouble is, their methods can often be potentially harmful to the environment and, more importantly, hazardous to themselves. *Note:* The extended family playing softball inside of a U.S. Forest Service campground in the Dixie National Forest is doing so on a campground road.

Creating an enjoyable play experience is in part a function of the kinds of equipment you buy, but the primary ingredient for a successful playground is design, which should attend to several factors. The first consideration is not to plan in a vacuum. Think about uses of surrounding areas. The relationship (for circulation)

Figure 6.19

between a picnic area and a playground shouldn't be the same as the connection between a playground and campsites. Campsites, for the sake of campers, need to be screened from adjacent uses. Picnickers may prefer to have a direct and easily accessible link between the playground and their table so they can keep an eye on their children.

We've discussed the use of the pod concept in relation to campsites in off-road vehicle areas and picnic sites. This also applies to playgrounds in two respects. First, a playground may be considered as one type of pod in a larger development that can relate to others in different ways, depending on its purpose. Second, you can view a playground as a collection of pods with different uses. One section within a playground might be devoted to gross motor skills, another for passive play, a third for cooperative and/or competitive play, and another for individual use. The key is to understand the needs of your users and plan for them.

Children aren't the only users you need to think about when designing play areas. Particularly when you provide play equipment for younger ones, you should understand that adults may accompany them. If a play area is comfortable for adults (e.g., well-formed benches with shade as opposed to a torture rack placed in the sun), you may find more youngsters using the equipment. Including some types of adult-play facilities such as tennis courts may also increase the use of both the playground and adult area. Just remember to place them near enough together for parents to watch their children and play at the same time. It's difficult to generalize too much about support facilities for playgrounds since areas vary so widely with respect to type and location. Children should have access to drinking water and toilet facilities, but it's pointless to install these in a neighborhood tot lot where none of the users will be more than a block from home or a friend's house. As usual, common sense is an excellent guide.

Beaches are another type of use zone to keep in mind when locating play equipment. Our basic reasoning here deals with attraction: People use beaches. Locating play equipment near (or in) beach zones provides activity alternatives for swimmers and nonswimmers alike. It makes sense to us to do all we can to enhance recreation experiences, and putting play opportunities where people will be anyway is one way of doing this. Here's a classic story to demonstrate this.

Figure 6.20

Once while visiting a beautiful Forest Service day-use area beach in Indiana to plan a visit during an upcoming workshop we were conducting, we suggested to the ranger with us what a perfect place this would be for a water volleyball net and standards. The beach was gently sloping, large, well-used and designated by PVC pipe buoys. His reply was more incredulous than supportive, "Why would anyone want something frivolous like that in a Forest Service area, of all places?!" We wrote the suggestion off as a lost cause and continued to plan for the workshop. Weeks later during our workshop visit to the beach, we saw a group of users—kids, teens and adults—playing water volleyball using the PVC buoy line as a divider between the two teams! When will people learn resource agencies expect beach users to study algae growth for entertainment?

One last aspect of playground design needs to be considered: *challenge*. While safety is always a primary concern, you should keep in mind that children need to be drawn to play areas and the equipment they contain. One excellent way to attract them is by challenging them with creative design and equipment. This is not the same as creating hazards. A challenge can come in the form of inviting a child to find different ways of moving through an area. Hills, tunnels, passageways, and climbing opportunities can all be used with imagination. Varied colors and forms can also stimulate vision and movement, alternating textures the tactile sense. Playgrounds should arouse as many of a child's senses as possible, in keeping with safe design. If you take an entirely businesslike approach to designing play spaces, you may defeat the purpose of the play experience.

The Americans With Disabilities Act (ADA). A friend of ours recently suggested the ADA will likely be legislated by lawsuit. The point is, no one really has too firm a purchase on the implications of the ADA for parks and recreation because the language of the act is not overly specific. There are, however, some things we know about the act worth mentioning at this point, both in general terms and as the act affects development of playscapes in particular. (Our thanks to Dr. Michael Crawford of the University of Missouri-Columbia who provided us with the following information.)

The ADA requires both accessibility and usability. Accessibility means the elimination of barriers that require efforts be undertaken to render the experience available in a meaningful way to the person with disabilities. As to usability, there are five major elements regarding ADA prohibition of discrimination based on disability. These include the following:

1. *Discriminatory Eligibility Criteria:* Places of public accommodation may not impose or apply eligibility criteria that screen out individuals with disability.
2. *Reasonable Modifications:* Places of public accommodation are required to make modifications to policies, practices or procedures to permit a person with disability to obtain the service, privilege or experience.
3. *Auxiliary Aids and Services:* Agencies or businesses must take steps necessary to assure participation, including ac-

quisition or modification of devices or equipment.
4. *Readily Achievable Barrier Removal in Existing Facilities:* Agencies or businesses must remove architectural barriers that are structural in nature in existing facilities where such removal is readily achievable.
5. *Alternative Methods:* Where measures to remove barriers are not required because an agency or business can demonstrate that they are not readily achievable, management must still make its goods, services, facilities and privileges available through "alternative methods" . . . if such methods are readily achievable. All newly constructed facilities and/or significant alterations of existing facilities must be accessible unless management can demonstrate that doing so is structurally impractical or that so doing would be disproportionate to the overall cost and scope of the project. (A disproportionate criterion has been suggested at 30 percent of total costs.) Existing facilities are only required to make structural changes that are "readily achievable"—defined to mean "easily accomplishable and able to be carried out without much difficulty or expense." This requires physical access that can be achieved without extensive restructuring or burdensome expense.

Four factors of the alternative methods are considered:

1. The nature and cost of the action needed.
2. The overall financial resources of the facility/operation.
3. The overall financial resources of the covered entity: size, number, type and location of its facilities.
4. The type of operation(s) of the covered entity and nature of fiscal relationship to the facility in question.

The determination of whether such action constitutes an undue burden will likely be made on a case-by-case basis by the courts. The limitation on "readily achievable" will fluctuate, with, for example, a higher standard being set for large businesses than for small, for large cities than small, and so on. It has been suggested that one to three percent of the facility's total worth be used to determine the undue burden criteria.

The accessible and usable standard does not require every part of every area of a facility to be accommodating. Nor does management have to provide services for persons with disabilities not available to able-bodied persons (e.g., rest rooms). Thus, if your playground has swings, climbers, and slides, you don't have to have a disabled equivalent for each; but you must provide some of them. However, you don't have to provide a spinner for children with disabilities if one doesn't exist for children without disabilities.

Public accommodations are prohibited from subjecting an individual with a disability to any of the following forms of discrimination:

1. Denying participation or benefit of an opportunity.
2. Affording participation an opportunity that is not equal to that made available to others.

3. Providing an opportunity that is different or separate unless such separation or difference is necessary to provide an individual with a disability an opportunity that is as effective as that provided to others. (If equipment design and/or safety factors preclude retrofitting of a playground's equipment then separate or parallel play stations for persons with disabilities might be considered.)

4. Providing opportunities that are not in the most integrated setting appropriate to the needs of the individual. (If an integrated option is possible at an equivalent cost then separate or parallel play stations would be precluded.)

5. Using standards or methods that perpetuate discrimination.

A few playgrounds will escape ADA requirements (e.g., small town or owner/operator day care where undue burden can be documented), some will argue for geographic/demographic stratification and site specific exemptions based upon financial exigency and undue burden arguments (e.g., public school yards, mid-size city parks and recreation departments), some will have to retrofit all existing playgrounds (e.g., state park systems, large cities), and many park systems will demolish old playgrounds rather than renovate or retrofit (convert back to open parkland).

How does ADA affect playgrounds? There are multiple problems with accessibility and usability based upon a number of factors, including the diversity of play structures, the diversity of children with disabilities, safety standards and safety problems:

I. Diversity of play structures
   A. Manufactured appliance era—freestanding iron, steel and wooden equipment for climbing, spinning, swinging and sliding. Based on the "amusement theory" of play, these structures have existed since the early 1900s.
   B. Novelty era—structures designed around a central theme such as western play, space travel or jungle animals—supposed to stimulate creative mental and social play. Introduced in the 1950s and 1960s.
   C. Modern era—modular wooden, cast aluminum and molded fiberglass, and plastic structures—interconnected play structures thought to heighten intensity and flow of play experience. Introduced in the early 1970s.

II. Diversity of children with disabilities
   A. Some children who require orthotic and prosthetic assistance can still utilize regular play equipment (e.g., Canadian crutches or Milwaukee brace). Others cannot due to medical conditions (e.g., spinal rods) and require the same accommodations as wheelchair-bound children.
   B. Classes of wheelchair children vary dramatically and may include traumatic injuries (in manually propelled chairs) such as spinal column, head injury, and traumatic or congenital amputee. Neurological and neuromuscular conditions (in manual chairs with atten-

dant or in electric chairs with joystick control) may include muscular dystrophy, multiple sclerosis or cerebral palsy (athetotic or ataxic type). Medically fragile (in custom-fit electric chairs with halo control features) may include spina bifida, cerebral palsy (rigid or spastic type), and spinal injury (C1 or C2 level).
   C. Providing accessibility, usability and a meaningful play experience for such a diverse group of children requires multiple design and feature accommodations. A 1989 report by the American Alliance for Leisure and Recreation Committee on Play (AALR) indicated that 85 percent of community park playground equipment surveyed provided neither accessibility to or usability of playground equipment.

III. Safety standards and safety problems

There are national safety standards for American playgrounds and play structures which have been in effect since 1981. Despite this, recent national studies by the AALR Committee on Play have shown that the majority of America's playgrounds, including day care, community park or elementary schoolyards, are accidents waiting to happen.

These yards feature structures with excessive height, insufficient or no safe fall-zone areas, and dangerous equipment design elements. The greatest area of difficulty between the Consumer Product Safety Commission (CPSC) safety standards and the accessibility factor for the ADA compliance for children with disabilities lies in the area of safety undersurfaces within the fall zone. The traditional materials used (sand, wood chips) and depth requirements (6 to 12 inches) needed for a safe fall zone preclude wheelchair access. A flood of new synthetic and manufactured surfaces to resolve this dilemma has hit the market—many are of questionable value, however, not in terms of accessibility but in their shock-absorbing characteristics, and most are also very expensive. Some approaches include:

- Interlocking rubber tiles,
- Plastic grid/grass combination grids,
- Layer cake gravel/fabric/mat systems,
- Milled wood fiber systems,
- Shredded rubber mulch systems,
- Rubber mat/air waffle systems, and
- Layered thickness rubber mat systems.

If play stations for children with disabilities are provided in a parallel configuration (as opposed to integrated) then a limited use of hardened pathways might provide access without compromising the fall safety zone of other equipment.

The greatest area of difficulty between the CPSC safety standards and the usability factor for ADA compliance for children with disabilities lies in the area of equipment access and egress. Retrofitting some traditional equipment is rather simple (e.g., wheelchair swings). Other retrofits are more challenging (e.g., providing ramped access to raised platforms, connecting bridges). Retrofitting some traditional equipment is next to impossible (e.g., slides). All retrofits of manufactured equipment require written notice and approval from the manufacturer. Without this approval, the agency or company making such retrofits bears legal responsibility for any injuries resulting from structural failures or flaws.

The ADA does provide for the use of alternative methods of providing playground experiences when retrofits of existing equipment are not practical—this can include providing equivalent experiences through custom-designed wheelchair equipment and/or substitute play experiences (e.g., sensory and social play zones as opposed to kinetic ones).

What are some of the equipment and design options available to playground designers interested in either retrofitting, providing alternative play stations, or designing new playgrounds for children with disabilities?

1. Stand-alone kinetic wheelchair equipment (for parallel or substitute configuration within able-bodied equipment): swings, spinners, rocker platforms, kinetic bridges, low-level slides.
2. Challenge activities/vita courses: pull-up station, sit-up station, stretch and flexibility stations, and leg-lift.
3. Sensory-stimulation/play stations: raised sandboxes, water play, light/color effect stations, hide-and-seek stations, touch and smell stations, musical bridges/chime walls, cargo net bed, ball play/auto return stations.

All of these approaches can be incorporated with modern-era modular equipment for a total, integrated playscape. These approaches can also be used in parallel play configurations and/or interspersed with traditional, stand-alone equipment.

Types of Play Areas

Tot Lots. Play areas or tot lots for smaller children should be planned with both the capabilities and the limitations of this age group in mind. Young children need to develop basic motor skills like coordination, balance and agility. In general, younger children also have shorter attention spans, so playgrounds using a variety of colors and equipment may be more successful in creating and maintaining play opportunities for them. By the time children are old enough to visit a tot lot, they have begun to reach the stage in their development where they can establish secondary relationships. That is, they can supplement the relationships they have with their parents by interacting with other individuals, particularly those their own age. Tot lots can encourage this type of social development if you include some space and equipment encouraging common use. Sandboxes, tunnels, areas for foursquare and similar facilities present situations for these social encounters. While some group spaces should stimulate competitive play, others should stress cooperation as well.

Most of our discussion about safety in playgrounds to this point has focused on areas and equipment that children can use without undue risk of injury. It's an unfortunate commentary on our society, but there is another type of safety you need to consider in designing play areas also. Play spaces,

especially those for young children, need to be secure. Since this isn't a text on social psychology, we won't enter into a discussion of deviant behavior except to point out it does exist. Areas to which children are attracted can also serve as magnets for disturbed individuals who may take advantage of the innocence and natural curiosity of children. Recreation professionals can't solve all the world's ills, but they can at least try to design and maintain safe areas by planning play spaces which can be supervised. This may mean sacrificing some visual variety and landscaping, but as you've heard before, form follows function, and safety is a functional consideration.

Planning play areas with supervision in mind is not difficult—it just takes a little foresight. Benches for adults are helpful, and you should place these where the play area can be scanned. Remember that when you site benches (determine where to put them), you need to consider the view an adult will have when seated rather than when standing. If you're planning an area where safety may be a problem, it may also help to allot a buffer zone of open space around the perimeter of the playground. In other words, avoid having the play area border immediately, for example, on a tree line that might afford hiding places. In some instances, it may be safer to fence a play space and provide a single entry/exit point. By gating, you may decrease opportunities for vandalism as well. Lighting may also help in these respects.

Playgrounds for Older Children. As is the case with tot lots, playgrounds for older children need to be designed with the question, Who is it for? in mind. Obviously, the scale of equipment should be larger to match the size of the children involved, but at times space limitations or cost constraints may preclude the opportunity to develop separate play areas for tots and older children. If this is the case, the principle of zoning use areas should be applied. A play area is no different from any other recreation space in zoning potential. If a single space is all you have at your disposal, it's appropriate to allocate some of the area for tots and another portion for older children. It may not be possible to physically force different age groups to stay in separate areas within a playground.

However, it is quite feasible to use techniques of design psychology to encourage segregation by age. For example, the flow or circulation from the entrance to a play area for children of all ages can move older children and tots in separate directions. Figure 6.21 demonstrates this concept. Just inside the entrance to a play area, you can place two pieces of play equipment, one of which is obviously designed—in terms of scale and function—for tots; let this apparatus pull younger children to it and push older kids away from it. Repeat this logic in the opposite direction with an apparatus for older children, perhaps a horizontal ladder with rungs too high for tots to reach. Each piece can then serve, in effect, as a secondary entranceway to two separate areas of the playground. This is an excellent example of how the concept of design psychology works to achieve your management goals.

Playgrounds, or the portions of them, devoted to older children can stress finer motor skills than areas designed for

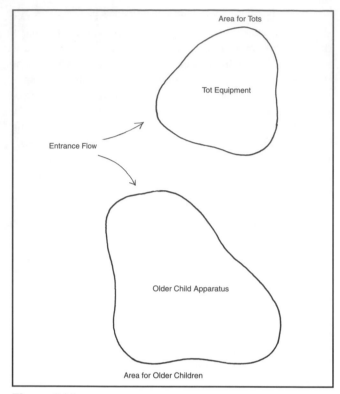

Area for Tots

Tot Equipment

Entrance Flow

Older Child Apparatus

Area for Older Children

Figure 6.21

tots since older children are better coordinated and stronger. Safety features for injury prevention are still an overriding concern, but the need for challenge increases. In fact, it may be safer to provide equipment that encourages this. Given the recklessness of youth, children at times seek some risk in their play. If they take risks on equipment not designed for this type of behavior, they are more likely to injure themselves than if they try difficult maneuvers on equipment designed to accommodate some element of perceived danger.

As with tot lots, some portions of play areas for older children should be free of equipment and devoted to open play. These spaces can be larger than their counterparts in tot lots to accommodate increased size, strength and speed. Playgrounds for older children should also include space for passive use—game areas and resting spots—but these quiet areas in particular should be visible from supervisory points. If you visit any playground containing secluded passive zones, we bet a month's salary (which really isn't much of a risk on our part) that you'll find cigarette butts, beer cans, or other signs of behavior we'd prefer to see avoided in playgrounds.

Although older children have longer attention spans, it may take more creativity on your part as a designer to attract and hold their interest in play equipment. With age comes sophistication, or at least the perception of it, so apparatus for older children may require more imaginative options. To some extent, manufacturers have addressed this problem for you in creative designs. It's still up to you, however, to buy the right equipment and then site individual pieces in such a way that encourages a total play experience.

You won't find a section in this chapter on playgrounds for children with disabilities. As mentioned in our discussion

of trails for the disabled in Chapter Three, we prefer to incorporate play opportunities for all children in all playgrounds. You should consult someone with training in therapeutic recreation before attempting barrier-free design in playgrounds, but don't make a point of isolating children with differing abilities. Common sense can help too. We once bought a wheelchair sandbox designed so children could pull their wheelchairs under an elevated, circular bin filled with sand. It worked fine until the first rain, at which point it became an excellent beach for birds. When we drilled holes in the bottom to drain the water, the sand ran out, so the sandbox is now in an equipment graveyard serving as a monument to our lack of foresight.

Play Areas for Adults. Our society seems to have the idea that play, in the traditional sense, is only for children. When recreation plans and designs consider the need for adult play space at all, the focus is generally on either competitive sports or passive areas for social experience, game tables and the like. Yet some play opportunities are as appropriate for adults as they are for children; it's simply a matter of designing to accommodate adult play. Children have wading pools; we don't typically encourage adults to use them, at least through design. Therefore adults—if they want to wade— either do so in fountains or, more likely, forego the experience. Children also have swings in parks, but adults are usually relegated to porch swings at home. An exception to this is Columbian Park in Lafayette, Indiana. Here, someone thought of adult play and built a number of porch-type swings suspended from A-frames. They get frequent use.

In general, we feel play areas should encourage people of all ages and not exclude individuals just because they happen to be adults. Some types of areas, such as the field archery course we'll discuss under the "skills areas," can be designed primarily with adults in mind. Because of the need for safety, certain sites may not be appropriate for children to use without adults present; thus, you may want to consider adult recreation needs beyond simply providing them with a place to sit. In fact, designing play areas for children with adjacent adult-use options nearby may help encourage families to pursue play together.

Play Courts and Play Fields. Most textbooks dealing with recreation planning and design include a section on play courts and play fields—sites for tennis, basketball, softball, and the like. We'd like to address these issues as well, but from a slightly different perspective. Let's start with an example of an "unmistake," a departure from the typical approach to planning. Generally, planners develop designs for recreation areas by considering the total area, looking at the entire resource base and trying to fit a variety of areas and facilities to it. This approach seems to make sense, but sometimes rules need to be broken.

Consider the case of Beech Lake Resort, a private family campground near Lexington, Tennessee. When this area was being planned, the developers had plenty of land—about 70 acres—but not much of it was flat. In fact, there was only one spot suitable for a softball field that wouldn't require extensive grading and leveling. The planning solution in this case was to "design the area in reverse." Instead of considering the entire area, the designer, in effect, said, "We've got one logical spot for a ball field, so let's assume it's going to go there and use that as the focal point of the plan." The approach worked. Instead of forcing a ball field on a spot to complement activities that didn't require flat land, the field was located first and the other uses added around it. To put it another way, the existing resource base suggested the only sensible approach to design, an offshoot of our principle of balancing resource needs with people needs. In retrospect, it sounds rather simplistic to say that it makes sense to put a ball field on flat ground. However, we've seen a lot of designers spend money unnecessarily trying to fit land to their plans rather than taking the reverse approach. This approach may be something of a departure from the traditional view of shaping the land to your needs, but it makes sense to us.

There are other instances when design of play courts and play fields should depart from the norm. Here we're going to be really blasphemous and suggest that not all courts and fields must conform to traditional standards and basic design principles. If you're charged with developing a softball complex where regulation or league play will occur, then by all means plan regulation fields. If, on the other hand, you're planning a softball field in a campground (and we'll try to convince you to do so in the chapter on programming), standards may not be quite so critical. In a campground setting, you might observe a pickup softball game with players ranging in age from six to 60. We've seen games with 20 players on the field for the same team at one time. These folks don't need 90-foot baselines, they need a place to have fun. We once saw a softball diamond on a piece of land about 100 feet too short with a five percent slope. The designer, probably not "trained" in recreation, put home plate at the low end of the field. Ground balls—hit uphill—didn't roll as far, the field worked, and the campers played. Sometimes, common sense is a better guide than a book on standards.

Play courts in some environments can depart from standards as well. If you build an asphalt basketball court a bit wider than suggested in the rule book, you may be able to put two sets of volleyball standards across it and create a second use. Adding a couple of area lights and an electrical outlet can transform it into a square dance surface. Or you can paint a foursquare surface on one end of a play court and add another dimension. The point is this: In some types of recreation areas, a departure from basics and standards can encourage new uses by increasing the variety of activities available. "Skinning" an infield for baseball or softball can enhance league play, but it may detract from soccer or football in areas where the real need is for a multipurpose play field.

One of the most frequent comments we hear from resource-oriented recreation staff is, "We'd like to provide play space, but we don't have the room or the money." Our response to this is, "Piffle!" In most parks and recreation areas, the resource necessary

for play courts is already there in the form of the parking lot someone designed at double the capacity it ever receives. Putting a basketball standard at one end of a parking lot doesn't decrease the parking space, it just increases the opportunity for taking full advantage of your resources. Volleyball standards consisting of the old tires, some cement and two posts can also be rolled onto a parking lot in no time. This kind of design doesn't require a large investment of funds, just a commitment to enhancing user experience and a little creativity.

In some instances there are "exceptions to our exceptions." If you provide horseshoe pits, it's a good idea to build to recommended size. Since these areas require a minimum amount of space (Figure 6.22), there's no reason to miss the opportunity for regulation play by trying to save a few feet. (We also suggest you use decorative fencing around your horseshoe pits for safety reasons.) If you're designing a field where baseball or softball will be played, you should consider orientation to sun. In general, regardless of the sport, the principle line of play should be perpendicular to the direction of the setting sun. The best choice for a line connecting home plate to the pitcher's mound is about 20° east of south (Figure 6.23). If the field is for multiple-use play, you may want to avoid a permanent home plate and pitcher's mound or rubber and instead suggest direction of play by placing a small backstop behind the point you intend for home plate.

If the site for a play field or play court does require grading and leveling, you can increase playability by center-crowning the land base to aid drainage during wet periods. Similarly, opportunities for using the space can be increased—funds permitting—by providing area lighting. If you do add lighting to a play area, remember the following: Be sure the play space is zoned so it won't cause conflicts as a result of night use. For example, don't site a lighted play court adjacent to or inside of a camping loop (as in Figure 6.24, originally shown as Figure 6.5). There are several problems with this design decision. First, don't be surprised if campers complain about the "noisy kids" ruining the camping experience. The children get blamed, but you know who's really at fault. Second, from a resource stewardship perspective, think about pedestrian impact. A play facility located inside a camp loop will attract participants from every campsite, leading to soil compaction and undesignated trails from as many directions as there are campsites. Finally, notice the campsite in Figure 6.24 is empty. A good axiom of design is to separate private

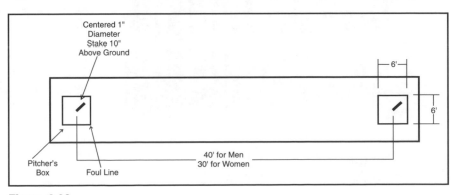

Figure 6.22

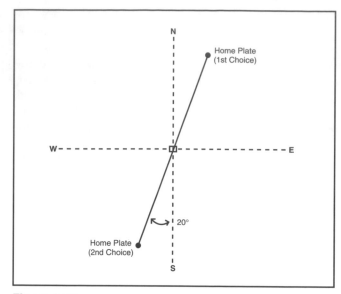

Figure 6.23

spaces, such as campsites, from public spaces such as playgrounds. Users of these various areas have different motives and recreational goals. Public and private use zones should both be a part of recreation areas, but apart from each other.

Be sure posts used for mounting lights are far enough removed from the play space that they don't cause a safety hazard during the heat of play. Recessed posts for basketball backboards are a good idea, too.

As we've suggested before, design is a matter of *balance*. The need for light posts far enough away for safety has to be balanced with the need for adequate light for after dark play. Lighting a play area for evening use, by the way, shouldn't stop there. People need to be able to find their way safely to and from these after dark areas, and pathways connecting play spaces with other zones should be lighted. Yet another "balancing act" needs to be applied here, at least in campgrounds. Pedestrians need lighted walkways, but you want to avoid lighting the entire area so it looks like downtown Manhattan. One solution is to use waist-high path side lights with downward-directed beams, as in Figure 6.25 (a planning version of having your cake and eating it too).

Figure 6.24

Shelter Buildings. The primary concern in designing shelter buildings is to make them programmable. Any construction crew worth their salt can, if you ask them, build a shelter for you. Your job as a planner is to serve as the link between program staff and the people responsible for the actual builders. Construction crews may know how to build and programmers may know how they want to use the shelter, but these two sets of knowns won't always fit together without a little attention to planning concerns. As a case in point, consider the portion of a TVA campground in Kentucky shown in Figure 6.26a.

The challenge for the planner here was one of potentially conflicting uses. Management and program staff decided there was a demand for an inexpensive, open-sided shelter building in the campground. From a zoning perspective, the logical location for the shelter was in the open field near the existing campfire theater. The problem concerned one anticipated use. The staff was familiar enough with the clientele in this campground to know that bluegrass music would be a popular program. Since this produces fairly high sound levels, and since the shelter was to be open-sided, a potential problem arose. Careless design and placement could preclude the opportunity to program the shelter and the campfire theater simultaneously.

The planners' solution (which adhered to the KISS principle) had two components. First, since there was a dense stand of trees and understory vegetation surrounding the theater, they were able to use this screening and physical distance to help attenuate the noise from the shelter. The "shouting and walking" technique described in Chapter Three worked here—one person stood at the campfire theater and shouted while another walked across the open field. When the walker could no longer hear the shouts, the planner determined the site for the shelter. KISS. The second part of the solution was also simple. Program staff wanted the shelter to include a stage for the bluegrass band and other programs. The planner's response accommodated this need and reduced the noise problem further by orienting the stage as shown in Figure 6.26b. By placing the stage in the corner of the shelter nearest the theater, the planner "pointed" the noise away from the theater. Enclosing the portions of the walls immediately behind the stage also contained sound.

The point is this: The shelter design itself was simple, but it took careful consideration and attention to detail on the part of the planner to make the zone functional from a programming standpoint. Shelter buildings don't need to be expensive, highly modernized facilities in order to work for you. They do, however, need to be incorporated, like other facilities, into the total design picture. Depending on intended uses, you can add other features like a barbecue pit or shuffleboard surfaces to encourage other program possibilities.

A shelter building can function as a focal point for programming. If zoning and other on-site conditions are favorable, it may be a good idea to locate it near the center of the program zone or near the point where most users will enter the program area. With these locations, an enclosed room at one end of the shelter can serve as an equipment storage and

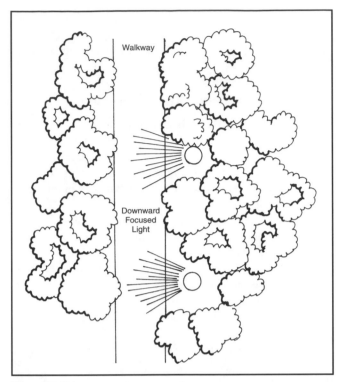

Figure 6.25

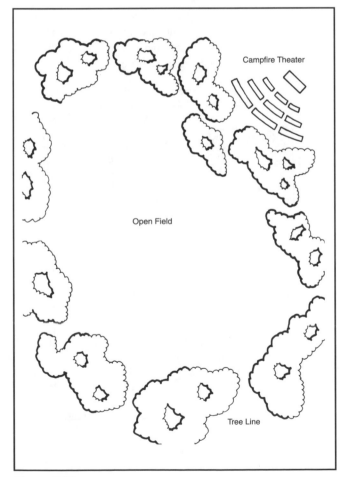

Figure 6.26a

checkout room for a variety of programs. We'll address this point further in the programming chapter.

Skills Courses

Although the "how" of this book centers around planning, the real focus, the "why," is on programming of recreation areas. One of the most successful types of programs we've seen in outdoor recreation areas, both in numbers of participants and enjoyment derived from activities, is skills enhancement. Think for a moment about what people do in developed recreation areas. Camping, fishing, hunting, bicycling, hiking and swimming are among the most popular forms of outdoor recreation. While all of these activities may not lend themselves to successful skills enhancement programs, several do—particularly bicycling, bow hunting and fishing. The logic, or justification, for skills programs is simple. People who use outdoor recreation areas already have an interest in the types of activities available in the out-of-doors, so you may have a built-in audience receptive to learning more about a given activity. Further, a broad spectrum of recreational programs can both enhance the visitor's experience and increase your use figures (see the programming chapter). Finally, the cost associated with skills development programs can be minimal.

Consider how various types of skills instruction are provided as part of all sorts of group camps—those for scouts, church groups, boys and girls clubs, for example. These programs include nature arts, crafts, sailing, fishing, swimming, canoeing, archery, shooting, rowing and more. However, we seldom hear of these sorts of skills being taught in family campgrounds; when this does happen, it greatly enhances the users' experience and increases campground use, which, in turn, increases revenues and reduces depreciative behavior.

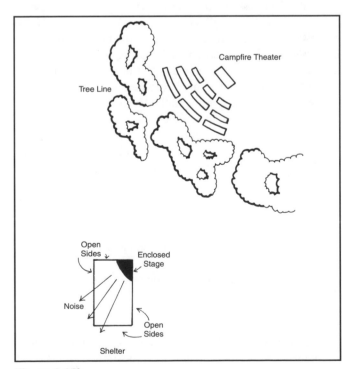

Figure 6.26b

Nothing in this world is easy, however. Providing programs of any type requires commitment, investment of time and energy, creativity, enthusiasm, positive attitude and the right "mind set" from staff and administration. These tend to be lacking in most public-resource management agencies, particularly on the state and federal levels, but no one says people like you can't be agents for positive change if you put your mind to it. We seem to be on our soapbox again, so let's step down and consider some specific types of skills development areas.

Bicycle Skills. Bike skills courses provide a good starting point for this discussion because they can function effectively in urban, suburban, or resource-based areas. It seems that wherever children are, bikes will be along as well. We once polled campers exiting a developed campground in Kentucky after a busy weekend and found that one out of every five individuals (adults included) had a bicycle with him or her. This figure may not sound too impressive, but there were 2,500 campers using the campground. Even we could figure out the potential for programming here.

One of the biggest advantages of a bike skills course is the low cost involved. If you have an existing hard surface like a multipurpose play court or parking lot, you can superimpose a course by adding a few painted lines and buying or borrowing a small number of orange plastic highway safety cones. If a suitable surface isn't available, the potential for programming associated with bicycle skills may help provide justification for adding a multipurpose court to your area. And if a court-type layout won't function effectively in your setting, you can design a bike skills zone like a miniature golf course, with progressive stations. Although this approach will probably require a bit more land, it does allow you to incorporate changes in elevation into your course for added challenge if rolling topography is available. Figure 6.27 shows one design of a bike skills course. Since this concept may be new to you, we've included, in the following section, an outline of how this particular course can be used. The parenthetical numbers after each skills test in the narrative correspond to the circled numbers in Figure 6.27. (Our thanks go to a former coworker of ours, Kathy Howard Cuddebeck, who developed this program a few years ago.)

Figure 6.28 shows a score sheet for the described course. You can use this design "as is" or modify it to meet your needs or creative urges. The only additional comments we have are these:

1. Stress the fun aspect of the program along with the safety and instructional elements of the activity (don't make it too much like school, or your audience will stay away in droves); and
2. You may increase participation and enhance enjoyment by providing some type of incentive with programs of this type.

An inexpensive "certificate of completion" will find its way to many a child's bedroom wall, especially if it's signed (stamped signature) by someone in authority (e.g., the direc-

tor of parks and the staff person or practicum student conducting the program). If this certificate has your agency or organization name and logo on it, we're also talking positive public relations here.

Bicycle Skills Course

I. OBJECTIVE: To test the riding skills, road knowledge and safety attitudes of cyclists of all ages while developing skills in bike handling and traffic awareness. This skills course is designed to teach cyclists the following:
   A. How to recognize unsafe mechanical conditions on the bicycle.
   B. The types of basic bicycle maneuvers, such as changes of speed and direction, obstacles, emergency stops, etc.
   C. The handling characteristics, capabilities and limitations of the rider's bike.
   D. An awareness of the actions of other road users.
   E. The self-confidence developed from knowledge and practice.
   F. The rules of safe cycling.

II. PROGRAM
   A. Introduction and instruction.
      1. Explain objectives of the program.
      2. Course instructions:
         a. With bicyclists lined up on the outside of the course, one leader will demonstrate each skill while another leader explains the rules and scoring procedure.

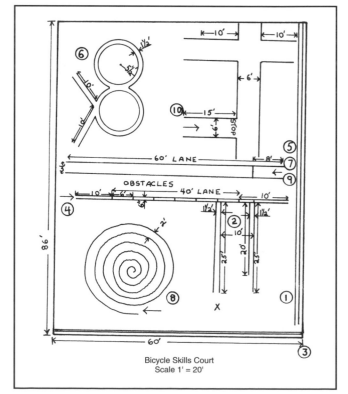

Bicycle Skills Court
Scale 1' = 20'

Figure 6.27

132

Bicycle Skills Score Sheet

Rider_____ Number_____ Age_____ Score 430_____

1.	Inspection	30 points_____		6.	Emergency Stop	30 points_____
	Size	3_____			Test	10_____
	Frame	3_____			Instructions	10_____
	Pedals	3_____			Stopped w/in 10–14"	10_____
	Handlebars	3_____			Stopped w/in 14–18"	5_____
	Front Wheel	3_____			Stopped w/in 18–20	3_____
	Rear Wheel	3_____			Stopped w/in 20–22"	2_____
	Brakes	3_____			Stopped w/in 22–24"	1_____
	Chain	3_____				
	Lights and Reflectors	3_____				
	Cleanliness	3_____		7.	Figure Eight	45 points_____
					Test	10_____
2.	Balance Test	30 points_____			Instructions	10_____
					Feet	10_____
	Test	10_____			Front Wheel	10_____
	Instructions	10_____			Control	5_____
	Wheels	5_____				
	Feet	5_____		8.	Weaving	35 points_____
					Test	10_____
3.	Short Radius Turn	35 points_____			Instructions	10_____
					Feet	5_____
	Test	10_____			Obstacles	5_____
	Instructions	10_____			Correct Direction	5_____
	Feet to the ground	5_____				
	Wheels	5_____		9.	Spiral	55 points_____
	Smoothness	5_____			Test	10_____
					Instructions	10_____
4.	Straight Line	45 points_____			Feet	10_____
					Front Wheel	10_____
	Test	10_____			Completes Spiral	10_____
	Instructions	10_____			Second Circle	5_____
					Third Circle	3_____
	Straight Line & Hand Signal				Fourth Circle	2_____
					Control	5_____
	Feet	3_____				
	Wheels	5_____		10.	Slow Speed	45 points_____
	Hand Signal	3_____			Test	10_____
					Instructions	10_____
	Straight Line & Right Hand				Pedals	5_____
					Feet	5_____
	Feet	2_____			Wheels	5_____
	Wheels	5_____			30 Seconds	10_____
					25–30 Seconds	5_____
	Straight Line & Left Hand				20–25 Seconds	3_____
					15–20 Seconds	2_____
	Feet	2_____			10–15 Seconds	1_____
	Wheel	5_____				
				11.	Road Test	40 points_____
5.	Avoiding Obstacles	35 points_____				
					Test	10_____
	Test	10_____			Instructions	10_____
	Instructions	10_____			Hand Signal	10_____
	Feet	5_____			Control	5_____
	Wheels	5_____			Wheels	5_____
	Obstacles	5_____				

Figure 6.28

b. Participants must go through each skill one at a time with a leader at each station.

3. Mechanical inspection: Leaders will help bicyclists inspect their bikes to score points for the following:

a. Size: test seat for weight, level, tightness, frame size. Can the rider straddle the frame with both feet flat on the ground? (3 points)

b. Frame: frame should be in line, bearings adjusted; no looseness or binding in rotation. (3 points)

c. Pedals: intact and tight; treads intact and tight. (3 points)

d. Handlebars: in line with wheel and tightly fitted, grips tight, ends plugged. (3 points)

e. Front wheel: runs true, side to side and round; check air, spokes, rim, tread. (3 points)

f. Rear wheel: runs true and round; check air, spokes, rim, tire tread. (3 points)

g. Brakes. (3 points)

h. Chain tension; $1/_2$" play. (3 points)

i. Lights and reflectors. (3 points)

j. Cleanliness: no rust or excessive buildup. (3 points)

4. Scoring: Total Possible Points (30)

III. SKILLS

A. Balance test (1). Purpose: To test the rider's primary sense of balance while showing the rider how a slight movement of the wheel can reinstitute balance
1. Rider must coast 45 feet on a straight line not more than six-inches wide with right foot pushing off on the left side of the bicycle.
2. Rider must stand erect with both hands on the handlebars and not sitting on the saddle.
3. Rider is allowed a 20-foot starting and a 15 foot-stopping distance.
4. Scoring: Total Possible Points (30)
   a. Completion of test. (10 points)
   b. Followed all verbal instructions capably. (Take 1 to 9 points off if the rider followed some instructions and not others.) (10 points)
   c. Rider stays in balance without letting wheels touch or go over line. (5 points)
   d. Rider in balance; both feet not on the ground at one time. (5 points)

B. Short Radius Turn (2). Purpose: To test the rider's ability to turn a bicycle around smoothly within a limited area such as a narrow street.
1. Rider must travel 25-feet down a lane $1\frac{1}{2}$-feet wide and turn within a 10-foot wide area into another 25-by-$1\frac{1}{2}$-feet lane.
2. An obstacle is placed four feet away from the turning area as turning marker.
3. Scoring: Total Possible Points (35)
   a. Completion of test. (10 points)
   b. Follows all verbal instructions. (10 points)
   c. Touches neither foot to the ground. (5 points)
   d. Touches neither borderline with wheel. (5 points)
   e. Makes smooth turn with no excessive braking. (5 points)

C. Riding a Straight Line (3). Purpose: To establish the ability to ride in a straight unwavering line in the street adjacent to a road edge.
1. Riders must travel down a 40-foot straight line six-inches wide with a 15-foot start and finish, making the appropriate hand signal as they exit the lane.
2. Riders must stay within the lane using their right hand and then their left hand only for steering.
3. Scoring: Total Possible Points (45)
   a. Completion of test. (10 points)
   b. Follows all verbal commands. (10 points)
   c. Straight line and hand signal: neither foot touches the ground (3 points); wheel does not touch either borderline (5 points); makes correct hand signal smoothly (3 points).
   d. Straight line and right-hand steering: touches neither foot to ground (2 points);

touches neither borderline with wheel (5 points).
   e. Straight line and left-hand steering: touches neither foot to ground (2 points); touches neither borderline with wheel (5 points).

D. Avoiding Obstacles (4). Purpose: To establish the ability to avoid objects in the riding path.
1. Rider must ride 40 feet within a six-inch space flanked at six-foot intervals on alternate sides with cans or flat stones.
2. Rider is allowed a 10-foot starting and eight-foot stopping distance.
3. Scoring: Total Possible Points (35)
   a. Completion of test. (10 points)
   b. Follows all verbal commands. (10 points)
   c. Touches neither foot to ground. (5 points)
   d. Touches neither borderline with wheel. (5 points)
   e. Touches none of the obstacles. (5 points)

E. Emergency Stop (5). Purpose: To learn change in balance and capability of bicycle for stopping in an emergency while testing visual reactions in relation to momentum.
1. Rider must ride 60 feet, stopping within 10–14 inches of finish line or obstacle such as a board.
2. Leader will measure distance from front tip of the tire to the obstacle.
3. Scoring: Total Possible Points (30)
   a. Completion of test. (10 points)
   b. Follows all verbal directions. (10 points)
   c. Stops within 10–14 inches of the obstacle. (10 points)
   d. Stops within 14–18 inches of the obstacle. (5 points)
   e. Stops within 18–20 inches of the obstacle. (3 points)
   f. Stops within 20–22 inches of the obstacle. (2 points)
   g. Stops within 22–24 inches of the obstacle. (1 point)

F. Figure Eight (6). Purpose: To test the rider's balance and sense of momentum as well as the changes in balance required by changes in direction. (Frequently a cyclist must swerve, shift, and balance to avoid a pedestrian or obstacles in the cyclist's path.)
1. Riders must ride around a figure eight, keeping their front tire within a lane $1\frac{1}{2}$-feet wide circling in both directions.
2. Scoring: Total Possible Points (45)
   a. Completion of test. (10 points)
   b. Follows instructions. (10 points)
   c. Completes test without touching a foot to the ground. (Take 2 points off each time foot touches the ground.) (10 points)
   d. Completes test without letting front tire go over either line. (Take 2 points off each time tire goes over line.) (10 points)

    e. Keeps control of bicycle at all times. (5 points)

G. Weaving Around Obstacles (7). Purpose: To test the rider's ability to change direction quickly which requires balance and judgment. (A rider often hits an object in the bike's path because the rider is watching it. This test teaches the rider to focus on the clear path rather than obstacles.)

    1. Rider must ride 60 feet at normal speed between obstacles placed six feet apart, going to the right and left alternately.

    2. Scoring: Total Possible Points (35)

        a. Completion of test. (10 points)

        b. Follows instructions. (10 points)

        c. Rider completes the course without touching a foot to the ground. (Take 1 or 2 points off each time.) (5 points)

        d. Rider does not touch obstacles. (Take 1 or 2 points off each time a cone is touched.) (5 points)

        e. Rider completes the test without missing an obstacle or making a wrong turn. (Take 1 or 2 points off each time.) (5 points)

H. Spiral (8). Purpose: To determine the rider's ability to balance a bicycle while changing speed and operating brakes. (Cyclists often have to change directions quickly and sharply to avoid an obstacle while controlling the bicycle to avoid skidding.)

    1. Rider must begin at the wide circle, following the lane until the circle gets so small the rider can go no further. At this point the rider must turn the bicycle around and head out of the circle, keeping within the travel lane.

    2. Riders must keep their front tire within the two-foot riding lane.

    3. Scoring: Total Possible Points (55)

        a. Completion of test. (10 points)

        b. Follows instructions. (10 points)

        c. Completes test without touching foot to ground. (Take 2 points off each time.) (10 points)

        d. Completes test without letting front tire touch either boundary line. (Take 2 points off each time.) (10 points)

        e. Rider completes spiral all the way into the center circle (10 points); rider stops within second circle (5 points); rider stops within third circle (3 points); rider stops within fourth circle (2 points).

        f. Rider keeps control of bicycle at all times. (5 points)

I. Slow Speed (9). Purpose: To have the rider demonstrate a skill in proper pedaling and braking motion at slow speeds, keeping the bicycle under control at all times. (A bicyclist, while riding along a street in heavy traffic conditions, will need to pedal slowly and brake often.)

    1. Riders must travel down a lane three-feet wide and 60-feet long within 30 seconds or more.

    2. Rider must keep feet parallel to the pavement while pedaling, using brakes when necessary.

    3. Leaders must time each rider and record time.

    4. Scoring: Total Possible Points (45)

        a. Completion of test. (10 points)

        b. Follows instructions. (10 points)

        c. Rider keeps balls of feet on pedals and pedals are kept parallel to the ground. (5 points)

        d. Rider completes test without touching either foot to ground. (5 points)

        e. Rider stays within three-foot boundary without touching wheels to the line. (5 points)

        f. Rider completes test within 30 seconds or more (10 points); 25–30 seconds time (5 points); 20–25 seconds time (3 points); 15–20 seconds time (2 points); and 10–15 seconds time (1 point).

J. Road Test (10). Purpose: To establish control of the bicycle with one hand on the handlebars and demonstrate knowledge of traffic signals and the ability to turn rapidly at intersections. (Other vehicles and pedestrians need to know in advance what a bicycle rider intends to do. It is very important that proper hand signals are used and that the rider has control of the bicycle at all times.)

    1. Rider must come to a complete stop at the first intersection, using the stop signal. Turning left with left-hand signal, the rider approaches the leader, who signals for the bicyclist to turn right or left at the second intersection using the appropriate hand signal.

    2. Rider must demonstrate all hand signals plainly before each movement.

    3. Scoring: Total Possible Points (40)

        a. Completion of test. (10 points)

        b. Follows all instructions. (10 points)

        c. Rider makes all hand signals plainly before each movement. (10 points)

        d. Rider keeps bicycle under control at all times. (5 points)

        e. Rider touches neither wheel to line. (5 points)

Archery Skills. The key question to consider when you think of designing an archery skills course is *safety*. If there are any concerns about adequate space, relationship of the course to other use areas, or circulation adjacent to the course, it's better to avoid development altogether. If safety issues can be addressed, an archery skills area can add a new dimension to your program for youths and adults alike. While it's possible to teach archery in a flat, open space, the program can be enhanced by designing a field archery course. You'll need, depending on topography, three to six acres for this approach. Figure 6.29 shows the basic components and target requirements for a 14 target field range. The archery skills program itself needs close supervision. However, with adequate regulations and safety requirements posted, such as not permitting broadhead hunting points, the course may be opened for independent target practice as well.

You need to consider a variety of factors, both for safety and programming, when designing a field archery course. The target sequence should be laid out in a loop, with internal circulation on the inside and targets to the outside as in Figure 6.30. The order of the shooting lanes can vary, but for skill enhancement alternate among short, long and intermediate distances with adjacent lanes. Target butts (arrow stops) should not be placed where paths or roads pass behind them at unsafe distances. The minimum distance between shooting lanes should be 50 feet, unless topography provides a barrier between lanes. For shorter lanes, allow 15° as a safety distance on either side of the target butt, and increase this arc to 30° on longer lanes. Use topography to your advantage, but avoid placing targets on hilltops. The clearing width of a shooting lane should be a minimum of eight feet. The clearing height should be eight to 10 feet, increasing for longer lanes to protect against arrow deflections from tree limbs. An area equal to one-quarter the shooting distance squared should be cleared in front of the target butt, with twice this space cleared behind the target.

Targets themselves can consist of bales of straw or excelsior. On 20- to 25-foot targets, two bales will suffice, while longer distances will require bales stacked three high. The bottom bale should rest on used tires to prevent moisture damage, and two wooden posts set behind the target will provide support. Attaching a sheet of fiber or rubber to the back of the bales with heavy wire will keep arrows from passing completely through. Polyethylene plastic tied over the upper portion of the top bale will extend the life of the target by affording some protection from rain.

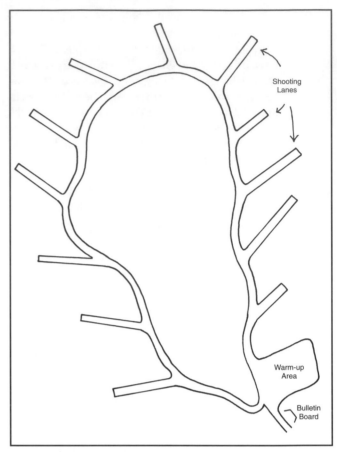

Figure 6.30

Shooting stations should have markers indicating target distances. Each station can be accompanied by a six-foot post for target numbers and a bow hanger. The National Field Archery Association in Redlands, California, can provide you with additional information on designing and building archery ranges.

As a final point about archery skills in particular (and what skills programs in general can do for your use and for your users), consider this: A year or so after Land Between the Lakes began teaching archery skills in campground summer programs, bow hunters, in great numbers, started camping in these areas *and* bringing their families with them; they found they could combine their enjoyment of hunting with a variety of other activities for both themselves and their spouses and children. These are the fruits of programming we continue to stress.

Fishing Skills Exercise

Often, part of the challenge of recreation planning and design is in developing a type of area or facility you haven't tackled before. We wouldn't want you to miss such an opportunity, so instead of telling you how we might design a fishing skills course (and program), we'll let you try it as this chapter's exercise. First, identify a suitable area—you'll have to have a program in mind, of course—and consider design needs. It would be nice to have a body of water to incorporate, but it really isn't necessary.

Field Archery Course Requirements

1. Practice targets
2. Garbage cans
3. Access road or path
4. One entrance sign
5. One regulations sign
6. 25–30 boundary signs
7. Bulletin board

Requirements for each 14-target unit follow:

Distance	Target Size
20–25–30–35 feet	6" (four-position target)
15 yards	12"
20 yards	12"
25 yards	12"
30 yards	12"
35–35–35–35 yards	18" (four-position target)
40 yards	18"
45 yards	18"
45–40–35–30 yards	18" (four-position target)
50 yards	18"
55 yards	24"
60 yards	24"
65 yards	24"
80–70–60–50 yards	24" (four-position target)

Figure 6.29

The challenge of this exercise is determining what skills to develop, and then designing an area for practice. We suggest you use a "course" approach similar to the bike skills area. You might design your stations by starting with simple pole casts, and move on to more difficult ones, such as placing a plug under a barrier representing overhanging brush. Old tires make excellent targets, too. The key element in this exercise is to fit your design to the site you select and to the program you develop. Try this project with a team approach; let one team member be a planner/designer, another a pro-grammer, and a third an administrator. Each of these positions has different responsibilities, so each member of your team should act accordingly. How, for example, would you as a programmer justify the purchase of a number of fishing rods to your administrator? What would you as an administrator require in the way of design alternatives? What would you as a planner ask of your programmer in terms of providing design sideboards or guidelines? We could provide you with more questions to ask each other about fishing skills areas, but we'd prefer to let you flounder.

Chapter Seven

The Many Campgrounds We Really Have (or Could Have)

As usual this chapter begins with a photo collage and some questions for you. We have selected eight "dandy" camp units from eight state park campgrounds in eight states (all taken since 1990). Those states are Connecticut, Kentucky, Pennsylvania, Alabama, Indiana, Michigan, California, and New Hampshire—from sea to shining sea! Try your hand at guessing which state parks are shown in Figures 7.1 to 7.8. Photos of similar environmental destruction could have been taken in campgrounds in most others states and in federal, county, municipal and private sector campgrounds throughout North America. What do you see in each photo? How, you say, can the environmental problems happen when our park profes-sionals are trained and highly skilled and experienced? How indeed!? Could it be we either don't know much about campground design and how it affects the environment or maybe professionals don't care? Many of our friends in the academic, environmental, research and even in the on-the-ground professional realms will think they see *overuse* in these photos. They will also stroke their chins and speak wisely of violations of physical carrying capacities; the need to eliminate camping (and people) from parks; the need for much more research; and the general worthlessness of campers, particularly those who aren't backpackers. Our response to these knowing musings is, "Phooey!"

Figure 7.1

Figure 7.3

Figure 7.2

Figure 7.4

Figure 7.5

Figure 7.8

Figure 7.6

Figure 7.7

Why did we begin our campground chapter in this manner? Three reasons come to mind. We wanted to shock you a little and we also like to stir up the smug rascals who like to lay the blame for our parks' problems on the user. However, the main reason is to make you aware of the nationwide campsite environmental impact problem and the simple solution to it. This solution is similar in all campgrounds from wilderness and backcountry areas with their dispersed sites to the private campgrounds where you may find 25 sites or more to the acre. You will have environmental destruction in all campsites (including those in wildlands) unless they are *defined* and *reinforced!*

Campers (particularly the nontenters) take the rap for these campsite disasters while the guilty folks (planners, designers, construction and maintenance personnel, and park administrators) continue their less than learned tripping through the woods. The week this chapter was being written the Secretary of the Interior told the National Park Service to eliminate 100 more campsites at Yosemite. "Overuse" and "new" concern for the environment were cited as the reasons. Again— Phooey! Forgive them, for they knoweth not what they are talking about! (This was at least a year before the 1997 flood destroyed the campground there.)

What sort of things did the authors see in Figures 7.1 through 7.8? We saw unfriendly campsites with mud aplenty when wet and dust aplenty when dry. We saw no site definition or boundaries and no site reinforcement. We saw exposed tree roots, stumps of once fine trees and low vigor in existing trees. We saw site compaction, soil loss, water and air infiltration rates drastically reduced. We saw either too much shade or not enough shade. On one site, we saw site furniture located above the parking space and another site with tons of rock separating the auto and camping vehicle from the worn-out bare campsite. What we did not see was *overuse!* Later in the chapter we will return to this topic.

Perhaps the most important reason the first edition of this book sold well to both students and practitioners was the information in the original campground chapter. We've traveled extensively throughout America since we wrote the first edition and have learned and imagineered many new things to share with you. We've added a second chapter on campgrounds but there is so much to learn we can't begin to compress the subject into two chapters in a book. Fact is, we conduct two or three 4$\frac{1}{2}$-day workshops per year for professionals on this subject and still don't cover it as well as we'd like. One or two chapters on campgrounds in anyone's book, including this one, can't begin to cover the subject adequately.

This chapter, as you'll see shortly, could have appropriately been called: "The Mini-Campgrounds We Really Have." Since such a title might have implied the discussion was going to focus on scale models of campgrounds, however, "mini" doesn't appear in the chapter heading. Even so, the reference to smallness would have been a true and unfortunate one. As Chapter One suggested, recreation planners, managers, and designers need to think big, plan big, and build big. For no other type of facility is this guideline more important than campgrounds. While there are some exceptions, which we'll discuss below, in general campgrounds must be large for three important reasons: management, users, and environment.

Management

Several management-oriented concerns can be addressed by building large campgrounds, and perhaps the most important among these is cost-effectiveness. Private campgrounds need to make a profit. Public campgrounds shouldn't have to be subsidized by tax dollars any more than necessary. In either case, more campsites mean more campers, and more campers mean a lower per capita expenditure for facilities. For example, assume we build an inexpensive shelter inside our campground for $15,000. If the area has 30 campsites, the per site share of the shelter is $500. If our campground has 300 units, the per site cost drops to $50, plus we now have the opportunity to attract enough campers to justify the expense of building a shelter in the first place. Add in the cost of paved roads, play areas, toilets/showers, trails, and other amenities, and the rationale becomes evident.

A second advantage of larger campgrounds for managerial folks is maintenance. We've said this before, but it bears repeating. If you plan and build 250 campsites at a lake, you'll have to operate and maintain 250 campsites. You can spread these units out over 10 or 12 areas and force garbage collectors, maintenance crews, management personnel, and visitor protection and program staff to drive up to several hundred miles to perform their tasks, or you can build one 250-unit campground and have all personnel work in one location. Again, the private sector must make a profit; the public sector, which usually charges smaller fees, should at least break even in terms of operation and maintenance. In other words, the cost of operation and maintenance should be offset by camper fees charged. In the public sector depending on agency policy, fee structure and development costs this break-even strategy requires at least 200 campsites per campground.

Another important size-related management concern is control. Most campgrounds tend to be "out in the boonies," particularly those developed by resource-oriented public agencies at the state and federal levels. If an agency can't afford or justify on-site management, the area will quickly become a target for vandalism and become a camper harassment hangout for rowdies, or both. Campground use will change and decrease. You'll have the good ol' boys like most of the federal sector and families will be scarce. While this may sound rather harsh and perhaps opinionated, we've seen and experienced these phenomena too many times to ignore them. Small campgrounds make it difficult to justify on-site management. Often the presence of official personnel is enough to deter most depreciative behavior, but a ranger-type person driving through a small, otherwise unprotected area once a day is not a meaningful substitute for on-site staff.

Another often ignored management advantage of large campgrounds is the potential for programming. In the first place, it's difficult to justify spending development dollars on program facilities for small areas. If your campground has a maximum capacity of 60 people (15 sites with four users per site), it's rather pointless to build a 200-seat campfire theater. In the second place, programs require staff to run them. Even if you take a low-cost approach, such as using intern students to develop and conduct programs, which we advocate, it just isn't worth the effort for a 15-unit campground. We wish campground size were the greatest impediment to provision of programs. Unfortunately this typically isn't the case, as you'll see here.

Users

If you've completed or are completing a degree in recreation, parks, or leisure studies, chances are good you'll have some background in programming. With this in mind, think about the campgrounds you've visited. If these are operated by a state Division of Natural Resources or state parks, you may have found a moderate number of programs. (The state of Virginia has numerous fun campground programs in its parks. These are quite scarce in other state park systems.) If you've visited campgrounds developed and maintained by federal agencies, you haven't seen much, if any, recreation programming. Note the choice of words—the National Park Service and, to a lesser extent, a few other agencies have some natural and historical interpretive programs in campgrounds, but rarely is the emphasis on recreation. Chapter Nine explores this problem in some depth, but for now consider this question: Where is it written that campgrounds shouldn't provide opportunities for fun? The Forest Service, Corps of Engineers, TVA, and other federal and state agencies provide recreation facilities but generally not programs. When asked why, they often respond, "It's not in our policy." This is a valid answer as far as it goes, but it's also somewhat analogous to saying that the turkey doesn't have stuffing in it because we didn't put it there. Those of us in the business of providing recreation opportunities have a professional obligation to maximize the experience of all users, campers included. Building large campgrounds provides the opportunity to provide programs, and doing so requires an attitude favorable to, and an interest in, recreation.

Moving to campground size, consider another user need: visitor protection. As the century comes to a close, we have observed a drastic change in what campers say is their greatest concern in selecting a campground. Research from the 1950s through the 1980s told us campers' greatest concern was for clean toilets and showers. Today and likely for some time to come their main concern is security. If it isn't available, then the families *will not come.* For this reason alone small unprotected campgrounds are extremely negative elements for most users and agencies.

Earlier in this book we suggested beginning all of your recreation planning (including campgrounds) with: Whom do you want to use your areas? If you want all types of families, minorities, persons with disabilities, international visitors, and teens camping with their families, it's obvious you should think *big,* plan *big,* build *big,* protect, and program. If you don't want the above users, continue thinking small!

There's no need to belabor the point we've made about control, but you should consider it from the user's standpoint as well; campgrounds should be protected environments for the sake of the campers. If I set up camp and then spend the day fishing on your lake, I have the right to expect my untouched camping equipment to be waiting for me when I return. Yet in recreation journals you'll find a host of studies and reports dealing with theft, vandalism and other negative behavior in campgrounds. Often these writings focus on the social and personal causes of such behavior, but more often than not most of these behaviors could be avoided if on-site supervision were provided. Again on-site supervision becomes easier to justify as campgrounds increase in size.

A final user-oriented consideration of campground size is *convenience.* Most individuals who participate in wilderness camping prefer to rough it. Those who prefer camping trailers and recreational vehicles (RVs) have different tastes. Hot showers, indoor toilets, and other convenience-oriented facilities cost money, but if there weren't a demand for these types of amenities, there wouldn't be a multimillion dollar RV industry. What you personally think of this kind of camping experience shouldn't have any bearing on the kinds of camping opportunities you provide as a professional. In order to provide convenience facilities in family campgrounds, the areas you build must simply be large enough to justify the expense. Running utility lines to a 20-unit campground is not economical, and building 20-unit campgrounds in order to avoid providing the amenities RV campers want and deserve is unprofessional.

Environment

If it weren't such a major concern, we'd suggest the development of small campgrounds was one of life's minor ironies. Consider campground size and design from this perspective: There exist few professions other than recreation and parks for which the environment is such a critical issue. We may build swimming pools, central-city playgrounds, and vest-pocket parks without too much concern for natural resources, but beyond these, the environment is our bread and butter.

One of the basic purposes of parks is to offer a natural setting for people to escape the constraints of a highly technological society. Yet in many cases the very areas park professionals develop to provide access to the natural environment end up becoming so severely degraded the benefit of the experience is lost.

One factor contributing to this degradation is our continuing tendency to build small areas. Because campgrounds are impact-intensive, from both vehicular and pedestrian standpoints, they are among the most likely areas to suffer environmental harm. Cost-effectiveness again enters the picture here since it costs money to reinforce areas of known impact. An environmentally protected universal camp unit, depending on who is building it and local site conditions, can cost $2,000 or more. Add in the expense of maintaining the surrounding environment through design psychology and preventative maintenance, and the cost of ecologically safe small areas becomes prohibitive. Further, as we discussed in Chapter Two, the best way to minimize impact is to localize it. A 250-unit campground may not take up any less space than 10 areas with 25 units each, but think about access: How many acres of land or miles of road does it take to provide the ingress/egress for one area versus 10? Think about use patterns. Will one well-designed, reinforced trail system radiating out from a large campground cause the same impact as unplanned user designed pathways surrounding 10 small areas? Ironically, here is another situation in which rabid environmentalists and the environmental educators (who have much to say but generally aren't family campers) come up with environmental damage–causing advice. They seem to prefer small campgrounds and undefined campsites to more manageable large areas with environmentally sound universal camp units. Fortunately, most real users of family campgrounds are not in these fringe groups.

Types of Campgrounds

Up to this point, it may sound as if all campgrounds should be the same, and the bigger the better, but neither of these statements is entirely accurate. Most of the topics we'll consider in the following sections are concerned with modernized, developed site campgrounds because the types of facilities and amenities found here are the types desired by the majority of people who camp. These are truly family campgrounds. Wilderness camping may have a more romantic appeal and certainly receives more press in both the public and professional literature, but it is simply not the experience sought by most campers.

Perhaps the best way to consider the point is to think of camping as existing on a continuum. At one end are the "purists," who consider equipment purchases by comparing the relative weight of two camp stoves in ounces. At the other end is the family with three children or the retired couple, who consider equipment purchases by comparing how many electrical outlets the RVs have, and how close the microwave is to the dining table and VCR. There's no point in trying to argue the relative merits of either camping preference.

Professionally, we'll continue to stress the need to provide opportunities for all users, though if 90 percent of the people who camp want developed sites, safety, fun, and convenience, it seems reasonable to channel 90 percent of your energy and resources into facilities for these folks. Similarly, we'll direct the bulk of our discussion toward these types of experiences. Unfortunately, providing for the majority is not what several large agencies—including the Forest Service, the Bureau of Land Management, and lately the National Park Service—have done. These agencies are eliminating or downsizing campgrounds rather than making them larger. Their "expertise" in campground design will be noted throughout this chapter.

Several hundred years ago, when we wrote the chapter on trails, we asked you to describe what makes a good one. We suggested the answer depended on two more questions: What kind of a trail is it, and for whom was it built? The same logic applies to campgrounds. Purpose and clientele determine planning criteria and design considerations. For example, one way of distinguishing campgrounds, regardless of the level of development or the tastes of the campers, is the intended length of stay. Some campgrounds should be developed for transient use, like an area along a parkway or an interstate highway where most users simply camp for the night and move on, as they would in a motel. These campgrounds need basic amenities like toilets/showers, sewage dumping stations, and high density, universal, reinforced camp units. To be successful the transient campgrounds should also have an abundance of pull-through campsites. A heavy emphasis on program support facilities, such as a comprehensive trails system or sports fields, isn't necessary as most group-oriented recreation seems to occur when campers spend enough time in an area to get to know their neighbors. This doesn't imply, however, that program opportunities should be ignored in transient campgrounds. Small group activity areas, such as horseshoe pits, beaches, and basketball goals, can work to your advantage. Campfire programs, for example, may be useful even if you experience a 70 percent turnover in clientele each night.

If you do a good enough job of providing enjoyment, you will find some of your transient campers will change their minds and be interested in a second general type of area: the destination camp. The destination camp is what it sounds like, a place where users go to make camp and stay for a period—a weekend or a few days. Developed destination camps are really the focus of discussion later in this chapter, so we'll put these on hold temporarily. First, turn your attention to other types of campgrounds, beginning at the other end of our camping continuum with the wilderness experience.

The Backcountry Camp

Does the planner/designer really need to enter the picture when the camping experience is wilderness oriented? As it turns out, we can apply the transient/destination distinction to the wilderness experience as well as to the developed camp. Inadequate planning and management in the backcountry can cause problems you wouldn't believe unless you'd seen them. All three of the authors have been wilderness campers.

Transient Backcountry Use: The Backpacking Experience. There tends to be a strong positive relationship between the desire for a wilderness experience and environmental fervor. Preservationists who want to rough it are often the most critical of developed site, modern campgrounds. These individuals sometimes think hot showers, flush toilets and recreation programs belong only in the city, that they ruin the out-of-doors for others who "really know how to enjoy nature," and that they degrade the environment. Many—probably most—developed campgrounds you'll see are environmentally unsound. As we'll see later in this book, however, modernized camping facilities don't have to damage the environment, and, as we've said before, are in demand by the majority of folks who camp.

Ironically, some of the most environmentally degraded and aesthetically unappealing camping areas we've seen are those used and misused by backcountry enthusiasts. In Chapter One, we discussed the concept of overuse, suggesting that much of the blame for site impact is erroneously leveled at users when the real fault lies with planners, designers, and managers. This concept holds true in the backcountry as well as in developed areas. You'll find backpackers cause damage similar to that caused by family campground users. Hike the Appalachian Trail or equally popular backcountry in your area and look for damage. Pay particular attention to sites near overnight shelters where users tend to camp on a regular basis. You'll see compacted soils and erosion. You won't see much dead and rotting wood providing needed nutrients for the soil because of the popularity of campfires. While we don't blame backpackers for poor planning and mismanagement, we do get a bit miffed when these users harp on the damage caused in developed campgrounds and remain oblivious to their own impact.

There may be no universal solutions to damage caused by wilderness camping, but you may consider some partial ones. The major source of impact in the backcountry seems to us to be management's designation of camping zones. In many wilderness areas, camping is prohibited except in specified areas, often spaced about a day's hike apart. These areas tend to receive the bulk of the use and, of course, the impact. In some areas, particularly where free-flowing streams are scarce, camping zones and shelters are adjacent to springs or other water points.

Obviously we have a problem. Campers need to replenish their water supplies and, in bear country, shelters are a good idea. Further, we've advocated the concept of localizing impact throughout this book. Now, it seems we're standing on shaky ground by suggesting that shelters be erected for users and that zoned areas harm the environment. However, if water points are plentiful and bears aren't a real concern, we suggest avoiding zones for camping. Most wilderness users are environmentally conscious, and if their overnight stays are spread along the length of a trail system, the impact they do have may tend to heal itself at least to some extent (particularly in the eastern and southern United States). If water points are limited, management may need to localize camping to a few designated sites. In these cases, we suggest reinforcing the spots designated for camping with fine gravel to minimize impact, as in other areas where use is intensified by design.

One other impact problem associated with the backcountry experience is worth mentioning here. If shelters for campers are provided, they should not be accessible by vehicles other than those used by management and maintenance personnel. It may be necessary to provide vehicular access to shelters for periodic cleaning and repairs, but access roads should always be physically and administratively closed. A few people may misuse or vandalize shelters if they can reach them by vehicle, so shelter access roads need to be controlled. Damage to these facilities can be further minimized by placing them at least a mile into the interior from points where trails cross roadways.

Destination Backcountry Use: An Often-Missed Opportunity. When is backcountry camping not backcountry camping, at least not in the traditional sense? Too often, recreation planners and managers seem to view camping as a dichotomous experience, a situation in which either all amenities and facilities are provided or all are absent. As we suggested earlier in this chapter, camping can be viewed as a continuum. Some users, for example, may want the isolation of a backcountry experience without the exertion of backpacking. With a little foresight and planning, it's possible to provide a facility for these individuals and add a new dimension to recreation opportunities. The backcountry destination camp fills this niche, and Figure 7.9 shows a potential layout for this type of area.

While the design for an area like this should be simple, you need to consider some aspects of development. The key to managing a functional backcountry camp is administration. One potential problem with this facility is misuse, allowing the site to become a party spot for local youths. Our recommendation is to use a reservation system in which camping parties call ahead to register for a particular time period. Drop-in use can be accepted for sites not reserved in advance as long as there is some controlled use. The best system we've seen involves a locked cable at the entrance to the camp. When users enter the park or recreation area, they go to an administrative office or staffed recreation site nearby, register, and pick up a key to the cable lock. They then drive to the backcountry camp, unlock the cable, enter, and lock it behind them. Upon departure, they deposit their key in a locked drop box at the cabled entry/exit point.

It isn't necessary to provide backcountry users with a host of amenities. One chemical toilet for every six to eight campsites and a trash dumpster near the entry/exit point are really the only facilities needed. If raccoons aren't a problem, it may be a good idea to issue a few plastic trash bags to camping parties when they register, preventing users from having to take their garbage to the dumpster until they are ready to leave the area for the last time. (We assume one of the criteria for renting a site is complete site cleanup by users.) One aspect that users of this type of area will appreciate is privacy,

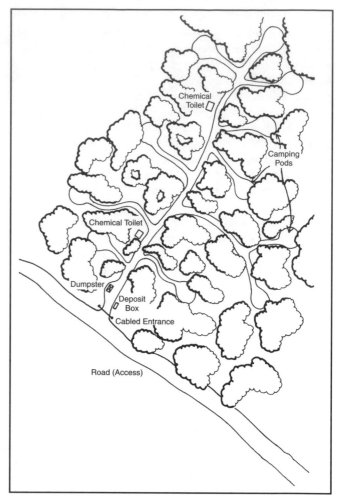

Figure 7.9

probably the primary reason people are attracted to a backcountry camp. For a large acreage-to-site ratio, allow a ratio of 20 to 25 acres per campsite. This amount can be reduced somewhat if steep topography and dense vegetation separate sites psychologically. The need for privacy raises another point. Land for recreation is at a premium, yet the use rate at backcountry camps will not be intensive and fees shouldn't be too high. Since management's dilemma is to provide a wilderness experience without excessive capital expenditures, the number of camp units at a backcountry camp should be kept low, both to provide a sense of wilderness and to hold down development costs. The major potential expense for this type of facility is a road system, so we also suggest that as you review alternative sites you look for an area where roads are already in place. A completed logging operation, or perhaps abandoned camps or summer home sites, can provide you with ready-made road systems.

Another concern associated with backcountry camps, as always, is impact. We recommend gravel roads into campsites to reduce vehicular impact at a cost less than paving. Once you decide the locations for the campsites, it's a good idea to build a reinforced camping pad for this type of user. A bit later, we'll discuss the universal campsite. A sizable variation of this type of camp unit would work well in the destination backcountry camp. Thin overstory vegetation somewhat to allow a good measure of sunlight to reach the ground. The backcountry experience, whether transient or destination, is a recreation activity planners and managers need to accommodate. To some extent the type of backcountry experience users desire is a function of geography. As a professional, you should make an effort to determine what needs exist in your area and act accordingly, remembering that backcountry is only one type of camping experience people seek.

The Boatel

Water-based recreation areas, particularly those on lakes large enough for fishing and other motorized boats, are among the most popular outdoor areas available. In keeping with our concept of developing facilities for a broad spectrum of users, we think it's a good idea to consider the inclusion of *boatels,* or boat-camping areas, in recreation management plans. The purpose of a boatel is to provide a camping opportunity for people who like to combine tent camping and boating but who don't need or want all the amenities associated with a developed campground (and the intensive use associated with these areas). It isn't necessary, or desirable, to develop a large number of boatels on a lake. Depending on the size of the lake and the amount of use, one to four boatels will probably suffice in most instances. Each should be small, with 10 to 15 campsites, and of relatively low density—no more than four or five campsites per acre. Since boatels are not built with wilderness users in mind, they should be constructed as developed facilities with universal campsites and basic amenities including tables and grills (see the section on camp unit design later in the book).

Figure 7.10 shows a schematic layout for a boatel. Basically, the area consists of a collection of individual camp units, each with a water orientation. The distinguishing characteristic of a boatel is inherent in its name, and its design for use by campers who arrive in boats raises two points. First, provision of a boatel (or a wrangler's camp or an OHV area) speaks to your professional commitment to provide facilities for a diversity of users. It's quite easy to avoid becoming involved in this type of venture, but being a professional means you should avoid avoiding involvement. Second, developing a special-use facility doesn't guarantee that it will be used. This is particularly true for boatels, which may go mostly unnoticed if you don't let folks know they exist. Part of recreation management is marketing. If you hide your light under the proverbial basket, life may be somewhat easier, but we'll never accuse you of behaving professionally, either. Planning and developing facilities must be coupled with concerted efforts to help people find out about them.

How should you go about developing a boatel? Since, by definition, use must be limited to those who arrive by boat, internal circulation is not really a design factor. Road access should be provided, but confined by a cable-and-post system for administrative use. Aspects of design you should consider include location, physical site characteristics, and ease of on-site development.

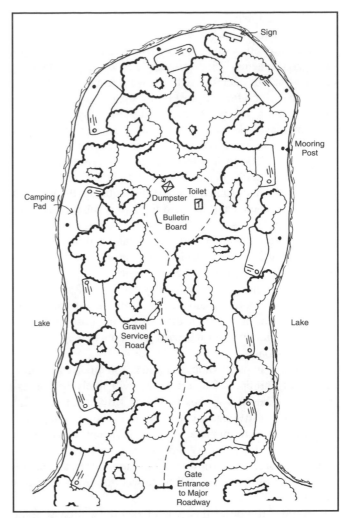

Figure 7.10

Wherever possible boatels should be located near other existing facilities. By placing a boatel close to a developed campground or use area you can minimize operations like collecting fees and garbage. You can also consider uses of adjacent stretches of water when choosing a location for a boatel. Heavily fished areas may attract people to a boatel. If the two are located near each other, it may be helpful to contact and work in cooperation with fisheries personnel when considering alternative locations.

Since water access is the only real requirement, it's possible to develop boatels on a variety of resource bases. Some shorelines, however, are more favorable than others. In surveying potential locations, look for narrow peninsulas like the one depicted in Figure 7.10. These land forms allow you to maximize shoreline use because you get double the water frontage with space for a double row of camp units. You should also look for sites where the vertical difference between the lake pool and the maximum elevation of developable land is minimized, an academic way of telling you to avoid steep shorelines. This criterion needs to be balanced, though, with the need for sites adjacent to water deep enough for craft with steep drafts, such as sailboats.

Once you select an area for a boatel, consider how to lay out camp units. Along with the general guidelines provided in the section on camp unit design, there are a few other specific requirements. First, provide a mooring post for each campsite at the water's edge to allow users a convenient spot for tying their craft. This post is also the place for a campsite number, and a reserved or occupied plastic clip. Since boat campers may seek out a boatel partly because of the privacy afforded by the area, screening between camp units and well-spaced sites (100 to 150 feet between units) should also be site design criteria. Place a sign that designates the area as a boatel (and names it) in a prominent spot facing the water. A dumpster, a chemical toilet, and perhaps a bulletin board for posting regulations and announcements about nearby recreation opportunities are the only additional facilities you need. It's a good idea to post a welcoming message here too. This lets them know who you are as an agency. It also gives them rules of use—how and when to pay for their sites and emergency information. Finally, it tells them you are pleased to have the opportunity to host them. After all, hosting and getting a bit of goodwill for it is what providing recreation facilities is all about.

Size of campsites should vary to accommodate more than one family group. This sort of use will likely beckon extended families and groups including Boy Scouts and Girl Scouts. We also suggest you tuck an on-the-ground grill in the corner of each campsite. And in this special area consider placing a *fixed* heavy-duty table on site near the fire place. Using movable tables in this lightly administered area will mean some of the tables will be moved to the shore line or even stolen.

Administration of this type of facility will cause some challenges and could be expensive. For instance, permits might have to be issued at different prices for different site sizes. The benefits, though, to your organization may well exceed the challenges.

Sporting Camps

Hunting and fishing are two of the more popular forms of outdoor recreation. Apparently these activities are so popular that some agencies seem to develop sporting camps to the exclusion of others. Which agencies? The Corps of Engineers, the Forest Service, the Tennessee Valley Authority, the Bureau of Land Management, most state forests, county parks, and some state parks. What many of these agencies call family campgrounds far too often fits our description of the sporting camp: a small five- to 30-unit camping area; no on-site management or at best a part-time, unpaid campground host; minimal user protection; and maximum impact both locally— since sites are often not reinforced—and regionally, since a dozen or more of these areas are often developed on a given resource base.

Hundreds of these small campgrounds we call sporting camps were built by the Forest Service in the Civilian Conservation Corps days and continued to be built up to the 1990s (one of the authors designed and built several early in his ca-

reer, but by the late 1960s was active in trying to eliminate as many of these areas as possible or in enlarging them). The campsites were generally small and difficult for anyone but tenters to use. A "million" expensive, unfriendly, and unnecessary barricades separated the campsite use area from the parking pad placed there (we said) to protect the precious lush site environment from the soil-compacting wheeled vehicles. The bulletin boards generally told folks 84 reasons why they shouldn't do something. Ranger-type folks visited the area once a day (usually when we weren't there) to help us. Law enforcement personnel seemed to be ever present to check out one of the six special permits or licenses we had to have if we wanted to fish.

The small campgrounds (sporting camps) were great places for local rowdies to have fun, particularly late at night. Clientele (before they were run off) were mom and dad and 1.8 youngsters whose average age was nine, or an older mom and dad whose teens found all sorts of reasons to stay at home. Some of the Forest Service Regions realized the small campgrounds were causing the agency lots of problems, so as early as the mid 1960s (particularly in the South) the Forest Service tried to eliminate and/or enlarge some of them. As we approach the year 2000, most Forest Service Regions continue to live with and even spend thousands of dollars renovating small sites. See, for example, the proposed rehabilitation of Big Elk Creek Campground in Figure 7.11. This "design" was presented by the Forest Service requesting grant money from a special grants program in the state of Idaho. Considering the "quality" of the renovation plan, what sort of disaster was the original campground? Fortunately for all of us, the grants committee said, "No way."

Who else built a surplus of small sites? Planners in the U.S. Army Corps of Engineers provided similar plans in the late 1950s on into the 1970s. Their reservoirs—particularly in the East and South—were littered with 15- to 30-unit sporting camps. These, like those in the Forest Service, were often combination campground/picnic areas adding to the manager's management problems. However, in the mid 1970s they changed leadership and policies, began building sizable, more manageable areas, eliminated hundreds of small sites, and selected the best for renovation and enlargement. Their personnel enthusiastically embraced continuing education efforts and as a result most of their professional personnel have been trained in area renovation and design.

The TVA didn't begin extensive outdoor recreation planning and development until the early 1970s. After having been thoroughly forewarned by the Forest Service and the Corps of Engineers concerning the agency and user negatives involved with building small sites, they built 140 small areas throughout their reservoir system. More often than not, day use was thoroughly mixed with camping. Their managers and users continue to live with those mistakes. Most of their planning staff was engineers (without recreation experience) in those early days. They were a bit difficult to train.

The National Park Service built most of their campgrounds in the 1950s and 1960s, and most designed and built later looked like those of the 1950s and 1960s. They made all

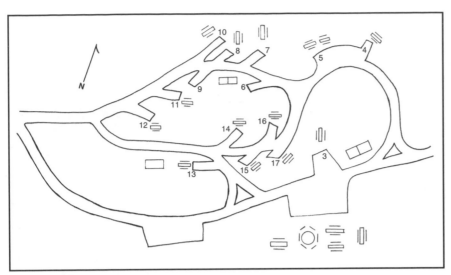

Figure 7.11

agencies have historically been unwilling to give. If we had written this book several decades ago, when public and private sectors were just beginning to provide camping facilities, our advice would have been, "don't build 'em small!" Unfortunately, hindsight is usually better than foresight, and we now have a host of small campgrounds to deal with. Many are in poor condition and most are difficult to manage and impossible to program. As a result, our advice is three-fold. First, avoid repeating mistakes by adding new areas too small to maintain. Second, when possible, phase some small areas out of existence. If, for example, you find yourself responsible for 10 areas with 20 units each, select one with potential for expansion. Over a period of several years, re-design it by adding units and support facilities gradually. (We'll tell you how to develop large areas later in this chapter.) As the one area is expanded, gradually close the other small areas and work to attract users to the newly enlarged campground. This will, by the way, likely meet with considerable resistance from some users, and some of your own staff, but remember your responsibility to provide for people and protect the environment.

Finally, for those small areas you simply can't close, practice rehabilitation measures. Develop new, impact-resistant universal campsites, realign roads when necessary, identify and reinforce areas of known impact, remove hazard trees, and try to cut your losses by managing these areas as effectively as you can. The good ol' boys will be pleased.

Family Campgrounds

The final, and by far the most important, category of camping areas is family campgrounds. As we saw in the beginning of this chapter, these are sizable areas (we suggest 200 units as a minimum) that have the amenities and programs to beckon *families*. If you don't want families, continue building small, unsafe, and unprogrammed areas. If you do want families, read on. Some years ago we developed a series of yes or no questions we think everyone should consider if they manage or build family campgrounds. These questions are shown in Figure 7.12. We call it: "The Do You Love Your Mother and Other Equally Thoughtful Questions" quiz.

During our numerous workshops and seminars we give these questions to the professional trainees. They generally give an enthusiastic "yes!" to questions one through six. Most reluctantly agree they should consider disabled folks who need electricity. And, some even say "yes" to question eight. Many, though, are uncomfortable with a full yes on question seven and some are offended by question nine. The authors take a dim view of these rascals.

As you can see, we think *people,* particularly families, should be your first concern with all sorts of park areas including campgrounds. The authors' basic rule (we've said

sorts of anti-user design errors that campers still enjoy but they didn't make the mistake of building tiny unmanageable campgrounds. We'll discuss some of their planning efforts later in this chapter and in the discussion on the Americans with Disabilities Act in Chapter Ten.

Ponder for a moment what you've read and then relate your thoughts to the facetious book title: *Planning Parks for People.* We hope you are beginning to understand why the authors don't think many wildland parks, particularly camping areas, were planned for people.

What about the largest of the land-managing agencies, the Bureau of Land Management (BLM)? They have some marvelous opportunities to build and manage sizable areas— base camps for users to visit their numerous attractions and those of other agencies (more on this later). Their areas, while built much later than those of the Forest Service, are relatively small sporting camps, too, with a large 1995 vintage one being about 35 campsites. Perhaps this will change, though we doubt it.

By now you should understand we don't advocate building large, large numbers of small, small areas! Because of the environmental degradation often associated with these sites and the lack of cost-effectiveness in trying to manage and program them, small campgrounds do not beckon family groups, although you'll often find families camped here because they have no place else to go. Consider a typical camping family. Let's say we have two parents, a teenager, and a five-year-old. Too many times we've seen situations where Pop goes off to fish or hunt and everyone else is left at the campsite with nothing to do! We say provide camping and other recreation areas for all people to enjoy the out-of-doors. Given the scenario described above, most folks probably enjoy about all of the out-of-doors they can stand in a few hours.

Our basic reason for advocating large family-oriented developed campgrounds is that they provide a sizable base camp for people who want to hunt, fish, and enjoy boating plus activity alternatives for people who don't! Again, this approach requires program provision that, unfortunately, many

Do You Love Your Mother and Other Equally Thoughtful Questions

In you agency's family campgrounds (not your little 5–20 unit sportsman's camps) do you want the following groups as campers?

1.   Yes   No   Do you want minorities such as African Americans, Hispanics, Asians, Native Americans? Do you have them?

2.   Yes   No   Do you want entire families, including teens, camping with their families? You don't have them now, do you?

3.   Yes   No   Do you really want persons with disabilities? There are 43 million of them. This may surprise you, but they all want to visit parks where they can do more than just go to the toilet.

4.   Yes   No   Do you want senior citizens who have need for hookups and special facilities? Do you have senior citizens now?

5.   Yes   No   Do you want the 21 percent of American families headed by single parents? Do you think your campgrounds beckon these folks (80 percent headed by women)? Likely they do not feel wanted, comfortable, or safe in your areas.

6.   Yes   No   Do you want your family campgrounds to be enjoyed by the ever increasing number of international vacationers?

7.   Yes   No   Do you beckon: campers who want electric fans in tents, or hot showers, or dump stations; campers who have 29-foot trailers, or those who need electricity to charge their trolling motors, electric wheelchairs, or a refrigerator for their medicine; or campers who want to have fun, play softball or water volleyball, dance, and see movies? Do you have them now?

8.   Yes   No   Do you want campers who expect to be protected from night- or day-riding thieves, vandals, noisemakers, rowdies, or rampaging cowboys?

OR

9.   Are you satisfied in your so-called family campgrounds to get the right sort of folks like hunters, fishermen, backpackers, the environmentalists, the tent camping folks, and the good ol' boys who don't ride in wheelchairs, or want or need security, water, electricity, dump stations, and fun programming?

Figure 7.12

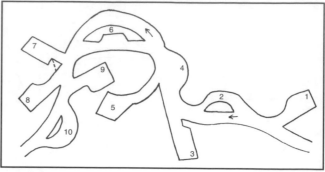

Figure 7.13

this before) is, first determine whom you want (in this case families in a family campground), then determine the kinds of programs you'll need to warmly beckon and host the users, and finally add the last ingredient—the hardware—such as toilets/showers, campsites, roads, ball fields, trails, beaches, and more.

A most important element of hardware is *campsites*. Thousands of these relatively simple features (campsites) have been poorly designed worldwide. The eight state park campsites in eight states at the beginning of this chapter are excellent examples of how not to design and build these facilities.

Family Campground Campsites

Campsites—there are a few good ones and numerous poor or bad ones. Do you know the difference? Here's a test for you.

Figure 7.13 shows 10 campsites located on a segment of one-way road which moves traffic from right to left. Your job is to determine what sort of campsite each one is and whether it is a good functional site. The answers are shown in Table 7.1.

Since you passed our easy test (which most planners don't) here's one—Figure 7.14—which may be a bit more difficult. In this figure, nine of the 50 units on Loop A are well-designed; the other 41 are poorly done. Which are which? On Wildcat Loop, seven of the 50 sites are poorly designed. Find them and indicate what's wrong with each. You'll find the answers in Appendix D. Incidentally, you wouldn't name camp loops "A" and "B", or "1" and "2"—or would you?!

Throughout the book, including this chapter, we've shown you photo collages which have far more wrong with them than right. It's time to shock you a bit with a six-photograph collage showing well-done facilities. Interestingly, all of the units we've selected to show you something well-done are located in U.S. Army Corps of Engineers (USCOE) campgrounds. This doesn't mean the private sector and other agencies haven't built some excellent, environment-protecting, people-pleasing, universal sites. The

SITE #	TYPE	REMARKS
1.	Back-in	Excellent, preferred by a slight majority of campers.
2.	Pull-through	Excellent, also a high camper preference; however, takes up much more space than a back-in if designed right! We suggest you build about 30–35 percent of your units as pull-throughs.
3.	Back-in	With rare exceptions, the back-in, with its living space located on the right side of the spur, is the only usable unit to place on the left side of a one-way road!
4.	Pull-off	Not a preferred unit, but it does function well.
5.	Back-in	Curved to the left to allow proper location of living space. A good camp unit. Owners of large trailers can easily back in on a left-turning curve. It is also quite a design help in locating the view from the living area away from other campsites and, where possible, towards water or scenery.
6.	Pull-through	One of the exceptions noted in 3. Living space is properly located for trailer doors which open on the right.
7.	Not Sure?	"Designers" meant this to be a back-in, but they didn't widen the throat of the spur. (See dashed line.) This has to be done if you design units that are 90° off the road.
8.	Pull-in	No! If your "designers" or planners locate a pull-in spur on their plan or field-locate it on site, shoot them!
9.	Back-in	This is used by many so-called designers, but the living space is located on the wrong side of the spur.
10.	Pull-through	Used by NPS, U.S. Corps of Engineers and others even though it functions poorly for the user. Trailer doors open on the right away from the living space.

If you said units 1 through 6 were OK, and units 7 through 10 were not, you know far more about campsite location than most park designers!

Table 7.1

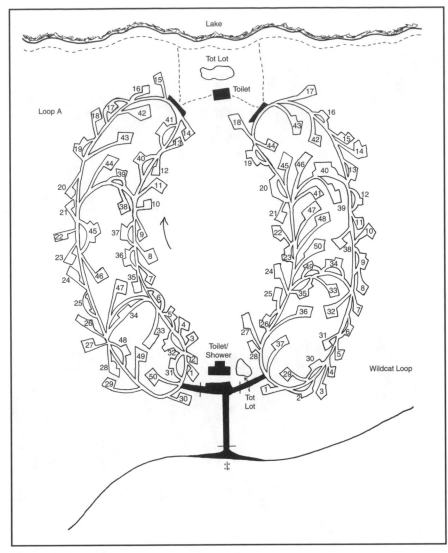

Figure 7.14

USCOE simply has the best ones we've seen (and we built a number of our own some years ago at Land Between the Lakes). Two of the campsites are pull-through units and three are back-ins. Figure 7.15 shows a defined, reinforced generous back-in campsite on Lake Barkley in Kentucky. It has an on-the-ground fireplace, six-foot portable movable wooden picnic table, and a short two-foot portable table used for food storage or as a convenient place for campers' cooking facilities (stoves). It also has water and electric service hookups. There is extra space for additional vehicles including boats and trailers. Campers know where their living space begins and ends. They also can "design" their own campsite living area. Note the vitality of near-site vegetation, 15 years after the heavily used campsites were built! The dashed line shows the edge of the one-way road.

Figure 7.16 shows a defined, reinforced generous back-in campsite at a USCOE campground on Lake Shelbyville in Illinois. The campsite living space is defined by a few concrete barriers while the paved campsite spur is self-defining. Campsite furniture consists of an electric hookup, portable combination wood and metal table, portable lantern-hanging

pole, and an on-the-ground grill tucked into the corner. It is obvious this is a field-designed unit using existing vegetation and an existing paved spur.

Figure 7.17 also shows a level, safe, generous, defined and reinforced campsite at Lake Cumberland in Kentucky. Campsite furniture consists of water and electric hookups, two fixed lantern hangers, a portable table, and an on-the-ground grill tucked into the corner of the defined site. There is adequate room for extra vehicles. This site, too, has been field designed around existing vegetation.

Figure 7.18 shows a unique, generous, level, defined pull-through campsite located in the same Cumberland Lake USCOE campground. It, too, has been beautifully and professionally field designed at the intersection of two campground roads. (The road in the foreground is two-way; the road to the left of the site is one-way with traffic moving toward the top of the picture. The two roads intersect in a "T" at the bottom left of the picture.) The site had been in use for a number of years, yet the intersite zone was in excellent environmental condition. There is adequate room for several vehicles and camping equipment. Campsite furniture includes a portable wooden table, water and electric hookups, on-the-ground grill and fixed lantern hanger.

Figure 7.19 shows another pull-through unit—defined, reinforced, safe, generous, level, and quite usable. The definition is the meeting of gravel and grass. Here we have the beginning of prairie land in eastern Kansas. There are no physical barriers and no crosstie definition, yet campers respect the psychological barriers and stay on the graveled surface. The table is portable and the in-the-ground grill is tucked

Figure 7.15

Figure 7.16

Figure 7.19

Figure 7.17

Figure 7.20

Figure 7.18

into the corner of the campsite. The gravel surface is generous enough to hold a sizable trailer, boat, and two or three extra vehicles. The pull-through is where it should be—on the right side of the paved one-way road.

The temporary sign (Figure 7.20), on-site administration, and the general size of the campsite in Figure 7.19 are the keys to keeping campers on the developed and reinforced campsites. The USCOE manager said the sign (which is near the entrance gate) can be taken down in about two years. By then, it seems his camping clientele will be accustomed to how and where they should camp. The key here, though, is on-site administration. The sign in Figure 7.20 reads "Camp on Designated Pads Only."

These five campsites were built by four different USCOE organizations on four reservoirs in three states. They used different techniques (for example, the number of crosstie definers), and built different sizes and kinds of shapes of campsites. Right? Right! All of the camp units were generous and level, with the living space located on the proper side of the camp spur; defined (I know where my territory is! You know where it is!); reinforced with fine gravel, usable, and desirable for any type of camper (including folks with tents, motor homes, or trailers, and persons with disabilities); and the surrounding vegetation is enhanced and protected. Note only the spur in Figure 7.16 is paved and it is a rehabilitated site utilizing an existing paved space. None of the other excellent units has paved parking spaces. They simply aren't needed at least on these sites on level land. Contrast the five campsites (and surrounding environments) with those from the eight state parks in eight states shown at the beginning of the chapter. Our two basic responsibilities in recreation are providing for people and protecting resources. The five quality USCOE campsites do both of these jobs quite well.

The Universal Campsite

The five USCOE campsites shown in Figures 7.15 through 7.19 fit our description of what we've long called *universal campsites*. To us this means anyone (tenter, wheeled-vehicle camper, and persons with disabilities) could use the site. There were no design or administrative differences saying tenters here, trailers there, or wheelchair users at a special (though more often than not poor) site next to a toilet. As you've seen in the five USCOE photographs, the campsites can be different sizes, shapes, and kinds but persons with varying needs—including an extended family with several vehicles—can physically get onto the defined site and they can design their own living space (Figure 7.21).

There are several common characteristics concerning universal campsites. The parking space is a part of (not separated from) the unit. You don't see a sea of expensive barricades (posts, rails, logs, or rocks) keeping users from using the site they've rented. The site isn't "overused" or muddy when wet or dusty when dry. Vegetation, including screening and larger trees, is in good condition between sites. Campers can place their tents, awnings, dining flys, cars, trucks, trailers, motor homes, bicycles, lawn furniture, camping supplies, and goodness knows what else anywhere they wish. Who would have thought the camper would park that car on the extreme left side of the site shown in Figure 7.21? Are they causing environmental or administrative problems? Nope. This is a great example of hosting through design.

Who appreciates the universal sites? Applied research tells us tent campers and wheeled campers alike have high preferences for them (both types of users cause tremendous site damage on undefined sites). Administrators like them since they mean various types of users don't have to be told where they can and can't go. Applied research tells us tent

Figure 7.21

campers (contrary to the opinion of many park managers) do like to camp amid wheeled-vehicle users—at least in family camping environments—so the universal site meets both user and manager needs. Those who are charged with resource protection prefer these sites since they protect the environment between sites. Fact is, if you rehabilitate a so-called overused campground using the defined universal type of campsite, you'll find healing and revegetation of the previously impacted intersite zones will occur throughout much of the United States with little or no work on your part. Maintenance personnel like the universal site because it requires a minimum of maintenance. Adding gravel to the site every three to four years and maintaining the site furniture and the defining railroad ties as they deteriorate eliminates the tremendous job of complete rehabilitation when universal sites aren't used.

We found an unusual group of critters who don't like the universal graveled campsites. Fire ants won't live there! That's a real plus for those of you who don't enjoy stinging fire ants being an intimate part of your camping experience. We'll likely be castigated by the fire ant lovers of the world and other similar environmental groups, but that's a price we're willing to pay!

Another big bonus users get when you provide universal sites is one of space. "I know where my site is located (I can see the 'private' boundaries), and you know where yours is located and where the boundaries of mine are" (a sort of territorial imperative of campers). This known space bonus is great for users and for the site environment.

Furniture on the site can vary but we suggest you consider an on-the-ground grill tucked into one corner, a movable table (preferably eight-feet long with one end cantilevered), and a fixed or movable lantern hanger. As you can see, this allows users considerable freedom concerning how they use the site. This is great hosting and being user-friendly.

Based on the overwhelming acceptance of the universal site by users and most managers, coupled with the fact thousands of the sites have been built across the country, we are pleased to have been the imagineers years ago of what we now call the universal campsite. It has been a contribution to serious environmental protection.

Original Purpose. Our basic reason for imagineering what we now call the universal campsite was quite simple. We wanted to build maintenance problems (site deterioration and what we then called overuse) out of campgrounds. The other benefits we've described—tent and wheeled-vehicle user preferences, user freedom to design their own space, high quality area for campers with disabilities, ease of administration, protection and enhancement of inner site zones, and fire ant discouragement—came not through design or our brilliance *but* by blundering into something exceptionally beneficial. We wish we could take all sorts of credit, but it isn't deserved!

Are the universal campsites savers of scarce maintenance dollars and protectors of the environment? For a dramatic answer, have a look at Figures 7.22 and 7.23. When we took these photographs, both of the campsites at Piney Campground in Land Between the Lakes had been in use for 20 years. The

Figure 7.22

understory and overstory vegetation around both campsites originally looked like the vegetation now surrounding the defined universal site. The campsite in Figure 7.22 was one of 30 already-built sites the oldest of the authors was asked (during an on-loan consulting visit from the Forest Service) to critique. His answer was the lack of reinforcement and definition together with the scattering of campsite furniture under shade would soon mean tremendous on-site impact, loss of understory vegetation, and eventual death of many on- and near-site trees (even though they were young, vigorous hardwoods). He further told them, the Forest Service, National Park Service, and all other agencies had built campsites like their 30 with similar disastrous results! Their question essentially was, "OK, you turkey, how should campsites be built?" He told them, and wonder of wonders, they took his advice, then designed and built the additional 70 sites—including the one shown in Figure 7.23. These became the original impact-resistant universal campsites. (Later, when the three authors worked there, the contrasting site types at Piney were a part of heralding LBL as a national outdoor recreation demonstration area.) All 100 sites, including the poorly designed 30, were opened to public use in 1968. The two photographs taken 20 years later tell the story of environmental destruction and true environmental protection. By the fall of 1970 (after only three years of use) on the undefined sites, the un-

Figure 7.23

derstory vegetation was gone; on-site soils were severely compacted; the undefined campsites had greatly enlarged; and trees were beginning to exhibit considerable dieback. Overuse? No! Poor design? Yes!

Problems in Campsite Land. Since the authors have done such a good job extolling the virtues of the universal campsite over 25 years, all of the students and professionals they've taught have done a great job building them! Right? Wrong! Most of the universal campsites we've seen have been good ones, particularly in recent years. But numerous mistakes have been made and continue to be made. These include separation of unit furniture from the parking pad by barricades or elevation, an overabundance of crosstie work, use of existing parking spaces where they don't always meet user needs, location of use areas and site furniture on the wrong side of the parking spur, nongenerous living space, leaving trees within the living area, and using pea gravel or crushed stone—which is too large for tenters and wheelchairs—on the living area. Review the characteristics of a well-done universal campsite again and describe the mistakes in Figures 7.24 through 7.31. All of these sites *were thought to be* well-done universal ones when they were built:

7.24. North Georgia USCOE camp unit on a two-way road. (Note where camper has to park.)
7.25. Tennessee State Park rehabilitated back-in site on the left side of a one-way road. Motor home on site (this one is a bit tricky).
7.26. Central Illinois USCOE site on left side of one-way road.
7.27. Southern California USCOE renovated back-in site on the left side on a one-way road. Note the extensive crosstie work on the road areas.
7.28. U.S. Forest Service back-in site in central Colorado.
7.29. U.S. Forest Service back-in site in central Colorado.
7.30. Back-in rehabilitated campsite on right side of a western Kentucky USCOE campground road. (Using the in-place, four-foot, large, round concrete table was their goal and that isn't the problem.)
7.31. Back-in site on the right side of a one-way road in a USCOE campground in California.

Remember, these are all examples of how not to build universal campsites!

Camp Unit Design

In the discussion of wrangler's camps in Chapter Five, we alluded briefly to a few considerations concerning camp unit design. Different types of campgrounds, because they attract specific kinds of users, require somewhat different approaches to laying out camp units. However, with the possible exception of backcountry or wilderness camps, some techniques should be common to camp unit design regardless of the type

Figure 7.24

Figure 7.25

Figure 7.26

Figure 7.27

Figure 7.28

Figure 7.29

of campground involved. Campsites in a family campground, due to management concerns and the amount of space and convenience users need and expect, probably require the most careful attention during field design. Thus in this section, we'll focus on the types of considerations you need to think about when designing or rehabilitating camp units in a family camping environment.

The techniques discussed here should provide you with a general set of guidelines for designing and building camp units in other types of areas as well. The differences in campsites

Figure 7.30

Figure 7.31

for other types of facilities depend mainly on size and level of development. For example, units in sporting camps can generally be somewhat smaller than those discussed here because of the types of vehicles and camping equipment hunting and fishing parties normally use. Campsites in group areas may need to be somewhat larger since groups consisting of more members than a single family may want to use a particular site. Wrangler's camps, OHV, and other special-use facilities normally won't need the intensive, on-site management, diversified program opportunities, or number of camp units found in a large family campground. Thus campsites in these special-use areas may or may not need the unit numbering system, electrical outlets, or sewer and water hookups often found in family campgrounds. Basic layout and construction methods are generally the same for all developed campsites, and these techniques are what we'd like to discuss next.

There are probably as many solutions to the challenge of how to design functional camp units as there are plots of developable land. Before you begin to think about specific layouts for campsites, however, you need to keep two general considerations in mind. First, campsites, like other recreation facilities, *should never be* exclusively paper or computer designed. It's simply not possible to develop a good camp unit

without the integral step of field design. Factors including shade, site aesthetics like scenic vistas, cuts and fills, location of units adjacent to the one you're designing, site type, size, density, and understory vegetation for screening must all be considered in final design and layout. These and other elements can be analyzed only after careful and frequent on-site inspections. Second, camp units, like the ball field at the private campground we discussed in Chapter Six, are best designed in reverse. Instead of beginning the design or rehabilitation process by saying, "Let's put the entrance zone here, maintenance yard here, campsites here," and so on, begin by determining what areas are most suitable for campsites. Let shade, type of vegetation, terrain, and potential for access serve as your primary guides here. We'll discuss these topics in more detail shortly.

For now, allow your resource base to lead you to decisions about unit placement; let unit placement lead you to traffic flow patterns, traffic flow to camp-loop road alignment, and loop road alignment to access to the camping zone. This may seem to be a backward approach to zoning. However, campsites (at least to users) are the focal points of campgrounds. From this perspective, we think it makes sense to locate units first and look at roads and other facilities as being supportive of the camping experience. We do suggest one exception to this approach. Can you guess what it is? To check your answer, turn to the design section of Chapter Nine.

Unit Site Selection—The Way It Should Be! Quality individual campsite locations should be determined first. These locations (control points) should determine the center line location of camp loop roads. Finally the main road is a linkage of those loop roads. You should know, however, campgrounds are rarely designed this way. Our engineers or planners locate the main road first, then the loop roads, and the remaining space—good or bad—is where they try to locate campsites.

Once areas within the campground complex have been earmarked for camp units, you can begin clearing the right-of-ways for the loop or access road on which units are to be built. (Remember, traffic flow should have already been determined.) After clearing the right-of-way, the planner, or preferably a design team, should go to the field and lay out individual units. Mark the perimeter of each unit with stakes and/or flagging tape, then clear the entire site, leaving all other understory vegetation between sites intact except for hazard trees. Once you've cleared these enclaves, stake the outline of each unit for construction, being particularly careful to indicate where corners of the campsite will fall.

Unit Size. During the early 1960s when many of our public campgrounds were designed and built, wheeled-vehicle camping (trailers, motor homes, van conversions, pop-up campers and more) and tent camping were nearly equal in popularity. By the late 1970s, however, tent camping made up 20 percent or less of the camping population. This percentage continues in most places today. Many of our public campgrounds have higher tent camping ratios simply because most of their campsites aren't usable by campers who have anything larger than a pop-up tent camper. Figure 7.32 takes

Figure 7.32

us back to the 1930s, when small cars and trailers like this one had difficulty finding adequate camping space on any of our public land campgrounds. The combination of car, hitch distance, and trailer was about 32-feet long. Compare this to Figure 7.33 in which the motor home and sizable boat trailer are 58-feet long! How large should the campsites of the late 1990s be? "Generous enough to meet the needs of most users," would be our answer.

A good unit size, *excluding the parking spur,* is an average of 35-feet long by 25-feet wide, or 875 square feet. Camp units don't have to be—in fact, shouldn't be—all the same size and shape. Different angles, lengths, and widths will add variety to your design and better accommodate the different types of equipment and vehicles campers have. A 35-by-25-foot site is a good benchmark figure, because a unit this size should be large enough to contain the equipment used by an "average" camping family (the one with 1.8 children). Make some campsites larger than this for dual family use or for those groups with more family members. Units smaller than 875 square feet are acceptable, and you may prefer them over the alternative of extensive cosmetic work on the land base.

In short, provide a diversity of unit sizes, shapes, and types. The field design process should give you different sizes and shapes. This approach allows you to accommodate dif-

ferent types and numbers of users, provide aesthetic appeal through variety, maximize the use of the resource base, and minimize the necessary amount of grading and other construction challenges.

Camp-Unit Density. At one time, the Forest Service recreation manual strongly suggested woodland areas contain no more than three camp units per acre. They were certain this is what their campers wanted. At the same time, National Park campgrounds are likely to feature 12 to 15 units per acre since their experts apparently feel this is what American campers want as a camping density. Unfortunately, undefined campsites in most of these Forest Service and Park Service campgrounds look like environmental disaster areas no matter what the density! But that is another story.

Three units per acre in a Forest Service "family" campground mean campers are at least 100 feet apart, that today's campers will likely be fearful of the heavy between unit screening, that a resource is wasted, that camper social needs haven't been considered, and that cost per unit for roads and sanitary facilities will be quite prohibitive. Further, most users prefer higher densities, although the National Park density may be a bit much for many (not most) users. Yet neither the Forest Service nor the National Park Service has designed loops of different densities to find out what users actually prefer! This is exactly what you should do.

Private campground owners would likely tell us the National Park Service density of 12 to 15 units per acre is low if you are at all concerned with land costs and profit margins. We've designed family campgrounds with densities from the ridiculous low of three units per acre to 35 units per acre, which is much too high considering the types and sizes of American camping equipment. Experience and applied research tell us campers have all sorts of preferences, and our advice is to design loops of different densities in your family campgrounds. The public park camping unit density might range from a low of seven units per acre to a high of 16.

One of the problems many planners have is not being able to visualize camp unit density. Figure 7.34 shows a universal campsite density of 10 units per acre. It also shows different unit types, sizes and shapes.

Figure 7.33

Figure 7.34

PARKS FOR PEOPLE

Since research tells us campers prefer camping on the outside of a camp loop rather than on the inside, you have an opportunity to design with density preferences as a primary criterion. One approach would be to locate most of your low density sites on the inside and high or higher density units on the outside.

Types of Camp Units. There are three functional types of camp units. These are the back-in, the pull-through, and the pull-off. Figure 7.35 shows several back-in units, the most space efficient you can build because you can maximize the

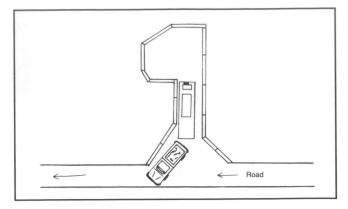

Figure 7.36

Figure 7.35

unit per acre density if this is a design goal. Further, roughly half the campers we've asked tell us they prefer back-in sites. Back-in units function well on either side of a camp loop road as long as the angle of the spur-to-road juncture is not greater than 90°. Occasionally, the lay of the land may dictate a 90° spur-to-road juncture. You can make a perpendicular back-in unit usable if you flare the spur wide where it meets the road (Figure 7.36). Depending on site conditions, this space may be better designed with a pull-through or a pull-off unit.

Any unit where the spur-to-road juncture is greater than 90° is a pull-in campsite (Figure 7.37). Do not build pull-in campsites! If campers have a nonmotorized RV like a trailer or fifth wheeler, they must pull into these sites with their tow vehicle *in front of* their camping rig. Then they can't leave the site without taking their camper with them. Manufacturers try to make camping trailers as convenient as possible,

but they do require some effort to set up for camp use, like using a leveling jack to make sure the trailer rests level. Pull-in sites require users to break camp and take their trailer with them every time they leave the unit. Then they must relevel their rig upon returning. Chances are, they'll simply drive the wrong way on your one-way roads so they can back into the unit, creating less-than-safe conditions and management headaches.

On a back-in unit, the spur should be a minimum of 12-feet wide, though lengths can vary considerably. Not all sites you select for camp units will have enough depth for you to provide 55-foot spurs without extensive grading, cutting or filling. Here are two solutions to this problem. One is not to worry about it. The other is not all users have 35-foot trailers, and as a result you can build some camp units with shorter spurs. Those who come in compact cars and camp in tents may need only 18–20 feet of spur for a functional site. Beyond this minimum, there is no set criterion for spur length. However, you should understand this: Where possible, make all camp units sizable and generous so anyone can camp on any campsite. Some site topography may call for 100–120 feet of spur to reach a good unit location. Spurs of different lengths also allow you to "stagger" adjacent camp units, letting you take maximum advantage of the land you have available. Compare the two designs in Figure 7.38. On the top portion of the drawing, we have two adjacent units with similar spur lengths. Note the one on the left is much larger than the one on the right. On the bottom portion, three units take the same amount of road space as those above because the spur lengths are varied. Staggered spur lengths also help pre-

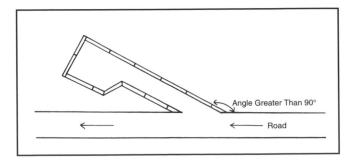

Figure 7.37

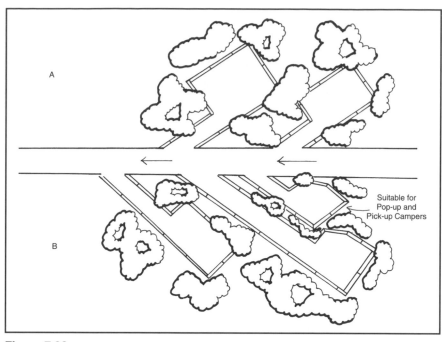

Figure 7.38

side of a one-way road. To understand the logic behind this design requirement, you need to know a bit about camping rigs. With the exception of pickup camper shells, which have rear exits, most camping vehicles like trailers and motor homes have doors on the right-hand, or passenger, side of the vehicle. Therefore one goal of camp unit design is to place the living space to the right of the parking spur as you face the direction of traffic flow. This applies to all camp units, regardless of type. Consider the four campsites in Figure 7.41. Sites A and B are functional for users because the doors to camping rigs parked on these sites open directly onto the living space. Sites C and D, however, because of their design, force users to walk around their camping vehicles to reach their living space. This design mistake—one we see in national parks and everywhere else—won't prevent campers from using the site, but why inconvenience folks when it's so

vent visual monotony among camp units. We call this an "up-and-back" principle of unit layout. This allows you to take maximum advantage of space while minimizing the amount of loop road needed.

Figure 7.39 shows three universal back-in sites designed using the up-and-back principle. The one on the left is near the road but is made more generous by having a wide throat on the short spur. A large middle unit tucks in behind the one on the left. The campsite on the right ramps down to a living area behind the middle site.

A second popular type of camp unit is the pull-through (Figure 7.40). The pull-through unit requires more linear, or roadside, space than the back-in, but often not as much depth. Also, since the pull-through doesn't require the user to enter the site in reverse gear, this may be the best type for inexperienced campers to negotiate. Pull-through sites function well on either side of a two-way road, but only on the right-hand

Figure 7.39

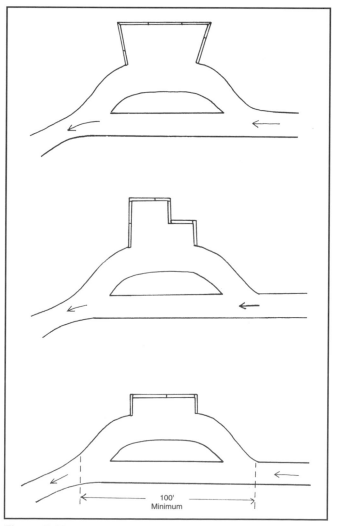

Figure 7.40

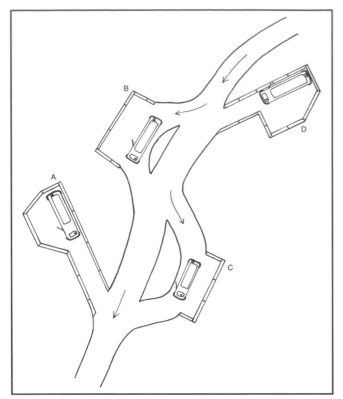

Figure 7.41

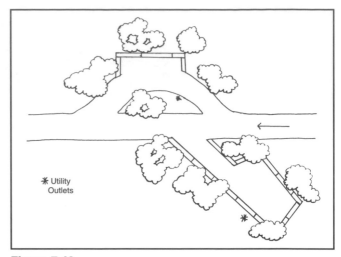

Figure 7.42

easy to design the site with the user in mind? Why, indeed, if you are a real professional?

Experience tells us the majority of older campers will not consider camping in your campground unless you have pull-through campsites available. Thus, we suggest both public and private sectors provide about 30–35 percent of their units as pull-throughs. If you don't have an abundance of pull-throughs, you are essentially telling older campers—including retirees—"We don't want you!" In our view this is not politically, socially, or financially smart.

As long as we're talking about user convenience, let's consider the correct location for utility hookups. On camping vehicles, the connections for electrical, water, and sewer hookups are on the rear of the left-hand, or driver's, side of the vehicle. This means that utility outlets, if you provide them, must be to the left of the parking spur as you face the direction of traffic flow. Figure 7.42 illustrates appropriate locations for utility outlets. (*Note:* Don't locate these hookups too close to the edge of the parking spur as camping rigs with slide outs may damage them or be damaged. Complicating your job is the fact that the location of these slide outs varies greatly.)

The third type of functional camp unit you can design is the pull-off (Figure 7.43). Essentially "abbreviated" versions of the pull-through site, pull-offs are suited for locations where you don't have enough depth to back in and too little linear space to pull through. Again like the pull-through, the pull-off unit will function on either side of a two-way road but only on the right-hand side of a one-way road. If the pull-off unit is on a loop where utility hookups are provided, placing

them to the left of the spur may increase the potential for collisions with utility outlet posts. Thus you should place utility hookups as Figure 7.43 shows.

On a related note, in order to minimize construction costs and allow managers to charge fees based on the types of amenities provided (electrical, water, sewer, or a combination of these), all units on a given loop should offer the same kinds of services; that is, one loop may have no utilities, while another has electricity only, another electricity and water, and so on. Separating loops by type of utilities provided is a good design technique. Conversely, separating different types of users—tent versus trailer campers, for example—is not a good idea. Tent and trailer campers in developed family campgrounds don't mind camping together, and trying to separate them into different zones creates a host of management problems.

One important factor in designing camp units is variety. A long series of identical units may give the user a feeling of being in a "rubber stamp" campground. "Cookie-cutter" designs create monotony and prevent users from selecting the type they prefer. This does not imply a particular type of unit should be forced onto a piece of land where it won't fit without extensive cosmetic work. Rather, unit types should be as varied as the land base permits. Altering the shapes and sizes of units of the same type (e.g., the back-in), helps reduce monotony as well, a practice which also helps you accommodate different types and sizes of camping rigs (Figure 7.44).

There are nine excellent campsites shown in Figure 7.44, including a pull-off, five back-ins with different sizes and

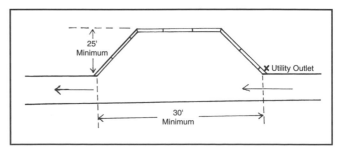

Figure 7.43

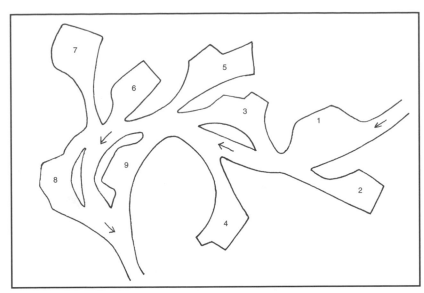

Figure 7.44

shapes, and three pull-throughs. Look carefully and see if you can find all three types of units.

Figure 7.45 shows an example of cookie-cutter campsite construction. The traffic flow throughout the loop is a bit strange but once you and the users "figure it out" you'll find all campsites are quite usable. Those on the left side of the one-way roads have the living spaces where they should be. There is some shade, lots of grass cutting, little or no screening between any units, and the loop isn't pointed toward the water (we'll explain this one in the next chapter) but our concern here is complete lack of camp unit variety. There are no older-camper beckoning pull-through units, and the campsites appear to be (other than perhaps some spur length differences) all the same size and shape making engineering and contracting easy, but lacking in the user-friendly realm.

Special Camp Unit Features

Before we go further we want to share four very special features about campsites:

1. An exception to the no pull-throughs on the left side of one-way road "rule;"
2. Buddy sites;
3. Extra parking space at campsites; and
4. The benefits of curved camping spurs.

Each of these special features is extremely important to campground design and administration as well as to beckoning and hosting users! They are also four important items most planners and designers, particularly consultants, have never heard about.

The Exception to the "No Pull-Throughs on the Left" Rule. Camp units eight and nine on Figure 7.44 are both pull-through units. They are excellent sites though one is on the left side of the one-way road. Since we've said pull-throughs don't function well on the left side of a one-way

road we appear to be contradicting ourselves. Not so. Figure 7.46 shows a well-done exception to our rule. This pull-through, like campsite nine of Figure 7.44, crosses the narrow upper end of a camp loop road. The generous living space is on the right side of the pull-through, located between it and the edge of the sharply curving end of a loop road. USCOE folks in Georgia have built a generous easy-to-use universal campsite. It has a portable table, on-the-ground grill and double fixed lantern hanger. The unit is defined by timbers that are flush or level with the ground. And, the site is covered with fine gravel—a dandy campsite.

This takes us into Chapter Eight—Family Campground Design—but it further shows how our exception can be used to add numerous pull-through units on a fatter than "normal" peanut loop. The authors call this their woolly worm design. Figure 7.47 illustrates this notion. Here, the campsites are medium-to-high density but the positioning of the motor home, car, or truck and trailer on the curved parking spur acts as or adds to the screening between the camper and the unit below. The vehicles of the campers above act as screening. Pull-through sites can also be located completely

Figure 7.45

Figure 7.46

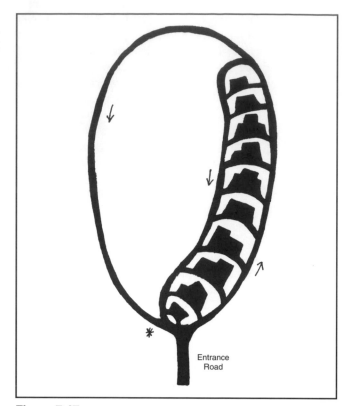

Figure 7.47

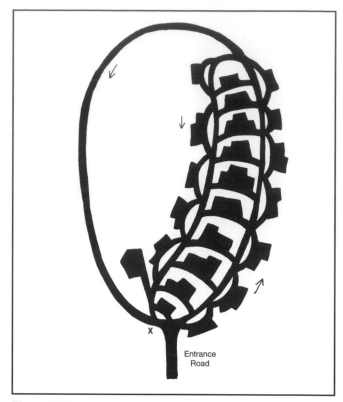

Figure 7.48

around the "worm" and the entire "worm" outline is the right side of a one-way road (Figure 7.48). One word of caution—make sure the exit point of the worm road is to the left of the main entrance road and curving toward it (see point X). If campers come in on the right side of the entrance, they will enjoy a version of perpetual motion.

Buddy Sites. The scene: A national forest campground in the far West (or anywhere else for that matter); campsites 100 feet apart with heavy screening between them; a short camp spur barricaded from site furniture which is six feet in elevation below the spur and 50 feet away from it; signs around the loop proclaim, "Only one camping vehicle/campsite"!

Early in this chapter we discussed "whom do you want" elements. These elements included extended families, minorities, single-parent families, persons with disabilities, families with teens, and more. The above scene isn't too beckoning to any of these folks or, in fact, to most other campers.

Some years ago when we were conducting numerous applied recreation research studies at LBL, we were surprised to find 37 percent of our camping use came as extended families (that's great) or family and friends camping together (that's great, too). Our campsite density, generous size of what was then the rare universal campsite, and beckoning programming were partial reasons for this. The basic reason, though, was families and friends like to camp together. How do we meet this challenge, and what is the national trend as we move nearer to the year 2000? Our response then was to begin building a series of double campsites in our campgrounds.

Part of the original study that gave us the 37 percent figure noted above was replicated early in the 1990s by Penn

State University at a sizable state campground in Indiana. At Leiber State Recreation Area the researcher found 44 percent of the campers came as a sizable extended family, or family and friend groups. That's quite a social finding and one that must be plugged into the design of new campgrounds and the rehabilitation of old ones. It appears the trend is toward more extended groups of campers. We've given this information to hundreds of participants at our campground workshops. Some folks have listened, particularly our friends in the U.S. Corps of Engineers. The Buddy Site sign idea shown in Figure 7.49 is a bit of imagineering by staff at USCOE Lake Shelbyville in Illinois. The "group of two only" may be confusing but the buddy idea is great. The double site in Figure 7.50 with a generous common entrance is on the left side of a

Figure 7.49

one-way road. (Note the paved road in the foreground is level with the ground.) There is some elevation difference between the two sites, which means they could also be used by campers who didn't know each other. Each site has a portable table, on-the-ground grill and electrical outlet. All sorts of trailers, cars, trucks and camping equipment brought by extended families could be placed in these 15-year-old universal campsites without harm to the environment. The two camping groups

A final excellent example is a ramped-up paved-spur buddy site on the Daniel Boone National Forest in Kentucky (Figure 7.52). Here again this site is well-laid out for use by a big camping family.

There are numerous ways to build sites designed to accommodate families camping together. One obvious way is to build sizable single sites. You can also use a combination of pull-throughs and back-ins, and if you're skilled and

Figure 7.50

Figure 7.52

shown could be camping together or perhaps not. In any event, the adjacent buddy sites work extremely well for large families. This again is great hosting.

Figure 7.51 shows a large motor home with auto carrier, and the front end of what appears to be a sizable van conversion on a buddy site at West Point Lake in west Georgia. The long, paved spur in the foreground is ramping down to the site while the more level and even longer spur (where the motor home is located) has a gravel surface. Someone has done some outstanding thinking here and the campers are the beneficiaries. It is obvious this was done in the field and not in some office! This is one of the best examples of field design and site construction on the buddy sites the authors have ever seen.

thoughtful enough, you can interface units of one camp loop with those of another. Buddy sites can be designed on both sides of one- or two-way roads. Design and build them, and they (the campers) will come!

Extra Parking. A vacation begins on a Tuesday morning with Mom and two children in their car pulling their camping trailer on their way to your campground on Lake Whoop De Doo. They arrive and find a dandy site with a water view. It's a bit snug and the car and trailer barely fit on the spur, but this is one of your largest and best sites and they enjoy camping. A common scenario follows: Dad and the oldest son have been working at the office or factory and they arrive late Friday evening with a pickup truck, boat, and trailer. The boat is filled with electronics and fishing treasures. They are

Figure 7.51

eager to see other family members and catch fish. The problem is there is no room for them to park with their family on *their* campsite. They are taken to a parking lot in the campground one-quarter mile away from their unit. And they are charged an additional camping fee. They are unhappy campers! If they don't unload all their fishing gear and take it to their campsite they know or fear it will be stolen. This tale could go on but it will have a less than pleasant ending. The problem here is the campground isn't designed to care for and beckon users, particularly if you want happy campers and return business. Figure 7.53 shows a generous universal site that more than adequately meets the needs of the family we described visiting a lakeside campground. They have a camping trailer (the tow vehicle is missing), boat, and trailer with pickup truck. Two additional USCOE innovations shown here include built-in benches on the left side of the living space and a portable cooking or serving table. Note here the movable table is located under the trailer awning. This is a highly user-friendly campsite.

Figure 7.54 features a paved back-in camping spur with extra parking on the left. This is a good site, though on this flat ground we don't recommend paving. They have also added an upright picnic grill which is quite unnecessary and nearly useless.

Figure 7.53

Figure 7.54

Figure 7.55 has an excellent back-in campsite on the left side of a one-way road (traffic moves toward the bottom of the photograph). The site has a lantern hanger, on-the-ground grill, portable table, and both water and electric hookups (placed properly). The necessary extra parking is provided. This USCOE campsite is on Lake Cumberland in Kentucky. They could have added even more space by placing the nearly flush crosstie border where we've added a dashed line.

Figure 7.55

The Curved Parking Spur

Earlier in the chapter we gave you a test asking if you knew which campsites were good and which weren't (Figure 7.14). Most of the planners and designers we've tried to train said the curved spur (Site 4 on Figure 7.44) was a bad one. They are wrong! Figure 7.56 shows three rehabilitated sites at a Tennessee state park campground. They aren't large sites (they were limited—as they should have been—by using an existing paved road), but they are large enough for the extra vehicles discussed in the previous paragraphs. One subtle design trick would have made these good universal campsites much better. Had each site been curved to the right, the campers would have had views of the lake rather than a straight

Figure 7.56

view of the trailer to the left. Curving the spur would also have given the campers more private space.

Figure 7.57 shows a 100-foot spur with a curved living space at the end. This means the living space on this universal site (one designed by an author years ago) has full orientation to the water. As with many of the things we've done, we blundered into another good idea. A camping friend who had a sizable trailer gave us the inspiration for this idea when he said he and others had no problem backing in on a curve with full use of his left-hand side mirror. The table is a fixed one here so it isn't as user friendly as we suggest now.

Figure 7.58 shows a beautiful USCOE site (again at West Point Lake) with a curved spur giving the camper privacy and a full orientation to the lake. Note this technique makes use of the camping vehicle as a privacy screen for the user. Site generosity gives plenty of room for the boat trailer and other vehicles brought by an extended family. The curved spur concept also allows the unit field designer to best position campsite living spaces to enhance views of all sorts, including mountains and other scenery. It is a marvelous technique—use it!

Figure 7.57

Universal Campsite Construction

First have a look at two campsites—one well-designed and well-built, the other a disaster. If you've studied the chapter to this point, you should know what's usable and good, and what isn't about both camp units. Take some time and list the good and bad. One (the disaster) was office designed by a planner/designer; the other was field designed by a manager and his maintenance foreman. One protects the environment in and between campsites and is highly desirable for camper use; the other isn't. Both sites are back-ins; only one, however, has the living area where it should be—on the passenger side of the trailer. One builds maintenance problems out of the site (Figure 7.59); the other builds in maintenance problems (Figure 7.60). Ironically, the more fragile of the two sites (before anything was built) was the poor one. Both campsites were paid for by your tax dollars. Shouldn't you expect quality work from all public employees? (Oh yes, one is Forest Service, the other is USCOE. Which is which?)

Figure 7.58

Figure 7.59

Figure 7.60

A Preconstruction Concern. One of the critical jobs which should be undertaken three or four years before you reach the construction stage of building roads and camp units is preconstruction tree removal. After you've determined you wish to build a campground and have budgeted funding to begin in three or four years, you should make sure all potential hazard trees, trees of low vigor, most large ones, and the shallow rooted ones that can't stand compaction and use pressure are removed. (This should occur where the campground is to be built and for at least 75 feet outside of the actual use zone.) Further, since research tells us a 50 percent overstory shade factor in young vigorous hardwoods is optimum for campground development, you should remove (if necessary) additional trees to reach this shade factor. (We'll talk more about trees and shade in Chapter Eight.) Most planners don't take this preconstruction thinning step and as a result most campground managers inherit costly tree removal problems not long after the campground opens and for years to come. Preconstruction tree removal three or four years before other work begins means much of the debris (tops and limbs) will—throughout at least two-thirds of the United States—rot or melt away. With today's explosive lumber prices it is also likely you'll make considerable money selling the logs of the unwanted trees.

Earlier we told you unit site selection should be a first priority. Once you determine (say on a ridge) where the best unit locations are, let these locations determine the control points of the center lines for loop roads. Assuming you've followed this procedure, flag the loop center line and clear it of trees and brush. Make sure you clear enough vegetation (beyond the road width) to eliminate tree limbs that might hit a camping vehicle. For instance, on a paved loop road 12-feet wide built flush with the ground, your minimum clearing limit should be 22-feet wide.

The next logical step is to flag or outline all of the units if clearing is to be done under contract (or at least be five or six units ahead of your own clearing crew). Make sure you cut enough to allow the equipment necessary to build the sites to function. Remove all trees and understory vegetation in these flagged areas. Make sure (at this time) to leave the vegetative screening material between camp units. This is most critical if your unit density is in the medium to high range (8–16 units per acre). Here again if you have good tree cover the logs from cleared units and roads may be quite valuable. In some cases the money can help build your campground.

Screening

There are two mistakes you can make between camp units: having too much screening (Figure 7.61, a Florida State Park campsite) or not having enough—or, for that matter, any—screening (Figure 7.62, an Indiana State Park campsite). There are all sorts of opinions and agency procedures concerning screening, and some applied research, though this needs to be updated and replicated. Figure 7.59 at the beginning of this section shows a well-done USCOE universal campsite with the understory screening intact between medium density sites (eight units per acre). This is extremely unusual for USCOE folks, as most of their campsites throughout the country have had the understory screening between sites completely removed with much emphasis on the growing and mowing of grass! Many of their managers will likely tell you screening isn't what their campers want. At the other extreme (this is another of those multiple realities) is the Forest Service. They

Figure 7.61

Figure 7.62

generally carve out their camp units 100 feet apart making sure they don't cut a twig between units. They will also tell you their campers really like such stuff. Complete screen removal or having screening so dense the city-originated user is afraid the bears or even Big Foot is about to "get 'im" are both wrong. Some years ago we found when given a choice (and that's critical in any research) a slim majority of users did have a desire for some screening between units. With today's emphasis on camper security plugged in as an important criterion in the screening thought process; as well as the need to open views of lakes, streams and mountains; and the element of varied unit density, we suggest you design loops and sections of loops with different screening densities—from none to a bunch. Obviously, this will beckon users with a wide spectrum of preferences for screening. One of the USFS campgrounds on the Ozark National Forest in the Southeast had several campsites located on the shore (within 20 feet) of a beautiful mountain lake. However, the understory screening vegetation was so heavy you couldn't see the lake from the campsite! This is extremely poor hosting.

Water, Sewage and Electric Service

It is beyond the scope of our limited knowledge to guide you through the legal and technical aspects of what kind of utilities to provide and how to go about providing them. This is mainly due to variations and peculiarities in the various state codes and regulations. Working with electricians, engineers and plumbers, or with a contractor experienced in these challenges is how you should proceed. (Don't depend on them, though, to design your campground and camp units!) In some states, water and electric lines can be laid in the same trench while sewage lines have to be located some distance from the potable water line. Questions such as whether to provide water at each site, provide both water and electric hookups, or have no hookups at all have to be answered in your planning phase.

To hook up or not to hook up? That is the question! It seems to us your answer to this goes back to the question: Whom do you want to visit your campground? For the most part, the private campground sector understands the social and financial opportunities concerning provision of at least water and 30-amp electric service at camp units. The public sector is more than a little confused about this issue.

For instance, the USFS has several campgrounds with electric hookups around the United States and a few 50-amp service electric hookups for the ever increasing numbers of large camping rigs that need it. However, in most places they consider themselves to be modern if they have pit toilets and hand pumps. They often provide their unpaid hosts with water and electric hookups while no other campsites in the campground have the nasty things. The USCOE has electricity at most camp units and water at many of them throughout the Southeast and Midwest while in the Northeast, few if any of their numerous park areas have utility hookups. We haven't seen a Bureau of Land Management campground with any sort of hookups. State parks throughout much of the country do provide electric hookups while again they don't in the Northeast. It is also interesting to note camping use is going down at public areas in the Northeast!

What do you think? Some years ago we asked a retired friend who camped three or four times each month what he thought. He had some health problems that required him to have ready access to refrigerated medicine. The reply of this mild-mannered man was, "If you don't have electricity available at each campsite, put a sign at the campground entrance saying, 'Folks with disabilities, we don't want you!'"

Another curious scenario goes like this. Perhaps the users of those big trailers (who many resource rascals say shouldn't be allowed in public parks anyhow) do need electricity and maybe even water. But we know fishermen, hunters, the good old boys, and tenters ("who are our main users") don't want or need much other than a place to park or maybe a table. Right? We don't think so.

Two Native-American children had just awakened and walked out of the tent shown in Figure 7.63 at a powwow area in Iowa. Note the fan and electric cord. Without the fan, getting the children to take a daytime nap that hot day would have been a real problem and the small children most likely would have been as well.

Figure 7.64 should give some planners a clue as to why most fishing parties need electricity. With any sort of use and no way to charge boat batteries, their trolling motors won't be too swift after the first camping/fishing day. Failing to provide the amenities these users need is, again, not user friendly.

Figure 7.65 shows a tent camping family at a northern Indiana state park campground. (The site is compacted a bit, isn't it?) It was 95° that day with high humidity. The family even needed the fan at their table cooling them as they were finishing lunch. "Do you folks really need electricity?" we facetiously asked. Their rather indignant reply was, "We like to camp and come here often but we couldn't do so if there were no place to plug in our fan. Did you ever try to sleep in a tent with children at night with 90° temperatures and no way to circulate air?" We said we understood and promptly moved away. Did you note the tent camping family camping next to the fifth wheel campers?

After reading the last few paragraphs many natural resource types will not believe what we've said or shown. They will conduct "research" of their own at their "family" campgrounds (where there are no hookups and few families). The answers they will get will likely confirm the majority of their clientele don't want hookups, as it will spoil the "wilderness flavor" of their experiences (or some other sort of thought). Once again, they haven't made an assessment of who's there and who isn't and seriously decided whom they want as campers. If it is the good old boys they want, the "research" *may be* valid. If not, it isn't.

Figure 7.63

Figure 7.64

Figure 7.65

Now Back to Universal Campsite Construction. We have just finished tree and brush removal from our campsites and loop roads. The next step is to lay out those various hookup lines, dig the trenches, install the wiring and piping, and fill and tamp the trench lines. Figure 7.42 shows where hookups should be located on back-in and pull-through campsites while Figure 7.66 shows a photograph of a properly located utility installation on a pull-through campsite. The unit living space is at the bottom and right of the photo. The water spigot is fixed to a post and has a defined gravel-filled sump at the bottom for drainage purposes. In the island you'll find the unit numbering post (facing traffic) which also has a plastic container/metal clip holder for the tag that indicates payment and the last paid camping date. The defined island shown here is quite small; it can be many times this large.

Parking Spurs. The next step is to grade the parking spur into the back edge of the living space. If the living zone is on or near the same level or contour as your roadway, your parking spur will also be level with the road. However, if the living zone is down grade from the road, your spur should ramp down to it. Conversely, if the living zone is above the level of the road, your parking spur would ramp up to the area. Since the entire living zone should be level, the last 25–

30 feet of the parking spur (on back-in units) should also be level as this space is part of the living zone. This up and down ramping technique will minimize the cuts and fills at each site.

Ramping up and Down. Figure 7.67 shows a Forest Service vehicle parked halfway up a paved parking spur that ramps up. The paving ends where the spur hits the living zone. This steep area is *one place* where paving at least a portion of your camping spur is an excellent technique. The one shown here has a six percent upgrade, which is about the maximum for backing a trailer or other large vehicle. The living zone is a well-built USFS universal campsite on the left side of a one-way road. If the grade on a ramped-up spur is three percent or less, it can be covered with road rock rather than being paved.

Figure 7.68 shows a sizable trailer with a slide-out side section and the tow vehicle at the leveled out living section of a paved ramped down parking spur. The planners have even curved the end slightly to minimize filling and to give better orientation to the water. This is a Corps of Engineers site in Georgia. They have rehabilitated a poor existing campsite using the fixed concrete table and base. As long as the spur is paved, you can ramp down as much as 12 percent to get to a desirable living area. Figure 7.69 shows in line form how to ramp up and down.

Figure 7.67

Figure 7.66

Figure 7.68

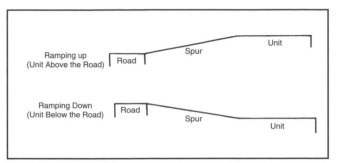

Figure 7.69

Ramping up and down is also a marvelous technique with pull-through universal sites. Remember, one of the main criteria making a site universal is the ability to get onto the living zone with your vehicle/camping trailer. The living zone isn't up or down a set of stairs. As an example, if the living space to be built is above the level of your road, you would ramp up and over to the site, make the spur zone level where it has contact with the living zone, and then ramp down to the roadway. A reverse of this would be true if the living zone is below the road grade.

Since we're discussing parking spurs, it's a good time to talk about paving or not paving them. Obviously, when you ramp up or down *over* a three percent grade, the spur should be paved to the juncture of the level unit living area. You pave a road in a campground for dust abatement purposes. Fine, powder-like dust covering your tent, trailer, camping gear, your food, and you doesn't provide the come-again experience most folks want. Figure 7.70 shows a cloud of dust on an interior gravel campground road. You can see from this photograph why campground roads need to be paved. Why pave the spur, though, since vehicular movement on it is so minimal? Paved spurs are expensive to build, add maintenance problems you don't need, and they cause campers considerable difficulty in leveling their trailers or motor homes (unless the parking portion of the spur is completely level). Blacktop also has to be used extensively or it loses its elasticity, and paved spurs don't get enough traffic use to maintain this elasticity. Blacktop must also have firm support against

its edges as it can't stand by itself without crumbling like concrete can. Figure 7.71 shows this type of problem. Where the blacktop edge has no weight against it chunks have begun to fall away. It looks as though there is a water undercutting problem here as well at this Michigan State Park campsite.

Would you like to know why many state park and federal folks continue to pave their parking spurs even on flat land? The answer is easy: "Because we've always done it that way!" This is an expensive and poorly thought out reason for doing so.

Living Space Construction. There are so many variables here it is impossible to cover all of the challenges you'll encounter. You've roughed out the spur through the living space, ramped up or down as needed between the last 25 feet of the spur and the site furniture or living zone, and now you need to make the cuts and fills necessary to make the site level. Please minimize your cutting and filling. Again, we'll say this has to be carefully done in the field, not in an office! There is a nationwide tendency to fill too much. One of the authors had initially picked out the exact location of the universal site shown in Figures 7.72 and 7.73. It was built by TVA several years later. It was designed as a *ramped-down* unit with a minimum of fill needed. However, when it was actually built, it received an extensive and expensive amount of fill material and ended up as a slightly ramped-up unit. This was a waste of the public's money. We have seen some fills 40-feet high where planners have office-designed a unit on a steep roadside and built it level with the road. This is no-brainer "professionalism."

This story is at the opposite end of the cut/fill spectrum. As they designed and built a sizable campground on a U.S. Army rest and relaxation area in southern Germany, planners were required (as you may be) to use an area that had heavy clay as the soil base. Sometimes a good clay base works in your favor; in this instance, there was little percolation through it. It had been used for informal camping for a number of years. After less than one-half inch of rain, the area became a tent-soaking quagmire. Placing campsites on rock fills was a less than satisfactory answer as the water problem would not have been solved. Likely as not the planners would have had

Figure 7.70

Figure 7.71

serious ponding between fills. A better solution was to totally excavate 10 to 12 inches of soil at each living area and fill this with one-inch or larger rock. They used concrete definers rather than wooden crossties because to do so there was less expensive. They then added two inches of fine gravel to the top of the larger material. This provided an excellent surface for tents and other types of camping. The sites treated in this manner acted as drainage sumps not only for the camping units but for the surrounding inner site zones. Two problems were solved at the same time and a former quagmire became a dandy camping area.

Soil types and depths, ground flatness or steepness, and even vegetative cover or the lack of it all combine to make the need for cutting and filling different at each site.

Once you get the living area of the campsite completely level, it's time (before you add rock) to carefully locate and install the defining crossties. For straight sides use a string line to keep your ties straight. We suggest you use treated six-by-eight hardwood ties 8- to 10-feet long. If no rot is present in them, used railroad ties will do the job. The six-inch side should face up and down. Butt each tie together and if some leveling support is needed shim under the joints with rough boards. Drive three six-inch pole-barn nails into the

Figure 7.72

Figure 7.73

joint area (two from one side and one from the other). It will help if you oil the nails and drill diagonal holes two inches deep near the end of the ties. You will have to cut some of the 8- to 10-foot ties and use short sections when necessary. Ties that are four feet or shorter should be made stationary by driving two three-foot long five-eighths-inch steel reinforcement bars (rebar) straight through the tie and into the ground. Locate the holes six inches from the tie ends. Drill the holes for the rebars using a one-half-inch drill which is smaller than the steel rebar diameter. Recess the rebar one inch below the level of the hole. With ties longer than eight feet, add one additional three-foot rebar in the middle of each tie. In some cases you may not have to define the spur from the road to the site. Area administration, existing trees, and screening will help determine such needs.

Rock Size. Once the crossties are in place you have a defined area about eight-inches deep. Fill this with six inches of crushed stone similar to that used for road surfacing. Move over this surface with a vibrating hand tamper at least twice. Then add two inches of fine gravel. This should bring the rock surface to or near the top of the crossties. This surface should also be tamped. Road surfacing should come to the edge of the living space which is covered with fine gravel. Figure 7.74 shows the two rock sizes. The person's right hand shows the largest rock size you should use for the top layer of stone. The rock in his left hand is much too large for tenters and wheelchair users. Even when tamped or compacted, the eight inches of rock will allow water and air to move through it to nurture the tree roots below the unit. Campers can also install tent pegs and pull them up with little difficulty in this material. On the outside of the ties, backfill with road rock or soil and slope as needed (Figure 7.75).

Earlier we said there were all sorts of site challenges when you build campsites. Where you have a flat space to build a campsite you may have to excavate some soil when you place the crossties. In this instance you'll also have to excavate several inches of soil inside the tie boundaries and fill this with gravel.

Another situation might arise with construction in an area with a clay base. Since clay allows some drainage, you may

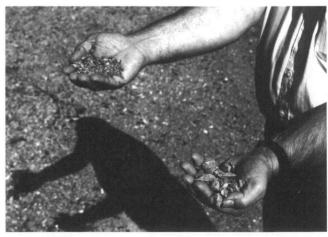

Figure 7.74

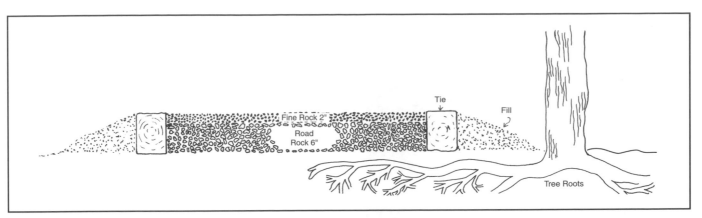

Figure 7.75

not need the six inches of road rock; instead use the clay as the subsurface of your units and simply add the two inches of fine rock surfacing.

The crosstie border on camp units gives you an opportunity for additional camper pleasing innovations. Note the bench attached to the crossties shown earlier in Figure 7.50. Here, a decorative separation between two buddy sites also serves as seating for the unit below. Occasionally the camp unit location you've selected is on a high place overlooking a lake or stream. Here it is a good idea to provide a safety rail around the steep facing part of the unit. This may keep a sleepy camper from tumbling down the hill. The safety rail can be anchored to the crosstie border. Figure 7.76 illustrates this sort of "safety" rail which is also a great place to dry dish towels and clothes and acts as a storage shelf for camper goodies. There was a tent camper on this site when this photograph was taken. Note the electric toaster on the shelf, meaning the tent camper used electricity. The pea gravel used was larger than the size we recommend, meaning wheelchairs would be difficult to use here.

Universal Campsite Furniture

There are three essential pieces of furniture on most campsites (a fourth would be some sort of human-made shade, like a ramada if no vegetative shade were available): a lantern hanger, grill, and portable table.

Lantern Hanger. Figure 7.76 showed two of the three items needed—a double lantern hanger and a grill (here, this is a portable camper-owned grill; more on this later). Why do we have to furnish something like a lantern hanger? There are two reasons: Campers need it and, if you don't provide it, they will likely hang lanterns on the nearby trees and harm them. Figure 7.77 shows a nail in a campsite tree with a lantern hanging on it. Earlier, we discussed preconstruction thinning and the percentage of shade you should have. It seems to us that you would want your remaining trees to be healthy and nurtured, right? That's why lantern hanging posts are needed in your campsites.

The nail itself doesn't hurt the tree; however, a lighted lantern hanging on that nail will kill the cambium—the growth layer of cells beneath the tree bark behind the hot lantern. Figure 7.78 shows a tree with at least one nail in it and several lantern scars. This sort of damage occurs wherever there are campsites with surrounding trees. The scar is an open wound that beckons infection and wood rot, sometimes resulting in tree death. The lantern hanging posts can be fixed as the one shown in Figure 7.76 or portable allowing the user to locate it anywhere on the campsite. Use them, and the precious trees surrounding your campsites will be protected.

Figure 7.76

Figure 7.77

169

Figure 7.78

Campsite Grill. The upright grill shown in Figure 7.79 is quite a useful piece of park furniture *in picnic areas*. It is a picnic grill, and is nearly useless and oftentimes harmful when provided on a campsite! Again, we often hear, "We use them because that's what we've always done." In Figure 7.76 we pointed out the sizable cooker brought by the user. Research tells us 95–99 percent of campers bring their own cooking facility with them. Research also tells us that even in the hottest months, over 70 percent of the campers want an evening campfire. That's a basic part of the camping experience. Why provide the upright grill if 95–99 percent of our campers don't need it and it doesn't function as a place where you can build an evening campfire? Why, indeed? In many campgrounds, the only fireplace provided at a campsite is an upright grill. It is there you will find unsightly and maintenance-producing fire circles built by campers all over the site. These add filth to the site and tree and shrub roots (if you aren't using a universal campsite) near the soil line under these fire spots will be damaged adding additional stress to nearly trees and shrubs.

Figure 7.80 does show one excellent use for the upright grill—it is a good place to use as a base for your portable camp stove. (If you'll look carefully at the nearby tree you'll see another solution to the lantern hanging challenge—a camper-owned commercially available lantern hanger.)

What sort of fireplace should be used at campsites? There are several good on-the-ground grills on the market.

Figure 7.79

The one shown in Figure 7.81 is called a tilt-back fireplace. You can cook on it if need be, and it is an excellent facility for the evening campfire. Years ago, we designed the circular base shown, as it better fits the configuration of a campfire than a square or rectangular base. The grill is hinged so it can tilt back, making it rest at the outside of the circular base. On a universal site, we suggest you tuck the grill into a corner of the defined area, making sure it is far enough away from the crosstie border so the fire won't damage the ties. It should also be located so it won't be under or even near a trailer awning. The grill should be installed so when the metal grill is tilted back, it does not block the campers' view of the campfire from the living area of the site. Your cleanup schedule should include periodic removal of campfire ashes.

Tables. In the first edition of this book the authors recommended you use a fixed concrete table with wooden benches on campsites. *Wrong!* Thinking like a manager attempting to minimize numerous real and imagined hassles with campers guided this recommendation. We weren't "planning parks for people" as we should have been. On the universal site you want users to "design" their own living space meaning a tent here, trailer there, awning over the table some place else, and the tow vehicle wherever they wish. The fixed table simply isn't as user friendly as it should be. So, we recommend portable tables on campsites. Like the on-the-ground grills, there are dozens of suitable tables on the market. You can also have local persons or the nearby technical high school build them. A word of caution here, though: Make them sturdy enough to accommodate extended use with table tops at least one-and-one-half-inches thick.

We suggest the portable table (wooden, metal and wooden, all metal, or whatever) be eight-feet long with six-foot benches and the top extended two feet beyond the benches on one end. This gives each one of your camp units a wheelchair-accessible table (on a universal campsite, campers in wheelchairs then have a choice of where they want to camp). The two-foot extended end also is a great place for campers to place their stoves, cook, and wash dishes without thumping their legs or knees on the seat ends. Since the tables are portable they can be taken to special events when necessary. If you must tie them down use a lengthy chain anchored on site and tied to the midpoint under the

Figure 7.80

Figure 7.81

table. This at least allows users some freedom to move the table somewhat and position it to suit their living space needs.

In Chapter Two we discussed the construction of 100 massive cantilevered campsites at a state park in Tennessee. Cost estimates for each site ranged from $10,000 to $40,000 (years ago). Obviously that's completely unreasonable! We, too, have built sites on steep slopes where numerous steps were needed to climb up or down from the parking site to the camping pad. In retrospect we think these carved-out campsites for tenters only are too expensive to build and maintain. The problem is where to draw the line on what can be called overbuilding of sites. We don't have an answer for you as there are so many factors to consider at each private or public campground. In some instances, there are less expensive solutions than the one we've built. The authors believe the excellent pull-through campsite in Figure 7.82 has at least two less-expensive solutions. We do not disagree the solution used at a beautiful water view site is a dandy; however, future maintenance costs and the high potential for accidental destruction of the wooden platform from burning are two serious considerations.

Solution One could be to move the pull-through spur several feet to the left—which would require the removal of the

Figure 7.82

sizable tree—then building a living zone where most of the existing pull-through parking area is located now. Some fill might be required but the resulting unit would not have the initial higher cost and many future maintenance challenges would be eliminated. Solution Two would be quite similar and would entail a back-in unit ramping down from the upper left and tucked into the bank. The tree may or may not need to be cut with this approach. We prefer Solution One.

Hydrants. In many campgrounds the hydrant will be a piece of individual campsite furniture. In others you may have one hydrant for every four to six camping units. Some things to consider include:

1. Make sure (if the hydrant is not at individual units) you don't locate it in or too near one of the several sites it serves.
2. Check water pressure to make sure it isn't high enough to damage valves in camping vehicles.
3. Where frost or freezing is a problem use anti-siphon frost-free self-draining hydrants.
4. Provide a rock sump under each hydrant similar to the one shown in Figure 7.83.
5. Make sure you have a gravel-reinforced surface (for pedestrian impact) from the roadside to the hydrant unless your hydrant is in an individual universal campsite.

Barriers. As you have likely determined by now the authors aren't big backers of barriers. The generous universal campsites coupled with prudent administration combine to eliminate the need for most of them. The defining crossties around the unit living spaces and (perhaps) placed the length of the parking spur serve as psychological barriers rather than physical ones. Most barriers we've seen around the country need not have been there. They are simply Jurassic remnants of a "this is how we've always done it" age, just like upright grills in campsites and paved parking spurs! Figure 7.84 shows the number of post barriers (we can count 40) around a USFS camp unit in north Florida. Campers could drive over the undefined "living area" with its characteristic exposed roots and stumps in spite of the 40 post barriers.

Figure 7.85 shows a barricaded paved parking spur on a USCOE area in California with unit furniture an unhandy 50 feet

Figure 7.83

Figure 7.84

Figure 7.85

Figure 7.86

from the spur end. There are some built-in erosion problems and damage to the left side of the paving. The barriers here keep the users from full enjoyment of their space. What a great place for a curved spur universal campsite!

Figure 7.86 shows a double spur (that's good) in a sizable USFS campground (on a lake) in central Colorado. The campers have maneuvered around the barricades to get where they want to be. Why do we make things so difficult and unfriendly for our users? If our objective for placing these barriers was to protect the living zone from compaction and "overuse," the exposed on-site roots and rocks and missing soil near the table tell us we haven't been too successful.

Campsites for Persons with Disabilities

There is a section in Chapter Ten covering most of our guidance for these sites. Obviously, if you build universal sites as we've suggested you'll have the kind of sites folks with disabilities need throughout your entire campground.

Chapter Seven Problem

At the end of most chapters we've given you some sort of problem, so here is one for you involving several extremely poor National Park Service (NPS) camping units. Some explanation is in order. The U.S. Department of the Interior's National Park Service personnel do some great work, particularly with living-history programs at national historic sites. Their professionals are generally outstanding even though they are low rated on the federal pay and promotion system. The three authors have always had a high regard for the NPS professionals and their work. However, in the developed campgrounds and picnic area realm, their parks are generally good examples of how not to provide visitor facilities and services!

There are several reasons for this:

- Lack of interest in the subject;
- Lack of training concerning developed site design and rehabilitation;
- Dependence on internal training rather than seeking help outside the agency;

- Their popular areas stay quite full (so they reason) so why spend the time and money building safe, generous, impact-resistant universal sites;
- No person or group we've encountered in the agency seems to have developed sites as a concern; and
- Their design work is all assigned to the designers at their Denver Service Center. They rarely use managerial ideas and are far less than knowledgable concerning campground design. Field design of campsites would likely be unthinkable!

We'd be pleased to be proven wrong here, but the environment in our national park campgrounds is being destroyed by lack of knowledge, apathy and/or poor husbandry. (Giving them more money without requiring extensive external training would mean a waste of that money.)

Over the years we've had limited opportunities to discuss our concern with NPS personnel. Their response each time we did was:

- Users have caused all this "overuse."
- We should eliminate most of the camping in our national parks (*Note:* our, not the public's, national parks).
- There's no money to fix anything anyhow.
- Why improve things when we have to turn users away?

From time to time, special funding has been available to the NPS for site rehabilitation and in a few instances new construction. Their new construction of campsites copies errors of the past and the site rehabilitation money was spent working on attempting to correct effects rather than trying to find cures to the causes. (For instance, trying to grow grass on a tri-level campsite rather than building universal campsites as the USCOE has done.)

For your Chapter Seven problem we have a 10-photo collage taken in three national park campgrounds. These are Acadia National Park in Maine, Mammoth Cave National Park in Kentucky, and Mesa Verde National Park in Colorado. All three parks are National Treasures and personnel generally do a fine job; however, their developed sites are typical of the quality we discussed earlier. Your assignment is to carefully critique each photo (Figures 7.87 through 7.96) and describe what's less than good. Here is some information on each one.

Figures 7.87 and 7.88 are in the Acadia campground in Maine. Figure 7.87 shows a small trailer owned by a retired camper parked in a back-in site. Aside from the on-site problems, this couple was not at all happy that the campground didn't have shower facilities. We were camped in a tent and were also not pleased there was no place to take a shower. Figure 7.88 shows a conversion van parked in another back-in site on the left side of a paved one-way road.

Figures 7.89 through 7.93 are at Mammoth Cave National Park campground. Figure 7.89 shows a paved one-way road moving toward you with paved pull-through spurs on both sides of the one-way road. The motor home with the open door is located on a pull-though campsite. Figure 7.90 is a back-in unit with a paved parking spur. Traffic flow is to the right on this one-way road placing the perpendicular unit on the left side of the road. Figure 7.91 shows a back-in on the left side of a one-way road. It is a classic view of what causes the myth of overuse and why tree stumps are common occurrences in the living zones of most nonuniversal sites. Figure 7.92 shows a number of less than good design items including the flush toilet being located in the center of the camp loop. Why do you suppose the trees had to be taken out? Figure 7.93 shows a back-in campsite on the right side of a one-way road. There are two or three serious problems and a subtle one described in the Universal Campsite Construction section of this chapter.

Figures 7.94 through 7.96 are in the Mesa Verde Campground in Colorado. Figure 7.94 was taken in a new section of their campground. The walk-in units are located above each of the "well-engineered" scalloped parking areas. We weren't sure if the road was one-way or two. Camping sites and furniture were above the parking pads on the right side and somewhere below on the left. Figure 7.95 shows the steps

Figure 7.87

Figure 7.89

Figure 7.88

Figure 7.90

Figure 7.91

Figure 7.94

Figure 7.92

left. The three pipes imbedded in concrete appear to be a location for a garbage can bag. None of these new campsites had any sort of surfacing.

If you've found numerous problems in, and provided solutions for, the 10 photographs you've obviously learned more about top-quality environment-protecting campsites than many plan-

Figure 7.95

ners (including consultants) understand. This includes those in the National Park Service!

Figure 7.93

up to one of the steeper areas on the right side of the road. A hint to consider in your critique of Figures 7.94 and 7.95 might include challenges for folks in wheelchairs. The flat living zone here could have been reached with a ramped-up spur. Figure 7.96 shows a narrow, extremely short pull-in spur. There was a cleared space behind the barriers. There's a small tent located to the right of the clearing and a table is on the

Figure 7.96

Family Campground Design

Historically, administrators and managers have inherited campgrounds which were either poorly planned, never planned, or outdated through continuously changing camping demands. As a result, our campgrounds *appear* overused, worn-out, and mismanaged. Rather than learning from research or lessons from the past planners and designers today (including consultants) continue to "invent the wheel" and to "design" dollar-grabbing maintenance monsters.

For the last 23 years we have conducted a five-day basic campground design, rehabilitation, and programming workshop in either Tennessee, Arkansas, or Kentucky. The paragraph above comes from the brochure heralding this training session. Indeed, millions of dollars have been spent in the private and public sectors designing, building, and trying to administer the monsters we've created! Managers and users have been the "beneficiaries" of our planning and designing mistakes. Our mission in the development of this chapter is to help you and others bypass these *mistakes,* minimize costs, simplify design, and truly provide the aura for beckoning all sorts of users.

Family Campground Design wasn't a full chapter in our first edition, though we did cover some of the information in the one chapter on campgrounds. Our travels throughout North America and Europe tell us most planners, designers, engineers, consultants, *and* college professors who are confronted with the need to guide or teach campground design do not have the background, skills, or interest to do a good job. As a result their versions of "inventing the wheel" litter the landscape.

Since you've waded through seven chapters to arrive at Chapter Eight, you likely have surmised *Planning Parks for People* isn't a text on planning. It's main purpose is to help you *after* you've taken the planning steps to decide whether you wish to build or extensively renovate a recreation facility, trail, picnic area, wrangler's camp, or family campground. Most texts and agency planning guides or manuals will take you through the planning process (including helping answer the environmental questions) onto the point of design and then say, OK, turkey—do it! This text essentially says, "You've done the planning and here's some guidance for the design of a quality final product."

Campground Planning Thoughts

In dealing with hundreds of family campgrounds (or that's what they're called), we've found many of the more basic monster-causing problems happen because we forget about, misunderstand, or don't concern ourselves with some common sense planning elements. The authors feel these should be discussed before we move into basic design.

Regional Planning

It seems to us a most basic planning criteria for everyone would be: What are other folks doing of a similar nature on a regional or statewide basis? This would include federal, state, and local governments (including Native Americans), and the private sector. How can what we do build on and enhance *what is needed* and what others are doing or planning to do in the near future? How can we work with them for the most prudent use of scarce dollars? If you are a college student, these are questions you might ask your *learned* professors and the professionals you meet while visiting parks. All of this is called cooperation and coordination with, and between a spectrum of, park folks. Problem is, being concerned about the plans of others and how they interface with ours rarely happens! Why? There are numerous reasons for this failure from "we don't care" to "it isn't standard procedure" to "the private sector's saying the public sector should get out of the park realm" to "agency policy" to "less than thoughtful environmental constraints" to politicians saying two divergent things at the same time.

As usual, we have a most interesting true-to-life illustration for you. Don't waste your time wondering who the good and bad guys are. There aren't any good ones!

Our story takes us to the extreme southwest corner of Utah to (they say) the fastest growing city in that state—St. George. It is located on an interstate highway, is near the Arizona state line, has palm trees and a warm winter climate, is a sizable center of Mormon religious activities, and is a retirement center. It is no more than an hour's drive from Zion National Park, several historical sites, Bureau of Land Management (BLM) and Dixie National Forest lands and parks, three to four state parks, the gambling casinos in Nevada, and more. Scenery varies from desert to mountain to lush forests all within a short drive. It is a destination for a sizable part of ever increasing international tourism because of the attractions and the mild winters.

Another prime attraction is (a new one for recreation planners) the sizable St. George Discount Shopping Mall. One of the big problems is the lack of either public or private campgrounds and campsites to meet current and expected user needs and to help continue growth. Land values have skyrocketed and environmental constraints are costly, meaning private campground development is nearly prohibitive. There are campsites available on public lands though *only the state parks* have hookups. National forest campsites on the Dixie National Forest are small and difficult to use. BLM sites are being upgraded to at least accommodate the camping clientele of today. (They even plan to use universal campsites!) The National Park Service campsites are small, undefined and, to our knowledge, they don't plan to upgrade or expand them. What is likely is the elimination of campsites there, as they are doing in other places.

The obvious answer is some *serious* regional planning including coordination, cooperation, and imagineering somewhere nearby on the *abundant* public lands! The good news is in 1968, Congress enacted the Governmental Cooperation Act which established procedures for coordination of plans and programs at federal, state, and local levels. This includes park planning. Considerable time is spent in lengthy meetings to try to accomplish great things! The bad news is likely nothing will happen, particularly in the park realm!

One of the most scenic of all treasures in the St. George region is a nearby state park called Snow Canyon. It is a desert park in a valley surrounded by giant sandstone formations with their sun-splashed, ever changing colors beckoning thousands of camera-clutching visitors each year. The state has a great need to expand visitor day-use facilities including pods of facilities for group use, particularly tour bus groups. Problem is where and how to do so? There is plenty of developable land in the park for expansion, but due to "great good fortune," it is nearly all inhabited by the desert tortoise. There are thousands of acres of desert tortoise habitat *locked* up throughout the arid parts of the west, including public lands in Utah. People should be concerned about an endangered species, however, not being able to carve out (or being afraid to try) 20 to 30 acres more *for people* in an established park is one of the reasons why we've previously stated the environmental movement has been detrimental to people and parks. One option to the urgent need for additional day-use acreage at the park is to eliminate the campground and increase day use there. As stated earlier, it has the *only* water and electric hookups on public lands!

Base Camp Concept

As we continue the story, it doesn't look as though the urgent need for camping space in the St. George region has many friends in the public sector. Right? Right! Remember we are discussing a missing piece of the recreation planning puzzle called *coordination.* It's time to share with you a concept which could have been listed in Chapter Seven: The Many Campgrounds We Really Have, though we think its better to share it with you here. We call it the *base camp concept.*

Essentially it is a sizable destination facility that doesn't have or doesn't need a drawing attraction of its own (lake, sizable stream, or beautiful scenery.) It's the sort of area, though, that can be a camping hub for numerous surrounding attractions (Figure 8.1). The circles marked *A* surrounding the base camp are attractions. In our view the amenity features and programs would be a viable part of such a campground design, though programming emphasis might be aimed even more at the evening hours than another type of family campground.

The campground should be sizable (built perhaps in phases) with 300 camp units as a *minimum.* Here is a great place for public-private interface with some facilities built by the government and some by a private campground company. The area would be under long-term lease to the company and would be managed by it. The state should be involved in financing as should the city of St. George as well as the federal agencies. Perhaps this is a proper place for a federal-state block grant. The campground should have water and electric hookups (some 50 amp) at all sites with some loops having full hookups including sewage.

Where should the base camp be located? The Snow Canyon State Park area with its pristine scenery, protected critters and excessive summer temperatures isn't the place. The Pine Valley area 30 minutes north of Snow Canyon is U.S. Forest Service country located along a mountain stream in a cool stand of large timber. It is also frequently snowed in several weeks during the winter. On top of that, the Forest Service isn't known for taking bold steps, particularly in the *family* camping realm. The obvious answer is a less than pristine

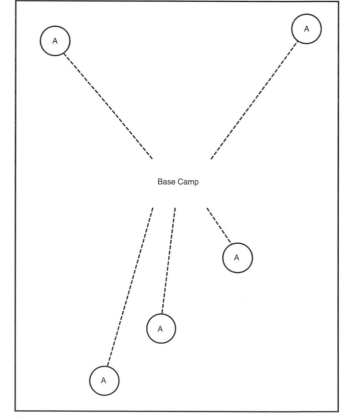

Figure 8.1

area near Baker Dam on BLM lands 15 minutes north of Snow Canyon. The sizable area has excellent access, some tree cover, and is flat and easy to develop. It is the location of a primitive campground now being enlarged to 30-plus universal camp units *without hookups or flush toilets/showers.* As such, it will have no impact on meeting the needs of the St. George region. The base camp campground would be a creative political plus for the BLM *and* an economic boon for the region. Is it likely to happen in light of the agency's mandate to coordinate and cooperate with others? No! Interestingly, the main reason for this negative answer is the local BLM resource area manager can say the upgraded primitive area with 30 units is enough!

This takes us to a *monumental* planning error of the current administration (1997), which is to move the power of federal agencies, including planning, to the lowest level possible. In this case, it's a BLM resource area manager. For the U.S. Forest Service, it's the local District Ranger. This makes a mockery of the regional planning process. If you believe these managers (however skilled) of relatively small federal land bases have the experience, knowledge, interest, or integrity to think or plan on a regional or statewide basis, the authors have several mountains and bridges to sell ya!

There are numerous similar areas around the United States where the base camp concept, with or without private-public cooperation, would work well. For example the Ocala National Forest near Disney World in Florida, the Shoshone National Forest near the entrance to Yellowstone National Park, the Pike National Forest near Colorado Springs, Colorado, the George Washington National Forest near the national capital, numerous now surplus military bases and other areas. The base camp concept, with public-private interface, in the southern Utah/St. George area makes so much sense that it will never happen. Prove us wrong!

Chapter Ten will have more to say about the harm done to people and parks by environmental regulations, the environmental movement, and the lack of integrity of some of its proponents, and what's happening in one agency as it moves the regional decision and planning process to the local action level. Before we move on to other planning concerns here's what we think should be done at Utah's Snow Canyon State Park. Expand—not eliminate—the campground (perhaps even relocate it) even if the BLM should embrace the base camp concept. Build four or five day- and overnight-use group pods and expand day-use facilities. If there are desert tortoises in the expansion zones, move the critters some distance away and at least consider people at the same value level of animals! (What a radical concept!)

Why Are They There?

Another big campground planning error we see in far too many state parks, Forest Service, and other areas, is the location of the campground some distance away from a lake or stream attraction. We've illustrated the problem with Figure 8.2—an area called Our Park on Lake Hultscott. The recreation area is located on the shore of a beautiful lake. Picnic area,

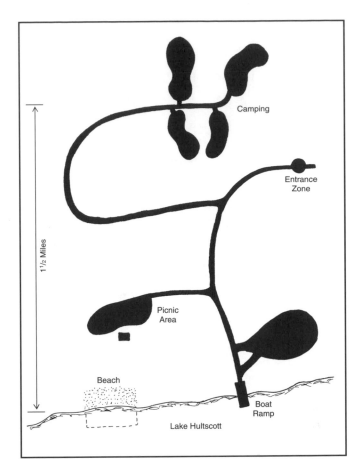

Figure 8.2

beach, and boat ramp all are oriented to the attracting shoreline. (That's particularly good planning for the beach and boat ramp, don't you think?) Where is the campground? It's located on a dry ridge $1\frac{1}{2}$ miles from the reason most campers would be beckoned to the campground—the lake! We understand that sometimes developable shoreline acreage is scarce and it has to be devoted to a beach, boating site, or other features. *However,* camping use is limited and the camping experience is diminished if there is lake view or lakeside land available and we fail to locate the campground there. In our view, this represents recreation planning at its worst!

Beware of Existing Roads

An existing road or transportation system oftentimes frightens most folks into poor park planning. An excellent illustration of this planning paralysis is Spring Lake Recreation Area on the Ozark National Forest in Arkansas. Figure 8.3 shows the sizable mountain lake, the existing gravel road transportation system and the location (near the dam) of the recreation area with picnicking, swimming, camping and boating sites. It's an old Civilian Conservation Corps park built with poorly zoned day-use and overnight-use areas. The campground has fewer than 15 camp units. Years ago, no one thought of the consequences of charging for one sort of use and not another, or about the zoning problems, or the difficulties of administration. Add to all this the steepness of much

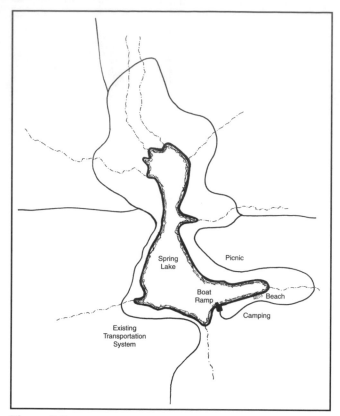

Figure 8.3

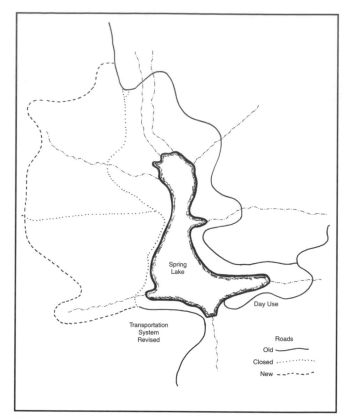

Figure 8.4

of the area around the use sites and you begin to see the problems.

The excellent location of this beautiful mountain lake and the environment around it cry out for a sizable campground to be built there. Assuming a 200-unit campground (minimum) is desirable and needed there, where should it be built? Since most of the area on the east side of the lake is flat and developable, we feel the sizable campground with amenities should be located on the shoreline there. Problem is the existing roads would cause numerous headaches. The obvious answer includes blocking or elimination of those roads and relocating a paved main road out of the potential developable area (Figure 8.4).

The roads to be eliminated are indicated by dotted lines while the new main road is shown with dashes. Please read and study this serious planning problem carefully! Existing roads are usually deterrents to quality park planning worldwide. The engineers, planners and others responsible for planning rarely seem to understand the design, administration and programming problems they cause. Your professional challenge is to explain the problem to the rascals. Good luck!

Figure 8.5 shows the existing area near the dam converted completely to day use while you now have a sizable campground with amenities located on the east side of the lake. There are seven camp loops all pointing to four flush toilets or toilets/showers. If you want to superimpose a sizable day-use event (an industrial or church picnic, for example) on the amenity zone, you can do so without penetrating any of the camp loops. Construction of the camp loops can be phased as needed with differing unit densities, degrees of screening, and

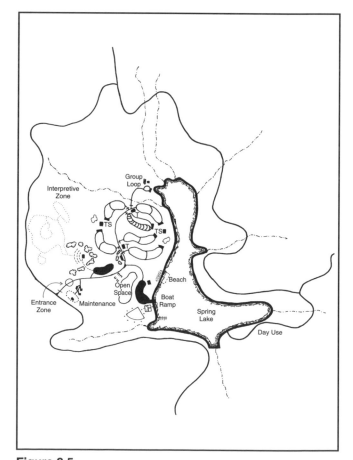

Figure 8.5

other things learned in the preceding chapter. We'll tell you again that while phasing the 250 units on the loops is a good idea, *don't phase the amenities.* Build them with your *first* camp loops and begin programming immediately.

This is a logical place for a public-private interface with a long-term lease as the budget constraints of most public agencies aren't likely to decrease as we enter the twenty-first century. If so, the two easternmost camp loops could well include seasonal campsites and cabins as well as a lodge.

You should be able to find many of the elements in this design we'll share with you later in this chapter. These include:

- Building something large enough to make someone (even the government) a profit;
- Control;
- Phasing capability;
- Zoning;
- Ease of administration;
- Opportunities to superimpose group day use without penetration of the campground by keeping camp loops free of amenities;
- Simple design psychology (all camp loops pointing at toilets/showers);
- An overall concern for the environment; and
- A beckoning area for all sorts of users.

Private-public interface in today's environment makes lots of sense to the authors. You'll note we've recommended it for several areas around the country. We also do so in our training sessions. However, we are certain it is *not* in the camping public's interest to turn over all existing and potential public *family campgrounds* to the private sector! Nor do we believe the public sector should *only* be involved with wilderness, backcountry, and primitive camping. Private campground associations—particularly those on the national scene—beat this drum incessantly. This bombast, like the rhetoric of the environmentalists, has had a negative impact on public park policy—in our view causing social problems and greatly reduced camping emphasis by families. More on this later.

Design of Family Campgrounds

Figures 8.6 through 8.14 are actual drawings of nine campgrounds though some include day use in the same area. They cross the nation again with areas from the Pacific Ocean on U.S. Highway 101 to Florida Bay just across U.S. Highway 1 from the Atlantic Ocean. Four of the nine are state park campgrounds in Oregon, Iowa, Illinois, and Georgia. Two are private sector campgrounds—one a sizable KOA. Another one is a U.S. Forest Service campground in Colorado, while another is a U.S. Corps of Engineers recreation area with camping in Arkansas. The final example is of a municipal park

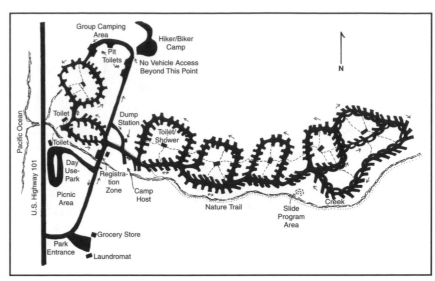

Figure 8.6 Oregon State Park

including a campground in North Dakota. We had a problem selecting these nine for your review as we have dozens of similar less than good designs from all over the United States and Canada to choose from. Many are even more interesting than these!

There are errors common to all nine designs. They are all poorly designed—some much more than others; they are user and management unfriendly; they have too many confusing roads; and each design causes environmental and social problems. Later in this chapter we will provide a new or

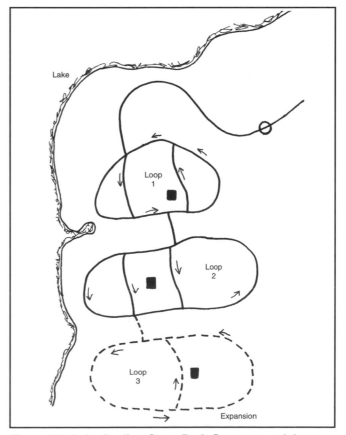

Figure 8.7 Lake Darling State Park Campground, Iowa

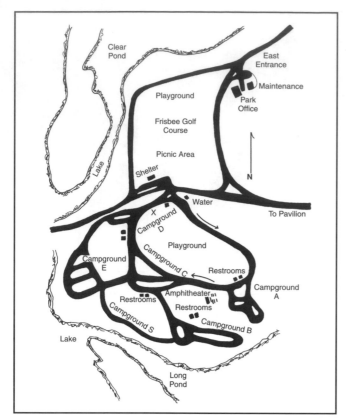

Figure 8.8 Kickapoo State Park, Illinois

improved design for all nine areas. At this time, however, you should carefully study each one, make a list of all the problems you find, and try your hand at redesigning each one to make it user and management friendly.

There are two things you should know about all nine areas: (1) The authors have visited and studied each of the areas at least once, and (2) poor planning and design doesn't mean campgrounds don't get heavy use. Each one of these areas has a history of excellent occupancy, particularly the KOA area and the Oregon State Park.

What is our description of a well-designed family campground, and are there good examples across the country we might visit to see great design? First we'll answer the second part of the question—we haven't seen a well-designed campground in the United States, Europe, Japan or Canada yet, but we're working on two or three now. Here are some of the items or criteria concerning good design. A well-designed family campground should be sizable with 200 camp units if you have the space. It should have a single entrance/exit with safe ingress and egress, and adequate signing to get you there. Entrance control station should be far enough from the highway to safely handle all traffic. Entrance control should have a minimum of two entrance lanes extending at least 200 feet before the

visitors get to the structure. A double sewage dumping station should be located near the entrance control structure with a horseshoe drive off of the main road.

Our campground would have a minimum of four loops with expansion potential as needed. This would likely require two flush toilet/shower structures (each with a family assist room for persons with disabilities) and two flush toilet structures. Camp units would vary in type and size as described in Chapter Seven.

The maintenance/housing complex would be zoned near the entrance control structure and preferably hidden from public view. Amenities such as a beach and boat ramp will not be located on or in any of the camp loops. Other amenities such as a campfire theater, multipurpose play court, recreation building and ball fields should all be located so as to be used for special day-use events as you choose to do so, without penetrating a camp loop. As the chapter develops further you'll see how these and other facilities and amenities fit together.

Campground Design Dos and Don'ts

First some family campground don'ts (they aren't prioritized):

1. Don't use too much road. Many private and public campgrounds have far more roads than are needed.
2. Don't mix day use and camping use. It's OK to design recreation areas with day- and overnight-use areas but don't mix them.
3. Don't put amenities (such as beaches, shelters and tot lots) or toilets/showers inside of camp loops.
4. Don't locate amenities in or on the edges of camp loops.
5. Don't move traffic from one camp loop into another and another.
6. Don't mix family campsites and seasonal campsites on the same camp loop.
7. Don't call your loops A or B, or 1 or 2—name them.
8. Don't assume engineers or landscape architects or planners or foresters or consulting firms or college profes-

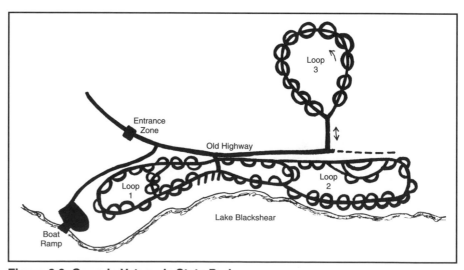

Figure 8.9 Georgia Veteran's State Park

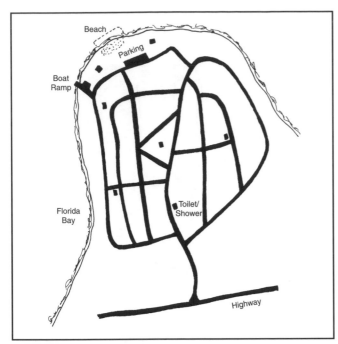

Figure 8.10 Florida KOA Campground

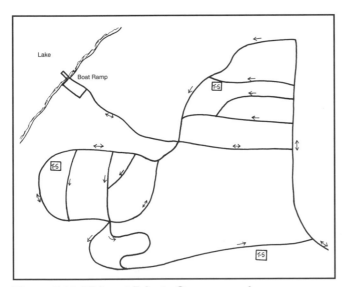

Figure 8.11 Midwest Private Campground

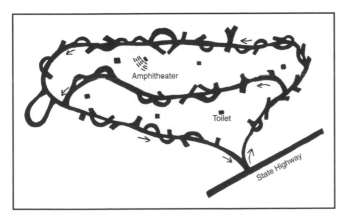

Figure 8.12 USFS Campground, Colorado

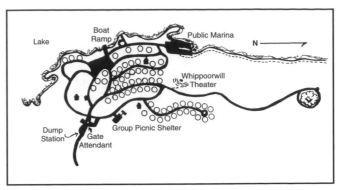

Figure 8.13 USCOE Shoal Bay Rec. Area, Arkansas

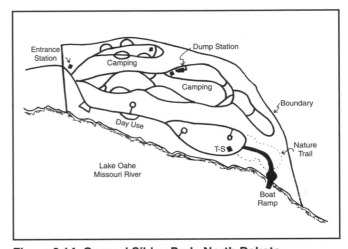

Figure 8.14 General Sibley Park, North Dakota

sors or other rascals know how to design campgrounds. It is quite likely they don't!

9. Don't locate your primary road between camp loops and the main attraction (lake or stream).

10. Don't (if at all possible) utilize many existing roads and facilities in a major renovation of a campground.

11. Don't make "third-class citizens" of campers by keeping them away from the lake or stream attraction, or by (unless shoreline acreage is quite limited) having them cross or move through day users to get to the attraction.

12. Don't design "overuse" impact potential into your campground.

13. Don't waste your land base by designing big fat loops.

14. Don't (if you are a designer) ask others (managers, maintenance folks or programmers) how they want you to design something; ask them how they want the design to function for them and users.

Here are some (not all) family campground design dos:

1. Do seek input from managers, maintenance personnel, planners, engineers, users, persons with disabilities, and other available specialists.

2. Do decide early on who you want to beckon to your family campground then design for those users.

3. Do think big, plan big, and build big.

4. Do consider (if this is a public area) the possibility of public-private cooperation.

5. Do design your campground so construction can be phased logically.

6. Do build the amenities with the first phase.

7. Do spend considerable time on site before you draw two or three alternative designs. Then, when a master plan is acceptable, field design your camping units and roads.

8. Do (in area rehabilitation) use sections of existing roads, toilet/shower structures (if they are in good condition) and other existing features if—and that's a *big* if—they enhance your design.

Some Frequently Used Designs and What's Wrong

With the don'ts and dos in mind, let's critique some typical designs. We've used the same generous gently sloped area for each illustration. The design in Figure 8.15 is one used frequently by consultants and both the public and private sectors. Campers move from loop to loop to loop and the toilets/showers are in the center of each loop. You wouldn't build or buy a three-bedroom home where you had no hallways (thus forcing you to move from one bedroom to another and another) would you? Yet, planners often do build this constraint into campground design. Don't name your loops A or B, or 2 or 3—give them names. Never travel from one loop to another to another as all traffic has to move through every one. Locating the toilet/shower structures (or anything else) in loop centers creates as many pathways as there are campsites. How would you solve this problem? This is a major cause of "overuse." Can you see why?

Consultants can help you if (and that's a *big* if) they are knowledgeable (though most aren't) concerning campground design. Remember two things: First, a nicely packaged and presented design does not mean you have a well-designed campground; second, consultants don't have to manage the products they design—you do. Make sure you get what you need from them rather than what they tell you you need.

If you are building a 200-unit or larger family campground you'll often have a sizable gently sloping area similar to the illustration in Figure 8.16 located between a steep side hill and the lake or stream attraction. It could also be a flat area

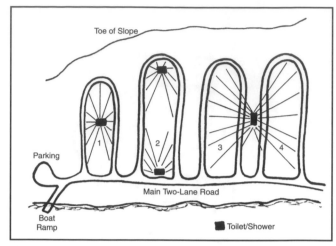

Figure 8.16

on a ridge top. Anyhow, quality design isn't too difficult but some agencies and designers make it so. Figure 8.16 shows four flat horseshoe-shaped loops with eight road junctions intersecting a main road which is located next to the attraction. State parks, the Forest Service and even the private sector seem to use this sort of design frequently. The four toilets/showers are all poorly located. They cause all sorts of people movement across, around, through, and between camp units. This causes camper unhappiness and the so-called "overuse" mentioned earlier. There are eight entrance/exits all requiring gates and added administration. The main road (which was likely planned before the camp loops) is located between the campers and the attraction, thus, you have designed in a safety problem just as the toilet/shower locations designed in the so-called overuse.

Your Chapter Seven problem and the National Park Service campsite photos acquainted you with their developed site work. Now have a look at Figure 8.17. They seem to use this design across America. One of the great tragedies of this is that other folks who believe the NPS knows how it is to be done far too often follow their leadership. Again, the toilets/showers (in truth they are far more likely to be just flush toilets in NPS areas) are located in the loop centers. Persons from up to three loops away may be crossing each other to use the toilet facility; here is a design that obviously causes serious environmental problems. Another problem is the wasted space caused by these fat loops. (NPS campgrounds can be sizable with a string of loops nearly one-half-mile long.) Today's land values and construction costs should tell us to utilize our parklands as carefully as possible. The traffic flow of a design like this creates problems for campers in terms of confusion (remember KISS). What you and the authors see in the drawing isn't what confronts users on the ground. Where are we? Where do we go now? Where is our campsite and how do we return to it? This design and the one following are what we call sign maker's delights as all sorts of arrow and directional signs are required to take folks where the designer intended for them to go.

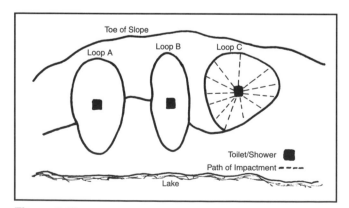

Figure 8.15

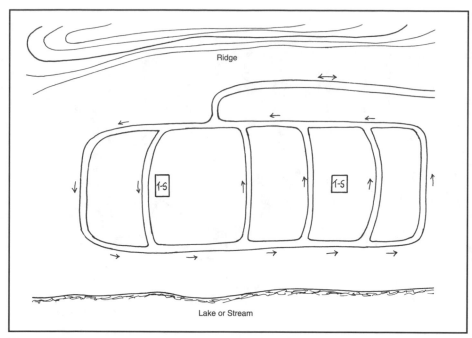

Figure 8.17

pits, campfire theater with interpretive trails, four boccie ball courts, hike 'n bike system, fishing piers, boat ramp, and more.

Included in the entrance zone would be a structure in the center of the road large enough for up to four persons plus office and communicating equipment, adequate road system, double sewage dumping station, maintenance structure and equipment storage yard, and campsites with full hookups for seasonal and volunteer staff.

Construction of the area could be done in two or three phases though as you'll remember we recommend the amenities be built with the initial camp loops. Which of the five campgrounds shown in Figures 8.15 through 8.19 would you prefer to own or manage, and which one is the most likely to beckon families?

Figure 8.18 shows an even worse design for the level generous site, yet both the public and private sectors use this sort of plan nationwide. It's your turn to describe the errors or don'ts. Are there any good things about the design? Following the arrows will cause headaches. What if you were camped in this monster and quickly had to find your way out? If you are camped at point X, how did the designer expect you to get there? For a real change of pace have a careful look at Figure 8.19. Here we have the same generous developable area between a steep ridge and a lakeshore as shown in the four previous designs. This time, however, the design helps users, managers and programmers rather than causing problems. The main road is located against the toe of the slope out of the developable area. There are five named camp loops all pointed at the toilets or toilets/showers and at the lakeside attraction. Through design psychology users move where they wish to go (and where you wish them to go) with a minimum of beckoning across loops and camp units. The manager can open or close various loops to meet his or her needs. A group loop with tot lot, small shelter, sand volleyball court and council circle meeting area gives management an excellent moneymaking "tool."

The sizable amenity zone is located near the entrance as a beckoning "agent" for potential campers and available for special event groups without camp loop penetration. The amenities or fun facilities include a lighted softball field, a sizable combination shelter/toilet/shower and concession/play equipment/checkout structure, group picnic facilities, beach with in-water volleyball standards, paved multipurpose play court, two tot lots, fenced horseshoe

Basic Loop Design

Before we get any deeper into fitting together the various puzzle pieces in campground design, let's take a brief look at a few general techniques for developing loops. Specifically, how would you respond if we were to ask you, "How wide (or narrow) should loops be?" or "How many (or few) camp units should you place on a single loop?" Answering these questions depends on a basic planning axiom: *know your users!* To make informed planning decisions, you need to understand what types of equipment recreationists use. While this holds true for all types of areas, we'll demonstrate the principle with camp loop design.

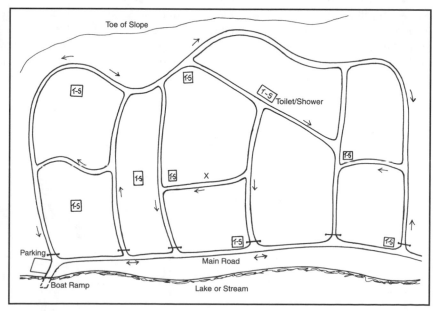

Figure 8.18

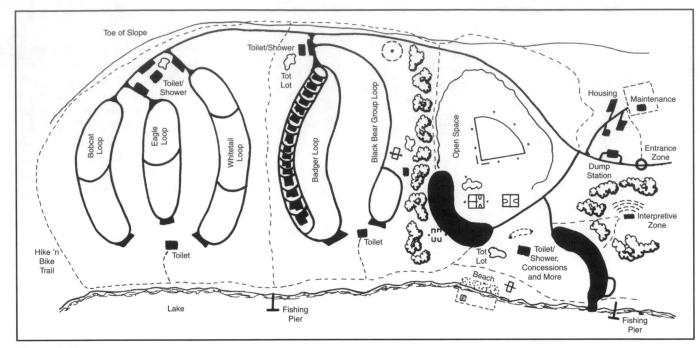

Figure 8.19

Camp loops should be between a minimum of 100-feet wide and a maximum of 120-feet wide (Figure 8.20). To justify this, consider the size of most recreation vehicles. By law, camping trailers can be up to 35 feet in length; otherwise, they must be licensed as permanent house trailers. Add another 20–25 feet for the length of a tow vehicle, and you'll find you need between 55 and 60 feet to park a camper on a camp unit. Since you don't want folks bumping into users parked on the opposite side of a loop, you'll need a minimum of 100 feet from a point on the inside to the point on the opposite *inside* of each loop. The answer is simple as long as you have the information about users' equipment you have to have. Conversely, you don't want to waste space by making loops too fat. If two 35-foot trailers with tow vehicles are parked opposite each other, the maximum space you'd need would be about 100 feet. Add to this a neutral intersite zone or buffer between the backs of the two sites of about 20 feet, and the most width necessary for a loop would be about 120 feet. So why build it any wider?

This information about camping equipment can also provide you with the necessary "knowns" to decide how far apart two loops should be. To accommodate the longest possible trailer and tow vehicle on a single site, you know you'll need about 60 feet. If you look at the schematic of the camp unit in Figure 8.21, you'll notice the site is not perpendicular to the loop road. Rather, the unit is angled at less than 90° to allow users an easier approach when backing a long rig onto the site. This angle also keeps the back of the camp unit less than 55 feet from the edge of the loop on a straight line, although the unit itself is 55-feet long. You can also stagger camp units on adjacent loops as shown, and not all of your units need to be large enough to accommodate the maximum trailer length. If acreage is limited, the ground is level, and you want to maximize the number of units per acre, loops can be located 100 feet apart. Actual distances will be determined by loop configurations, existing vegetation, topography and the unit density of various loops.

Peanuts or Hot Dogs

As you likely have already discovered the authors favor peanut- or hot dog–shaped loops for campgrounds. Why? They are space and land base conservers; they can be bent and shaped to fit existing vegetation and topography; you can point them at your toilet/shower structure and at your attraction (lake or stream) thus moving pedestrian traffic up and down roadways to those attractions through design psychology; therefore they can minimize "overuse" and enhance user comfort. Peanut loops can be small or large as needed. Don't use the peanut shape where it doesn't fit—on a narrow ridge for ex-

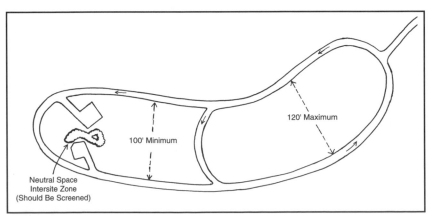

Figure 8.20

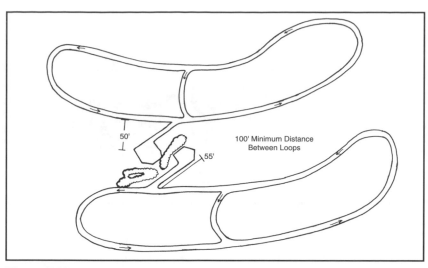

Figure 8.21

ample—or doesn't meet your design needs such as for special group loops (see the Black Bear group loop in Figure 8.19).

Some Peanut Ideas

Figure 8.22 shows four types of peanut applications. The three-loop combo is particularly good for a variety of needs. Obviously there are differing combinations of toilets and showers you might use. For instance the upper and lower structure in the cluster illustration could be simple flush toilets while the center structure could be a toilet/shower.

Figure 8.23 shows three peanut loops with something inside of each loop. These somethings can be found in peanut and other loop centers wherever campgrounds exist. *Toi-*

lets, tot lots, shelters and/or other facilities don't belong in loop centers! By now you should know why this is so.

Figure 8.24 shows two sets of loops located on a lakeshore attraction. One is correctly designed, the other (the No! example) functions if the only user-attracting feature is your toilet/shower. Since the main attraction, though, is the lake, the extreme configuration means some users will cross though each other to get to that attraction. The design on the right corrects this problem.

Figure 8.25 gives a classic example of the "you can't win them all" syndrome. Here is both a pleasant and highly profitable "problem." The area to be used is a ridge 200-feet wide penetrating out into a lake. Obviously any campsites built here will be highly desirable for users and could command user fees higher than less choice campsites in other parts of the campground. However, the lakeshore is an attractive magnet which will pull users toward it from all directions. If there is, for instance, excellent fishing at points X and Y, users will be pulled toward those sites. (We've shown a few units to emphasize the challenge.) Since the 100-foot wide peanut loop is well-suited to maximum utilization of this developable peninsula, use it and do your thoughtful best to cope with the less than desirable expected people movement. Adding numerous reinforced connecting trails from the loop road to the lakeshore trail will minimize problems and, from experience, we know the defined universal campsites will—by simply being there—keep most folks from crossing through actual campsites.

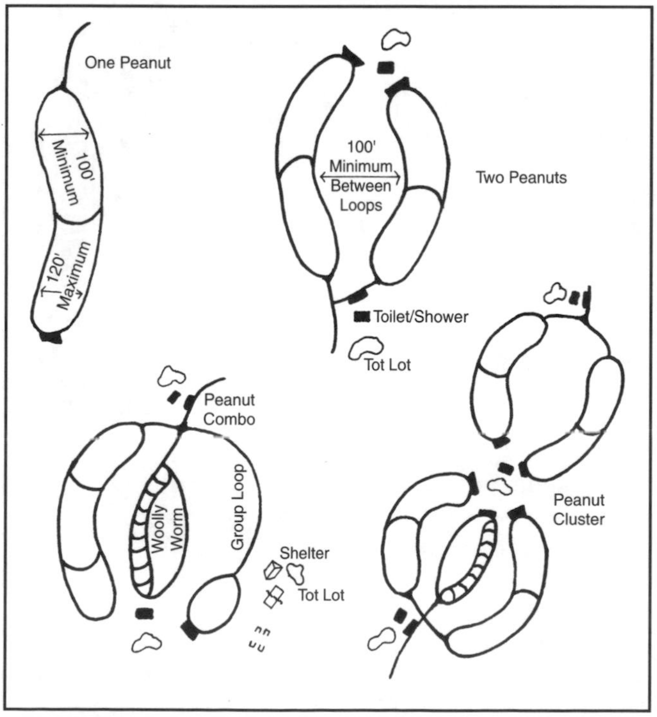

Figure 8.22

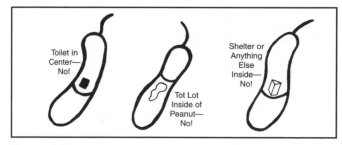

Figure 8.23

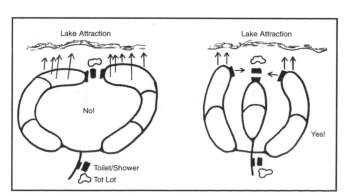

Figure 8.24

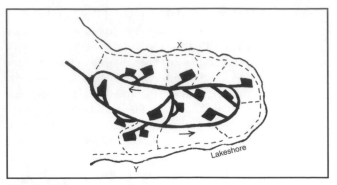

Figure 8.25

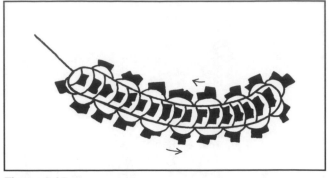

Figure 8.27

Figure 8.26 shows a reasonably good unit layout system for a peanut loop. It includes back-in sites, pull-throughs, buddy sites, high- and medium-density sites, varied spur lengths, and extra spur width and some larger units to provide additional parking. Note the bending ability of the peanut allowing *you* to point the ends where you wish.

If, as we advise you to do, you want to provide some or several loops with a majority of pull-through sites giving you a campground with 30–35 percent or more pull-throughs, think both skinny and fat. In one private campground we designed, the managers wanted a high percentage of pull-through campsites in a small developable area. This forced us to think skinny.

Figure 8.27 shows one of those skinny peanut loops. At both ends of the loop it should bulb out to 100-feet wide while it can be narrower throughout much of its length (75–80 feet). All of the units on this one are pull-throughs and they vary in size and shape. It's a good variation on design though we would be more satisfied to use some back-ins on the outside of the loop.

Our preference between skinny and fat peanuts to help give you more pull-through campsites is to use what we've called the woolly worm. In Chapter Seven we said, with limited exception, a pull-through campsite is nonfunctional on the left side of a one-way loop road. See the inside left end of the typical peanut site layout (Figure 8.26) for the one exception. A fat peanut (at least 175-feet wide) will give you the opportunity to design a "woolly worm" feature inside of the loop's fatness (Figure 8.28).

Obviously this is the exception to the rule saying pull-through sites are nonfunctional on the left side of a one-way road. Make sure your exit to the woolly worm curves into the

exit road before it connects with the double track entrance/exit road (see point X). The units should be different sizes and shapes (don't forget the extra parking) and you can vary the unit density. Make sure your junction of the pull-through parking spur (see point Y) has a smooth drivable transition with the exit road.

Figure 8.29 shows the loop completely designed with emphasis on adding pull-through campsites. Use of the interior woolly worm gives you maximum lineal one-way road footage of right side variety to properly use the pull-through sites. Note the five curved back-in sites inside of the loop on the only "left side" road surface available. If the unit density here is too high for you, eliminate several units to meet your needs.

The left side of the fat peanut loop with a woolly worm inside shown in Figure 8.30 demonstrates the authors' preference for campsite selection. Mixing back-in units (including some sizable ones and a large back-in buddy site) gives better utilization of the developable area than does full use of the pull-through sites in the previous figure. We hope you remember here the Chapter Seven admonition to field design all camp units! Note the graveled linkages or trails (marked with a T) showing some of the numerous ways you can provide buddy sites. While the authors confess we are the imagineers—in recent years—of the woolly worm design to increase your opportunity to add the needed pull-through camp units, we know we haven't thought out the many, many

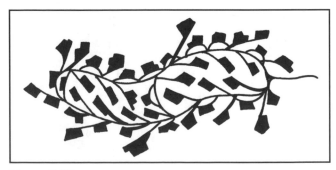

Figure 8.26

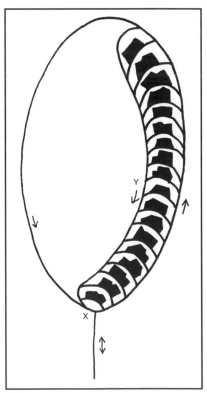

Figure 8.28

Figure 8.29

ways it could be used. Figure 8.31 with its three drawings gives you a few more ideas. As long as your total units per camp loop are a maximum of 50 to 55, we're sure there are dozens of ways to use the woolly worm concept. You should understand a well-designed pull-through campsite takes up considerable space; thus we recommend your using a mixture of back-ins, double or buddy sites, and pull-throughs.

As you can see, the peanut with all of its variations should meet most—though not all—of your camp loop design needs. There are areas, such as narrow ridges and narrow flat areas between a lakeshore or stream and a steep area, where the peanut—even a skinny one—is simply too much road for the available land base. If, for instance, the flat ridge extending out into the lake in Figure 8.25 were only 80- to 120-feet wide, a standard peanut would mean too much road. Where this challenge occurs we suggest a "loop" with a double lane road ending in a turnaround diameter of at least 100 feet (Figure 8.32). Oftentimes these will have fewer units than a standard (if there is one) peanut. They can vary from 10 to 30 units.

The illustration has 20. The road should be curvilinear and also should, at its origin, point to a flush toilet or toilet/shower. Since traffic flows both ways on the double track road, pull-throughs will work on either side.

This type of "loop" gives you some excellent versatility, particularly as group use is becoming more in demand. Groups come in all sizes and kinds from a family reunion where the 10-unit "loop" would be excellent to 30 units and even on up to a peanut with 50 units for camping clubs.

Figure 8.30

Campers within groups also want to be camped close together so high density is the way to go here. Our example caters to a group by adding a few group amenities such as a small shelter, tot lot, horseshoe pits, sand volleyball court, council circle meeting place and even a boccie ball court. Don't put the amenities inside of that turning circle; locate them off to the side of the loop away from camp units so the noise would be at a minimum for days when the loop isn't rented to groups. We

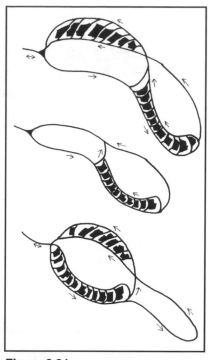

Figure 8.31

like the group "loop" idea so much we recommend you add a few to your design even if the land base doesn't have narrow ridges or other places to demand their use.

As usual, you should realize there are design challenges that *allow you* to combine different types of loops. A narrow ridge that flattens out and gets wider is a good example, and a flat area 300-feet wide would be another.

Figure 8.33 shows a narrow ridge top that widens out at the end. The combination of double track road section and small peanut works well here. Note the toilet near the center of the design will also be in a good location where users will walk the roads to get to it. If the ridge were even wider at its right end you could consider use of a fat peanut and woolly worm.

Figure 8.34 shows a ridge or a peninsula 300-feet wide, and the combination of lengthy peanut 100-feet wide and a double track road with turnaround as a solution. Obviously another solution would be a fat peanut with a woolly worm. Both are correct although the woolly worm on this large an area might exceed 50 camp units.

Return to the nine areas (Figures 8.6 through 8.14) you visited and critiqued earlier in the chapter. What's wrong with them; how could they be

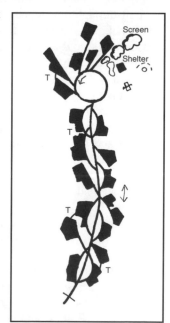

Figure 8.32

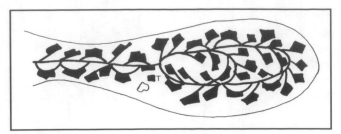

Figure 8.33

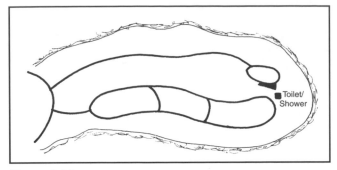

Toilet/
Shower

Figure 8.34

rehabilitated; or how could they have been better designed initially? Rather than having to refer back to each of the nine areas, here they are again. Since you've studied the dos and don'ts, and the elements of peanut design, you should be able to provide a serious critique of all nine areas.

Figure 8.35 is the Oregon State Park (originally shown as Figure 8.6) located just across U.S. Highway 101 from the Pacific Ocean. What an attraction! Here are a few of the less-than-good design items we see: toilets/showers in centers of loops; camping spurs 90° off loop roads; fat loops; main road between loops and the stream attraction; cookie-cutter unit design; group campers having to travel through family loops; and no play amenities. At first glance, some of the pull-through units appear to be non-functional. However—and this is quite unusual for so old an area—each of the pull-throughs is on the right side of a one-way road.

In Figure 8.36 we show what might have been. The area now has numerous loops which point at the toilets, toilets/ showers and the stream attraction. All campers don't move through most others as in the original. Amenities such as a lighted ball field, multipurpose play court, playground, shelter, and open space together with a screened campfire theater will provide the program elements to beckon the families we've previously discussed. We see ways to improve our plan, such as the addition of two or three group loops. How else would you improve it?

Figure 8.37 shows an Iowa State Park campground in southeastern Iowa (first

shown as Figure 8.7). Some of the things we see that are less than good include moving from one loop to another, adding traffic and safety problems for most campers; loops named 1, 2 and 3; toilets in loop centers; nothing much to do; and space-wasting fat loops. Our revision of the Iowa area (Figure 8.38) utilizes the two existing fat loops by adding two woolly worm features giving them the needed pull-through units. We also added two peanut loops and a group loop pointing to the lake and gave critter names to all five loops. We've eliminated the two toilets in the loop centers and relocated a new toilet and a toilet/shower structure with a family assist room for persons with disabilities. The location of the entrance zone makes it possible for fee collection personnel (at low- to medium-use times) to dispense the play equipment needed in the activity zone. What would be needed in the activity area to beckon families? Since the activity area is out of the camp loop zone, the manager or programmer could superimpose a special day-use event there with little or no impact on the campers.

Kickapoo State Park in east central Illinois (Figure 8.39, originally shown as Figure 8.8) is one of the most interesting areas we've seen, experienced, or ever heard of! Earlier in the chapter we asked you to determine what's wrong with this design. Let's just say you had plenty to work with. The current manager of this park is an old professional friend and he, like hundreds of his follow managers across North America, inherited this mess from park managers and planners of years gone by. (Unlike most managers, our friend took on the State Park higher-ups and the designers and at the writing of this story, a well-designed campground is replacing the mess he inherited.) The campground is typical of "the way it happened" in both the private and public sectors. It started with a few campsites then grew and grew some more. A manager plunked some sites here and a planner plunked some sites there while neither had a clue concerning decent master planning. There are ways to redesign or disentangle this mess but we've taken the easiest pathway and designed a new area.

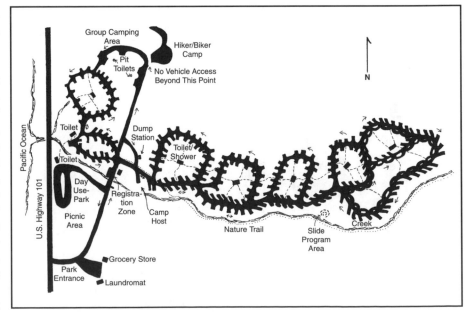

Figure 8.35 Oregon State Park

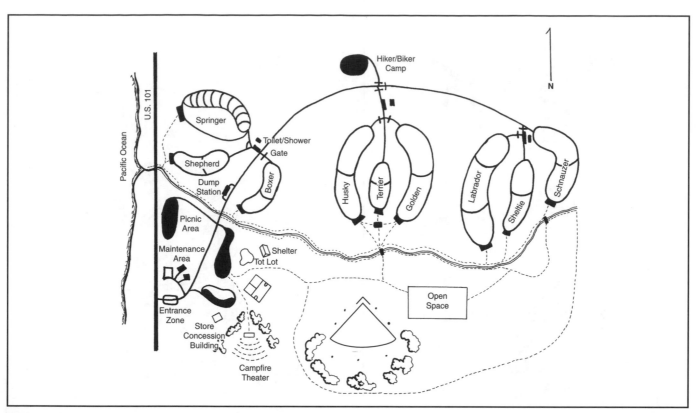

Figure 8.36

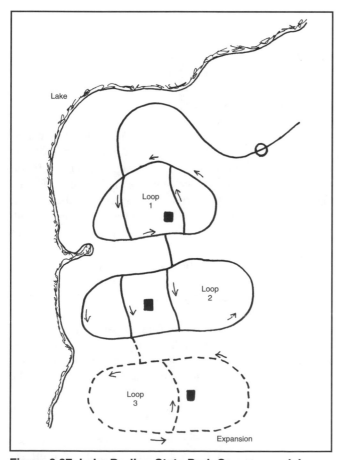

Figure 8.37 Lake Darling State Park Campground, Iowa

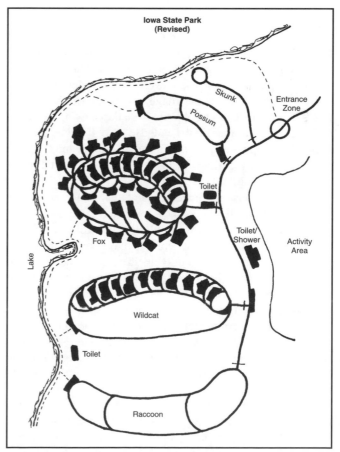

Figure 8.38

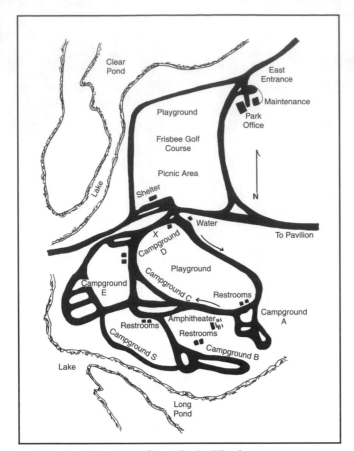

Figure 8.39 Kickapoo State Park, Illinois

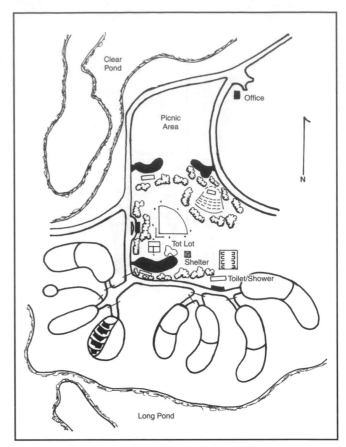

Figure 8.40

What's wrong with the old one? It's a monster to manage! An early warning clue to problems is the left traffic flow at the campground entrance. "Where are we and how do we get out of this place?" Folks here even had a problem with their ABC's since the loops are imaginatively named A, B, C, E and S. If you are camped at point X on the drawing (which is quite near the entrance) and decided to leave the campground, your return trip takes you to or through loops A and C, and if you're not lucky perhaps even E. And that's not the user-friendly way it should be!

Figure 8.40 is our version of how it all might have been. Here and now we'll let you know it is *much* easier to design a new campground than it is to redesign and salvage a poorly designed old one. Our point here is to make your campground designers design for you, not them. There are eight loops in this plan and each cluster of four points to a nearby sizable toilet/shower and to the lake. The manager can open or close various loops as needed. He has one group loop but could use any of the others as group size dictates. The fun section is located like the one in Iowa—outside of the camp loop zone, but inside of the entrance control station. Note, too, the camp loops all point toward the fun or amenity zone, thus people move—through design psychology—where you want them to go. We haven't named each loop but have given you this challenge. Loop names are one more special nuance to beckon folks to return again and again to your campground. They also help you do some creative programming such as prize

drawings or contests between the Dasey May loop campers and the Joy Juice loop folks. Use all the tools of the trade to beckon users! Loop names might include animals, state names, U.S. presidents, sports teams, cities, historical sites, events or figures, and countless others, such as Confederate generals as shown in the next design.

Figure 8.41 is the Georgia Veteran's State Park campground you first saw as Figure 8.9. You likely have determined several of the less than good design items here. If not, we'll point out a few. In our view, the planners committed a sizable error (which dictated some poor design to them) when they used the old highway as their entrance and main road. The nearness of that road to the lake makes good design for users, managers and the environment ("overuse" again) an impossibility. Aside from that, it doesn't appear their designers knew much about quality loop and camp unit design. Loops parallel to the shoreline mean campers move through each other to get to the attraction. Here again we have great loop names: 1, 2 and 3. We've used Confederate generals as loop names in our redesign, though it likely would be a better historical tie-in to the Georgia Veteran's organization to use Confederate generals who were residents of Georgia. Note the pull-through sites on all three loops on the left sides of their one-way roads. Finally, where are the family-beckoning fun facilities?

Figure 8.42 is our version of how this campground could have been better planned. We ignored or eliminated the ex-

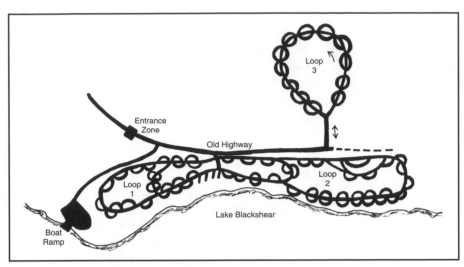

Figure 8.41 Georgia Veteran's State Park

isting road. Note how most of our road systems minimize straight lines. For several reasons curvilinear roads are well-suited to most park designs. The Hampton and Forrest loops would host groups and should have special play amenities on each loop. The Jackson loop, which is tied into the boat ramp and the beach toilet/shower, is designed for special winter use meaning other parts (or at least the other six loops) of the area could be winterized and closed. Again, the amenity zone, including a campfire theater with interpretive theme trails, could be used for sizable (and profitable) special events or industrial day-use groups.

At this point it's time to let you know there are dozens of potential solutions to the design or rehabilitation problems we are presenting. Many are likely far better than ours. Whatever you do, make sure your designs fit your user, manager, and other design needs.

A sizable private KOA campground located on U.S. Highway 1 in the Florida Keys is shown in Figure 8.43 (originally Figure 8.10). It has many things for users to do and gets extremely heavy use. They have a large swimming pool, bi-

cycle rentals, a small camp store, and several creative places for campers including shelters designed in pie-shaped individual sections for those who don't have wheeled camping vehicles or tents. Many of their sites are seasonal, meaning near permanence in location (more on this later). What they don't have is a well-designed area. Fact is, it's quite difficult to find a well-designed private or public campground anywhere!

The maze of roads which are parallel to the shoreline and each other means potential safety problems and users moving through these undefined units to get to the Florida Bay attraction and to the toilets/showers. If the manager wished, in slow times (if there are any slow times here), to close some areas he could do so *if* (and that's a *big* if) he had lots of cables, chains and gates. Since seasonal and overnight campsites are mixed together, closing some parts of this campground will be almost impossible.

Our redesign (Figure 8.44) provides a curvilinear main road and loop roads, two areas with six seasonal camp loops and four loops for family camping use. The maintenance and housing complex is, as it should be, a part of yet apart from the campground. One sizable activity area is located near the entrance to attract potential users. The other activity area—with swimming pool, natural beach, and boat ramp—is located on the tip of the land base. Again, which area would you prefer to own and manage?

The authors understand that if this area had initially been well-designed, it likely would not have received more use than it has gotten! Access and attraction here, like the state park on the Oregon coast (Figure 8.36), are so outstanding they negate most design mistakes. Also, since campers have rarely been exposed to good design (including universal campsites) they don't expect it and likely would only be subconsciously aware of such unusual stuff anyhow. However, good design in parks (including private campgrounds) can and should provide easier administration, less damage to the environment, less confusion to users, and improved programming ability. Because campers and others know or care little about good design doesn't give license to you or us to continue to do it poorly!

Figure 8.45 (originally shown as Figure 8.11) shows another private campground in the Midwest. Day use, including boat launching, was allowed to penetrate the camping zone. Several of the roads, such as the one at the bottom of the drawing, had units only on the inside of the road. Location of the three toilet/shower buildings causes movement between and

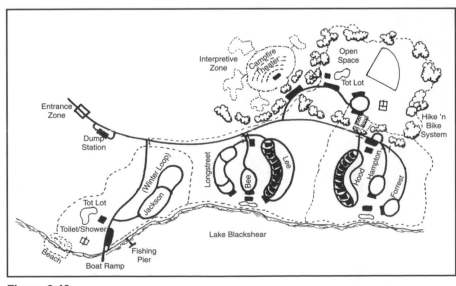

Figure 8.42

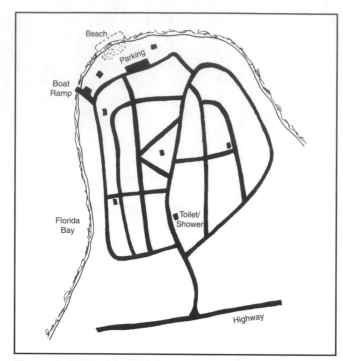

Figure 8.43 Florida KOA Campground

across units and roads. There is considerable wasted space in the design, too many straight roads, and too much road for the space used. What other less than good design features do you see? You might begin with "where are the amenities?"

Figure 8.46 shows one solution to the private campground design problem. It provides two family camping loops with woolly worm features and lots of potential for pull-through

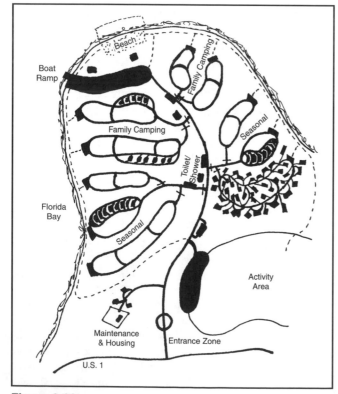

Figure 8.44

sites. (The initial design only had back-in or pull-in camp units.) There is also a small group loop. We've given you a complete unit layout for one loop. There are two sizable toilet/shower structures with all loops pointing at them. Note also how four of the loops point at the lake attraction. The activity area is located away from the campground off the boat ramp road again making it available for sizable daytime group use. We've also added two seasonal campsite loops. With adequate amenities, including a beach or swimming pool, this well-zoned campground would be a real moneymaker. Shouldn't this be a goal of campground design?

Figure 8.47 shows the campground you saw originally as Figure 8.12. We ran onto this 63-unit Forest Service campground between Colorado Springs and Pike's Peak. There was a lake and day-use area down the road and to the left which would have made a fantastic group day-use area with theme pods (but that's another story). Nearby there were also two other small Forest Service campgrounds which could be eliminated thus giving the Forest Service a sizable expansion of this one. Earlier in the chapter we shared a concept about development of a base camp which didn't have an on-site attraction but could be a hub for numerous others. This "large" area—which is only about one-third the size it should be—is an excellent example of a potentially profitable base camp. What did you find wrong with this area?

We hope you carefully critiqued all of the camp units to find the usable ones. (Remember our recent discussion about campers' scant exposure to good design? This area is a great example of that truism!) The things we found that were less than good include: The units included pull-throughs on the wrong side of one-way roads; pull-ins; no buddy sites or extra parking; short spurs; and 90° spurs off the road. Toilets were in the center of the fat (wasted space) loops as was the campfire theater. There were no other amenities or on-site programs. The sharp "V" at the entrance doesn't allow campers to (as almost all campers will) look over all the open campsites and easily make the turn back through the area to pick their special site! The campground host told us users had to *exit* the campground, drive a half mile down the road to turn

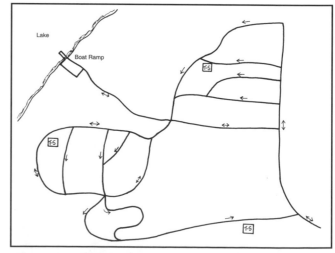

Figure 8.45 Midwest Private Campground

around in the day-use area, and return to the campground to find their preferred campsite. Suppose you were that person and while you were making the user-unfriendly trip to return to your campsite some other person moved into the empty site!? User-unfriendly design is rampant here! The check-in area was located just after you entered the campground, meaning there was an inadequate space for several campers to enter and register. Someone stopped there for any reason also blocked the road which added to camper unhappiness and caused an unnecessary visitor safety problem. Somewhere along the way we hope you're asking yourself and others how some of these obvious and serious mistakes were allowed to happen. There are lots of reasons, including taking untrained (academic or otherwise) persons such as foresters, wildlife graduates, and other rascals, and making them instant experts; thinking that landscape architects or recreation planners have the academic training to do a good job; and having persons in authority, who supervise those folks, who know little about what they're doing either. In any event the parks, the users and taxpayers have all been shortchanged. The three authors have some skills now after 70-plus years (cumulative) working with parks and people; however none of them were trained adequately when they finished college.

Consider the design in Figure 8.48. It took a little courage, but we finally decided to take an existing area and rehabilitate it using as much of the existing road network as possible. Wherever you see an ellipsis (. . .), we've used a section of the USFS existing road. We named the base camp Haunted Hollow and designed five loops including a group loop with a few amenities.

All the loops have interesting names, perhaps not what you'd select, but interesting. The entrance road extends several hundred feet to provide a safe entering environment. It also is double width on the right of the center line from the highway to the entrance structure to provide for back up traffic and for those who have already checked in. There is one sizable flush toilet and a large toilet/shower. The toilet/shower is located with all loops pointing to it and near the amenity

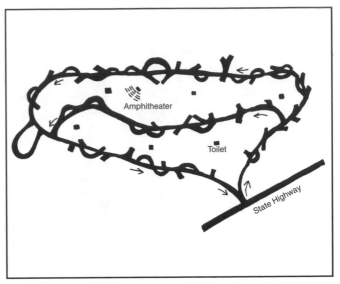

Figure 8.47 USFS Campground, Colorado

zone. The five loops should provide 170 potential campsites. A future planned loop will provide 40 more units meaning the campground can have over 200 units which should give them a base for public-private profit. We've also included a maintenance yard and seasonal housing zone for staff close to the entrance station. Having the five loops will give the Forest Service an opportunity to use different unit densities, shade factors, screening densities, buddy sites, extra parking, the woolly worm, and all sorts of items you and they have learned in Chapters Seven and Eight, assuming Forest Service personnel read the book. The group loop will add to that versatility. Figure 8.49 shows the amenity or fun zone for Haunted Hollow Campground. We've used an existing road to get to the parking areas. The screened Finger Bone Loop is located near the amenities. It will be an attraction to those most

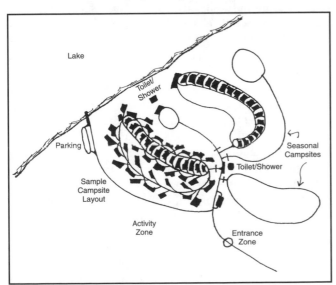

Figure 8.46

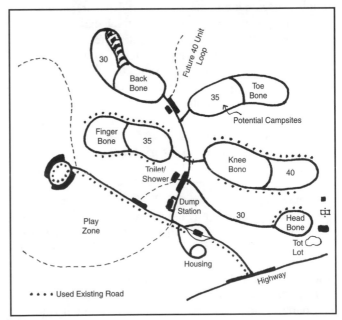

Figure 8.48

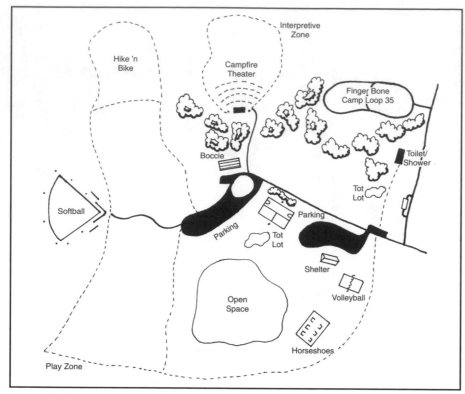

Figure 8.49

campers have to cross one or several roads to get to the lake or anywhere else. The gate attendant can only guess where folks go when they pass the fee booth. Poorly planned and designed (though heavily used) areas like Shoal Bay Recreation Area in Arkansas litter our North American continent. In most agencies, managers have little to say before and even after the areas get built. Part of this is caused by managerial lack of knowledge and/or disinterest, so it's easy for the planning rascals to "assume" managers aren't interested. On the other side of the coin, a high-level agency planner once told us managers and programmers had no business telling his trained and competent staff how something should be designed. That's how you, us and the public end up with all of the dandy plans and parks we've shared with you. In our training of hundreds of working practitioners we've found they rarely have taken the time (even in a major rehabilitation) to see if they could improve a messed-up area. The previously discussed Forest Service area in Colorado is a good example. If you want to improve visitor safety, minimize confusion, give yourself a better chance to manage your area, zone various features, move users where you want them to safely go, upgrade camp loops and more, take the time to overlay and replan some of the monsters planners and others have given you and see how at least some of the problems can be eliminated. Three or four quick attempts at replanning can give you wonderful results. Try it, you won't be disappointed. Also, don't wait for your planners and designers to correct their mistakes or you are likely to have a long wait.

interested in sports, games, and programs while the other loops will be far from the screened noise and excitement.

The activity area is also zoned with screening into active and passive areas. Included are lighted softball field, multipurpose play court, boccie ball and horseshoe areas, shelter and equipment checkout structure, hike and bike trails, open space, and a 400–450 person campfire theater with a set of theme interpretive trails. Again, the manager can superimpose a sizable day-use group on this amenity zone (or day camping, or nursing home group, or whatever) on this area without loop penetration. Note also the location of the entrance control structure allows the staff there to see and control where users go. Campers can have fun, play, or otherwise enjoy themselves until 2:00 or 3:00 A.M. in the lighted softball area, multipurpose play court, and other lighted area without causing noise problems for sleeping campers.

Much of the amenity zone can be seen from the highway meaning it is a beckoning element, particularly for children, in getting folks interested in experiencing your campground (design psychology again). Finally, we ask "our" question— "Which of the two campgrounds would you prefer to manage or have an enjoyable vacation in?" (In this progressive Forest Service Region this might happen!)

Figure 8.50 shows the U.S. Corps of Engineers park originally discussed in Figure 8.13. Earlier we said this type of heavily used area was difficult to administer. We hope you described several of the major problems. The mixing of traffic from day-use picnicking, two boat launching sites, a sizable public marina, and group picnickers all going through various camp loops should give you a clue. Almost all of the

As you can see in Figure 8.51, we've taken the easiest pathway again and designed the area almost as if nothing were there, though we utilized their boating site, marina, and roadway to the trails area. Again, there could be a number of acceptable solutions to the original design problem and ours is but one of these.

From the entrance gate the attendant can see where most cars and tow vehicles go. If, for instance, there is no charge, or a reduced one for visitors moving to the public marina, the attendant can tell them to turn right and watch them do it. Only campers and their visitors should be entering the nearby campground road at the left, while boaters and day users (if you want day users here) should drive straight ahead. There are some flaws in all of this, but the gate person does have considerable opportunity for control.

Since the land base is small, our campground would likely be a maximum of 150 units (which is nearly twice as many as the original) with four versatile loops all pointing to the lake and to the sizable toilet/shower. The campground play zone could be mostly for campers only or could be available for

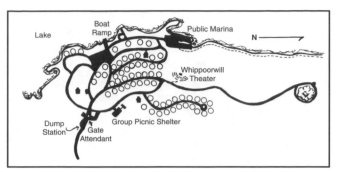

Figure 8.50 USCOE Shoal Bay Rec. Area, Arkansas

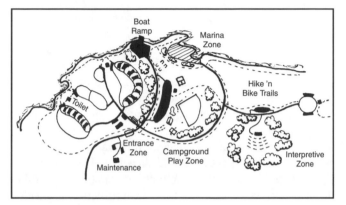

Figure 8.51

special events. We've added an interpretive zone to the screened campfire theater.

Our last example (Figure 8.52; originally Figure 8.14) is the poorly designed municipal General Sibley Park area with sizable campground in North Dakota. What's wrong here? Yes, it appears they (likely by accident) used a form of peanut design. The loops look a bit strange with all of the roads crossing in, around, and through and they obviously don't point at the river attraction or at the toilets/showers. The big mistake here, in our view, is the "third-class citizenship" designers give to campers. Everyone will move to the river or lake attraction. This means campers will walk through other camper spaces and through various day users to get to the

Figure 8.53

water. This is not a user-friendly design. It means many users cross many roads causing confusion and safety problems.

Years ago, when we visited the area, the campsite environment was in trouble because of the unregulated foot traffic. There was no campsite definition which added to compaction throughout the area. At the area entrance (Figure 8.53) visitors were zapped with 16 signs essentially telling them what they couldn't do. This is an example of user unfriendliness and unbeckoning design psychology.

Our design (Figure 8.54) moves the main campground road to the back boundary line out of the developable area. It also leads to a camping zone with six loops, all but one of which point at the lake and to the toilets/showers. The manager can open and close loops as the demand arises. Several loops could be used for groups though three are specifically designed for them. The play zone could serve a dual purpose meeting both day-use and campground programming needs. We're not sure a beach would work here though we know it's possible in places on Lake Oahe. We've made sure the gate attendant has some control, and the campers, like the day users, are all "first-class citizens."

An interesting story evolved while we were writing this chapter. One of the three authors got a call from a person interested in building a private campground on land he had bought on Lake Oahe near General Sibley Park. Problem

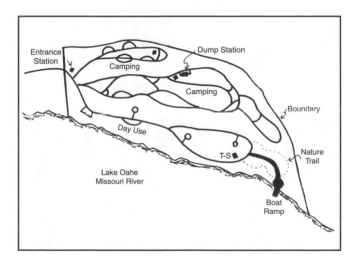

Figure 8.52 General Sibley Park, North Dakota

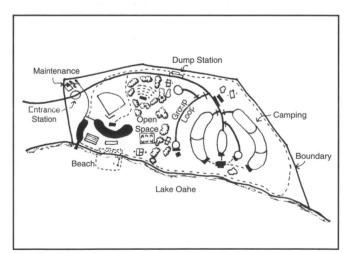

Figure 8.54

was, he wasn't sure how a quality campground should be built. He believed the logical thing for him to do was to talk with and learn from a nearby recreation vehicle dealer. It would seem logical such a person would know something about campground design, as quality public and private campgrounds with well-designed universal campsites, buddy sites, extra parking, and all that good stuff would be of paramount concern to him. (Not!) Anyhow, the dealer took him to General Sibley campground and said, "Do it like this, as this is state-of-the-art park planning." Fortunately the person didn't quite believe all of this and looked for more help.

This story is a tragic one in that logic tells us recreation vehicle dealers and manufacturers should be interested in promoting and helping improve what obviously is their basic resource—campgrounds and campsites. Experience tells us logic is wrong here in that neither the dealers' organization nor the manufacturers have ever exhibited an interest in supporting campground design, research, or even spending time learning about the basics of good campground and campsite design. Why? We don't know! (Finding the scope of this problem and recommending a few ways to improve it would seem to be good thesis topics for graduate students.)

Family Campground Design

Seasonal Campsites. Our discussion of Native-American parks introduced you to seasonal campsites (Figure 5.55). We also added two seasonal site loops to our revision of the Midwestern private campground in Figure 8.46 earlier in this chapter. What are seasonal campsites? Are they a good idea for public and private campgrounds? Why haven't we heard of them before?

The advent nationally of the seasonal campsite is new to some parts of the United States. Essentially these are sites leased or rented to a camper for the season's length. In some places this would be all 12 months while in others it may only be for a five- to six-month period. Unlike most new occurrences it seems to have started in the eastern United States and moved west. The campsites may be rented or leased for as little as $400 per season to $3,000 or higher. This depends on the attraction, section of the county, and location on or away from a lake or stream. The private sector has pioneered these sites but the public sector, particularly counties and municipalities who have considerable flexibility (and are likely better attuned to the public and making money than federal or state folks), is beginning to understand the demand for and profitability of seasonal campsites.

The campground may be entirely seasonal with no weekday or week-long use or it may be partially so. The main benefits for the park owner are the up-front lump sum payment made early in the year and the ability to use campsite locations which couldn't be used by the short time in and out family camper. The benefits to the seasonal campsite renter or lessee are numerous. This site is available to them, their friends and relatives anytime they wish to use it. They don't have to drive or tow their motor home, trailer or other camping rig to the site (oftentimes great distances) each time they

wish to use it. They will likely take many more trips there than if they didn't have a permanent site or faced the towing challenge each time. (A good research topic.) In some cases local city ordinances don't allow a camping trailer or motor home to be located on a person's private lot. (We take a dim view of this!) Since, it has to be stored someplace; why not in a campground? And, they have a little corner of the oftentimes expensive out-of-doors with all the hookups they need without buying, upgrading, maintaining, and governmental hassles of outright property ownership. Many of the seasonal campgrounds we've visited are similar to the base camp concept we described earlier in the chapter in that there is no particular on-site or even nearby attraction. (We were somewhat surprised at this although we've seen seasonal attractionless campgrounds in the Midwest and far West.) The campers want that wildland place of their own and will travel away from their campsites some distance to attractions.

What the users get for their rental fee varies even within the same campground. Some owners rent or lease small, defined, and staked plots of ground, and have a sample site or two to show users how their plot may be designed. Some have this system with an allowance for some gravel. Others actually build different sizes and shapes of universal campsites before they offer them for rent. All can be successful if the owner/manager has a strict set of guidelines covering plot layout sideboards, on-site facilities, and rules of use including who may use the site other than the renter. In most instances the users can have small gardens, decks, storage buildings, fireplaces or fire circles, boats, trailers, and extra parking for guests. Standard practice is to allow the user to rent the same space year after year.

Figure 8.55 shows two water view units with decks in a seasonal area on Kentucky Lake in Kentucky. Note the quality of each unit and the cleanliness of the grounds. Figure 8.56 shows a more elaborate site on a private seasonal-only campground in Indiana. They have built a universal site with privacy fence, landscaping and sizable deck. Several of the rented plots in that small campground (45 sites) had similar quality features. (For those who might question seasonal site

Figure 8.55

quality compare this one with the eight campsites in eight state parks in eight states at the beginning of Chapter Seven!)

Figure 8.57 takes us back to the campground on Kentucky Lake. Here is a narrow peninsula jutting out into the lake. It has a dead-end road (laid out by one of the authors) through the center and plots located all along the shoreline. A conventional loop road or even a road with a 100-foot radius turnaround at the end which is needed for overnight users won't work here as the peninsula isn't wide enough. However, the 15–20 units are real moneymakers for the owners. Since the camping rigs are brought in once a season (or even less) the hassle of maneuvering them into position isn't a big problem. Most campground owners (as a part of the rental fee) will use their own equipment (Figure 8.58, a tractor moving a trailer) to carefully place the trailer on site. Then there is no problem for users to visit the area with their personal autos, vans, and trucks. This is likely a bonus, too, to older users who are uncomfortable towing and maneuvering their expensive sizable equipment in public and private nonseasonal campgrounds that rarely have safe, generous, level, defined, highly desirable campsites.

The Kentucky campground has 115 seasonal campsites. Each site has water, sewage, and electric hookups furnished by the owner (electric service was metered). In addition, the renters also had access to phone and TV cable service. The

Figure 8.58

area has several cabins, activity zone with swimming pool (and program staff!), sizable protected marina, and restaurant. Fortunately, the semiprivate seasonal sites were on a large peninsula beyond the other features (in other words, by accident the area was well-zoned!). So administration was simple in that those who had the rented sites and a few family members were issued a plastic card they could use to activate the electronic gate and enter the area (Figure 8.59).

Figure 8.60 shows the exit approach to the same gate with its explanatory sign. There are all sorts of electronic gates

Figure 8.56

Figure 8.59

Figure 8.57

Figure 8.60

available including those with a changeable punch-in combination. If you are considering seasonal sites in a campground here are some recommendations:

1. Build or require the user to build impact-resistant universal sites.
2. In general, use as many back-in sites as possible. The pull-throughs take up considerable space and you don't have the necessity of providing easier entry for older campers and larger equipment as you can move their trailers on site once a season or less. (As you can see, the design constraints aren't the same as those for overnight camping.) Long back-ins can also get to those nooks and crannies easier than other unit types.
3. Don't mix seasonal sites on loops with overnight or week-long camping folks. (This results in numerous problems.) Have loops with seasonals and separate loops for other types of users.
4. Don't give the seasonals your best attraction-oriented camp loop and campsite locations. They can be a part of your loop overall system but away from heavy activity and overnight use. (See Figure 8.5, the sizable seven-loop campground on Spring Lake. Here, the two easternmost peanut camp loops pointing to the toilet/shower should be the location of your seasonal site loops.)
5. Do zone your seasonal loops so users there have excellent access to play amenities and programs.
6. Do consider the use of seasonal campsites. We expect demand for such sites will increase as we enter the next century.

Sanitation

Included briefly under this heading will be flush toilets, toilets/showers, dumping stations, lagoons, treatment plants, garbage collection facilities and recycling. Again, we aren't versed in the local state and federal constraints and guidelines you will face for all these facilities. However, this section will provide you some guidance into mistakes you can avoid and sideboards you should consider. For those who continue to pump out vault toilets or have need to provide sanitation where water isn't available or at elevations where freezing is a possibility in any month we have two brief bits of advice:

1. If you need or must use vault toilets we suggest you consider one devised by USDA sanitation research folks called the Sweet Smelling Toilet System. *If* (that's a big if again) they are built, installed, oriented, and maintained properly they will provide a viable option for you. Your best bet is to contact any U.S. Forest Service office for information. Their regional office division of engineering will have this information.
2. If you have short seasons with threats of freezing, another good system is the Clivis Maultrem System. Again, the U.S. Forest Service will have information for you as will the company. Neither of the two systems mentioned

is inexpensive. Our recommendation for most public and private family campgrounds is flush toilets and showers.

Flush Toilets and Toilets/Showers

Since you should have considerable knowledge of our campground design philosophy, you should now know how to properly locate these facilities. (Remember peanut loops and where they should point, how to move folks where you want them to go and how to combat the myth of overuse?) Have another look at Figure 8.51 on the redesign of Shoal Bay Park. There are four camp loops, two flush toilets, and one sizable toilet/ shower. Obviously, the three structures could all have been toilets/showers, though we don't think it is necessary. We've even seen a successful system in a large USCOE campground where there was an adequate number of flush toilets on the camp loops and a large shower building with toilet facilities located near the entrance station (Figure 8.61). If folks want a shower they will *walk or drive* to the one large shower facility. We prefer a system similar to the ones shown for the entire (say, eight loop) campground. If you do use the one sizable shower/toilet structure near the entrance you can also locate it close to the amenity play and program area which could eliminate the need for an additional structure. (Hope you can see that all of this advice will require you, designers, and engineers to think a bit!)

The amount and kind of "furniture" or facilities inside (shower stalls, commodes, urinals, toilets, mirrors, shelves, lights, clothes hanging pegs, and more) will be determined in part by state and local laws and regulations, and persons serviced. We don't know about the proper ratio of facilities on the men's and women's sides in campgrounds though we suggest at least 25 percent more toilet facilities on the women's side than on the men's. (For day-use areas this should be much higher.) Again, what an opportunity for applied master's degree research to find out what's really wanted and needed! Perhaps on the men's side a shower room without individual stalls would work and be less expensive than shower stalls which are the best choice for women.

Make sure your toilets/showers have plenty of light with either electric or a combination of skylights and electric, and

Figure 8.61

an air movement system (vents or fans or both). All facilities should be as vandal-proof and as safe as possible. We also don't recommend heavy shade around these or other campground structures. There are numerous user-friendly and unfriendly toilet/shower items you should consider. (Again we will save most of our recommendations and thoughts about persons with disabilities for a section in Chapter Ten.)

1. Provide a clean entrance environment preferably with generous concrete walkways around the structure.
2. If there are no gutters on the building make sure the water runoff from the roof falls into a dissipating rock sump. Mud holes around toilets/showers are quite common and unappreciated.
3. Have stalls separating urinals from wash basins. Suppose you were brushing your teeth at the wash basin in Figure 8.62 when someone rushed in and used the urinal? Most folks would not consider this user friendly. See Figure 8.63 for a better solution.
4. Provide a nonslip floor surface.
5. Provide adequate drainage. Standing in two inches of water as you shower or shave isn't a user-friendly experience.

6. Provide adequate shelf or counter space for gear, glasses and blow dryers and more. Note there is no such space in Figures 8.62 and 8.63.
7. Make sure your vents are designed so as to prohibit children and perverts from viewing unclothed folks.
8. Provide adequate—indeed generous and safe-substantive—pegs or hangers for clothing and towels. The providers of toilet facilities (without showers) we used in a sizable NPS Acadia campground in Maine and a majority of other campgrounds, both public and private, don't seem to consider such things as being necessary (Figure 8.64). Note here, too, the less-than-generous space provided for shaving kits, wash cloths, and glasses. The light fixtures weren't great places to hang towels but they were the only places.
9. Provide adequate bench spaces for dressing both at the entrance to the shower stalls and shower room, and where the wash basins are located.
10. Don't—we repeat, *don't*—be talked into putting coin-operated showers in your structure. The experiences of naked, soap-covered authors who didn't have another quarter either on their person or in their *far off* pockets have given us most intimate feelings of user unfriendliness of these **#@#!&&**!!
11. Do inspect your toilets/showers several times each day and keep them clean.
12. Since toilets/showers are obvious focal points that most campers visit on a regular basis, make use of them in several other ways. Figure 8.65 shows a facility in an Indiana state park. Note the convenient pay phone and drink machines. This is also a great place for a bulletin board announcing your numerous programs (we certainly recommend lots of programs), what to do and who to contact in an emergency, location of nearby churches, hospitals, and other attractions. *Note:* In seasonal campsite loops where all users have sewage hookups, and in family camping loops with full hookups, it seems to us the number of shower facilities, urinals, and toilets could be cut back somewhat. (Again, a dandy research topic.)

Figure 8.62

Figure 8.63

Figure 8.64

Figure 8.65

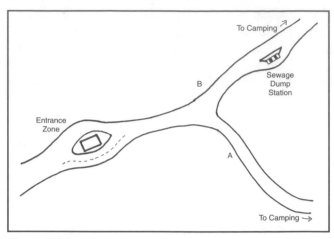

Figure 8.66

Sewage Dumping Stations

If you do want to beckon all sorts of family campers, including older persons, one critical feature to have in your campground is a sewage dumping station. As we've tried to stress before, you should know the needs of your users and how their equipment functions. Waste disposal facilities provide an excellent example of these principles.

Many RVs, built as they are for user convenience, have *sewage holding tanks.* These tanks are designed to hold several days' worth of raw sewage, drain on a gravity flow basis, and be flushed out with water when emptied. Let's take a test here. In the preceding sentence, we've given you the basic facts you need to *zone, design* and *build* a sewage dumping station. Did you get them? You probably need a little more to go on. Since sewage holding tanks will contain several day's worth of raw sewage, campers will empty their tanks at one of two times: on their way *into* or *out of* a campground. Consider the location of the sewage dumping station in Figure 8.66. Here campers using the camp loops within the area designated A will have to drive out of their way to reach the dumping station. You also may need to place an additional sign at point B indicating where the station is. Placing the dumping station as shown in Figure 8.66 causes an inconvenience for campers, costs you a few bucks for an extra sign, and violates the principle of zoning use areas. Figure 8.67 shows a simple alternative to avoid these problems. With this location, the dumping station is easy to find and convenient to campers, although from an aesthetic standpoint you should screen it. Another plus for this location is that it's a possible turnaround zone for people who, after reaching the entry station, decide they want to leave the area.

From a design perspective, you need to remember the connection for draining an RV holding or septic tank is on the left-hand or driver's side of the vehicle. Figure 8.68 shows the proper location of a sewage dumping station on the driver's side of the vehicle. The picture showing how not to do it in Figure 8.69 is courtesy of our old friend, the National Park Service. Users solved this problem just as they oftentimes do on campground roads—they entered at the exit and exited at

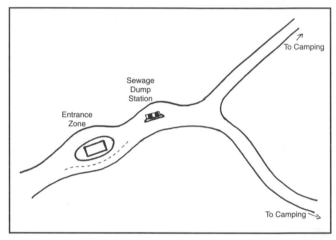

Figure 8.67

the entrance. Doing something properly is rarely more costly than doing the same thing poorly!

Since the dumping station you provide is designed around a large underground holding tank, campers need to be able to pull alongside it. The whole operation is rather like the design of a pump island at a gas station, and Figure 8.70 shows

Figure 8.68

one way of designing a double dumping station. With this layout, campers can reach the drain points from either side of the island, which means they have the convenience of emptying their holding tanks as they enter or exit your campground. Between the two drain points a hose, or flushing outlet, lets them flush out their holding tanks. Since the tip of this hose may come in contact with raw sewage, you should sign the outlet for cleaning purposes only (not to be used to replenish drinking supplies).

Because RV holding tanks drain on gravity flow, the portion of road adjacent to the drain points needs to be *insloped* two to three percent, as shown in Figure 8.71, for complete draining. The concrete slab housing the drains themselves should be slightly *concave,* with the drains placed at the *lowest point* on the surface so any spillage will run downhill into the drain. Get help from your engineering staff, but don't assume they have all the answers.

"If we locate it near the toilet/shower our costs will be less!" We often hear this blurb, particularly from engineers. However, locating a sewage dumping station on a loop road near a toilet/shower is poor design and poor hosting (Figure 8.72). A facility which could malfunction or have accidental spillage should be located apart of *yet* apart from general public view. Several years ago—while visiting a southern state park—we had the unique experience of seeing another combination toilet/shower/dumping station where the drain was the *highest point* on the concrete slab. Spillage had run across and down the road and children were playing in the runoff with sticks! Gross? Yes! Gross incompetence? Even more so!

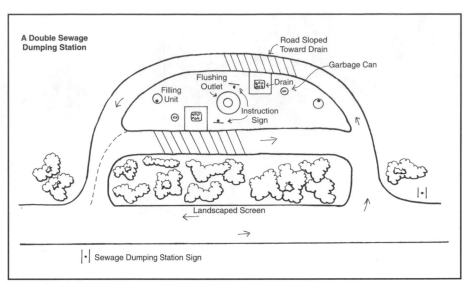

Figure 8.70

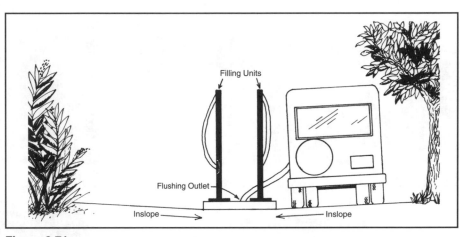

Figure 8.71

Figure 8.69

Sewage Treatment

If your campground soils have an adequate absorption capacity your best and least expensive facility is septic tanks and drain fields. And if your drain field can be located near the toilet/shower that, too, is best for you. Sometimes a toilet needs to be located where an adjacent drain field can't be located. Here you'll likely need (if the available drain field is uphill from this and other flush toilets) one or more sewage lift stations. If environmental regulations or lack of adequate soil absorption are a problem your next best sewage disposal facility is a lagoon (Figure 8.73). *As a last resort* you may have to go to a dollar-gobbling sewage treatment plant which costs big bucks to build, operate and maintain. If your engineers tell you this is the only option, get a second opinion.

Dumping stations, lagoons, treatment plants and any other sewage treatment facility other than a drain field should be zoned away from public view. Figure 8.74 (originally Figure 2.47) shows a TVA/LBL sewage facility with an almost never used (though universal) campsite snuggled against it. Removal of all campsite screening and constant mowing add to the distasteful insensitivity.

Figure 8.72

Figure 8.74

Figure 8.73

Figure 8.75

Garbage Collection

We've seen and had to administer several systems from individual containers (often times poorly placed at each campsite) to a pack-it-in/pack-it-out policy which more and more park systems feel compelled to use today. From a *user-friendly perspective* we suggest you consider a system of dumpsters with no more than two per camp loop. Some years ago we recommended can clusters located to service three to five campsites. With the quality and expense of today's work force this is not economically feasible. So dumpsters appear to be the answer. We do however suggest they be screened either with plant materials or in a wooden enclosure as shown in Figures 8.75 and 8.76. If you want the garbage to be bagged your best bet is to provide the plastic bag for users. Give them their first one as they check in, and others at the entrance station as they are needed.

Recycling

Some chapters ago we spoke about recycling drink cans at a U.S. Forest Service recreation area. The wire basket idea was a good one as folks would likely have placed garbage along with cans in a closed container. Recycling these cans offers the opportunity to work with a civic organization which would

Figure 8.76

give the USFS a much needed friend in building a recreation power base (Figure 8.77).

Depending on your recycling emphasis and who does it (your staff or a civic organization), you can be more or less sophisticated including having some educational-fun programs. (An appropriately dressed Mr. or Ms. Trashmore would be an avenue to explore as well as Sergeant Litter Getter.) The recycling effort at an Arkansas state park calls for separation of recyclable items (Figure 8.78). We have been in

Figure 8.77

Figure 8.78

Figure 8.79

Figure 8.81 takes you to the Midwest to an Indiana state park where they've done a little better—but not much. This is still not a beckoning entrance zone. Many of the wildlife and forestry rascals we've tried to teach (who now are recreation "experts") snicker a bit at our advice to be user-friendly all different kinds of ways, particularly at entrances. At the same time the rabid environmentalists (unfortunately we get a few in our courses) say they like the dark entrance zones and would rather those insensitive campers in their trailers didn't come into their parks anyhow. We aren't being facetious here, we *are* trying to condition you to the problems you'll face in trying to plan campgrounds for people.

There is quite a contrast between the dark, foreboding entrance zones in the previous three illustrations and the beckoning open zones in the next two. Figure 8.82 takes you to a beautifully landscaped open entrance zone at Wind Creek State Park in Alabama. This says, "Folks come right on in and enjoy yourselves. We really want you here!"

Beech Lake Family Camping Resort (Figure 8.83) is a sizable private campground in west Tennessee. The private campground owners came to our basic workshop, learned and listened, and obviously decided to do all they could to beckon users. Their simple sign was attractive, landscaped, and not

public campgrounds where considerable time, expense, and manpower was devoted to recycling while absolutely *no effort* went into family beckoning Fun Programming. This is another example of how the environmental movement has had a negative effect on family camping and a measure of how far we've strayed from seriously doing things for people!

Campground Entrance Zones

Way back in Chapter Two we discussed how you might beckon or repulse users at park entrances. Remember, most of the users visiting your campground will be from cities and towns rather than farms and ranches. You may like the deep dark woods with trailing, hanging vines, and the aura of a potential camper-biting critter lurking therein *but*—and again that's a *big* but—the city folks likely don't share your enthusiasm. Therefore you should—in your design, administration and programming—strive to make a gentle transition from the lights and open areas of cities to the somewhat frightening wonders of the woodland. Figure 8.79 shows a gated entrance to a county campground in southern Washington—Big Foot is *there!* Even if the gate is open, the entrance is dark and dreary. Figure 8.80 takes us across America to a state park with camping on the Florida Keys. It is not quite as "Boogery" as the one in Washington state, but nearly so. Here the gators'll get ya!

Figure 8.80

Figure 8.81

Figure 8.83

"garbaged up" with extra boards telling potential users propane or worms were available therein. Their landscape materials (which were then small) have matured and now enhance the zone. Figure 8.84 shows their varied road clearing limits including generous open space where their road junctions with the country road. Their road was curvilinear throughout the area adding a sense of wonderment to the user experience. Why not use all the "tools" at your disposal to enhance visitor enjoyment?

If you have a large park or recreation area where camping is but one component, we suggest you consider locating the park office near the main park entrance. Contractors, persons bringing supplies, those seeking or providing information, public safety, and visitor protection personnel will visit here. Providing service here will lessen the visitor impact at your busy campground entrance station. We also suggest two other helpful features. The first is to make sure your parking lot at this office facility is generous and has space for tow vehicles and trailers, or large motor homes, or boats and trailers to park *and* turn around. It should be quite easy for these folks and commercial vehicles to enter and exit. Having dead-end parking lots at park offices is an inexcusable lack of professionalism! The second feature you should consider at your office complex is a sizable paved landing pad for Emergency Medical Technician (EMT) and other helicopter use.

Campground Entrance Stations

We are assuming your campground is a sizable family campground with the need for an adequately staffed entrance facility. If you are upgrading an inadequate facility or building a new one we suggest you talk to your own staff about design requirements and visit four or five campgrounds with staffed entrances, and ask the entrance staff at these facilities all sorts of questions. Is their building functional? Are there any problems in the building's design or the entrance/exit lanes? When are the peak use times? How many staff folks are needed at peak times (likely Friday afternoon and evening, and Sunday

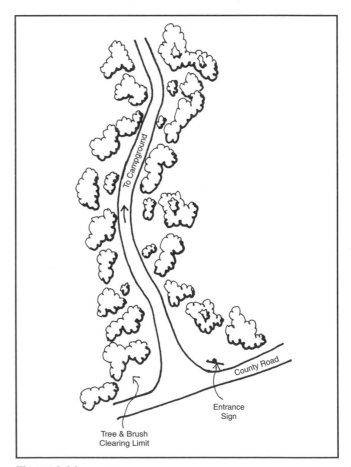

Figure 8.84

Figure 8.82

afternoon)? Are viewing areas on both sides, as well as forward and behind, adequate? Do you need a toilet, wash basin, refrigerator, stove, and kitchen facilities, or computer in the building, or radio contact with the main office or other sites? Don't ask these folks how to design various things. Do ask them how they function and how to improve the process.

Historically, entrance stations have been poorly designed because designers aren't required to know about various functions. Other things to consider are: Can the entrance structure function as a play equipment checkout facility during low use times? Will there be an effort to conduct applied research and interview some or all users at times as they exit? How much parking space is necessary for trucks and trailers whose owners want or need a visitor parking area easily seen from the entrance station?

The entrance structure shown in Figure 8.85 is located at McCormick's Creek State Park campground in Indiana. It has two lanes entering on the right and two lanes exiting on the left. Four signs are located on a cable near the top of the photo. These light up for late evening and night viewing, telling users which lane to use. As you are moving toward the entrance, the sign on the far right reads, "Reentry lane." (Note the open lane on the right of the persons being registered.) Next is the Registration Lane sign for the lane which carries most of the registration use. Both signs to the left of the entrance station normally read, "Exit do not enter"; however, the lane next to the building can be used as a peak time registration lane. At such times three persons will staff the booth; one to direct traffic to the right or left registration lane (both lanes will have lighted signs) and the other two to move already registered persons to the right reentry lane. This now is a most user-friendly entrance though it wasn't always so.

Obviously there are all sorts of variations for entrances which would be adequate. One example is shown in Figure 8.86. Remember, this zone is likely your first impression contact point with campers. Courteous and friendly contact persons and convenient design are all keys to the beginning of a delightful camping experience.

Campground Roads

Throughout Chapter Seven and most of this chapter we've related numerous thoughts about campground roads. These included clearing limits, road elimination, minimizing the amount you build, peanut and other designs, and why campground roads should be paved while most parking spurs shouldn't. Obviously, again, we realize various agencies and divisions within agencies have their own standards. We'll discuss some minimum standards for your consideration and will, as usual, show some mistakes and how to avoid them.

Figure 8.85

As for paved campground loop road surfacing we suggest your single track (one-way) roads be 12-feet wide. The clearing limit width would be a minimum of 22 feet. Make sure you also have a clearing height of 16 feet to avoid damaging fifth-wheel campers and other tall rigs.

Double track interior campground roads should have a minimum of 20 feet paving, meaning your clearing width or limit would be 30 feet. Entrance roads which may cover considerable distance from the state or county road should be 22- to 24-feet wide. The clearing width here would be variable with a minimum of 34- to 36-feet wide. The variety is another part of the hosting process creating a subconscious user enjoyment factor.

One of the greatest problems we find (worldwide) concerning campground or park road development is turning road design completely over to what should be a *service* (only) group—the engineers. We've worked in engineering organizations and know many engineers who are knowledgeable, or will listen to advice, about park roads.

However, three *big* problems frequently happen:

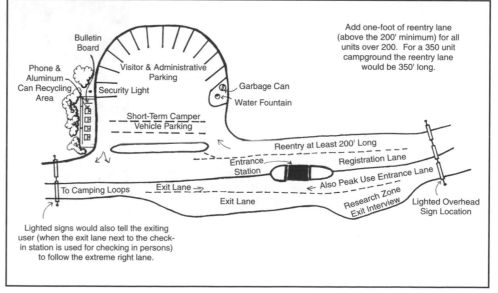

Figure 8.86

1. We don't take the time to tell them exactly what we want (such as deciding where camp units should go; this being the guide or control points for interior camp loop road location; and finally locating the main road is but a linkage of these elements).
2. Many engineers think they don't need and know they don't want input from planners or even administrators.
3. In many public agencies the engineers are in another section or division of "equal" rank with the parks division. This can work quite well with everyone striving for the best product possible. Far too often it doesn't though, and the engineers and architects dominate, telling park folks to use their plans or else!

Tangents (straight road sections) and culverts are examples of the above. Long tangents in parks and campgrounds cause all sorts of administrative and visitor safety problems. We often try to correct such mistakes with speed limit signs and speed bumps. The former don't work well and the latter make most users quite unhappy. If you need speed bumps in your campground your road designers have failed you! The straight road or long tangent in a public park in Indiana (Figure 8.87, originally Figure 2.48) may thrill a design engineer but it's a *big* negative in the park. This in our view is extremely poor "professional" work! One good thing about it is that it is built flush with the ground.

Often previous mistakes can be the "nursery bed" of others. Recently the same public park in Indiana had a sizable campground expansion. Long tangents and the short radius curves connecting them were in the finished product. Figure 8.88 illustrates the problem. We don't know why these things continue to happen, they just do!

The private sector is not without similar problems. Here, overall experience (or the perception of it) likely weighs heavy on the design scales as it's easier and cheaper and less mind straining to build straight roads than to build curved ones. Figure 8.89 shows a straight, unpaved road extending as least as far as the one in the previous photo. Problems in this Indiana private campground would be compounded with road-generated dust.

Obviously we are big backers of curvilinear park road design. We suggest you check this again by having a look at our design and redesign of the nine poorly designed parks illustrated early in this chapter. The road in a southern Indiana state park could have been straight as a tight string from the bottom of Figure 8.90 to the top. It wasn't, and the end product is well-done!

In several illustrations throughout Chapters Seven and Eight we have suggested your campground roads should not only be curvilinear and field-designed, but also built flush with the ground level. The USCOE manager-located road in Kentucky does just that (Figure 8.91). An extensive fill through this rolling topography would have caused drainage problems and the addition of unnecessary culverts. (One problem is obvious—or should be—in that the clearing limits should be a bit more generous.) Don't use ditches and culverts or other drainage structures that are expensive to con-

Figure 8.87

Figure 8.88

Figure 8.89

struct and expensive to maintain if you don't need them. Even minor drainages can be crossed with long, paved dips rather than using fills and culverts.

Now have a look at one of the most interesting campground roads and campgrounds we've ever "enjoyed" (Figure 8.92): one designed by an inexperienced professional at an Alabama state park. Take the time to see what you can

Figure 8.90

Figure 8.91

Figure 8.92

For a final look at roads let's visit the White Mountain National Forest in New Hampshire (Figure 8.93). The campground was small (though one of their larger ones.) Campsites were about 100 feet apart with short barricaded spurs and unit furniture down slope some distance from the user's vehicle. There didn't appear to be any programs for users. You couldn't see folks at the next campsite. An author's son and vehicle may "clearly be seen" at the left halfway down on the main road between two campsites. (Can't you see the van and boy?) And if vegetation on the roadside had ever been cleared, it wasn't in this decade. Hope you see several user-unfriendly elements here including the possibility bears will eat you and yours any minute now. The mistakes are different than in the Alabama photo but nearly as serious. It is no wonder camping use is down considerably in the public and private campgrounds in the eastern United States!

Maintenance Yards

Some years ago two of the authors enjoyed building a maintenance structure and equipment storage yard at a (then) 200-unit campground. Jobs at the maintenance center included minor maintenance of mowers (TVA folks really liked to mow lots and lots of grass), storage of supplies (including

find less than well-done here. Some years ago we angered an engineering participant at one of our continuing education efforts. "Everyone knows," he indignantly said, "that all roads have to have ditches and culverts." We didn't change what mind he had that week! Anyhow, this sort of rascal must have been one of the primary advisors to the landscape architect in charge of the Alabama design. (Note the land slopes ever so gently from right to left.) With the exception of the short radius curves at road ends almost all of the loop roads were *long, long* tangents. They dug a ditch down both sides of the road which was on nearly flat ground. Then they made all spurs level with the loop road and installed culverts with concrete head walls under all parking spurs. (Note the plugged culvert in the foreground and the chipped head wall likely done by a now-damaged mower!) Obviously all spurs could have and should have been level with the ground even with a bit of ramping up and down. No ditches or culverts were needed! Campsite furniture (particularly on the sites at the down slope [left] side of the road) was *below* the level of the flat spur. They used upright grills and had no screening between any units. All of this required a team of folks who knew little about campground design. Hope you can see why we "enjoyed" this one!

Figure 8.93

yard storage of extra tables and grills), different rock sizes, crossties, and other equipment. There was a small meeting room with a mini-kitchen, office with two or three desks, and a toilet/shower. A small building was also available for chemicals, insect sprays, and gasoline for the mowers and other equipment. During the planning phase we asked our campground manager and the maintenance crew members what they thought was needed (building size and layout, crew comforts, yard-size fencing, and more.) Since we weren't "experts" concerning maintenance building and yard needs, we asked folks who were. This process provided all of us with a quality facility to which everyone there had contributed. You should do this with all of your park design from entrance stations to toilets/showers to layout of a campfire theater.

A word of caution, though, is in order. Some of the advice you get will be far less than good or usable. For instance, we didn't ask *where* the maintenance facility should be located. (Here we should also say that the two or three trailers housing our intern student program staff were also located at this site.) Our campground maintenance chief strongly suggested the new building, student housing, and fenced area should be located in the center of the campground. It seems this was the best location for directing his ever working mowing crew.

Maintenance structures and fenced yards are a basic necessity in most large campgrounds. They should, however, be located away from public view. They certainly shouldn't be located inside of a camp loop as is true at some public campgrounds.

Remember the maintenance structure in Figure 5.39? It is the first building you see as you enter this church camp area in the Midwest. Fact is, it is located where the entrance double-track road ends and you move to the right on a single-track road.

Our solution to the maintenance complex location at TVA's Land Between the Lakes is shown in Figure 8.94. The area is a part of, yet apart from, the campground. Here we located it before you get to the round-the-clock staffed entrance control structure. Thus suppliers, crews and intern students can come and go without adding traffic through the entrance station. We feel the off-duty intern students and even some hosts and volunteers need a quiet place for after hour relaxation. This location provides that privacy. Note the curve leading into the zone is sharp enough and the screen vegetation is dense enough to eliminate the housing, building and yard from public view.

Trees and Shade

In Chapter Seven we briefly discussed tree removal, overstory shade factors and desirable screening. We think trees and shade are so important to a beckoning campground we want to share a few more important tree related thoughts with you. Fact is, we even writ some poetry for ya. (With sincere apologies to the memory of Sergeant Joyce Kilmer.)

We hope that we will never see;
    a camping site without a tree!
A tree who's leafy bows are bent;
    to shade my bald head bone and my tent.
"What kind," you say, "of tree to use?
    And are there some species we should not choose?"
Not a hemlock, white pine, beech, scarlet oak or aspen—
    so shallow-rooted they quickly die of compaction.
"Should we cut trees or should we relent?"
    Research tells us shade should be about 50 percent.
Some trees die young, soon after planted;
    while others have long life—if camper-granted.
They live in spite of camper hatchet, knife, lantern and nail;
    or Mother Nature's lightning, fire and hail.
Yes, God does mighty things from A to Z;
    but man sure made a mess of this "poet-tree."

As you can see, the few skills we have don't include writing poetry. Trees in campgrounds: Do campers want shade? "You Bet!" over 90 percent of them say. This is true all across North America from Maine and Ontario to Oregon and British Columbia. Why, then, do we see so many private and public campgrounds with little or no shade? We don't mean in places where trees don't normally grow, but in three-fourths or more of our states and provinces where they will grow! A shadeless campground in summer in a grass-covered bare field causes unhappy campers and income problems aplenty!

The main challenges you face with shade are having too much (you already know you should have about a 50 percent

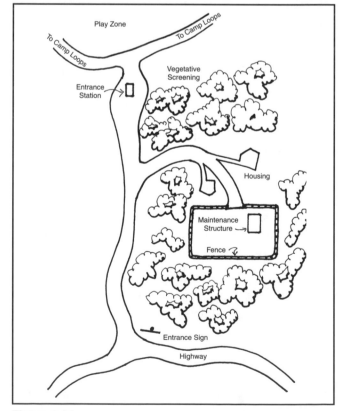

Figure 8.94

shade factor) and not having enough. Not having enough requires some planting. (Can you tie this into the hosting process?) Pines aren't a good choice but deep-rooted, young, vigorous hardwoods are. Stay away from shallow-rooted species like Douglas fir, aspen, white pine, hemlock, and some oaks. Figure 8.95 shows the lack of root depth of a sizable, shallow-rooted tree like a scarlet oak. Obviously any sort of construction work and people impact around trees like this causes big problems including quick tree mortality. Which species rank best for pedestrian impact in campgrounds? For the eastern United States, some research of 30-plus years ago ranks the following:

Species Ability to Withstand Recreation Impact
(Listed in Decreasing Order)[3]

Hardwoods		Conifers
1. Hickories	12. Red Maple	1. Shortleaf Pine
2. Persimmon	13. American Holly	2. Hemlocks
3. Sycamore	14. Sourwood	3. White Pine
4. White Ash	15. Black Birch	4. Pitch Pine
5. Beech	16. White Oaks	5. Virginia Pine
6. Sassafras	17. Black Walnut	
7. Buckeye	18. Red Oaks	
8. Yellow Poplar	19. Black Locust	
9. Dogwood	20. Magnolia	
10. Blackgum	21. Black Cherry	
11. Yellow Birch	22. Blue Beech	

There are several problems with this impact ranking, including the lack of follow-up replication. As far as it went, this was an excellent applied research study. One of the authors' main sources of unhappiness (and we all have been extensively involved with applied research and researchers) is that researchers don't tell us what their findings mean, and give us a simple one, two and three list, of recommendations regarding correction of the problems. This is one of the basic reasons why *most* recreation research isn't and hasn't been used by planners, designers, and managers. Many of the research rascals will tell you recommending solutions isn't what they do. That's right, but it's wrong!

With the possible exception of shortleaf pine, the other conifers in the above list rank quite low in impact resistance compared to most of the hardwoods. Though we question American beech because of its shallow root system and propensity for users to carve their initials in its smooth bark, what the listing tells us is when you thin your trees to a 50 percent shade factor (at the same time striving to eliminate the large slow-growing trees), you should not remove the species ranked high on the list. Any of the hickory species with their deep tap roots are great. What about the central, southwestern, and western United States? Which species are best there? We don't know. To the best of our knowledge, those doing forestry-related recreation research aren't interested, or more

[3]U.S. Forest Service. (1962). *Tree and Shrub Response to Recreation Use* (Experiment Station Research Note 171). T.H. Ripley, Project Leader.

Figure 8.95

likely haven't been forcefully asked, to find these answers. Your best bet is to select the deeper-rooted species.

The environmental experts aren't too helpful in advising you concerning shade factors in family campgrounds either. Cutting trees is not their thing, and you remember the impact-resistant, site-protecting, universal campsites aren't what they like either. These antimanagement thoughts by the environmentalists are also highly antienvironment.

Planners haven't helped much either for if (when planning or locating a new park area) they have a choice between a heavy stand of old growth trees and a light stand of young hardwoods, planners will invariably pick the big tree grove. They will "plunk" their park facilities into such an area with a minimum of tree removal and, more often than not, planners will prescribe nonreinforced campsites, leaving the condemned trees to the bewildered manager who then will spend lots of your money trying to save the trees from those horrible overuse-causing campers! Figure 8.96 shows the results of this sort of thought (or lack of thought) in an Indiana state park campground. The campground is in a shallow-rooted white pine stand, and universal sites, though well-known to Indiana folks, weren't used. Overuse? *No!* Poor park practice? *Yes!*

Interestingly, thousands of Indiana taxpayer dollars were spent (two years after we camped there and took this photo) in extensive area rehabilitation. This included bringing in topsoil, rototilling, liming, and seeding,

Figure 8.96

but not replacing the undefined sites with maintenance-saving, environment-improving, impact-resistant universal sites! This sort of maintenance money waste goes on all across our country.

If you wish to build a campground or parts of one where there is little or no shade available we suggest the following:

1. Assuming you have a few years of potential growth time, randomly plant fast-growing species throughout the area. These should be planted about 40-feet apart, but not in straight lines. Follow this with a planting of longer lasting species, such as hickory or bald cypress (depending on where your area is located; consult with forestry folks on this one).

2. If you are building now and opening soon, lay out your roads and campsites and concentrate on trying to provide at least some afternoon shade around your sites. A good tree to consider planting in such an area is the recently developed Carolina poplar which can grow up to 10 feet a year. It also can be used across much of the country (Figure 8.97).

Hybrid poplars can be planted as 8- to 10-inch unrooted cuttings or as small rooted trees. Cost is minimal—about 25 cents per unrooted cutting. (Find one or plant a few and in three years you'll have all the cutting material you need.) Again, you should also plant slower-growing species throughout the area.

One final thought about shade: When you build those defined universal campsites, field design them using available shade around the *outside* of the unit. Don't leave trees inside of the defined area. While the gravel surface will protect roots of such trees, they often limit the ability of users to maneuver throughout the site placing their equipment anywhere they wish. The well-done generous universal campsite on the USCOE in Kentucky (Figure 8.98) would be even better with the removal of the sizable oak tree. This is another spot where the USCOE has added two user pleasing benches along the crosstie definers.

Storm Clouds in Campground Land

Earlier in this book we shared our concern about the numerous negatives and indeed disasters befalling parks and park users particularly in outdoor recreation. We plan to explore the subject further in Chapter Eleven. If you have closely read this chapter and Chapter Seven, you are aware of several of those challenges (including self-inflicted ones) involving campgrounds.

The self-inflicted ones include lack of training for those responsible for designing, building and managing campgrounds; the strong resource emphasis of many so-called recreation professionals (biologists, foresters, wildlife specialists) with corresponding antipeople skills; almost no emphasis on applied recreation research; disinterest shown by the recreation vehicle industry and the Recreation Vehicle Dealer's Association; diminished emphasis (which was never great any-

how) in the academic community; and a general disdain for vehicle campers!

Storm Cloud 1. Public versus Private—and the winner is? In our view one of the greatest detriments to providing parks and campgrounds, and programs for "all Americans" has been the nearly continual clamor by segments of the private campground industry to eliminate, drastically reduce, or even take over

Figure 8.97

public campgrounds. Since this chapter needs to end sometime soon we can't develop this problem to its fullest extent.

Take time to read again Figure 7.12 "Do You Love Your Mother and Other Equally Thoughtful Questions," asking you who you want to use family campgrounds. According to some folks, public campgrounds should only be for the good ol' boy primitive campers. No showers or flush toilets or hookups or programs; maybe something for persons with disabilities (but not much) is what they prescribe. To this we say, "Phooey!" The losers in all of this have been the users (particularly families), the public sector, camping industries, and yes, even *the private sector itself*. For many years we couldn't determine any winners, and then we realized de-emphasis on family campground upgrading and development in the public sector turned resource managers' attention even more to appeasing the environmentalists and wilderness (lock-it-all-up) rascals. So there is a winner, though it likely isn't you.

In the 1960s and early 1970s when there was considerable public development, overnight campsite rental fees on

Figure 8.98

public lands were low—in many places likely too low. (This is not often the case now. We recently saw buddy sites in a National Forest campground in North Carolina *without hookups* renting for $22 per night! We didn't see any rented ones!) The low rental fees of 30 years ago had, however, a big, bodacious benefit: They made it possible for almost everyone (even those with low incomes) to camp throughout America if they wished. And they did. The more expensive private campgrounds benefited greatly as the users moved up to more sophisticated equipment and wanted more services than the public sector provided. This was never understood by most folks, and the shrill cries from the small in number, but vocal, private sector made the public sector dramatically raise prices. (Which caused a continuing upward spiral in all prices.) The major effect of all this was to drastically curtail and/or eliminate those young families on the lower end of the discretionary income scale meaning elimination of the user base for most campgrounds, *including the private sector.* People still camp but the users are getting older and older (particularly in the eastern United States) with only a few "seed source" younger folks following their footsteps. This is particularly true in the camping clubs like the National Campers and Hikers Association. We liken this to the fisheries chain shown in Figure 8.99. If you eliminate or kill the small plants and animals, the big fish won't be harmed right away. When they do mature and die, however, there will be no small ones to replace them and the entire chain is gone. Unless we *all* begin to think and act maturely and responsibly, family camping is in big trouble. What is needed is millions of warm bodies enjoying family camping. We've worked for numerous folks in the private sector and most of them want public-private cooperation and competition. If private campground owners have quality, generous universal campsites and beckoning programming then they need not worry about competition! Problem is many of them blame their lack of use on the nearby public park.

Storm Cloud 2. Another storm cloud involves who's good and who isn't. This is primarily a public sector problem as most of the private sector folks are too smart to concern themselves with such foolishness. Experience tells us there is a sizable number of recreation resource "professionals" in-

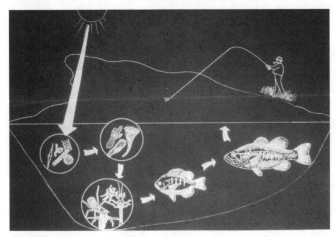

Figure 8.99

cluding our environmental education "friends" who have interesting ideas (though sick ones) involving who should be allowed into or who they would prefer in *their* parks. The good folks seem to be backpackers, hikers, wilderness users, hunters and fishermen, tent campers, and just maybe even campers who have pop-up tent campers. The bad folks (those who certainly aren't interested in the environment or such good stuff) are those who insist on bringing trailers, motor homes, fifth-wheel campers, and other unnatural things into *our* campgrounds. These folks often want clean showers, generous campsites close to each other (not 100 feet apart), roads they can safely navigate, programs, and security. How bad can you get?! By the way, at the writing of this book all three authors enjoy both tent and RV camping—guess that makes us good, bad, or indifferent (or is it just ugly).

Storm Cloud 3. Writers of liberal newspaper columns and even some outdoor writers also are famous for causing anti-camping storm clouds. All three authors have lived in an environmental Mecca—with an over abundance of "aginners" (we're agin this and we're agin that too)—called Bloomington, Indiana. Two newspaper writers (one who writes a caustic daily editorial) have had interesting things to say about the bad campers discussed earlier. When the daily writer got behind an older person who was pulling a trailer in rugged (for Indiana) Brown County, he was upset with the slowness of the older person's (and everyone like his) driving. His disdain for these older campers (who couldn't possibly be environmentally pure) was expressed when he wrote a lengthy article calling them Road Maggots. His partner, who masquerades as the outdoor editor, was quite upset with the number of wheeled-vehicle users and their wants when he camped in the nearby Hoosier National Forest. He thought the Hoosier National Forest shouldn't allow such people there, and what did these campers mean by asking for more electric outlets and higher voltages?! The Forest Service should remove the 10 outlets they mistakenly put in there anyhow, and maybe something extra should be done for folks with disabilities but not much.

Do you begin to get a glimmer of your challenge?

Storm Cloud 4. Another storm cloud (though we could write at least one sizable chapter on this subject) is the public meeting process agencies now use to find out just what a *majority* of the public wants, then act accordingly. For many years public agencies did their own thing without any public input. The environmental movement stopped all of this and rightly so. (Hey, we said something good about the rascals.) The public meeting process was essentially to follow this pathway: The agencies would draft four or five proposals for some new facility or process or program and let interested parties know all about them. The next step was to have a public meeting where everyone had the opportunity to comment. If all went as planned, the agencies would follow the guidance of the majority. Sounds politically correct and great, doesn't it? *Wrong!* Early on the environmental groups saw this was a dandy way to curtail, stop, and/or control. Many folks in their groups found this was the way they could stop any proposal, thus providing them with an unusual source of power. "We stopped the building of that horse trail, the campground expansion, the recreation plan," or whatever has become quite a game for these environmental groups. The public meetings were stuffed with environmental groupies from the Sierra Club, Audubon Society, National Wildlife Federation, and more. Real users—the family campers—have never been big attendees of such meetings so they rarely show up and certainly aren't organized to do so. When they do show up, they are called all sorts of less-than-nice names. This makes sure they don't subject themselves to further harassment so the agency is left with the "majority" being against nearly everything and in most cases they don't have the courage to plan parks for people!

Storm Cloud 5. Another storm cloud to be concerned about is today's rush to turn over many public parks, including campgrounds, to concessionaires. You should be aware at this time that the authors like the idea of long-term private sector leases for many parks on public lands. We even propose that governments should pay for some basic features such as major roads and bridges and bringing in electric power. Some years ago, the oldest of the three authors had administration of the entire southern region of the U.S. Forest Service concessionaires as a part of his responsibility. There were only a dozen or so—all real problem causers to users, to the Forest Service, and oftentimes to the short-term concessionaire. A good part of the problem was that the number and kind of camp units and amenities the concessionaire had available didn't really provide a sound economic venture. Size of area, lack of hookups, poor unit layout, and more all were contributors to the problem. Many of the concessionaires were less than good at running the area as well. So the author worked to eliminate concessionaires and almost had the job done when he transferred to TVA.

As often happens, about the same time a new group of foresters took over the U.S. Forest Service's Washington Office recreation organization. (We understand a similar crop of rascals is again in the Washington Office!) Their new and great idea was to strongly emphasize short-term concessionaire operation throughout the service. (The wheel of ignorance made another full turn, and is turning ever faster today!)

Today's budget challenges have set the stage for another and even greater Forest Service emphasis on concessionaires. It may be the right way to go in limited instances though we doubt it. Our measure will be how it affects the user. Time will tell.

Storm Cloud 6. Beware of consultants, for they likely knoweth not! Most consulting organizations with their engineers, architects, and landscape architects know little or nothing about campground planning or design and even less about operating such areas. A good example of what we mean is shown in Figure 8.100. It is early August at an east Tennessee state park campground. There are water and electric hookups at each "well-engineered" campsite. Most of the camp units had little or no shade, unit furniture or table, and tent pad locations were at least 30 feet from the paved parking spur. The road was a series of long tangents and short radius

Figure 8.100

curves. The toilet/shower was in the center of the loop. There were no fun program amenities and there was one camper on the back side of the loop located under the only available shade tree. Why he was there, we don't know. With the knowledge you've gained from these last two chapters *you* know what's wrong with this area and you know far more than the expensive consulting firm did.

State and federal agencies quite often have money limits regarding who can and can't design and build their areas. If, for instance, a total job is less than $250,000, it may be done in-house by park staff and they can, if needed, hire a knowledgeable person to advise them. If it is more than this dollar figure or whatever magic amount is determined by the agency "wise men," the entire construction job—including design—has to move through the bid process and a consulting firm selected, more often than not, by lowest bid. Typically, these firms know nothing about campgrounds. What's the answer to all this foolish waste of money? We're not sure, but buying this book or borrowing it free from the local library; requiring contractor attendance at one of our workshops; or hiring you or one of us to guide the process would certainly give the park system a better product than they normally get. In fairness to engineering or landscape architectural firms, so seldom does designing and building campgrounds happen, that it is unrealistic to expect them to initially know what you know now.

Chapter Eight Problem

As usual we'll take a different approach with this chapter. For at least the last 15 years, public agencies have conducted countless hours of "How to Be a Good Host" training. This included hiring training consultants skilled at hosting; providing extensive training for special persons within the agencies to conduct training for others, pounds of written material and expensive video tapes. How to greet visitors, learning all about your parks or whatever so you can warmly welcome users there, how to answer the telephone, and more wonderful stuff is all part of that extensive training. There is even a recent presidential Executive Order issued to all federal agencies saying, "thou shalt treat folks good." While this is all delightful stuff, the hosting process rarely ever concerns itself with beckoning users, and designing facilities and programs that do a great job seriously hosting users. Your problem for this chapter is to create a list of tangible actions you would take as a park manager (with responsibility for both day use and camping) to host users effectively. Your list should be divided into sections on planning and design, administration, programming, and maintenance. If you've read carefully, your list should be quite lengthy.

Chapter Nine

Outdoor Recreation Programming or Yes, Virginia, Camping Can (and Should) Be Fun!

In several of the preceding chapters, we've discussed the importance of recreation programming as well as the lack of it in most of the nation's resource-based parks. This chapter concerns itself entirely with programming—programming in family campgrounds where you want (or should want) families to visit. If you aren't an advocate of attracting family groups—including extended families, families headed by single parents, families with young children, and teens—then this chapter will be wasted on you. If, however, having campers other than the good ol' boys, vandals and rowdies interests you, read on.

Figures 9.1 through 9.8 cover much of the campground programming story. Figure 9.1 shows a preteen excited out of his mind (or is it boredom?) over the prospect of attending yet another scintillating ranger presentation on the diet of the spotted owl or a really jazzy discussion of fire management. In all seriousness, these sorts of programs (which, by the way, the authors enjoy from time to time) are more often than not the only planned activities available in campgrounds—if there are any programs at all. Figure 9.2 depicts the same youth trying to pull a limb from a mulberry tree, a likely outcome of our failure to provide campers with fun activities. Out of boredom comes depreciative behavior. Figure 9.3 shows the typical park manager's response to such behavior, which is to bring in the rangers and blow those mud-sucking campers away. While generally well-meaning, most park managers and staff haven't figured out that campers, especially kids and teens, just might not be entirely satisfied simply watching moss grow, listening to fish breathe, or hearing about these wonderful phenomena from an interpretive naturalist. This lack of sensitivity to user needs means we really don't know (or care) about camp-

ing families and their needs as we move toward the year 2000.

Figure 9.4 shows the grinning 'gator product of five folks who had fun as a family in a campground's sand sculpture contest. They won first prize, and the odds are good they will continue to return to this Indiana State Reservoir campground as a camping family for many years to come. Figure 9.5

Figure 9.2

Figure 9.1

Figure 9.3

Figure 9.4

Figure 9.7

Figure 9.5

Figure 9.8

Figure 9.6

shows a group of teens and younger children about to gang up on a "green submarine"—a greased watermelon. How about the two young (at heart) roundballers in Figure 9.6? Did you see any bored campers in Figures 9.4 through 9.6? How about vandalism? What we're really saying here, quite simply, is this: People go camping to enjoy themselves and have fun. Provide fun programming and lots of recreational opportunities (like basketball and water volleyball), and fami-

lies will come to your campgrounds. What is it about fun that park managers don't understand?

Figures 9.7 and 9.8 shoot some holes in the arguments of those who say, "Campers don't want to play ball and have fun, and besides, we simply can't afford to provide recreational opportunities and programs." As Figure 9.7 shows, the extended family playing ball in the curve of a campground road in Utah's Dixie National Forest was having fun in spite of the agency's lack of attention to programming (ironically, an excellent site for a ball field, a meadow adjacent to the campground, if it were mowed, was about 50 yards away). The woman mowing grass in Figure 9.8 was working as part of the Older Americans program on Tennessee's Cherokee National Forest. She could have done far more good for campers, and for the Forest Service, by checking out play equipment and helping conduct programs in a large campground located near the site where this photograph was taken, where at least that summer day there were no programs and few campers. An attitude change about the need to beckon and host campers is probably the most critical missing element in recreation resource management nationwide.

Earlier you were left with two challenges. One was to rehabilitate the poorly designed campground shown in Figure 1.17. The other, less straightforward issue was to determine the real problem with the area. If you haven't figured out what this was, don't feel too bad. Most outdoor recreation professionals—managers, support staff, and academics—"missed the boat" on this question as well. As you've heard before, errors can be in both commission and omission. The poor design was committed; to fix it would require an investment of funds and some knowledge of rehabilitation techniques. The omission would be harder to correct, for the missing element in this campground, as is too often the case, was programming. There were neither the facilities—play courts, play fields, campfire theater, and the like—to support a diversified array of programs nor the supportive attitude of a staff to make a move to correct such a lack. The campground beckoned the good ol' boys but wasn't a great place for families, especially those with teens.

To understand this second point, you need to see an expanded view of the facilities in Figure 1.17, and Figure 9.9 provides this view. The campground was adjacent to a large swimming pool, open from noon to 7:00 P.M., and both facilities were managed by the same agency. When we first visited the area, however, we learned that no attempts had been made to use the pool as a program element for the campground. Campers could use the pool, but only in the same way as all other visitors to the park: on a pay-as-you-go basis. We see several things here: a missed opportunity for the agency to increase use of the pool, perhaps through early and late hour swimming sessions for campground users at a reduced entry fee; and less exercise and fun because of the lack of incentives to use the pool (decreased fees, organized programs directed toward them, or both). Mostly, we see an unfortunate attitude, one that suggests a management philosophy of indifference to programs. We don't try to hide being opinionated,

but we think the lack of outdoor recreation programming is the most serious shortcoming in the profession today.

A big part of the problem is the attitude responsible for it. A few years ago, one of the authors was a guest speaker at a large recreation and park meeting (400 participants for $3\frac{1}{2}$ days) in the western United States. The U.S. Forest Service—an organization that claims to have the greatest use among all federal agencies—was the host. Most of the participants were with the Forest Service although there were invitees from other agencies. Interestingly, there was only one presentation (by the author) on developed sites, which is where most of the Forest Service's use actually occurs. Millions of dollars were then being allocated and spent in what was called the President's Initiative. These funds were to be used to upgrade developed sites. As a condition for giving the developed site lecture, the author asked to be allowed to speak for at least one hour on a topic all three of the authors are enthusiastic about: how to beckon users, particularly families, to wildland parks with programming.

After the lecture, three different women approached the author at three different times, all with essentially the same lament. Their stories sounded like this: "I'm a Forest Service employee responsible for all developed sites in my ranger district. I'm also a single parent with two children. I was shocked when I finally realized the campgrounds I was managing were not places I would want to take my children and they were not places my children would want to visit. When I shared this sacrilegious sentiment with my ranger, he [or she] questioned my loyalty to the agency, my integrity, and my sanity." Tragically, this is a true story, repeated three times. The rangers' reactions were, in our view, typical. We've hosted workshops, symposia, and consortia for thousands of resource and environmental "professionals," and the vast majority of them would respond just as the rangers in this tale did. Probably much of the reason for this stems from the resource-oriented, as opposed to people-oriented, background of most professionals working in outdoor recreation. How serious and widespread is the problem? Think back to your last few visits to resource-based parks and recreation areas, particularly those managed by state or federal agencies. How much recreation programming do you remember? (We aren't talking here of environmental or historical interpretation programs. That discussion comes later.) Chances are good that you won't remember much because, with a few notable exceptions, these programs simply aren't offered. Why? Carefully read the following scenarios, all of which we've encountered in visits to parks and recreation areas in the last few years.

Once upon a time we talked with a young National Park Service ranger who had been chewed out by his superiors for suggesting campers be allowed to play softball at a Grand Canyon National Park campground; it seems some campers had asked his permission to play. You can read this reprimand as, "Visitors to national parks shouldn't even want to play softball."

Once upon a time a U.S. Forest Service assistant ranger in a southern U.S. National Forest committed heresy by mowing a half-acre space near his largest campground so campers

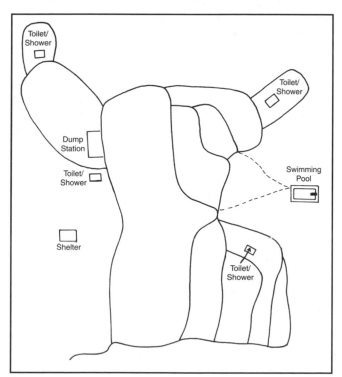

Figure 9.9

could play badminton and throw Frisbees. Read this as a heresy because it suggests visitors are not happy just hugging trees and smelling flowers when they visit National Forests.

Once upon a time we spoke to a U.S. Army Recreation Service Officer who was upset because young children in her travel camp in Italy were playing in and bringing dirt into the campground shower building. Read this as a problem resulting from a lack of anything else for the youngsters or other campers to do. This was a surprise, as the U.S. Army usually has excellent programming.

Once upon a time a private campground owner told a professor friend of ours that she didn't require research into user needs because she knew what her campers wanted—and it wasn't fun and games. Read this as a head-in-the-sand attitude some private sector folks had better abandon before they start waking up to empty campgrounds. Her campground stayed far less than full. (That, of course, was someone else's fault!)

Once upon a time a seasonal interpretive specialist with the U.S. Army Corps of Engineers got a reluctant OK to play softball with youngsters in her campground *providing* and *only providing* she first interpret the wooden bat the children were using as a product of natural resources management. Read this as a management assumption that the only reason people, including children, visit (or should be allowed to visit) the out-of-doors is to soak up as much environmental education as they can.

Once upon a time a lady in a campground rest room in an Indiana state park that lacked programming overheard teenage boys daring each other to run into the ladies room. (Three did so and were quickly stopped.) Read this as a cause-and-effect relationship between boredom and unsociable behavior. At the writing of this paragraph, there are still no programs at that large compound.

These grim fairy tales tell us failing to program outdoor recreation areas is, in essence, failing to meet the needs of users; thus, we—not the users—cause the ever increasing depreciative behavior we see in wildland parks. Several years ago, a number of federal recreation agencies had their collective hands smacked by the General Accounting Office (GAO) for "double counting" users (reporting inflated use figures). The reprimand by GAO resulted in new methods for tracking visitation rates—a positive step as far as it went. However, this situation reminds us of one you've seen before: fighting effects rather than causes. Since budget allocations are in part tied to quantitative measures (numbers of users), agencies needed to show high levels of use, thus many figures got inflated. Could the cause of low use levels—then and now—be tied to programs? When we travel, we keep a log of what we see in campgrounds.

Consider the following "confessions of a campground snooper" during a recent summer:

July 7: A National Park Service campground on Missouri's Current River, 300 units, 290 built in the open without shade; no play equipment for children; program-

ming limited to nature walks on weekends; no utility hookups; four units occupied.

July 22 (a Friday afternoon): An Arkansas state park 40 miles from Memphis, Tennessee; 100 units, all in the sun; parking spurs barricaded from unit furniture (which was in the shade); water and electric hookups provided; play amenities for young children only; all activities nature-oriented; three units occupied. The park manager asked us why his sites weren't full. Why, indeed!

September 2 (the Friday before Labor Day): Seven hundred camping units in three family campgrounds in a U.S. Corps of Engineers area in southern Illinois; 70 percent of the units built in the sun; nature programs only; 100 units occupied. (Remember that Labor Day is one of the "big three" holidays for peak use.)

August 12 (another Friday): Backbone Rock Campground on the Cherokee National Forest; 20 units; a free area; no security or protection; no utilities; no programming; no campers.

We could go on, but the song remains the same. Obviously these areas and other, similar ones worldwide, suffer from a variety of problems, many of which are design-related. But we're talking about programming here. Consider the situation at a campground in Virginia's Hungry Mother State Park. Here the area was poorly designed and suffered from compacted soil, erosion, and dying trees. It had a trampled-on, no-grass, "overused" appearance *and* it was *full* of camping families enjoying themselves. Why? The campground also offers a broad spectrum of recreation programs—programs which are fun for folks of all ages. There's a message here.

Over the past few decades, we've been involved in a host of different aspects of outdoor recreation—planning, design, administration, teaching, interpretation, and, unlike many planners, extensive participation. As a result, we've come to appreciate the benefits of all sorts of facilities and programs in campgrounds. Both personally and professionally, we're "up" on all elements of the outdoor realm and have discovered the following truisms:

1. Most resource-based recreation areas are "out in the boonies," removed from urban environments.
2. Most of the use in these areas originates from municipal settings; most of our park visitors are city folks.
3. Most of the recreation programs you'll find in cities and towns are flavored with fun; league sports, arts and crafts activities, dances, puppet shows, and similar activities for people from three to 93.
4. When you go to campgrounds in resource-based settings, you typically find one of two things: either no programming at all or only interpretive programs, usually limited to weekends and daylight hours (a nature walk on Wednesday and a dandy program on boater safety on Saturday night). Whoop-de-doo!

To make the point of this list clear, here are two more stories for you. The first involves a visit we once made to a California state park in the Big Sur area. The campground was in the redwoods, but it was old, suffering from impact and poor design, and mostly devoid of campers. We did, however, see a campfire theater and asked a staff person we encountered if programs were held there. "Occasionally," he replied. "Next weekend, a Forest Service Ranger is coming in to tell the story of a forest fire." Isn't that user beckoning?

Just plain fun is the key to campground programming, and the focus of our next story. Sitting in an Indiana restaurant, we overheard a conversation between two men who appeared to be in their forties. One was telling the other about how his two teenage children had recently ruined the family vacation. It seems that two days after arriving in a state park campground, the teens wanted to go home. Why? They had nothing to do or at least nothing they could relate to. The next day the family left, spoiling Dad's vacation, and reducing the number of visitor days the park could report at year's end. (Indiana State Park management personnel have the most outstanding/successful park programming team in the United States in one of their parks. Their activities have brought national attention, yet all of this happens *in spite of* Indiana State Park leadership!)

These stories raise two questions you need to consider. First, why? Why hasn't recreation programming been a big deal in campgrounds? We feel there are three reasons for this. First, although it's not really their fault, in one sense the culprit is the National Park Service (oh, my!). TVA, the Corps of Engineers, the Forest Service, and many state park systems have followed the programming lead of the national parks. In general, NPS interpretive and living-history programs are excellent, attracting millions of visitors each year. But where? And why? Visitors go to Appomattox, Gettysburg, Shiloh, and other similar Park Service areas because of their historical significance and to see the NPS living-history programs. They go to nature centers and interpretive trails to learn about the environment. They want to be informed, to be educated, or they wouldn't stop in at these areas. But here's the kicker: Visitors go to our campgrounds to relax, refresh, and recreate, to rest their minds, not to tax them. In other words, to have fun! Personally, we think well-conceived historical and environmental programs are great. Professionally, we simply can't afford an attitude like, "If I like it, it must be right for everybody." Interpretive programming was only moderately successful at the height of the environmental movement in the 1960s, and although not all interpretive programming is environmentally oriented, the state of the environmental movement today helps to illustrate our point: As we write this section, the Sierra Club is losing members and is millions of dollars in debt. In the 1990s, interpretive programs are considerably less successful than they were 30 years ago.

Here's an example. A few years back, we attended a mid-September "camper's fair" weekend, a three-day special event in a campground where recreation programs were in effect. The potential audience for programs consisted of over 1,000 campers ranging in age from tots to senior citizens. One pro-

gram, a puppet show put on by teenagers from a local church, attracted over 600 campers. Two nature walks, both of which were conducted by professionals, attracted a total of three campers (one of whom was one of the authors, another was his wife). We aren't suggesting campers never attend nature programs; obviously they occasionally do. We do know, though, if given a choice, they prefer something else. However, the real message in this story addresses two other points. One, provide the choice. Schedule interpretive programs, certainly, but *make them a small piece of your programming pie.* Second, and this is the focus of Chapter Nine, camping should be fun! Campers visit most of our parks to enjoy themselves. Park professionals don't have to teach everyone who visits their campgrounds something in order to justify their existence. Far too often in our programs, we've tragically transposed ideas appropriate for historical sites and nature centers into campgrounds where most users simply aren't interested. Camping should be fun, and given the success of recreation-oriented programs in municipal settings, what "logic" tells us not to transpose programs into campgrounds for the same users who attend programs at home?

A second reason that recreation programming hasn't been successful in campgrounds refers back to a topic we discussed in Chapter Seven: what the typical "campground" really is. With few exceptions, what most public agencies and some private concerns call "campgrounds" are really sporting camps, small areas of perhaps 10 to 30 units where services are limited to access and attraction (roads and the natural environment). On one hand, these areas are too small to justify either on-site programming personnel or the diversity of facilities you should have in order to offer a broad spectrum of recreation programs.

From a second perspective, think about the users of these areas. In large, developed site family campgrounds where a variety of programs and support facilities are available, it has been our experience to find only about 60 percent of the visitors are interested in attending programs of any type. Therefore, if an average camping party consists of four people, you might, in a 300-unit campground, have over 700 people as a potential market for programs. In a 25-unit campground, the corresponding number would be 60 if the clientele were the same. At the opposite end of the spectrum, in small sporting camps a sizable proportion of the users is usually comprised of hunting and/or fishing parties or the good ol' boys, folks who mostly want you and your staff to let them alone to do their own thing. They are not the kind of clientele where recreation or interpretive programs are likely to succeed.

This situation is another argument for, as we suggested in Chapter One, thinking, planning, and building big, and developing areas large enough to protect, manage, maintain and program for families. The Forest Service, Corps of Engineers, and TVA have all tried interpretive programming in small sporting camps. All three "enjoyed" the same negative results, all three couldn't understand why, and all three canceled programs in sporting camps and family campgrounds.

A final reason we feel recreation programming is not more evident in campgrounds brings us back to the point we raised earlier about attitudes toward programs. This point is best illustrated by another experience we encountered while camping in a Corps of Engineers area in North Dakota. Although the campground was relatively full, only a few campers appeared at an evening interpretive program we attended. After the program was over, we approached the naturalist who had conducted it and asked her if interpretive programs were the only type of activity offered and if the low attendance had been typical. Her response was, "Yes, this is all we offer, and I'm just doing my job—I don't care whether people come or not." Too bad, and all too typical of many "professionals" in many agencies.

Hopefully this was an extreme example, though likely it wasn't. However, we do frequently discover attitudes that reflect a lack of introspection relative to campers' program preferences. Managers and support staff, it seems, either don't know or, as in our example, don't care to know what campers want.

Early in this chapter you saw a photograph of an extended family trying to play ball on a campground road in the Dixie National Forest. As we mentioned then, there was a grass and brush covered "field" near the road that, if cleaned up, would have been an excellent safe place for softball, volleyball, Frisbee throwing, and other games. Even if the resource rascals couldn't make the connection between the recreational preferences of campers used to urban park programming and woodland recreational needs, clearing the field with a bush hog would have gone a long way toward making sure campers could have had an enjoyable experience. It's a good thing Forest Service law enforcement personnel weren't with us when we happened onto this large family, for the pine fuzz would likely have taken a dim view of campers having fun on a road.

Later that day, we took the photograph shown in Figure 9.10 of the young boy playing with his remote controlled car on the same road. The ball game and the fun with the car—both of which are potentially dangerous on a road—should have given the agency a clue concerning the need for programming. We doubt it though, as evidenced by Figures 9.11 and 9.12, both taken on national forests in Colorado. What

Figure 9.11

do you suppose the two posts with an eight-foot tall net (next to the ranger station sign!) in Figure 9.11 represent? Seems station personnel like to play volleyball in the woods. What would you guess, though, is the opportunity for campers to play volleyball in a large developed recreation site (recreation, as in fun) with 75 camping units less than two miles away and operated by the folks in this ranger station? If you said zero, you'd be right on target.

Why, you say, can't these agency folks make the logical connection between what they themselves enjoy and what their customers might enjoy too? Figure 9.12 shows two visitors enjoying a relatively new game called washer toss, which is fun for both youngsters and adults. This homemade set was located at the campsite of a Forest Service campground host who said campers from all over the campground joined him in the evening to play. The two folks shown here playing aren't campers; they are Forest Service employees (not from the forest being visited). It appears they are enjoying themselves. Wonder if they thought their campers might enjoy such an opportunity?

We've picked on the Forest Ser-

Figure 9.12

vice for a bit, so let's ask: Are other agencies in the resource realm as antiprogram? A few state park organizations (Virginia, for example) do understand and respond to camper recreational needs and preferences, but most federal and state agencies don't. The basketball goal shown in Figure 9.13 is

Figure 9.10

in the park maintenance yard of a western state park and is for park staff—not users. Interestingly, this is the only basketball goal we saw in the park! Again, wildland park professionals can't seem to make what should be a simple and logical linkage.

The antirecreation program stance of state park systems like Indiana's is quite surprising if you consider how programming is a proven, low cost way to greatly enhance campground use and revenue, and state park systems in the 1990s certainly need this infusion of users and revenue!

Figure 9.13

In some agencies—mainly the Corps—there have been spotty efforts to provide all sorts of playscapes (including tennis courts, paved volleyball and basketball courts, and lighted ball fields) in campgrounds in various parts of the country, and this often included program personnel, but there doesn't seem to be any nationwide effort or planning directive to do so. Look closely at Figure 9.14, and you'll see two young boys throwing a softball on a campground road at a USCOE park in Pennsylvania. The campground was heavily used (though we saw few teenagers) and we later heard they were conducting a "carrying capacity" study on the lake, *but* fun programming and program facilities weren't there. We'll let you draw your own conclusions on this one.

Finally, we found an extended family playing boccie ball in a Corps campground in Texas (Figure 9.15). Their camp-

site wasn't built for that purpose, but this didn't deter the campers. In this instance, the park manager saw the campers playing and (wonder of wonders!) didn't arrest or chasten the folks (including children) having the fun. Fact is, he now intends to add a boccie ball area to his numerous camper recreation facilities and at one time hired seasonal recreation programmers. What a delightful and logical surprise!

Before we leave this section on the agency nonresponse to programming, there is a bright side we can relate to you. One of our workshop participants in the early 1990s was a Forest Service district ranger on the Nebraska National Forest. After hearing the lecture on the hows and whys of programming, he told us, "Hey, I'm a camper and I've always been less than excited about the extent of our concern for families. Fact is, I don't camp at National Forest campgrounds because they're boring. I'm going to hire a recreation person and start programming next summer." And he did (with fantastic results). The point is, field-level management folks in most agencies have the authority to make the personnel and budget changes required to be a better host. The problem is not funding or management constraints, but attitudinal: Most managers either don't want to make the effort to program or simply don't believe in it. Remember the danger of the "If I like it, it must be right for everyone." mentality. You'll find this forest ranger listed in the Hero section of Chapter Eleven.

In part, this lack of introspection may harken back to the training outdoor recreation professionals get while in school. In general, folks trained in forestry or other resource disciplines (if they take a programming course at all) learn resource interpretation—period. Conversely, program courses in most "people-oriented" curricula, Health, Physical Education, and Recreation (HPER) or education, teach fun programming, but don't consider resource-based recreation areas as a medium for this message of enjoyment. Earlier we suggested you should think about two questions. The first was why recreation programming hasn't been an integral part of the campground services we provide, but the second was even more important: So what? What difference does it make if recreation programs aren't a big deal in campgrounds?

It seems to us that there are three responses to this question, each of which deals with an aspect of "planning parks

Figure 9.14

Figure 9.15

for people" you've heard before—users, management and the environment. The advantage of programming in campgrounds from the user's perspective is quite simple: Programs provide opportunities for enjoyment, and maximizing the potential benefits of any recreation experience is a worthy goal for our profession. Offering a broad spectrum of recreation programs is one means of working toward this goal. From a management perspective, programming is an excellent way to *enhance use figures and revenue* in anyone's campground. If people enjoy a particular recreation experience, they're inclined to do two things: Repeat it and tell their friends about it. Over time, return visits and word-of-mouth will build a clientele for you.

From the standpoint of protecting the environment, programs also offer an alternative to negative pastimes in campgrounds. The philosophy of service provision limited to access and attraction has reaped a harvest of depreciative behavior in campgrounds worldwide. We've seen seven-year-olds sitting near their campsites aimlessly hacking on a tree with a hatchet. If we don't provide opportunities for enjoyment, users will try to entertain themselves, and, whether from ignorance or malice, much of this behavior ends up harming the environment and/or our facilities. Typically, we respond with more rules and more emphasis on law enforcement, and end up fighting effects rather than causes.

As we dig a little deeper into the implications of failing to provide a diversity of campground programs, consider a couple of seemingly unrelated topics—demographics and squirrels. First, demographics leads to consideration of camping-group composition. Who are our campers? If you drive through a typical campground without recreation programming, you'll see retirees, adults, and young children. Generally you won't see teenagers. Small children camp with their families because they have to. Teens, if given a choice, tend to avoid most campgrounds. It may be a painful revelation for resource-oriented professionals, but our experience tells us teenagers, for the most part, are bored in a forest environment. Let's offer them nature programs, the professionals say? We say these teens go to school nine months of the year; the last thing they want is an eager naturalist pushing educational programs at them.

We've talked to families of campers all over the country and what we find is this: Less than 20 percent of the teenagers in these families camp with their parents. In other words, for every five camping households with teens, we may get one teenager in our campgrounds. In facilities where recreation programs are offered on a regular basis, we've seen through applied recreation research studies the percentage of teens camping with their families rises to between 80 and 90 percent. It's true that teens *don't* camp with their families. It's not true teens *won't* camp with them!

We suggested earlier that slightly less than two-thirds of the adults are interested in campground programs. After asking teens in a large, program-oriented campground the same question one summer, we found that 87 percent said they attended at least one recreation activity each day they camped. The important point here, we feel, is a matter of family unity.

If fun-oriented programs motivate teenagers to camp—and research tells us they do—you can encourage entire families to recreate together. Maybe we're old-fashioned, but this strikes us as being a pretty nifty objective for recreation professionals.

Speaking of objectives, do agencies you are aware of have objectives? Some years ago while attending a professional recreation and park meeting in Illinois, we heard an Illinois park district manager say, "The basic objective of our park district is helping visitors have fun!" Well said! As students, you should quiz all sorts of park personnel regarding their recreation objectives. If helping users have fun isn't part of their basic objective (and it likely won't be), question the rascals a bit more. Ask them why not. Ask them what recreation personnel should do. Ask them why people shouldn't have fun in resource areas as well as in cities, towns, and suburbs. Ask them if they love their mothers and apple pie. Ask them if they wouldn't rather be having fun than answering your questions. Then tell them their users would probably rather be having fun, too. You may not make too much of an impact, but at least you'll be having fun watching them squirm.

If you are currently a professional and your agency doesn't mention helping users have fun as an objective, work toward making this needed professional change. The oldest of your three authors remembers the basic purpose of the Forest Service Visitor Information Services (VIS) program (their vehicle for campground programs) was to try to sell visitors on the virtues of the multiple-use act—about as entertaining as watching sidewalks crack. It's no wonder they are a bit slow embracing enjoyable and beckoning programming.

Squirrels? Maybe this is stretching literary license a bit thin, but we're trying to get your attention on an important point here. Squirrels gather nuts and store them in anticipation of bleak times ahead. Similarly, recreation professionals need to think about "putting up a harvest" for the future. If teenagers don't go to campgrounds now, or go and don't enjoy themselves, who will be our campers in the next generation? We aren't suggesting campgrounds are on the road to extinction without recreation programs, although camping use in both the public and private sectors is down across the eastern United States and Canada; however, we are convinced programs can lead to increased numbers of campers both now and in the years to come. Programming is a means of beckoning people to our campgrounds throughout their lives; this coupled with more enjoyment and positive behavior justifies a commitment to programming. "Secondary" benefits would also be increased camping gear sales and increased revenue from user fees in both the public and private sectors.

In Chapter Seven, we shared some "do you love your mother" questions with you. Single-parent families, extended families, retirees, minorities, persons with disabilities, and families with teens were all mentioned. When we discuss these folks with groups of park managers, they are almost unanimously in favor of wanting all these folks to visit the parks they manage. To attract these groups to family campgrounds, however, requires fun programming and visitor protection. Leave these two elements out and you exclude most potential family use.

Ask yourself a series of questions. Do you want people to enjoy themselves in campgrounds? Would you like to encourage entire families to camp together? Do you want campers to feel welcome in your areas? If you like the idea of building positive public relations, increasing your use rates and revenue, discouraging depreciative behavior, minimizing the money you spend on law enforcement, and enhancing the fun people have in your campgrounds, then program. We've given numerous lectures across the country, heralding the exciting benefits of fun programming. Those in our audiences who have changed their less than successful nature dockets to fun activities have been delighted with the results.

Types of Campground Programs

The critical element involved in campground programming is diversity. In subsequent sections of this chapter, we'll discuss kinds of facilities helpful, though not indispensable, for successful programs; planning and design considerations for programming; and program promotion and conduct. Most important, however, is a broad spectrum of activity opportunities for all users: retirees, mature adults, young adults, teens, and preteens. Some programs, such as grocery bingo or shuffleboard tournaments, may appeal to more than one age group. Others, such as a bicycle race, may generate interest from a smaller proportion of your campers.

This raises two points you should consider. First, don't try to develop all your programs for "universal appeal." Getting entire families to enjoy a program together is great, but some simply won't attract all age groups. Therefore you should focus some of your efforts on specific target audiences. Second, successful programs aren't entirely dependent on maximum attendance. As we've suggested before, some campers will want to "do their own thing" and are perfectly happy whether you program or not. Shortly we'll talk about ways to increase the proportion of campers who attend programs, but attempting to "hard sell" or force activities on an entire camping clientele is both futile and aggravating.

The potential range of individual programs is limited only by the imagination and enthusiasm of the programmer. We can, though, classify most programs into one of six categories, including active, passive, interpretive, skills, nature arts and crafts, and a broad classification of activities we can refer to as special events.

Active Programs. Figures 9.16 through 9.22 illustrate some of the potential range of active programs we've seen succeed in campgrounds. Programs such as egg tosses (Figure 9.16) and pet shows (Figure 9.17) work well for young children. Field or court games like basketball (Figure 9.18) and games adapted to water such as volleyball (Figure 9.19) and tug of war (Figure 9.20) are examples of active programs with appeal to younger adults, teens, and preteens. Square dances (Figure 9.21) and washer toss (Figure 9.22) attract older adults and senior citizens. Other types of programs, such as family Olympics, live entertainment, and carnivals are good for bringing multiple age groups together.

Figure 9.16

Figure 9.17

Figure 9.18

Conducting active programs requires you to integrate all aspects of campground management into a comprehensive plan for providing user services. We've seen teenagers, when given the opportunity, play volleyball on a lighted play court until 2:00 A.M. We've also seen campground regulations enforcing a 9:00 P.M. curfew on activities. While quiet hours are

Figure 9.19

Figure 9.20

Figure 9.21

Figure 9.22

night and their parents don't object, managers, by enforcing early quiet hours, say, "Your needs aren't as important as those of other campers." Potentially noisy active programs can coexist with quiet evenings if the facilities designed for these activities are zoned away from campground "bedroom areas" where quiet, at least after 10:30 or 11:00 P.M., should be a management goal.

Passive Programs. Storytelling, board games, campfire programs, grocery bingo (Figure 9.23), and other "quiet" activities are examples of passive programs. Depending on what you offer, these may appeal to a specific age group (fairy tales for children, a senior citizen checkers tournament) or a broader clientele (a "film festival" at your campfire theater with movies borrowed from the local public library). Passive programs can help salvage a camping trip dampened by poor weather, when "cabin fever" sets in quickly after one or two rainy days. An activity at a shelter building can be a welcome change from sitting inside a camping trailer wondering if the sun will ever come out again. Passive programs also provide an alternative to more strenuous activities. It may not be quite so difficult to explain to a six-year-old why he or she can't swim immediately after lunch if there's a toe-painting contest at the campfire theater at 1:30 P.M.

Interpretive Programs. We have several comments to make about interpretation in campgrounds, most of which are philosophical. First, many of our earlier statements may have led you to conclude that we view interpretive programs negatively. We hope this isn't the case, because we strongly support a reasonable ratio of well-thought-out environmental and historical presentations. Our concern is your approach to these activities. Nature hikes, lectures on forest products, and talks about the nearby Civil War battlefield are typical of the activities many professionals think of when the subject of interpretation arises. This is unfortunate. Some "traditional" interpretive programs in campgrounds are well-received; some campers, us included, will get up at 6:00 A.M. to go on an early-morning songbird walk. The problem with limiting interpretive programs to this approach is that most campers won't participate. For the majority of campground users, we feel traditional methods of attempting to educate through programs

an excellent management policy since many early risers retire early, simply enforcing a "no noise after 9:00 P.M." rule suggests managers and planners don't consider all campers. Campers are there to enjoy themselves. Going to bed and getting up when they want should be their decision as long as you plan areas where they can do their own thing without disturbing others. If teenagers want to stay up until after mid-

Figure 9.23

simply don't have much appeal. To test our point, don't look at the number of campers you attract to a typical interpretive program; take a look at the proportion of users who don't attend.

In one respect, interpretive specialists are similar to some college professors we know; they may understand their material inside out and be terribly enthusiastic about it, but conveying this information and excitement is another matter. Just because you thrill over a woodpecker at work at dawn or the 37 most fascinating facts about the honeybee (Figure 9.24) doesn't mean your campers will. Interpretive programs can make campers more conscious of the environment and their cultural heritage. Thus we advocate including these programs in the activities you offer. But camping should be fun, and this philosophy extends to educational programs as well.

We feel traditional approaches to interpretation in campgrounds should be continued, with moderation, for the small percentage of campers who are inclined to learn for the sake of knowledge itself. Remember, however, the following guidelines. First, these programs should be only one dimension of a much broader spectrum of activity opportunities you provide; please don't assume everyone has a burning desire to learn. No matter how important you think it is for people to appreciate nature and culture, you simply can't force-feed these topics to everyone. Offering only traditional interpretive programs attempts a strategy you've heard before: You can lead a horse to water. . . .

Second, with a little creativity, even traditional programs can be entertaining for many campers. Instead of a lecture on cultural heritage, a living-history program (Figure 9.25) can be both informative and enjoyable. Nature interpretation can be enhanced with interactive approaches that involve the camper. The tree finder, shown in Figure 9.26, demonstrates this principle. Here, a stationary disk, mounted on a four-by-four post, contains 8 to 10 cards with information about different tree species. A second disk, mounted on top of the first, rotates 360° via a handle. This top disk has a Plexiglas window through which the information on the cards is read. When a particular card is beneath the Plexiglas, a sight on the

Figure 9.25

top disk points to the tree described on the card. The post can be any height you want; it could be set for children, adults in wheelchairs, or ambulatory adults. The trick to placing a tree finder is to make sure you have a good variety of species located in (generally) a circular configuration. You can, of course, use "tree finders" to interpret rock formations, cacti, shrubs or other natural features besides trees. We think the best messages are ones that identify the object and then briefly describe how people or animals use it (for example, noting a hole in a saguaro cactus as the home of a cactus wren).

A third consideration concerns potential alternatives to traditional approaches to interpretation, and we know of

Figure 9.24

Figure 9.26

two you may find useful. First, conduct recreation programs with an undertone of interpretation. An excellent example of this is to plan a bike hike on which you have five to seven scheduled rest stops (Figure 9.27). Make your first rest stop in the shade of a tree where squirrels nest (squirrels again?). Here you might talk about "homes in the forest" while participants stretch their legs and get a drink. Have your next stop planned under a bird's nest and ask riders if they see any other forest dwellings. In other words, keep the educational aspect of the ride low-key and secondary to the outing itself. Then users will enjoy themselves and learn a little in the process.

Figure 9.27

Another alternative to traditional interpretive programs is to conduct a "real" interpretive program around a fun theme. One of the most popular activities we've ever seen in a campground is one you've probably never heard of: the critter crawl. The critter crawl is a two-stage program. In the first stage, you meet with participants and tell them to find a critter in the woods—a frog, a turtle, or an insect—most any small critter will do as long as it can't fly. At this point, you should remind campers not to hurt the animal and use this as a springboard for an informative talk (not a lecture) on the need to protect natural resources. Next, give everyone half an hour to search. After they return with their discoveries, or even at a somewhat later time, the critter crawl begins. To conduct this part of the program, mark a small circle perhaps three feet in diameter inside a larger circle about 10 feet in diameter. Contestants place their critters on the ground within the inner circle and, at a signal, release their animals (Figure 9.28). The first critter that crosses the outer circle wins. You may need a few "ground rules," like any critter that eats another is disqualified. We've seen this happen, but a good interpreter can seize this opportunity to talk about the food chain. After the crawl, there's time to talk about returning the critters to the woods, again with the potential for "soft" interpretation. (There were over 300 campers watching and enjoying the critter crawl that day.)

Another method of infusing fun into interpretive programs is to develop interpretive skits in which your program staff dress up as (for example) animals or insects. They can script and act out things as they occur in nature, adding a humorous slant to the message (Figure 9.29).

With these programs, you can plan around the common denominator of fun. If your programmer is a capable interpreter, participants will learn a few things, but the learning environments won't be "painful."

Figure 9.28

Skills Programs. In Chapter Six, we discussed planning facilities for bicycling and archery skills development and asked you to design an area for teaching fishing techniques. (Pictures of a bicycle skills area, superimposed on a paved parking lot, are shown in Figures 9.30 and 9.31). In addition to these activities, a camp skills program can include tips on outdoor cooking and canoeing. Outdoor-cooking programs are a good way of "easing into" skills-development activities because they don't require much in the way of support facilities or equipment. A small open space for a campfire, a programmer who has had a bit of experience in camping, and a few cooking utensils are all you need. By asking campers to provide their own foodstuffs in advance, you can also minimize expenses. As with many, but not all other campground programs, outdoor cooking activities offer some opportunities to incorporate low-key interpretive lessons: "This is how the pioneers did it," or "Don't cut live saplings for firewood."

Figure 9.29

Figure 9.30

Figure 9.31

Canoeing skills programs may require more of an investment, but costs can be kept low with a little foresight. You don't need new, expensive canoes since secondhand aluminum ones will work quite well. As an alternative, it may be possible to work out a cooperative agreement with a local outfitter. During slow, midweek periods, canoe-rental businesses may be willing to rent you several at reduced rates, or even loan them to you in exchange for some free advertisement.

There are two points to consider here. First, programming creativity doesn't stop with thinking of good programs; the how, as well as the what takes some thought and effort. Second, programs can create opportunities for positive recreation experience beyond the "now" of a camping trip. If you teach an eight-year-old child how to canoe, he or she may develop a lifelong avocation.

Skills programs, regardless of the activity, can also function as an effective means of getting families to recreate together. If one of the main reasons a family visits your campground is for Dad to fish, you may be able to use his interest as a bridge to promote a family activity in a fishing skills program (Figure 9.32). For example, when we worked for TVA, we saw an interesting phenomenon occur. Traditionally, deer hunters who camped in Land Between the Lakes

Figure 9.32

used the small sporting camps the agency provided. When programmers in the neighboring developed campgrounds started offering archery skills programs, some of these hunters began, for the first time, to camp in these areas and brought their families with them. Since a variety of other programs was offered, all family members could enjoy the hunting trip, not just the hunters. The skills program attracted users, who brought other users, who attended other programs, which . . . hmm, there seems to be a ripple effect here.

Nature Arts and Crafts. Activities such as rock painting, and making dolls from corn shucks and cobs and other natural materials are examples of nature arts and crafts programs. These activities can be directed to a specific age group like preteens, or focus on a broader campground population. As with skills-development programs, nature arts and crafts offer the opportunity for low-key interpretive messages. Depending on funds and staffing availability and limitations, nature arts and crafts can be organized with an extensive array of supplies or operated, if necessary, on a shoestring budget. Most of the materials you'll need occur naturally; acorns, pine cones, sweet-gum balls, leaves, stones, and similar supplies can be picked up by participants before or during the program. This points out an important aspect of program provision. While it's nice to have a well-funded budget for recreation programming, it really isn't a requirement. The only things you really need to operate a successful activities program are a little creativity and a lot of enthusiasm.

Special Programs. The activities we've discussed to this point are by no means exhaustive, but with the preceding discussion as a guideline, you should be able to develop a much broader set of program offerings. The types of activities described here also have one thing in common; they are examples of programs that you can conduct on an ongoing, everyday basis in campgrounds. However, a good programmer shouldn't stop with the "ordinary." To make visiting your campground a special occasion—one users will remember—it's a good idea to plan and conduct some programs which are, well, special—not a very scientific description but a fitting one.

The range of opportunities for special programs is limited only by your imagination, though to ensure successful programs it helps to know who your users are. People who camp in developed site, family campgrounds tend to be just "folks." You'll find chemical engineers and college professors camped next to retired janitors and 20-year-old maintenance workers. Demographic and socioeconomic variables are interesting to social scientists, but for you as a programmer or a planner who supports programming, there's a more basic variable at work here. Many people, regardless of their education, income, and career, simply enjoy camping in developed site campgrounds. These individuals are basically down-to-earth, regardless of their real-life roles. We once spent several minutes explaining understory vegetation to an unshaven, middle-aged camper who, we learned later, had a doctoral degree in forestry. He never said a word to discourage our less-than-learned lecture.

Special programs can be centered around a specific theme like a square-dance weekend, a special event like a stargazing outing to view shooting stars, a particular group like a National Campers and Hikers Association retreat, a "contrived occasion" like Christmas in July, or simply a collection of programs like the Camper's Fair we mentioned earlier. Flea markets, auctions, food fairs, and cleanup weekends are other examples of special occasions—ones the user will remember. We once attended a successful weekend centered around pulling nails out of trees and installing lantern-hanging devices. The weekend worked because it was well-advertised and organized, and offered a broad spectrum of fun activities throughout. By working with current and potential user groups, you can develop special programs to complement just about any interest, enhance the experience campers have, and boost your use figures considerably. While programming isn't difficult, it does take a commitment from management, hard work, and a little foresight. Turn your attention now to some campground features and facilities you can use to your advantage in activity programs.

Program Support Facilities

Return with us again to Figure 9.9 and review the story of a campground without play facilities or programs. Is it possible to renovate this campground to eliminate user confusion and administrative problems? Our version of how this might be done is shown in Figure 9.33. We've also added several play facilities.

The Chapter One illustration "happened" over many years and is similar to hundreds of happenings worldwide. It grew and grew and then grew again until

the final "design" was gruesome! What was needed was a master plan for the entire area with built-in playing capabilities. Figure 9.34 takes one final look at the potential this campground could have had if the person had designed the area for programming, administration, and different types of users.

The new campground has six peanut loops, three group loops with their own program amenities, three toilet showers (one with a companion care room) and numerous program amenities. As usual, the play zones are located so a manager could superimpose a sizable day use group without harming the numerous camp loops. This is a sizable campground with at least 300 camping units. The manager could pick a combination of three loops out of the nine then build them and the amenities in the first phase. He could then, as needed, build additional loops.

Play or program facilities here include: campfire theater with interpretive zone, fenced horseshoe pits, boccie ball courts, paved multipurpose play court, tot lot, sizable shelter with toilet facilities, a stage (pointing away from the campfire theater), equipment checkout/office room, and softball field (with lights for night use).

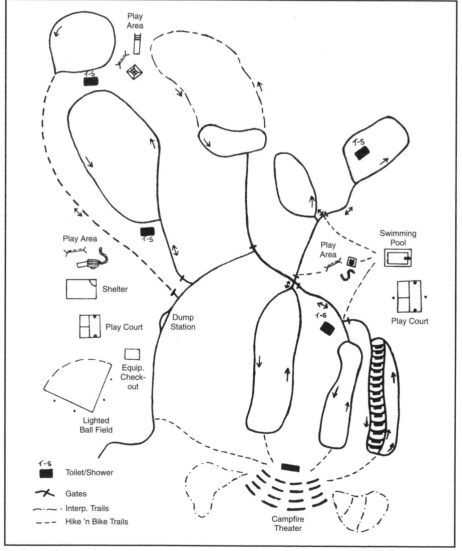

Figure 9.33

228

Assuming a quality programming effort here, this campground would beckon families with teens or without teens, retirees, single parent families, minorities, international visitors, and group use. Isn't that great? And isn't that what should happen in all family campgrounds?

We'll leave it to you to name the camp loops and to identify the many other positive aspects of this solution. (*Hint:* Think about control, circulation, design psychology, and reducing impact.) We'd like to focus now on the features it's desirable to have in a campground from a programming perspective. Note that we said, "desirable." All you really need to conduct programs is an audience and a desire to help users enjoy themselves. However, a few support facilities like the following will make life easier for program staff.

Play Courts. If we were asked to choose one single program-support facility, it would be the multipurpose play court. If well-designed and zoned, this facility can support basketball, volleyball, children's games, teen dances, square dances, skills programs and a host of other activities. Figure 9.35 shows a layout for a multipurpose play court. Ideally, it should be designed and built as a program facility with a paved sur-

face, and should be lighted for evening play. If development dollars are limited, however, there are alternatives. Ball courts may be "superimposed" on an existing paved parking lot by painting lines for court boundaries on the lot surface and erecting standards for nets and goals. Whichever approach you use, remember to orient the direction of play along a north-south axis. A flat, grassy area can be used as a volleyball court (Figure 9.36), though if the selected site is shaded you should scrape the turf and provide a 50-50 mixture of sand and soil packed smooth and graded. The value or utility of a multipurpose play court can also be extended by adding lighting and electrical outlets. When deciding where to site a play court, don't forget our discussions of screening, separation of conflicting uses, and the difference between regulation league play and the less structured form of play in campgrounds.

Campfire Theaters. Campfire theaters or amphitheaters are to passive programs what multipurpose courts are to active programs; they serve a variety of uses. Evening programs, daytime story hours, and staging areas for interpretive walks are a few examples of their various applications. Campfire theaters also offer us an excellent opportunity to talk about

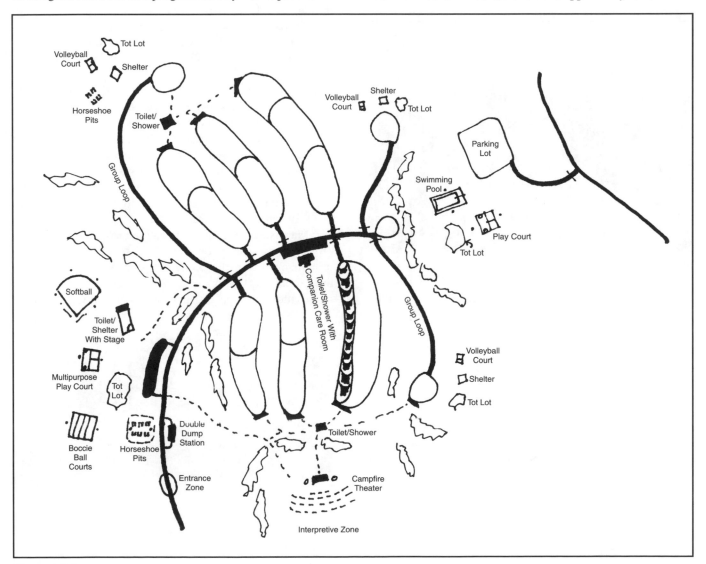

Figure 9.34

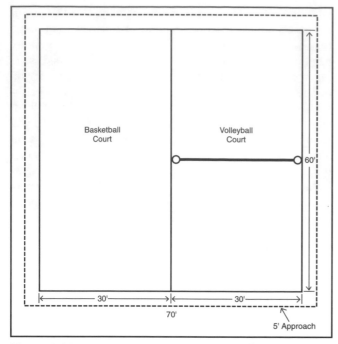

Figure 9.35

Figure 9.36

how design decisions should be made, regardless of the type of facility involved. Consider this scenario: You've just been hired as the assistant manager of Cornfed State Park in Nebraska. Your first assignment is to supervise the development of a new campfire theater for the campground. The campground has 250 units and, because recreation programs are emphasized, use is quite high. Our question to you is: How many linear feet of seating space should you provide? What we're really asking is how you should justify this decision from a planning standpoint. Put more simply, we're asking why. As we've said before, you should always be able to justify the planning decisions you make. Here, as usual, your decision should be based on minimizing costs balanced with meeting the needs of your users. We're sure you know the answer to this question as a good planner, but for the dummies seated next to you, we'll walk them through the logic you used to arrive at the solution:

1. You knew the campground had a maximum capacity of 1,000 people (remember PAOT?) based on 250 units times four users per site.
2. You knew from looking at program records that only about 50 percent of your campers attended evening programs.
3. You knew from books on standards that the average adult needs about two feet of seating space, but since many of your campers are children, you amended this figure to $1\frac{1}{2}$ feet.
4. You then developed a simple formula which states that units times users per site times potential audience times individual seating space equals necessary seating space. Thus, using the numbers from Cornfed Campground, you multiplied 250 units times 4 users times 50 percent times $1\frac{1}{2}$ feet ($250 \times 4 \times 0.5 \times 1.5$) to arrive at 750 linear feet of seating space. As a conscientious planner, this is the kind of approach you should always take.

You should also consider a few other design aspects of campfire theaters. First, it's a good idea to provide both barrier-free seating and ramped access to the stage area of the theater. You should also allow for user involvement in campfire programs because an inaccessible stage may exclude some from participating. Access trails from the rest of the campground to the theater should be barrier-free as well and, if at all possible, choose natural slopes as locations for theaters to enhance the view of the program area or stage (Figure 9.37). If you don't have this option, you should elevate the stage so people seated in the rear of the theater will have unobstructed views. Within a campground, distance from camp units to the theater doesn't seem to be a factor in determining who attends programs there. However, you shouldn't, as many state parks, the National Park Service and the Forest Service do, locate a theater outside the campground and expect high levels of camper attendance.

Many state parks have recreation buildings and evening programming near their park lodges, and these are often two or more miles from the family campground. Since programs open to all park visitors are scheduled at night in the recreation building, it appears that managers and programmers feel

Figure 9.37

campers have an opportunity to participate and if they don't, they must not be interested. We see this as another failure to plan parks for people. Campers, even those interested in programming, are quite difficult to "lure" from their sites at night. Thus we recommend you program with enthusiasm at well-zoned program facilities *inside or at the edge of your campgrounds*. This doesn't imply you should stop programming at facilities outside the campground; you just shouldn't expect to attract a large proportion of your campers to these activities.

From an administrative standpoint, it may or may not be a good idea to bring noncampers into a campground for programming, or you'll have an admission-control problem. If you're building a new area or adding program features to an existing park, one solution is to zone new program amenities on the edge of the campground nearest other park facilities so they can be reached on foot from both within and outside the campground.

Campfire theaters should be zoned away from active areas where noise may conflict with your quieter programs. For example, vegetative screening and a "buffer zone" of a system of interpretive trails can help reduce conflicts between programs going on simultaneously in the theater and an adjacent active area. If you provide parking for the theater, be sure either the lot is oriented away from the stage area of the theater, or you build an earthen berm to prevent vehicle headlights from shining onto the stage. You should provide stage lights, however, to allow program staff the flexibility for a variety of activities. Since planning is a support function, work closely with program staff to develop the facilities they will need; a projection stand in the seating area with electrical outlet, for example.

Play Fields. Play fields serve as a good example of how recreation programs in campgrounds can be implemented without major outlays of dollars. A relatively flat, open field, cleared with a bush hog, can serve as a program zone for a variety of activities. Note in Figure 9.38 how the Corps of Engineers in Kansas have zoned a ball field, volleyball court, tot lot, horseshoe pits, and shelter together to provide for multiple activities. (Numerous USCOE folks have told us this can't be done!) Soccer, touch football, softball, Frisbee, golf, a variety of children's games, and a number of other activities

don't require expensive equipment or regulation play space. It isn't an environmentally sound practice to use a groundhog for home plate, but you don't have to provide major league-quality bases either. As we suggested in Chapter Six, a perfectly level field isn't even a necessity. Gradually sloping terrain may drain more effectively and can shorten the distance balls will roll if you're short on space.

To reinforce a point we made earlier, regulation play and competition are not as important to campers as the opportunity to participate and have a little fun. If you have the funds available to build a backstop, do so. We feel it's more important, however, to provide an enthusiastic program person who has a little creativity. A good programmer can create activities with little in the way of support, whereas a well-designed play zone may go mostly unused unless someone is there to organize programs.

Shelter Buildings. If you have access to an architect, shelter buildings are easy to design. They aren't quite as simple to plan. The distinction we're making here is one of recreation use. If you commit the funds to build a shelter, you should make sure that what you get is what your programmer and users need. To determine what these needs are, it's critical to talk to the people who use your campground. A well-designed shelter may mean one with a good roof, a floor, and support beams. A well-planned shelter might include shuffleboard-court surfacing, a large grill for group cookouts, and other program amenities aimed at the types of users who come to your campground. The shelter shown in Figure 9.39 has shuffleboard and a stage built for bluegrass bands. The expansion joints run the length of the paved floor rather than the width in order to provide the smooth surface needed for shuffleboard. A member of the crew constructing this shelter played in a bluegrass band and was largely responsible for the stage design—how many electrical outlets, where to put them, stage size, and so on.

In addition to serving as an activity zone, the shelter can be a focal point of your programming efforts. If it is centrally located, if possible, it can double as an equipment checkout building. Providing inexpensive and durable equipment—aluminum bats, Frisbees, balls, and the like—preferably free to users, can create activity opportunities. The shelter can additionally serve as a gathering point for hikes, nature walks,

Figure 9.38

Figure 9.39

and other "diffused" programs. One advantage of using shelters for this purpose is getting your users to a protected spot should the weather turn nasty. Once you have a congregation, you can always substitute an indoor activity for the rained-out hike.

Fishing Piers. As we suggested earlier, some campers won't be interested in the campground programs you develop, and fishing piers are a good example of unorganized offerings. Designing and building a fishing pier creates the chance for campers to use an amenity without a formal program (Figure 9.40). While everyone may not be interested in an evening campfire program, for example, your campground may have a water attraction like a lake or a stream that a large percentage of your users take advantage of. (Fact is they are likely

Figure 9.40

camping at your area because of that lake or stream!) By providing a fishing pier you have, in effect, provided a program. There's nothing to stop you from developing a planned activity around the pier or another facility, but these programs require on-site staff to function successfully.

If you build a pier, be sure to locate it fairly close to your other campground facilities for use in organized programs. It should only be zoned just far enough away from beaches and boat ramps so these activities won't interfere with the quiet needed for fishing. You can sink fish attractors made from brush or other materials in the surrounding water (Figure 9.41).

It's a good idea to coordinate the location of your fishing pier with fisheries and/or wildlife staff, *but* the final decision on where to place it should be based on recreation program needs. (This will come as quite a shock to most wildlife and fisheries rascals.)

Beaches. We've already discussed the need to consider user safety and environmental protection when you locate beaches. Aside from these and the other basic concerns you found in the chapter on day-use areas, one important aspect of locating beaches in campgrounds is our old friend, zoning. Beaches need to be zoned so they are convenient to, but not intrusive upon, camp units. This is true of all program amenities, but planners seem to violate this principle more frequently with beaches.

Figure 9.41

Figures 9.42 and 9.43 show two ways of designing a beach zone combined with a camping-loop zone. While the design in Figure 9.42 uses less road, it has a negative impact on campers using the loop shown here since users from other loops located further away from the water must travel through this one to reach the beach. Furthermore, campers on the upper part of this loop—those farther away from the lake—are beckoned to move through the units nearer the water to get to the lake. Because managers can't control traffic to the beach without barricading the camp-loop road, an administrative problem results as well. Our message here is, "keep loop roads 'clean.'" Don't rely on camping roads to provide access to program (or other) support facilities. On a tangential note, be sure to tilt the parking lot slightly (two to three percent) away from the beach or take other measures, such as a filter strip, or ditch and berm combination between the lot and the beach to keep water runoff from washing automotive pollutants into the beach zone. Note also the toilet/shower at the top of the three camp loops (Figure 9.43) does double duty as the sanitary/shower facility for the beach.

Often, you'll find campgrounds and other recreation facilities on lakes used for transportation. For instance, the TVA system of reservoirs and many USCOE lakes have a steady flow of barge traffic, whose wave action can destroy a beach and be hazardous to weak swimmers. Barge traffic also provides an example of how complex recreation planning can

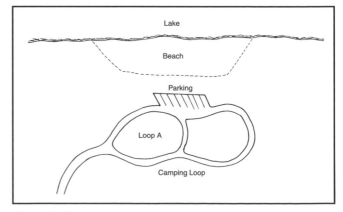

Figure 9.42

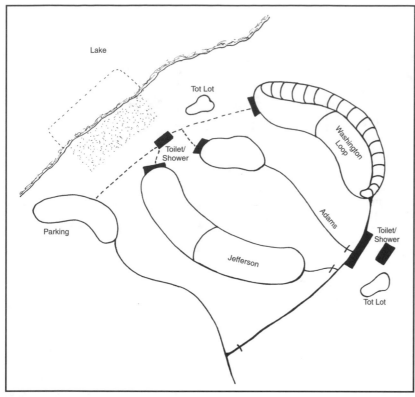

Figure 9.43

be. We once found a perfect location for a campfire theater—a natural bowl, well-zoned, overlooking a lake. It was perfect until we camped on the site and experienced barge traffic all night long with its flashing lights and noises. The lights and noise would have destroyed a passive campfire program. Remember then, that off-site conditions can really have an impact on your designs.

Trails. Although they may not be perceived as program zones, many campgrounds have a variety of natural amenities capable of supporting recreation activities, and a trails system is one example. Existing trails can be used for hikes, nature walks, scavenger hunts, and other programs. But since many organized groups, such as the National Campers and Hikers Association, award patches and other incentives for service projects, a little creative programming can turn a periodic trails-maintenance job into a theme weekend. This will result in a reduced work load for your maintenance crew, an activity for campers, an increase in your attendance figures, additional program opportunities, and a positive piece of public relations. With a little cooperation from local media, the weekend can even become something of a local "event" that provides you with free advertising. One trick we've learned over the years in organizing "joint venture" programs such as this is to take a back seat to other groups; let the camping club have the limelight for the work they do with a mention of your agency or organization as cosponsor. You'll accrue the benefits you need, but it's good to make user groups feel important as well. This is a lesson the authors learned while working for TVA. It's too bad TVA didn't learn the same lesson.

If you're considering the addition of a trails system to a campground, remember to avoid mixing trails with conflicting uses, as we discussed in Chapter Three. If your campground already has a number of trails for hiking, biking, and circulation, you'll always be better off building an additional trail for interpretation than trying to superimpose this use on existing ones. The initial cost may be higher, but you'll save maintenance dollars over time because of reduced vandalism. A separate interpretive system will also enhance the experience for all trail users. (Don't mix hiking and interpretation! We've said that before, haven't we?)

Whenever you consider developing trails—particularly in campgrounds—keep in mind the potential for program development. For specific tips on trail design and layout, refer back to Chapter Three.

Skills and Crafts Sites. In addition to the facilities for archery, fishing, canoeing, and bicycling we discussed previously, a central location for skills and nature crafts can add another dimension to programming. You can use a shelter building as a focal point for activities such as cooking skills and nature crafts, but if a shelter is zoned to serve as the center of your active program feature, these activities may conflict with more passive skills, arts, and crafts programs. By adding a separate zone for the latter, you can create the opportunity to offer concurrent programs. Thus campers not interested in a midmorning volleyball game can choose to attend a program on outdoor cooking or an activity focusing on nature art.

Many public recreation areas contain property formerly held by the private sector, like old farm buildings in various stages of disrepair. Using materials from these buildings, it's frequently possible to build a crafts cabin. Log or rustic wooden structures fit a campground environment, appeal to children and adults, and can provide you with a relatively inexpensive focal point for programs ranging from storytelling to crafts.

Putting the Pieces Together

To this point, we've focused the discussion on justifying programming in campgrounds and highlighting a variety of programs and support features. Now, you need to consider the how. Once you've decided (and we hope you have) that programming is an integral part of campground management, how do you go about doing it? We can break this process down into three general stages: design, program planning and preparation, and cost.

Design. There are two interrelated aspects of designing program facilities for campgrounds. One of these is zoning. Program areas need to be zoned so they won't conflict with each other or with the camping experience itself. Program facilities like tot lots should be built close to the toilets/showers near camping loops so young children can reach them without parental concern for safety. You should locate play courts and fields and other active program zones centrally, if possible, but certainly far enough away from camping loops and passive-program areas so noise won't interfere with other activities. Then campers can enjoy the 50-person softball game until 1:30 A.M. without causing problems for others. Where you place beaches, boat launch sites, fishing piers and other water dependent facilities depends on location of good water, access without encroachment on camping-loop roads, and proposed sites for other program zones. As Figure 9.44 suggests graphically, the potential complexity of a good fit for all campground amenities, including program facilities can be quite puzzling. The proper fit of all items is where design folks flop and fail and fall frequently. This also points out the need for a second design consideration: sequencing.

In Chapter Seven we suggested a good design technique is to "work backwards." Instead of locating your main road first, determine where camping loops can best be placed (remembering the unit locations) and then add the access road and circulation. Figures 9.45 and 9.46 illustrate this principle. Let's assume for a moment the land base shown in these figures is flat enough so topography isn't a limiting factor, but the beach and boating site must be located as they appear in Figure 9.46. Ignoring programming for a moment, the campground in Figure 9.46 will work from several perspectives. There is a single entry/exit point and good potential for controlling loop use, the design prevents confusion and keeps boating and beach traffic away from loops for users, the loops are designed with environmental protection in mind, and the sewage-dumping station and maintenance complex are well-zoned. But we don't want to ignore programming.

To allow us to include potential programs in our campground, we need to carry the concept of sequencing one step further and first determine where the major active and passive program zones should go. Let's say the best locations are shown in Figure 9.47.

With these fixed, preferably with two or three alternatives, it's now possible to begin to "plug in" camping loops so all the zones begin to complement each other. Figure 9.48 shows this next step in the progression.

Finally, we can work out the optimum circulation system to move users into and through the various zones, add support features like toilets/showers, and fine-tune program zones. Figure 9.49 shows the completed campground.

Figure 9.44

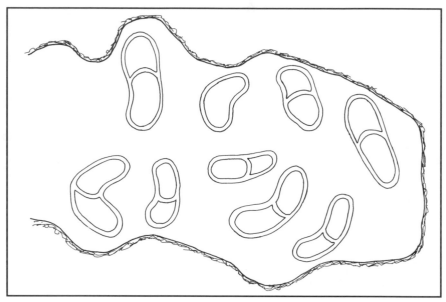

Figure 9.45

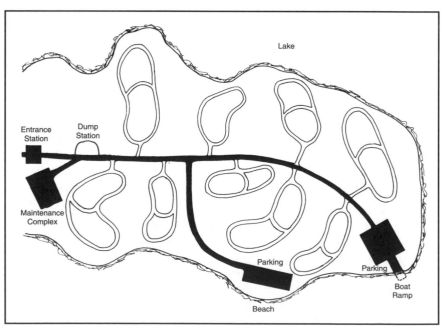

Figure 9.46

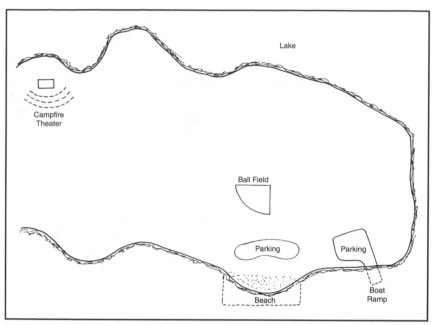

Figure 9.47

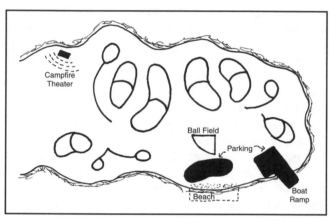

Figure 9.48

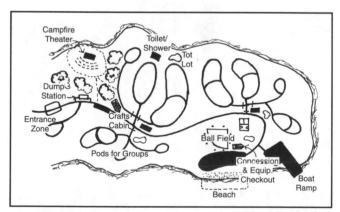

Figure 9.49

Using a sequencing approach, the design challenge becomes a logical process as opposed to a guessing game. The main road is *one of the last features* you should plan. It is truly a subordinate piece of "hardware" rather than, as is usu-

ally the case, a poorly engineered dominant feature. From a programming perspective, contrast the final location of the main and subordinate roads in Figure 9.49 with the ones less well-done in Figure 9.46. Note also you can superimpose special day use programs on your activity zones without camp loop penetration.

Program Planning and Preparation. Planning and developing a broad spectrum of campground programs isn't especially difficult or too different from organizing recreation activities in a municipal setting. Recreation programs, regardless of environment, depend in part on four things: types of facilities available, suitability of resource base, capabilities and talents of program staff, and kinds of programs emphasized, keeping in mind the needs of all users. There is a "psychology of programming" with respect to activities in campgrounds, however, and some aspects you'll want to consider include the following:

Preferences. Part of the challenge (and the fun) of working in a people-oriented profession is differences among people. What might be an excellent program for teens might flop with young adults. A superb program in a campground near Washington, D.C., could fail miserably in the state of Washington. Therefore the programs that you offer need to be based in part on who your campers are. You should find out what interests your users and give them what they want, not what you think they need. Various means of determining user preferences include talking informally to campers, developing and conducting a formal survey (graduate students in recreation-related curricula are always looking for research topics), and simply trying various programs over the course of a few use seasons to see which types of activities best suit your users' needs.

Timing. The simplest way to maximize attendance at different activities is to program where people go when they are there. For example, you can plan a beach-oriented activity like a water volleyball game in the hot, early afternoon hours when people will congregate in this zone without any outside motivation. Conversely, some activities such as active games for young children should be planned for early morning and early evening hours to avoid excessive exposure to sun and high temperatures. Knowing your campers' habits is important to timing. We used to assume campers ate at 8:00 A.M., noon, and 6:00 P.M., until we asked them. Our guesses were an hour early for each meal. (The correct times were 9:00 A.M., 1:00 P.M. and 7:00 P.M.)

Advertising. Like any other "product," campground programs can enjoy maximum success only if you make potential users aware of what you have to offer. Place eye-catching, up-to-date signs where people are most likely to see them: in rest rooms (Figure 9.50), on shower doors, at the campground entrance station, the equipment checkout structure (Figure 9.51), in program zones, and on bulletin boards (Figure 9.52; notice how nicely prepared bulletin boards attract

Figure 9.50

Figure 9.52

particularly desirable campers like the ones shown here). Do make sure bulletin boards avoid looking overly cluttered and are not neglected like the one shown in Figure 9.53. Please don't, as most folks do, use the entire space to tell your guests 63 things they can't do. These boards should be "designed" with a central focus for all information. Two excellent techniques involve using brightly colored construction paper and signs reading, "Don't look under here," with program announcements beneath.

Program schedules available at the entrance station covering a seven-day period give campers an idea of what activities are pending. These can be posted and given to users when they check into the campground. If they have programming at all, most of the state and federal campgrounds we've visited design a brochure for the entire summer season. This allows people to do the same things at the same hours of the same days all summer! Such an "enthusiastic" approach to creative programming is discouraging. Whenever you conduct a program, announce the times and locations of the next few activities to build a repeat clientele. Near mealtimes, programmers can drive, pedal or walk through camping areas to invite, not force, users to attend upcoming activities.

Naming. Use creative names for your programs, particularly those aimed at young children. You're more likely to attract youngsters to a "Water World Series" than to a program imaginatively entitled "Beach Activity." We know a programmer who periodically held "Green Submarine Hunts" at her beach, and people often came to find out what it was—a greased watermelon tossed into a shallow swimming area for contestants to try and capture. Wouldn't it be awful to hear teens and other youngsters shouting and having fun chasing a greased watermelon at a beach in a National Forest or National Park campground when they could be learning the differences between parasitic and symbiotic relationships in the natural environment?

Certificates and Awards. Although some might disagree, we recommend against using awards as program participation incentives. Ours is a highly competitive society, and recreational settings should offer a change of pace from this norm. It isn't necessary to have a "winner" in a critter-crawl contest; if you do, you have to have perhaps 20 or 30 losers as well, many of whom may be quite young, and you don't want the negative feelings that go with losing in your campground. The alternative we prefer is to provide certificates of enthusiastic participation, such as the one shown in Figure 9.54, given to all who join in the activity. These can be printed in bulk with blank spaces for the programmer to fill in name of participant and activity. By printing colorful certificates with your logo, you can provide a memento of the occasion not tied to competition and a fantastic source of advertisement for your campground. (By the way, did you

Figure 9.51

Figure 9.53

Figure 9.54

- A bike repair workshop,
- A bicycle safety program,
- A bike "show,"
- A family bike hike,
- A bicycle exhibition in cooperation with local retailers,
- A bike-decorating contest,
- First aid for bike-related injuries,
- A cross-country biking workshop (packing, touring, maps),
- A road rally,
- Bicycle games (follow the leader, Frisbee tag),
- A bike Olympics,
- An overnight bike trip, or
- A bicycle "weekend" centered around bike-related activities.

know the vast majority of campers come to both public and private campgrounds through word-of-mouth recommendations?) If you do offer competitive programs like horseshoe tournaments, trophy and athletic supply houses normally stock inexpensive ribbons for awards; you can buy these in quantity. Your logo can go on these, too. You can also, with a good word processor, printer and a little clip art, produce your own awards, like the one shown in Figure 9.55.

Cost. The issue of expense—the cost involved in providing campground activities—often seems to be a stumbling block in programming. "We'd like to provide programs, but the budget's too tight," is a frequent comment. Yet successful programming doesn't have to be tied to major outlays of funds. Consider two examples: bicycles and bingo. As we suggested earlier, many campers tend to bring bicycles with them. In addition to the bicycle skills program we mentioned in Chapter Six, you can center more than a dozen others around bikes, none of which requires much in the way of special facilities or equipment:

The cost of an inexpensive bingo game can provide all the support you need for an evening program popular enough to conduct two or three times a week. (Remember that campground populations "turn over" frequently.) One of the best and cheapest bingo games we've seen is grocery bingo. Prior to this event, post advertisements asking campers to attend and bring with them as an "entry fee" some item of food: a bottle of soda, can of beans, piece of fruit, or box of crackers. To begin the game, issue a bingo card in exchange for each food item, placing the collected goods on a table (Figure 9.23). The winner of each round then gets to select two or more food "prizes." We've seen a program like this run successfully for two hours with 50 participants. Once the game gets started, a volunteer camper can keep it going, allowing your program person to move on to conducting other programs. Conducted twice a week for 15 weeks, this would work out to 3,000 person hours of entertainment for a capital outlay of perhaps six or seven dollars. Expensive programming?

Building a complete inventory of program support equipment (games, sports equipment, arts and crafts supplies and the like) will require some funding, but there are ways of keeping costs low. Some expenses can be reduced by buying in quantity. Often you may also be able to find sporting-goods stores and other suppliers with factory seconds available; a blemished basketball will save you money and function perfectly well in a campground environment. Your agency or company may already have audiovisual equipment available for campfire movies and slide shows. Some programs such as a "trash scavenger hunt" don't need support equipment and can even save you money for ongoing maintenance tasks. Several years ago, before can manufacturers started producing ringless tabs, we attended a campground carnival where the "admission" for each of several programs was two pop-tops. The program collected seven large grocery bags of "fees." You should also consider developing cooperative agreements with local merchants. If Wilbur, Jr., wins a coupon for a double-dip cone at the Tastee Possum, the rest of the family may spend several dollars there. Local businesses benefit, your campers are happy, and you earn some positive public relations.

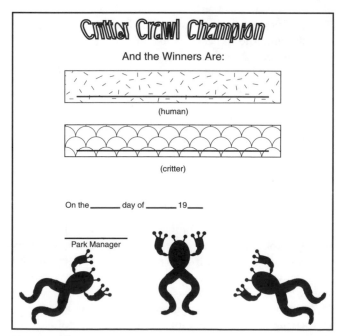

Figure 9.55

Sources of Programs. A creative friend of ours once programmed a campground alone for a summer. On many occasions, he had three or four activities running concurrently. He'd start contestants hunting for critters for a critter crawl, organize a softball game and a volleyball game with two poles and a rope for a net, begin a grocery bingo game and leave a willing camper in charge, and return in time to conduct the critter crawl. Enthusiasm? You bet. Buying a hat full of goodwill and eliminating depreciative behavior? You bet some more! It helps to have several people involved in programming, but there are ways of getting free support from several sources. "Cruising" for talent in your campground can produce a wealth of activities. Since programmers will spend considerable time with your camping population, they should continually look for campers with program talents and a willingness to perform or share their skills; an entire evening campfire program might be planned around a camper with a guitar. Often older campers also have skills such as whittling which appeal to campers young and old. When you do develop programs using the talents of your visitors, get their names and addresses to write them a letter of thanks on your letterhead stationery.

Other recreation agencies in your area may also have programs you can use. We once worked out an agreement with the superintendent of a nearby National Park Service park to conduct living-history programs in our campgrounds. The programs were well-received and they beckoned many of our campers to the NPS area where they originated. Churches and local civic organizations are other sources of activities at little or no cost. For example, local manufacturers of fishing or camping equipment are often more than willing to cosponsor demonstration programs. And special-interest groups such as bass clubs, archery clubs, or a parachute club are often willing to conduct demonstrations.

You can create successful programs with little more than a fertile imagination. For instance, you'd be surprised at the interest campers will have in a dog show. Dog-food companies have, at times, provided free kits with instructions, rules and ribbons. In fact, if you dig a bit, there are all types of "freebies" available to conduct all sorts of programs.

Staffing. Probably the least expensive means of providing programming personnel is working through college and university intern programs. While there are several ways of coordinating an intern program, we recommend the following procedures:

1. Each year, several months in advance of the camping season, you and your staff should determine the number of students needed and the various types of talents you want. The intent here is to provide each program area with a balanced mix of expertise. For example, if a campground has three intern positions, you might look for students with respective backgrounds in urban community centers and playgrounds, natural resources and interpretation, and skills certification. A spin-off benefit of this approach is the opportunity to let the students share their talents with coworkers, thus broadening the background

of each. By pairing students from different schools together, you can also expand the teaching experience the students receive. Hundreds of two- and four-year curricula across America include recreation. Many of these require their students to complete 8–18 week internship experiences in park settings.

2. After determining the required number of students and the talent you want, initiate the hiring process with university intern supervisors, or contact professors. We recommend against hiring students directly. By developing close working relationships with faculty, you make arrangements with individuals who will be more familiar than you with the potential and limitations of particular students. Faculty should also be familiar with university internship requirements, and once a professor knows you and your needs, he or she can match your requirements to specific students. Because of placement, early enrollment, competition for top students, and other considerations, it's important to start the hiring process well in advance of the use season.

If you hire students with backgrounds in recreation, it isn't difficult to teach them the actual programming techniques they need. Thus the most important qualities to seek in potential students are *enthusiasm* and *initiative*. These intangibles are often difficult to identify in a resume or a brief interview, which reinforces the need to establish a relationship with faculty representatives. We also recommend having a formal orientation to familiarize incoming intern students with your policies, goals, objectives, management practices, and particular programming approaches. Once they are oriented, students should be able to develop and conduct programs with minimal day-to-day supervision.

3. Once you select specific students, you should initiate a service contract with the university—not the student—that allows him or her to be employed by the school rather than your agency or company. From your standpoint, this simplifies procedural matters such as insurance and wage-and-tax reporting. It also formalizes the relationship between you and the school involved. With this arrangement, direct payment for services enables schools to handle student requirements according to their policies. A few schools do not allow students to be paid for an internship; others compute taxes and handle the payments as a salary, and still others treat the payment as a cost of living stipend and make few, if any, deductions.

Problems and Challenges

Consider the series of photographs shown in Figures 9.56 through 9.60. They depict some of the problems you may have with programming from the standpoint of trying to cope with the challenges planners and designers can cause you. Figure 9.56 shows an auto parked in a Forest Service parking lot in Indiana. The lot is adjacent to a campfire theater (you can see the screen for showing movies to the left of the car). Because of the placement of the parking lot relative to the

Figure 9.56

Figure 9.58

theater, the designer has caused the programmer to try to deal with serious headlight and noise problems during evening programs. As in many other cases, the designers simply neglected to think about the relationship between the support facility (the parking lot) and the program zone (the theater). In other words, the designer didn't attend to how the facility would function.

Figure 9.57 shows a shelter building in the center of a camp loop in a municipal campground in Alabama. Although the location seems, at first thought, to be convenient, the shelter placement causes environmental damage (people access the shelter from as many directions as there are individual campsites around the loop) and use conflicts (between people who want to relax in quiet on their campsites and those who want to attend programs and socialize).

Figure 9.58 shows a compounded program/design error at a LBL campground in Kentucky. Here, the designer—again without thought to function—zoned a shelter, a multipurpose play court and a campfire theater all together. Consider the difficulty of trying to program this zone for multiple groups with different interests at the same time. For example, it's a good idea to conduct evening court sports—basketball and volleyball—for teenagers at the same time you schedule a movie with appeal to young children and their parents; this technique separates users with diverse interests and keeps

everyone happy. (Fact is, we think conducting two to four programs at the same time is great—particularly during evening hours.) With the design shown here, the programmer simply can't meet this objective (believe us—the three authors have tried).

Figure 9.59 shows this same sort of dandy design dilemma at a Corps of Engineers area in Georgia. Here, the theater was located next to a tot lot and both are located on the main campground road across from a busy toilet/shower structure. Do you see any potential problems with this layout? The designer obviously didn't.

Planners and designers aren't programmers (most don't even have backgrounds in recreation). Few have the skills and/or the interest to provide proper locations for program features. Designers, planners, engineers, and architects (including landscape architects) should play a service role relative to programmers and managers. More often than not, though, they tell you where program and support features must go rather than asking how the users and program staff function. In fairness, these folks get to share the blame with programmers and managers for not demanding to be wrapped into the design process. Consider this analogy: If you decided to build a million dollar home (like we plan to do with the profits from revising this book), would you let the architect tell you you must put all your bedrooms off of the kitchen

Figure 9.57

Figure 9.59

or you have to have a combined living/dining room instead of separate rooms? We hope not. What you should expect is a set of alternative ideas, each complete with the cost and layout implications. With this information in hand, you can then make informed decisions about the best use of your resources. Why should your users expect anything different from you as a professional?

Another issue to keep in mind when developing campground programming zones and strategies is timing. Prime programming time in campgrounds is from around 8:00 P.M. until 11:00 P.M. Most casual (i.e., informal) recreation—swimming, fishing, sailing, sightseeing, and the like—occurs during the day. By mid-evening, most campers have finished with dinner and are prime candidates for something to occupy their time. This is when you should program intensively. We recently saw an example of *how not to do this* in a large private campground in Indiana. The area had a large recreation building, swimming pool, multipurpose play court, tennis courts, a large horseshoe complex, and more. The amenity area was zoned well away from most campsites. Sounds ideal, but there were two problems. One was lighting—or the lack of it—everywhere except the recreation building. This problem could be solved if it hadn't been for the second problem: attitude (strange in the for-profit sector). The evening we visited, they started a bingo game at 7:00 P.M. and finished at 7:30. There were no other programs offered that evening. It was early August and the campground was perhaps 40 percent occupied. When we asked why there weren't other programs, we got three answers. First, mind your own business (we hear that a lot); second, our campers don't have time for programs after dark; and third, our campers simply aren't interested in programs. To some extent, this last answer may be correct. What would be fun to find out, however, is whether the people who stay away from this campground might camp there if more programs were offered. A well-zoned and managed recreation program can beckon people who want programs without interfering with those who don't. To us, the issue is rather like the commercials for Mounds and Almond Joy; sometimes you feel like a nut, sometimes you don't. Point is, the candy company gets your business either way by offering you a choice. Seems to the authors there's a lesson here.

Another programming concern deals with what can happen if you embrace recreation programming and then, for whatever reason, move away from it. The following story illustrates this point and its potential for impact on visitation. Our story concerns the Kentucky State Parks system and Land Between the Lakes. In the early 1970s, Kentucky's state system was the nation's leader in campground programming. In fact, we stole some of our programming ideas for Land Between the Lakes from them. Our results and theirs were similar; at one point, we were providing upwards of 100 programs per week in each of our three large campgrounds, and use by family groups (including teens) in our areas and those managed by the state parks increased tremendously. One survey indicated nearly 90 percent of the teens of camping families had joined their parents in our campgrounds. Vandalism dropped considerably and revenues—especially during mid-

week when most campgrounds have more staff than visitors—were way up. Then . . . enter the politicians and environmental educators. The politicians got the state parks. They decided to eliminate the state office program staff and cut budgets in individual parks by getting rid of on-site programmers. Campground use dropped and—more significantly—changed from extended families and teens to older, childless couples and young parents who "force" their young children (preteens) to camp with them. In the early 1990s, Kentucky reintroduced fun programming into state parks. Since then, use figures have gradually begun to increase. This tells us three things. First, recreation programming attracts campers. Second, this attraction does not materialize overnight. Finally, if you stop fun programming you'll see a sharp drop in use and your clientele will change. Sophisticated (and expensive) marketing plans aside, we believe the best way to advertise your facilities is word of mouth. Campers know a good (or a bad) thing when they see it and tell their friends. Do it right and, eventually, users will find out about and find your campground.

At Land Between the Lakes it wasn't the politicians, but the environmental educators who zapped recreation programming. Some shifts in personnel and management responsibilities in the late 1970s resulted in recreation moving under the auspices of these folks. Within a short time, they had gone from 100-plus programs per week to fewer than 10, most of which were oriented toward environmental education. The results mirrored those in the Kentucky state parks: decreased usage coupled with increases in vandalism and other forms of depreciative behavior such as shown in Figure 9.60. The environmental indoctrinators still rule there with the same anticamping family results. Seems to us there's yet another lesson here.

Figure 9.60

Conclusions

A well-planned and conducted array of recreation programs in a campground is similar to a three-ring circus; campers choose from a variety of diversions to make their stay in your area more enjoyable. The key to successful programming is twofold, and the first critical element is the programmer.

Whether you use practicum students, seasonal employees, volunteers, or full-time staff, programmers must be enthusiastic, creative and imaginative. Support facilities and well-funded program budgets are nice to have, but the people responsible for programs and your supportive attitude, including careful and unannounced critiques, will ultimately determine the success of your activities. The second aspect necessary for good programs is an understanding that activities must build a bridge between the known and unknown. To many urban-oriented recreationists, camping is a somewhat unfamiliar, foreign, and perhaps frightening experience. If you want to beckon minorities and other "nonusers" that agencies would like to host but rarely entice, you can do so. By providing activities from municipal recreation settings that these users recognize and are comfortable with, and then carefully adding a *few* fun-flavored nature goodies, you can bridge the gap between the familiar and the unfamiliar. To us, failing to recognize the potential of fun-oriented recreation programs in outdoor recreation settings represents one of the biggest missed opportunities in the profession today. If you're serious about wanting all types of users—young and old; male and female; black, brown, red, yellow, and white; disabled and not; wealthy and poor; and the "unforgotten" majority of average campers—give fun programming a try. If you aren't interested in these folks, don't program; you'll still have the environmentalists, fishing parties, and good ol' boys. You'll also have empty units and depreciative behavior, but what else is new?

Hopefully, you won't miss the opportunity to program. Aside from the tips we've provided here, Woodall's (the camp-ground guide publisher) sells an excellent source of information about how to program in campgrounds with much more emphasis given to conducting programs, step-by-step instructions and necessary support materials. To give you a chance to try your creative hand at programming, here's an exercise for you. Haunted Hollow Campground is located in a large Western state park. The campground has a shelter building, beach, skills court, play court, playground, interpretive trail, archery range, fishing pier, lighted ball field, boat ramp, activity building, campfire theater, log cabin, horseshoe pits, boccie ball court, and hike 'n bike trail system. Your assignment is to plan a week-long activity calendar for the campground. You have three practicum students as programmers, each of whom needs two consecutive off days during the week (not on Fridays and Saturdays when use is heaviest). You should plan a broad spectrum of programs—some for all users and some for specific age groups—including as many as four concurrent programs for campers with varying interests. We've included a sample calendar as Appendix E, but you should also use the information in this chapter to develop a strategy for advertising that involves users and finds other program sources. You can assume you have a good inventory of support equipment. You can also assume you can do better than we did since we're just planners. (Interestingly enough one of the authors was once told by an assistant director of the Washington state park system that he had asked his campground users if they wanted fun programs and they didn't! Who's there, who isn't, and who do you want, are all questions they failed to answer or consider.)

Chapter Ten

Miscellaneous Goodies

Two of the monumental things we've learned in rewriting this book are it has taken far more time to do so and is much more difficult a task to accomplish than was the first edition. We should have known this as we do know it is much more difficult to redesign a park than it is to design a new one. Rather than months, the task consumed over three years. Some of this extra time was health related but most involved over *10 years* additional accumulation of knowledge, of concern for, and alarm about subjects. What to eliminate, what to revise, what new thoughts and concerns to add gave us quite a challenge.

The problem again was each of the previous chapters could have been much more lengthy than they turned out. Entire texts have been written about trails, or group camps, and certainly about programming. We could have written several more pages in both of the campground chapters (Chapters Seven and Eight). The twin difficulties we had were finding stopping points while at the same time giving you a foundation in the nuts and bolts of planning parks for people. The basic purpose of this chapter is to touch briefly on a few more of the many important topics related to planning, designing and programming functional and pleasing parks and recreation areas. As usual, our approach includes how to avoid some of the many pits and snake holes most of your predecessors (including the authors) have flopped into.

Chapter Ten topics will include multiple-use management as it relates (or doesn't relate) to recreation, signing dos and don'ts, pitfalls in planning parks for persons with disabilities, park safety, the rise and fall and flop of outdoor recreation research, carrying capacities and other wonderful ideas, customer service, and a few thoughts on maintenance.

Multiple-Use Management
(As It Relates to Outdoor Recreation)

Simply said, multiple-use management means the harmonious management of water, timber, wildlife, forage (grazing), and recreation resources on a wildland base. This *doesn't* mean all resources are or should be managed on all areas. At one time, multiple-use management referred to the U.S. Forest Service and the Congressional Multiple Use Act of 1960. On paper this act gave recreation the same legal status emphasis as the other major resources which it hadn't previously had. The problem was (and oftentimes still is) the majority of Forest Service foresters—untrained in people and recreation skills—never considered developed site recreation and the users it brought (particularly campers in wheeled vehicles) as

being too important. In the last three decades wilderness, winter sports, dispersed use, and the "wonders" of scenic resource management received considerable staff and budgetary emphasis while developed site use was actually deemphasized. (The *big* "new" Forest Service push to farm out as many developed sites to concessionaires is quite synonymous with their further disinterest.)

The authors believe multiple-use management of *renewable* resources is an excellent concept. Water, timber, forage, wildlife, and recreation *can* and *should be managed* for the benefit of all. (This, too, is not a popular concept with the "lock-it-all-up-for-me" environmentalists and their leaders—the environmental indoctrinators.)[4]

In our view multiple-use management requires: managing resources by allocating varying degrees of emphasis to recreation, forage (or range), wildlife, watershed, and timber. For example, a management plan might have recreation as a primary focus in a given resource base "unit" with a secondary emphasis on wildlife and watershed while allocating an adjacent unit primarily for timber with a subsidiary purpose of forage.

Various textbooks focus on the "hows" of this aspect of resource management. Here we want to consider a second implication of the concept: *resource coordination.* By this we mean opportunities and shortcomings in planning and administration techniques to ensure that all components receive equitable emphasis in management plans. Note we didn't say *equal* emphasis. Some resources, because of unsuitability or the need to stress other aspects of multiple-use management, shouldn't focus on recreation. Since this is a text about recreation, let's start by using this aspect of multiple-use management to demonstrate the need for a *comprehensive* approach to allocating resources.

Recreation

One of the underlying concepts we've tried to stress throughout this book is the need to plan and manage recreation resources to meet the needs of *all* users—from the backpacker

---

[4]At the writing of this chapter the Multiple Use Act of 1960 and the once viable multiple-use concept hangs in the Forest Service by a thread. Games played by the environmentalists, wilderness advocates and considerable attempts at appeasement by the Forest Service have stalled and, in many places, stopped wise management of natural resources including most forms of recreation on the 200-million acres once called "lands of many uses." They are now "lands of mini-uses!"

to the RV camper. An extension of this approach should be the philosophical basis for multiple-use management: using resources to meet the needs of the entire *community* of plants, animals, *and* people. Aldo Leopold probably stated the case most eloquently in *A Sand County Almanac* when he spoke of the land ethic. Our concern, limited here to the topic of recreation, is for what we feel is a failure on the part of resource managers to consider the spectrum of recreationists. Perhaps a more basic problem is what we feel is the cause of this failure: Far too many outdoor recreation professionals aren't "people persons." Fact is, they aren't recreation professionals!

To demonstrate this point, consider the following story. We once represented TVA at a meeting to discuss the recreational use of a whitewater river that was also being used to produce hydroelectric power. Participants at the meeting included staff from two federal agencies, several state offices, commercial rafting outfitters, and river users. After driving for two hours to reach the town where the meeting was to be held, we had dinner with the TVA representative who was to chair the meeting. We finished our meal 10 minutes *before* the 7:00 P.M. meeting time, yet the person in charge of the meeting sat and drank coffee until 7:15. When we suggested leaving the restaurant, his response was, "Hell, they can't start without me—I'm running the show."

We aren't suggesting this is a typical occurrence, but it does point out the distinction between a public servant and a slob, it does speak to the issue of professionalism, and it does demonstrate the lack of sensitivity, in an extreme case, some recreation "professionals" have for the need to work *for* and *with* people.

Although this insensitivity rarely occurs in such a direct fashion, we feel outdoor recreation today often suffers from an undercurrent of the same attitude responsible for the behavior of the person in our story. Such behavior can negatively affect users several ways. For example, in Chapter One we suggested outdoor recreation professionals need to be concerned with people and the environment. In looking at the situation in outdoor recreation today, we feel concern for the *environment* has been confused with violent reaction to environmental rhetoric.

This is a difficult point to make, because it seems to imply that the authors are antienvironmental and we aren't. Simply put, we feel the management direction most resource-based recreation agencies take today stresses environmentally oriented use or no use *at the expense of neglecting the needs of users interested in many forms of recreation.* The problem with this approach occurs because, quite frankly, the majority of people who recreate in the out-of-doors simply aren't the users at whom this environmental emphasis is directed. Our "community" of outdoor recreationists is made up in large part of people who don't want to "rough it," yet our allocation of resources, both fiscal and physical, emphasizes wilderness use. This strikes us as being an inequitable distribution of resources which, aside from failing to address the needs of all users, causes considerable harm to the public relations of the agencies involved. We will have more to say in Chapter Eleven about wilderness emphasis and the harm done to users and developed site recreation.

Particularly in times when social programs receive less governmental emphasis, those public agencies involved in service delivery must address the interests of all segments of the population. To fulfill their purpose effectively, we think public recreation agencies, particularly those with a resource emphasis, *must* develop goals and objectives with a stronger social orientation. The planning process should begin with people—what sort of users do we want? Agency personnel need to understand the demographics of outdoor recreation and the social forces and motivations leading to recreation behavior. The mission of public recreation should be to help people have fun and to meet the demands of all users—minorities, the aged, the disabled, and the "forgotten majority" of mainstream recreationists as well as those with a preference for backcountry camping. This is what we mean by an equitable distribution of resources focusing on a broad spectrum of people.

Accomplishing this mission requires a coordination of resources to ensure we take into account all members of the outdoor recreation community. If reading this book does nothing else than motivate you to ask all sorts of questions as you visit parks, then we will feel greatly rewarded. Ask national forest, state park, national park, and other park personnel to describe their recreation mission to you. If they haven't included fun programming and have few teens in their parks; if they've failed to host senior citizens who need refrigerated medicine by not providing electrical hookups; if they've ignored "mainstream" campers and persons with disabilities by overemphasizing wilderness use; if they're eliminating camping facilities because of "overuse;" if they're placing their areas under concessionaires; or if they've conveniently "forgotten" certain legitimate recreation pursuits like off-road riding, ask *why*. Your question may make resource-oriented professionals think—some, perhaps, for the first time ever! Expanding on this theme of resource coordination, let's briefly consider the other components of multiple-use management.

Forage

Just as efforts *within* recreation need to be coordinated to provide a judicious approach to service delivery, planners and managers need to balance strategies *between* recreation and other components of multiple-use management. To illustrate this point, consider the situation Figure 10.1 depicts. In this example, the TVA planned a beach at point B on our drawing. From a *recreation standpoint* only, point B might have been an acceptable location for a beach.

Thinking back to the chapter on day-use areas, you could assess this location from such perspectives as slope, erosion potential, safety, water quality, and adjacent recreation use zones. If all these factors "check out," however, you still would need to consider other aspects of multiple-use management. In this case, the critical factors were watershed, pollution, and forage. As it turned out, point B was unacceptable, although TVA actually planned the beach at that location, because: (1) point B was at the base of a watershed, where surface water drained into the lake; and (2) point A at the upper end of the

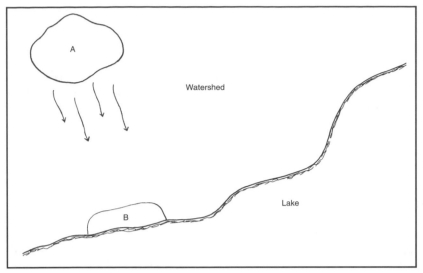

Figure 10.1

Figure 10.2

watershed in Figure 10.1 happened to be a hog lot and feeding area. All quite bare and eroded (Figure 10.2).

In many areas of the western United States, ranchers have grazing allotments on public lands. While we realize there is some controversy about this, we believe grazing to be a viable use of most public lands *if* it is monitored and carefully regulated. However longhorns, campgrounds, and campers aren't compatible, so for visitor health and safety purposes, recreation areas in open range lands should be enclosed with suitable fencing and cattle guards. Figure 10.3 shows an entrance sign inside of a fenced BLM recreation area in western Arizona.

Wildlife

If individuals, agencies, and corporations involved in multiple-use management practice resource coordination, the results can benefit more than one activity. For example, fishing is a wildlife-management opportunity valuable from a recreational perspective as well. Building fish attractors can enhance the fish population in a lake and may increase potential

angling (remember Figure 9.41). Yet in our experience, we've found wildlife-management efforts that benefit recreation are too often *incidental* and quite often accidental. Fish attractors may enhance fishing, but rarely have we seen efforts to place them coordinated with recreation planners, managers or programmers. This problem stems from the tendency of most resource-oriented professionals, particularly wildlife biologists, to be arrogant toward recreation, though notable exceptions exist. We've seen this attitude create problems and limit opportunities for recreation staff time and time again. Consider our example of fish attractors. If fisheries or wildlife staff fail to coordinate placement of these with recreational personnel, a missed opportunity may result. Hypothetically, a fisheries biologist might have two locations—A and B—acceptable for an attractor. If the biologist places it at point A when point B is adjacent to a stretch of shoreline with excellent potential for a fishing pier in a group camp, what happens? The fisheries program reaps the same benefit in either case, but an enhanced recreation program falls by the wayside.

Recreation professionals must understand yet another idea when dealing with most resource-trained folks: The belief that users, if they are of any value, visit our nation's wildland parks either to hunt or to fish. Further, many resource people believe any camping associated with hunting or fishing is acceptable *but* that it's inconceivable people would want to camp for fun or a social vacation with fishing as a small bonus. These kinds of less-than-desirable city dwellers should "stay away from *my* forest, *my* lakes, and *my* streams," the resource people imply. (See Chapter Eight for the good guy–bad guy explanation of this issue.)

We aren't suggesting the resource professional *purposely* takes steps to limit potential recreation, but failures to coordinate efforts with others whose work may be affected by their decisions is still a breech of professionalism. The resource arrogance we're discussing may be a matter of perspective. Unfortunately, some of these professionals tend to view their work as "hard science" when compared to the "soft science"

Figure 10.3

of people-oriented disciplines such as recreation. In one sense, the point is well-taken. Generally the physical sciences, which include resource disciplines, are more exact than the social sciences. If we introduce a given quantity of the pesticide rotenone into a lake embayment, we can predict with some accuracy the resulting fishkill percentage. Conversely, if we superimpose water skiing on a lake previously limited to fishing, it's much more difficult to predict the social implications (though as ardent fans of fishing we know who will be quite unhappy). Although recreation, because of this element of uncertainty, may be more challenging, it is in an absolute sense a "softer" science.

When resource professionals adopt the attitude that, "We're scientists, and recreation workers are baby-sitters," we still have a problem. We once drew up plans for a campground at Land Between the Lakes which was to have been built several years in the future. Part of the proposed campground had once been farmed thus there were several acres of grass and weed covered ground. The plan anticipated a five-year growth on several young trees and shrubs which, by the time the campground was built, would have provided shade and screening for camp units. In order to get the benefit of public involvement and to save the taxpayers (that's you) a bit of money, we purchased several hundred inexpensive small hardwood trees and worked with a group of volunteers from the National Campers and Hikers Association to plant them. (We can tell you this wasn't the "normal" way TVA did things!) Wildlife staff had been informed of the planting and knew this work had been done but were not pleased recreation was interested (at some future time) in building a sizable campground in one of *their* areas.

The following year wildlife staff had the area bush-hogged as part of a wildlife "enhancement" program for the good ol' boys. The young seedlings planted by the large camping club were all cut off at ground level. The wildlife staff *and* upper management were quite amused by our reaction, and didn't even understand why we and the camping group were angry over their actions. Shortly after this interesting bit of sanctioned "coordination" occurred, outdoor recreation was deemphasized there, recreation staff was cut by half, fun programs by 70 percent, and a bit later wildlife staff took over recreation at Land Between the Lakes. Later recreation was turned over to the environmental educators! (Cutting the budget because of fund shortages wasn't a part of the problem.) TVA's initial promises that LBL would be quickly built to ultimately beckon 10-million visitors per year and thus have a tremendous economic impact in the region were broken at this time. Coordination is oftentimes a difficult challenge. We hope your efforts to work with others aren't as difficult as the unique challenges we once faced. (When pigs fly is also when we expect the bush-hogged campground to be built!)

Resource coordination is a necessity in successful multiple-use management. Wildlife watering holes and woods openings that create the "edge effect" beneficial to wildlife can, if well-placed, enhance the aesthetics of roads and trails traveled by recreationists. Cover plantings of shrubs and co-

niferous trees for deer and upland game birds can provide screening helpful in separating conflicting recreation zones. Salt licks can aid wildlife as well as serve as observation points for people interested in viewing animals. These examples and other wildlife management techniques can be useful from a recreation perspective if they are coordinated with the appropriate staff. In fairness, recreation developments created in a vacuum can be harmful to wildlife management. You owe it to coworkers to keep them informed of your plans; you should expect the same in return.

Watershed

Watershed management can affect recreation in a variety of ways. We've already discussed the potential for erosion and siltation around beaches, other waterfront zones, trails, campsites, and play amenities if planners ignore preventative maintenance measures. However, let's dig a little deeper and explore other water-related concerns planners must consider relative to recreation. In general, water can be harmful to recreation when there is too much of it *or* not enough. Typically, we tend to recognize the former problem more frequently since the results of erosion, siltation, and facility damage are usually quite evident.

Often, however, the problem of too much water isn't solved as readily as it should be. In many cases this seems to result from planners' *reluctance* to cope with the situation. In most instances the solution to too much water is channelization: altering the land base to provide drainage patterns compatible with recreation development. Figure 10.4 shows some minor drainage routing or channelization around and between two campsites which were being renovated. (We did this one.) Figure 10.5 shows a far more sophisticated—excellent—watershed or water movement strategy at the edge of two buddy campsites at a U.S. Army campground at Tennessee's Fort Campbell. The campsite table at the upper part of the photo is two feet in elevation below the camp loop road at the bottom of the photo. Since drainage from 20 percent of the campground came in this direction, recreation folks there designed a rock sump/energy-dissipating water collection area near the road, added a paved ditch with a curved and

Figure 10.4

Figure 10.5

raised retaining wall (which also served as a seating area for the campsite), and placed another cluster of energy-dissipating larger rock below the paved ditch. (Professionalism in the U.S. Army was one of the bright spots in the federal recreation sector in the 1980s.)

Here's an axiom of design for you: *Directing water runoff where you need it to go in parks is not a sin against nature.* If you make a decision to develop a given resource base for recreation, you've already committed to changing the site environment. (The same would be true of implementing a program of cover plantings for wildlife.) The challenge is to make the changes in ways not harmful to resources.

Channelization (ditching) has suffered in some cases because self-styled environmentalists have criticized the practice. Ditching does alter the landscape, but if a potential for damage or a site design problem exists without it, the technique is a positive measure. The point to remember is more often than not, people sincerely concerned with environmental protection will make judgments based on personal opinions and superficial appearances rather than professional knowledge. Part of professionalism is living with criticism when you know your decisions are based on accepted management techniques, one of which is channeling water runoff to prevent damage. We remember a situation in Kentucky where a local judge criticized a mowing program *because he said it was harming wildlife.* The purpose of the mowing was to create the edge environment necessary for wildlife, yet the criticism originated entirely from a position of resource management ignorance, resulted in negative public relations for the agency involved, and slowed the mowing program which, ironically and tragically, affected wildlife negatively.

Picnic shelters and other roofed structures in our parks are also small watersheds. Gutters and downspouts work well for some of these buildings while for others rock sumps from the paved floor out beyond the drip line will do the job (Figure 10.6). Where we don't cope with the potential "blasting" effects of water running off roofs we find mud holes, lots of bare soil, erosion, and a less than good experience for users. Have a close look at shelter zones in parks near you and see if we're right or wrong. Paving of ditches along roads is another good practice as is the location of berms and

sodded ditches to move water around facilities like campfire theaters, ball fields and play courts (Figures 10.7 and 10.8).

A second and often less evident problem with recreational water is a lack of it. To demonstrate this point, consider the following two examples. During the planning stage of a living-history complex at LBL in Tennessee, interpretive staff (the same folks who, in Chapter Three,

Figure 10.6

"planned" the Blue-Gray Trail) decided to designate a spring near the reconstructed homestead as the focal point of the interpretive zone. The spring had a history of heavy to moderate flow but within two years after the living-history farm

Figure 10.7

Figure 10.8

was opened to the public, the spring went dry. Water then had to be piped in at considerable cost to make the now fake spring *spring* (so to speak). What the interpretive staff didn't understand was how the once lightly shaded and grassy hillside above the spring was now covered with brush and larger trees. This problem was the result of a phenomenon known as *evapotransporation*. The heavy tree cover on the ridge literally pumped the available water out of the watershed serving the spring. The mistake was a failure to recognize the effect watershed and timber considerations can have on recreation developments. Removing some of the trees and brush would have helped.

Our second example takes us to a campground and beach area on a human-made lake in the Jefferson National Forest in West Virginia. Here, as elsewhere, ponds and lakes need a sizable watershed behind them feeding a year-round flowing stream in order to provide an adequate water supply for the lake during the hotter months of the year. In this instance the lake water, including the swimming area at a beach, became stagnant since evaporation and evapotransporation combined to reduce the inflow of water from the watershed to the beach zone. In fact, there was no summer inflow. The answer here was to have a timber sale in the headwaters of the lake and remove most of the larger trees. Watershed experiments have shown this would add thousands of gallons per acre per year of extra water to this lake each year. This sort of challenge occurs nationwide without a realization of why by most recreation professionals. Add to this lack of knowledge on the part of the professionals the common environmentalist's cry to do nothing to this "wilderness" of *second growth trees* (catch the irony here?) and we have *recreational/watershed* shooting-your-own-foot problems aplenty!

Next, consider a situation in which attention to resource coordination and watershed considerations can enhance recreation and other components of multiple-use management, in this case, fisheries. Figure 10.9 shows two ponds created by damming two points along a stream. If our objective is to enhance both recreation use and fisheries, we could devote pond A to recreation, and implement fisheries management techniques, including fertilization, on pond B. This approach would work if the water in the stream remained clean and clear at all times. If water quality and siltation, however, were problems, a solution would be to add a third pond as shown in Figure 10.10. Here, pond A serves as a *filter* in which sediments will settle. Pond B, for recreation, will now have a higher water quality, and pond C can be intensively managed for fisheries, which require a heavy fertilization and dark green water. The critical element in this approach is understanding the interrelationships among the components of multiple-use management and *coordinating* them in a comprehensive way.

Both ponds A and B in Figure 10.10 would have some fishing capability—particularly if fishing piers (earthen and other) and fish attractors

were used. We have seen a two-pond scenario where extensive fisheries work was being conducted (green algae and all that good stuff) on the *upper* lake meaning overflow into the downstream recreation lake causes serious problems there. This and similar instances like it in resource coordination mean as a recreation professional you have to know enough about management of water, timber, wildlife, and grazing resources *or* those resource rascals will have a delightful time rolling over the top of you and us! Fact is, even if you do have some expertise in other resource activities you likely won't escape the flattening.

Timber

Outdoor recreation without trees would be like, as the song goes, a day without sunshine. Trees provide parks with shade, cooling, screening, interpretive opportunities, erosion control, food and homes for wildlife, and aesthetic value. They also exemplify the complexity involved in coordinating resources in multiple-use management. Consider just one species: the scarlet oak. It provides a heavy mast crop (acorns or food) for wildlife; it's a fast-growing tree and, while not particularly useful for lumber, it produces a good cubic volume for pulpwood so foresters like it; it has good fall color and is a well-formed tree. But when it comes to intensive recreation development, it is a poor tree indeed! The scarlet oak is quite shallow rooted, which means it won't stand up under the impact associated with intensive recreation use. On the other hand, it makes an aesthetically pleasing "background" tree with a beautiful dark red color in the fall when removed from zones where people and vehicles will circulate. Thus, planners need to know about and balance several factors with respect to *only the scarlet oak:* where intensive use zones will be; which trees can be left to avoid unnecessary cutting; and which trees should be cut prior to construction to avoid maintenance problems and potential hazards later on. (What do you know about all the other trees you'll encounter?)

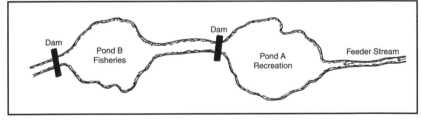

Figure 10.9

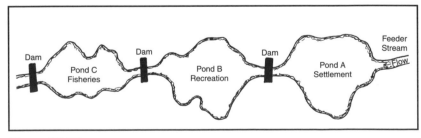

Figure 10.10

This last issue—preconstruction thinning—can be a problem in itself. Planners worldwide are often reluctant to cut trees for recreation development. While you shouldn't cut trees indiscriminately, you should learn when it is appropriate to cut and do so. To complicate matters, there is no standard or simple answer we can give you. As an example, think about the Douglas fir for a moment. If you happen to be working in the Rocky Mountain section of the country, the Douglas fir is considerably shorter and stockier than its relatives to the west, and, in general, it isn't a bad tree for recreation. In the far Pacific Northwest, however, the taller, more slender version of the tree causes planners problems. Western Douglas firs, which are also shallow rooted, depend on the branches of adjacent trees for support. When you thin a stand for recreation development, taking away the fir's support, it becomes susceptible to wind damage. Thus, part of understanding the relationship between the timber and recreation components of multiple-use management is knowing when not to cut, when to cut quite heavily, and when to keep intensive use areas out of certain stands of trees.

In the West, planners often build campgrounds and other recreation areas in groves of aspen. Since aspen is a rather short-lived species with a low tolerance for people and impact, these areas often end up without trees. In general, old-growth or mature trees don't withstand impact as well as young, vigorous ones, and this raises two points. First, you need to know which trees and species to leave and which to cut. Second—and this is critical—resource management practices, including timber thinning and new plantings, need your attention *several years* in advance of actual development. This aspect of design points directly to the need for long-range master planning. Strangely enough, we've found that foresters who make a living harvesting timber are almost as reluctant as environmentalists with regard to cutting trees in *park* areas.

Recreation planning and management aren't just "now" activities. They both require *advance work* in the form of master planning and foresight in the form of discovering the *future implications* of designs you implement. If you don't plant in advance, you may have to live without shade and screening and adequate revenues when you open an area. If you don't consider the implications of your design relative to impact, you may have to live without shade and screening a few years after you open an area. Since this isn't a text on master planning or resource management, we'll leave these topics at this point. The important element for you to remember is recreation doesn't and can't exist in a vacuum. You may have a personal and professional bias toward the importance of recreation, but downplaying the importance of the other components of multiple-use management can result in problems we'd rather not have to face. One final sobering thought: Even if other resource personnel (foresters, biologists, and wildlife specialists) are eager to work carefully with you, *don't assume* they have the recreation-flavored skills to do so! For instance, foresters likely won't know about shade and screening factors, or why large trees are problems, or which tree species will best withstand use pressures. Know-

ing these sideboards and dozens of others is all part of being a real outdoor recreation professional and a planner of quality parks for people.

Forage, wildlife, watershed, timber, and recreation, as we've considered them in this chapter, are rarely easy to interrelate. It would be helpful to us all if *coordination* were a required course in resource and recreation curricula. The elements of multiple-use management often conflict with each other, but they can also coexist as long as managers make *informed* judgments about how to allocate resources equitably. Perhaps the "saving grace" of multiple-use management is the potential for and the solutions to most problems are for the most part tangible. If you know, for example, that white pine is a shallow-rooted species, you can avoid a headache by coping with it through design and preconstruction cuts. The really difficult problems in recreation, as in life, are the intangible ones. We will discuss several of these in Chapter Eleven.

Signing

Earlier in the text you read about possible problems resulting from the buildup of gases, oils, and waxes on parking lots. This was potential *physical* pollution about which recreation planners should be concerned. Signing in parks can cause another type of pollution, too, one that is *psychological* and often harder to correct because it is less apparent. We've seen sign pollution in the city (Figure 10.11); sign pollution on the way to the park (Figure 10.12); and sign pollution in the park itself (Figure 10.13). (This is an example of attempting to administer small areas by too much signing and not enough personnel; you by now should be aware of our advice on this challenge.) One of the biggest problems with poor signing in recreation areas is once someone installs a sign it seems to take an act of Congress (or an act of vandalism) to take it down. Since signs cost big bucks, there seems to be a tendency on the part of park managers to leave them in place. Thus, as is the case with other planning decisions, you should ask yourself whether or not a sign is necessary in the first place.

You need signs in parks to *inform, instruct,* and *warn* visitors. A well-designed sign can enhance user convenience as long as you remember three concerns. First, signs should

Figure 10.11

Figure 10.12

Figure 10.13

support a visual experience rather than *dominate* it. Second, an overdependence on signs may point to a more basic problem of poor design. If an area is confusing in terms of circulation, for example chances are good that signs will multiply like rabbits. Another author axiom is if a park is difficult to sign it is likely to be poorly designed. Finally, if you don't need a sign, don't install it. This last point may seem to be overstating the obvious, but many signing mistakes result from precisely this problem. Did you know, for instance, what the purpose of the support facility in Figure 10.14 was *before* you read the accompanying sign?

Figure 10.14

Admittedly there may be instances when some seemingly evident situations require signing, as in some primitive parks where you need to warn visitors about water unsafe for drinking. Again, however, we must ask if you knew the purpose of the container in Figure 10.15 without having to read the sign. Humorous, yes; expensive, yes; necessary, no. It is another one of these instances where it was done that way, because that's the way it's always been done. While it's unfortunate, signing is occasionally necessary to remind visitors of the obvious. Such is the case with no-litter signs in parks like the one in the picnic area in Figure 10.16. Do you think, however, that the planner needed to go to the lengths shown in an expanded view of this area in Figure 10.17? The antilitter signs once littered every picnic site in this Ohio rest area! Signing mistakes fill a continuum from obvious errors to subconscious problems. To illustrate this point, let's consider a few of these.

Figure 10.15

Figure 10.16

Spelling

People who work in recreation have different types and levels of intelligence. We've known maintenance workers barely able to read who could rebuild an engine without having to think about it. Closer to home, two of the authors are excellent spellers while the third has "consederabble" spelling problems! Thus, while it seems unlikely, it's not impossible to

Figure 10.17

find signing errors resulting from someone's inability to spell, as in Figure 10.18. The important point illustrated here is the need to pay *close attention to detail.* If you assume something will be done correctly just because *you* know how to do it, the results can be embarrassing. In recreation planning, *never take anything for granted.*

At times, human nature being what it is, people have a tendency to *see what they expect to see.* If you've ever proofread a term paper half a dozen times and then had someone point out a typing error, you'll know what we mean. After taking the picture of the sign in Figure 10.19, we asked the

Figure 10.18

Figure 10.19

ranger accompanying us how long it had been in place. It turned out the sign had been installed three years earlier and that no one had noticed the misspelled word. People—users and management alike—saw the word "scenic" because it was what they *expected* to see. The same thing is true with the sign in Figure 10.20. Normally there is a "k" in the word picnicking but not here in this Georgia State Park. It wasn't a recently installed sign!

In addition to paying attention to detail, you need to train yourself to look for problems and head them of at the the pass. (We assume you saw the incorrect spelling of the word

Figure 10.20

"off," but did you catch the double "the" as well?) Years ago, one of the authors had signing of a 14-state U.S. Forest Service region and technical direction of the region's sign making shop as his major assignment. Shop personnel had a history of producing quality signs. One day during a shop visit he asked the shop foreman if his crew had ever made a mistrake on a big expensive routed wooden sign. An indignant, *"Never,"* was the foreman's answer. As luck would have it later the same morning the author found a large, finished, ready-to-be-shipped wooden sign with "Garden's Bluff Campground" routed in large letters on both sides. Unfortunately for the foreman, the author knew the campground (a poorly designed one) was Cardens Bluff not Garden's Bluff—for it seems the author had designed the area! "Something must be wrong with the order form!" said the foreman. No, it was "Cardens" on the order form—they had *read* and *routed wrongly!* The embarrassed crew likely made *another* deposit to the handy, fuel-gobbling wood stove where we suspect other similar goodies had found a safe home. The point is, making mistakes is common practice with anyone who does anything in the work realm or, in fact, the act of living from day to day. The sign foreman's nonacceptance of his making mistakes was a shock to the author. Such nonacceptance, or blaming *our* errors on something *or* someone else *or* on circumstances is another of those *big* problems we face today. *Being a real park professional means accepting responsibility for what you do.* Obviously this is also a piece of the integrity/honesty dilemma which is under attack today. More on this later.

Readability

In addition to conveying correctly spelled information, signs in recreation areas must be *legible*. Therefore the size of the lettering you use is a consideration, particularly as it relates to *distance* and *scale of motion*. Signs placed a few feet away from a trail to reduce incidental damage must have lettering large enough to read. Lettering on signs you expect people to see from a car traveling at 45 miles per hour should be larger than lettering read from a stationary position. The type of sign you use can have a positive or negative effect on legibility as well. For example, the slat sign in Figure 10.21 is quite difficult to read because you have a tendency to try and focus on both the foreground—the sign itself—and the background visible between the slats.

When installing a sign, you need to consider not only how legible it is now but how easy it will be to read *later*. For instance, you could argue the problem in Figure 10.22 was caused by poor maintenance, and our response would be that better maintenance would have cured the *effects* of the problem. The *cause,* however, can be attributed to poor signing techniques since sign installations must be high enough to *prevent* problems like this from occurring in the first place. As we've tried to point out to you on other occasions, design decisions are always a matter of *balance:* too much balanced

with not enough; too expensive with too cheap; and, in this case, too low with too high. You *should* place signs high enough to keep weeds from obscuring them in the future. Poor maintenance can cause readability problems. Did you see the pine limb growing over the important messages on the sizable flag-draped entrance sign in Figure 10.23? The USCOE park employee who drove us into the area hadn't seen the limbs, yet you are looking at two to three years of growth.

While readability can be influenced by physical factors like sign height, psychological considerations play a part as well. When we discussed displays in visitor centers, we suggested a good rule of thumb for message length was a maximum reading time of 20 seconds. This holds true for most signing situations. One of the most popular attractions at TVA's Land Between the Lakes is a buffalo range. When we worked there, we *rarely* saw anyone take the time to read the sign in Figure 10.24. Now contrast the message in Figure 10.24 with the one in Figure 10.25. From a psychological perspective, which would you be more likely to read? Neither topic was likely to attract many visitors, yet the Forest Service sign was well-done; the TVA sign wasn't. (It, too, was designed by the folks responsible for the Blue-Gray Trail!) Remember, in order for people to *learn* from your signs, they have to read them. It makes more sense to tell folks two or three things and have them remember one or two than to try

Figure 10.21

Figure 10.23

Figure 10.22

Figure 10.24

Figure 10.25

and tell them 20 things and "turn them off" to reading anything at all.

Sign Psychology

Signs are not simply signs. They are part of an environment visitors perceive when they use parks and recreation areas. As a result, you need to go beyond limiting your attention to signs themselves and think about sign *placement*. For example, the directional sign in Figure 10.26 is perfectly *functional*. Directly and simplistically it conveys the information users need. However, what does the environment in which the sign is placed *say* to users, from a psychological perspective, about the recreational experience awaiting them? The dumpster or the sign needs to be moved. Contrast the majestic sign environment in Figure 10.27 with the less than majestic setting in Figure 10.26. Which would you prefer?

The *shape* of signs can have a positive or a negative effect as well. The best example of the positive effects we've seen is the sign (Figure 10.28) you'll see at the entrance to most Idaho state parks. It also "speaks to" the value of "expectability" or recognizability. While it's physically possible to frame a square sign, the psychological effect on viewers is quite negative. Your eyes have a tendency to look for *dominance* in what you see, and a rectangular sign like the one in Figure 10.29 lets you perceive either a vertical or a horizontal dominance, depending on which way the sign is oriented. A square sign appears to be out of balance because there is no dominant direction for your eyes to follow.

Even when information on signs doesn't conflict with other messages the results can be puzzling to the public. Consider the message on the sign in Figure 10.30. How can you launch your boat if you have to stay clear of the ramp? One of the more interesting signs with confusing messages is shown in Figure 10.31. While we think park folks there knew what they wanted to say, we couldn't figure it all out. Likely though, our lack of smarts

Figure 10.27

Figure 10.28

Figure 10.26

Figure 10.29

Figure 10.30

Figure 10.33

Figure 10.31

caused our sign problem. Avoid signs with incongruous meanings. Even when the message on a sign isn't confusing, the impact can be negative. For example, what kind of a mental picture do you get of the gardens in Figure 10.32?

The gardens' sign also points out another common problem; in this case, adding a slat with a different color to the first one. We've seen posts with as many as four or five color, size and shape variations. We call this garbaging. Another common form of garbaging is shown in Figure 10.33. We

Figure 10.32

doubt the need for, or the desirability of, the grocery and restaurant slat and question the discordant guide service addition to a sizable and expensive private resort sign. Your major entrance sign shouldn't be littered with other signs heralding the purchase possibility of worms, propane, or even turnips! (We saw the big sign again recently and the Guide Service garbaging is no more.) Note the dandy signs in Figures 10.30 and 10.31 have bits of unreadable garbaging, too.

Sign messages like those on bulletin boards can impart the warm fuzzies to users or can make them unhappy with the park and you. The "No washing of anything" sign (Figure 10.34) is a good example: "All I wanted to do was wash my little girl's hands." Not all signing errors result from too much verbiage or too many sign installations. Sometimes "not enough" can be a culprit as well. Consider the blank back of the sign in Figure 10.35. Essentially, this is wasted space. Sign installations are expensive and too many of them tend to clutter the environment, so you can reduce costs and minimize the number of sign installations you need by taking advantage of both sides of signs like this one. Since the road appears to lead into the darkness of the "Black Forest" (we've visited The Black Forest), why not proclaim "Big Foot is here [or near] and waiting for you" in big letters on the blank sign? (Facetious? *Yes!* Do something positive with a blank sign like this one!) The sign back in Figure 10.36 contributes to both a good use of the installation

Figure 10.34

Figure 10.35

Figure 10.38

Figure 10.36

Figure 10.39

and your efforts to have visitors experience a positive feeling about your area.

One of the most frequent signing mistakes we see results from designers assuming every sign needs a sign post. The camp unit number sign in Figure 10.37 may be necessary from a management perspective; the sign *post* isn't. Figure 10.38 shows an alternative solution if your campsites are electrified: place the unit number sign on the electrical outlet post. If this isn't a possibility, try the solution in Figure 10.39. Put

the unit number on the side of the picnic table (which we recommend be portable, unlike the one shown) facing the loop road. Make sure your camp unit number signs aren't located where campers have even the *remotest* opportunity to run over them. Also don't tack the numbers to the campsite trees. Sign installations can be minimized further by *stenciling* information directly on paved roads or trails, as Figure 10.40 demonstrates. If sign posts are necessary, and the information isn't conflicting or confusing, it's possible to reduce the number of

Figure 10.37

Figure 10.40

installations by *stacking* several signs on the same post as in Figure 10.41. We advise you to combine these into one metal sign as shown here rather than four individual signs. This installation also demonstrates the best way we know to reduce verbiage: using *symbols.* Consider the sign in Figure 10.42. There isn't any wording at all, yet the message should be clear to anyone.

In an earlier chapter we discussed the importance of *lines, forms, textures,* and *colors* in

Figure 10.41

recreation design, which you can use quite effectively in signing parks. Figure 10.43 shows an excellent application of line in signing. The linear shape of the sign reinforces the line of the message contained on it. Similarly, the *form* of the sign in Figure 10.44 is aesthetically pleasing and conjures up an image of the physical resource to which it refers. The sign

in Figure 10.45 carries this technique a step further. Here the sign installation reinforces the form of the sign. In Figure 10.46 the sign makes good use of *texture,* giving the message a sense of depth. You can clarify information on signs by using color as well. Colors contrast effectively and make the message as well as the sign attractive. As a final sign, the authors have chosen what we think is another attractive entrance sign at Vernon L. Richards Riverbend Park—one of the Lower Colorado River Authority's areas in Texas (Figure 10.47).

Figure 10.44

Figure 10.42

Figure 10.45

Figure 10.43

Figure 10.46

Figure 10.47

Pitfalls in Planning Parks for Persons With Disabilities

The Americans with Disabilities Act (ADA) of 1990 set the stage for all sorts of happenings, many good and some not so good. Pounds of "how-to" books, guidelines, regulations, and suggestions are available to you from numerous sources. Consultants, too, have popped up like toadstools in a freshly mown lawn to share their "vast knowledge" with all of us (for nominal fees, of course). As usual, our contribution to all this confusing knowledge comes from the mistakes realm; some from things we did sincerely but poorly.

The authors are not therapeutic recreation specialists or teachers of this subject. We have worked with and hosted numerous groups of persons with disabilities, including people with limited visual abilities, adults and children with mental disabilities, dyslexia, muscular dystrophy, and persons from nursing homes. Most of our experience in this arena is centered on use at developed recreation areas: campgrounds and picnic areas.

Prior to ADA, the major congressional act impacting public recreation (as it concerns persons with disabilities) was the Architectural Barriers Act of 1968. Most agencies were in minimum compliance by making sure their new toilets/ showers were accessible. The problem here was while the toilet *was* accessible (once you got to the front door) there was a less than sincere attempt by *many* agencies to see to it a person with a disability could easily get to the front door! The flush toilet at a Southern state park picnic area shown in Figure 10.48 has accessible facilities inside though there is an obvious challenge for a person in a wheelchair to *get* inside. Our extensive coast-to-coast travels found this to have been quite a common practice throughout America. In our view— then as now—this signals a lack of honesty and integrity by anyone who did it!

Before we go further *you* should understand something (it's obvious many park folks *don't*): *Persons with disabilities visit parks to enjoy themselves—not to go to the toilet!* As you have no doubt already determined, our various experiences while working for TVA gave us numerous examples

of how things shouldn't be done and we've shared many of these with you. In fairness, most of the toilet/shower facilities TVA built throughout their park systems were accessible inside and users could easily get to the front doors.

Our first attempt (some 20-plus years ago) at going beyond providing accessible toilets/ showers was the signed, cabled,

Figure 10.48

and partially paved campsite we designed next to a new toilet/shower in a sizable campground expansion. The campsite (Figure 10.42) was a generous universal back-in with a short, paved connecting trail to the adjacent toilet/shower. We used an eight-foot fixed concrete table with six-foot benches. This allowed the user (Figure 10.49) adequate space to roll under the extended table end. Without knowing why or why not we paved part of the site including the table zone and a trail around the back edge of the site. Our method of administration was to have our attendants at the 24-hour per day staffed gate be on the alert for people in need of a site like this and furnish them a key to the locked cable.

To our surprise use came almost immediately and we responded by adding additional sites. Within a few weeks we had a surprise visit from a representative of the state office of the Easter Seal Society. The person was delighted with our special units *but* his greatest delight (ours too) was in saying "*all* of your campsites are accessible to the folks we represent!" This, he said, meant they weren't confined to a unit next to a toilet (which oftentimes isn't the choice unit in anyone's campground). He further

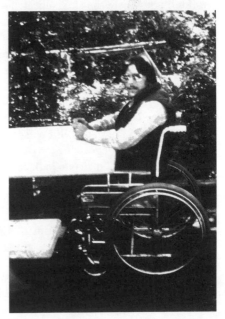

Figure 10.49

257

said the paving wasn't needed on any part of the campsite. The universal, gravel-covered campsites allowed persons with disabilities the same choice as all other campers in selection of their just right campsite. We were concerned and sincere 20 years ago with our first attempt but concern and sincerity don't add up to competence and correctness. Partial camp unit paving, site location next to the toilet/shower, and the fixed concrete table were wrong then and they are wrong today! We compounded these errors by sharing them with others in the first edition of this book. As you can see we have considerable experience at making mistakes.

Take time now to return to the early part of Chapter Seven to review which kinds of camp units are functional, which aren't, and why. In our discussion of camping units for persons with disabilities we will be referring to camp units 1–10 in Figure 10.50 (originally shown as Figure 7.13). We hope you remembered units 1–6 are usable and functional, and 7–10 aren't. The first site we built (Figure 10.42) would be a unit similar to unit 1.

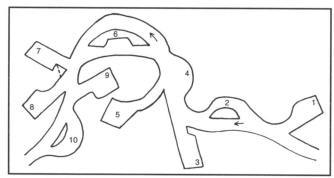

Figure 10.50

It's test-your-skills time again with the following six-photo collage of campsites provided for persons with disabilities. What's right or wrong with each campsite? To help, we'll tell you where the site is located *and* the 1-10 category as shown in Figure 10.50.

1. Figure 10.51 is a Division of Forestry campground in Indiana. This one is a bit difficult to categorize though we'll say category 9.
2. Figure 10.52 is in an Illinois state park campground. The category is somewhere between 1 and 7.
3. Figure 10.53 is in a U.S. Forest Service campground in California. Category 9.
4. Figure 10.54 is in a state park campground in Colorado. Category 9.
5. Figure 10.55 is a campsite in a South Dakota state campground. Close to category 1.
6. Figure 10.56 is a U.S. Corps of Engineers campsite at Lake Shelbyville, Illinois. Category 1.

All six of these sites likely were sincere efforts to provide a quality living area for persons with physical disabilities. The least expensive example—6—is the *only one* that correctly and fully meets the needs of these individuals.

Figure 10.51

Figure 10.52

Figure 10.53

Here are *some* things we see wrong with the first five campsites:

1. *The Indiana Division of Forestry Site* (Figure 10.51). With its asphalt surface, this unit will absorb the full heat of the sun since there is no on-site shade. In southern Indiana in the humid summertime, this is not beckoning to anyone including a person with disabilities. You will "en-

Figure 10.54

Figure 10.55

Figure 10.56

joy" the unwanted heat absorbed by the blacktop several hours after sundown. This campsite has a 90° back-in off of a two-way road. (Note the barrier where the parking is supposed to happen.) Where is the door on the trailer? Why does the special site (built by a consulting firm in the early 1990s) have to be located at the toilet/ shower? This is the way others do it; therefore it must be good! The table is portable and that's a plus.

2. *The Illinois State Park Campsite* (Figure 10.52). This site, which is perpendicular to its road like the previous one, is the new (1995) standard in Illinois state parks at least for those in engineering who oversee contracts. (Most of the Illinois park managers know better but have little or no control over planning or contracting.) It is just as warm and humid in summer in Illinois as it is in Indiana and the fully paved campsites (again located near the toilets/showers) are just as "enjoyable" in the heat. Here they seemed to have selected a less than level site which compounds the challenges. As you'll remember, paving parking spurs and campsite living area zones is a poor idea we see far too frequently.

3. *The U.S. Forest Service Back-in Campsite in California* (Figure 10.53). Here, the campsite zone and parking spur are paved. (Why?) Back your trailer in to this one and— again—where is your trailer door? Why the tons of barrier rocks? The table isn't cantilevered but a wheelchair could come close on this one. There are two grills: one is a picnic grill and the other is an on-the-ground cooking/fire pit. Considerable time and effort have been spent (wasted, we think)—particularly in the Forest Service— debating and worrying about the proper type of grill to provide for persons with disabilities. If more than 95 percent of campers bring their own cooking facility with them, why all the hand wringing? The upright picnic grill (as you already have learned) is a waste of money in campgrounds anyplace. On sites where you want to beckon paraplegics in wheelchairs this type of grill is an *extreme hazard!* It's easy to roll under these upright grills and receive severe leg burns from unseen falling ashes. Paraplegics don't have feeling in their legs, so they don't know they're being burned, and—due to circulatory problems—have a difficult challenge in healing wounds they do receive. *Please remember this!*

4. *The Colorado State Park Back-in Campsite* (Figure 10.54). When we described this unit as a category 9 type that alone should have given you a big negative clue. Here is another instance where an engineering consulting firm has zapped us. Full blacktop and concrete paving and the upright, unsafe grill are also no-nos. They do have a portable cantilevered table which is good but doesn't overcome the expensive mistakes.

5. *The South Dakota State Park Campsite* (Figure 10.55). This unit has a special personal trail to the toilet which (as many of these do) likely moves other campers through their "private" site. At least the site furniture is on the proper side of the unit (unlike examples 3 and 4). They have the unnecessary paving and the unsafe grill. There is an excellent movable table suitable on either end for wheelchair use.

6. *The Defined, Graveled Universal Campsite on a USCOE Area at Lake Shelbyville in Illinois* (Figure 10.56). This unit has an on-the-ground grill tucked into an out-of-the-way corner and a portable cantilevered table which means anyone, including persons with disabilities, can use the site. When users back their rig in, the trailer door opens

toward the furniture. You can locate your tent or any-thing else anywhere you wish on site (you can't do so—at least as easily—on pavement). Let's talk about the sign—is it needed?

We've previously said universal sites provide great camp-ing environments anyplace in most campgrounds (with the exception of steep road sections) and campers with disabili-ties appreciate them. Why then is a sign necessary on any of the universal campsites? As you will see later in this section the gurus, experts, and consultants—including those who rep-resent one or another of the disabled organizations (gover-nors' staffs and federal agency employees too)—often pre-scribe, dictate, and even praise without having a clue about good or bad design. Even if all of your camp units are of the universal type usable by everyone, some legalistic turkey may say you aren't in compliance because you don't have a sign on two or three campsites. They won't even notice the signed and unsigned units are exactly alike! The authors aren't pleased to understand this problem and to recommend what in reality should be an unnecessary sign but the arrogance and ignorance of some folks with a little authority causes us to do so.

Three common threads link Figures 10.51 through 10.55: They are all poorly done *and* our professionals likely don't know what's wrong or how to correct the mistakes. If you are a young inexperienced student, doesn't all of this make you wonder a bit about "experienced" professionals? We certainly spend time pondering the whys of it all.

While you are in this wondering and pondering mode have a look at some even deeper pits you and those afore-mentioned professionals can fall into. The next one takes us to a National Park campground in Colorado: at the Black Canyon of the Gunnison National Monument. First, though, you should know all sorts of well-intentioned facilities have been built, some by volunteers and many by agencies all across the United States. Several of them have been built under the government's new partnership umbrella. We think partner-ships are great but far too often—particularly in the realm of providing for persons with disabilities—the results are poorly located, seldom programmed and poorly designed. Everyone involved is generally quite proud of these cooperative efforts. From experience the authors know being critical of these "good" works puts you in the bad guy corner! Another chal-lenge (a tough one, too) is the disabled volunteer who has a "wonderful" idea he'd like to help you design and build.

The concrete *unloading dock camp unit* in Figure 10.57 is the result of such help. It is a back-in site (or is it a pull-off?) on the left side of a paved one-way campground road. It seems the "design" worked well for the volunteer and his van. The expensive concrete dock doesn't work well for tenters, trailer owners, or other wheeled-vehicle campers. Why build things poorly when, with just a small amount of knowledge and considerably less money, you can build universal sites with less environmental impact usable by *anyone?* Even if all labor and materials for this site were free it is still quite poor. We realize this is a tough situation to tackle but if you

Figure 10.57

have some skills you should be able to direct sincere enthusi-asm like this into positive results.

We ran into the award-winning site (Figures 10.58 and 10.59) at a state park in west central Arkansas. In fact, we visited it two or three times and on all occasions it was occu-pied. (Remember there appears to be no correlation between high or low occupancy and poor design!) The campsite is a category 8 on Figure 10.50—a pull-in campsite! Several chap-

Figure 10.58

Figure 10.59

ters ago we told you pull-in campsites were bad news and those who design and build them should be *exterminated* (or something of this sort). This is a good place to stop and say park people seem to focus on poorly designed campsites *nationally* when they select a site to retrofit for persons with disabilities! What a tragedy! The motor home in Figure 10.58 had no problem pulling into the site. As you'd expect the door or doors (other than the driver's) opened to the passenger side of the site away from the table. The state and their volunteer organization got help and materials from a local wood product specialties group and the site was built at little or no cost to the state. Note the separated terraced areas and the challenge of moving between different levels. This is an exceptionally challenging site for any person in a wheelchair. Figure 10.59 shows a trailer backed into the paved parking spur meaning the driver had to go around the camp loop the wrong way in order to use the site. (The designer should be ashamed!)

During one of our workshop visits, park staff proudly told us about this cooperative effort and about the statewide award they received. We didn't have the on-site courage to point out what should have been obvious. One good thing to report is the table is a good one. (We hope you learned students are still scratching your heads and wondering about us and the park staff.)

Figures 10.60 and 10.61 take us to a state park in southern Nevada. We stopped at a back-in camp unit (category 9 again) on the left side of a fat, one-way loop road. Note the beautiful toilet/shower is in the center of that loop. (Hope you've read Chapter Seven and understand why this is poor design.) Where does the trailer door open and why—again—did they pick such a poor site? The wide-paved trail through this campsite is a draw for at least 20 percent of the campground meaning other folks are beckoned, through poor design, to walk through this special site. The table located between the two upright posts under the ramada doesn't allow space for a wheelchair. We also believe the spaces between the posts and the edges of the paving aren't generous enough for *safe* passage of a wheelchair around either end! The upright grill (though designed a bit differently) still is unsafe

Figure 10.61

and unnecessary. We suspect park folks are proud of this site and likely have been praised by the disabled community.

Figure 10.62 takes us back to the Colorado state park campground where we found something which at first (in our ignorance) we weren't sure we liked—the 12-by-12-foot raised wooden tent platform. Before we discuss it, have a look at the campsite (Figure 10.63). There we go again! We've picked as a special site for persons with disabilities—a category 10

Figure 10.62

Figure 10.60

Figure 10.63

pull-through campsite on the left side of a one-way road. (Oh no!) The parking spur is paved, the eating zone is paved, they've added one of those upright grills, and the gravel in the nonpaved zone is too large for ease of wheelchair movement. The difficulty of wheelchair movement through sizable rock was pointed out to us recently when we tent camped at a Missouri KOA next to a family with a severely disabled youngster. The father (a big guy) could manage the chair in the on-site rock; however, the mother and the two eight- and 12-year-old brothers couldn't. (The gravel we recommend for all universal campsites allows easy movement for crutches and wheelchairs.) The on-site portable cantilevered table in Figure 10.63 on the Colorado campsite was a good one. (You should be pondering again.)

We had heard about the special camping platform (a version of those built in group camps years ago to keep tents and campers out of the nongravel reinforced mud) for tenters with disabilities, particularly those in wheelchairs, but were, as usual, skeptical. The tent platform in Figure 10.62 is a well-built sturdy 12-by-12-feet wide and about 14-inches high built with two-inch treated lumber. The 14-inch height is that of the bottom of a child's wheelchair. While an adult wheelchair height (bottom of chair) varies from 16 to 19 inches, adults who are a bit heavier than they'd like to be often select the 14-inch height for comfort. So, while there is likely to be debate from the "legalists," the 14-inch platform height may be correct, or at least a good compromise.

There were four recessed metal hangers located on each side of the platform to hold tent ropes securely. Gravel width around the platform should be a minimum of three feet to allow for chair movement. When you, as a professional, don't know what's best for users, *find someone who does!* This is another of those author axioms you should warmly embrace. Since, to our knowledge, there isn't any applied research on the desirability and use of those raised platforms we went to an even better source—a tent-camping paraplegic friend of ours named Janet. She was excited about the special raised wooden tent platform and had high hopes that Indiana state park folks would—in her camping lifetime—provide some universal campsites with platforms included. (We hope so too!) She further told us having to get out of her wheelchair and onto a ground level tent floor was not only difficult, but made her and other camping paraplegics feel like a "whale out of water." "Moving onto and off of the platform at either 14 or 16 inches would be quite easy," she said.

It seems to us, as a minimum, one of those signed, generous universal campsites should be selected in each camp loop with one of those recently developed 30-inch fire pits (with cooking capability) and a 12-by-12-foot (or larger) wooden tent platform added. You might consider cabling and locking the signed site and giving a key to those who request it. As usual, your *other* universal sites with the cantilevered table on each one would give *all* persons an opportunity to camp where they wish. It was, incidentally, a joy to write about a well-done good idea (the tent platform) amid having to point out the far too numerous mistakes we, as professionals, have all made!

Now, back to reality. The first tent platform for persons with disabilities we had seen was on an undefined, barricaded, *pull-in* Forest Service site in southern Colorado. (It's no wonder we were somewhat skeptical.) The campsite was unlevel, getting from the short barricaded spur to the platform and the table for a person in a wheelchair was nearly impossible, and the table wasn't suitable. It was also a *pull-in* site! Aside from the poor camp unit, they are up to their old tricks of seeing something they think is good and, without brain in gear, plunking it down someplace. This seems to happen even more as we scramble frantically to do great things in the name of ADA.

Retrofitting. One of the biggest physical and financial challenges park managers have today is in making sure as many of their existing parks as are reasonably feasible are now accessible to persons with disabilities. Can the users easily and safely get to your facilities? Are the structures accessible once you're inside? A good example of making something more accessible is the blacktop at an entrance to a TVA toilet/shower. There was a $1\frac{1}{2}$-inch concrete lip where the concrete slab met the paved trail (Figure 10.64). The blacktop wedge was an answer to the problem and likely cured a tripping hazard too.

Most of the upgrading and retrofitting in wildland parks we've seen is centered on making the toilets/ showers accessible. However, since disabled persons come to these parks to enjoy themselves you should make certain they can get to as many program areas as possible. (Our wild assumption here is that the campground has programs and areas.) This varies from accessible paved areas among

Figure 10.64

the benches in campfire theaters, to play equipment, to beaches, to shelters and to play courts like the one shown in Figure 10.65. In one of our visits to a far western state park, the manager there proudly showed us the accessibility improvements and retrofitting he had made to his campground's flush toilets/showers. The improvements were good, but we pointed out he hadn't provided for safe access to a nearby campfire theater. He was quite upset he hadn't, as they were providing evening programs there. As you can see we can't seem to think beyond toilets!

The paraplegic man and his family (Figure 10.66) had heard of our providing access at LBL to toilets/showers, camp-

Figure 10.65

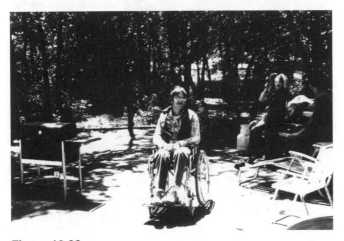

Figure 10.66

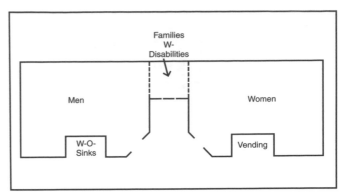

Figure 10.67

sites, *and* program areas, so they traveled 150 miles from southern Missouri, bypassing other federal, state and private parks to a place where they felt like the family was wanted, welcomed, and could be involved. It all goes back to our questions about whom do you want, doesn't it? (Also note the cooking grill he and the other 95 percent of campers bring with them.)

At least 10 years ago Tennessee state park personnel came up with a marvelous idea as they struggled to retrofit a toilet/shower building in their Montgomery Bell State Park campground. It seemed to be a near physical and financial impossibility to build a toilet and a shower stall in either the women's or men's side of their building. (This was at least 10 years or more before ADA.) Some wise person said, "Why not take the generous laundry room built between the two sides and make it into a sort of 'families with disabilities room'" (Figure 10.67). Those who needed to use this sort of private room could get a key at the registration desk. This was a fantastic idea for all sorts of persons with disabilities and various family members who might help with their care.

A father could take all of his children camping even if one were a teenage girl in a wheelchair. The same is true with a mother and teenage son. Obviously in campgrounds without this sort of special room the two single parents mentioned

would have challenges helping their son or daughter in the men's or women's rest rooms. The combinations of special family opportunities are numerous including a wife helping her husband or a husband helping his wife. We took this idea to our friend who was so enthusiastic about the special tent platform and she was again delighted. We went a step further and asked, "Even when you find quality, easy-to-use facilities in women's rest rooms, aren't you a bit uncomfortable and/or embarrassed in using them?" "*Yes,*" was her answer and she said the special room would eliminate these feelings and give her and any family member privacy. She also said no park person had ever asked her or any of her friends how they could do a better job for them in his or her park. Shame on you and us.

In our work as lecturers and consultants in the family campground realm, we strongly advise both the public and private sectors to build and administer what folks now call family assist or companion care rooms (Figure 10.68). In our view these facilities will beckon many users you wouldn't get, would increase park revenue, bring tons of goodwill to your park and agency, and, most importantly, provide an opportunity (and motivation) for families with their special family members to participate in outdoor recreation. We wish we had blundered into creating the family assist room idea! Figures 10.69, 10.70 and 10.71 give you an idea of some of the

Figure 10.68

fixtures needed in such a room. Note the pull-down baby-changing table and the double shower head (one at wheelchair height.) Water temperature should be checked often to make certain it isn't too hot or cold. We'd also suggest a three-foot high screen be located in front of the toilet (locate screen far enough from the stool to allow chair movement between it and the toilet) to give some privacy,

Figure 10.69

a wash basin with a generous counter space for towels and shaving items, electrical outlets for blow dryers, a comfortable bench seating area across the room for family members, adequate and sturdy hangers along one wall for towels and clothing, and adequate lighting and ventilation be included.

It is interesting to note while other agencies take considerable credit for their leadership in providing facilities for person with disabilities, the U.S. Forest Service—particularly in their southern region—is responsible for several new family assist rooms including the one shown in the last three figures.

In the 1970s and 1980s before the ADA legislation became law there were many good things happening including complete areas devoted to persons with disabilities (like the one on a national forest in Florida), numerous trails and all sorts of fishing piers. Our main concern (other than poor design) over the years was that most park agencies continued to consider provision of the physical hardware (e.g., trail or fishing pier) all they needed to do. (This ain't necessarily so.) Beckoning persons with disabilities—particularly groups to use those sincerely provided trails and fishing piers requires extra public relations efforts and a close relation-

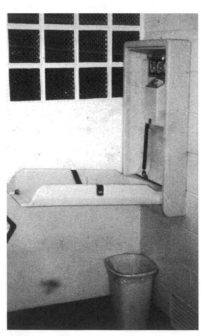

Figure 10.70

ship with special groups, nursing homes, and the Kennedy Foundation.

Bringing heavy use to a facility means someone has to help plan, provide transportation, consider feeding and sanitation, and arrange for one-on-one help. In sharing this thought with federal park administrators who had provided a facility we oftentimes generate the glossy stare of incomprehension.

Figure 10.71

As a modest step forward (*a giant one* for most resource related park folks) we suggest you move (at least in campgrounds) beyond providing hardware to developing some innovative programming. Campground visitors with disabilities can participate in skills and puppet shows; enter their mutts in your dog shows; be big time winners at grocery bingo; go on *short* interpretive "walks;" use a tree finder (Figure 10.72); win a prize with their radio-controlled boat, truck or car; play softball, volleyball or badminton (Figure 10.73); make sweet gum and other nature crafts; and more and more and more. (Sort of like the rest of your users, eh?)

Or you can bore them to death as we've done with a generation of youngsters by having no programs, thus making sure camping isn't on their list of future exciting lifetime things they'll pursue. If (and that's a *big* if) you do put forth a little extra effort by providing something fun to do, *you* can change the young boy's frown (Figure 10.74) to a great *big* grin (Figure 10.75). Isn't that what outdoor recreation and being a real professional *should be* all about?

Figure 10.72

Figure 10.73

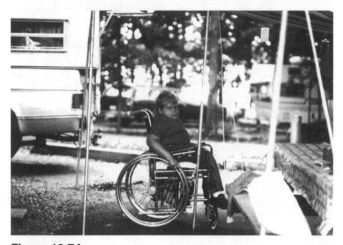

Figure 10.74

Park Safety

The following axiom from the Hultscott (the authors') realm is the most important one in this entire book. *You should manage parks as though there is a shyster lawyer behind each rock and tree!* (You will also find a few of the rascals *under* some of those rocks.) Facetious? Perhaps a bit, but we don't exaggerate by much. Visitor health and safety in parks should be of *utmost concern to all park personnel.* Why? There are lots of reasons for this including:

Figure 10.75

1. Common decency and integrity, which justifiably head the list! A park experience includes the expectation users will enjoy themselves and be relatively safe while doing so. There are all sorts of risks people expect when they visit wildland parks, from bee and mosquito stings and bites to snake bites, encounters with skunks and bears and other less than friendly critters, to stepping in a stump hole, and even falling off of a trail. One of the authors was once mashed flat into a large rhododendron plant by a 250-pound hiker in slick-soled slippers on a paved and somewhat steep trail. Fortunately the then-flat author and the sizable hiker weren't hurt. They did walk away from one destroyed rhododendron. (The fall was the larger hiker's fault and she didn't sue the author or the U.S. Forest Service.) Anyhow visitors don't expect to be injured by your negligence or your hazardous facilities.

2. There are lots of folks looking for opportunities to make big bucks taking you to court. Unfortunately in the last 30 years, our culture has also fostered a lack of responsibility for our own actions so when we do something stupid we look for someone other than us to blame. Park agencies and private organizations all too often settle the most absurd lawsuits out of court just to curb their legal fees. The jury system too sometimes makes less than sensible decisions likely brought about by the skillful manipulation of lawyers. Included here is the ever increasing tendency to sock it to the "wealthy" private company.

3. Those behind-the-trees and under-the-rocks lawyers who with *all their hearts* wish "to help injured people" are out there in ever increasing numbers. They "charge no fees until *you* get paid and will protect *you* from those greedy insurance companies." Oh, yes, it is a comfort to know they have a 24-hour phone number with prerecorded advice.

Add 3 to 2, and park folks can get into hot water. (At which point, we suppose we could sue McDonald's for not warning us that hot coffee might burn us.) As consultants in the recreation and park realm we are sometimes asked to be "expert" witnesses at pretrial sessions. A few times the lawyer who contacted us has wisely decided not to hire us and have us testify. One case involved a heavyweight man and wife (both well over 225 pounds) who placed bowls of hot food on a six-foot wooden picnic table and then both sat down on the *same* side. Up, up went the hot, hot food and down, down went the less than bright, hot food–covered couple. The only thing to do was bring suit against the private campground owner! Their lawyer asked us to say less than kind things about the table and the private campground owner. We said they had best look for other "expert" witnesses. (Obviously this is one of those lack of responsibility cases).

A case we did take was one in which a family had brought a metal grill to place over and cook with charcoal on a ground level fire circle. The circle was a longtime standard Forest Service campfire ring. Hundreds are in use by agencies all over the country. After finishing their meal, they took the metal grill off the fire pit but didn't extinguish the hot coals.

(Which is OK for most folks.) However, they had a small child with them who was just learning to walk. She was (and had been) moving around the campsite in a walker. You guessed it; during an after-meal discussion the campers didn't watch their child closely and she rolled face first into the pit. The park personnel, the authors and the agency attorneys felt it was a clear case of negligence on the part of the family. In the final analysis the government agency settled the claim out-of-court rather than risk (even with a solid case) what might have been done by a jury. In our view this again was a case involving lack of responsibility. We cite these cases to show what can happen even if your park appears to be safety problem free.

Now, take a look at some photos that do show some safety problems—some obvious, some perhaps not. We found the first five the last time we visited TVA's Land Between the Lakes. What do you see? Figure 10.76 shows a corrugated metal culvert across a trail hit at one time (or more) by a mower. Figure 10.77 shows a blacktop trail touching a foot bridge. Figure 10.78 shows steps in a campfire theater. Figure 10.79 shows benches in the same campfire theater with clumps of some sort of plant growing under them. Figure 10.80 shows a well-used and well-worn play apparatus.

Figure 10.76

Figure 10.77

Figure 10.78

Figure 10.79

Figure 10.80

It wasn't surprising to find these safety problems during even a quick visit as recreation had been deemphasized *and* staff there had always had problems seeing what was obvious to the authors. Here's what we saw:

- Figure 10.76: The once gravel-covered culvert across a trail was a hazard in two ways. There were sharp, jagged metal edges and a sizable hole people—particularly children—could step into.

- Figure 10.77: Note the unsupported blacktop at the bridge-blacktop junction has broken, leaving an unexpected hole; a hazard when someone steps from the bridge to the trail. This is a heavily used trail providing night access to the campground's main programming shelter. Walkers at night wouldn't expect the trail tread to have a sizable hole in it.

- Figure 10.78: Steps in a campfire theater are necessary, expected and commonly found there. The settling of soil and gravel is also a common occurrence which should be remedied in the early spring. The photo was taken in midsummer and the previous winter's settling hadn't been corrected meaning a serious tripping hazard wasn't seen and repaired.

- Figure 10.79: The previously mentioned vegetation under the campfire theater benches is poison ivy. Since they are sizable clumps they have been there for *at least* three seasons. (The invitations to campers dressed in shorts to enjoy their campfire programs will include a user-unfriendly "bonus.")

- Figure 10.80: You likely had some difficulty seeing the raised and hazardous nail heads in the photo. They were far more obvious to us and the TVA staff person with us. When we asked why these and other obvious safety problems hadn't been observed and eliminated the reply was they were *scheduled for correction the following year!*

The first and foremost expenditure of *any park maintenance funds* should always go to visitor health and safety problems! If a safety problem occurs or is found today it should be corrected *today!* If it can't be addressed until tomorrow the safety problem should at least be removed from use by temporary signs and plastic safety construction tape. This is true if you have funds for correction or not!

Now have a look at five additional figures showing safety problems unseen by park personnel. What do you see? There is a common thread linking all five. What is it? Figure 10.81 shows a fire-damaged butt of a yellow poplar tree on a campsite in an Indiana state forest. Wind could topple this at any time. Fig-

Figure 10.81

ure 10.82 shows a sizable damaged and dying walnut tree which was next to a play apparatus in an Indiana state park. Here we may be looking at a "save the tree" environmentalist challenge as well as a hazard. Figure 10.83 is our old "friend," poison ivy again—this time at the edge of a camp unit in an Indiana state park. Poison ivy between camp units may be OK, but it is an unprofes-

Figure 10.82

sional hazard at the edge of a camp unit. Our city-born users likely don't know poison ivy vines from passion flower vines. (Do you?) Figure 10.84 shows a severely damaged and scarred maple tree at the edge of a camp unit in a Tennessee state park. It could snap off in even a moderate wind. The background shows a root sprung tree held up by others between camp units. It, too, is a hazard which should be seen and removed. Figure 10.85 is a large hackberry tree showing considerable damage in a U.S. Corps of Engineers picnic area in Kentucky.

The common thread tying these five figures together is they all show hazardous plants. If a visitor were to be injured by any one of the hazards in the preceding figures it would be an obvious case of negligence, and if a lawsuit were filed you/we would likely lose it big time.

The next five figures are safety problems on public parks both east and west. Two are difficult to see but all five are quite hazardous. What do you see?

Figure 10.86 is of an entrance sign to a U.S. Forest Service campground in Colorado. The entrance/exit road to the campground is just to the left edge of the sign. We took the

Figure 10.83

Figure 10.84

Figure 10.85

Figure 10.86

Figure 10.87

Figure 10.88

photo from our car window. The sign face is quite near the road surface meaning you must (with most vehicles) move slightly out into the road to see around the sign.

In the area shown in Figure 10.87, someone had taken the unnecessary barrier log off the two concrete posts in another U.S. Forest Service area. However, the hazardous upright bolts are still there waiting for someone—perhaps a child—to run, fall, and impale himself or herself! (What a great spot for a universal campsite!)

Figure 10.88 is a photo of an obviously forgotten campsite along Boulder Creek on U.S. Forest Service lands in Colorado. The concrete bench hanging over the upright *is not attached* in any way to the two uprights. If it were to fall on anyone, particularly a small child . . . well, you figure it out.

Figure 10.89 is in a cabin rental area in an Arkansas state park. See the unmarked guy wire to an unseen light pole? It is difficult to see in daylight. What about the hazard at night? What should be done about correcting the safety problem?

We found the remains of this structure in Figure 10.90 in an Indiana *county park*. It was at the far edge of a camp loop (likely marked A or B or C). The vines growing over parts of the roof tell us this has been there for at least the better part of the summer and perhaps much longer. Note the bolts sticking out of the concrete and the numerous sharp nails in the plywood and the two-by-fours! This is extremely hazardous.

The next three figures show unseen safety problems in private campgrounds. What do you see and what's wrong? (Two of them are a bit difficult.)

Figure 10.91 shows the front porch of a rustic cabin we rented in a campground in southern Ontario. Rustic and unsafe don't necessarily go together though they did here. Several of the boards at mid-photo were nearly rotted through. Had one of our fishing friends (who weighs over 250 pounds) stepped on any of those, he would likely have been injured.

Figure 10.92 is a bit subtle. The metal camp unit

Figure 10.89

number sign in this Indiana private campground has sharp pointed corners. These could cause problems for a running child or in fact anyone who walked into them. A few moments rounding the corners on a grinder would have solved this problem.

Figure 10.93 shows a double shuffleboard court in the same Indiana private campground with at least two safety problems. In some places it's at least 14 inches off the ground. During a spirited game it wouldn't take much for players to fall off the edges. Those boards at the far end of the right side were there to keep the pucks from falling off the side and rolling into the nearby algae-covered lagoon. The problem is several boards are missing yet parts of three of the upright bolts which once held the boards are still there. Quite hazardous? Yes!

Figures 10.76 to 10.93 show you 18 safety problems park personnel didn't see or weren't worried about or both. Most of them would have required minimal maintenance action early on. We aren't sure why the corrective work wasn't performed. *Most* park managers worldwide are quite concerned about safety and make sure prompt action is taken to correct problems. The federal agency we believe to be most concerned about park and visitor safety is the U.S. Corps of Engineers. In 30 years of seeing their work, we've noted few problems with safety. The agency we feel to be the least concerned with safety is the TVA.

When the oldest author transferred from the U.S. Forest Service to TVA in 1970 he was conditioned to be concerned about safety. The Forest Service then stressed safety in all its work. Safety briefing meetings were held weekly and when different types of projects were undertaken. Frequently, office staff as well as field personnel were included in these sessions. He was quite surprised to find TVA didn't have similar concerns or training sessions.

Figure 10.91

Figure 10.92

Figure 10.90

Figure 10.93

From our visits to all of the Forest Service regions (other than Alaska) our view in the 1990s is safety problems have greatly increased in this agency rather than remaining an exception like safety problems in the U.S. Corps of Engineers. In the case of TVA it should be noted this agency is a highly unionized organization including their "professionals" and that they were consumed in the 1970s and 1980s with concerns about equal opportunity hiring quotas, higher salaries, and diversity. The U.S. Forest Service wasn't heavily involved *then* with unions, quotas and diversity but they are now. Add these challenges to a Forest Service de-emphasis on developed outdoor recreation sites and programs and you may well understand why they are having safety and image problems today.

Health and Safety Activities in Travis County, Texas

There are several big bonuses from doing consulting work in the recreation and park realm. Traveling over this great country, meeting new and interesting people, getting a greater perspective of the scope of recreation challenges, and having the opportunity to learn are four of these bonuses. One recent lengthy assignment we had involved helping guide the recreation planning process of Travis County in Texas. This included master planning and on-the-ground site layout. This system now has 25 parks and nearly 3,000 acres. Many of these are on Lake Travis which is part of the lower Colorado River chain of lakes. The sizable lake and its nearness to Austin mean heavy use of both the parklands and the lake. A few years ago the county leased several existing primitive areas from the Lower Colorado River Authority. The major planning emphasis now is on upgrading all of these heavily used and poorly designed parks. How does any of this fit into the visitor safety and health realms?

The remarkable answer is that Travis County's concern for park visitor health and safety is the best we've seen any place in the public park realm! Their initial emphasis *hasn't* been on multimillion dollar expansion and upgrading of facilities, but on providing quality customer service *and* a trained staff to provide visitor protection and medical help of all sorts! (What a contrast to some of the other systems we've discussed with you!) All of their rangers are trained and certified EMTs (Emergency Medical Technicians), and trained and certified peace officers. In addition, they also have staff paramedics and at heavy use times they use temporary EMTs and paramedics from other agencies' off-duty personnel.

A check of the weekly incident summaries for 14 weeks (spring through early fall of 1995), revealed the on-site visitor medical incidents included broken arms, legs, elbows, and ankles; ant bites and bee stings (they have county bee hot line personnel available); numerous seizures; burned toes, arms, and legs; cut chins, feet, arms, thighs, knees, and heads; hyperventilations; dislocated shoulders; jet ski accidents including cut hands, feet, heads, and injured backs; dog and cat bites; heat stroke; allergic reactions; labor pains; fish hooks in feet, hands, legs, and abdomens; two near drownings; and two

deaths by drowning (Figure 10.94). Their rangers administered first aid, requested additional help from their own and other county paramedics, prepared persons to be transported, and called in medevac helicopters numerous times.

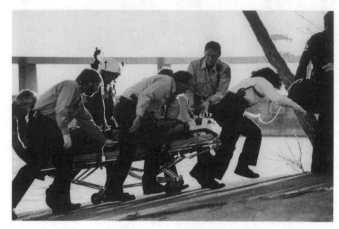

Figure 10.94

Since their rangers wear at least two certified hats they also got involved (during the same 14-week period) with challenges such as lost children, boating accidents, rescue of persons on sinking boats, verbal disturbances, bicycle accidents, speeding, theft, fights, intoxicated individuals, collisions, motor vehicle accidents (and deaths), catching and arresting a naked jet skier, and helping the sheriff with a murder at a nearby factory.

We were with them on a Labor Day boat tour when they quickly responded to a serious injury at their sizable vertical (yes, that's straight up and straight down) "beach." A person had fallen from a ledge, hit his head on rocks on the way down and ended up bleeding and floating in deep water. The crew worked their way through the crowd of hundreds of swimmers (it was national splash day there), put the person on a buddy board (immobilizing him), hauled him on board, administered first aid (a paramedic was on board), and transported him across the lake to a waiting ambulance. We were impressed and the crew got a spontaneous round of applause from hundreds of splash day participants as the crew slowly worked their way through the crowd! On board they had a cardiac monitor, life pack and defibrillator among the other medical aids available. (Oh, yes, the beach was the nationally famous Hippie Hollow, a clothing optional beach.)

They have designated helispots throughout their park system (a park may have several). Helicopters *do not* land at boat ramps, beaches or other heavily populated facilities for they know such landings would cause chaos and safety problems among the users. The director there says the obvious concern for the health and well-being of their customers by all staff has done several good things including:

- Overcome some of the obvious need to improve all of their parks (an ongoing expensive process);
- Created an extremely positive patron image of their parks;

- Created big park backers of the county judge *and* county commissioners; and
- Helped increase family use including single parent families.

Earlier we told you Travis County ranger training includes being certified peace officers. (See the Forest Service negative "peace" officer activities under the Customer Service section of this chapter.) According to the park director their peace officers are "de-fanged" community-helping, people-focused, good-guy type folks—or else! What a contrast this park system is to some of our federal park agencies who are doing everything possible to have *minimal contact* with developed site visitors or to arrest many of those they *do* see! (Ponder this one a bit, too!)

The authors also found the following after-action report to be quite interesting. It deals with a potential visitor hazard which had happened the *day before*. The direct quote is:

Richard Moya Park—Park staff discovered a large tree limb had fallen on the picnic area near shelter one. Staff cordoned off the affected area and cut the limb that afternoon. The debris was immediately removed.

Again, *contrast* this with any of those examples listed or shown in the maintenance section of this chapter. What was done here isn't remarkable—it's what should be done by all park personnel in all parks.

The Rise and Flop of Outdoor Recreation Research

Several years ago we participated in a unique gathering of researchers (from both universities and resource management agencies) and practitioners. It was hosted at Estes Park, Colorado, by two USDA agencies (Extension Service and Soil Conservation Service) and the National Recreation and Park Association's (NRPA) American Park and Recreation Society. The idea was a good one—to create some badly needed dialogue between researchers and managers. One big problem in the session was the managers were there for the entire program but—as usual—the researchers didn't stay beyond their presentation times. The researchers presented their dandy research projects and their findings (as usual without recommendations to the "less smart" managers) and, with little discussion and "littler" inclination to *learn,* promptly departed. It was clear, early on, that dialogue with manager types wasn't a big priority with researchers!

One group of two young researchers near the end of the presentations was forced to listen to the frustrations of the managers. The group had made an animated, coordinated presentation on the virtues of two modeling schemes, and were quite impressed with *their* work when they finished. While the participating author admits to less than great smarts and understanding little of what had been said, he strongly suspected his bewilderment was shared with a majority (perhaps all) of the managers. An exasperated manager of a sizable municipal park system said he appreciated their enthusiastic presentations, *but* just what were they talking about and how could their research help him or anyone else? The young researchers were shocked at these two "unethical" questions but tried without success to give answers. It was obvious questions like this weren't expected and shouldn't be asked. This should give you an overview of some of your research challenges. You also need to understand how research has been conducted in the resource realm. Generally, this research has been conducted either by universities or by the agencies themselves and we need to consider each of these scenarios.

What about useful applied park management needs research conducted by universities? There has never been a concerted effort on the part of the universities to seek and to do low budget applied research for park managers. (It seems to us this would be standard operating procedure at all universities). If considerable research money were involved, university administrations oftentimes gobbled up 50 percent or more of this for "overhead." This practice has had a negative effect on creating agency buy-in—getting agencies to seek out university research. More importantly (and more harmful to the advancement of knowledge in outdoor recreation) is the nature of most of the research conducted by university faculty. Plainly put, it generally has had little or no relevance to practitioners.

In defense of recreation educators, we need to share with you what we feel is one of the major problems these folks face: the university rewards system. Basically, the problem is too many universities don't reward faculty activities with value to most professionals. To understand this point, you need to consider the nature of the term "value." In essence, there are two kinds, intrinsic and extrinsic, and most things can be judged according to either type. A wedding ring, for example, can be evaluated extrinsically by how much it costs and intrinsically by the significance of the marriage it symbolizes. Similarly, the activities of a faculty member can be judged extrinsically by how well he or she prepares students for professional careers and researches topics relevant to professionals and intrinsically by publications in basic research journals.

In our opinion, the rewards of tenure and promotion associated with academic productivity are too often tied to activities judged on the basis of intrinsic value. We know faculty members who have been granted tenure because of success in publishing articles, yet they are less than good teachers and they don't really understand the needs of professionals. We know others who have been denied tenure (i.e., fired) because they devoted time and energy to excellence in teaching and professional service but failed to publish regularly.

This is a touchy issue, and we should qualify our position with two comments. First, good teaching and valuable research are not mutually exclusive activities. As a friend of ours, Tony Mobley, had said, "Research is to teaching like sin is to confession: If you don't do the first, you don't have much to talk about at the second." Universities have the right to expect their faculty to be both scholars and teachers. Unfortunately most schools seem to reward scholarship far more readily than teaching.

271

Our second qualification deals with the research for which faculty are rewarded. From the perspective of outdoor recreation professionals, we feel the most serious problem with research today is a lack of applicability. In other words, the results of much of the research being conducted are, for various reasons, of little utility to managers, planners, and programmers trying to improve the facilities and services they provide for the public. The way university reward systems are set up, research doesn't count for much unless and until it gets published, and for the most part leisure journals tend to publish basic research instead of applied findings. In order to publish—and win tenure points—most academics are encouraged to do basic research. Thus field-level professionals don't find much to interest them in journals, tend not to read them, and miss out on most of the applied information that is available.

These institutional obstacles notwithstanding, there are some barriers to providing usable and useful research findings that university faculty could overcome if they put their hearts into it. For example, the applied journals—those with "implications for management" sections—could do a better job of compelling authors to address managerial needs. This is, incidentally, self-criticism in part, for one of the authors is finishing a second three-year term as editor of the oldest applied journal in the field.

Another problem with application is the way in which researchers write results. Any scientific discipline, ours included, has its own jargon and style. Most recreation journals thrive on terms such as "statistical significance," "regression coefficients" and "orthogonal factors." Research reports also tend to be formatted with an introduction, a methods section, a review of results, and a discussion. From a research standpoint, this is both desirable and necessary for the advancement of knowledge. If another researcher can scan a journal article and learn how a particular variable explains only six percent of the variance of the dependent measure, he or she will learn something from it. But it probably doesn't help the average manager very much. For research to be useful to the practitioner, it must lay out, in plain English, a set of *recommendations* based on research results for consideration. If, for example, a study finds that "perceived isolation" is one of the most important factors in choosing a campsite, the researcher should recommend leaving vegetation growing between some camp units. However, this bridge between results and recommendations is neglected far too often.

Another barrier to research application we can blame on university researchers is the lack of understanding they often have for the problems facing the practitioner. When we were with TVA, we were called by a well-known researcher from a northeastern university. He asked us to serve as state coordinators and distribute a research-needs questionnaire to resort owners, federal and state administrators, user groups, and recreation equipment suppliers. We agreed. The questionnaires arrived on June 16 with a note saying they were to be returned by the respondents by June 20! Remember that the pre-Fourth of July period is the professionals' busiest season. The researcher simply didn't understand this.

Too often also, university researchers decide what they want to study without adequate input from professionals. If you asked managerial folks why they don't pay more attention to research, most would probably tell you it's because the studies don't help them do their jobs. If you asked them why not, they'd probably tell you they aren't asked what they need to have researched. This is partly the fault of the professional for not seeking help from academic types by letting researchers know their needs. Partly, though, researchers are to blame for not seeking input from practitioners as they develop topics to investigate. (We hope that you are shocked by this lack of concern!)

Let's turn our attention now to the other primary source of recreation research: the agencies themselves. Several of the larger federal agencies, including the National Park Service, U.S. Forest Service, TVA, and U.S. Corps of Engineers, established outdoor research staffs. Some good things came from these staffs and the millions of dollars spent, but the basic problems we discussed earlier occurred here, too. Essentially, researchers decided what sorts of problems or questions needed their attention without adequate input from managerial types, wrote in language for each other rather than for field-level personnel, and failed to address recommendations for management actions. Thus the usefulness or relevance of their reports for managers and others who wanted answers was missing.

The U.S. Forest Service at their research stations moved with considerable vigor in the late 1950s into the recreation research realm. Considerable numbers of people with advanced degrees were hired and a few good things happened. However, while researchers should have become a service (support) group to managers—it never happened. The blame for this can be shared equally with management and research staffs. One of the authors was once head of recreation design, administration, and budgeting for the National Forest Service Southern Region, which comprised 33 forests. As a part of this job he and the Deputy Regional Forester met every other year with recreation research staff from the nearby research station. In all instances the research folks presented a list of studies they planned to conduct in the next two years. There was never an attempt to find out what was needed or wanted by management; just an explanation of what they (with funding from the National Forests) were planning to *do* for us. Obviously the author was an accomplice as he should have said, "No, no, you aren't researching what needs to be researched, so let's work together with some of our rangers and come up with real needs." It never happened!

In those days some of the studies included a concern for which grass grows best under picnic tables (none does), the effects of fenced enclosures (keep the offending users out of our areas), rest and rotation theories (close Campground A this season to let it recuperate from all the overuse), and numerous studies on "overuse" itself. (All tragic examples of *your* money flowing down the drain.) There were no social concerns at that time and there was also a refusal on the part of researchers to write reports in understandable language *and* to make "do this, this and this" type serious recommendations.

The U.S. Corps of Engineers became involved in research several years after the Forest Service and concentrated its limited staff at the Vicksburg, Mississippi, Waterways Experiment Station. The problem was, they picked up several bad habits from the Forest Service mainly by charting their own research path with little management input. We will describe some of their efforts in this chapter's section on carrying capacity. While writing this section we were pleased to learn USCOE management now directs most of what their outdoor recreation researchers do.

The National Park Service has (like some other agencies) neglected developed sites and developed site use in recreation research but has been quite active and successful in trying to define socially acceptable levels of use on their river ways.

In summary, for anything positive to happen in the realm of applied outdoor recreation research, there must be more communication among field professionals, agency researchers, and academic types. Unfortunately we don't anticipate this happening given the current university rewards system and the tendency of many academics and agency researchers to remain arrogantly aloof to the needs of the practitioner.

The three authors have considerable experience in park planning, administration, programming, visitor protection, extension, continuing education, actual participation in outdoor recreation opportunities, and—*we think*—recreation research. The fact is, we've guided, funded and nurtured studies from a socioeconomic study of Appalachian Trail users on seven southern national forests, to what types of camp units users prefer, to teenage participation in family camping, to how tent and trailer campers feel about camping next to each other, and even to what times of day campers eat to optimize program schedules. At the end of the writing of this section our involvement also included participation in an NRPA-funded effort to determine the outcomes of youth participation in recreation. The studies we've guided have involved persons gathering doctorate and master's thesis data, intern student mini-reports, and overnight or weekend data gathering by our own staff to seek urgently needed answers. We also conducted an in-house yearlong visitor use study by land, water, and air, finding out just who did visit Land Between the Lakes and what they did while they were there. Interestingly enough the results of this $50,000 study were never revealed to the public as 69 percent of total use was in camping. This finding *did not* please most staff folks (particularly the wildlife specialists and interpretation rascals) or the managers there.

Since Land Between the Lakes was established by President Kennedy as the nation's only outdoor recreation demonstration area (not a wildlife or an environmental education area or a national recreation area), we decided to make it so by designing research capability into our facilities and programs and then, through university research, measure what was happening. We used the information found in these studies to upgrade our design, management, and programming. Our recreation folks at LBL functioned as a linkage between the academic community and leisure products and services

companies using the Land Between the Lakes area as a research base. In a small way we tried to cope with the manager/professor/user products community research challenge. Included as fund providers then were the Coleman Company, Inc., the American Motorcyclist Association, and the Motorcycle Industry Council. It all worked well when we made sure the right school with the right attitude was paired with a mini-funding source. We had to approach the schools with proposals, though, rather than being approached by them. This became the basis for beckoning and hosting hundreds of college students per year and gave us the opportunity to train them *and their professors*. We particularly treasure a visiting professor who said, "It's unbelievable—you set the stage for and conduct applied research and then use the results to manage facilities and programs. It's unheard of!" Unfortunately he was right! The gathering of applied research information was not a main concern of TVA including most folks as LBL and was quickly deemphasized when we were no longer there.

It seems to us responsible professionals would have, as standard operating procedure, frequent measurements of what they do. It's all a part of the integrity business. The problem is it rarely happens. (You students should ask all of us, *why?*)

Where is outdoor recreation research today? The NPS and a few USCOE researchers continue to do perceived needed recreation research and are moving slowly into the social realm. The U.S. Forest Service outdoor recreation research team is now quite small. They never made the management-researcher linkage to gain the backing needed to remain viable. They also have hurt themselves by saying, "Hey, we've done it all," meaning all the necessary research on camping, picnicking, trails, and other use areas has already been done. That's unfortunate as they never really had a good beginning. Their work still is quite self-generated.

If you've carefully read the preceding chapters you are aware we've pointed out numerous research needs. These include replication of previous studies (in different parts of the country), for example, overstory shade and screening densities, numbers of facilities to be placed in men's and women's toilet/shower buildings, who's using camping areas and who isn't, unit density studies, who uses various types of trails (and how and why), and a host of studies on users with disabilities. One *most urgent* study the Forest Service and *any other* park system with *unpaid campground* hosts needs to undertake is a serious (undercover) study of the good and bad elements or effects of using these folks. USCOE campground hosts are paid under contract and are closely monitored. We don't think the free hosts are real pluses to the other agencies. (Research would prove us right or wrong!) The opportunities and needs for applied research are limitless. You should also be aware (as most researchers aren't) that research capability has to be designed into facilities before research is done. You can't, for instance, find out user preferences for types of campsites or unit densities without designing those differences into your area. Since we strongly feel our activities in parks should be measured and frequently checked for trend changes (and since we know manager's perceptions of what's happening or what users want have a habit of being far less than right), outdoor recreation research must be continued, strengthened, encouraged, and funded.

For this to happen we should:

- Create a professional attitude which says we must frequently measure how we're doing and, if it is less than good, seek ways to do it better. (How can park persons call themselves professionals and not do this?)
- Never be satisfied with our work.
- Make sure researchers and managers are on the same team.
- Seek ways to minimize research costs and to emphasize applied rather than long-term and costly basic research.

In our view the only reasonable answer is a strong linkage between public and private park managers and owners with much improved responsive help from the academic community (colleges and universities). Building big research staffs within agencies makes no sense now and it really never did. If, for instance, *all* intern students were required to gather data (and gain extra credit) during their fieldwork experiences before graduation, the *parks,* the *universities,* and the *students* would benefit at little or no cost to anyone. Since the university would be gathering the data they would have considerable credibility. This model would also force park folks to think about looking for problems and finding some real answers—a process quite new to most of them. We are also convinced the leisure products and services communities can and should be involved with some limited financial help and guidance. Creating such a model should be the function of both universities and park managers.

Finally—and this is a tough one—the publish-or-perish syndrome in universities should be drastically changed (and the so-called reward system too) by making sure:

- Most recreation research is tied to real applied professional needs;
- Emphasis is placed on helping managers;
- The research products faculty and students produce are written in language managers can understand; and
- Researchers make tangible and applicable recommendations based on their research findings.

To help this process along we suggest generating research possibilities and needs from park practitioners be an *important* task of at least one person on university recreation and park faculties. The key word is important, so the task should be given to an *enthusiastic* faculty person (preferably one with *both* practical and academic experience). Identifying increased numbers of manager-identified opportunities for students to generate applied research studies should be a primary goal of this person!

Carrying Capacities and Other Wonderful Stuff

As you already know we disagree in this edition with several things we recommended in the first edition. These include calling for fixed tables in campsites, camp units with some blacktop surfacing for persons with disabilities, and camp units placed next to toilets/showers for those same folks. We now confess an even bigger *mistake*—we wrote a little about carrying capacities without questioning them and without giving you serious guidance on this topic. There has been a big push over the last several years for professionals to embrace all sorts of guidance on physical and social carrying capacities, and we all fell into that academic trap. Today researchers have come up with several more types of capacities including economic areas and even more academic emphasis on carrying capacities.

Carrying capacity is a concept pioneered by range or grazing experts. Essentially, the idea is a given land base can sustain a certain number of horned critters for a certain time. If the number of critters is exceeded over time (without management action such as mooving—ouch—the critters to another piece of land) the entire environment can suffer. A factor in all of this in some places is overstory shade removal. If you want *more* cows and *more* grass you have to begin overstory shade removal. Wildlife folks bought into the carrying capacity realm and finally recreation and park folks made the move. It all seems a bit logical, doesn't it?

Before we proceed further with this discussion you should review several items:

- We do not believe in the myth of physical overuse when applied to human use of recreation areas.
- If you build campsites in primitive campgrounds, wilderness areas, or family campgrounds, and they receive use, they must have site reinforcement or the environment there will be destroyed!
- Users have several preferences for unit densities though most prefer the 8–12 unit per acre medium range.
- Public parks belong to the public.
- Site hardening, facility and furniture location, and overstory shade removal are excellent people-pleasing, environment-protecting tools.
- Paving camp and picnic sites on level ground makes no sense even for persons with disabilities.

Many years ago the USCOE Waterways Experiment Station contracted with a research and development corporation to come up with a method for determining physical and social carrying capacities. It seems resource "overuse" and user overcrowding were the focal issues. The 104-page report called *Recreation Carrying Capacity Handbook: Methods and Techniques for Planning, Design and Management* was issued in July of 1980. There were several good ideas in the book and numerous bad ones. The problem is, few folks recognized the bad ones.

The research group had heard of impact-resistant campsites but felt these weren't needed everywhere. With the guidance you've previously received you should question the following findings and recommendations:

- Build numerous small areas instead of a few large ones. This disperses the use and cuts down on overuse. (Oh!) We say think *big,* plan *big* and build *big!*
- Close portions of areas or entire areas for a year or more so the *overused* areas will heal. We say rest and rotation theories do not work!
- Increase maintenance funding of areas receiving overuse. We say spending that money simply throws good money after bad.
- Charge more to curtail use. Well, this works on use but not on impact.
- Restrict the numbers of users per campsite (this includes vehicles). This approach leaves out user wishes completely *and* doesn't help impact problems.
- Pave campsites to eliminate overuse. What about user needs, heat, initial expense, and maintenance costs?

In the report's redesign drawings showing how to eliminate overuse or at least minimize it, they ended up with more impact than the poor original! Examples of this include:

- Fat loops placed parallel to the lakeshore, meaning persons from all parts of the loop walked through the shoreline-oriented sites.
- Toilets/showers in loop centers!
- Moving traffic from one loop onto another.
- Units located 90° off one-way roads.
- Pull-through units on the left sides of one-way roads.
- Speed bumps on roads.

There was no mention of varied unit density, use of buddy sites, the up-and-back principle to minimize roads, or curtailing the USCOE propensity to eliminate screening between units and grow and mow more grass.

As we said, the expensive product presented several interesting items, but completely fell apart in application. The authors have seen the same problems occur with *all* attempts to prescribe physical carrying capacity standards. Perhaps it can be done, but the efforts to date have, in our view, caused far more problems than they've cured. Remember, for instance, that all camp and picnic units that receive use need to have site reinforcement! For best results, the universal type site reinforcement is far better than hardening with asphalt or concrete. Therefore, prescribing unreinforced primitive low density sites is as poor a practice as not hardening sites where the density is 10 units or more per acre. If you want to build parks for people use the numerous tools and techniques we've given you. Don't spend your time (as many folks do today) dinking around with theories and schemes involving physical carrying capacity!

As far as social carrying capacities go, well, maybe, but common sense such as understanding what folks want in backcountry areas, family campgrounds, seasonal sites, and trails will help determine guidelines to increase or decrease use. If, for instance, too many folks are using a trail system, elimination of some access points and/or parking spaces are obvious answers.

Social carrying capacity guidelines (which also in many cases mean increased use) *have* helped with boating and people use on lakes and streams. Increasing or decreasing access points, boating slips, parking places, and even hours for certain use are all good tools. So, the authors can buy into some social carrying capacity schemes—but not the numerous physical capacity types of guidance for recreation use.

Obviously what we've just said and what you've just read will not help us into the elite realm of the researcher academic worlds. That's OK. As long as *you* get some guidance, we are well paid. Some 25 years ago a U.S. Forest Service associate came up with a resource planning scheme which to date has cost the American public millions of dollars to try to implement *and* nearly stopped developed site construction (for families) in the Forest Service. Tragically, some folks in the Bureau of Land Management have also bought the product. What is it? It's the heralded and greatly ballyhooed *Recreation Opportunity Spectrum* (ROS). Essentially it ties all recreation use to seven basic categories (though there can be numerous others added). These categories go from Primitive (P) to Semi-Primitive/Nonmotorized (SPNM) to Roaded Natural (RN) to Rural (R) to Urban (U). Depending on the type of experience a user wants (and we certainly question these), lands are allocated to one or another of the seven categories.

All of this good stuff is based on the idea that the "goal of the recreationist is to have satisfying experiences." (We wonder where having *fun* and being together with family and friends fits in.) Why haven't the authors bought into the ROS concept? Here are several reasons:

- The process has encouraged Forest Service personnel to think rustic, primitive, and small. If you've read the three preceding chapters, you'll understand this causes both people *and* environmental problems.
- The concept perpetuates the antienvironmental theory that low-density campsites can be built and used without site reinforcement. This is not so in wilderness or anyplace else.
- The number one concern today in camping is visitor protection. Those scattered small sites not only harm the environment, they discourage family use.
- Who's there and who isn't is not a concern in ROS. In fact, users, particularly families of all types, aren't a big ROS concern.
- The elements we've shared with you—site design, design psychology, buddy sites, extra parking, universal sites, complete reinforcement of areas of known impact, amenities for older users and persons with disabilities, and family beckoning programming—aren't a part of ROS.
- ROS makes it easy for Forest Service planners to lean to the elitist left and provide for wilderness types rather than

for "all Americans." (The number of Urban-type campgrounds and other facilities they've designed and built in the last 10 to 15 years, or the lack of numbers, proves our contention.)

Just to make sure the authors' concern about carrying capacities, ROS, and other similar wonders aren't out in left field, we ran our sacrilegious thoughts by four or five folks who have lots of recreation and park expertise, smarts, and common sense. We were both relieved and surprised they all agreed with our serious questioning. We and they also agree ROS is not a usable process *and* the physical carrying capacity quest may still be a good one. But, to date, we haven't arrived at making it work in the field with *simple, workable,* and *user-benefiting* guidelines!

If that quest is someday successful we believe the results will have to come from a team of knowledgeable *managers* with *some* input from the academic research realm. If you haven't had several years experience at running the train (managing parks for real people) you quite likely don't know much about how a train runneth. (That's kinda profound, ain't it!)

One final thought about ROS: We were pleased to find this U.S. Forest Service concept, while extensively (and expensively) used on *your* 200 million acres of Forest Service–managed lands, has not been warmly embraced by other agencies—even the BLM. State and county parks and numerous federal agencies, particularly the heavily visited U.S. Corps of Engineers, aren't involved. This is good news for developed site users which make up the bulk of use on public lands.

The agencies, with help from researchers, have tied all this together with carrying capacities. Their latest tie-in was a sizable study and manual for recreation use for persons with disabilities. The concept and the rationale for ROS and the guidelines evolved after the Forest Service moved away from their progress with developed sites and programs including some early pioneering imagineering for persons with disabilities *and* turned their full attention to appeasement of the environmentalists and wilderness folk. It is interesting to note as we move to the year 2000 there is still much rhetoric from those noise makers of the 1970s *but* ever decreasing use!

Of all the Hultscott axioms, advice, guidance and opinions in this book, our disdain for ROS goodies and physical carrying capacity guidance will—we believe—bring us the most flack. So be it!

Customer Service

Back in the mid 1960s when the oldest of the authors was assistant supervisor of the Cherokee National Forest in Tennessee he had a forest supervisor who was exceptionally interested in good public and good neighbor relations. (Even then this was quite unusual.) The author's duties also included being recreation staff officer *and* forest public relations officer. One of the things he did in wearing that PR hat was (on his visits to the six ranger districts) to go to several local backcountry, old-time general stores. This was done at break times, and for cheese and cracker lunches. The break time

snack included an RC Cola, a moon pie, and some *serious conversation* with the store owner. These store owners (and those in more modern but similar positions today) were the *key* contacts to let us know what was or wasn't happening, including who was or wasn't pleased with the Forest Service in those mountain valleys. Numerous problems and misconceptions were unearthed and repaired during those visits and, even more importantly, many new Forest Service friends were made.

Fifteen years later (when the oldest of the authors was working for TVA at Land Between the Lakes), the second oldest of the authors chanced to visit one of those same RC Cola and moon pie mountain grocery stores. By that time he had been "promoted" and was working out of east Tennessee in TVA's Natural Resource Division. Most of the PR training he had received while at LBL had made sense to him, so he told the store owner he was from TVA and wanted to help him if he could. You should understand that trusting outsiders (particularly government types) and believing them early on aren't traits of Appalachian Mountain folk. Mountain folk are wonderful people but it takes considerable time and sincerity to gain their confidence. The store owner's response was splashed with laughter at the thought that a government person—particularly anyone from TVA—was there to help him or the community! He had asked for TVA help before and it had been promised on several occasions but never materialized. Then he said the only person ever to have helped them was a Forest Service person (the oldest author) and that was years ago. For as long as he worked for TVA, the other author provided the maps and other information the store owner and his clientele needed. Both authors made new friends for their agencies and provided the customer service *all* government personnel should provide (simply by doing the *right and decent thing*).

Earlier we told the story concerning a lack of safety emphasis found when an author transferred from the Forest Service to TVA. The same sort of finding was true about making friends (and building a public relations power base) with local folks at and near Land Between the Lakes. This just wasn't a standard operating procedure in TVA. Experience tells us emphasis on building such a base was far more prevalent (years ago) in the Forest Service South than it was in the West. We have reason to believe this, while in lessening degree, is also true as we near the year 2000.

The Sagebrush Rebellion in the far West, government officials being threatened and actually shot at, having to travel in teams, and the general public's being upset (rightly or wrongly) with "public servants" who tell them in no uncertain terms what they can or can't do, even on their own private lands do not describe an aura where, "I'm from the government and I'm sincerely here to help *you!" Whatever happened to the golden rule?*

There are numerous public servants who do and have done conscientious work with local folks (their neighbors) and the general public. The fact is, the best park professional at customer service *and* at building a strong, local power base we've ever known is Don Albeitz of Indiana's Lieber State Recreation Area. We've mentioned his work two or three times previously. Local shop owners for miles around actually *get upset with him* if his staff *doesn't* ask them to donate to one or another of his numerous programs. His program fund got an anonymous donation of (guess what) $300,000 because of his work. Do you know of any other park professional with this sort of record?

Early in President Clinton's administration he showed "concern" for the government's obvious lack of quality public service when he issued Executive Order 12862, *Setting Customer Service Standards*. It called for "ensuring that the federal government provides the highest quality service possible to the American People." Furthermore, it was to require continual reform of the executive branch's management practices and operations to provide service to the public "that matches or exceeds the best service available in the private sector." ("Matching or exceeding!" Oh my!)

"Sounds good—tastes great." *But* will it happen particularly with the current public dislike and distrust of things government and considerable federal employee disdain for the public? We doubt it! Here are three true examples to make you ponder. Two of the examples happened in the U.S. Forest Service. Both were due to out of control or beyond control law enforcement personnel and both happened *before* the Executive Order was issued. The third example occurred at TVA's Land Between the Lakes—*after* issuance of the order.

Example 1. Location: A recreation area on a southern national forest. An elderly Kansas couple, having heard of the wonders of national forest camping facilities, decided to make their *first visit* and were excited about the prospects. They drove all day and arrived somewhere near their destination in the early evening. Since the route to the small recreation area was poorly signed, they arrived well after dark, couldn't find the campground loop, were exhausted and discouraged; and parked their truck and trailer in an empty day-use picnic area parking lot. At 2 A.M. (that's 2 o'clock in the morning!) they were rudely awakened by a persistent *pounding* on their trailer door. They had no way of knowing who might be there to rob or harm them and they were completely frightened! Initially they decided to keep the door locked but the pounding increased in intensity so in great fear they opened the door. At 2:10 A.M., in an empty parking lot, a uniformed U.S. Forest Service law enforcement officer informed them it was against Forest Service rules to camp overnight in that day-use parking lot and they were to leave—pronto (that means now). Later they wrote the Forest Service and complained about the "customer service" they received. A greatly embarrassed official answered their letter with a sincere apology and the wish that they would return for a better (as the USFS says) "experience." To date those folks haven't—surprise—returned.

If you find this to be an example of poor public service, read on. In recent years the USFS has adopted a new motto: "Caring for the land *and* serving people." We think they do a far better job in land caring (though their wilderness friends even question that) than they do in serving people, particularly "all Americans."

Example 2. Location: A small campground on a western national forest. An older couple with a large camping rig arrives late in the evening at a small Forest Service "sporting camp." They knew about the campground *and reserved* the only campsite in the campground suitable to their use weeks before. They, too, were excited about camping near a mountain trout stream on *their* national forest, and they looked forward to quickly setting up camp, having a meal, and enjoying some relaxation. However, the unpaid campground "host" had decided he and his camping vehicle should have the large site and was camped and entrenched thereon! (The plot thickens.) The camper asked the "host" (we use the term loosely here) to move and after a heated discussion the "host" said no way and if they couldn't find another suitable campsite, they could leave! The camper who had the *guaranteed* reservation did just that. Since it was quite late they drove a short distance and camped that night near the edge of the paved road. (This story goes on.) Early the next morning a uniformed "compliance" checker (another law enforcement rascal) knocked on their door and cited them for parking where they shouldn't be parked. This was not a warning but a citation! The compliance checker had no sympathy for what had happened earlier. (That ain't all folks). The camper complained to the district ranger who backed his personnel as did the next highest level. Sometime later the amazing *un-hosting* story found its way to the Regional Office Recreation Division *and* the regional forester. They put a stop to at least that bit of foolishness and issued a sincere apology. The damage to the Forest Service from this *one* tragic incident is incalculable! What must visitors think of the "professionals" who run *their* parks? What do you think?

Example 3. The scene: The western Kentucky Big Lakes resort country. A middle-aged married couple (one a federal employee) takes a few days early spring vacation and visits some of the state parks, restaurants, private resorts and other areas including a brief visit to the north end of Land Between the Lakes (where, as you know, years ago all three authors were employees). Their first destination was the LBL visitor center. Since it was early spring and midmorning they were the only visitors there. They entered the visitor center expecting to be greeted by, or smiled at, or in some manner acknowledged by the *two* on-duty staff persons (why two at that time?). None of the above happened! The two staff persons behind a counter were deep in conversation about "important" night before personnel happenings and at no time welcomed or said anything to their *only two visitors!* The visitors walked around and viewed the numerous exhibits, giving the two staff people ample opportunity to greet them and be helped—and after a 20-minute less-than-delightful visit—walked out. The federal employee and his wife were both *completely disgusted* with TVA and those two staff persons. Interestingly, teaching permanent and seasonal staff skills in quality *sincere* customer service is one of the responsibilities of the federal employee who "enjoyed" the TVA visitor center. Are we to believe this disgraceful example "provides service to the public that matches or exceeds the best service available in the private sector" called for in the executive order?!

In the three examples, you read the work of several government employees including two law enforcement officers (storm trooper types), a campground "host" who as a czar-like character rules the park, and two TVA staff persons whose pay wouldn't change if they did greet visitors warmly *and* whose union would fight mightily if they were reprimanded. We think all five persons should be terminated or at least hung by their thumbs. What do you think? Four of the five folks are *your* federal employees paid for by *your* taxes. The free host is no bargain either. When will we grow tired of this sort of treatment, and when will we expect *our* employees to do a day's work for their high pay?

The authors believe the executive order is a step in the right direction, though it is likely a political gambit. We liken this action to giving a Band-Aid to a person who has just lost half of a leg. The authors believe customer service involves careful park planning, design, construction, management (including visitor protection), and programming, *as well as* how a park staff greet visitors. As you should by this time have been aware, though, there are countless roadblocks the previously mentioned executive order Band-Aid doesn't cover. For instance, have a closer look at those Forest Service law enforcement folks. When they first came onto the scene in the early 1960s, they were of tremendous help to users and the Forest Service. Back then, they were directly assigned to a forest supervisor and responsible to him for their actions. Any hint of a storm trooper–type treatment of visitors called for and received immediate attitude adjustment. For the last several years, though, they all have been directly assigned to the Washington, D.C., office. There is no supervision by the regional forester or forest supervisor or anyone for that matter. They are not a part of a team and can (and often do) run amuck. (Recently a disgusted USFS recreation planner told us the storm troopers now have arrest or citation quotas, and the most convenient place to fill those quotas and harass the campers is at developed sites.) Whoever made this sort of "antiserving people" decision deserves the dodo of the year award. This further highlights the disdain the U.S. Forest Service now has (particularly in its national office) for developed site users!

The problem we gave you at the end of Chapter Eight should have given you dozens of reasons why many parks lack good hosting and quality customer service. Examples here were small area size, no on-site management, no programming, no protection, small campsites, and on and on. The good visitor and bad visitor thought process mentioned as a storm cloud in the same chapter is also part of the problem. Tied in, too, is a federal government employee de-emphasis in measurement of quality and quantity of work with its direct linkage to pay scale and promotion. "Why do much if it won't, for one reason or another, benefit me?" We hope some of what we've said will cause you to make sure *at least you* approach a potentially rewarding park career with enthusiasm, honesty, integrity, and an acceptance of responsibility. Unless things change drastically, you will be unique.

Some Thoughts on Park Maintenance

The importance of park maintenance is woven throughout this book. There are college texts on maintenance and for at least the last 20 years the National Recreation and Park Association has, with others, hosted three to five park maintenance workshops each year. In our view these workshops are well worth the time and money required to attend. This is not a maintenance textbook so our additional thoughts will be brief. Sprinkled through the remaining text will also be a few more axioms.

Axiom 1. If at all possible, build maintenance problems *out* of your parks rather than building them in. Two excellent examples of this are shown in Figures 10.95 and 10.96. Figure 10.95 shows erosion prevention on a ditch at an Indiana state recreation area. Figure 10.96 shows a defined rock sump that catches the rainwater from a USCOE visitor center roof in Kentucky.

Figure 10.95

Figure 10.96

Axiom 2. Far too many of our maintenance dollars are spent curing effects rather than causes. Figure 10.97 shows a nonuniversal campsite at a municipal campground in Virginia in early spring and the leaf litter covers up most of the sizable area of bare soil. If they decide to rehabilitate the campsite by rototilling, fertilizing and seeding they will, as most folks do, be wasting

Figure 10.97

Figure 10.99

Figure 10.100

your money. The use of the universal defined and gravel reinforced campsite here (as in other places) is a money and environment saver.

Axiom 3. If you allow your facilities to deteriorate like the Warwoman Dell sign of long ago you will be asking for vandalism and added maintenance woes. Ol' Zack Cravey lost that election. His posters didn't deface the cracked, blanched and paint-peeled sign; if anything they made it look better (Figure 10.98).

Axiom 4. If a maintenance challenge occurs, take action as soon as possible. If you don't, users will think you don't care and will contribute negatively to your problems. Someone or some critter has dumped the garbage can at the toilet/shower shown in Figure 10.99. If you don't pick up the trash and clean the walkway *pronto* you'll be asking for more of a mess.

Axiom 5. Building on and encouraging foot traffic on areas that aren't level causes extra maintenance problems. (Figure 10.100 is a Georgia State Park campsite.) The undefined and unlevel parking spur at the right of the photo ends at (not on) the tent pad. The pad was costly to build and is another safety hazard. The upright grill encourages those campfire spots around the site adding filth and tree root damage. And the piece of play equipment in the center of the loop adds to the impact-maintenance challenge. (Other than the things we've mentioned, it's a "wonnerful" campsite.)

Axiom 6. Minimize maintenance challenges *and* dollars needed by being smart. The sign post and both signs at a toilet/shower facility at a USFS area in Florida (Figure 10.101) are costly, unnecessary, and vandal beckoning. The showerhead symbol and the women's side could have been stenciled on the building. Note the shower symbol has already been vandalized and the upper sign is cupped and bent.

What sort of maintenance problems do you see in Figures 10.102, 10.103 and 10.104? Figure 10.102 shows a tree with an already dead top in an Indiana county park dayuse area parking lot. The "save the trees" folks are at it again. It will be far more expensive to remove the tree

Figure 10.98

Figure 10.101

Figure 10.102

and stump and crossties (and you *will* have to do so eventually) than it would to have eliminated it when the lot was built. It wasn't an island of trees in the center of the lot worthy to be saved; it was a thoughtless problem-causing mistake!

Figures 10.103 and 10.104 have a similar problem although one is in California and the other is in North Carolina. The problem is vegetation has grown where it shouldn't be and we haven't seen it happen. Not seeing maintenance problems (and safety problems)

Figure 10.103

Figure 10.104

is some sort of obviously incurable malady all across America. The vegetative growth happened over at least a three-year period. Why didn't we see it?

Axiom 7. Make sure what you build is built to a reasonable standard with proper quality materials. The new asphalt-paved parking spur with full hookups located in all of the wrong places is in a new private campground in Mississippi (Figure 10.105). The asphalt is raised off the *sand base* meaning there is no side support *and* the sand base will move and shift as heavy wheels park on the asphalt. (There was no rock base under the paved spurs.) So maintenance problems aplenty are built into this new site. To add to the challenges here all of the paved parking spurs are at a 90° angle to the road meaning backing challenges big time for users. This is another instance where an engineering consulting firm has been less than knowledgeable.

Many years ago when we worked for TVA at LBL their construction crew paved a sizable parking lot at a new group camp. Part of the lot had a rock base under it but a sizable part didn't. The part that didn't provided maintenance work soon after the parking lot was open to traffic. (The blacktop without a base quickly failed.) We found that experience to be quite interesting, expensive, lacking in integrity and typical of TVA.

While TVA is fresh on our (your) mind have a look at the maintenance problems in Figures 10.106 and 10.107. Both were in the same campground. The commercial wooden structure in Figure 10.106 has obviously been vandalized and partially burned weeks or months before the photo was taken. Note, the crosstie-sized piece laying in the center also has a safety problem—a steel bolt sticking up through it. The vandalism by spray paint on Figure 10.107 also had been done some time ago. Again, when you don't immediately attend to vandalism maintenance problems, you are asking for more!

If you'll look closely at the flood lights over the table at the left of the photo in Figure 10.107 you'll see they are lit. All of the lights around the softball field, which is near the multipurpose play court, were also brightly shining. Since the photo was taken at 2:30 P.M. on a sunny day, all of the lights had been on at least since the evening before. Government waste? Yes! Your dollars? Yes again!

Figure 10.105

Figure 10.106

Figure 10.107

Most of the problems mentioned in the safety section of this chapter could have been eliminated or greatly improved by prompt maintenance action. The main problems are seeing them and promptly taking remedial action. Each individual working for you—including laborers—must be trained to see maintenance problems *and* must have the integrity to want quality work done. This should be true of public and private facilities. In today's society, however, what "should be" many times isn't.

This chapter, with its eight sections, has been a challenging chapter to write and rewrite. There is some linkage between most of the sections but there is no dominate thread running through all of them. If we haven't said it before, as we arrive near the end of *Planning Parks for People,* we need to say it now: The authors do not expect students, on-the-ground professionals, or professors to agree with us on all or even a majority of what we've written. If we've made you mad a few times and you have disagreed on numerous points we've at least gotten you to think.

You likely have had major challenges and problems aplenty with Chapter Ten. (At least we hope so!) As a reward for putting up with your many problems we aren't giving you a chapter-ending real problem. We do suggest you carefully read the chapter again to better understand what we've tried to give you.

Chapter Eleven

Access to a Heritage: Roadblocks or Assurances?

The outdoors lies deep in American tradition. It has had immeasurable impact on the Nation's character and on those who made its history. . . . When an American looks for the meaning of his past, he seeks it not in ancient ruins, but more likely in mountains and forests, by a river, or at the edge of the sea. . . . Today's challenge is to assure all Americans permanent access to their outdoor heritage.

At the beginning of Chapter One we provided you with what we called the foundation of our recreation philosophy—the above quotation from all volumes of the Outdoors Recreation Resources Review Commission (ORRRC) report. Since you have arrived at this last chapter we'll assume you've read and perhaps studied the other 10 chapters.

The authors didn't give you a specific problem at the end of Chapter Ten so here's a *Planning Parks for People* problem given at the beginning of the final chapter. Based on what you've read—up to this page in the book—give us your assessment of the job we've (park folks across America) done in "assuring *all* Americans permanent access to *their* outdoor heritage." Again, the key words are *all* and *their*. We'll leave the details or sideboards of this assignment up to you. Keep in mind, though, developed sites of all types hold the key to provision of areas and activities for the broadest spectrum of users.

Thirty-six years have swiftly gone by since the ORRRC report was published. All three authors have enjoyed (and continue to enjoy) exciting, rewarding, and oftentimes frustrating careers. During those years many, many good things have happened in the outdoor recreation realm and, at the same time, numerous occurrences (mostly political) have been far less than good. In contrast to the first edition of *Planning Parks for People* wherein we discussed serious problems only in the last chapters, we've tried to point many of them out chapter by chapter beginning in Chapter One. The main purpose of this final chapter is to share additional problems and concerns (as we see them) you'll face as you take us to the year 2000 and beyond.

Have the American park professionals (including educators) striven to "assure access" (particularly in the last 20 years) or have we created roadblocks impeding maximum enjoyment of the out-of-doors by all Americans? You likely have already found out what we think, but just in case, we believe we've taken dozens of steps backwards in providing outdoor recreation facilities and programs for most people.

Please keep in mind as you read this last chapter we are giving you our perspective on several volatile issues. We do so out of care and concern for existing and potential park users, for you, and for our profession. Our comments may anger some of you, your professors, and more than a few professionals. We do not have all the answers; in fact there may be no answers to several of our problems and questions. Since many of our readers are students, we'll begin our problem discussion with *you*.

Today's Student, Tomorrow's Professional (That Is, If He or She Can Get a Job)

Numerous things have happened in the academic realm in recent years. Curricula teaching any sort of recreation have dropped from 400 (20 years ago) to about 175 today. Academic emphasis on planning, designing, programming, and managing developed sites was never too strong and is now almost nonexistent while teaching about the virtues of wilderness (even as wilderness use is rapidly declining) continues to increase. Emphasis on diversity and affirmative action in the federal park realm has meant most of the already scarce jobs aren't available now to a sizable percentage of park and recreation graduates. Budget cuts in most government park providing agencies have also dimmed job prospects. Park systems turning to concessionaire operations and management add to the problem.

During the last 20 turbulent years we've had the opportunity to interact on a rather close basis with perhaps 5,000 recreation students. If we were in the place of an outdoor recreation manager looking to hire a staff assistant, we would consider hiring maybe—maybe—five percent of this group. In fairness to students, part of the blame for this situation falls on curricula. As we've discussed before, there are basically two types of university departments turning out recreation majors: the department housed in a school or college of health, physical education and recreation (HPER), and the department housed in a school of forestry or natural resources. In general, HPER schools do a reasonably good job of teaching "people-oriented" skills such as programming and administration. However, most of these departments don't have the faculty expertise (or the inclination) to teach courses relevant to resource management; courses like dendrology, hydrology, soil science, park planning, and the like.

How many of you who are HPER students, for example, would recognize a scarlet oak? Without a course in dendrology, you might not even think about the need to consider the properties of this tree relative to recreation. Try, however, putting a campground or picnic area in a stand of scarlet oaks and watch how quickly your shade disappears because these shallow-rooted trees simply can't withstand nearby construction and compaction. On the other hand, graduates of resource-oriented schools might know these things, but they almost always fail to learn how to provide a *people-oriented* experience and fun in outdoor recreation areas. What we don't seem to understand is the city folks who enjoy the sports and games and other activities hosted by HPER types *in the city* are the same folks who visit our wildland parks. There the resource folks fail quickly to interest these visitors with "exciting" talks about fuzzy sycamore leaves or a boating safety program.

While part of the "student problem" lies with curricula, students aren't blameless either. We've seen far too many undergraduates *and* graduate students interested only in a quick-fix education with attitudes like, "I'll take easy courses for less work and a higher GPA." We've seen graduating seniors who are literally incapable of writing a grammatically correct, much less comprehensible, report; who don't even know the names of our professional journals, let alone read them; and who seem to feel the profession "owes" them a job just because they have a degree. We aren't so old to not remember how tough it can be to get through school, and we are quite aware of your difficulties in finding jobs. If you want to market yourself, you need to be ready to make some sacrifices.

Try to find summer work in recreation settings. You may make less money, but you can pick up some great experience and make some good contacts. Join professional societies and *get involved* in them. Volunteer to serve on committees, help organize conferences and attend meetings. Professional societies don't exist *for* you, they exist *because* of you. Talk to teachers *and professionals* and find out the kinds of skills you need to have to function effectively—then go get them. Take courses in technical writing, business administration, and computer skills. Your grade point average may suffer a little, but you'll be a better professional for it. Finally, demonstrate that you're capable of being a professional by acting like one. For example, don't simply read articles and editorials in professional tabloids, magazines, and journals because they're assigned. Read them because it's your responsibility to know what's happening in the field!

Perhaps you feel what we've been saying doesn't apply to you. If you're right, you're the type of student we'd want to hire. If you can look at yourself and say, "I've honestly done all I can to get the most out of my education," then good for you. If you have challenged yourself (and your professors), congratulations. If you've taken people- and resource-oriented courses and management classes to prepare for a career in outdoor recreation, you should feel positive about yourself. If you are eager and willing to learn, you are already thinking like a professional should. Add to these excellent attributes *bountiful enthusiasm,* a willingness to sometimes work (without pay) far beyond the eight-hour day, generous measures of honesty and integrity and if you fit this description, we'd feel pretty good about you, too! But, we would also guess, you represent a minority of students.

"Professoring" and Outdoor Recreation

Let's turn our attention now to the individuals primarily responsible for training recreation students: university professors. Although there are exceptions, most of the academicians we know are intelligent, well-meaning, and personable. When it comes to outdoor recreation, many professors have problems understanding it, teaching it, and researching it. The fact is, being intelligent, well-meaning and personable, while commendable, doesn't qualify someone to teach or research a particular area. You also need a sensitivity to, and an understanding of, the subject at hand. Too many academicians we have met over the years lack these qualities in relation to outdoor recreation. Part of the problem, as we perceive it, stems from professors receiving their training in either an HPER or a resource-oriented curriculum—the same problem that detracts from the capabilities of their students.

Back in the early and mid 1960s, many forestry schools made the decision to climb aboard the recreation bandwagon. Unfortunately for the profession and the students they were to instruct, many of the forestry school professors selected to teach outdoor recreation were not trained to do so, and some were quite upset at being given this challenge. Others were excited about their new assignments, and these folks did all they could to fill in the gaps in their knowledge. Still others decided not to invest the time or energy to learn their trade, and this lack of background (and interest) had been quite harmful to the "production" of enthusiastic, well-trained, outdoor recreation resource professionals. Curiously, too, many of the graduates they produced were extremely mainstream environmentalists—a result contributing measurably to the many parks which haven't been planned for people. Lots of those professors have retired or are about to retire now. They either aren't being replaced or are being replaced by persons as qualified and interested as they were!?

"What sort of serious knowledge does a person really have to have to design simple facilities like trails, camp and picnic sites, or group areas anyhow?" This attitude has always been a problem and is likely more so today. When you add to this our increasing dependence on computers to do "wonderful" planning for us, the plot thickens.

Another factor contributing to the deficiencies of outdoor recreation-oriented educators is the discrepancy between academic environments and the "real world" of recreation management. The faculty members we feel are "good" in the sense of being concerned with the needs of professionals are those who work closely with field-level personnel and keep abreast of the issues facing these folks. The academic types we have problems with are the ones who teach about and profess an expertise in outdoor recreation without ever having worked in a professional setting or who haven't kept up with what happens in the field.

To make our point, let us share a couple of stories with you. When we worked for the TVA, our office once received a "windfall appropriation." In other words, we had about $90,000 dumped into our laps that we weren't expecting to get. The only catch was that we got it on June 15 and had to either spend it by the end of our fiscal year or lose it. Our fiscal year ended on June 30.

Now every planning course we've ever taken or taught has said you first conduct a needs assignment, then prepare a master plan, then devise site plans, work up alternative designs, select the best option from among the alternatives, and lay out the design in the field. The day we found out about the money we had a staff meeting to decide how to spend it. At 7:00 A.M. the next morning, we were flagging a hike and bike trail. At 7:30, a truck unloaded a bulldozer, and two weeks later, the trail was finished. The hike and bike trail has been an excellent facility heavily used by young and old and disabled alike as well as functioning some years ago as a teaching tool for countless outdoor recreation college classes. This wasn't an ideal situation, but it was the real world, and sometimes the classroom is a long way from it. Today, before any sort of work began, you'd have to have an environmental impact statement (EIS) and survey, a team of archeologists would have to ponder and approve it, and the local save-the-environment groups would likely oppose it anyhow. Thus, what occurred then and the lasting benefits that followed would never have happened, *and* the $90,000 for outdoor recreation would likely have gone to a failed public housing project or something else of that sort. We wonder at the "blessings" of progress and yearn for a return of President John F. Kennedy who provided agencies with millions of dollars of accelerated public works money, gave them three or four days to plan their work, and had manpower waiting to begin public works work the following week.

Our second story also stems from our TVA days. In the mid 1970s, we were involved in planning an outdoor recreation consortium for five university recreation departments. While the TVA was to host the event, it was up to the university faculty to develop the objectives and curriculum for the consortium the way they felt it should be done. We met for two days. By suppertime on the second day, with our available time drawing to a close, we had managed to agree on a statement of purpose and a handful of objectives for the consortium—and hadn't even discussed the curriculum. We put that together rather quickly the last evening before we left. What happened? The purpose and objectives were important, but not—in our view—as important as what subjects we were going to teach, who would teach them, where would we go in LBL and outside for our field trip, what sort of outside speakers did we want, and who could contact them? Oftentimes academicians tend to think in lofty terms and forget the nuts and bolts in the process. As our friend Tony Tinsley suggested by quoting Sir Francis Bacon, people who dwell in ivory towers sometimes have heads made of the same material. *Note:* LBL became internationally famous mainly because of the hundreds of students and faculty we worked with in the four consortia and other workshops hosted each year.

They are no longer being conducted at LBL—what a shame—as they were the most outstanding programs ever conducted there.

The shortcomings in outdoor recreation knowledge of most of those assigned to teach it could be overcome if they attended a few *substantive* workshops, but in our 20-plus years of providing this training for hundreds of professionals we've had fewer than 10 professors in our classes. Perhaps that isn't all bad as one of the less than 10 was a recreation professor from a heralded California school. He was in the class with practitioners with all sorts of backgrounds, including maintenance folks, and he was the *only person* at the end who couldn't begin to unscrew a simple field problem!

Professional Issues: Telling It Like (We Think) It Is!

We will present several issues for you with our assessment of what has happened or is happening all with the criterion of "assuring all Americans permanent access to their outdoor heritage." You, like us, are welcome to your own opinion. We suggest what we have to say in this section will be grist for great debate with your professors and classmates.

The Political Scene

In Chapter Two we hinted at giving an outdoor recreation rating or ABC grade (based on the above criterion) to all presidents this half century. Here they are. *Note:* Seven of the ten presidents have held office less than a month in the last year of the service. (Presidents take office in late January). President Nixon resigned, President Kennedy was killed, and President Clinton is still with us at the writing of this chapter.

1950–January 1953 (actually 1945–1953) Truman: C. He was wrapping up one war and involved in the Korean Conflict so his contributions to parks for all Americans were few. He did see to it work began on upgrading federal parks that had seen no upgrading since the beginning of World War II.

1953–1961 Eisenhower: A. Some accomplishments include Mission 66 of the National Park Service; Operation Outdoors in the USFS (providing extensive funding to upgrade park facilities); Multiple Use Act of 1960 giving recreation (at least on paper) the same status as other USFS resources; the interstate highway system providing excellent access across America; and establishment of the ORRR Commission.

1961–1963 Kennedy: A++. Unfortunately his time in office was quite short but he did more in developed site recreation for "all Americans" then all presidents since. He completed ORRRC and instituted numerous programs including establishment of the Bureau of Outdoor Recreation (BOR); National Recreation Areas (NRA); help for private developers through USDA Soil Conservation Service and Extension services; National Recreation Trails; provision of funding for extensive development in the Federal Sector; accelerated public works program; creation of a national outdoor recreation demonstration area at Land Between the Lakes; and more and more!

1963–1969 Johnson: A+. Continued excellent work of former president; kept the top notch secretaries of Interior and Agriculture and the Accelerated Public Works Programs; both secretaries actually visited, used, and were big backers of public developed sites; 1964 Wilderness Act and establishment of millions of acres of *true* wilderness.

1969–1974 Nixon: B. Outdoor recreation division established in U.S. Army and tremendous emphasis on improved sites and increased staff in the U.S. Corps of Engineers; continued funding for developments in the public and private sectors; executive order requiring federal agencies to consider and, if possible, provide for off-road vehicle use on public lands.

1974–1977 Ford: C-. Very little done for recreation for all Americans though some funding was continued.

1977–1981 Carter: F+. De-emphasized developed sites and areas in the federal sector; demoralized agency personnel with special hiring of minorities (experienced and greatly inexperienced); packed the U.S. Department of Agriculture and U.S. Department of the Interior with lock-it-up environmentalists; increased wilderness expansion greatly, particularly in the eastern United States where most lands did not meet the establishment criteria of the Wilderness Act of 1964; changed the BOR to HCRS (the Heritage Conservation and [oh yes] Recreation Service); and more and more!

1981–1989 Reagan: B. Greatly expanded funding for outdoor recreation in all military services in the United States and overseas; eliminated HCRS; put brakes on wilderness expansion and purchase of additional private lands for nonpark purposes; established The President's Commission on Americans Outdoors.

1989–1993 Bush: C. Like Truman, had to contend with a war. Also had opposite party Congress throughout his four years; began President's Initiative which provided millions of dollars to the U.S. Forest Service to upgrade park facilities; signed landmark Americans with Disabilities Act.

1993–present Clinton: F (that's only because there isn't a lower grade). Is a Carter clone (regarding emphasis on programs for special interests with zip for others) with a lock-it-all-up-for-us environmentalist Vice President; big backers of concessionaire operation of public facilities; extremely active in making (or trying to make) major American park treasures (Yosemite, Grand Canyon) beyond the economic bounds of average folks. "Why shouldn't entrance to the Grand Canyon cost at least as much as entrance to Disney World?" asked the Secretary of the Interior in May, 1996; severe cutback of all federal park personnel and programs; pushed for more and more wilderness including a shady preelection lockup of 1.7 million *more* acres in Utah.

That's our list with these rankings: Truman, C; Eisenhower, A; Kennedy, A++; Johnson, A+; Nixon, B; Ford, C-; Carter, F+; Reagan, B; Bush, C; and Clinton, F. Wouldn't it be great for all American park users if the next two presidents we elect could be like Kennedy and Johnson? Note the top two rated presidents are Democrats *and* so are the bottom two!

History and the media tell us Republicans are generally big on helping rich folks while the Democrats do great things for poor folks and the common man. We won't get into this argument but will say the last two Democrats have certainly not fit the mold as they provide—in recreation—for the elite, the wealthy and special interests; not for most Americans!

Issue: The Special-Interest Syndrome

As you know we haven't been too kind throughout the book concerning what the special interests have done. Here is further background.

The 1960s and '70s were a time of tremendous upheaval. These days were also the era of "movements," from civil rights to antiwar to environmental protection. Causes became the "in" thing, and we must admit some of what happened was good. American society began to correct, or at least become aware of, prejudices based on race, beliefs, or gender; the immorality of a military-industrial approach to foreign policy; the disdain for the environment of self-serving corporate interests; and other problems inherent in a society pushed too quickly into the future. Relative to our discussion here, one problem stemmed from the realization by a variety of special-interest groups of their power with the news media. In effect, nearly any issue could become a celebrated cause if its proponents argued loud enough to attract media attention. The question of whether "movements make news" or "news makes movements" is one for journalism classes. The point for us to consider is the effects special-interest groups have had on outdoor recreation. Essentially the progress toward outdoor recreation for *all* Americans halted when special-interest groups began demanding more than their fair share of the pie.

The Environmentalists. The extremely vocal environmental movement gave added voice and political clout to proponents of wilderness use. This halted all sorts of development-oriented recreation activities in most of the federal sector. Anything not connected with the wilderness was bad, bad, bad. The National Park Service, U.S. Forest Service and other agencies backed away from development and closed, or tried to close, some of their park and recreation areas (particularly campgrounds) to all sorts of legitimate users while increasing manyfold their money and emphasis on wilderness and the environment. The Forest Service now heralds wilderness and winter sports as their main recreation components, yet history and research have both shown these activities to be the pursuits of the *wealthy,* the *well-educated,* the *young,* and the *physically fit.* This hardly includes all Americans—in fact, it excludes most of them. We are not antiwilderness; we are simply opposed to emphasizing wilderness use *at the expense* of the silent majority of Americans who are either unable or not inclined to carry their recreation gear on their backs. A tangible example of this de-emphasis on opportunities for all Americans is the almost exclusive policy of the National Park Service, the Bureau of Land Management, and the Forest Service of providing no electrical hookups in their campgrounds. To those individuals, including many older Americans, who need refrigerated medicine or a booster charge for their electric wheelchair or air conditioning because of health problems, this policy says, "We don't want you!"

Issue: Causes and the Aginners

The environmental movement, which early on seemed to have a sincere desire to improve management of resources on public lands, didn't take long to realize their togetherness and noise (mixed with ever increasing doses of truth stretching) could stop all sorts of things. "Stop the _____" (add here almost anything wildland managers wish to do) became the banner heading for hundreds of self-proclaimed environmental saver type groups—the "aginners," or those who are agin everything instead of being "fur" some things.

Earlier in the book we said all three authors lived (all three have finally escaped) in Bloomington, Indiana—home of Indiana University and hundreds of "stop the" type rascals or aginners. Figures 11.1 and 11.2 tell part of the story. The "Don't Pave Paradise" concert advertised in Figure 11.1 was part of the wild uproar stopping Brown County from paving an existing extremely narrow and rough road into the small lake and picnic area on the nearby Yellowwood State Forest (not state park or wilderness area). The road was needed to help young families and older people drive safely to a delightful area. It was stopped mainly by folks who looked and acted like those shown on their poster! The losers were those young families, older folks, and *you*. "Stop the Highway" posters littered the landscape throughout Bloomington (Figure 11.2). What they didn't want was the proposed interstate from the Great Lakes to Texas which would be of tremendous help to the economy of depressed southern Indiana. According to the EIS, the section in Indiana would have minimal impact on the environment. To date the environmentalists haven't stopped the highway but our money is on their loud noises. As we began this chapter a longhaired fellow showed up at our door wanting us to sign a petition condemning the road. As usual he could not explain his "fact" sheet! He was also glad to leave after we seriously quizzed him.

Other examples near Bloomington include: "Don't build the horse trail," "Don't salvage the blown-down timber," "Don't allow a concessionaire to host fun programs in a campground," "Don't add water *and* electricity to the campground (and remove the 10 hookup sites already blemishing the area)," "Restrict horseback riding in the wilderness." (Oh, what a dandy wilderness!) All of these barbs were aimed at the beleaguered folks on the nearby Hoosier National Forest. In our view the "lock-it-all-up-for-me aginner crowd" has destroyed multiple use management on that national forest. Unless a miracle occurs soon the environmental indoctrinators will see to it your other 156 National Forests will follow the sad Hoosier National Forest example.

The tragic part of this story is you'll find the anti-everything aginners all across America. The heaviest concentrations, though, are in the Washington, D.C., area and around liberal universities. Oftentimes groups will join together to provide additional clout. Such a group is the Hoosier Environmental Council (HEC) made up of 2,200-plus members in 50 organizations (or so their always questionable propaganda tells us). Included in the 50 are the Audubon Society, Sierra Club, and the Isaak Walton League. A paid staff person showed up one day asking the Bloomington author to join his wonderful group. (The ever present petition was there to sign.) He showed the author their registration form, a sheet showing their "accomplishments" and a fact sheet about the nearby Hoosier National Forest. Of the six "facts," four were completely false and the other two were distortions. If the author was reasonably intelligent but not knowledgeable about Hoosier National Forest management, *and* believed the fact sheet and the HEC (including the so-called prestigious environmental organizations) he too would, as many had done, have signed their petition condemning Hoosier National Forest management. He did not sign or join but asked the *paid* employee to carefully explain his facts. He couldn't, didn't, and, amid some sweating, quickly retreated.

We are quite aware National Forest management folks have made (like you and us) all sorts of mistakes, particularly in recreation. We are also aware the current administration has helped destroy that agency. In their second term, the USFS will likely see horrendous further changes. (See what we think under our predictions section *and* also do some research concerning what has happened to the USFS in recent years.)

One of the problems of the USFS nationwide and particularly in Indiana is the failure to *continually educate* and *inform* the public through radio, TV and the printed media

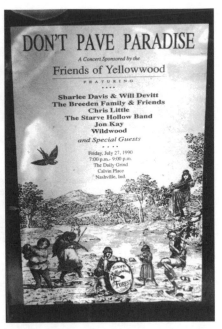

Figure 11.1

Figure 11.2

287

concerning all sorts of happenings. One of the authors was once an information and education (I and E) officer on a national forest where the public was informed at least weekly in one or more media forms about happenings and things to do on the Cherokee National Forest. It's a tremendous job involving long hours, *but* it provides the power base and the means to combat the untruth garbage given to the media by groups like the HEC.

The media with its leftist leanings is also part of the problem. The Bloomington "paper" (in our view) hit a new integrity low when it printed a rare Hoosier National Forest press release but editorialized and commented throughout the release. They also inserted comments therein by the local aginners. Resource-educated folks are rarely trained, inclined or skilled enough in public relations to fend off the frantic foolishness. You and we and "all Americans" are the losers!

Throughout the first 10 chapters we've shared tragic stories with you. Here are two more. Within an hour's drive of Bloomington is one of the most heavily visited parks in America. It is Brown County State Park near Nashville, Indiana. It is a sizable heavily wooded park in Indiana's unique unglaciated big hill country. Problem is and has been for at least 10 years, the tremendous deer herd is destroying the park. You can look through the once dense understory and see little or no young vegetation throughout much of the park. The deer also have suffered from a near starvation diet. They are quite small for their age and have little or no fat on them. While hunting hasn't been allowed in Indiana state parks, the only *feasible* remedial action to take was a series of carefully controlled hunts. Reluctantly the Department of Natural Resources decided that to *save* the park's *diminishing environment* a hunt was necessary. As usual the environmental crowd was ready to help the environment, *right? Wrong* again, you turkey!

The environmental aginners joined hands with the animal rights folks and stopped the first hunt. A year later the destruction had greatly increased and, fearing disease would infest the herd, the state politicians allowed the hunts to begin. Department of National Resources folks (like the USFS) became targets of the environmental crowd. An animal rights "expert" declared the deer were small because they were a dwarf subspecies of the white-tailed deer, and the aginners also threatened to dress like deer and be shot on opening day. We won't touch this one but hope you begin to see the extent these folks will go to have their way!

Story number two takes us back to the Yellowwood State Forest. In keeping with forest management needs, foresters marked some mature timber as well as some trees that would be helped by thinning (a sort of weeding process). The marking included a paint spot or line at about breast height and a spot on the stump. With a cry of "you can't do that to our wilderness," a group of lawless environmentalists drove several steel spikes in all of the marked trees. This renders them unfit for sale to anyone. Like the Watergate incident, the ends justified any means necessary to stop the timber cutting. What happened then was even more interesting. The local newspaper printed a half page article complete with drawings on just how spiking trees was or could be done. Oh yes, at the end they did say this sort of thing shouldn't happen *and* quoted representatives from local environmental groups saying they were innocent! The authors don't believe these folks are or were "innocent."

Many of the ardent environmentalists of today are the hippies from the '60s. They have haircuts and suits and look like regular folks. They are also the educators of today's youth. Ever wonder why students are far less educated today than in yesteryears in spite of skyrocketing educational costs? Much of the "education" they get is indoctrination of all sorts particularly in the antiestablishment and antiresource management realms. This includes such items as trees should never be cut, animals should never be hunted, and fish should never be caught.

Teachers are bombarded with politically correct environmental guidance (including delightful posters) from the National Wildlife Federation, Sierra Club, and other similar groups. Even the *Weekly Reader* now brings antimanagement guidance to youngsters supplied by the environmentalists.

It is our belief a person can become an overnight expert environmentalist by sending his or her check to the Sierra Club (remember, we once got a commendation from them though when and if this gets printed we don't expect to be overcome with similar awards!) or the Wilderness Society, or the HEC, and by picking up their anti-everything cardboard sign and bash-the-resource-rascals scarf or tie and gold card permit. They need not have knowledge, training, experience, or common sense to get this card. In fact, it seems the less people know the better and the more sheep-like they are in character the easier they are to lead. Add to this the opportunity this gives some powerless folks to wield power in stopping something and you have today's challenge to quality park provision.

One of the tactics practiced by the aginners regarding agencies such as the USFS is, while being against almost all resource use, they say they want the land strictly for recreation purposes. Don't be fooled by this rhetoric. For example, have another look at the list of things listed here that the aginners didn't want—most of these are recreation flavored. The "recreation" they are for is not developed site use for all Americans. Their recreation is wilderness.

As students of different sorts and backgrounds, you will be pushed and pulled and tugged and clobbered and asked to espouse this or that sort of cause. Please before you do so, let your integrity and honesty and your quest for truth guide what you do. Some causes are great, many aren't. We leave the choices to you.

Issue: Wilderness

The three authors enjoy and have enjoyed true wilderness recreation though age and other challenges have (as they have with the public throughout our country) diminished this interest and use. (Or perhaps broadened them—this passage is being written on a laptop PC in a 26-foot fifth wheeler powered by a 30-amp hookup in a KOA in Utah as the author is returning home from a five-day solo backpack in northern Idaho.) We are not antiwilderness!

At the writing of this chapter (mid 1996) how many acres of *your* public lands have been dedicated or locked up for wilderness use? Are more and more Americans using the wilderness? (We've already given you this answer.) Is the figure 25,000,000 acres? Is it a tremendous 50,000,000 (that's 50 million) acres? Is it a stupendous 75,000,000 acres? Or is it now a horrendous 100,000,000 acres and growing? If you knew or guessed at 100 million-plus acres, you are right on. The current administration is pushing for millions of acres more, particularly in Utah and other western states, where additional lock up of lands causes the states tremendous financial tax base hardship. We suggest that 100,000,000 acres is enough particularly as use is declining.

The Wilderness Society, Sierra Club, and other similar organizations have the opposite view. It isn't based on use; it is based on a curious philosophy and the need to get more and more members and more and more money for their sizable staffs. The curious philosophy says, "We don't want public lands to have other uses, including timber management, grazing, or even developed site recreation use. We want the Congressional designation and lock up because the feds aren't to be trusted to manage it properly" (as they define properly). The decline in actual wilderness use across this country gives them a real dilemma in money collection so this is why much of the deception issue-causing rhetoric goes on in even greater measures today.

When the Reagan administration took over from Carter folks, brakes were applied to the rampaging wilderness lockup of public lands. This required new strategies and schemes by the environmentalists. And so was born (in our view) an already existing bird called the spotted owl. The critter had been in the Pacific Northwest, for who knows how long, breeding in old growth *and* second growth timber stands, and otherwise minding its own business. As a possible way to lock up millions more acres of wilderness, the environmental "scientific" community said the little critter was nearing extinction because all old growth was being cut and the owl could *only* breed successfully in old growth virgin timber! This is simply not true! (Remember the "dwarf" white-tailed deer invented by the environmentalists earlier in this chapter?) Battle lines were drawn and the fake wilderness grab using the Endangered Species Act built up steam. When the team of Clinton and Gore made the scene, the big time land lockup took off again. One of their first hatchet jobs was to wipe out the hierarchy of the USFS and install a nonmanagement-trained wildlife researcher (friendly to the spotted owl) as chief. With this done the takeover was easy.

One quick result of the stoppage of old growth timber cutting was a doubling or more of structural timber costs *and* increased costs of new home construction throughout America. Another was the economic destruction of countless small towns dependent on timber harvesting in Washington and Oregon. Remember there are 100 million acres already locked up including numerous old growth stands in the Pacific Northwest. If the spotted owl were dependent on old growth and *all* other old growth were cut, the little spotted bird would still have millions of acres in which to frolic. The spotted owl land grab, in our view, is the most blatant of examples of deception we've yet seen the environmentalists employ. Stay tuned for further negative developments!

Issue: Career Challenges— Is There a Safe, Clear, Obstacle-Free Pathway to the Top?

The answer is yes for special people but no for most of you. Attempting to deal with the demands and the deceptive actions of special-interest groups is indeed a major impediment for outdoor recreation professionals. For the most part, however, these groups represent "outside interests" and are at least easy to identify. A more difficult problem arises when factors impeding "access for all Americans" are internal to the profession. This is the topic we'd like to discuss now: situations existing under the general heading of personnel-related issues.

Top Dogs. The bottom line is the top; ultimately the decisions affecting recreation policy rest with the individuals responsible for managing agencies involved in the profession. Consider some parallel situations. If you check into a hospital, presumably you would expect and feel more secure if the person in charge has a medical background. Similarly, academic institutions need educators with management and personnel experience in decision-making positions. Somehow this logic has escaped many public agencies involved in providing outdoor recreation areas and facilities. For the most part, the "top slots" in many agencies which manage recreation resources are not filled with people who have backgrounds in recreation (particularly federal agencies). In a Corps of Engineers district, personnel are ultimately responsible to a career military officer, usually a colonel. They typically stay in that position for two to three years. Directly under this individual and responsible for day-to-day operations, you'll find a district engineer. This person typically has engineers as assistants. Perhaps at the next level down (the fourth from the top), you'll find a recreation-trained person; more often, however, even these slots are filled with foresters or wildlife biologists.

We aren't picking on the Corps. Similar situations exist in the Forest Service, TVA, and other federal and state agencies. We aren't even being generally critical of the individuals involved; many of these folks are competent and well-meaning. *But* they generally aren't recreation oriented. Regardless of how professional or how nice an individual is, he or she is going to have personal and discipline-oriented biases that will influence decision making. Simply stated, we feel outdoor recreation interests—access for all Americans— would be better served if most of the people responsible for recreation management were trained in recreation. (This, too, we realize is quite a radical thought.)

First-Level Positions: No Jobs or Snow Job? If you follow the job markets at regional and national conventions

289

and watch job announcement bulletins, you'll find far fewer openings advertised for outdoor recreation positions than any other branch of the profession. One of the obvious reasons for this is the government job situation in general. Whether you agree or disagree with administration policy, there are fewer jobs available today in the public sector. We feel, however, that there is another reason behind the lack of entry-level positions available to graduates of recreation curricula; we perceive a disdain for these graduates—probably you included—on the part of resource-oriented agencies. Historically, recreation jobs in these agencies, for example the Forest Service, were filled with resource-trained individuals. One of the three authors became an overnight instant expert in outdoor recreation. (He might have amounted to something had he been recreation trained.) In the "early days" of recreation—the 1950s and early 1960s—this was more understandable since there were problems. In some instances, Forest Service recreation jobs were used as "dumping grounds" for individuals perceived as incompetent by their supervisors. In the 1990s many of the same jobs are filled with surplus timber specialists thanks to the spotted owl and the environmental rascals!

Today, however, available recreation graduates rarely find their way into the few existing job openings. People get promoted, retire or leave public service, so jobs open up and we don't object to seeing foresters, landscape architects, and wildlife biologists get them. We do object to seeing these individuals get *recreation* jobs because the hiring decisions are made by foresters, landscape architects, and wildlife biologists. (More later on the logic of this as it applies to affirmative action and diversity.)

Watch Where You Step: The Career Ladder. To put it bluntly, recreation-related jobs in resource-oriented agencies tend not to be career-structured. Ideally, professions such as recreation should have *career ladders*. Under these circumstances, an individual fresh out of college with a degree in recreation is hired in an entry-level position. After some on-the-job training and experience, our now-seasoned professional moves up the career ladder to a mid-level recreation position (assuming he or she deserves the promotion). After several more years, the more talented individuals with equal parts of enthusiasm, dedication, creativity, and willingness to work hard, become the next generation of decision makers.

Such a system perpetuates excellence for two reasons. First, people learn as they grow professionally, becoming more competent. Second, promotions create new entry-level positions which can be filled by younger folks who can then be helped along by those who preceded them. Problem is, things rarely work this way in practice. Recreation jobs in many public agencies have tended to evolve into stepping stones for administrative careers. Instead of moving *vertically* up a career ladder in recreation, people are often "stairstepped," moved up *and* over to recreation temporarily from another discipline within the same agency. Then they stairstep back up and over to an administrative position.

In addition to defeating the purpose of the career ladder, the real problem stemming from this practice is that recreation expertise never materializes. If you take a forester or other resource-oriented individual and place him or her in a mid-level recreation position for a year or two and then promote this person to an administrative position, there isn't much time and even less inclination to learn recreation (been there, experienced that!). Thus when the people answering to this "temporary" recreation person make mistakes, (and those mistakes litter the United States), particularly in their guidance or critiques of lower level personnel, we shouldn't be too surprised to see the results of these mistakes become reality in our parks and recreation areas. Using recreation positions as stepping stones rather than creating a career ladder accounts for many of the planning, designing, and management mistakes we've described throughout this book.

Strange Bedfellows. Another personnel-related issue in recreation is the question of unionism. Should recreation professionals belong to and support them? Our perspective on the matter is an emphatic, big time *no!* For many workers, unions, particularly through the first half of the twentieth century, were a source of salvation. Poor and often hazardous working conditions, low pay, and insufficient benefits all received attention and were largely eliminated for many workers due in significant part to the efforts of unions. There is, however, a basic difference between workers and recreation professionals. The difference is professionalism. Until the early 1970s, the unionization of recreation professionals was a rare occurrence. Then, starting with maintenance personnel, unions slowly began working their way through recreation programs in both municipal and resource-based agencies. Some years ago we heard the recreation director of a large western city tell us and others how disgusting and distasteful it was to deal with unionizing "professionals." It seems they wanted more and more pay for less and less supervision and even less work for that pay. According to him those "professionals" seemed to have little or no interest in providing exciting top notch programs for the people of their community.

We can't argue recreation professionals haven't been benefited personally from the growth of unions; they tend to bargain from positions of strength. Our concern is for what we feel is a resulting decline in both the quality and quantity of professional work. Unions tend to breed self-interest, and individuals who become concerned with increasing wages, more benefits, and the fruits of seniority have less time to devote to quality work. Requiring that professionals be promoted because of seniority rather than expertise and diligence works against the progression of a profession. In a very real sense, unionism and professionalism work at cross-purposes. Unions are by definition formed to advance self-interests; professionals are dedicated to advancing society through selflessness.

TVA's "professionals" had a union (none of the three authors belonged) and by now you should be aware of their work quality! In most states school teachers are unionized and they consider themselves to be highly professional. You be the judge of what's happening in education. We are not saying if you are a so-called nonprofessional person being unionized is good for both you and the country. Most post office employees belong to their union and certainly you are aware post office services have declined while postage has gone up, up, up. Another example of an agency immersed in unionism is the Social Security Administration. This would be another issue into which students should look.

Ours will quite likely be an unpopular opinion, but we continually hear recreation workers lamenting they are not looked upon and respected as professionals. Auto assembly line workers unionize and aren't viewed by the public as professionals, doctors don't unionize and are! Thus, you are what you are perceived to be.

The Spoils System. Recently a long time friend of ours—a state park director who was doing an outstanding job—was fired, terminated, zapped. He had worked his way up through the park ranks and, what's most important, had the respect of his personnel. Why was he fired when the Democratic Party was reelected? The incoming governor paid a debt to a person with no experience in the park realm, that's why.

The spoils system—rewarding campaign assistance with jobs—has been around for some time; however, this doesn't make it any more palatable from a professional perspective. Early in his career, one of the authors aspired to a resource position with the USFS. As it turned out, there was no opportunity for the aspiration to become reality, for the individual who approved the selections filled those slots with candidates who just happened to have the same religious affiliation as his. Being fired through the spoils system or not being considered because you aren't religiously correct are both shoddy things to experience.

In our view being hired or promoted because of race, gender, or anything else other than competence are shoddy too; in fact, they are un-American! How would you feel or respond if you were told you couldn't be considered or were fired because you were the *wrong color?* On April 20, 1996, a press release from Oakland, California, reported a $7.6 million jury award to a black man who was reportedly fired by a company branch manager because he was "the wrong color for the industrial market." While the award might be high and the case is being appealed, *no one, including this man, should be told he or she is the wrong color! Right? You bet!* Yet, one of the authors was told the same thing near the end of the Carter administration. Surprisingly and strangely, a need for GS-15 assistant directors of all Heritage, Conservation and Recreation Service regions (remember them?) was announced to the recreation world. Since the author had considerable experience, he applied for two of the jobs. There was no reply from one region. In the other, where the director was a personal friend, the author was told, and we quote: "You would make an outstanding assistant for me and I'd hire you, *but* these jobs were established strictly for minorities and you are the wrong color." Unlike the black man, the author had no opportunity to seek help anyplace.

Affirmative action requiring persons be hired for racial or other purposes has stocked the federal government with many special persons who were untrained and unqualified for their entry and many subsequent higher level jobs. If, as we hope and suspect, pushed by a vast majority of the American public, affirmative action finally gets struck down by the courts, the legacy of special hirings will still be with us for decades because it's likely de facto affirmative action will be difficult to erase.

Shortly after the special-person hiring emphasis began, many of those hired perceived themselves to be special and immune from work performance and other standards. (It is an even more unfortunate fact of life today.) This leads to countless personnel problems. When some were pushed to do acceptable work, cries of racial discrimination filled the air. Anyone accused of that was or is, automatically "guilty," all of which meant supervisors oftentimes backed away from even blatant problems to salvage their own careers. By that time the equal employment opportunity staffs were nearly all minorities and this caused additional problems aplenty. During this time (the Carter years and later) there was a noticeable decline in federal employee morale and work productivity. (Been there, experienced that!) This continues at an ever increasing rate today.

Gender Hiring: A Tale of Two Federal Agencies— The U.S. Corps of Engineers and the U.S. Forest Service. First, let's look at gender and the politically correct diversity in the USCOE. In the early 1970s, a high-level manager in the USCOE Nashville District took a critical look at his district staff and those under him on the numerous USCOE lakes. He saw a capable staff but it did not include women in ranger and other professional jobs, including recreation. The few women they did have were secretaries and clerks in the business and personnel offices. Since he knew the resource and HPER universities were beginning just then to graduate numbers of women trained with the skills his agency needed, he quietly began to consider women as well as men for his new hires. At the same time the USCOE (we've previously discussed their dramatic upward thrust in the recreation realm) began expanding their reservoir staff on old areas and on the lakes then being built for public use. Since we worked closely with him, *we know* he had the opportunity to pick women with topnotch credentials helping assure the success of what was then both a courageous and bold step for a federal agency. Were there problems? Yes, but they were carefully and quickly overcome. The outstanding nature of those women chosen greatly helped the process. During the middle and late 1970s though, one *big* problem did arise which stayed with the USCOE for several years. Guess what? Our environmental "friends" entered the picture *again* telling anyone who would listen (particularly college students) the U.S. Corps of Engineers was public enemy number one as an environmental destroyer. This caused some recruitment problems early on, but the key to solving the problem turned out to be quite simple. The agency let those young, topnotch female rangers visit university classes and simply tell students the truth. (What a contrast to the antics of the environmentalists!) We made sure each student consortium group hosted then at LBL got to hear from and interface with one or more of these motivated women. (Been there, saw, and enjoyed that!)

The success of this boldness quickly found favor throughout the agency (which, we think, is by far the best outdoor recreation delivery agency in the federal government) *and* the results have been excellent for the USCOE, for *you, us,* and the *American public.* Women performed ranger and other jobs as well as, and oftentimes better than, men. There was no sort of quota or *you must hire* rhetoric and the USCOE continues to this day to consider the *best qualified persons*—including men, women, and minorities for new hires and promotions. (What a novel procedure for a federal agency to follow!) That USCOE manager went on to be chief of recreation in Washington, D.C., and had other challenging assignments in the South. Look for him in our "heroes" section of this chapter! USCOE employee morale is the highest we've experienced for any federal agency, though the recent drastic cutbacks in personnel and the continued push to have someone else take over USCOE recreation activities are beginning to harm even this group.

Now let's have a look at gender hiring in the U.S. Forest Service. It was also an agency with few (extremely few!) women in their professional ranks at least until 10 to 15 years ago. One of the reasons for this was the "nature of the beast." Most of their employees in the natural resources realm were foresters and few college forestry graduates (until say 1970) were women. This is not an excuse but a fact. Another problem with the USFS then was they were limited by civil service code in just what sort of recreation degree a person had to have to be eligible for hire. If you were a forestry school recreation graduate (male or female), you were a "good folk;" if you weren't, you weren't! The previously mentioned USFS career ladder for those in recreation also caused problems. The biggest problem, though, was there was no bold person or persons spearheading the hiring of women or no great agency desire to do so. (Remember this, like most other comments in our texts, is our view.) Then along came the federal judge in California in 1973 who, when the Forest Service's lack of women was pointed out to him, took a dim view of such antics. The regional forester was told to make changes pronto and when he didn't move fast enough, the judge threatened to jail him. This and other challenges finally got the attention of the chief and his upper staff and all sorts of things happened—and continue to happen. One of the first reactions was to notify universities the USFS was going to hire scores of new employees, of course without discrimination due to color or gender or anything else. And they did so, *but* the new hires were women and minorities, not white males.

Since there was no special funding for hiring this sizable group each resource was assessed in each Forest Service region, meaning a sizable cut for recreation and other activities. This assessment went into a Work Force Diversity Fund. As mentioned, recreation contributed to this fund but few recreation trained persons were ever hired. Unlike the USCOE situation, the USFS couldn't spend much time seeing to it they got all top-crop folks. So, dozens of women and minorities (many who hadn't been able to find a job) found themselves new hires on ranger districts across the country.

The sizable influx of women not "traditionally" forestry trained imposed on a previously all male organization caused resentment problems early on meaning all sorts of new and old unhappy employees. Rapid promotion of those new folks (minorities and women) to the near exclusion of white males in the process saw morale drop drastically. In a short time (at least based on previous Forest Service history) women and minorities became assistant rangers and rangers years earlier than had been done by previous training and promotion practices. Along with the resentment and morale problems came one equally as disastrous—this involved placement of folks in jobs for which they weren't carefully trained to *successfully* accomplish.

Throughout these turbulent times we have had the opportunity to meet with and provide recreation training for dozens of these women. (Most have been topnotch folks!) In informal discussions with them across the country we were pleased to learn most Forest Service women take a dim view of both gender and any other special hiring practices. They don't mind competing one-on-one with anyone. They are also quite aware of the resentment caused by the quota-like actions. We and they realize they are not responsible for those problems and are actually victims just like the white males.

Add all this to the severe downsizing of the Forest Service, the continual pounding they get from the environmentalists and wilderness folks, the strangulation of environmental regulations, and the current administration's microenvironmental management emphasis and you have a nearly dysfunctional agency! This is particularly sad as the USFS has the best nationwide outdoor recreation land base of any agency. It seems to us we are all guilty for allowing this disaster to happen. It's your turn now to contrast the two federal agencies. We know which one did it best. We don't know how to help rescue the USFS.

Federal Salaries

Many years ago the salaries in the federal sector were adequate but far from excessive. Today we think they are greatly excessive. As a for instance, the beginning salary of a high-level GS-14 in 1970 was about $20,000 per year. In mid 1996 it was $62,000 and there are many more GS-14s in the agencies than in 1970. The $20,000 GS-14 salary of 1970 is what a beginning GS-5 makes today. (Interestingly enough, TVA job salaries are much higher than those in other federal agencies—been there, saw that!)

Anyhow, it seems to us that the American public is the shortchanged recipient of all of this social engineering and political payback foolishness. We believe federal—and for that matter, *any*—public sector jobs should be filled with the *best candidates possible.* Race, religion, gender, political affiliation, and other personal factors should all be irrelevant. Until we demand this from the political parties, government outputs will continue to decline. What think you?

Measuring Park Work. Figure 11.3 (a rather strange photo) shows a rose bush without its leaves in winter and its shadow and four measuring sticks. They are a foot-long en-

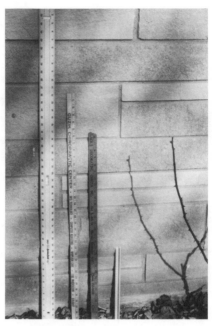

Figure 11.3

gineering scale, a broken yardstick less than three-feet long, a full yardstick and one four-feet long. All three of the authors toiled in TVA, an agency where the work output of different folks was measured and rewarded by "sticks of different lengths." Like telling someone they are the wrong color, this is shoddy! (One of the nicer words we've used.) If the foot-long instrument is the preferable measuring tool, use it for everyone: women, men, whites, minorities, and anyone else. Don't use special measuring sticks for special people. (We suggest you have a quick look at Proverbs 20:10.)

Predictions

The authors believe the greatest problem confronting developed site recreation for all Americans is simply the fact most users—including the 50 million persons reported to be camping today—have no strong organization or power base. The politicians hear strident groups and respond but rarely "listen" to the quiet majority. We do not believe this will change. It is with this as background that we make most of the following predictions:

- The backlog of park rehabilitation work on federal park areas is now in the multibillion-dollar range. This will continue to increase. Rather than providing the funding, the government will likely eliminate more and more facilities like campgrounds in parks.
- Affirmative action as we have experienced it will likely be eliminated but de facto hiring and promotion will continue.
- Camping club and organization members will continue to get older and fewer.
- Recreation research will see little improvement and will continue to have a disdain for management needs.
- Volunteerism will continue to be pushed in the public sector. The total results will be negative *and* we will see continued fund reduction.
- The private campground sector hierarchy will not understand why camping (particularly in the eastern United

States) is declining and will continue to blame it on the public sector ("I am their leader. Which way did they go?!"). The percent of private campground owners who understand what really is happening, however, will increase.
- Wilderness use will decline at an ever increasing rate while the frantic rhetoric to add more and more acres will increase.
- Wilderness proponents aided by the environmentalists will replace the highly "successful" spotted owl with other critters both real and imagined.
- The U.S. Corps of Engineers will continue to do quality work on developed sites but it isn't likely to happen in the other federal agencies.
- Counties like St. Joseph in Indiana, Mecosta in Michigan, Travis in Texas, and several of the county systems in Iowa will take over some of the park efforts dropped by the feds. They will also upgrade their outdoor recreation skills with workshops and other substantive continuing education programs.
- Utility companies such as Georgia Power and the Lower Colorado River Authority will follow the lead of the previously mentioned counties.
- Cities with outdoor recreation lands and challenges such as Edmond, Oklahoma, will mirror the successes of the above counties and will also make sure staff attends substantive park design and programming workshops.
- Since the Clinton administration got another four years, the demoralized U.S. Forest Service will be moved to the Department of the Interior where parks for common people have a low priority.
- If some drastic changes don't happen for the better, the United States will follow Japan's example of providing numerous public parks for lookers only (in our case carefully regulated wilderness-type use, too). The private sector will flourish but high prices for going there will eliminate most Americans from enjoying a family fun experience anywhere! (Been to Japan—experienced that!)

Planning Parks for People: 2nd Edition—Book Predictions

This book will be quite controversial—praised by those who want to see more and better parks for "all Americans" and condemned by the wilderness and environmental crowds, some researchers, and those who believe in the spoils system, unionized "professionals," and affirmative action.

Sales will be far greater than those of the first edition and in-the-field practitioners will likely be the cause.

We will have forgotten a few heroes and heroines, and failed to name countless of the more villainous rascals.

Heroes, Heroines and Villains

First, our listing of heroes and heroines. Over the years we've had the privilege of working with several topnotch persons—many were or are recreation professionals. Here are a few. Forgive us if we've failed to add you to our list.

Who	Organization	Why
Ralph C. Wilson**	USDA, Soil Conservation Service	Ralph has a special rating far above our hero classification. Find out why by turning to the text dedication page near the front of this book. We suggest you learn from and follow his example.

ALL OF THE FOLLOWING HEROES AND HEROINES ARE LISTED IN ALPHABETICAL ORDER (Retired*/Deceased**)

Who	Organization	Why
Don Albietz	Leiber State Recreation Area Park Manager, Indiana	Took over as manager of a park with a large, poorly designed campground and a history of rowdyism and vandalism. Began recreation—fun—programming, changed type of users to families (with teens), and increased use and revenue greatly. Pioneer in bringing group day users from all around the state.
Vicki Albietz	Leiber State Recreation Area Recreation Director, Indiana	Imagineered all sorts of enjoyable recreation programs for Leiber and has taken her own brand of enjoyable environmental education throughout Indiana and several other states.
Bill Brown*	USCOE Lake Barkley, Kentucky, Assistant Project Manager	Attended our pilot campground workshop 23 years ago; asked us to design a workshop for USCOE personnel resulting in hundreds of trained persons across the country; also built first USCOE universal campsites and got forgiveness later.
Janet Carter	Church secretary, paraplegic housewife, mother and outdoor person	The person we've turned to concerning ADA designs, mistakes and answers. When we were off base she told us so. When the park folks and disabled community did foolish things she said so.
Robert Chapman and Larry South	USCOE Project Manager and assistant in Texas (Larry is now in Oregon)	Did and are doing outstanding things in recreation design, group use, and programming that "can't be done in the USCOE."
Dr. Ken Chilman*	Forestry professor at Southern Illinois University	Has a 25-year history of finding low budget applied research answers to meet *manager* needs. Does so in understandable language! Also does an outstanding job teaching outdoor recreation planning and applied research methods. (Now that Ken has retired, we hope the university will replace him with an outstanding recreation planner/common-sense researcher!)
Kathy (Howard) Cuddeback*	TVA at Land Between the Lakes and USCOE, Washington County, Iowa	Kathy was our chief recreation program staff person at LBL and was the imagineer of fun programming blended wisely with interpretation and outdoor skills. Moved to an USCOE position in Iowa, married, and became the programmer/naturalist in an Iowa county park system. She now battles daily for her life with Lyme disease she contracted while at LBL—an inspiration to all of us.
Mack Deveraux*	USFS Ranger, Nebraska National Forest	Attended one of our sessions; said he was a longtime trailer camper, didn't camp in Forest Service areas because they were boring, and the Forest Service campsites were almost all too small and without hookups. Within a year he was doing programming and building large universal sites—some with 50-amp service. Who says it can't be done?

Who	Organization	Why
Yvonne Ferrell	Director, Department of Parks and Recreation for the state of Idaho	In our view, Mrs. Ferrell has been the most outstanding State Park Director in the United States in the decade of the 1990s. She gets things done; looks for new and better ways to provide parks for people; makes changes and corrections when needed; maintains high staff enthusiasm; and constantly courts members of the state legislature.
Luis Garcia	USCOE Maintenance Foreman, West Point Lake, Georgia	Luis came to one of our workshops; went back to his job, field designed and built (with other USCOE help) universal campsites far better than any we ever designed or built.
Bonnie Godbey**	Officer, Venture Publishing, Inc.	Bonnie insisted we get off our duffs and write this second edition. She also agreed we should really tell it like it is. We miss her!
Ken Guston*	Ozark National Forest Recreational Planner	Ken attended our basic workshop years ago when he was a technician. Returned to the Ozark forest and talked them into sponsoring a two-day session for them and *three other forests*. Has helped us in later years as an instructor in our programs.
Frank Kinsman*	U.S. Army Chief of Outdoor Recreation, Washington, D.C.	Frank took over a new program; asked for help when he didn't have the needed experience, and overviewed excellent work on bases in the United States and for NATO in Europe.
Dr. Philip Lavely	Professor at the University of Tennessee at Martin	For teaching hundreds of students sound basics in park planning, design *and* fun programming. Also, for providing substantive continuing education for hundreds of professionals.
Al Lookofsky and Winston Campbell	USCOE, Lake Shelbyville, Illinois	Hosts of our advanced workshop and longtime innovators in the realm of park design, universal campsites and programming. They even field designed an entire campground! (This, too, can't be done in the USCOE!?) Their reservoir property has become known nationwide as a national demonstration in campground and day-use design.
Dr. Frank Lupton*	Professor and Chair, Western Illinois University, Recreation, Park, and Tourism Administration	Outstanding broad-based educator from environmental education through all forms of recreation. Winner of numerous national awards. Big backer of undergraduate students, consortia, and our good friend.
Brian Plawer**	Manager, Kickapoo State Park, Illinois	Chapter Eight introduced you to the disaster of Kickapoo State Park. Brian wasn't happy with his poorly designed facilities; overcame internal and external park problems; pushed hard for funding and got it! He attended our advanced park design workshop to make sure he knew how to guide park designers, and helped us conduct two other sessions. *Note:* shortly before this book was published, Brian was killed by a bomb.
Gerald Purvis*	U.S. Corps of Engineers	The fellow who long ago began hiring women in the Nashville District of the USCOE and made sure the process moved throughout the United States.
Winston Smith	U.S. Forest Service, Southern Region	Longtime coworker, listener, provider of information on the public sector, and critiquer of our programs and our textbook.

Who	Organization	Why
Stan Specht	Chief Landscape Architect, U.S. Forest Service, Denver Region	During the Bush years, he was responsible for $200 million of campground rehab work. Personnel in the Forest Service there were spending time and money poorly, so he asked us to conduct training sessions across his region. They switched immediately to universal campsites, peanut design, and *even* recreation program facilities and a few programs. We know it took courage to ask us for help!
Reed Stalder	Bureau of Land Management, Utah State Office	Reed got his conservative agency to sponsor two workshops, to begin building universal sites, and to start thinking about fun programming.
Robert Strosnider*	U.S. Forest Service, Daniel Boone National Forest	Bob visited us at LBL soon after he moved to the DBNF and decided they would build universal campsites with electricity, would add amenity zones, *and* begin fun programming—and over the years *they did.* He got in trouble at all levels in the Forest Service for doing so.
Joe and Ellen Grace Utley	Ardent campers from Paducah, Kentucky	As users, Joe and his wife gave us all sorts of asked-for and not-asked-for advice on camping, campsites, how to work with users, and made sure we listened. Thanks for all your help!

Note a common thread runs through almost all of our park heroes and heroines: They accomplished great things in outdoor recreation for all Americans in spite of peer criticism and agency harassment.

General Heroes

- College professors who attend substantive continuing education programs.
- College professors who have the courage *and* background knowledge to use this book as a text.
- Organizations that hire and promote employees only because they are highly qualified.
- Northern Cheyenne Agency and Tribe (Montana) for their excellent indoor and outdoor recreation programs and facilities for children and young adults.
- White Mountain Apache Tribe (Whiteriver, Arizona) for their business-like marketing, quality facilities, and their emphasis on tourist promotion. Their Rent-A-Lake for a day is a good example!

Villains

Countless folks and organizations have harmed or hindered doing things for "all Americans" and we've made sure you already have been acquainted with some of the rascals. Here is a short list—far more should be named. (Have we missed you?)

Organization or Group	Villainy
The environmental extremists and the environmental indoctrinators	You already know why.
Recreation Vehicle Industry (RVIA) and Recreation Vehicle Dealers (RVDA)	It makes no economic sense that they *do not* help with making the best campsites possible available in both the public and private sectors.
National Association of Recreation Vehicle Parks and Campgrounds (ARVC)	For not understanding both public and private campgrounds' need to be built, expanded, renovated, and programmed to beckon warm bodies. Blaming the public sector for lack of use or declining use in their campgrounds is foolish.
Indiana state parks	For refusing to follow Don Albietz's economic and family-beckoning leadership.
Presidents Carter and Clinton	We realize they are heroes to the fringe groups, but they were and are disastrous to developed site recreation for families and "all Americans."

Organization or Group	Villainy
Public park providers in the Northeast	Somehow they have joined together and decided fun programming, water, and electric hookups shouldn't be provided in parks belonging not to them, but the American people. They all discourage family use and contribute to ever declining camp use there.
Park Organizations	Who hire or promote staff because of gender, age, religion, party affiliation, or race.
Park Organizations	Those who don't have the following written or implied in their recreation mission statement: "Providing fun for visitors."
Park Organizations	Who talk and write much about planning for persons with disabilities while doing little or nothing or the wrong things in their parks.
The National Park Service	For their lack of interest in their developed sites and their reluctance to seek substantive park design training outside of the agency.
Any current or former TVA staff person at the Land Between the Lakes if they had a part in:	Turning the nation's only outdoor recreation demonstration area (once called the Nation's Outdoor Recreation experiment station by Ralph Wilson) into the morass it is today! *Gone* are the college student consortia. *Gone* is the recreation research and demonstration emphasis. *Gone* are the 75–100 programs each week in family campgrounds. *Gone* is the high percentage (85–90%) of teens camping with their families. *Gone* also is the extensive emphasis on family use. *Gone* is the high-use generated economic nucleus so needed by the local economy. *Gone* also are the extensive programs and staff emphasis on numerous groups of persons with disabilities. Doubled is the deer herd for the good ol' boys *and* with it came a further increase (millions) in disease-carrying ticks. All of the Gones, they say, came about by budget cuts. We disagree!

Conclusion

This has been a difficult chapter—and book—to rewrite, primarily because we think recreation is such a positive phenomenon and we felt a need to take a negative approach at times to make the points we wanted to make. We made several mistakes 10 years ago with the first edition. Obviously the greatest one of these was our failure to foresee and tell you about the harm being done by numerous entities to providing parks and programs for all of us. Our purpose in writing this book has been to share mistakes we and others have made in the hope of keeping you from repeating these and similar errors.

Ours is an ever changing, dynamic profession. New opportunities for service provision appear almost daily, and with these comes the chance to improve access to our heritage of recreation *and* the potential for making further errors.

Mistakes will continue to occur. The only *real* mistake—however, the only one you shouldn't accept—is perpetuating the errors of those who have gone before you. Whether you agree with our arguments or not; whether you've found our discussions and our stories meaningful or "just another assignment to read;" whether you learn from us or someone else, we hope you will at least accept a challenge: *Plan parks for people.*

P.S.—We couldn't leave you without one more environmental story. This one concerns our majestic national bird, the bald eagle. Because of some well-done environmental action this once endangered bird (we love to watch them fish) is now flourishing all across America. It, like the spotted owl, doesn't need zillions of acres to thrive. A few years ago we visited Cape Canaveral. As the shuttle bus made the final turn toward the launch site the driver's main point of interest was a mother eagle and her young looking down on us from her nest in a tall roadside pine. It seems she returns there amid the rocket firings and tourist traffic each year. There appears to be a lesson here—you decide what it is.

Appendix A

Figure 2.1 Mistakes

Entrance Zone

1. Three entrances (loss of administrative control)
2. Entrance zones placed too near a curve (safety hazard)
3. Full tree canopy over one entrance (too much tunnel effect)
4. Long straightaway on entrance instead of curvilinear layout

Road Design

5. Existing road dictates design
6. Requires driving through campground to get to picnic area
7. Too much road on day-use area

Program

8. Passive and active areas zoned together instead of apart
9. Tot lots located immediately adjacent to main road (safety hazard)
10. Hike 'n bike trail crosses main park road at entrance (safety hazard)
11. Baseball field aligned on an east-west axis (should be north-south to keep sun from batter's and pitcher's eyes)
12. The parking lot adjacent to the campfire theater is aligned so headlights will shine on the theater stage
13. All picnic sites are located in heavy shade (some sun needed for cooler weather)

Water-Related Facilities

14. Need to drive through camping loop to reach boat ramp
15. Boat ramp is adjacent to beach (pollutants and possible safety hazard)
16. Parking slots in area serving boat ramp are not designed for boat trailers
17. Boat ramp is single-lane only (most boating ends just before darkness arrives—a "rush hour" situation results)
18. Swimming area on east facing shore (south or west facing preferred)

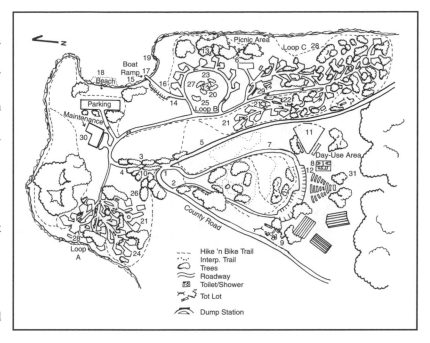

19. Boating area in back of a cove (needs to be located so wind and wave action won't fill launch area with silt)

Camping Area

20. Toilet/shower located in center of loop (increased impact)
21. Pull-in campsite
22. Pull-through campsite on wrong side of road
23. Too much shade surrounding toilet/shower (poor ventilation)
24. Living space on wrong side of parking spur
25. Camping loop too fat (wasted space)
26. Parking spur detached from living area of site
27. No campsites on inside of loop (wasted space)
28. Camp loops called A, B and C

Support Facilities

29. Sewage dumping station on camping loop (inconvenience for campers on other loops)
30. Maintenance building placed near entrance of complex
31. No comfort facilities in day-use area

Appendix B

One Solution to Figure 3.56 Trails Exercise

As we suggested at the end of Chapter Three, there is no single correct solution to planning a comprehensive system of trails for the campground shown in Figure 3.56. A good solution should address circulation, access and recreation needs; should include at least one innovative concept (we added a water-oriented interpretive trail to take advantage of the otherwise inaccessible limestone bluffs); and should provide support facilities as needed (did you think to include bicycle racks at program areas?). As a follow-up to this design exercise, you might try to "sell" your plan to others in your class. What would be your reaction to aspects of the plan they don't accept?

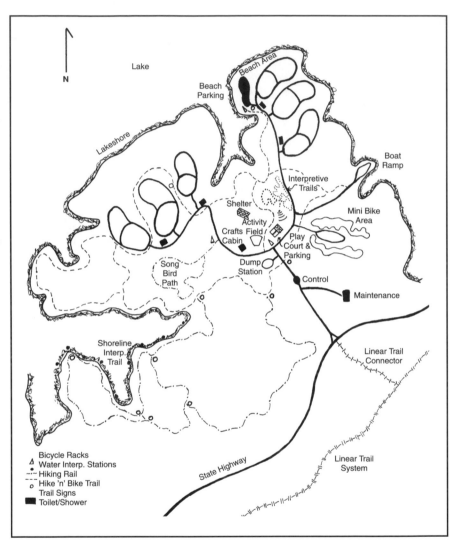

Appendix C

Possible Solution to Figure 4.39 Problem

The primary constraints you faced in this exercise were to develop program facilities to serve both overnight and day uses and to access the property from the county road. For administrative control, you should separate campers and day users as soon after they enter the complex as possible. Compare your plan and our solution. How can they both be improved? We've located a day-use group pod in the area zoned somewhat away from other uses and users yet close enough for groups to use the play amenities.

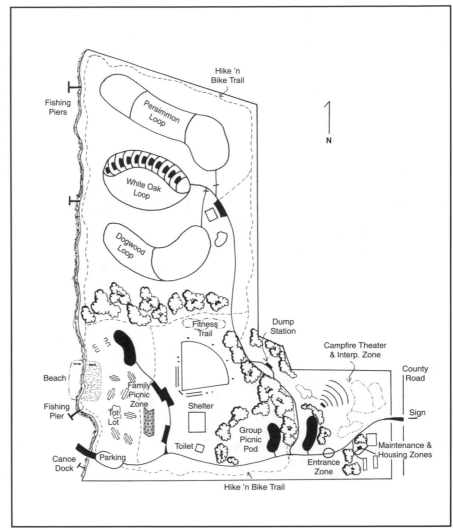

Appendix D

Answers to Figure 7.14 Unit Design Quiz

Loop A Good Units

Unit #	Unit Type
5	Pull-through (living space on right-hand side of spur)
8	Back-in (living space on right-hand side of spur)
16	Back-in (living space on right-hand side of spur)
19	Pull-through (living space on right-hand side of spur)
33	Back-in (living space on right-hand side of spur)
34	Pull-through (living space on right-hand side of spur)
39	Pull-through (living space on right-hand side of spur)
43	Back-in (living space on right-hand side of the spur)
50	Back-in (living space on right-hand space of the spur)

Wildcat Loop Poor Units

Unit #	Unit Type
1	Back-in (living space on left-hand side of spur)
10	Pull-in (always a no-no)
21	Pull-in
30	Pull-through (living space on left-hand side of spur)
35	Pull-through (living space on left-hand side of spur)
41	Back-in (living space on left-hand side of spur)
44	Pull-in

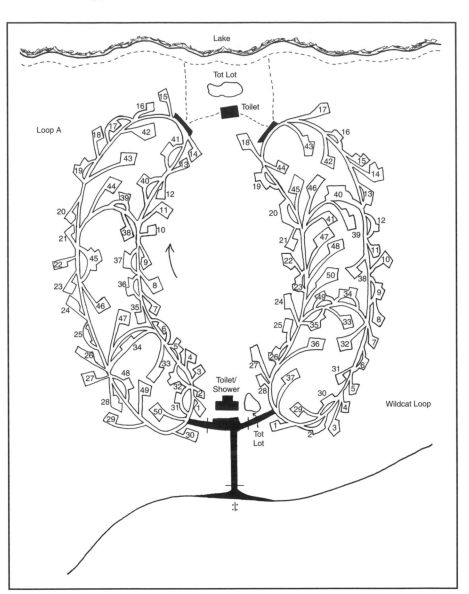

Appendix E

Sample Program Calendar

Haunted Hollow Campground Program Schedule

Week of June 21-27

Facility or area code*:

S – shelter, B – beach, SC – skills court, PC – play court, P – playground, IT – interpretive trail, A – archery range, F – fishing pier, BF – ball field, G – entrance gate, R – boat ramp, AB – activity building, CT – campfire theater, LC – log cabin, HP – horseshoe pits, BBC – boccie ball court

*Code indicates where program begins.

Monday, June 21
6:30 A.M.	Bicycle Hike for Wildlife (S)
7:00 A.M.	Early Bird Jog (G)
9:00 A.M.	Fishing Skills (F) (For children 13 and under)
10:00 A.M.	Nature Crafts (S)
11:00 A.M.	Critter Gathering (G)
2:00 P.M.	Critter Races (S)
2:00 P.M.	Water Volleyball & Tug of War (B)
3:30 P.M.	Green Submarine Hunt (B)
7:00 P.M.	Soccer Skills (BF)
8:30 P.M.	Cartoons for Little Folks (CT)
9:00 P.M.	Teen Dance (S)
9:00 P.M.	Karaoke (CT)
10:00 P.M.	Family Softball (BF)

Tuesday, June 22
8:30 A.M.	Archery Skills (A) (For teens)
9:00 A.M.	Scavenger Hunt (G) (For those 12 and under)
9:30 A.M.	Checker Tournament (S) (All ages)
10:00 A.M.	Paint an Intern Student (CT)
11:00 A.M.	Cooking Skills for Dads (LC)
2:00 P.M.	Raft Races (B)
2:00 P.M.	Water Volleyball (B)
2:00 P.M.	Storytelling (S)
3:30 P.M.	Nature Crafts (S)
5:00 P.M.	Bike Hike (G)
7:30 P.M.	Puppet Show (CT)
8:30 P.M.	Line Dance Skills (SC)
8:30 P.M.	Cartoons for Kids (ST)
9:00 P.M.	Grocery Bingo (S)

9:00 P.M.	Teen Volleyball (PC)
10:30 P.M.	Teen Coffeehouse (S) Bring your guitar!

Wednesday, June 23
8:00 A.M.	Rowing Skills (R)
9:00 A.M.	Solar Food Drying (S)
9:00 A.M.	Archery Skills (A) (Dads and children under 13)
10:00 A.M.	Blind Rowboat Races (R)
11:00 A.M.	Horseshoe Tournament (HP)
2:00 P.M.	Water Volleyball & Tug of War (B)
2:00 P.M.	Outdoor Cooking (LC) (For teens)
3:00 P.M.	Dog Show (CT)
3:30 P.M.	Bicycle Skills (SC)
4:30 P.M.	Sandcastle Creations (B)
6:30 P.M.	Pillow Polo (BF)
8:00 P.M.	Paris Fashions (CT)
8:30 P.M.	Remote-Controlled Vehicle Races (R)
8:30 P.M.	Grocery Bingo (AB)
9:00 P.M.	Karaoke (CT)
10:30 P.M.	Family Softball (BF)

Thursday, June 24
7:00 A.M.	Early Bird Jog (G)
8:30 A.M.	5-Mile Family Bike Hike (C)
9:00 A.M.	Canoe Skills (B)
9:00 A.M.	Sack Races (BF)
10:00 A.M.	Badminton (PC)
11:00 A.M.	Raft Races (R)
2:00 P.M.	Water Volleyball & Tug of War (B)
2:00 P.M.	Rowing Races (R)
4:00 P.M.	Storytelling (AB)
7:00 P.M.	Bait-Casting Contest (F)
7:00 P.M.	Tug of War (Moms and Sons versus Dads and Daughters; B)
8:30 P.M.	Square Dance (PC)
8:30 P.M.	Boccie Ball (BBC)
9:00 P.M.	Teen Dance (S) Bring Your Own Music!
9:00 P.M.	Nature Campfire Program (CT)
10:30 P.M.	Family Volleyball (PC)

Friday, June 25
6:30 A.M.	Early Morning Hike & Nature Walk (G)
9:00 A.M.	Scavenger Hunt (Moms and Sons; AB)
9:30 A.M.	Egg Fight (BF) Bring Your Own Boiled Eggs.
10:30 A.M.	Nature Crafts (AB)

10:30 A.M.	Critter Gathering (G)
11:00 A.M.	Water Frisbee (B)
2:00 P.M.	Critter Races (S)
2:00 P.M.	Green Submarine Hunt (B)
3:00 P.M.	Water Volleyball (B)
4:00 P.M.	Learn to Swim (B)
5:00 P.M.	Bicycle Skills (SC)
7:00 P.M.	3-on-3 Basketball (PC)
7:00 P.M.	Horseshoe Tournament (SC)
8:00 P.M.	Living-History Program (CT)
8:30 P.M.	Square Dance (PC)
9:30 P.M.	Monster Movie (CT)
10:30 P.M.	Family Softball (BF)
11:00 P.M.–?	Insomnia Theater with John Wayne

Saturday, June 26

9:00 A.M.	Badminton (PC)
9:00 A.M.	Rock and Seed Crafts (AB)
10:00 A.M.	Storytelling (CT)
11:00 A.M.	Water-Balloon Toss & Tug of War (B)
2:00 P.M.	Water Wiffle Ball (B)
2:00 P.M.	Canoe Races (B)
2:00–7:00 P.M.	Camper Flea Market (S)
4:00 P.M.	Adult Learn to Swim (B)
7:30 P.M.	New Town Band (CT)
8:30 P.M.	Karaoke (CT)
9:30 P.M.	Teen Dance (S)
10:00 P.M.	Saturday Night Movies (CT)

10:30 P.M.	Teen Volleyball (PC)
10:30 P.M.	Family Softball (BF)

Sunday, June 27

8:30 A.M.	Worship Service (CT)
10:00 A.M.	Family Swim Time (B)
11:00 A.M.	Water Volleyball (Moms and Dads against children; B)
11:00 A.M.	Shuffleboard Contest (S)
2:00 P.M.	Beach Games (B)
2:00 P.M.	Fishing Skills (F)
3:00 P.M.	Nature Walk (IT)
7:30 P.M.	Remote-Controlled Vehicle Races (R)
8:00 P.M.	Boccie Ball Contest (BBC)
8:30 P.M.	Grocery Bingo (CT)
9:00 P.M.	Family Softball (BF)

You are invited to learn and have fun throughout the day and evening with all sorts of activities. College students who are majoring in parks and recreation from several universities and local senior citizen volunteers are your program hosts. The students receive credit and are carefully graded during their 12- to 15-week practicum experience.

A variety of outdoor play equipment is available without cost for your use at the equipment checkout building. Hours are 9:00 A.M.–noon; 3:00 P.M.–5:00 P.M.; and 6:00 P.M.–10:00 P.M. each day.

Enjoy your stay at Haunted Hollow and please come again!

Other Books From Venture Publishing

The A•B•Cs of Behavior Change: Skills for Working With Behavior Problems in Nursing Homes
    by Margaret D. Cohn, Michael A. Smyer and Ann L. Horgas
Activity Experiences and Programming Within Long-Term Care
    by Ted Tedrick and Elaine R. Green
The Activity Gourmet
    by Peggy Powers
Advanced Concepts for Geriatric Nursing Assistants
    by Carolyn A. McDonald
Adventure Education
    edited by John C. Miles and Simon Priest
Aerobics of the Mind: Keeping the Mind Active in Aging—A New Perspective on Programming for Older Adults
    by Marge Engelman
Assessment: The Cornerstone of Activity Programs
    by Ruth Perschbacher
Behavior Modification in Therapeutic Recreation: An Introductory Manual
    by John Datillo and William D. Murphy
Benefits of Leisure
    edited by B. L. Driver, Perry J. Brown and George L. Peterson
Benefits of Recreation Research Update
    by Judy M. Sefton and W. Kerry Mummery
Beyond Bingo: Innovative Programs for the New Senior
    by Sal Arrigo, Jr., Ann Lewis and Hank Mattimore
Beyond Bingo 2: More Innovative Programs for the New Senior
    by Sal Arrigo, Jr.
Both Gains and Gaps: Feminist Perspectives on Women's Leisure
    by Karla Henderson, M. Deborah Bialeschki, Susan M. Shaw and Valeria J. Freysinger
Dimensions of Choice: A Qualitative Approach to Recreation, Parks, and Leisure Research
    by Karla A. Henderson
Effective Management in Therapeutic Recreation Service
    by Gerald S. O'Morrow and Marcia Jean Carter
Evaluating Leisure Services: Making Enlightened Decisions
    by Karla A. Henderson with M. Deborah Bialeschki
The Evolution of Leisure: Historical and Philosophical Perspectives (Second Printing)
    by Thomas Goodale and Geoffrey Godbey
File o' Fun: A Recreation Planner for Games & Activities—Third Edition
    by Jane Harris Ericson and Diane Ruth Albright
The Game Finder—A Leader's Guide to Great Activities
    by Annette C. Moore
Getting People Involved in Life and Activities: Effective Motivating Techniques
    by Jeanne Adams
Great Special Events and Activities
    by Annie Morton, Angie Prosser and Sue Spangler
Inclusive Leisure Services: Responding to the Rights of People With Disabilities
    by John Dattilo
Internships in Recreation and Leisure Services: A Practical Guide for Students (Second Edition)
    by Edward E. Seagle, Jr., Ralph W. Smith and Lola M. Dalton
Interpretation of Cultural and Natural Resources
    by Douglas M. Knudson, Ted T. Cable and Larry Beck
Introduction to Leisure Services—7th Edition
    by H. Douglas Sessoms and Karla A. Henderson

Leadership and Administration of Outdoor Pursuits, Second Edition
        by Phyllis Ford and James Blanchard
Leadership in Leisure Services: Making a Difference
        by Debra J. Jordan
Leisure and Family Fun (LAFF)
        by Mary Atteberry-Rogers
Leisure and Leisure Services in the 21st Century
        by Geoffrey Godbey
Leisure Diagnostic Battery Computer Software
        by Gary Ellis and Peter A. Witt
The Leisure Diagnostic Battery: Users Manual and Sample Forms
        by Peter A. Witt and Gary Ellis
Leisure Education: A Manual of Activities and Resources
        by Norma J. Stumbo and Steven R. Thompson
Leisure Education II: More Activities and Resources
        by Norma J. Stumbo
Leisure Education III: More Goal-Oriented Activities
        by Norma J. Stumbo
Leisure Education IV: Activities for Individuals With Substance Addictions
        by Norma J. Stumbo
Leisure Education Program Planning: A Systematic Approach
        by John Dattilo and William D. Murphy
Leisure in Your Life: An Exploration—Fourth Edition
        by Geoffrey Godbey
Leisure Services in Canada: An Introduction
        by Mark S. Searle and Russell E. Brayley
The Lifestory Re-Play Circle: A Manual of Activities and Techniques
        by Rosilyn Wilder
Marketing for Parks, Recreation, and Leisure
        by Ellen L. O'Sullivan
Models of Change in Municipal Parks and Recreation: A Book of Innovative Case Studies
        edited by Mark E. Havitz
More Than a Game: A New Focus on Senior Activity Services
        by Brenda Corbett
Nature and the Human Spirit: Toward an Expanded Land Management Ethic
        edited by B. L. Driver, Daniel Dustin, Tony Baltic, Gary Elsner, and George Peterson
Outdoor Recreation Management: Theory and Application, Third Edition
        by Alan Jubenville and Ben Twight
Planning Parks for People
        by John Hultsman, Richard L. Cottrell and Wendy Hultsman
Private and Commercial Recreation
        edited by Arlin Epperson
The Process of Recreation Programming Theory and Technique, Third Edition
        by Patricia Farrell and Herberta M. Lundegren
Protocols for Recreation Therapy Programs
        edited by Jill Kelland, along with the Recreation Therapy Staff at Alberta Hospital Edmonton
Quality Management: Applications for Therapeutic Recreation
        edited by Bob Riley
Recreation and Leisure: Issues in an Era of Change, Third Edition
        edited by Thomas Goodale and Peter A. Witt
Recreation Economic Decisions: Comparing Benefits and Costs (Second Edition)
        by John B. Loomis and Richard G. Walsh

Recreation Programming and Activities for Older Adults
        by Jerold E. Elliott and Judith A. Sorg-Elliott
Recreation Programs That Work for At-Risk Youth: The Challenge of Shaping the Future
        by Peter A. Witt and John L. Crompton
Reference Manual for Writing Rehabilitation Therapy Treatment Plans
        by Penny Hogberg and Mary Johnson
Research in Therapeutic Recreation: Concepts and Methods
        edited by Marjorie J. Malkin and Christine Z. Howe
A Social History of Leisure Since 1600
        by Gary Cross
A Social Psychology of Leisure
        by Roger C. Mannell and Douglas A. Kleiber
The Sociology of Leisure
        by John R. Kelly and Geoffrey Godbey
Therapeutic Activity Intervention With the Elderly: Foundations & Practices
        by Barbara A. Hawkins, Marti E. May and Nancy Brattain Rogers
Therapeutic Recreation: Cases and Exercises
        by Barbara C. Wilhite and M. Jean Keller
Therapeutic Recreation in the Nursing Home
        by Linda Buettner and Shelley L. Martin
Therapeutic Recreation Protocol for Treatment of Substance Addictions
        by Rozanne W. Faulkner
Time for Life: The Surprising Ways Americans Use Their Time
        by John P. Robinson and Geoffrey Godbey
A Training Manual for Americans With Disabilities Act Compliance in Parks and Recreation Settings
        by Carol Stensrud